CW01263590

The Life and Travels of Xavier Marmier (1808–1892):
Bringing World Literature to France

Xavier Marmier, c. 1855. Print from drawing by Auguste Lemoine. Reproduced by the Musée municipal de Pontarlier from the original held in their collection.

The Life and Travels of Xavier Marmier (1808–1892)

Bringing World Literature to France

by
Wendy S. Mercer

*A British Academy
Postdoctoral Fellowship Monograph*

Published for THE BRITISH ACADEMY
by OXFORD UNIVERSITY PRESS

Oxford University Press, Great Clarendon Street, Oxford OX2 6DP

Oxford New York

Auckland Cape Town Dar es Salaam Hong Kong Karachi
Kuala Lumpur Madrid Melbourne Mexico City Nairobi
New Delhi Shanghai Taipei Toronto

With offices in
Argentina Austria Brazil Chile Czech Republic France Greece
Guatemala Hungary Italy Japan Poland Portugal Singapore
South Korea Switzerland Thailand Turkey Ukraine Vietnam

Published in the United States
by Oxford University Press Inc., New York

© The British Academy 2007

Database right The British Academy (maker)

First published 2007

British Library Cataloguing in Publication Data
Data available

Library of Congress Cataloging in Publication Data
Data available

Typeset by J&L Composition, Filey, North Yorkshire
Printed in Great Britain
on acid-free paper by
The Cromwell Press Limited
Trowbridge, Wilts

ISBN 978–0–19–726388–4

For Johnny and Manka;
and in memory of my parents and grandparents

Contents

Plates

Abbreviations

For libraries, archives, and other manuscript material:

AnF	Archives Nationales [de France], Paris
AAf	Archives de l'Académie française, Paris
BIF	Bibliothèque de l'Institut de France, Paris
BmB	Bibliothèque municipale de Besançon
BnF	Bibliothèque nationale de France, Paris
BSG, Fn	Bibliothèque Sainte-Geneviève, Fonds nordique, Paris
PV	Procès-Verbaux

For periodicals and reviews:

NRg	*Nouvelle Revue germanique*
RDM	*Revue des Deux Mondes*
Rg	*Revue germanique*
RP	*Revue de Paris*

For works by Xavier Marmier:

EB	*Un été au bord de la Baltique et de la mer du Nord*, 2nd edn. (Paris: Hachette, 1883).
EG	*Études sur Goethe* (Paris and Strasbourg: Levrault, 1835).
En Franche-Comté	*En Franche-Comté: histoires et paysages. Nouvelle édition* (Paris: Lecoffre, 1885).
Franche-Comté	*Nouveaux souvenirs de voyage et traditions populaires: Franche-Comté* (Paris: Charpentier, 1845).
HI	*Histoire de l'Islande* (Paris: Arthus Bertrand, 1840).
HLDS	*Histoire de la littérature en Danemark et en Suède* (Paris: Bonnaire, 1839).
HLS	*Histoire de la littérature scandinave* (Paris: Arthus Bertrand, 1848).
Journal	*Journal*, ed. Eldon Kaye, 2 vols. (Geneva: Droz, 1968).
LA	*Lettres sur l'Algérie* (Paris: Arthus Bertrand, [1847]).
LAC	*Lettres sur l'Amérique: Canada, États-Unis, Havane, Rio de la Plata*, 2 vols. (Paris: Arthus Bertrand, 1851).
LAM	*Lettres sur l'Adriatique et le Monténégro*, 2 vols. (Paris: Arthus Bertrand, 1854).
LH	*Lettres sur la Hollande* (Paris: Delloye, 1841).
LI	*Lettres sur l'Islande* (Brussels: N.-J. Grégoir, V. Wouters et Cie, 1841).

LN   *Lettres sur le Nord (Danemark, Suède, Norvège, Laponie et Spitzberg)*, 2 vols. (Brussels: N.-J. Grégoir, V. Wouters et Cie, 1841).

LR   *Lettres sur la Russie, la Finlande et la Pologne*, 2 vols. (Paris: Delloye, 1843).

RN   *Du Rhin au Nil*, 2 vols. (Paris: Arthus Bertrand, [1846]).

SV   *Souvenirs d'un voyageur*, 2nd edn. (Paris: Didier, 1867)

VCN   *Voyages de la Commission scientifique du Nord en Scandinavie, en Laponie, au Spitzberg et au Feroë pendant les années 1838, 1839 et 1840 sur la corvette La Recherche commandée par M. Fabvre, publiés par ordre du roi sous la direction de M. Paul Gaimard. Relation du voyage, par M. Xavier Marmier*, 2 vols. (Paris: Arthus Bertrand, [1844–7]).

Voyage pittoresque   *Voyage pittoresque en Allemagne*, 2 vols. (Paris: Morizot, 1859–60).

Voyages de Nils   *Les Voyages de Nils à la recherche de l'idéal* (Paris: Hachette, 1869).

Chronology of Selected Publications by Xavier Marmier[1]

1830   *Esquisses poétiques, par X. Marmier* (Paris: Guyonnet).

1831   *Nouvelles Esquisses poétiques, par X. Marmier* (Vesoul: Zaepffel; Paris: chez les marchands de nouveautés).

1833   *Feuilles volantes: Souvenirs d'Allemagne* (Berlin: Haude et Spener).

         Pierre, ou les Suites de l'ignorance, imité de l'allemand [de Christophe Schmid] *par X. Marmier* (Paris and Strasbourg: Levrault).

         [translation] Friedrich Krummacher, *Choix de paraboles de F. Krummacher, par X. Marmier* (Paris: Levrault).

1834   *Maître Pierre, ou le Savant de village* (Paris: Levrault).

         Visites à une école de petits enfants, ouvrage imité de l'anglais (Strasbourg: Levrault).

         [translation] Adam Oehlenschläger, *Corrège, tragédie en 5 actes, par A. Oehlenschläger, traduite par X. Marmier* (Paris and Strasbourg: Levrault).

         [translation] Michel Beer, *Le Paria, tragédie en un acte, par Michel Beer, traduite par Xavier Marmier* (Strasbourg: Levrault).

         [translation] August Koberstein, *Manuel de l'histoire de la littérature nationale allemande* (Paris and Strasbourg: Levrault).

         [translation] Friedrich Krummacher, *Nouveau choix de paraboles de F. Krummacher* (Paris: Levrault).

1835   *Études sur Goethe* (Paris and Strasbourg: Levrault).

         [translation] *Choix de fables et de contes, traduits de divers auteurs anglais et allemands* (Paris and Strasbourg: Levrault).

         [translation] Ludwig Tieck, 'La Vie et la mort du petit chaperon rouge', in *Théâtre européen* [. . .] *Théâtre allemand*, 2nd ser., vol. 3 (Paris: Guérin).

         [translation] Theodor Körner, 'Le Garde de nuit', in *Théâtre européen* [. . .] *Théâtre allemand*, 2nd ser., vol. 3 (Paris: Guérin).

         [translation] L. Holberg, 'Le Potier d'étain politique', in *Théâtre européen* [. . .] *Théâtres danois et suédois* (Paris: Guérin).

         [translation] Ludwig Tieck, 'Les Etoiles', in *Théâtre européen* [. . .] *Théâtre allemand*, 2nd ser., vol. 3 (Paris: Guérin).

1836   [translation] *L'Ami des petits enfans, maximes morales et religieuses. Traduit du hollandais par X. Marmier* (Paris and Strasbourg: Levrault).

         [translation] *La Mère de famille, traduit de l'anglais* [de John S. C. Abbott] (Paris and Strasbourg: Levrault).

---

[1] Undated volumes are listed by date most likely according to available information.

1837   *Lettres sur l'Islande* (Paris: Bonnaire).
        [translation] Goethe, *Hermann et Dorothée* (Paris: Heideloff).
1838   [translation] Carl Christian Rafn, *Mémoire sur la découverte de l'Amérique, traduit par Xavier Marmier* (Paris: Arthus Bertrand).
1839   *Histoire de la littérature en Danemark et en Suède* (Paris: Bonnaire).
        [editor] Mme de Staël, *De l'Allemagne, nouvelle édition, avec une préface par M. X. Marmier* (Paris: Charpentier).
        [translation] *Théâtre de Goethe, traduction nouvelle, revue, corrigée et augmentée de notices et d'une préface par M. X. Marmier* (Paris: Charpentier).
1840   *Histoire de l'Islande* (Paris: Arthus Bertrand).
        Lettres sur le Nord, Danemark, Suède, Norvège, Laponie et Spitzberg, 2 vols. (Paris: Delloye).
1841   *Lettres sur la Hollande* (Paris: Delloye).
        Souvenirs de voyages et traditions populaires (Paris: Masgana).
        [translation] *Théâtre de Schiller, traduction nouvelle, précédée d'une notice sur sa vie et ses ouvrages par X. Marmier* (Paris: Charpentier).
1842   *Chants populaires du Nord* (Paris: Charpentier).
1843   *Lettres sur la Russie, la Finlande et la Pologne*, 2 vols. (Paris: Delloye).
        Littérature islandaise, 2 vols. (Paris: Arthus Bertrand).
        [translation] E. T. A. Hoffmann, *Contes fantastiques d'Hoffmann, traduction nouvelle de M. X. Marmier, précédée d'une notice par le traducteur* (Paris: Charpentier).
1844   *Poésies d'un voyageur* (Paris: Félix Locquin).
        Voyages de la Commission scientifique du Nord en Scandinavie, en Laponie, au Spitzberg et au Feröe pendant les années 1838, 1839 et 1840 sur la corvette La Recherche commandée par M. Fabvre, publiés par ordre du roi sous la direction de M. Paul Gaimard. Relation du voyage, par M. Xavier Marmier, 2 vols. (Paris: Arthus Bertrand, [1844–7]).
        [translation] *Poésies de Schiller, traduction nouvelle par M. X. Marmier, précédée d'une introduction par le traducteur* (Paris: Charpentier).
1845   *Nouveaux souvenirs de voyage et traditions populaires: Franche-Comté* (Paris: Charpentier).
        [translation] Johann Georg von Zimmermann, *La Solitude, traduction nouvelle, précédée d'une notice sur la vie de l'auteur, par X. Marmier* (Paris: Charpentier).
1846   *Du Rhin au Nil*, 2 vols. (Paris: Arthus Bertrand).
        Pontarlier (Paris: Claye, Taillefer et Cie).
1847   *Lettres sur l'Algérie* (Paris: Arthus Bertrand).
        [translation] *Nouvelles allemandes, par Zschokke, Chamisso, Hauff, Arnim, Auerbach, etc., traduites par X. Marmier* (Paris: Charpentier).
1848   *Histoire de la littérature scandinave, par M. Xavier Marmier* (Paris: Arthus Bertrand).
        Une conversion, nouvelle franc-comtoise (Paris: Pioux et Cie).
1849   *Deux émigrés en Suède* (Paris: Administration du journal *Le Pays*).
        Voyages de la Commission scientifique du Nord en Scandinavie, en Laponie, au Spitzberg et aux Iles Féröe, pendant les années 1838, 1839 et 1840, sur la corvette La Recherche commandée par M. Fabvre, publiés par ordre du roi

sous la direction de M. Paul Gaimard. Littérature scandinave, par M. Xavier Marmier (Paris: Arthus Bertrand).

[translation] Edwin Bryant, *Voyage en Californie, description de son sol, de son climat, de ses mines d'or, par Ed. Bryant, traduit par X. Marmier* (Paris: Arthus Bertrand).

1851 *Les Ames en peine, contes d'un voyageur* (Paris: Arthus Bertrand).

Les Voyageurs nouveaux, 3 vols. (Paris: Arthus Bertrand).

Lettres sur l'Amérique: Canada, États-Unis, Havane, Rio de la Plata, 2 vols. (Paris: Arthus Bertrand).

1854 *Du Danube au Caucase, voyages et littérature* (Paris: Garnier).

Lettres sur l'Adriatique et le Monténégro, 2 vols. (Paris: Arthus Bertrand).

Voyages de la Commission scientifique du Nord en Scandinavie, en Laponie, au Spitzberg et aux Iles Féröe, pendant les années 1838, 1839 et 1840, sur la corvette La Recherche commandée par M. Fabvre, publiés par ordre du gouvernement sous la direction de M. Paul Gaimard. Histoire de la Scandinavie (Paris: Arthus Bertrand).

[translation] *Les Perce-Neige, nouvelles du Nord traduites par X. Marmier* (Paris: Garnier).

1855 [translation] Friedrich Gerstäcker, *Aventures d'une colonie d'émigrants en Amérique, traduites de l'allemand par Xavier Marmier* (Paris: Hachette).

[preface] Gábor Prónay, *Esquisses de la vie populaire en Hongrie* (Pesth: Geibel).

1856 *Un été au bord de la Baltique et de la mer du Nord* (Paris: Hachette).

[preface] Hans Christian Andersen, *Contes d'Andersen, traduits du danois par D. Soldi avec une notice biographique par X. Marmier,* 6th edn. (Paris: Hachette).

[translation] *Au bord de la Néva: contes russes traduits par X. Marmier* (Paris: Michel Lévy).

1857 *Les Quatre Ages* (Paris: Jules Tardieu).

[translation] *Le Tentateur* (Leipzig: Dürr).

[translation] *Les Drames intimes: contes russes, par X. Marmier* (Paris: Michel Lévy).

1858 *La Forêt noire* (Paris: Charles Douniol).

Les Fiancés du Spitzberg (Paris: Hachette).

[translation] Ivan Turgenev, *Scènes de la vie russe: par M. J. Tourgueneff, nouvelles russes, traduites avec l'autorisation de l'auteur par M. X. Marmier* (Paris: Hachette).

1859 *Voyage pittoresque en Allemagne,* 2 vols. (Paris: Morizot, 1859–60).

[translation] *Nouvelles danoises, traduites par Xavier Marmier* (Paris: Hachette).

[translation] Vasilii Vonliarliarski, *Une grande dame russe: par B. A. Vonliarliarski, traduit du russe par X. Marmier* (Paris: Michel Lévy).

1860 *En Amérique et en Europe* (Paris: Hachette).

Gazida (Paris: Hachette).

Histoires allemandes et scandinaves par X. Marmier (Paris: Michel Lévy).

1861 *Voyage en Suisse* (Paris: Morizot).

1862 *Hélène et Suzanne* (Paris: Hachette).

Voyages et littérature (Paris: Morizot).

1863   *En Alsace: L'Avare et son trésor* (Paris: Hachette).
1864   *Le Roman d'un héritier* (Paris: Hachette).
        Les Mémoires d'un orphelin (Paris: Hachette).
        [translation] *En chemin de fer, nouvelles de l'Est et de l'Ouest, traduites par X. Marmier* (Paris: Michel Lévy).
1865   [translation] *Sous les sapins, nouvelles du Nord traduites par X. Marmier* (Paris: Hachette).
1866   *Histoire d'un pauvre musicien* (Paris: Hachette).
1867   *De l'est à l'ouest, voyages et littérature* (Paris: Hachette).
        Souvenirs d'un voyageur, 2nd edn. (Paris: Didier). Curiously, I have never found any trace of a first edition (either in library catalogues or in the *Bibliographie de la France*).
1868   *Les Hasards de la vie, contes et nouvelles* (Paris: Brunet).
        [translation] *Les Drames du cœur* (Paris: Michel Lévy).
1869   *Dernières Glanes* (Paris: Simon Raçon).
        Les Voyages de Nils à la recherche de l'idéal (Paris: Hachette).
1871   *L'Arbre de Noël, contes et légendes recueillis par X. Marmier et illustrés par Bertall* (Paris: Hachette).
        Institut de France, Académie française, *Discours prononcés dans la séance publique tenue par l'Académie française pour la réception de M. X. Marmier le 3 décembre 1871* (Paris: Firmin Didot).
1872   [translation] Henry Wadsworth Longfellow, *Drames et poésies, traduits avec l'autorisation de l'auteur, par X. Marmier* (Paris: Hachette).
1873   *Impressions et souvenirs d'un voyageur chrétien* (Tours: Alfred Mame).
        Robert Bruce: comment on reconquiert un royaume (Paris: Hachette).
        Trois jours de la vie d'une reine (1770–1793) (Tours: Alfred Mame).
        Institut de France, Académie française, *Discours prononcés dans la séance publique tenue par l'Académie française pour la réception de M. Le Baron de Viel-Castel, le 27 novembre 1873* (Paris: Firmin Didot).
1874   *Les États-Unis et le Canada* (Tours: Alfred Mame).
        Poésies d'un voyageur 1834–1874 (Paris: Simon Raçon).
        Récits américains (Tours: Alfred Mame).
1876   *En pays lointains* (Paris: Hachette).
        La Maison (Paris and Lyon: Lecoffre fils).
        La Vie dans la maison (Paris and Lyon: Lecoffre).
1879   *Nouveaux récits de voyage* (Paris: Hachette).
1880   *Antonia (1745), nouvelle historique, imitée de l'anglais* (Paris: Sauton).
        Paroisse Sainte-Clotilde, Ecole paroissiale libre, tenue par les frères des écoles chrétiennes, *Discours prononcé à la distribution des prix par M. Xavier Marmier de l'Académie française* (Paris: Imprimerie de l'œuvre de Saint-Paul, Soussens et Cie).
        'Réponse de M. Xavier Marmier, Directeur de l'Académie française, au discours de M. Henri Martin', *Recueil des discours, rapports et pièces diverses lus dans les séances publiques et particulières de l'Académie française, 1870–1879*, 2 vols. (Paris: Firmin Didot), 2, 447–76.
        [translation] *Contes populaires de différents pays, recueillis et traduits par Xavier Marmier de l'Académie française* (Paris: Hachette).

1881 [translation] Adam Oehlenschläger, *Théâtre choisi de Oehlenschläger et de Holberg, traduction de MM. Xavier Marmier et David Soldi* (Paris: Didier).

1882 *Légendes des plantes et des oiseaux* (Paris: Hachette).

    [translation] *Nouvelles du Nord, traduites du russe, du suédois, du danois, de l'allemand et de l'anglais* (Paris: Hachette).

1883 *A la maison, études et souvenirs* (Paris: Hachette).

    [preface] F. Bart, *Scènes et tableaux de la vie actuelle en Orient* (Limoges: Barbou).

1884 *Allocution de M. Xavier Marmier [. . .] prononcée à l'assemblée annuelle de l'œuvre de l'hospitalité de nuit, le 16 mars 1884* (Paris: Éthiou-Pérou).

    Le Succès par la persévérance, douze histoires et un conte (Paris: Hachette).

1885 *En Franche-Comté: histoires et paysages. Nouvelle édition* (Paris: Lecoffre).

    [translation] *A la ville et à la campagne, nouvelles traduites de l'anglais, du danois, du suédois et de l'allemand* (Paris: Hachette).

1887 *Rêveries et réflexions d'un voyageur* (Paris: Lahure).

    [translation] Alfred Tennyson, *Enoch Arden* (Paris: Lemerre).

1888 *Contes populaires de différents pays, recueillis et traduits par Xavier Marmier de l'Académie française*, 2nd ser. (Paris: Hachette).

1889 *A travers les tropiques* (Paris: Hachette).

1890 *Au sud et au nord* (Paris: Hachette).

    Prose et vers 1836–1886 (Paris: Lahure).

1891 *Contes des grand'mères* (Paris: Furne).

    En divers pays (Paris: Firmin Didot).

    [translation] *Histoires russes. Polevoï, Lioudmila [. . .]* (Paris, Calmann Lévy).

1893 *A travers le monde: diverses curiosités* (Paris: Firmin Didot).

    Le Danger d'une intervention. L'Aurore de pourpre (Paris: Gautier).

1

Introduction

The death of Xavier Marmier in 1892 made front-page news in most of the major newspapers and reviews in France, quality and popular press alike. Something of a celebrity in nineteenth-century France, Marmier had made a name for himself in quite a number of fields: as a traveller, translator, comparatist, journalist, novelist, poet, lecturer, linguist, literary critic, ethnologist, social historian, and latterly an outspoken member of the Académie française. He was also, in his later years, a member of the most elite social circles. In retrospect, his greatest achievement was probably as an initiator in bringing an awareness of foreign literatures and cultures to France; but his contribution is so vast that it is impossible to summarise it succinctly.

In many ways, Marmier epitomises a generation of Frenchmen born around the turn of the eighteenth and nineteenth centuries, growing up under the Empire and the Restoration, and coming of age with the advent of the July Monarchy. Born in 1808 to a family which had lost its modest property during the Revolution, Marmier was one of thousands of young men who made their way to Paris from the provinces hoping to make their fame and fortune. He was lucky enough to have influential contacts when he arrived in Paris; these put him in touch with some of the leading lights of the Romantic generation, including Vigny, Hugo, Lamartine, and Sainte-Beuve. Some of his earliest openings were positions in journalism, made possible by the rapid expansion of the press which had been inhibited under Charles X but facilitated by the relative freedom of the laws when Louis-Philippe came to the throne. Thus far, Marmier's early career follows a common pattern, and one which is familiar to, for instance, readers of Balzacian novels which capture so vividly the social and demographic changes of the era. Perhaps unlike a number of his contemporaries, however, Marmier had not had the benefit of a university education. Yet he was sufficiently astute and determined to build on a love of literature and an exceptional linguistic talent to carve a niche for himself that was virtually unique.

His first important foreign travel was to Germany. The destination could hardly have been better chosen in terms of timing—and in terms of his future career. Prior to the nineteenth century, the French had been convinced of their own cultural supremacy and had shown very little interest in things German. However, the success in France of Goethe's *Werther* towards the end of the eighteenth century, followed by the publication of Mme de Staël's *De la littérature considérée dans ses rapports avec les institutions sociales* and *De l'Allemagne*, had aroused general curiosity about life on the other side of the Rhine.[1] Isolated authors or works such as the tales of E. T. A. Hoffmann or Goethe's *Faust I* had penetrated in the late 1820s; but very little else was known about German life or letters. Without knowing a word of German, Marmier set out for Leipzig in the early days of the July Monarchy, and spent most of the next four years travelling around Germany. He learned German with alacrity, and during this period produced an outstanding array of articles, translations, and books, which together provide a comprehensive overview of contemporary literary activity in Germany; much of the work from this phase of his life already shows marked originality.

After this period in Germany, his travels took him to Iceland, Denmark, Sweden, Norway, Lapland, Finland, Russia, Poland, Holland, Switzerland, Austria, Italy, Hungary, Romania, Bulgaria, Moldavia, Turkey, Palestine, Syria, Egypt, Algeria, the USA, Canada, Argentina, Uruguay, and several of the Balkan states. The languages he learned included English, German, Danish, Swedish, Norwegian, Icelandic, Sami, Dutch, Spanish, Russian, Serbo-Croat, and Italian; he also read Anglo-Saxon, and when all else failed, conversed in Latin.

These achievements were all the more remarkable in an age when transport was slow, expensive, uncomfortable, often difficult to organise, and frequently dangerous. His early overland journeys were made before the advent of rail travel, whilst sea crossings were still effected by sailing boat. Even his ventures into neighbouring Germany in the 1830s took him several days, travelling by stagecoach. A useful point of comparison in modern-day terms is the relatively short journey from Paris to Lyon, which today takes some two hours by TGV. In the 1830s, this journey would have taken about three days by stagecoach. This, of course, was a well-worn route with regular and relatively efficient lines of communication. To appreciate the rigour of the longer journeys, account has to be taken not only of the vastly longer distances involved but also of the lack of public highways or organised public transport in many regions. The distances he managed to cover in these con-

---

[1] *De la littérature* was published in 1800 and *De l'Allemagne* first appeared in 1810, although both incurred Napoleon's displeasure. The first edition of *De l'Allemagne* was seized and destroyed, and Mme de Staël was sent into exile. The influence of her work was therefore not fully felt until after the fall of Napoleon.

ditions bear witness not only to his courage and determination, but also to his exceptional physical stamina. Learning foreign languages was also more difficult, in that for many languages no bilingual dictionaries were available; those that were tended to be unreliable. And yet, even in the relatively short periods of time available to him, Marmier managed not only to learn the languages, but to study the culture, institutions, and literatures of the countries he visited, often offering insights that were new within the countries themselves. His publications include over a hundred volumes and countless articles published both in France and abroad. His efforts received public recognition from a number of foreign governments and institutions, including the award of an honorary doctorate from the University of Leipzig; he was made a Knight of the Order of the Danebrog in Denmark, of the Order of the Northern Star in Sweden, and of the Order of King Charles III of Spain. He became a Chevalier and then an Officier de la Légion d'Honneur in France.

Colonial expansion in the nineteenth century and the simultaneous birth of the tourist industry doubtless accounted for some of the popularity of Marmier's work. Yet it would be quite wrong to see him simply as a prototype tourist. The regions he chose to visit were, for the most part, regions not widely known in France, and for which little documentation was readily available. Those who were the real 'prototype tourists' in this early era would usually choose destinations such as Switzerland, Greece, or, for the more adventurous, the Middle East. These travellers would tend to be well off, accompanied by servants, guides, and interpreters, and generally preserved their familiar home comforts wherever possible. They would travel in order to observe landscape or local traditions from the safe vantage point of their own privilege, rather than abandoning this 'outsider' status in order to experience life as lived in the country. Marmier opted for the latter mode of travel: 'Que les grands seigneurs s'en aillent avec leurs palanquins, leurs valets et leur office de restaurant à travers les montagnes de l'Inde et les sables de l'Egypte; pour moi, je n'envie point leur luxe stérile'.[2] He would not only learn the language of the country to be visited and study all that was available in print on the subject, but would deliberately surrender his position as privileged observer to enter into a relationship of exchange and respect, sharing the lives and experiences of the people. Significantly, he was most successful in this when visiting countries which had not been well documented in France (which was the case for most of the countries on which

---

[2] *Du Rhin au Nil*, 2 vols. (Paris: Arthus Bertrand, [1846]) (cited hereafter as *RN*), 2, 36. The title page gives no publication date; in such cases, I have included the date in square brackets if I have been able to locate it in the *Journal général de l'imprimerie* (or similar).

he based his travel narratives). His writings on, for example, the Scandinavian countries, Holland or Russia, are far more interesting than his accounts of his visits to Algeria or the Middle East, in which he constructs himself very much in the mould of 'traveller-as-coloniser'.[3] A further factor which enhances his work is the exceptional quality of his writing. The wealth of information, impressions, and new perspectives on foreign literatures and cultures which he gathered on his travels is conveyed in a style which is scholarly but still accessible; precise yet elegant; and at once scientific and highly poetic.

His motivation to travel is not clear-cut, but appears to have been the result of a combination of factors, or is at least expressed in slightly different ways at different times. The young hero of one of Marmier's novels sets out on a Romantic quest inspired by the tale of the 'fleur de l'air', whose roots do not touch the ground and which takes its sustenance from the dew and flourishes only in pure light. This flower appears to him as 'l'emblème des sentiments les plus élevés, l'emblème de l'idéal' and, he continues, 'je voudrais pouvoir observer cet idéal de la pensée humaine en différentes contrées, et rapporter comme un trophée de mon voyage cette fleur de l'air'.[4] It would seem, however, that Marmier's own impulse to travel and learn about new cultures was determined first and foremost by a love of literature. Doubtless influenced by Mme de Staël, he believed that

> toute littérature est dans sa partie essentielle l'image la plus saisissable d'un caractère national et dans ses formes diverses l'expression plus ou moins durable des circonstances qui agissent sur un pays. Pour en comprendre l'esprit et le développement, pour la suivre dans ses jours de progrès et ses jours de décadence, il faut nécessairement remonter de l'effet aux causes, étudier la nature du peuple dont elle doit refléter la physionomie, et les événements glorieux ou tristes qui doivent la dominer et souvent lui imprimer une autre direction.[5]

Elsewhere, he speaks (in vaguely Baudelairean terms) of travel as an antidote to 'ennui', portraying the individual who does not travel as 'rivé à une

---

[3] These points are amplified in the relevant chapters. Much critical theory has been produced in recent years on travel writing. Further clarification on the 'traveller-as-coloniser' can be found notably in the works of Edward Said (see particularly *Orientalism* (London: Routledge and Kegan Paul, 1979)), and in Mary Louise Pratt's *Imperial Eyes: Travel Writing and Transculturation* (London: Routledge, 1992). See also Gillian Rose, *Feminism and Geography: The Limits of Geographical Knowledge* (Cambridge: Polity Press, 1993).

[4] *Les Voyages de Nils à la recherche de l'idéal* (Paris: Hachette, 1869) (cited hereafter as *Voyages de Nils*), 6.

[5] *Lettres sur la Hollande* (Paris: Delloye, 1841) (cited hereafter as *LH*), pp. x–xi. This volume is now extremely rare: the only copies I have been able to locate are held at the Bibliothèque municipale de Besançon and the Bibliothèque Sainte-Geneviève in Paris.

chaîne qui lui serre les flancs'. Significantly, he adds, travel permits the individual to 's'oublier lui-même'.[6] The fact of identifying with and actually becoming a part of a foreign culture may be seen as an extension of 's'oublier lui-même'. Indeed, a major fascination for Marmier seems to have been difference or other-ness. The majority of European travellers in this period would retain their distance and judge everything by their own national norms, often using difference as a means of imposing their own superiority. Marmier, on the other hand, loved to learn about, and actually become a part of, that which was different. For him, that which was different was almost infallibly something to be respected and cherished (except, notably, where he encountered practices which he considered to infringe basic human rights; his texts are outspoken on issues such as corporal punishment or the abusive treatment of women). He was hostile to anything which we would now call 'globalisation': anything which would tend to diminish or eradicate that essential 'difference' between one people and another. Thus he disliked, for example, the adoption of Parisian fashions and the abandonment of national dress in other countries; he was deeply concerned about the potential consequences of travel by rail or steamboat when they were introduced; he lamented the abandonment of native languages—particularly when this was a facet of colonisation. His strong criticism of colonisation—particularly by England or Russia, but also, for example, the Danish rule of Iceland—is evident everywhere in his work. And yet, despite all this, he remained deeply favourable to French colonisation, apparently unable to reconstruct himself in colonies, or potential colonies, as anything other than a French coloniser. This leads to a number of inconsistencies and apparent paradoxes in Marmier's work which emerge as one of the most fascinating aspects of his life.

Perhaps one of the most fundamental of these paradoxes is his attitude to national identity, but also problematic is his attitude to capitalism. He was broadly against the capitalist ethos, which for a nineteenth-century Catholic and monarchist was not surprising. Capitalism allowed for social mobility and reward for initiative; this was obviously antipathetic to those of the more right-wing persuasion, who believed in a society in which wealth and social position were inherited, having been thus ordained by God. For Marmier, unbridled capitalism led to an obsession with materialism and to self-centred greed, to the detriment of other more worthwhile values. He witnessed it in a mild form amongst the merchants of Hamburg, who shocked him by their lack of interest in art and literature; but nothing

---

[6] *Prose et vers 1836–1886* (Paris: Lahure, 1890), 118–19.

prepared him for his experiences in the United States of America in 1849–50, where it seemed that everything, including human life, was sacrificed to financial profit. Henceforth, the concepts of capitalism and republicanism were indissolubly linked in his mind, and he became intransigent in his right-wing views, denouncing ideas of democracy and universal suffrage. He was never to forgive individuals such as Lamartine and Hugo for their stance in 1848. Yet he himself came from a humble background, and he benefited from the social mobility of the July Monarchy. Indeed, he was profoundly attached to Louis-Philippe and his family and all they stood for, despite the fact that this was a time of increasing capitalist activity in France. It may be that for him, as for so many other French people, the July Monarchy did represent the 'juste milieu'. Certainly he was able, to a large extent, to resolve these problems in his personal life, and to use the climate to pursue a career which he found satisfying, whilst generally rejecting the materialist ethos. Although he was successful and earned enough money to live on, he was not tempted by the fashionable trappings of wealth such as ostentatious apartments, furnishings, carriages, and clothes. His only luxury was his splendid collection of books, but his interest in these was for their content rather than their monetary value; indeed, one of his favourite pastimes was searching for bargains at the stalls of the 'bouquinistes' along the Seine.

A further incongruity in the views expressed and lived can be detected in his attitudes to poverty: in his writing, Marmier is often outspoken about exploitation of the working classes, their living conditions, poverty, and lack of freedom. He was particularly shocked by the poverty and living conditions of workers in England, notably Liverpool, Manchester, and the East End of London. Although his comments are less detailed, they are comparable in force to those made by the radical socialist Flora Tristan in her *Promenades dans Londres*.[7] The grandeur of the architecture of Liverpool, its superb docks, and the riches it produces were worthless in his eyes because of the cost in human terms: 'Moi, j'y ai vu les misères de l'industrie et j'en ai ressenti une tristesse inexprimable'.[8] The discrepancy between rich and poor was something that always shocked him on his travels; it was obviously a universal phenomenon, but the distance between the two was to him a gauge of social justice. Nowhere was he more horrified by the contrast than in England. The hero of one of his novels writes with passionate admiration of the splendours of the West End of London:

---

[7] Flora Tristan, *Promenades dans Londres* (Paris: Delloye, 1840).
[8] *Voyages de Nils*, 282.

Mais, en face de cette sphère lumineuse, les ombres sinistres de l'East-End, les malheureux ateliers de Spitalfields, de Bothnal-Green [*sic*], les allées tortueuses, les cours méphitiques de White-Chapel, les horribles repaires de Saint-Giles. Quand on a pénétré dans ce gouffre de misère et de corruption, dans cet enfer de deux mille âmes, on ne peut plus se complaire dans l'aspect des charmantes habitations de Cavendish-square et de Belgravia. On n'éprouve qu'un sentiment de douleur et de révolte, en songeant que sur le même sol, sous le même gouvernement, dans l'agglomération d'une même race, une telle splendeur rayonne près d'un tel abîme de fortune.[9]

But he seems to have been unable to see these social problems clearly in political terms, despite being generous to a fault with his own money. Anecdotes abound about acts of kindness and charity of the most discreet nature towards those less fortunate than himself; and a number of clauses in his will left money to charitable organisations.

A further and much more marked paradox in his character appears in his relationships with his French contemporaries. Marmier was a charming and handsome man who made friends easily in all ranks of society, and found numerous protectors. His correspondence shows him to have been an affectionate friend and a grateful protégé—at least on the surface. He was generally accepted at face value, and had relatively few known enemies. Yet his personal papers, many of which were bequeathed to the Académie des Sciences, Belles Lettres et Arts de Besançon, and some of which are appropriately entitled *The Night Side of Society*, reveal an unexpected side to his character. Returning home from his dinners with the cream of high society, he would confide to his diary his secret opinions, often highly critical, and record gossip about goings-on amongst his acquaintants. Even long-standing friends such as Sainte-Beuve are not spared. To judge from the evidence, few of his relationships with his contemporaries were based on genuine affection or respect. This may perhaps be explained in part by the fact that these comments were written after 1848, and mostly during the Second Empire or later; they may well bear the mark of Marmier's disillusionment about the lack of loyalty to the July Monarchy on the part of those who sought positions and favours from the new regimes. Even so, his reactions verge on the extreme in some cases. He was clearly aware of this 'étrange assemblage de dispositions totalement contradictoires'[10] in his personality. He noted in his diary the contrast between his 'bienveillance naturelle, [son] désir de complaire à tous' and the 'déplorable faculté pour saisir le côté vicieux ou ridicule [. . .] pour découvrir les prétentions de la vanité sous le

---

[9] *Ibid.*, 309. The first sentence here is printed without a verb.
[10] *Journal*, ed. Eldon Kaye, 2 vols. (Geneva: Droz, 1968) (cited hereafter as *Journal*), 1, 172.

langage de l'honnêteté, l'hypocrisie sous le voile doré de la vertu'.[11] Yet he does not seem to have registered his own frequent hypocrisy: erstwhile friends, mentors, and protectors are as often as not savaged in his private papers. A notable exception to this rule is his family and particularly his parents, who are consistently referred to with veneration.

Here is another apparent paradox: in all his diaries and personal papers, which are the closest we can expect to find to sincere expression, he constantly voices regret at not seeing his family more often. On many of his travels, he wrote of homesickness, his yearning to return to France, and in particular to his native Franche-Comté. And yet he was unable to settle in France, even when circumstances were favourable. In 1838, for example, he was appointed to the newly created post of 'professeur de littérature étrangère' at the University of Rennes, where he proved to be a tremendous success, attracting huge crowds to his lectures. The position also gave him a financial security which he had not previously experienced. Yet he handed in his notice after only a few months in order to join a new expedition to Spitzbergen.

The same trait can be seen in his relationships with women. In terms of his private life, he was a handsome and popular man, and had numerous affairs. He claims to have fallen in love several times, and writes sentimentally about a number of his lovers. He even became engaged once to Maria Oehlenschläger, the daughter of the Danish poet Adam Gottlob Oehlenschläger. But he was unable to commit himself and continued his roving bachelor existence until 1843, when he married Eugénie Pourchet, a young woman from his native Pontarlier. She died in childbirth less than a year later. Marmier was obviously profoundly distressed by her death and never remarried, although he had many more relationships. In his early years, he fathered at least one illegitimate child, but no mention is ever made in his correspondence or his personal papers of this child or of the mother (whom he had left in Iceland several months before the birth). It is tempting to see this unattractive feature of his personality as symptomatic of the social mobility of his era. He recognised that although his 'meilleurs sentiments' drew him to those of more humble origin, 'lorsque je redescends dans les réalités d'un autre échelon social, je suis choqué de ses habitudes et de ses préoccupations vulgaires. [. . .] [J]e dois m'avouer que je ne pourrais me marier dans une de ses familles bourgeoises'.[12] This rather snobbish admission (which is similar in tone to Raphaël's famous admission in *La Peau de chagrin*, although perhaps less materialist in its nature) is not, how-

---

[11] *Journal*, 1, 172.
[12] Ibid., 1,167.

ever, the whole story. He certainly had a number of lovers in the most elite social circles; and yet, despite his own apparent snobbery in the matter, he could not abide pretentiousness on the part of his lovers. In his private papers, he recalls an affair ('la plus triste des amours'[13]) with a marquise who refused to visit him at home in the Latin quarter, both on account of his modest lodgings at that time being on the fifth floor, and because she could not take her carriage into the narrow streets there. She would not consider taking a cab, let alone walking, even accompanied by a servant (walking in Paris at this time suggested poverty and carried a social stigma). Marmier was hurt by this incident, and his next lover was a 'gentille ouvrière'[14] called Anna from the rue de l'Odéon (in the heart of the Latin quarter) who had no objection to climbing his five flights of stairs, and with whom he subsequently remained on good terms. But even the most unpretentious wife would have inhibited that urge to travel and reconstruct his identity in different social and cultural contexts which seems to have been fundamental to his existence. In his published works, references to women can be seen in two ways. On the one hand, general physical descriptions—of ethnic groups, for example—tend to present women in terms of masculine desire, as was common in that era. Comments on individuals, however, are normally characterised by sympathy and respect. Particularly remarkable are his presentations of the achievements of women writers and intellectuals, which, given the attitudes prevalent in France at that time, are exceptionally positive and open-minded.

Marmier's vast output, the variety of his achievements, and his celebrity status made him an influential figure in nineteenth-century France. Although he is now generally neglected, his name still occurs quite frequently, most often in studies of comparative literature analysing the introduction of a particular author or culture to France.[15] Some of his travel narratives are slowly being recognised today as important social documents of the ways in which people lived in particular countries.[16] The (highly inaccurate) edition of a selection of Marmier's private papers from the

---

[13] Ibid.   [14] Ibid.

[15] See, for example, Marguerite Wieser, *La Fortune d'Uhland en France* (Paris: Nizet, 1972); Elizabeth Teichmann, *La Fortune d'Hoffmann en France* (Paris: Minard, 1961); Edmond Eggli, *Schiller et le romantisme français*, 2 vols. (Paris: Librairie Universitaire, J. Gamber éditeur, 1927). Such references are too frequent to list exhaustively here, but are cited in relevant chapters.

[16] Numerous examples will be found throughout the volume. But see, for example, Liljana Todorova's appreciation of Marmier's eyewitness accounts of the various ethnic groups in the Balkan states in his *Lettres sur l'Adriatique et le Monténégro*: L. Todorova, 'Xavier Marmier et les Slaves du Sud: A l'occasion du 80ᵉ anniversaire de sa mort', in Académie des Sciences, Belles Lettres et Arts de Besançon, *Procès-Verbaux et mémoires*, 180, années 1972–3 (1974), 186–98 (193).

post-1848 period partially highlighted the importance of his later career in France,[17] but no one has as yet provided an accurate biography.[18]

The compilation of the building blocks for such a biography is a considerable undertaking, in view not only of the lack of precedent (which can obviate much of the spadework) but also of the great amount of material, both published and in manuscript, to be located and read, and the variety of types of material involving a number of different languages and cultures. Since the achievements which make Marmier such an outstanding figure are now largely forgotten, a greater part of this biography is devoted to a critical assessment of his work than would have been the case if his name were still common currency today. Because his career was largely defined by his travels, the peregrinations of his early years were to be decisive in many respects: they also therefore form an important part of this book.

The research for this biography began with the location and the reading of Marmier's vast published output; this task was made more difficult by the fact that no comprehensive bibliography has ever been compiled, as well as by the fact that many of the works, particularly the earlier ones, have become rare and difficult to track down, necessitating journeys to libraries in different parts of France.[19] The diversity of subject matter covered entailed an equivalent amount of secondary reading in order to give a fair assessment of his achievement in the different subject areas: here, I am indebted to a number of colleagues and friends for their expertise and advice. In a second stage of research, I read as much of Marmier's correspondence as I was able to locate in both published and manuscript form. Marmier's private papers and diaries are conserved in a number of archives

---

[17] *Journal*, ed. Eldon Kaye (see above, n. 10). On the alarming extent of Kaye's inaccuracies, see Wendy Mercer, 'Xavier Marmier and the Contraband Vegetables: Notes on the Published Version of Marmier's *Journal*', *Australian Journal of French Studies*, 28/1 (1991), 29–38. References to Kaye's edition are cited as *Journal*; when there are clear errors in his transcription, references to the manuscripts will be cited in the notes. The nine manuscripts concerned are entitled *Memorandum 1, Memorandum 2, Night Side of Society* 1, 2, 3, 4, 5, 6, and *Common Place Book 2*. The latter volume is conserved at the Bibliothèque Sainte-Geneviève in Paris in the Fonds nordique (MS 3893); the first eight volumes were bequeathed to the Académie des Sciences, Belles Lettres et Arts de Besançon where they are now held (no classification at time of writing). Consultation is usually arranged at the Bibliothèque municipale de Besançon.

[18] Two biographies have been published: Alexandre Estignard, *Xavier Marmier, sa vie et ses œuvres* (Paris: Champion, 1893); and Camille Aymonier, *Xavier Marmier: sa vie, son œuvre* (Besançon: Séquania, 1928). Both are enthusiastic and contain odd pieces of useful information; but both are short and very patchy in terms of Marmier's life and achievements, both contain numerous inaccuracies, and neither has any system of references.

[19] A list of major works appeared previously in Wendy Mercer, *Xavier Marmier: 1808–1892* [exhibition catalogue] (Pontarlier: Les Amis du Musée de Pontarlier, 1992), pp. ii–vii; this has been updated to form the 'Chronology of Selected Publications by Xavier Marmier' at pp. xiii–xvii in this volume.

and libraries in France and abroad, and his own personal library, left in his will to the town of Pontarlier, contains books with many informative dedications, annotations, and inscriptions; several also have letters bound into them. References to Marmier in the correspondence and diaries of his contemporaries have also been useful.

It is my pleasure here to record my thanks to the individuals and institutions who have facilitated my research in one way or another: the British Academy, and in particular the Publications Committee; the Bibliothèque nationale de France; the British Library; the Bibliothèque Sainte-Geneviève and the Bibliothèque nordique; the Archives nationales de France; the Bibliothèque and the Archives de l'Institut de France; the Bibliothèque municipale de Besançon; the Académie des Sciences, Belles Lettres et Arts de Besançon; the National Library of Iceland; the Musée municipal de Pontarlier; the Archives municipales de Pontarlier; the Mairie de Pontarlier; the Archives départementales du Doubs in Besançon; the Archives départementales de la Haute Saône in Vesoul; the library of University College London; Robin Aizlewood; Lucien Bôle; André Damien; François-Xavier Dillmann; Joël Guiraud; Azzedine Haddour; the late Eileen Le Breton; Tom Lundskær-Nielsen; Francesco Manzini; Thomas Munch-Petersen; Svanhildur Óskarsdóttir; Claudine and Jacques Reichard; Jannie Roed; Michael Worton. I would also like to thank all those who have helped me with specific pieces of information, which I have acknowledged in the notes wherever possible. I am particularly grateful to my meticulous copy-editor, Jo Pearce, to Diana Tyson for her advice and support, and to my academic editor, Alison Finch, for her careful reading and her constructive suggestions. The portraits of Marmier are reproduced by courtesy of the Musée municipal de Pontarlier from originals held in their collections, and the photographs of the engravings depicting the expeditions of the Commission du Nord are reproduced by courtesy of the British Library.

2

Formative Years in the Franche-Comté (1808–31)

'Vous me demandez où je suis né', Marmier wrote in 1835. 'Mon Dieu, vous allez trouver cela bien étrange, mais à vrai dire, je ne saurais affirmer si c'est à Nods ou à Pontarlier. Je crois pourtant que c'est à Pontarlier.'[1] If the death of Jean-Marie Xavier Marmier in 1892 made headline news in the national press, the date and place of his birth were certainly not common knowledge, and have given rise to multitudinous biographical errors.[2] The reason for this confusion is not hard to discern. The second of six children, he was born to parents descended from long-established Franche-Comté families with strong Catholic and royalist sympathies. The Marmier family was one of the oldest families of Frasne (Haut-Doubs), a small village which today boasts the smallest TGV station in France (and still counts a number of Marmiers on the electoral register, although none are direct descendants of Jean-Marie Xavier).

Marmier's great-grandfather was one of three brothers who owned some of the best land in Frasne, land which they farmed themselves.[3] The three brothers married three sisters of the Alix family, one of the most influential in the village. The three couples lived together until the size of the families made it impossible for them to continue under one roof. The com-

---

[1] Bibliothèque municipale de Besançon (hereafter BmB), Collection Estignard, MS 1907, Correspondance de Charles Weiss, Lettres de X. Marmier, fo. 815.

[2] Kaye seems to have been the first researcher to have found Marmier's correct dates, although some of the data he gives for siblings are incorrect (see below, nn. 18 and 19). Alexandre Estignard gives 26 June 1808 in *Xavier Marmier, sa vie et ses œuvres* (Paris: Champion, 1893), 12; and Camille Aymonier says 24 June 1808 in *Xavier Marmier: sa vie, son œuvre* (Besançon: Séquania, 1928), 15. Even critics who have written about Marmier relatively recently have tended to perpetuate the early errors; A. Thierry, for example, gives 1808–90 in 'Littérature', in P. Gresser, C. Royer, C. Dondaine, A. Thierry, J. C. Wieber, and J. Boichard, *Franche-Comté* (Paris: Christine Bonneton, 1983), 223–59 (245); M.-F. Briselance gives 1809–93 in *Voyage en Franche-Comté littéraire* (Besançon: Cêtre, 1991), 157.

[3] The information about the family background is gleaned from the following sources: François-Xavier Marmier, *Souvenirs de famille pour mes enfans* (Paris: Plon, 1896); Jean-Marie Thiébaud, 'Les Quartiers de Xavier Marmier, de Pontarlier, membre de l'Académie française' (Pontarlier, 1990: unpublished; conserved in the Archives municipales de Pontarlier); and various other sources, as indicated.

munal existence of this extended family is probably referred to in Marmier's novel *Hélène et Suzanne*:

> On a vu une fois, dans ce village de Frasnes, trois frères épouser les trois sœurs et s'établir ensemble dans la même demeure. Au bout d'un an, il y avait dans la maison trois berceaux. Si un enfant pleurait, celle des jeunes femmes qui se trouvait là, le prenait dans ses bras, l'allaitait, l'endormait.[4]

Marmier's grandfather was one of five boys, two of whom died when they were young without having married. One was considered a wastrel; and one was a priest, who became curate of Villeneuve. Marmier's grandfather, Jean-Louis Marmier, had a difficult life. His land and property were confiscated during the Revolution and, according to Marmier's father, he had to endure a great deal of gratuitous harassment from 'des monstres qui administraient alors et qui se disaient patriotes'.[5] Marmier's father, François-Xavier Marmier, was the godson of his uncle the curate, and it was hoped that he would enter the Church and succeed his uncle. He was sent to school in 1789 and made a promising start to an academic career which would come to an untimely end with the Revolution. His teachers refused to take the new oath imposed on them, and the school was closed, leaving François-Xavier to return to his native village of Frasne to work as a labourer (the family land having been confiscated). Essentially a victim of historical circumstance, he found himself in an impossible situation 'entre le désir d'acquérir de l'instruction et l'impossibilité d'étudier, balancé par les principes sévères que j'avais reçus et d'un autre côté par la licence qui régnait alors'.[6] He was called up to serve in the army, and at first was a willing conscript, since he had been unable to settle to his new life in Frasne. After taking part in one campaign, however, he realised that this life was not for him: 'nous étions les soldats des terroristes et souvent la guillotine tranchait la tête d'un père dont le fils était à l'armée'.[7] Thanks to a fellow conscript named Loiseau, who was studying law in Besançon, François-Xavier Marmier managed to be posted as secretary to the commander of the garrison in Besançon. When Napoleon came to power, it became possible to buy out of the army, and François-Xavier paid a young man named Gloriod from Pontarlier 600 francs to take his place. Gloriod became a captain and an Officier de la Légion d'Honneur, but lost one of his legs in battle.

Unable to settle to life as a labourer, however, François-Xavier found himself a non-stipendiary position as a clerk to a lawyer in Pontarlier, who offered him food and lodging in return for three years' service. It was during

---

[4] *Hélène et Suzanne* (Paris: Hachette, 1862), 132.   [5] F.-X. Marmier, *Souvenirs*, 9.
[6] Ibid., 10.   [7] Ibid.

this period that he met his future wife, Marie-Gabrielle-Honorine Maillot.[8] Her mother, the descendant of a very well-to-do family from Vuillafans, was the widow of the 'procureur du roi' in Pontarlier, Nicolas Maillot, who had died during the Revolution after a period of imprisonment at the Fort de Joux. Mme Maillot took François-Xavier under her wing, and he recalls her in his *Souvenirs* as a 'bonne dame' and a 'tendre mère'.[9] Estignard argues that Marmier probably learned his aristocratic manners from his maternal grandmother,[10] and both Estignard[11] and Aymonier[12] see the character of Mme Martelle in his novel *Les Mémoires d'un orphelin* as a portrait of her:

> Veuve d'un ancien magistrat, elle n'avait pour toute ressource qu'une modique pension de l'État et son petit domaine de la Doye. Dans son chétif état de fortune, elle gardait une fierté naturelle qui n'offusquait personne et que chacun respectait. Le dimanche, quand elle se rendait à l'eglise avec ses vêtements d'apparât, [. . .] on eût dit la dame châtelaine de la paroisse.[13]

Another fictional widowed Mme Maillot, this time originating from Lons-le-Saunier, appears in *Les Voyages de Nils* and is described in terms of her 'grâce modeste'.[14] Although Marmier would not have remembered his maternal grandfather, he may have drawn on family reminiscences of him for the portrait of M. Maillot in *Hélène et Suzanne*, who, apart from sharing the same name, is described as an 'ancien lieutenant au bailliage de Pontarlier'[15] and as an

> homme de cœur, qui était le père des pauvres et qui a été traduit devant le tribunal révolutionnaire. Un de ses accusateurs disait qu'il fallait le condamner comme on avait condamné un citoyen de Paris, par la raison que, en faisant des charités, il pensait moins aux sans-culottes qu'à son Dieu, et qu'il humiliait le peuple par ses prétendus bienfaits.[16]

Despite François-Xavier's temporary lack of paid employment and his lack of personal fortune, he successfully courted Mlle Maillot, and the couple were married in Pontarlier on 30 November 1803.[17] Their first child,

---

[8] The spelling varies between 'Gabriel' and 'Gabrielle' in official documents, the former tending to predominate in the earlier papers.

[9] F.-X. Marmier, *Souvenirs*, 12.   [10] Estignard, *Xavier Marmier*, 228.

[11] Ibid., 227–8.   [12] Aymonier, *Xavier Marmier*, 9–10.

[13] See *Les Mémoires d'un orphelin*, 2nd edn. (Paris: Hachette, 1890), 16–17.

[14] *Voyages de Nils*, 115.   [15] *Hélène et Suzanne*, 159.   [16] Ibid.

[17] 'L'an douze de la République française, le premier frimaire, acte de mariage du Citoyen Jean François Xavier Marmier Practicien demeurant à Pontarlier âgé de vingt-cinq ans né à Frasne [. . .] Et Delle Marie Gabriel Honorine Maillot [. . .]' (extract of marriage certificate). The records office dates this as 30 November 1803, although most calculations would place it on 23 November 1803 (see, for example, <http://www.gefrance.com/calrep/calXII.htm>, accessed 1 December 2005).

Maria Louise Honorine, was born on 30 June 1804 in Pontarlier, followed by Jean-Marie Xavier Marmier on 22 June 1808.[18] The family had to be supported by Mme Maillot for most of this time. At the end of his 'articles', François-Xavier had acquired the necessary experience and qualifications for a legal position, for which he duly applied; his application was strongly supported with glowing references. The 'procureur impérial', however, an uncle of Mme Maillot named Maire, considered it improper to have another member of the family in the same office, and instead of appointing François-Xavier as a solicitor made him a customs officer, although he had to wait some eighteen months before a post actually became vacant. Shortly before Xavier's birth, François-Xavier was sent to Nods to take up a post as 'Receveur des Douanes Impériales' (hence, perhaps, Marmier's early confusion about his birthplace). One of Xavier's earliest memories is of being carried in his mother's arms to the church at Doubs, a small village close to Pontarlier. Shortly afterwards, he and his mother moved to Nods to join François-Xavier, leaving Maria in Pontarlier with her grandmother, where she stayed until Mme Maillot died, in 1816. On 9 September 1812, a younger brother, Claude-Marie Hyacinthe (Mami, or Hyacinthe), was born in Nods.[19] The family obviously spent a lot of time around this period travelling back and forth between Nods and Pontarlier. In 1814, the Austrians marched across the border creating terror amongst the local population. The following year, the young Xavier (now about seven years old), obviously already revealing an innate predilection for foreign travel, decided to visit Switzerland, and without saying a word to his family, set off for the border. A kindly Austrian soldier found him and delivered him safely back home to Pontarlier, to his parents' intense relief.[20]

---

[18] Kaye, in his edition of the *Journal*, claims that Maria was born in 1803, but this is not the case: her birth certificate states 'Le onze Messidor an douze est née le jour d'hier à trois heures de relevée MARIE LOUISE HONORINE MARMIER, fille de Monsieur Jean François Xavier Marmier [. . .] et de Dame Marie Gabrielle Honorine Maillot demeurant à Pontarlier [. . .]'. Although the certificate gives 'Marie' as a first name, she is always referred to as 'Maria' by family (see, for example, F.-X. Marmier, *Souvenirs*).

[19] Much confusion has arisen about the places and dates of birth of the other Marmier children, possibly from the erroneous footnotes inserted by Ulysse Robert in the published version of François-Xavier Marmier's *Souvenirs de famille pour mes enfans* (Paris: Plon, 1896). He asserts that Hyacinthe was born at Dambelin, and that Joseph was born on 20 November; no mention is made of the birth of Léocadie. The dates and places given here are taken from the respective birth certificates (Archives municipales de Pontarlier for Maria and Xavier and Archives départementales du Doubs for the other Marmier children). The error concerning Joseph's birth is repeated by Kaye (*Journal*, 1, 12).

[20] This anecdote is frequently recounted by his contemporaries. See, for example, Louis Peyen, *Xavier Marmier, poème couronné au concours de poésie pour 1895, par l'Académie des Sciences, Belles-Lettres et Arts de Besançon* (Besançon: Jacquin, 1895), 3.

In fact, the legacy of the travel associated with the Napoleonic cam-
paigns may well have proved a determining factor in Marmier's formative
years. In retrospect, he attributed his penchant for foreign travel to an early
contact:

> Dans mon enfance, j'étais le favori d'un vieil officier balafré, qui avait fait les
> campagnes d'Égypte, d'Allemagne et de Russie, et qui me racontait, en
> fumant sa pipe, des choses merveilleuses de la terre d'Orient et des régions du
> Nord. C'est peut-être cette impression première qui a éveillé en moi l'amour
> des voyages.[21]

The theme of an aged military mentor for a young man growing up in the
Franche-Comté who would eventually leave for Paris to seek his fortune is a
familiar one, not only through Stendhal's portrait of the young Julien Sorel
in *Le Rouge et le Noir*, but also through Balzac's numerous accounts of
young men coming to Paris from the provinces with similar ambitions.
These literary portraits were based on reality and reflect the demographic
shift of the time. The population of Paris actually doubled over the course
of the first half of the nineteenth century, and this despite high infant mortality and the ravages caused by malnutrition and disease (most notably, the
cholera epidemic of 1830–1).

Certain other memories can be seen in retrospect to relate to determining factors for the direction of his future career. A reference to 'ma chère
Franche-Comté, où jadis, aux veillées, sous le manteau de la vaste cheminée,
j'ai entendu raconter tant de pieuses traditions et de contes féériques, tant
d'histoires de sorcellerie et d'aventures divertissantes'[22] well befits the future
professor of foreign literature at the University of Rennes, whose inaugural
lecture was a study of comparative folklore of different countries; or the
future honorary president of the Société des traditions populaires, whose
works 'révélèrent au public français des richesses populaires et poétiques
qu'il ne soupçonnait pas'.[23]

On a more general level, a number of his reminiscences of Franche-
Comté life in the early decades of the century help us to understand—partially, at least—the unusual way in which he was later able to form
relationships built on respect with others from all social classes. In particular, they illustrate the way in which wealth or social status were not elements
which would normally preclude social interaction. Indeed, the lack of
respect accorded to those perceived to be inferior in some circles in France

---

[21] *Prose et vers 1836–1886* (Paris: Lahure, 1890), 92.
[22] *A la maison, études et souvenirs* (Paris: Hachette, 1883), 231.
[23] P. S., 'Nécrologie. Xavier Marmier', *Revue des traditions populaires*, 7ᵉ année, 7/11 (1892), 701–2
(702).

is implicitly criticised. For example, he recalls that in his native region, the whole family would sit down at mealtimes to eat together: husband, wife, children, grandchildren, and servants: 'car le domestique n'est point dans nos campagnes, comme dans les villes, un être en dehors du cercle intérieur, que l'on sonne quand on a un ordre à lui donner, et que l'on renvoie à l'antichambre ou à la cuisine'.[24] Nor was this extended family limited to the inclusion of servants:

> Outre les pauvres ambulants, auxquels on ne manquait jamais de donner l'aumône, chaque maison aisée avait ses pauvres attitrés, qui venaient quand bon leur semblait s'asseoir au foyer commun, qui en hiver s'installaient là parfois pendant des semaines, des mois entiers, et que l'on considérait, pour ainsi dire, comme des membres de la famille.[25]

A childhood memory of Nods illustrates the attitudes fostered by his family towards those less fortunate than themselves:

> Dès mon enfance, ma bonne mère m'avait inspiré la charité qui était une de ses vertus. Je me souviens alors de la joie qu'elle éprouva dans notre village de Nods, un dimanche qu'elle avait acheté une grappe de raisin, et qu'elle me vit remettre cette grappe à un pauvre enfant en haillons qui, debout sur le seuil de notre porte, me regardait d'un air suppliant. J'avais alors huit ans.[26]

At the age of eight, he also met his first girlfriend, whose name was Nellie. The two children went out together blackberrying or searching for birds' nests. They missed classes at school, without a scruple, in search of new adventures. When they received presents or treats they shared them. If he upset her, he hated to see her sulk, and preferred to be scolded or hit; they exchanged furtive kisses and promised to marry. In the end, however, she left him for someone with more money![27] From Xavier's recollections of his days at primary school, it is perhaps not surprising that he preferred to escape to have fun with Nellie: in a speech at the annual prize-giving ceremony at the École paroissiale de Sainte-Clotilde in Paris in 1880 he recalls an

> école élémentaire, une pauvre école de village, où nous apprenions péniblement à lire, à écrire, un peu d'arithmétique, un peu de grammaire. C'était tout ce que notre instituteur savait. Très hautaine pourtant était sa voix, très dure

---

[24] *En Franche-Comté: histoires et paysages. Nouvelle édition* (Paris: Lecoffre, 1885) (cited hereafter as *En Franche-Comté*), 19. This work was first published as *Nouveaux souvenirs de voyage et traditions populaires: Franche-Comté* (Paris: Charpentier, 1845) (cited hereafter as *Franche-Comté*).
[25] *En Franche-Comté*, 23.　　[26] *Journal*, 1, 173.
[27] *Esquisses poétiques, par X. Marmier* (Paris: Guyonnet, 1830), 27–31.

sa main armée d'un martinet, et formidable sa colère, surtout quand il
essayait de nous faire comprendre la règle des participes.[28]

As an old man in 1885, Xavier recalls the pleasure of school holidays: 'les
coteaux de Pontarlier, où je courais impétueusement à la recherche d'un nid
d'oiseau [. . .] le village de Frasnes et l'affectueuse maison de Forbonnet
où chaque année j'allais passer une partie de mes joyeuses vacances de
collège'.[29]

If he does not record many agreeable memories of his schooldays, his
childhood otherwise was by all accounts a happy one, despite the frequent
moves occasioned by his father's work, the changing political system, and
the lack of money. The rare reminiscences suggest an emotionally stable and
loving environment. In 1876, for example, he recalls the family home: 'pas
grande, pas brillante, non, mais si douce en son étroite enceinte, et si riche
dans sa pauvreté, si riche par les effusions du cœur, par les tendres enseignements et les innocentes joies de chaque jour'.[30] In his personal papers, he
recalls the 'joies du foyer, du pauvre humble foyer où nous revenions avec tant
de bonheur nous abriter comme des oiseaux'.[31] His father is remembered as
'le meilleur père, le cœur le plus tendre, qui ne vivait que par nous et pour
nous, qui, pour nous élever, avait souffert tant de privations'.[32] He wor-
shipped his mother, who is consistently referred to in reverential terms: 'ma
sainte mère', 'la douce, tendre, sainte femme'.[33]

From Nods, the family moved to Dambelin (Doubs), still leaving Maria
with her maternal grandmother, Mme Maillot, in Pontarlier. In Dambelin,
a second brother, Louis-Marie Joseph Adrien (Louis), was born on 22
September 1815. He was followed by a sister, Léocadie Joséphine (Léa),
born on 31 October 1817. From here, the family moved again to
Blancheroche (Doubs), where another brother, Marie-François Joseph
(Joseph) was born on 16 November 1820. Blancheroche is described by
Marmier in *Hélène et Suzanne* as an 'intéressant village' situated on a
plateau with stunning views over the Doubs valley. Its inhabitants are 'une
communauté d'une centaine de familles, en partie dispersées comme des
familles d'oiseaux dans les prés, au fond des ravins, sur la lisière des bois,
population laboureuse et perspicace, un des types remarquables de la race
de nos montagnards'.[34] François-Xavier recalls that while they were living

---

[28] Paroisse Sainte-Clotilde, École paroissiale libre, tenue par les frères des écoles chrétiennes,
Discours prononcé à la distribution des prix par M. Xavier Marmier de l'Académie française (Paris:
Imprimerie de l'œuvre de Saint-Paul, Soussens et Cⁱᵉ, 1880), 3.
[29] *En Franche-Comté*, 295.
[30] *La Maison* (Paris and Lyon: Lecoffre fils, 1876), 5.
[31] *Journal*, 1, 164.   [32] Ibid.   [33] Ibid., 1, 173 and 168.   [34] *Hélène et Suzanne*, 88.

here, he was demoted because of certain (unspecified) political opinions expressed at the time of the Restoration, and his salary reduced from 1,000 to 800 francs.[35] He recalls that Xavier was to suffer more from this instability than his other sons. Hyacinthe, Louis, and Joseph were to attend a school in Lons-le-Saunier as day pupils, cared for by their sister Maria, in order to minimise the strain on the family's modest income.

The story of Maria seems to be a particularly sad one; although neither sister apparently received any formal education, Maria, as an eldest daughter, seems to have spent most of her life caring for others. She lived with her grandmother in Pontarlier until the death of the latter in 1816; she then went to keep house for her younger brothers at Lons-le-Saunier until they had completed their education (probably around 1838 when Joseph, the youngest son, joined his parents in Colmar). She subsequently spent her winters caring for an elderly aunt until she died. By this time, Maria was too old to marry and have a family of her own. She moved back to stay with her parents as they approached the age of retirement and then cared for them. It is clear that the Marmier siblings were all brought up with a strong sense of family, and they all maintained contact over the years despite their lives taking different courses. Hyacinthe was to serve in the army in Algeria (where he met his wife) and then in the Franco-Prussian War. Louis taught philosophy and then became an 'inspecteur d'Académie' in Dijon; he had a daughter (Marthe) who became a nun in the order of Saint-Vincent de Paul and founded hospitals and orphanages in Santiago, Bethlehem, and Montevideo, where she died. Joseph attended the École Normale and became a teacher; he also took holy orders and acted as chaplain to the forces in the Franco-Prussian War shortly before his death. Léocadie married a well-known local magistrate called Guichard from Lons-le-Saunier and had three children, including a son named Xavier after his uncle, who became a priest in Dôle; one daughter became a nun, and the other married, but died young.[36]

Xavier, in the meantime, began his education at the seminary in Nozeroy (Jura) under the auspices of the priest, M. Épenoy, an old friend of the family. Here Xavier apparently distinguished himself in his first year by winning several prizes, but left the establishment in the course of his second year, much to his father's dismay.[37] François-Xavier, however, recognised his

---

[35] F.-X. Marmier, *Souvenirs*, 14.

[36] See André Pidoux de Maduère, *Le Bon Curé de Dôle 1892–1925. Le Chanoine Xavier Guichard 1849–1925* (Dôle: Edition de la Vie dôloise, 1926), 7–8. I would like to thank M. André Damien, Membre de l'Institut, and a distant descendant of the Marmier family, for bringing this work to my attention.

[37] Marmier eventually left 3,000 francs to this establishment in his will.

son's talent, the 'désir ardent qu'il avait de s'instruire [...], la facilité prodigieuse qu'il possédait',[38] and placed him as a day-pupil at a small school in nearby Cerneux-Monnot (the father, at this stage, still being employed at Blancheroche). He subsequently attended the seminary at Belvoir, where he constantly won the first prizes, and then the seminary at Ornans, where he took a second year of rhetoric. One teacher from this school, Father d'Artois, encouraged Marmier and gave him extra reading.[39] He did not settle here, either, and left (according to his father) because of his 'imagination trop vive, trop ardente'.[40]

It is tempting also to see an influence on the future young traveller in the form of his family's frequent upheavals during his formative years. Many of these moves, moreover, in view of the family's modest income, necessitated a good deal of travel by the cheapest means available: usually by foot. The eldest daughter, Maria, would accompany Hyacinthe, Louis, and Joseph from Lons-le-Saunier to visit their parents in Lorraine for the summer holidays (François-Xavier was appointed to Saulnes in the late 1820s). Xavier recalls walking from Besançon to Pontarlier during his holidays; fortunately, this was a mode of travel he enjoyed:

> En 18.., je m'en allais de Besançon visiter de nouveau mes montagnes natales. Je voyageais seul à pied, avec le bâton de houx à la main et la valise d'étudiant sur l'épaule. L'exiguïté de ma bourse m'eût forcé d'adopter ce mode de pérégrination, s'il n'eût été d'ailleurs d'accord avec mes goûts et mes rêveries nomades. Je n'avais d'autre but, d'autre désir que de suivre lentement tous les détours des sentiers les plus pittoresques, de contempler à mon aise, dans la naïve effervescence de mon imagination, les sites les plus frais et les plus grandioses, de revoir pas à pas les lieux chers à mon enfance, et consacrés pour moi par les souvenirs de ma famille.[41]

This experience was obviously to stand him in good stead for his arduous adventures later on in life: walking, for example, from Cattaro to Montenegro, or crossing Lapland largely on foot. His constant urge to move on to pastures new was to characterise his entire career until old age limited his physical mobility.

In 1828, now aged nineteen, Xavier Marmier left home for Besançon, capital of the Franche-Comté. In the same year, he was introduced to the Académie des Sciences, Belles Lettres et Arts de Besançon by Charles

---

[38] F.-X. Marmier, *Souvenirs*, 15.

[39] See *RN*, 2, 41 and *Impressions et souvenirs d'un voyageur chrétien*, 7th edn. (Tours: Alfred Mame, 1881), 153.

[40] F.-X. Marmier, *Souvenirs*, 15.

[41] *En Franche-Comté*, 295.

Viancin. At a meeting on 8 May he was invited by the president of the Academy to read a poem. The young Marmier explained to the assembled company that the poem had been written to accompany a sum of money which had been collected by a group of young people in the Franche-Comté to help an old man from the area who had worked hard all his life, but who found himself, at eighty years old, in a state of utter destitution.[42] The Academy found that 'ce petit poème, rempli des plus doux sentiments, honore surtout l'âme de son jeune auteur'.[43] It was also noted that 'Quelques observations critiques sur plusieurs passages de cette composition ont été reçues par le jeune poète avec autant de candeur que de reconnaissance'.[44] On 5 June, Marmier appeared again before the Academy to read a poem, this time accompanied by Auguste Demesmay, another young man from Pontarlier (who would later become its Member of Parliament). This second piece was entitled *La Jeune Fille*. F.-J. Genisset, in the official report of the session, noted that in the poem, 'on [. . .] trouve cette douceur de mœurs et de sentiments, cette aimable mélancolie qui fait comme le fond du caractère du jeune poète et l'âme de ses compositions'.[45]

Some weeks later, at a meeting on 3 July, Marmier was admitted for a third time, to read a new poem, entitled *Le Retour*. The secretary noted in the minutes of the meeting that 'On y a remarqué, avec l'imagination et le sentiment qui se trouvent d'ordinaire associés dans les compositions de l'auteur, une plus grande correction de style que dans ses pièces précédentes'.[46] *Le Retour* was published in the Mémoires of the Besançon Academy in 1828.[47]

Through his contacts with Charles Viancin and the Academy, Marmier also met Charles Weiss, curator of the Bibliothèque municipale de Besançon, who was to become his lifelong friend and protector.[48] Weiss offered him a modest position as assistant librarian which he accepted; once again, however, he was unable to settle. His letter of resignation to Weiss is revealing:

> Les nouvelles dispositions de M. le Maire de Besançon viennent de détruire en un instant toutes mes espérances. Après avoir épuisé les ressources de

---

[42] Alfred Ducat, *Les Débuts littéraires de Xavier Marmier* (Besançon: Jacquin, 1893), 6.
[43] Ibid., 7. [44] Ibid. [45] Ibid., 8. [46] Ibid., 11.
[47] ' "Le Retour", stances, par M. Marmier, de Pontarlier' in Académie des Sciences, Belles Lettres et Arts de Besançon, *Séances publiques des 28 janvier et 24 août 1829* [*sic*] [for *Séances publiques des 28 janvier 1828 et 25 août 1828*] (Besançon: Daclin, 1829), 165–6.
[48] Charles Weiss (1779–1867), bibliophile, bibliographer, and man of letters. He became a member of the Besançon Academy in 1807, and was appointed curator of the library in 1812. He became a corresponding member of the Académie des Inscriptions et Belles-Lettres in 1832.

mes amis et prolongé bien trop avant les sacrifices de mes parents, je ne suis pas décidé à les solliciter encore et je ne veux pas promettre de vivre avec 400F.

Je ne vous tromperai donc pas. J'aurais pu travailler avec vous et attendre une occasion favorable de prendre un meilleur parti, mais non, cette conduite répugne autant à ma délicatesse qu'elle pourrait répugner à vous-même. Si l'on veut me nommer, ne me faites pas nommer. Je n'accepterais pas. Cette place convient à tout jeune homme qui aura un peu de fortune et qui aimera les lettres, et je l'aurais embrassée avec ardeur, si j'avais été dans une autre position.

Mon parti est bien pris. Et je le suivrai. J'irai chercher ailleurs un moyen d'existence qui me fuit ici depuis 5 ans. J'entrerai dans une vie aventureuse, dans une carrière vaste mais pénible, un autre avenir que celui qu'aurait pu me donner Besançon, et si je dois échouer, si je dois vivre pauvre, misérable, j'aime mieux l'être dans un autre pays que dans le mien. Et puis, il n'est pas défendu d'oser, et quand on est jeune et qu'on a du courage, il vaut mieux l'employer à gravir une montagne qu'à se traîner dans les sentiers des autres.

Vous devez deviner mon but et mon projet. Il est peut-être téméraire, extravagant. Mais j'ai 20 ans, et dussé-je, comme Gilbert, mourir dans un hôpital, que la volonté de Dieu soit faite!

Je n'ai pas osé vous dire tout ceci, mais si je puis encore vous être utile, je ne demande pas mieux que de vous consacrer tout le temps possible. J'attends d'ailleurs de l'intérêt de votre part, quoique je sente combien je vous fais souffrir. Mais moi je souffre encore bien plus de me trouver sans existence au moment où je devrais me croire tranquille. Et si cette année n'avait pas été employée au service d'un ami, n'aurais-je pas encore le droit de souffrir pour avoir perdu tant de belles heures inutilement?

Adieu. Quelle que soit l'idée que je vous donne, et la part que vous preniez à ma position, je vous aimerai toujours comme le premier homme qui ait jeté dans mon âme de nobles idées de gloire et de vertu. Je vous regretterai toujours, ainsi que Viancin, parce que votre amitié désintéressée m'a souvent rendu très heureux. Je vous consacrerais encore toute ma vie si elle pouvait vous être de quelque prix, mais je ne puis pas croire que vous ne fassiez un meilleur choix pour vous et que vous ne soyez plus content d'un jeune homme laborieux que d'un cerveau exalté qui n'a que des idées de poésie et d'imagination en vue.

Adieu. Je ne serai pas chez moi aujourd'hui, mais quand j'y rentrerai, je serai[s?] content d'y trouver une lettre de vous.[49]

The main reason for his resignation appears, on the surface at least, to have been the humble salary. Four hundred francs a year was not a great deal of money, even in those days: the average pay at this time was about two francs a day for a male worker and one franc for a female worker. Since he was

---

[49] BmB, Collection Estignard, MS 1907, Correspondance de Charles Weiss, Lettres de X. Marmier, fo. 731.

single, he would probably just have managed on this income, since the absolute minimum necessary for a family of three to survive was estimated at 800 francs a year; but he would have been on the breadline. There is also, however, a strong sense of restlessness, and the desire to leave the provinces and head for the capital. The decision to resign was obviously not an easy one: Marmier was patently aware of the risk he was taking in leaving a secure if humble position in the library. Growing numbers of ambitious young men anxious to make fame and fortune through their writing flocked to Paris at this period. The figure of the young artist struggling in a garret was not only a symbol of the Romantic generation, but was firmly based in reality. Those without any private income struggled to survive, and significant numbers perished after failing to establish themselves in the literary world.[50]

He was furthermore fully conscious of the extent of his debt to Weiss for the confidence expressed in his abilities as much as for the actual post in the library. In fact, the experience gained at the Besançon library must have stood him in good stead for his later posts as librarian first at the Ministère de l'Instruction publique, and then at the Bibliothèque Sainte-Geneviève. It may also have been decisive in forming that love of books which is illustrated by his own personal library, now conserved at Pontarlier. The gratitude to Weiss was never forgotten, and the two were to become close friends over the years. In the early days, Marmier would send books purchased on his travels to enhance the library's collections; in subsequent years, he would dine with Weiss every time he returned to the Franche-Comté, and the two men maintained a regular correspondence, much of which is conserved at the Bibliothèque municipale de Besançon. Weiss is one of the very few individuals close to Marmier to have escaped the savage criticism which almost always appears as the reverse side of gratitude on Marmier's part. Weiss seems to have been aware of this unattractive side of Marmier's personality quite early on. In his journal for 1833 he notes that although the young man has 'esprit', 'il a peu de délicatesse et de sensibilité'. In particular, he recalls in terms of strong disapproval that at the time when Viancin introduced Marmier to the Besançon Academy, treating him like a son, Marmier amused himself by making 'des propos plus qu'indécents sur son bienfaiteur' and pouring scorn on Viancin's own poetry. Together with an accomplice named Renaud, Weiss judges, 'ils débutent mal mais ils peuvent encore se corriger'.[51]

---

[50] For example, Jacques-Imbert Galloix, Hégésippe Moreau, and Aloysius Bertrand, amongst others.

[51] Charles Weiss, *Journal 1823–1833*, ed. Suzanne Lepin, Cahier d'études comtoises 29, Annales littéraires de l'Université de Besançon 257 (Paris: Les Belles Lettres 1981), 319–20.

A further letter written to Weiss, presumably the following week in response to a letter of reply to the above-mentioned resignation letter, contains many similar elements of drama and hyperbole:

Mardi.

Je n'ai pas pu aller vous voir à la bibliothèque lundi, mon bon Monsieur Weiss. Lundi, je ne voulais pas voir le monde que j'y suppose, et le soir, je ne savais si vous pourriez me recevoir chez vous. J'y suis allé aujourd'hui, mais vous n'y étiez pas. J'ai pourtant tant de choses à vous dire qu'il me tarde de vous voir.

Vous n'avez donc pas eu besoin de moi, vous m'auriez fait dire d'aller travailler avec vous; j'y aurais volé. Je ne sais quel moyen je pourrais trouver pour vous prouver combien je vous aime et combien je suis reconnaissant de ce que vous avez fait pour moi. Quoique je vous quitte, vous êtes encore tout ce que j'estime le plus au monde, tout ce que je voudrais le plus tâcher d'approcher. Soyez-en sûr, vos principes grandiront dans mon âme, votre souvenir, vos conseils, me donneront un élan qui répondra peut-être à votre désir. Oui, je me formerai un beau caractère, je deviendrai grand par mes sentiments, et si je meurs sans gloire, je ne veux pas mourir sans emporter les regrets de l'estime. Mon langage ressemble à de la flatterie, et dans la position où je suis, abandonné sans ressource, vous flatter pour vous intéresser à moi serait si lâche. Non, non, ne le croyez pas, vous êtes mon maître, mon père, ce nom me permet tout; oubliez-moi, rejetez-moi, vous le serez encore, et jamais je n'oublierai combien j'étais heureux et plein d'espoir quand je vous le donnai et combien je fus fier quand vous l'acceptâtes.

Je pars demain pour un voyage de quelques jours, c'est le dernier que je fais dans mon pays; après cela, après cela!!! Adieu pour longtemps, mon beau pays, adieu notre Franche-Comté. Oh! que le ciel me protège! je voudrais mourir pour donner un nom de plus à notre histoire, pour qu'un ami, pour qu'un Franc-Comtois puisse dire avec plaisir qu'il m'a connu.

Exaltation, témérité, espoir et découragement, tout se ballotte dans cette tête qui s'est longtemps échauffée dans le silence, et qui éclate maintenant, mais je ne compte ni sur mes talents, ni sur aucune ressource étrangère, je compte sur mon courage. Je veux vivre—vivre dans toute l'étendue de ce mot, de cette vie de l'âme, de cette existence intellectuelle, ou héroïque qui animait tous ces hommes envoyés à la postérité.

Adieu, vous me plaignez peut-être—oui, il faut me plaindre, car je me crois arrivé à un moment de crise où toute ma vie va se décider, où le sort va juger si je dois être enfin un homme ou une brute. Il faut me plaindre, il faut m'aider; malgré cette fermentation d'idées qui m'éloigne de tant d'êtres, je sens combien je serais heureux de m'asseoir près de quelqu'un qui me comprendrait, de lui ouvrir mon cœur, de lui parler avec cette ardeur qui me ronge, de lui demander encore ses conseils, ses vœux, tout ce qu'il pourrait me donner.[52]

---

[52] BmB, Collection Estignard, MS 1907, Correspondance de Charles Weiss, Lettres de X. Marmier, fos. 733–4.

Charles Weiss was a close friend of Charles Nodier, who also hailed from the Franche-Comté, then employed as chief librarian at the Arsenal library in Paris. Nodier was at this time a highly influential figure in the literary world: his salon at the Arsenal was an important centre of literary life in the capital where, in a relaxed atmosphere, influential figures of the Romantic movement were welcomed alongside promising young talents who included, in their turn, Balzac, Dumas, and Musset. When Weiss visited Nodier in September 1828, he had taken with him a letter from Marmier, which does not seem to have made a very favourable impression on Nodier. Weiss nevertheless, anxious as to what might become of Marmier in Paris, wrote to Nodier on 10 February 1829 about Marmier's imminent arrival in the capital:

> Le jeune Marmier, dont je t'ai porté au mois de septembre une lettre que tu as trouvée extravagante, vient de quitter brusquement la bibliothèque, où je lui avais procuré une petite place de 400fr, en attendant mieux, pour aller à Paris tenter les aventures. Je crains que tu n'aies deviné le sort qui attend ce malheureux jeune homme, quand tu m'en parlais dans une de nos promenades sur le boulevard; je soupçonne que c'est le propriétaire du *Voleur* qui l'a mandé à Paris, en lui promettant de l'associer à cette entreprise. En partant, il m'a laissé une lettre dans laquelle il me dit que je n'entendrai jamais parler de lui, s'il ne parvient pas à se faire un nom honorable dans les lettres. Je suppose qu'il ira te voir. Fais à cet égard ce que tu croiras convenable.[53]

Obviously this last conjecture was confirmed, and Nodier decided to take the young man under his wing. Three weeks later, Weiss wrote to Nodier thanking him for the interest he had taken in Marmier, and for the intention he expressed of finding him a position which would pay him enough to live on while leaving him sufficient free time to pursue his literary interests.[54]

Through Nodier, Marmier made a number of highly important contacts, among them Alfred de Vigny, and Paul Lacroix the bibilophile, later to become librarian at the Arsenal. Vigny was obviously impressed by Marmier and undertook to find him a post, at first with little success. On 7 August 1829, he wrote to Édouard de La Grange:

> Vous me faites grand plaisir en me témoignant tant de contentement de ce bon petit Mr Marmier. Je fais tout au monde pour lui trouver l'emploi dont il est si digne et je ne trouve que des gens à argent qui n'ont point d'idées à dicter,

---

[53] Léonce Pingaud, 'Lettres de Weiss à Charles Nodier', Académie des Sciences, Belles Lettres et Arts de Besançon, Année 1887 (Besançon: Jacquin), 265, letter 36. This letter is also quoted by Kaye (also giving Pingaud as his source) who transcribes the first line as 'dont je t'ai parlé au mois de septembre dans une lettre que tu as trouvée extravagante' (*Journal*, 1, 15). This transcription is incorrect.

[54] Pingaud, 'Lettres de Weiss à Charles Nodier', 267, letter 37.

ou des gens à idées qui n'ont point d'argent à donner. Cela me fâche bien.
Pourtant je ne me décourage pas.[55]

Thanks to this letter, it was in fact Édouard de La Grange who eventually
found employment for Marmier as secretary and librarian to his father-
in-law, the comte de Caumont-La-Force, in Normandy. François-Philibert-
Bertrand, comte de Caumont-La-Force, later took the title of 'duc' after the
death of his elder brother, Louis-Joseph Nompar, in 1838. Marmier recalls
the elder brother as being 'un gentilhomme de l'ancien régime, élégant, poli,
généreux, hospitalier, et toujours fort endetté'.[56] The younger brother,
Marmier's employer, on the other hand, is described as being 'dur,
cauteleux, rapace, avare':[57] he engaged in all kinds of dubious speculations
in order to increase his wealth. He also had a sharp tongue. Marmier
describes his experiences at Chanday as having been 'pénibles'.[58] His only
pleasant contact there would appear to have been with his employer's second son, who used to visit Marmier with requests for poems to present to
his mistresses, usually actresses at the Vaudeville or Gymnase theatres in
Paris! This, however, contrasts strongly with the picture drawn of life at
Chanday in Marmier's first collection of poems, the *Esquisses poétiques*. In
a poem simply entitled 'Chanday' and dedicated to his employer ('A M. le
Comte de Caumont'), he refers to 'mes hôtes si bons que j'aimerai toujours',
their 'gaieté folâtre' and their 'sages discours'. The end of his period of
employment there is regretted in the poem and apostrophised as a 'doux
repos que j'avais ici reçu des cieux'.[59] Even allowing for a certain degree of
prudent flattery for a young man seeking his fortune, the difference in tone
between his poem and his later recollections is pronounced, and suggests a
more hypocritical side to the effusive young man of the early correspondence
and poetry.

At any rate, the employment with Caumont-La-Force clearly left
Marmier with time on his hands to write poetry. 1830 saw the publication
of his first collection, *Esquisses poétiques*, and a copy preserved at the
Bibliothèque Spoelberch de Lovenjoul (now at the Institut de France) bears
the inscription: 'A notre charmant poète, à mon protecteur et ami: M.
Alfred de Vigny. Hommage de l'auteur'. A letter addressed to Vigny
expresses his gratitude: 'C'est vous qui m'avez aidé! qui m'avez soutenu, qui
m'avez mis où je suis . . . J'attends à vous voir, pour me retremper de nouveau l'âme et reprendre espoir et courage'.[60] A note in the *Revue de Paris*,

---

[55] *Œuvres complètes de Alfred de Vigny. Correspondance (1816–1835)* (Paris: Louis Conard, 1933),
186–7.
[56] *Journal*, 1, 222.   [57] Ibid., 1, 223.   [58] Ibid.   [59] *Esquisses poétiques*, 51–8.
[60] Vigny, *Correspondance (1816–1835)*, 233.

which both Aymonier and Dupuy believe to have been either inspired or dictated by Vigny, alerts its readers to the fact that 'un très-jeune homme, M. Marmier, vient de publier un recueil de poésies où l'on remarque un talent incontestable'.[61]

The collection was reviewed by Sainte-Beuve in *Le Globe*. The tone of the review is predominantly favourable, and Sainte-Beuve writes of 'des vers harmonieux' and 'beaucoup de pièces pleines de grâce et de naturel'. Marmier, he says, 'a exprimé ces sortes de rêves avec une vérité douce et vive de fraîcheur'. He finishes, however, on a note of caution for the young poet: 'Cette source d'inspiration est bien monotone et ne tarde pas à s'épuiser'.[62] An undated letter to Sainte-Beuve referring to a work by the latter, illustrates the importance of this early review for the young Marmier:

> Mon cher ami,
>
> Ce matin, dans une de mes expéditions journalières de bouquinotage, une de mes dernières passions, si ce n'est la toute dernière, j'ai trouvé un délicieux volume: Vie, poésies et pensées de Joseph Delorme, Delangles, 1829. Il est rare, ce livre, très rare, et tout de suite, je l'ai acheté, sans marchander, avec un tressaillement de cœur, comme si j'achetais en même temps l'année lointaine, l'année de jeunesse, où j'allais, pauvre rimeur, mon humble recueil à la main, chercher rue Notre-Dame-des-Champs, mon maître.[63]

This review was to mark the start of a long friendship between the two men: Marmier would spend a great deal of time with Sainte-Beuve when he was in Paris. He wrote, in the early years at least, lengthy letters from travels, frequently including confidential details of love affairs and his own, often as yet unpublished, translations of the literature he discovered; many of these were to have a direct influence on Sainte-Beuve's own writing.[64] This did not, however, prevent Marmier from judging his friend's private life rather harshly, noting that he was

> l'un des hommes les plus lubriques que j'aie jamais connus, d'une lubricité qui, ne pouvant pas s'apaiser par l'action physique, reste dans le cerveau et le tourmente. Un de ses malheurs aussi est d'être affligé d'une figure qui ne

---

[61] [Anonymous], 'Chronique', *Revue de Paris* (cited hereafter as *RP*), 24 (1831), 186–92 (192). Both Aymonier (*Xavier Marmier*, 169) and Ernest Dupuy (*Alfred de Vigny, ses amitiés, son rôle littéraire*, 2 vols. (Paris: Société française d'imprimerie et de librairie, 1912), 2, 171) quote the review, although without any references.

[62] Charles Augustin Sainte-Beuve, *Premiers Lundis*, 3 vols. (Paris: Michel Lévy, 1874), 2, 61–2. The article originally appeared in 'Esquisses poétiques, par X. Marmier', *Le Globe*, 7e année, no. 81 (1831), 324.

[63] Spoelberch de Lovenjoul (now at the Bibliothèque de l'Institut de France (hereafter BIF)), D606, X, Lettres adressées à Sainte-Beuve, fo. 153.

[64] See Wendy Mercer, 'Xavier Marmier and the German Influences in the Work of Sainte-Beuve', *Revue de littérature comparée*, 60 (1986), 307–20.

s'accorde point avec ses galantes ardeurs [. . .] S'il est malheureux, c'est une
punition du ciel.[65]

In the meantime, towards the end of 1829, Marmier's father was
appointed to a post at Tellancourt, a move which necessitated a difficult
journey in the harsh winter. Marmier recalls visiting the family there in
1830, 'un vilain morose village de la Moselle'.[66] Shortly afterwards, the family was forced to move again when Marmier senior was transferred to
Saulnes, where he spent many happy years, having finally achieved the promotion for which he had worked so hard. Marmier visited the family in
Saulnes, a 'joli petit endroit au fond d'une pittoresque vallée'[67] and went for
walks to Longwy, where he had a girlfriend named Louise Hébert ('pauvre
chère Louise'[68]). The young couple were very much in love but, according to
Marmier, marriage was out of the question since neither of them had any
money to establish a household. He left Saulnes for Paris, and from there set
off on his travels; she married someone else, and later died of a chest ailment. A handsome and obviously charming individual, Marmier had a considerable number of romantic attachments over the years: in a letter to
Weiss, he claims that 'j'ai eu mon premier amour à 8 ans! je commençais de
bonne heure!'.[69]

The July Revolution of 1830, which brought Louis-Philippe to the
throne in place of the increasingly reactionary Charles X, proved decisive in
a number of ways for the Marmier family. Looking back on events, Marmier
recalled it as a moment of tremendous optimism:

> En 1830, encore quelle joie! Et quelle confiance dans un nouvel avenir! [. . .]
> C'était une nouvelle ère qui s'ouvrait sous de plus riantes couleurs. C'était une
> royauté libérale qui succédait à une monarchie rejetée par la majorité de la
> nation. [. . .] En très peu de temps, la confiance était rétablie, les affaires
> avaient repris leurs cours, et personne ne craignait ni pour sa sécurité, ni pour
> ses biens.[70]

It was in the early days of the July Monarchy, rather than under the
Restoration, that Marmier senior, much to his surprise, obtained his long-
awaited promotion. For Xavier too it was important. The press, which had
suffered massive censorship under the last days of Charles X, began to
flourish. On 3 May 1831, a new newspaper was founded, *L'Indépendant,
journal constitutionnel de la Haute-Saône*. It was to appear twice weekly,

[65] *Journal*, 1, 308.
[66] Ibid., 1, 253.   [67] Ibid.   [68] Ibid.
[69] BmB, Collection Estignard, MS 1907, Correspondance de Charles Weiss, Lettres de X. Marmier,
fo. 801.
[70] *Journal*, 1, 63–4.

and Marmier, who had been in Vesoul since April, was taken on as editor.[71] The town possessed only one printing press, so the existing weekly, the *Journal de la Haute-Saône*, had to be suspended. *L'Indépendant*, however, survived for only thirty issues, unable to compete with the flourishing Parisian press, and folded on 16 August. While in Vesoul, Marmier obviously had some time on his hands, for he wrote a number of poems which completed the slim volume of *Nouvelles Esquisses poétiques*, published towards the end of 1831.[72] Spending the remainder of August and September 1831 in Vesoul, Marmier then returned to Besançon where he was appointed as editor and ran *L'Impartial* from 6 November 1831 for approximately six months.[73] This had been a paper of the opposition until the July Revolution, and had been suspended immediately prior to that revolution (as had many other papers and reviews, under the draconian censorship of the last days of Charles X). The July Revolution allowed its reinstatement. However, in a letter to his father dated 17 May 1832 (quoted by Estignard but now lost), Marmier states his intention of resigning from the newspaper on moral grounds. It appears that he was given very little editorial independence, and that decisions regarding the political line of the newspaper were taken by shareholders 'qui n'écoutent que leurs passions et leur intérêt'.[74] This scenario is also familiar from, for example, such novels as Balzac's *La Peau de chagrin*; but here Marmier's career diverges from that of the typical Balzacian hero in that he refuses to be associated with the more sordid aspects of journalism.

During this period in Besançon, he spent time teaching himself Italian,[75] and he must also have spent some time on historical research, for he entered a competition organised by the Besançon Academy. This involved writing an essay on the following subject: 'Quels sont les événements qui ont eu lieu en Franche-Comté, depuis la réunion de cette province au duché de Bourgogne, opérée par le mariage de Marguerite de Flandres avec Philippe le Hardi, jusqu'à la fin de la domination des ducs de Bourgogne de la maison de Valois, c'est-à-dire depuis l'an 1369 jusqu'à l'an 1482, époque de la mort de

---

[71] This post is mentioned by Estignard (*Xavier Marmier*, 25), who wrongly entitles it *L'Indépendance*. The information given here is gleaned from the copies of the newspaper held at the Archives départementales de la Haute-Saône in Vesoul.

[72] *Nouvelles Esquisses poétiques,* par X. Marmier (Vesoul: Zaepffel; Paris: chez les marchands de nouveautés, 1831).

[73] Marcel Vogne, *La Presse périodique en Franche-Comté des origines à 1870*, 7 vols. (Vanves: M. Vogne, 1977–81), 3 (1978), 431. According to Vogne, Marmier was officially in charge of the newspaper until 30 September 1832, but it would seem from other sources (see chapter 3) that he left somewhat earlier.

[74] Estignard, *Xavier Marmier*, 26.   [75] *Journal*, 1, 170.

Marie de Bourgogne, épouse de l'empereur Maximilien?'. At a meeting of the Academy on 16 August 1832, the secretary, Bourgon, read out the verdict on the winning essay:

> L'auteur du no. 1 n'a pas consulté toutes les sources et n'a pas indiqué celles où il a puisé; son mémoire présente trop de généralités et n'est pas assez local. Il paraît avoir soigné la forme plus que le fond; mais cette négligence est abondamment rachetée par l'intérêt qui s'attache à ses récits, par la vérité des portraits, le mouvement varié des tableaux et l'élégance du style.[76]

A public announcement was made on 24 August by the Secretary of the Academy to the effect that Xavier Marmier, editor of *L'Impartial*, had been awarded first prize in the competition.

Thus ends the early phase of Marmier's career. His next move was to pack his bags and set off for Germany—a trip that would determine the path of his future career.

---

[76] Ducat, *Les Débuts littéraires*, 16.

3

Germany (1832–5): 'la rêveuse, la poétique, la mélancolique Allemagne'[1]

'Je suis à Leipzig depuis trois mois', Marmier wrote to the bibliophile Paul Lacroix, 'mon but n'est autre chose que d'apprendre au fond l'allemand, de connaître aussi bien que je pourrai l'Allemagne, et de retourner en France'.[2] In point of fact, Marmier was to spend some two years in the German-speaking world, with Leipzig as his base, returning only briefly to France in the intervening period. Immersing himself in the language and culture of these countries, Marmier would meet a number of the great literary figures of the day (including Tieck, Schwab, Uhland, the brothers Grimm, Chamisso, Holtei, and many others[3]). The publications resulting from his work here established his reputation as an exceptional linguist, travel writer, literary critic, and translator: in retrospect, he must be viewed as the most influential figure in Franco-German literary relations of the era.

In the early 1830s when Marmier first arrived there, Germany did not exist so much as a country per se, but rather as some thirty-eight different states and free towns united only by the German Confederation, which had been set up at the Congress of Vienna in 1815 under the auspices of Austria. Austria at this point was at the heart of the mighty Austro-Hungarian empire. Poland was divided between Russia, Austria, and Prussia. In 1828 the Zollverein had begun to take shape, although at this stage only a part of Hesse and some smaller states had been absorbed. During Marmier's first visit, Saxony, Bavaria, Baden, and Württemberg were all independent, but

---

[1] *Un été au bord de la Baltique et de la mer du Nord* (Paris: Hachette, 1856), 1.

[2] Bibliothèque de l'Arsenal, Fonds Paul Lacroix, M848, letter 1. This letter is dated 12 January 1832 (the letter is mentioned by Kaye in his edition of the *Journal* (1, 18), who mistakenly dates it 14 January) but as all the evidence suggests that Marmier was elsewhere in 1831 and early 1832, it would seem that Marmier may have written 1832 in error for 1833.

[3] Ludwig Tieck (1773–1853) was probably the most eminent of Marmier's German contacts: a highly prolific and influential author and thinker, he was one of the foremost early Romantics. Gustav Schwab (1792–1850) was a literary editor, anthologist, and poet (although his poetry is now largely forgotten). Ludwig Uhland (1787–1862) is remembered as one of the founders of philological and literary studies in German and as a prominent Romantic poet of the Swabian School. Adelbert (sometimes written Adalbert) von Chamisso (1781–1838) was a natural scientist and Romantic author of French origin. Karl von Holtei (1798–1880) was an actor, dramatist, poet, and novelist.

joined the union in the course of the next two years. It was during 1834 and
subsequently with the development of the German railways that the union
really came into being. Marmier was there to witness some of these
changes, although the full force of their political significance seems to have
struck him only a few years later.

In the meantime, however, Marmier was wholeheartedly embracing the
task he had set himself. Intellectual activity notwithstanding, he covered a
great deal of ground in physical terms alone between 1832 and 1833, taking
in Weimar, Leipzig, Dresden, Potsdam, Berlin, Bamberg, Nüremberg,
Stuttgart, and Jena. He appears to have spent the final months of 1833 in
France before returning to spend a further year in the region: this time, in
addition to returning to many of his earlier haunts, he also visited
Augsburg, München, Vienna, Göttingen, Baden-Baden, and the Rhineland.
Although his visits to Germany were to become less frequent after 1835 as
he ventured to other parts of the world, he was to retain a particular affection for the German-speaking countries. He travelled through Germany in
1837 on the way to Copenhagen, and in 1838 on his return from Sweden. He
passed through Germany in 1839, and again in 1840, staying in Leipzig on
both occasions: in 1839, he was awarded an honorary doctorate from the
University of Leipzig. An inscription in a book conserved in his library
shows that he visited Cologne in 1843, and he travelled through Austria
again in 1845. He spent the winter of 1852–3 in Hamburg, returning in the
spring through Bavaria and the Tyrol. He also spent the summer of 1855 visiting Berlin, Danzig, Rügen, Hamburg, and Heligoland. This is the journey
upon which *Un été au bord de la Baltique et de la mer du Nord* (1856) is
based, and also a significant part of the *Voyage pittoresque en Allemagne*
(1859–60).[4] In 1856, he made an excursion to the Black Forest with his long-
standing mistress, Ebba.[5] A simple inscription in a book in his library tells
us that he was in Leipzig at some point during 1863, and an entry in his private papers tells us that in 1864 he travelled to Copenhagen via the Mosel
and Saar valleys, Koblenz, Cologne, and Hamburg. Before returning to
Paris, he visited Ludwigslust, Leipzig, and Frankfurt.[6] This journey formed
the basis for his *Souvenirs d'un voyageur* (1867).[7]

---

[4] *Voyage pittoresque en Allemagne*, 2 vols. (Paris: Morizot, 1859–60) (cited hereafter as *Voyage pittoresque*).

[5] This presumably formed the basis for *La Forêt noire* (Paris: Charles Douniol, 1858).

[6] *Journal*, 1, 312.

[7] *Souvenirs d'un voyageur*, 2nd edn. (Paris: Didier, 1867) (cited hereafter as *SV*). Curiously, I have never found any trace of a first edition (either in library catalogues or in the *Bibliographie de la France*).

The timing of his departure to Germany, albeit 'sans savoir un mot d'allemand',[8] was providential: never before had the French been so avid to learn about foreign literatures and cultures—and Germany was a particular focus of attention. Prior to the nineteenth century, the French had shown very little interest in things German. Various factors, however, including the success of Goethe's *Werther* and later *Faust I*, Mme de Staël's *De l'Allemagne*, and the Hoffmann vogue which began in the late 1820s, had all created a new demand for information about German life and letters. In 1826, a new review, the *Bibliothèque allemande*, was founded to cater exclusively for this new-found interest. In 1827 it became known as the *Revue germanique*, and between 1829 and 1834 it adopted the title *Nouvelle Revue germanique*: it was this review which published the bulk of Marmier's early articles. It would seem that Marmier was probably introduced to the review by Édouard de La Grange, the Germanist of Dutch extraction who had been instrumental in finding Marmier his post with Caumont-La-Force at Vigny's behest.

Marmier's first article in the review, published in August 1832, was sent from Weimar.[9] From here, he must have made his way to Leipzig, where he took lodgings on the fourth floor of a house on the market square. Not yet having mastered the language, his negotiations with his prospective landlady were made through an interpreter. In later years, he recalled the early stages of his language-learning process:

> Quand j'en vins à pouvoir nouer l'un à l'autre quelques verbes et quelques substantifs du vocabulaire germanique, et à pouvoir échanger avec elle quelques mots, elle encourageait mes efforts avec une patiente bonté, elle répétait les paroles que je venais de prononcer, pour leur donner leur juste accent, et achevait la phrase que j'avais commencée.[10]

With his characteristic determination, however, Marmier made rapid progress:

> à force de chercher les mots dans le dictionnaire et à force d'entendre prononcer, j'en vins bientôt à en savoir assez pour traduire des contes populaires que la maison Levrault, de Strasbourg, voulut bien imprimer et vendre à mon profit. Avec le produit de ce travail, je pus visiter une partie de l'Allemagne du Nord.[11]

The volume in question was Krummacher's *Paraboles*.[12] The preface to this collection is dated 'Leipzig, 15 Mars 1833', suggesting that he had translated

[8] *Impressions et souvenirs d'un voyageur chrétien*, 7th edn. (Tours: Mame et fils, 1881), 11.

[9] 'Weimar', *Nouvelle Revue germanique* (cited hereafter as *NRg*), 11/44 (1832), 367–71.

[10] *Voyage pittoresque*, 2, 77.   [11] *Impressions et souvenirs*, 11.

[12] Friedrich Krummacher, *Choix de paraboles de F. Krummacher, par X. Marmier* (Paris: Levrault, 1833).

the work after having spent only eight months in the country. Further testimony to his progress in learning the language is given by the poet and dramatist Karl von Holtei, who recalls that on first meeting Marmier in 1833, the Frenchman 'hinreichend unsere Sprache verstand, um einem deutschen Schauspiele folgen zu können', and furthermore that in discussion after rehearsals, 'Marmier kämpfte diese Kämpfe alle redlich mit uns durch und spie Zorn, Feuer und Flammen'.[13] In the same year Marmier also published an anthology (in French) entitled *Feuilles volantes: Souvenirs d'Allemagne*.[14] The following year, a *Nouveau choix de paraboles*[15] appeared, along with a translation of Koberstein's *Manuel de l'histoire de la littérature nationale allemande*.[16] The latter was supplemented by a preface written by Marmier covering developments in German literature since 1812. His best-known work from this period was the *Études sur Goethe*, published in 1835.[17] Other volumes based on his work in Germany during this early period include translations of Goethe's *Hermann und Dorothea* (1837),[18] the theatre of Goethe (1839)[19] and Schiller (1841),[20] Schiller's poetry (1844),[21] a collection of tales by E. T. A. Hoffmann (1843),[22] and a volume of stories for children translated from German and English sources.[23] He also published a new edition of Mme de Staël's *De l'Allemagne* in 1839.[24]

In the meantime, Marmier had undertaken a series of articles which were to be published for the most part in the *Nouvelle Revue germanique*, but also, increasingly, in the prestigious *Revue des Deux Mondes* and the *Revue de Paris*. The earliest articles from Leipzig, which were published in

---

[13] Karl von Holtei, *Vierzig Jahre*, 8 vols. (Berlin: Buchhandlung des Berliner Lesekabinetts und W. Adolf; Breslau: August Schulz, 1843–50), 5, 335 and 338.

[14] *Feuilles volantes: Souvenirs d'Allemagne* (Berlin: Haude et Spener, 1833).

[15] Friedrich Krummacher, *Nouveau choix de paraboles de F. Krummacher* (Paris: Levrault, 1834).

[16] August Koberstein, *Manuel de l'histoire de la littérature nationale allemande* (Paris and Strasbourg: Levrault, 1834).

[17] *Études sur Goethe* (Paris and Strasbourg: Levrault, 1835) (cited hereafter as *EG*).

[18] *Hermann et Dorothée* (Paris: Heideloff, 1837).

[19] *Théâtre de Goethe, traduction nouvelle, revue, corrigée et augmentée de notices et d'une préface par M. X. Marmier* (Paris: Charpentier, 1839).

[20] *Théâtre de Schiller, traduction nouvelle, précédée d'une notice sur sa vie et ses ouvrages par X. Marmier* (Paris: Charpentier, 1841).

[21] *Poésies de Schiller, traduction nouvelle par M. X. Marmier, précédée d'une introduction par le traducteur* (Paris: Charpentier, 1844).

[22] *Contes fantastiques d'Hoffmann, traduction nouvelle de M. X. Marmier, précédée d'une notice par le traducteur* (Paris: Charpentier, 1843).

[23] *Choix de fables et de contes, traduits de divers auteurs anglais et allemands* (Paris and Strasbourg: Levrault, 1835).

[24] Mme de Staël, *De l'Allemagne, nouvelle édition, avec une préface par M. X. Marmier* (Paris: Charpentier, 1839).

the *Nouvelle Revue germanique*, were based on his experiences there, and presented details of domestic life in Germany. In January 1833 he initiated a series of 'Études biographiques', beginning with Hoffmann and treating a new author almost every month until 1835. Some of these authors, like Hoffmann, were already known and appreciated in France (although even in these cases, Marmier often succeeded in finding a new aspect or angle on the author in question), whilst others were unknown in France and virtually unrecognised in Germany. He also sent numerous translations and articles on his travels and observations of life in Germany. His articles soon came to dominate the review, although a letter to Charles Weiss reveals that this had not been his intention, and that he had in fact come under a good deal of pressure: 'Notre pauvre revue est bien en retard. Les collaborateurs, et surtout les bons collaborateurs, nous manquent. Je suis obligé de composer la plus grande partie des numéros, et j'ai déjà voulu plusieurs fois abdiquer une fonction qui me gêne sous bien des rapports'.[25]

Other articles by Marmier appeared in *La France littéraire*, *Le Monde dramatique*, and *Le Théâtre européen*. A number of pieces also appeared in *Le Voleur*, *Le Cabinet de lecture*, and *Le Magasin pittoresque*. These last three were publications aimed at a wide readership, and the fact that Marmier's work appeared here as well as in the more prestigious reviews indicates that his efforts brought German culture not only to a sophisticated elite, but also to the less privileged. In all, Marmier's work in Germany resulted in well over a hundred articles published in the various reviews cited, as well as the volumes of translations and criticism: it was one of the most prolific periods of his career.

For Marmier (as indeed for Mme de Staël), a survey of the literature of a country was incomplete without a simultaneous study of the people and manners of that country.[26] This is a precept which he was to apply to all his later studies, but which was of particular importance in Germany. A vital premise of Marmier's presentation of German literature is that it is 'une littérature vraiment nationale',[27] its sources generally being German in origin rather than foreign models. The German author, he says, 'puise ses sujets

---

[25] BmB, Collection Estignard, MS 1907, Correspondance de Charles Weiss, Lettres de X. Marmier, fos. 794–5.

[26] Despite his great admiration for Mme de Staël's work, Marmier does not accept everything she writes at face value. Even in the preface to his own edition of *De l'Allemagne* he says that she presents everything in a rather rosy light (de Staël, *De l'Allemagne*, 8). In 'Critique littéraire. Allemagne et Italie, de M. Edgar Quinet' (*RP*, 3rd ser., 4 (1839), 49–55, 52) he is rather more forceful about the issue.

[27] 'Littérature. Études sur Goethe. Goetz de Berlichingen. Egmont', *NRg*, 2nd ser., 2/7 (1834), 195–223 (195).

dans l'histoire de sa nation et sa poésie dans son cœur'.[28] Furthermore, since
the models are taken from the country and its people and their history,
rather than from extraneous sources, that literature is also for the people,
rather than being the domain of an intellectual elite. Marmier was
extremely impressed by the general awareness of literature which he found
amongst the German people: 'J'ai vu des ouvriers qui menaient une rude
vie, et qui connaissaient par cœur les plus belles tragédies de Goethe', he
commented in 1835.[29] A further reminiscence compared popular intellectual
activity in Germany and France: 'Je me souviens qu'un soir, en rentrant dans
ma demeure, je trouvais le *Hausknecht*, un portier de troisième ordre, ten-
ant sur ses genoux un gros livre qu'il lisait avec une profonde attention.
C'étaient les œuvres de Schiller. À Paris, nos portiers ne lisent que les plus
mauvais romans'.[30]

Some of this difference is also attributed to the high standards of public
education in the German-speaking countries, and much attention is devoted
to this aspect of German life. In 1834, for example, he remarks that in
Austria, 'le plus pauvre apprenti, le plus obscur berger, sait au moins lire et
écrire; si l'instruction du peuple ne s'élève guères plus haut, c'est qu'il ne le
veut pas'.[31] In the same year, an article appeared in the *Revue des Deux
Mondes* about the University of Göttingen, and another on Leipzig and the
German publishing trade: both of these stress the high value placed on
learning.[32] A good proportion of the later *Voyage pittoresque en Allemagne*
is devoted to the educational institutions of the German-speaking countries.
This work provides a general survey of the history and scope of German
universities, and a chronological list of their foundation dates serves to
underline the deep-rooted traditions of scholarship in the country.
Particularly detailed descriptions are given of the universities of Tübingen,
Prague, Leipzig, Breslau, Königsberg, Göttingen, Jena, and Würzburg.
Closely associated with the traditions of scholarship and the appreciation
of literature for Marmier is the exceptional rate of literary production.
Germany, he writes, is an 'immense Schriftstellerei', and is 'de tous les pays
de l'Europe celui où l'on compte le plus grand nombre d'écrivains'.[33]
Writing, like reading, seems to Marmier to be enjoyed by all: 'J'ai vu parfois

---

[28] 'Littérature. Études sur Goethe. Goetz de Berlichingen. Egmont', 196.
[29] [Introduction], *Revue germanique* (cited hereafter as *Rg*), 3rd ser., 1/1 (1835), 3–21 (11).
[30] *Voyage pittoresque*, 2, 85.
[31] 'Journal de voyage. Vienne', *NRg*, 2nd ser., 1/4 (1834), 359–77 (364).
[32] 'Les Universités allemandes—Goettingue', *Revue des Deux Mondes* (cited hereafter as *RDM*),
3rd ser., 3 (1834), 434–48; 'Leipzig et la librairie allemande', *RDM*, 3rd ser., 3 (1834), 93–105.
[33] *Voyage pittoresque*, 1, 95.

des réunions où l'on ne buvait que de bien mauvais vin, mais où l'on n'arrivait pas sans apporter son sonnet ou sa cantate'.[34] As this remark suggests, music is also shown to be present in all social situations and in all social ranks, from the 'musique des postillons assis sur leur siège d'Eilwagen ou d'Extrapost',[35] through the 'troupes d'étudians, comme vous les a si bien dépeintes Mme de Staël, qui s'en vont le soir, en chantant, à travers les rues',[36] the 'musique des orchestres à toutes les tables d'hôte',[37] and the 'musique de la flûte et du piano dans le salon de famille'.[38]

Both music and literature in Germany are closely associated in these early articles for Marmier with domestic harmony. In one of the earliest articles, 'Des soirées d'Allemagne', he recalls sitting down for the evening with his host family to read Krummacher, Goethe's *Hermann und Dorothea*, and Uhland.[39] At other junctures he links domestic life in Germany with Voss and Goethe.[40] Together with these literary images are numerous adjectives and expressions suggesting peace in the household ('chambre tranquille',[41] 'doux asyle',[42] 'paisibles intérieurs'[43]). In his second article to be published in 1832 in the *Nouvelle Revue germanique*, he reports on 'les vertus domestiques, la simplicité et la candeur dans les relations, la paix et l'union dans l'intérieur des familles'.[44] Closely connected to this love of the home for Marmier is the open, hospitable nature of the people, who welcome even strangers into their homes with open arms.

Domestic harmony was in Marmier's eyes a feature of that religious observance which he noted amongst those living in the German-speaking countries and which he found to be a part of everyday life: 'ils ont le bonheur le plus vrai et le plus durable, celui qui naît de la simplicité des habitudes, de la paix d'une honnête conscience et de l'expression d'une franche et ouverte nature'.[45] Although he distinguishes between the Protestantism of the northern countries and the virtues of Catholicism in the south, both are shown to have an impact on the quality of life: the exceptionally low rates of crime in the Tyrol, for example, are attributed to the latter.[46]

Another rather different type of religious thought which was to reach France from Germany is presented by Marmier in a poem first published in

---

[34] [Introduction], *Rg*, 3rd ser., 1/1 (1835), 10.
[35] *SV*, 91.   [36] [Introduction], *Rg*, 3rd ser., 1/1 (1835), 13.   [37] *SV*, 91.   [38] Ibid.
[39] 'Des soirées d'Allemagne', *NRg*, 15/57 & 58 (joint issue), 161–73 (163).
[40] e.g. *Voyage pittoresque*, 2, 51.
[41] 'Soirée allemande', in *Poésies d'un voyageur* (Paris: Félix Locquin, 1844), 55.   [42] Ibid.
[43] *Voyage pittoresque*, 2, 51.
[44] 'Mœurs de l'Allemagne. Premier article: le dimanche', *NRg*, 12/47 (1832), 266–77 (266).
[45] *Voyage pittoresque*, 1, 116.   [46] Ibid., 1, 148.

La France littéraire in 1834, simply entitled 'Panthéisme'.[47] For Marmier, the concept of pantheism, 'ce culte mystérieux de la nature', 'cette espèce de panthéisme secret dont le moyen âge a toujours admis le principe sans jamais le formuler', is profoundly German in character, and has its roots in the ancient mythological traditions of the country.[48] This was a subject which fascinated him. Two articles entitled 'Traditions d'Allemagne' were published in 1836 and 1837 in the *Revue de Paris*; they would be reprinted a number of times.[49]

Even in the nineteenth century, Marmier noted, Germany was a land of folklore:

> Ici, toutes les plaines ont leurs génies, toutes les montagnes leurs grottes mystérieuses, tous les lacs leurs palais de cristal; ici, toutes les fées ne sont pas mortes, et tous les sylphes n'ont pas dépouillé leurs ailes d'or; ici, quand la nuit silencieuse s'abaisse sur la terre, les flots de l'Elbe et du Rhin ont encore des soupirs d'amour, les arbres frissonnent au souffle des esprits [. . .].[50]

Distinguishing between myth and legend, he presents mythological figures according to the element or natural phenomenon with which they are normally associated, and also attempts to explain symbolism wherever this is possible. Legends are divided into those associated with particular locations (for example Rolandseck or the Lorelay); those associated with religion; and those connected with the devil, which he presents in a humorous manner:

> Quand on lit toutes ces histoires des déceptions du diable, répandues à travers les plus beaux monuments de l'Europe, depuis la merveilleuse cathédrale de Cologne, jusqu'à celle de Lund, en Suède, on est vraiment tenté de plaindre le malheureux artisan de tant d'œuvres si difficiles dont il a tiré si peu de bénéfice, et il me semble tout naturel de croire que de là vient la dénomination de pauvre diable appliquée à l'homme qui se trompe dans toutes ses tentatives.[51]

Whilst noting that most examples of folklore cited appear to be German in origin, he emphasises the fact that many variations are to be found elsewhere (for example in Brittany, Scotland, Iceland, Denmark, and in the Mediterranean countries). He suggests that it would be interesting to 'constater, par des rapprochements nombreux, leur parenté avec celles des autres

---

[47] 'Panthéisme', *La France littéraire*, 14 (1834), 185–6. This is an outstanding poem; the rest of Marmier's poetry is (save a few notable exceptions) generally mediocre.

[48] *Souvenirs de voyages et traditions populaires* (Paris: Masgana, 1841), 204.

[49] 'Traditions d'Allemagne', *RP*, 36 (1836), 246–64 and 38 (1837), 177–91. The section entitled 'Traditions d'Allemagne' in *Souvenirs de voyages et traditions populaires* is a reprint of these articles. The material appears again, albeit with some slighly altered wording, in the fourth chapter of *Voyage pittoresque*, this time under the title 'Les Légendes d'Allemagne'. All quotations given here are to be found in all the publications mentioned.

[50] *Voyage pittoresque*, 1, 57.   [51] Ibid., 1, 313.

peuples, et leurs transformations successives'.[52] Thus from an early stage in his career, Marmier (building on the earlier work of Mme de Staël) was a comparatist before the discipline of comparative literature was born; his work would also influence the awakening French interest in folklore.

The material presented was gathered from a number of sources. Where possible, Marmier preferred to learn from local people on his travels, and supplemented this with reading (his sources are given as Brentano, Büsching, Gerle, Massmann, Schreiber, Geib, and Grimm). He was also fortunate enough to be able to consult experts such as Schwab, or the brothers Grimm, whom he met in Göttingen.[53]

Marmier's peregrinations and his choice of authors for presentation in the French press were (intially, at any rate) largely dictated by the introductions which took him from one German man of letters to another. Most of these contacts can be traced back indirectly to Heinrich Heine, who was living in Paris at that time.[54] The initial contact between the two seems to have been warm, and published correspondence shows Heine making sympathetic enquiries of his friends in Germany as to Marmier's progress and whereabouts. Marmier briefly mentions Heine's lyric poetry 'qu'il faut placer au premier rang' in the introduction to his translation of Koberstein.[55] A turning point occurred in 1835, when an article by Marmier in *Le Monde dramatique* entitled 'Les Tragédies de Henri Heine' criticises the German:

> Je lui en veux d'avoir parlé avec si peu de respect d'Auguste Schlegel, le philologue, de Tieck le poète, et de ne nous avoir montré que sous leur face ridicule, plusieurs idées tout allemandes et admirables à voir du beau côté. Mais je lui en veux surtout d'avoir si vite quitté le paradis poétique, où il était entré de si bonne heure, pour retomber dans les sentiers épineux de la critique.[56]

In view of the date and reference, it would seem that Marmier is referring to the publication in France of Heine's *De l'Allemagne* in 1835, where Schlegel is discussed in part 5, chapter 1 and Tieck in part 5, chapter 2.[57] The antipathy thereafter degenerates to a personal level. In 1836, he wrote

[52] Ibid., 1, 58.

[53] A handwritten inscription in his copy of Jacob Grimm's *Deutsche Mythologie* reads: 'Acheté le 6 juillet 1886 [. . .], heureux de retrouver une des œuvres de ces deux savants si justement renommés qui en 1834 à Göttingen furent si bons pour moi'. Marmier's relationship with Schwab is discussed later in this chapter.

[54] Heinrich Heine (1797–1856) was a prolific writer and thinker who had settled in Paris in 1831 (inspired by the July Revolution of 1830). He is best remembered now for his fine poetry.

[55] Koberstein, *Manuel*, p. xv.

[56] 'Les Tragédies de Henri Heine', *Le Monde dramatique*, 2 (1835), 110–12 (110).

[57] Heinrich Heine, *Œuvres de Henri Heine. De l'Allemagne*, 2 vols. (Paris: E. Renduel, 1835). I have not seen a copy of this 1835 edition. Relevant references from a later edition are: Heinrich Heine, *De l'Allemagne*, 2 vols. (Paris: Michel Lévy frères, 1855), 1, 253–74 and 1, 275–93 respectively.

to the marquis de La Grange that 'Heine est revenu de son voyage dans le midi jaune de haine et de colère, criant contre tout le monde et proclamant partout qu'il a connu la femme de Loève Weimar [*sic*], qu'elle est vieille, laide, et n'a pas le sou'.[58] The following year, on reading in a German news-paper that Heine had left the *Revue des Deux Mondes* for the *Revue du XIXe siècle*, Marmier wrote to François Buloz that 'si cela est vrai, je puis vous assurer que c'est une perte qui ne vous fera pas grand tort'.[59] In later years the anger towards Heine continues unabated in his review of *Heinrich Heine über Ludwig Börne* in the *Revue des Deux Mondes*;[60] in 1860 he descends atypically into unveiled racism, describing Heine and Börne as 'deux acerbes juifs'.[61]

However, Heine originally wrote a letter of introduction on Marmier's behalf to Karl von Holtei.[62] Holtei, in his autobiography, demonstrates that preconceived notions of 'Frenchness' could also have affected the way that Marmier was perceived abroad. On their first meeting, Holtei's impression of Marmier was rather negative: his appearance immediately suggested to Holtei the stereotype of the travelling Frenchman: black-haired, elegant and blasé. On the second, he was delighted to find Marmier as enthusiastic and passionate as he had thought only a blond-haired German could be.[63] The two men became close during Marmier's stay; Holtei records how in 1833, Marmier's presence helped him through a bad spell of depression and describes the prospect of his new friend's imminent departure as 'painful' ('schmerzlich').[64] The following year, 1834, he recalls his delight at the return of the man described as 'unser Wandervogel aus Frankreich, der all-beliebte Marmier'.[65] Holtei is mentioned briefly by Marmier in his intro-duction to Koberstein under the section on dramatic poetry.[66] In 1835, Marmier wrote an article on Holtei's first wife, an actress, entitled simply 'Louise de Holtei' which was published in *Le Monde dramatique*.[67] Holtei

---

[58] Heinrich Heine, *Briefe*, Erste Gesamtausgabe nach den Handschriften herausgegeben, eingeleitet und erläutert von Friedrich Hirth, 6 vols. (Mainz: Florian Kupferberg, 1948[–1957]), 5, 185.

[59] Marie-Louise Pailleron, *François Buloz et ses amis: la vie littéraire sous Louis-Philippe* (Paris: Calmann Lévy, 1919), 154. The date of the letter is given here as 16 September 1837, whereas Hirth, editor of Heine's *Briefe*, suggests January 1838 (Heine, *Briefe*, 5, 237).

[60] 'Revue littéraire de l'Allemagne', *RDM*, 36 (1841), 627–55 (640). Many Germans shared Marmier's view of this book: for instance the editor of *Ludwig Börnes Urtheil über Heinrich Heine* (Frankfurt: Sauerländer, 1840) refers to the 'verwegnen und gemeinen Angriffe, durch welche Herr H. Heine nach Börnes Tode die Erinnerung an ihn zu entheiligen suchte' (*Ludwig Börnes Urtheil*, 1). Börne's review is found in the *Gesammelte Schriften*, 12 vols. (Vienna: Tendler, 1868), 7, 139.

[61] *Voyage pittoresque*, 2, 147.

[62] See Heine, *Briefe*, 3, 50; and Holtei, *Simmelsammelsusurium, aus Briefen, gedrückten Büchern, aus dem Leben, und aus ihm selbst*, 2 vols. (Breslau: Trewendt, 1872), 2, 62.

[63] Holtei, *Vierzig Jahre*, 5, 336–9.   [64] Ibid., 5, 339.   [65] Ibid., 6, 6.   [66] Koberstein, *Manuel*, xij.

[67] 'Louise de Holtei', *Le Monde dramatique*, 2 (1835), 119–21.

in his turn introduced Marmier to the historian Friedrich von Raumer,[68] who was presented in the 'Études biographiques' in 1833,[69] and to whom the anthology of *Feuilles volantes* is dedicated.

As well as introducing Marmier to Holtei, Heine probably also indirectly brought about his introduction to the scholar Adolf Wagner, who is presented in the 'Études biographiques' in April 1833.[70] Wagner was to become a close friend of Marmier's. He encouraged him to study the works of Goethe,[71] and also introduced him to a number of important figures in the literary world, including Schwab (who then introduced him to Uhland), Tieck, and the Stieglitz.

Schwab's poetry is not widely acclaimed today, but he was popular in Germany at that time: he was nonetheless virtually unknown to the French public before Marmier's translation of 'Erinnerung' appeared in the *Nouvelle Revue germanique* in 1833.[72] His importance is perhaps slightly overestimated by Marmier who, in his introduction to Koberstein and also in the *Études sur Goethe*, divides the modern genre of lyric poetry into four schools, one of which, according to Marmier, is headed by Schwab.[73] Schwab contributed indirectly to Marmier's works on Schiller, for most of the information contained in the biographical study which first appeared as an article in the *Revue des Deux Mondes*,[74] and then as an introduction to his translation of Schiller's theatre, was taken from Schwab's newly published *Schillers Leben* (1840). Another aspect of Schwab's work which undoubtedly influenced Marmier was his work on folklore: he is best remembered these days for his *Buch der schönsten Geschichten und Sagen* (1836–7) and we know from two different references that Schwab recounted '[des] traditions populaires' to Marmier during the time they spent together.[75]

Schwab moreover introduced Marmier to Uhland, whose work was to have considerable following in France.[76] Uhland was based in Stuttgart, and the two men dined together or took strolls along the banks of the river

---

[68] Holtei, *Vierzig Jahre*, 5, 339.

[69] 'Études biographiques: Frédéric L. G. de Raumer', *NRg*, 14/53 (1833), 1–18.

[70] 'Études biographiques: Adolphe Wagner', *NRg*, 13/52 (1833), 289–304.

[71] *SV*, 190; and an inscription in a copy of *Faust* in Marmier's personal library, the Bibliothèque Xavier Marmier in Pontarlier.

[72] *NRg*, 14/54 (1833), 188; this translation is reproduced in *Poésies d'un voyageur*, 26.

[73] Koberstein, *Manuel*, p. xv; *EG*, 428.   [74] 'Vie de Schiller', *RDM*, 24 (1840), 48–85.

[75] 'Études biographiques: Louis Uhland', *NRg*, 2nd ser., 1/1 (1834), 3–20 (4); *Voyage pittoresque*, 1, 39.

[76] See Marguerite Wieser, *La Fortune d'Uhland en France* (Paris: Nizet, 1972). Details of Schwab's introduction of Marmier to Uhland appear in *SV*, 113–14.

Neckar together in July 1833. Marmier recalls Uhland as being approximately fifty years old, with 'une figure grave, des traits accentués, mais réguliers, le front haut et découvert, les yeux lumineux, un sourire doux et fin, une aimable simplicité de forme et de langage. Tout ce que je remarquai de prime abord en lui était en parfait accord avec le caractère de ses poésies'.[77] The publications resulting from the meetings between the two were to prove highly influential in the introduction of Uhland's work to France.[78] Five poems translated by Marmier appeared in the *Nouvelle Revue germanique* in the course of 1833, and the same review published his 'Étude biographique' in 1834 (which contains translations of several more poems). This would appear to have been the first study in France not concerned solely with the lyric poetry, but giving an overview of the man and his work, his political views, his tragedies, and his study of Walther von der Vogelweide. For Marmier, Uhland is 'comme une réapparition d'un de ces vieux Meistersänger' by virtue of 'la même douceur de rythme, la même pureté d'âme, surtout la même loyauté de caractère'.[79] Uhland's poetry is characterised by the poet's 'vive imagination', which allows him to depict nature 'd'une manière fidèle, mais en y joignant toujours quelques-unes des couleurs brillantes du prisme à travers lequel il la regarde'.[80] Of the four main schools identified in Marmier's analysis of contemporary German lyric poetry in the *Études sur Goethe* (1835),

> celle d'Uhland [. . .] de toutes est peut-être la plus large et la plus vraie; [elle] admet aussi ce que le passé lui rappelle, ce que le présent lui offre, [elle] chante Dieu et la nature, l'amour et les joies du monde, retrace la ballade du Minnesänger, et combat aujourd'hui pour les libertés du peuple.[81]

In Stuttgart, Schwab also introduced Marmier to Menzel and Dannecker.[82] Knowing that the former had been dubbed the 'Franzosenfresser', Marmier met him with some trepidation, but was relieved to find that rather than

---

[77] *SV*, 116.

[78] See Wieser, *La Fortune d'Uhland*, esp. 66. Her assessment of Marmier's role is generally fair, although a number of his publications and details of the contacts between the two men are not mentioned.

[79] 'Études biographiques: Louis Uhland', 5.

[80] Ibid., 9. This comment is interesting not only for the description of Uhland, but also in terms of the history of criticism (compare, for example, Baudelaire's writing on the imagination in the *Salon de 1859*).

[81] *EG*, 428.

[82] Wolfgang Menzel (1798–1873) was an opponent of both Heine and Börne, an author and journalist with strong nationalistic and reactionary opinions. Johann Heinrich von Dannecker (1758–1841) was one of the most celebrated German sculptors of the era. The Christ figure mentioned now stands in the choir of the mortuary chapel in the cloister of St Emmeram, Thurn und Taxis, Regensburg.

showing any inclination to eat him, he in fact invited him to dinner. Dannecker also invited them to visit his studio and showed them his masterpiece, his figure of Christ.

Adolf Wagner also introduced Marmier to Charlotte Stieglitz and her husband Heinrich in Berlin.[83] Although of lesser literary significance than some of the other figures he had met, Marmier was fascinated by their curious saga, which caused a public sensation in Germany. Charlotte Stieglitz stabbed herself to death in order to give her husband a tragic experience which she hoped would inspire his writing (in this, the gesture was ineffectual!). Marmier related the tale in one of his 'Études biographiques' in 1835,[84] and it was a theme to which he returned a quarter of a century later in the *Voyage pittoresque*[85] and again in the *Souvenirs d'un voyageur*.[86] He dined with the couple and spent many interesting evenings with them in Berlin in 1833, then visited them again in 1834, not for a moment suspecting that he would never see Charlotte again. He recalled her as being friendly and attractive, if a little prone to melancholy: 'mais d'une mélancolie douce et poétique qui ne faisait point prévoir une si triste fin'.[87] Heinrich, he recalls, was sad, but 'affectueux et bon garçon'.[88]

In addition to meeting Holtei, Raumer, and the Stieglitz in Berlin, Marmier also made a number of other significant contacts. These included the journalists Albrecht, Josephi, and Lehmann; the philosophers Steffens (who was 'doux' and 'sympathique'[89]) and Hegel ('que je ne pouvais comprendre, mais qui attirait à lui une quantité de disciples'[90]). In the world of art and letters he met Hitzig, Raupach (the dramatist), Häring (the novelist), Rauch ('le charmant artiste'[91]), Kugler (the art historian), the Humboldt brothers, and Wilken (the historian) as well as Chamisso. In an article devoted to Chamisso, Marmier claims to have met him at a meeting of the 'société littéraire' in Berlin.[92] A later reminiscence suggests that these meetings took place at the home of Hitzig.[93] These two pieces of information combined would imply that Marmier had gained access to the 'Mittwochgesellschaft', one of the most influential literary circles in Berlin. Formed by Hitzig in 1824, the group, which also included Eichendorff in the days prior to Marmier's visit, and W. Alexis (Häring), was an important centre of the Romantic movement. (This circle also stimulated the

---

[83] *SV*, 189–92.

[84] 'Études biographiques: Charlotte Stieglitz', *Rg*, 3rd ser., 4/10, 62–71.

[85] *Voyage pittoresque*, 2, 187–91.   [86] *SV*, 189–92.

[87] Manuscript inscription in Anonymous [T. Mundt], *Charlotte Stieglitz: ein Denkmal* (Berlin: Veit, [1836]); copy in Bibliothèque Xavier Marmier, Pontarlier (no folio nos.).

[88] Ibid.   [89] *SV*, 103.   [90] Ibid.   [91] Ibid.   [92] 'Visite à un poète', *RP*, 36 (1836), 140–6 (146).

[93] *Voyage pittoresque*, 2, 185.

formation by Saphir of 'Der Tunnel über der Spree' as a form of negative reaction to its ideals.) Marmier's presence at these meetings is highly significant, for it confirms first that he was involved at the heart of literary activity in Germany, and second that he was at the forefront of new developments; it also shows how his ideas on German literature were formed and explains, at least in part, his later hostility to 'das junge Deutschland'.

Marmier also had a specific reason for wanting to visit Hitzig while he was in Berlin. Hitzig was the famous friend and biographer of the late E. T. A. Hoffmann. Hoffmann's tales had been translated into French and achieved phenomenal success in the 1820s.[94] On his travels in Germany, Marmier assiduously sought out the places and the individuals who had become associated with Hoffmann in the French literary consciousness.[95] His friend and mentor Adolf Wagner had known Hoffmann while he was living in Leipzig and supplied Marmier with copious details, both literary and biographical (the latter were in fact probably as influential as the former, since a great deal of the French interest in Hoffmann had sprung up around the legendary figure whose life appeared to the French to personify the eccentric but misunderstood Romantic who was also the 'complete' artist). Some of the anecdotes recounted by Wagner reinforced this image:

> Un jour le docteur Wagner rencontre la femme de Hoffmann, qui l'engage à aller chez elle passer la soirée. [. . .] Ils ouvrent la porte, et aperçoivent une femme qui, tout occupée de l'inspiration musicale à laquelle elle s'abandonne, ne les entend point venir, et continue à faire voltiger les doigts sur les touches avec une chaleur et une rapidité qui laissent deviner ce qui se passe au fond de son âme. Les deux curieux s'approchent sur la pointe du pied, arrivent auprès du piano, et sous un large chapeau de taffetas découvrent la figure de Hoffmann.[96]

Although Marmier was able to offer new anecdotal biographical information about Hoffmann, this is not where the true originality of his contribution to an understanding of Hoffmann in France lay. He published four articles on Hoffmann altogether,[97] and a collection of the tales in translation appeared in 1843.[98] In her study of Hoffmann's reception in France, Elizabeth Teichmann shows that by the time Marmier had reached Germany, the Hoffmann vogue was well under way in France; apart from

---

[94] The reception of Hoffmann's work in France has been studied by Elizabeth Teichmann in *La Fortune d'Hoffmann en France* (Paris: Minard, 1961).

[95] See 'Hoffmann et Devrient', *RDM*, 2nd ser., 4 (1833), 466–73, esp. 468; and 'Souvenirs de voyage. La cave de Hoffmann à Berlin', *NRg*, 13/52 (1833), 340–56.

[96] 'Études biographiques: Hoffmann', *NRg*, 13/49, 1833, 12–29 (23).

[97] The fourth article was 'Les Don Juan', *RP*, 2nd ser., 6 (1834), 73–82.

[98] *Contes fantastiques d'Hoffmann* (see above, n. 22).

the early translations, she singles out a number of early articles of criticism as the most important. These include an article by J.-J. Ampère, who introduced the concept of 'le merveilleux naturel', and an article by the major translator of Hoffmann, Loève-Veimars, entitled 'Les Dernières Années et la mort d'Hoffmann' (building on and catering for the fascination with Hoffmann's life story).[99] Both Ampère and Loève-Veimars, however, tended to sensationalise the rumours about Hoffmann's drinking habits. Ampère describes the German author in terms such as 'monstrueux', 'capricieux', 'intempérance' and 'débauche', concluding that Hoffmann 'se laisse entraîner à un genre de vie déplorable'.[100] Loève-Veimars comments that 'ce goût d'Hoffmann pour le vin se développa de bonne heure, et on ne saurait l'excuser',[101] and concludes that 'dans les dernières années de sa vie, l'ivrognerie prit chez lui un caractère qui est en quelque sorte le perfectionnement du vice'.[102] By 1833, when Marmier's first articles appeared, it would seem that the insistence on Hoffmann's drinking habits by the press might be causing interest in the author to wane: indeed, criticisms of excessive drinking were used as an argument against the acceptability of his work by the *Edinburgh Review* in an article which was reproduced in translation in the influential *Revue britannique*.[103] Marmier's articles, however, treat the question in a far more sensitive and perceptive manner, demonstrating a sound knowledge and understanding of the texts (in particular, here, 'Höchst zerstreute Gedanken' from the *Kreisleriana*) in terms foreshadowing Baudelaire's adaptation of the theme in the next decade:

> Ce n'est pas qu'il ait soif, ce n'est pas qu'il cherche ce plaisir brutal qu'ont les gens du peuple de boire pour s'enivrer; ce n'est pas le vin qu'il aime. [. . .] c'est cette nouvelle chaleur que le vin lui donne; c'est la fumée de Johannisberg qui lui monte au cerveau, c'est son imagination [. . .]. Alors toutes ses facultés sont tendues et mises en jeu, alors le peintre apporte ses couleurs vives et tranchantes, le poète ses mobiles sensations, le musicien l'exercice de son art [. . .]. C'est une terre toute neuve, et que l'on foule avec un singulier mélange d'étonnement et de plaisir [. . .]; c'est un concert auquel il se mêle toujours quelque chose de fascinant, de magique.[104]

---

[99] J.-J. Ampère, 'Hoffmann. Aus Hoffmanns Leben und Nachlass, herausgegeben von Hitzig, Berlin, 1822', *Globe*, 6/81 (1828), 588–9; Loève-Veimars, 'Les Dernières Années et la mort d'Hoffmann', *RP*, 7 (1829), 248–63.

[100] Ampère, 'Hoffman', 588–9.   [101] Loève-Veimars, 'Les Dernières Années', 250.

[102] Ibid.

[103] Anonymous, 'French literature. Recent novelists [. . .]', *Edinburgh Review*, 67 (1833), 330–57; Anonymous, 'Jugement de la Revue d'Edimbourg sur la littérature française contemporaine', *Revue britannique*, 3rd ser., 2 (1833), 193–218.

[104] 'Études biographiques: Hoffmann', 25–6.

Marmier's fourth article on Hoffmann, 'Les Don Juan', appeared just as a season of *Don Giovanni* at the Paris opera had turned the public attention to the musical aspects of the tales. In this article, Marmier studies the 'Don Juan' theme in different literatures, and concludes that Hoffmann 'a mis en récit ce que Mozart mettait en musique; il a dépeint Don Juan de manière à ce qu'on n'y ajoute plus rien'.[105] Teichmann does not comment on Marmier's contribution; it is, however, clear that he did succeed in finding some areas of originality despite the already considerable Hoffmann vogue in France.[106]

Probably the most significant introduction effected by Wagner on Marmier's behalf was to Tieck, whom he was to visit in Dresden early in 1833. The encounter was to provide Marmier with an abundance of material for presentation in France. Tieck was one of the great German Romantics, and unlike Uhland or Schwab, his work had been made public in France much earlier by Mme de Staël, in *De l'Allemagne*.[107] Her presentation was, however, double-edged: whilst making the French aware of Tieck's work, her reservations about it acted as a brake to its introduction, and it had never captured the French imagination in the same way as Hoffmann's work had done. The first translation of *Sternbald* had appeared in 1823 and was followed by various individual items until 1832 when the complete works began to appear in translation.[108]

Marmier's first passing reference to Tieck in the French press appears in 1832.[109] By March 1833 he had visited Tieck in Dresden and was fired with enthusiasm. In the resulting 'Étude biographique', Tieck is described as

> l'homme de génie, l'homme qui va sur la terre comme un élu du ciel, l'homme qui a la lyre mélancolique du poète et la lyre inspirée du prophète, l'homme qui reflète en soi le passé et devance le présent [. . .] l'homme, enfin, qui doit être le point marquant de son époque, et le maître encore des temps à venir.[110]

---

[105] 'Les Don Juan', 75.

[106] Teichmann's only significant remark about any of his articles is a mistaken one, for she maintains (*La Fortune d'Hoffmann en France*, 123) that the 'Hoffmann et Devrient' article was a reprint of one entitled 'La Cave d'Hoffmann' [*sic*] (presumably here referring to the article 'Souvenirs de voyage. La cave de Hoffmann à Berlin (see above, n. 95)). This is quite unfounded. It is true, however, that the 'Hoffmann et Devrient' article is very similar to the 'Notice' to the translations: she may have confused these two texts.

[107] Mme de Staël, *De l'Allemagne*, ed. Jean de Pange, 5 vols. (Paris: Hachette, 1960), 3, 177–9, 200–1, 203–5, 205–6, 267–70.

[108] Ludwig Tieck, *Sternbald, ou le peintre voyageur*, trans. anonymous (Paris: Librairie nationale et étrangère, 1823); Ludwig Tieck, *Œuvres complètes*, trans. L. H. Martin (Paris: Vimont, 1832–4).

[109] 'Mœurs d'Allemagne', *NRg*, 12/47 (1832), 266–77. Reproduced in *Le Cabinet de lecture*, 244 (1833), 9–11.

[110] 'Études biographiques: Louis Tieck', *NRg*, 13/51 (1833), 193–215 (194).

Given its concise nature, the monograph is surprisingly comprehensive. Marmier not only mentions those works already known in France, but also a number of early works which were not particularly well-known in Germany at the time, such as the early novels *Abdallah* and *William Lovell*, which are compared to *Sternbald*. He insists, however, that the version of *Sternbald* currently available in France does not do justice to the original. The major pieces such as *Phantasus*, *Der blonde Eckbert*, *Der getreue Eckart*, and *Die wundersame Liebesgeschichte* are presented in some detail, as are the 'Märchendramen' (*Der gestiefelte Kater*, *Die verkehrte Welt*, and *Leben und Tod des kleinen Rotkäppchens*). Two plays in particular, *Kaiser Octavianus* and *Leben und Tod der heiligen Genoveva*, are singled out as 'ce qui doit tenir le premier rang, ce qui peut donner la plus haute idée de son génie'.[111] Tieck's poetry is expressed in terms which would almost seem to foreshadow Baudelaire's 'Correspondances':

> C'est une manière vive, profonde, saillante, d'envisager la nature et de représenter ses tableaux. C'est plus que cela, c'est un art indéfinissable de vivifier cette nature, de donner à tout ce qu'il embrasse l'animation, la pensée, le sentiment, en sorte que le poète se place au milieu des prairies, des bois, des coteaux, et que les prairies, les bois, les coteaux, les fleurs qui s'y épanouissent, les abeilles qui s'y reposent, les oiseaux qui les traversent, ont pour lui une voix mystérieuse, une voix qu'il comprend et à laquelle il répond en frère, en ami, en poète. Ce n'est pas l'idylle, car l'idylle admet quelque chose de faux.[112]

In his preface to Koberstein, Marmier also mentions Tieck at some length in the sections on contemporary drama, poetry, and the novel.[113]

In 1835 Marmier published translations of Tieck's *Leben und Tod der heiligen Genoveva* in *Le Monde dramatique*;[114] and of *Leben und Tod des kleinen Rotkäppchens* and *Die Nacht* in the popular 'Théâtre européen'.[115] The latter also appeared in the same year in Marmier's *Choix de fables et de contes* and was to reappear in 1842 in *Le Magasin pittoresque*.[116] After 1835, however, general interest in Tieck's work began to wane in France, and relatively few references to his work appeared after this date. It would seem that Tieck's work was associated with Marmier in the minds of his contemporaries. In May 1835, for example, the sculptor David d'Angers made Marmier a gift of a bust of Tieck, which he proudly placed on his

[111] Ibid., 209.
[112] Ibid., 205.   [113] Koberstein, *Manuel*, pp. xiii and xv.
[114] 'La Vie et la mort de Sainte-Geneviève [*sic*]', *Le Monde dramatique*, 1 (1835) 63–4, 187–209.
[115] Ludwig Tieck, 'La Vie et la mort du petit chaperon rouge' and 'Les Etoiles', in *Théâtre européen* [. . .] *Théâtre allemand*, 2nd ser., vol. 3 (Paris: Guérin, 1835).
[116] *Choix de fables et de contes* (see above, n. 23); and in *Le Magasin pittoresque*, 10 (1842), 258.

mantelpiece. Later in the month, Marmier himself would sit for David to model the medallion which now adorns his grave in Pontarlier.[117] The subject of Tieck's reception in France has been studied by J. Lambert.[118] Although Lambert (with some justification) does not rate the quality of Marmier's translations very highly, he nonetheless compares Marmier's achievement in popularising Tieck with that of Loève-Veimars in popularising Hoffmann in France. The comparison is not altogether a solid one (in that, as already suggested, Hoffmann achieved an infinitely wider popularity in France than Tieck ever did), but it gives an idea of Marmier's significance as an intermediary in this sphere.

Tieck furthermore furnished Marmier with material for an important article on Novalis, which also appeared in the series of 'Études biographiques'.[119] Tieck had become very close to Novalis not long before his death in 1801, and was jointly responsible, along with F. Schlegel, for publication of his collected works in 1802. Marmier cites Tieck at a number of junctures; for example with regard to the overall plan of *Heinrich von Ofterdingen* (the major unfinished work of Novalis), which Marmier describes as 'un livre de la plus haute conception, un roman allégorique, dans lequel Novalis eût jeté à pleines mains tous les trésors de son imagination [. . .], l'épopée même de la poésie, le livre aux aventures de l'âme'.[120] Approximately three pages are devoted to translations of extracts and a discussion of the plans for the second part. *Die Lehrlinge zu Saïs* is mentioned in terms which, once again, perhaps foreshadow some of the concepts to be elaborated in subsequent years by Baudelaire:[121]

> Mais ceux qui aiment vraiment la nature, c'est le peintre qui la contemple, assidument, avec toutes ses variétés de dessin, ses tons et ses couleurs; c'est le poète qui la comprend avec toutes ses harmonies; le poète qui ne la regarde plus comme un vain assemblage de plantes, d'eau, de pierres, mais comme un grand tout qu'une chaîne mystérieuse unit au ciel, en prenant l'homme pour intermédiaire; c'est le poète qui devine la liaison intime du monde extérieur avec le monde intérieur, et qui entend le langage des arbres, le langage des fleurs et le choeur solonnel des astres.[122]

---

[117] *David d'Angers et ses relations littéraires*, ed. H. Jouin (Paris: Plon, 1890), 92, letter 139.

[118] J. Lambert, *Ludwig Tieck dans les lettres françaises* (Paris: Didier, 1976). See also E. Teichmann 'Tieck in Frankreich, oder "Die Fahrt ins Blaue hinein", 1800–1850', *Revue de littérature comparée*, 37 (1963), 513–39.

[119] 'Études biographiques: Novalis (Frédéric de Hardenberg)', *NRg*, 15/57 & 58 (joint issue) (1833), 1–22.

[120] Ibid., 10.

[121] See, for example, Baudelaire's *Salon de 1846*, ch. 3 and *Salon de 1859*, ch. 7; or 'Correspondances' or 'Élévation' in *Les Fleurs du mal*.

[122] 'Études biographiques: Novalis', 19.

The *Geistliche Lieder* are covered briefly, and the *Hymnen an die Nacht*, of which Marmier published an extract in translation in July 1833, are commented on with particular reference to their 'prose harmonieuse, cadencée, qui ne fait pas regretter la mélodie du rythme'.[123] The final page of the article is devoted to Novalis's philosophical writings, especially the *Fragmente* of which Marmier had published a highly abridged version the previous month in the *Nouvelle Revue germanique*.[124]

Other important articles by Marmier appeared on a number of eminent literary figures. In May 1834, he published a monograph on Rahel Varnhagen von Ense, the prominent literary hostess in Berlin, just a few months after her death.[125] He had known her quite well, and maintained contact with her husband for some time later. In the same year, an article appeared on Michael Beer, a dramatist who had died in 1833. Michael Beer was the brother of the composer Meyerbeer; another brother, Wilhelm Beer, whom Marmier met in Berlin, gave Marmier access to a number of unpublished papers which he used to produce some highly original work. Beer's work is not widely read nowadays, but Marmier presents his work with a tremendous enthusiasm (*Struensee*, for example, is described as 'sans contredit un des beaux drames que l'Allemagne possède'[126] and compared to works of both Schiller and Goethe). The 'Étude' in the *Nouvelle Revue germanique* was followed by a translation of *Der Paria*, and this appeared simultaneously in another edition.[127] In 1835–6, the *Revue germanique* published Marmier's translation of *Struensee*.[128]

Marmier also presented the first comprehensive study of the works of Theodor Körner,[129] and wrote a very important monograph on Heinrich von Kleist, an author at that time little known in France and not fully

---

[123] Ibid., 21.

[124] 'Pensées traduites des Fragmens de Novalis', *NRg*, 14/56, 1833, 345–64.

[125] 'Études biographiques: Mme Rahel Frédérique Varnhagen von Ense', *NRg*, 2nd ser., 2/5 (1834), 3–14.

[126] 'Études biographiques: Michel Beer', *NRg*, 2nd ser., 1/4 (1834), 291–304 (304).

[127] 'Le Paria, tragédie en un acte, traduite de Michel Beer', *NRg*, 2nd ser., 2/6 (1834), 99–127; *Le Paria, tragédie en un acte, par Michel Beer, traduite par Xavier Marmier* (Strasbourg: Levrault, 1834). This translation reappeared the following year, prefaced by a slightly abridged version of the monograph.

[128] 'Struensee, tragédie en 5 actes, par Michel Beer', *Rg*, 3rd ser., 4/11 (1835), 141–91; and 5/13 (1836), 55–106.

[129] Theodor Körner, 'Le Garde de nuit', in *Théâtre européen* [. . .] *Théâtre allemand*, 2nd ser., vol. 3 (Paris: Guérin, 1835). The 'notice', which precedes the translation, follows the format of the 'Études biographiques' series.

appreciated in Germany.[130] The penultimate number in the 'Études biographiques' series is an article on Lenz.[131] At the time of writing, Lenz was no longer popular in either Germany or France. Despite expressing reservations about a number of features which he finds unacceptable, Marmier nonetheless identifies some of the finer works (*Der Landprediger*, for example). Significantly, he quotes Goethe's condemnation of Lenz in *Dichtung und Wahrheit*, which he finds to be unjust. This foreshadows a new respect and sympathy for Lenz, both in the immediate future, in the form of Büchner's novelle, and also, later, on the part of the Naturalists, of whom Lenz was a forerunner. It is perhaps slightly curious that whilst Marmier was able to present new and original work on authors he had not been privileged to meet, he passed over the opportunity to write about Grillparzer, with whom he had 'longues et amicales causeries' in Vienna.[132] In the Austrian capital, he also met two outstanding women: Edith Pfeiffer, to whom he refers rather patronisingly as 'rêvant à ses intrépides voyages en faisant humblement son ménage',[133] but whose work is presented very positively and in some detail in *Les Voyageurs nouveaux*;[134] and Karoline Pichler, whom he apparently found writing her novels 'au milieu de ses petits enfants, qui venaient à tout instant la tirer par sa robe pour lui montrer leurs soldats meurtris ou leurs poupées endommagées'.[135]

For a critic as keen as Marmier, no literary survey of Germany could be complete without reference to the great giants, Schiller and Goethe, both of whom had been known in France for some time. Marmier's work on the former comprises a collection of the major dramatic works in translation, which appeared in 1841, and a collection of poetry, published in 1844.[136] Both translations bear a preface; the preface to the drama, which is essentially a biography, is the reproduction of an article which he had published in the *Revue des Deux Mondes* in 1840.[137] This piece contains biographical information from Schwab's newly published *Schillers Leben*, which had not

---

[130] 'Études biographiques: Henri de Kleist', *NRg*, 14/54 (1833), 99–119. For an assessment of the importance of Marmier's work on Kleist, see Wendy Mercer, 'A Neglected Link in the Introduction of the Works of Heinrich von Kleist to France: Xavier Marmier', *New Comparison*, 17 (1994), 3–10.
[131] 'Études biographiques: Jacques Michel Lenz', *NRg*, 2nd ser., 3/11 (1834), 199–216.
[132] *SV*, 112.   [133] Ibid., 111.
[134] 'Voyage d'une femme autour du monde', *Les Voyageurs nouveaux*, 3 vols. (Paris: Arthus Bertrand, 1851), 3, 1–39.
[135] *SV*, 111–12. Although such statements do come across as rather patronising nowadays, in the nineteenth-century context this is perhaps a little harsh on Marmier. Women who wrote (whether in France or in Germany) came in for a large amount of unveiled and sometimes rather brutal criticism; here Marmier's implication is that a woman who is a housewife and/or mother may also have an intellectual life (and vice versa).
[136] See above, nn. 20 and 21.   [137] See above, n. 74.

been available in France previously, but no major contribution to an appreciation of Schiller's work. The preface to the poetry, on the other hand, is considered by Eggli, in his study *Schiller et le romantisme français*, to be 'l'étude la plus documentée qui eût encore paru en France sur l'œuvre de Schiller'.[138] The new material which impresses Eggli so greatly is largely that which contributes to the understanding of the work from a biographical angle. The preface is, however, remarkable also for its clear-sightedness in placing Schiller's lyric poetry within its generic context in both national and international terms, and for the balanced approach adopted by Marmier, who gives similar weight to the biographical, historical, generic and thematic aspects. The latter are treated in a comparative manner which would become a trademark of Marmier's literary criticism, and which he had pioneered in his *Études sur Goethe*. The treatment of individual poems by this method involved a wide knowledge of different literatures ('Schiller empruntait le sujet de ces ballades à diverses contrées et à diverses traditions'[139]); detailed discussion is limited to 'Der Taucher', 'Der Handschuh', and 'Das Lied von der Glocke', although early versions of other poems are mentioned in summary.[140] Lamartine uses Marmier's translation of 'Das Lied von der Glocke' in 'Entretien XLI' of his *Cours familier de littérature*; in that same 'Entretien', he also acknowledges Marmier as the source of his brief biography of Schiller.[141]

But it was Marmier's work on Goethe which really sealed his reputation as a literary critic in France. Goethe was already well known in France by the time Marmier went to Germany, mainly through *Werther*, which had achieved tremendous popularity following its rapid translation into French in 1776, and then through *Faust I*, of which Nerval had published his famous translation in 1828. Marmier's first article from Germany was an article on Weimar, where he had stopped off en route for Leipzig when he first arrived in Germany, hoping to meet Goethe. Unfortunately, he arrived too late, as Goethe had died shortly before. Despite this disappointment, Marmier set to studying Goethe's work in his little room in Leipzig with the help of his friend and mentor Adolf Wagner, and in 1833 he published translations of *Mignonslied* and *Erlkönig*.[142] It may well be that his translation of *Mignonslied* was a major source of inspiration for Baudelaire's

---

[138] Edmond Eggli, *Schiller et le romantisme français*, 2 vols. (Paris: Librairie Universitaire, J. Gamber éditeur, 1927), 2, 550.

[139] *Poésies de Schiller*, p. xxix.   [140] Ibid., pp. xxx–xxxi.

[141] 'dans une préface de sa traduction de ce grand homme', thus implying familiarity with Marmier's translations of Schiller's dramatic works as well as his translations of the poetry. See Lamartine, *Cours familier de littérature* (Paris: Firmin Didot, 1859), 346 and 318.

[142] *NRg*, 13/52 (1833), 360 and 14/55 (1833), 275 respectively.

'L'Invitation au voyage'.[143] It would also appear highly probable that his translation of 'Selbstbetrug' was the main source of inspiration for Musset's 'Le Rideau de ma voisine'.[144] More importantly, he was on the spot for the posthumous publication of *Faust II* in 1832; Marmier's commentary on this piece in his *Études sur Goethe* (1835) was one of the first to appear in either German or French. In 1837 he published a translation of the epic *Hermann und Dorothea*, which achieved considerable success, and this was followed in 1839 by a translation of Goethe's theatre. The latter was not one of Marmier's more creditable achievements: although the fact does not appear to have been noted by other critics, Marmier's translation is a mere reproduction of the translations published by Stapfer between 1821 and 1825.[145] His preface, on the other hand, is certainly original, and this, combined with his other critical work on Goethe, represents an important step forward in Goethe criticism.

The *Études sur Goethe* was effectively the first work published in France to offer a critical appreciation of the quasi-totality of Goethe's œuvre. Its publication was heralded by an efficient publicity campaign in the press lasting almost eighteen months. It took the form of extracts published in various reviews (principally the *Revue de Paris* and the *Nouvelle Revue germanique*) accompanied by a few lines announcing the imminent publication of the volume.[146] All the indications are that when it finally appeared at the end of August 1835, it was a resounding success. *La France littéraire* noted that 'ce livre a obtenu les suffrages de la presse'.[147] Two whole pages of *Le Monde dramatique* were dedicated to a review which singled out for particular attention the historical and comparative study of the Faust legend, and the quality of the translations contained in the volume.[148] With typical modesty, Marmier wrote to Weiss on 12 September, asking him to

---

[143] On the possible importance of the *Mignonslied* translation, see Wendy Mercer, '*Wilhelm Meister* in France: "Mignonslied" and "L'Invitation au voyage"', in Carol Tully (ed.), *Romantik and Romance: Cultural Interanimation in European Romanticism*, Strathclyde Modern Language Studies (New Series), 4 (Glasgow: University of Strathclyde, 2000), 59–78.

[144] See Wendy Mercer, 'Le Rôle de Xavier Marmier (1808–1892) dans l'introduction de l'œuvre de Goethe en France', in Peter J. Edwards (ed.), *Poésie et poétique en France 1830–1890: Hommage à Eileen Souffrin-Le Breton* (New York: Peter Lang, 2001), 21–37 (26–7).

[145] *Œuvres dramatiques de J. W. Goethe, traduites de l'allemand, précédées d'une notice biographique et littéraire sur Goethe* (Paris: Bobée et Sautelet, 1821–5).

[146] The first announcement seems to have been in the *Revue de Paris* in April 1834 ('Album', *RP*, 2nd ser., 4 (1834), 192). The following month, the same review published 'La chronique du magicien Faust' and then 'Chronique de Goetz de Berlichingen' (*RP*, 2nd ser., 5 (1834), 34–8 and *RP*, 2nd ser., 8 (1834), 250–66 respectively). See also 'Études sur Goethe: Goetz de Berlichingen, Egmont', *NRg*, 2nd ser., 2/7 & 8 (1834), 195–223 and 291–367.

[147] 'Budget littéraire', *La France littéraire*, 22 (1835), 369.

[148] 'Bibliographie. Études sur Goethe, par M. X. Marmier', *Le Monde dramatique*, 1 (1835), 41–2.

read the book, but imploring him: 'Ne le jugez pas d'avance d'après ce que plusieurs journaux en ont dit, on m'a traité avec beaucoup trop de bienveillance'.[149]

Despite the originality of many of his insights Marmier was not writing for an educated elite. His avowed aim was to 'faire passer dans l'esprit de quelques lecteurs l'admiration sincère que j'éprouve pour le grand homme de l'Allemagne; si je puis leur inspirer au moins le désir de le connaître, de l'étudier, le but que j'avais en commençant cet ouvrage sera rempli'.[150] From the outset he describes the critical methodology adopted, namely to 'remonter à l'idée première d'où Goethe était parti pour composer un drame, une comédie; [. . .] voir comment il s'était emparé de cette idée, comment il avait su la faire ployer au gré de son génie, l'élever, l'étendre, l'ennoblir, la travailler avec art dans ses détails et la poser avec majesté dans l'ensemble'.[151] Thus, for example, he examines the legend of Faust from its origins through the dramas of Klingsor, Calderón, Marlowe, Byron, Lessing, Lenz, Chamisso, Schink, Grabbe, Holtei, Klingemann, and particularly Müller; through the novels of Seybold, Bechstein, Gerle, and Klinger; and through Spohr's opera, in order to demonstrate 'comment une même pensée peut être prise de tant de manières différentes, comment chaque poète a pu prêter à Faust sa propre individualité'.[152] In effect, he was working his way towards what we would now term a study in comparative criticism.

The book contains sections on Goethe's drama, novels, and epic and lyric poetry. The latter traces the history of the genre in Germany through the Minnesänger up to the present (1835), taking in Luther, Fleming, Günther, Gellert, Gleim; Uz, Hölty, Bürger and the *Göttinger Hain*; and Klopstock. He argues that after Klopstock, four different schools of lyric poetry were formed, Goethe heading the first. Goethe's poetry, he argues, is the most difficult to translate or to introduce to another nation since so much of its beauty lies in the form. The comparatist is again to the fore in the presentation of the pastoral idyll as Marmier traces and describes the history of the genre in Germany, comparing it favourably to its Italian, Spanish, and especially French counterparts. *Hermann und Dorothea*, he concludes, although essentially German in character, 'n'en est pas moins un modèle pour toutes les nations', and in particular, 'l'un des meilleurs livres à introduire dans notre littérature'.[153] The work had been translated into French earlier, but with no notable success; Marmier's translation of 1837 was reprinted at least eleven times, the last print run being in 1881. A large

---

[149] BmB, Collection Estignard, MS 1907, Correspondance de Charles Weiss, Lettres de X. Marmier, fo. 378.
[150] *EG*, p. vi.   [151] Ibid., pp. v–vi.   [152] Ibid., 141.   [153] Ibid., 424.

proportion of the section on dramatic art is devoted to the two parts of
Faust, not only through the history of the Faust legend through the ages, but
also through a detailed analysis of the newly published *Faust II* and translations of a number of extracts. A number of useful readings of the
encounter between Helen and Faust, and of the significance of Euphorion
are given. Neo-classical aspects of Goethe's other major plays are also highlighted in the analyses of *Iphigenie auf Tauris*, *Torquato Tasso*, and *Die
natürliche Tochter*. *Iphigenie* had been published in 1787 in Germany; but
despite translations appearing in France in 1821 and 1827 it remained virtually unknown there. Marmier underlines the purity of form and the difference between the concept of classical tragedy as it is generally understood
in France, 'froidement calquée sur des interprétations à demi fausses
d'Aristote', and that to be found in *Iphigenie*, 'la tragédie antique, conçue
dans sa grâce la plus pure'.[154] The form of *Iphigenie* is dicussed in terms of
its 'beaux contours' and its 'mouvements harmonieux'.[155] *Die natürliche
Tochter*, a play also little-known in France before the publication of the
Études, 'a la beauté et le poli du marbre, si l'on veut, mais elle en a aussi la
froideur'.[156] In the preface to his translation of Goethe's theatre, he characterises what he terms the third phase of Goethe's dramatic work as displaying 'les suaves contours, les doux reflets et l'attitude majestueuse d'un bon
marbre antique'.[157] Such remarks foreshadow the Parnassian aesthetic
which would develop over the coming decade.

The literary was not the only area in which Marmier was able to antici-
pate developments in Germany. In the early years of the decade, it is difficult to find any negative comments in Marmier's numerous publications.
Yet by the late 1830s, he was beginning to feel a definite sense of unease and
apprehension about political developments in the country, an unease which
would be confirmed and magnified by his visits there in the late 1850s and
1860s. In 1839, Marmier reviewed Quinet's *Allemagne et Italie* for the *Revue
de Paris*.[158] In this review, Marmier speaks for the first time of 'les haines tra-
ditionnelles cachées sous le manteau du stoïcisme', and the 'misères politiques voilées par le voile d'or de la poésie'.[159] He recognises that 1813 has
not been forgotten, and that there is a strong feeling towards unification in
Germany. Even from this relatively early date in his career, he expresses misgivings about the way this might be achieved. By 1841, he was able to focus
his misgivings more clearly: no longer is 'l'Allemagne' as such the source of
his anxiety, but more specifically, 'la Prusse'. In his 'Revue littéraire' in the

---

[154] *EG*, 341.   [155] Ibid.   [156] Ibid., 380.   [157] *Théâtre de Goethe*, p. xi.
[158] 'Critique littéraire. Allemagne et Italie, de M. Edgar Quinet', *RP*, 3rd ser., 4 (1839), 49–55.
[159] Ibid., 52.

Revue des Deux Mondes, he reviews anti-French pamphlets, which he claims have been far more numerous in recent weeks than any other form of publication.[160] The Prussian authors of such works, according to Marmier, 'se distinguent entre tous par leur ton tranchant et leurs paroles hautaines'.[161] He writes about their ominously aggressive patriotism, and warns about Prussia's strengths and intentions in no uncertain terms. He insists on the significance of its geographical position in relation to other countries and the danger this implies: 'Étendue comme un long cordon militaire du nord au sud, de la Pologne à la France, resserrée entre deux lignes de royaumes et de principautés, il faut nécessairement qu'elle s'élargisse sous peine d'être écrasée, et certes elle a bien montré qu'elle comprenait sa situation'.[162] The warnings for France become even clearer as he underlines the insidious way in which Prussia has acted to annex neighbouring states: 'Elle se les assimile peu à peu par des tentatives *dont elle seule peut-être comprend d'abord toute la portée*, aujourd'hui par son système monétaire, demain par son réseau de douanes'.[163] In the event of war, he warns, 'qui sait quels fruits porterait alors cette longue et patiente infiltration des idées prussiennes répandues de côté et d'autre?'.[164]

This, however, was written in 1841; although he had travelled through Germany and visited friends there on his way to other countries, he had not 'lived' in the country properly speaking since 1835, the year when the *Études sur Goethe* was published. The intervening years would see him visit Iceland, Denmark, Sweden, Holland, and Russia, as well as joining an expedition to Spitzbergen, and becoming something of a cult figure in France.

---

[160] 'Revue littéraire de l'Allemagne', *RDM*, 26 (1841), 627–55.
[161] Ibid., 630.
[162] Ibid.   [163] Ibid., my italics.   [164] Ibid., 631.

4

Iceland (1836): 'L'Invitation au voyage'

The year 1836 was to be an important year for Marmier, for it marked his first expedition with the Commission du Nord on board the corvette *La Recherche* to the Scandinavian countries. These prestigious expeditions had been initiated in 1835 with two objectives. The first of these was to search for the gunboat *La Lilloise*, commanded by Jules de Blosseville, which had gone missing in the area.[1] *La Lilloise* had been dispatched in 1833 to protect French fishing vessels in Icelandic waters. Blosseville had for some time wanted to visit Greenland, and this mission provided him with the ideal opportunity to combine both tasks. In May 1833, he sent a report to the ministry outlining a preliminary visit to the east coast of Greenland. The last news of the ship received in France was a letter to his brother written on 6 August. In 1834, the gunboat *La Bordelaise* was sent to search for the missing vessel and its crew, but returned without having succeeded. The following year (1835), *La Recherche* set sail for Iceland under the command of François-Thomas Tréhouart[2] with the same mission; this time, however, Paul Gaimard[3] and the geologist Eugène Robert were attached to the expedition, partly to help with making inquiries into the fate of *La Lilloise*, but also to explore Iceland. Leaving Gaimard and Robert in Iceland, Tréhouart went on to Greenland, but still failed to find any trace of *La Lilloise*. In September 1835, the party arrived back in France. Despite having failed in their primary objective, the secondary one surpassed all expectations: Gaimard and Robert returned with an impressive collection of objets d'art and scientific specimens. Although little was known about Iceland in France during the earlier part of the nineteenth century, the Romantic fascination

---

[1] Jules Alphonse René Poret, baron de Blosseville (1808–33), French navigator and geographer. At the age of twenty, he took part in a scientific expedition on board *La Coquille*; in 1827 he undertook a voyage of discovery in the seas of India and China.

[2] François-Thomas Tréhouart (1798–1873); this was an early stage in a dazzling naval career: he was promoted to the rank of 'lieutenant de vaisseau' in 1827; 'capitaine de corvette' in 1837; and finished his career as admiral.

[3] Paul Gaimard (1790–1858) was a French explorer, naturalist, and doctor. Between 1826 and 1829 he took part in the famous expedition of *L'Astrolabe* to the South Sea Islands. In the early 1830s he documented the spread of the cholera epidemic in Europe and Russia. As president of the Commission du Nord, he was a well-known and highly influential public figure, and Marmier owed much to his patronage.

with the Northern countries had led to the emergence of a hazy but enthusiastic perception of the Scandinavian countries; this perception was based
largely on received ideas, but fed into the literary and artistic production of
the era.[4] The expedition was thus timely, and the findings brought back by
Gaimard and Robert attracted a good deal of interest, both among the
general public and in the scientific world.

Encouraged by the success of this expedition, Admiral Duperré,[5] the
Ministre de la Marine, organised a second expedition to Iceland, to be led
by Gaimard.[6] Robert was to continue his geological studies; Victor Lottin[7]
was to be responsible for observation of magnetic variations and hydrography; Raoul Anglès was to study the meteorology of Iceland. Auguste Mayer[8]
and Louis Bévalet were attached to the expedition as artists (a particularly
important role prior to the era of photography): the former was to take on
landscapes and portraits; the latter was responsible for medical and scientific subjects; he also contributed notes on ornithology and entomology,
and caught and preserved a large number of specimens. On 15 March
1836, Gaimard wrote to the baron Pelet de la Lozère, then Ministre de
l'Instruction publique, with two requests. One was for a scholarship to edu-
cate a deserving young Icelander in France; the other, which occupies the
major part of the letter, is a request for permission to recruit a specialist in
philology and literature. His preferred candidate for the post was Marmier.
The choice of Marmier is justified by: the latter's knowledge of English,
German, Dutch, and Danish (this last possibly being slightly premature,
since Marmier was at that very time in the process of teaching himself
Danish); his *Études sur Goethe*; his articles in various reviews, particularly

---

[4] See, for example, Hugo's *Han d'Islande*. Much of the early interest in the Northern countries had
of course been aroused by Mme de Staël.

[5] Victor Guy Duperré, baron (1775–1846) was made a baron under the Empire after distinguishing
himself in the struggle against the English, particularly in the West Indies. He took part in the siege
of Cádiz (1823), then in the expedition of Algiers (July 1830). He became a 'pair de France' under
Charles X, then admiral under Louis-Philippe and served as Ministre de la Marine between 1834
and 1843.

[6] From reading the unpublished correspondence connected with the expedition, it would appear
that Gaimard organised everything virtually single-handed, from research projects to funding and
public relations. He comes across not only as a dynamic and efficient coordinator of all the
research projects undertaken by the members of the commission on behalf of numerous scientific
institutions, but also as a generous and compassionate human being.

[7] Victor Charles Lottin (1795–1858) had participated in the expedition of *L'Astrolabe* in 1826 and
was known for his research on magnetic variations and meteors.

[8] Étienne-François Auguste Mayer (or Meyer as he sometimes signs himself) was born in 1805 in
Brest and lived until 1890. From an early age, he specialised in marine painting. As well as being
attached to the voyages of the Commission du Nord, he also travelled to Holland and to the East.
Although he worked at tremendous speed on this expedition, often completing several pictures in a
day, many of his studies are of an exceptional quality.

the *Revue des Deux Mondes*; his translation of Koberstein's history of German literature; and his translations of drama by Oehlenschläger and Holberg.[9] A letter simply dated 'Mars 1836' from Marmier to Gaimard, and which probably predates Gaimard's letter to Pelet de la Lozère, shows that Gaimard had already spoken to Marmier about the research to be done on Icelandic language and literature, and about the possibility of his inclusion in the commission. Marmier's letter in fact constitutes a detailed research proposal, and reveals evidence of a good deal of preliminary investigation on his own part.[10] The request was approved: Marmier was granted a free passage and dining rights. No funds were available, however, for any supplementary allowance, and Marmier was not a young man of independent means. On 5 May, Gaimard addressed the following letter to the Académie française:

> Messieurs,
>
> Une nouvelle expédition à la recherche de *La Lilloise* doit aller incessamment visiter un peuple bon et hospitalier qui cultive les lettres avec distinction sous le cercle polaire. M^r l'Amiral Duperré, n'ayant voulu rien négliger pour le succès de cette exploration, a pris, dans l'intérêt de la littérature, et sur ma demande, une détermination qu'aucun de ses devanciers n'avait prise encore: il a autorisé un jeune et habile littérateur, Mr Xavier Marmier, à faire partie de la Commission d'Islande et de Groënland. Mr Marmier, par ordre de l'Amiral, sera admis à la table de l'État-Major et recevra le même traitement que les officiers de *La Recherche*.
>
> Mais quelques dépenses seront inévitables avant le départ et pendant le séjour en Islande. Déjà plusieurs fois vous avez fait, Messieurs, un noble usage des dotations que possède l'Académie. J'ai l'honneur de vous proposer de vouloir bien employer, pour faciliter les recherches de Mr Marmier, une petite part des libéralités de Mr Montyon. La somme de mille francs serait suffisante; et l'Académie en recevrait la récompense par les travaux qu'exécuterait, sur son patronage, un littérateur plein de zèle et de dévouement.
>
> J'ose espérer, Messieurs, que vous accueillerez favorablement une demande faite au nom de l'honneur national, et que l'Académie voudra bien s'associer à une bonne action: la recherche périlleuse de malheureux naufragés. C'est presque de la vertu pour un homme qui n'est point habitué à naviguer; et le vœu du testament sera rempli. [. . .][11]

The Academy moved with outstanding alacrity to approve the request; a formal decision was made the very day the letter was written, and forwarded to the minister; two days later (7 May), royal assent was requested.[12] The

---

[9] Archives nationales de France (hereafter AnF), 5JJ179.   [10] AnF, 5JJ180.
[11] Archives de l'Académie française (hereafter AAf), Correspondance à l'Académie française, 5B15, 1836.
[12] Ibid.

application was supported by a dazzling array of referees, including Guizot, one of the most influential politicians of the era,[13] Villemain,[14] de Ségur, Raynouard, Tissot, and also by the baron Hector d'Aunay, father of one of the victims of the presumed *Lilloise* disaster. Villemain wrote to Marmier to inform him of the Academy's decision to support Gaimard's application for his funding; but the departure date was imminent, and approval had not yet been obtained either from the Ministre de l'Instruction publique, or from Louis-Philippe. Marmier, however, had obviously invested too much of his time, energy, and enthusiasm in the venture to allow his participation to depend on the outcome of the application. On 8 May, he wrote to Villemain requesting that the final decision be communicated to the publisher and bookseller Pitois-Levrault, at 81 rue de la Harpe, in his absence. As it turned out, the request was probably unnecessary, since on 6 May, a letter was sent to the minister, Pelet de la Lozère, for approval; and on 7 May, a document allocating 1,000 francs to Marmier from the Montyon fund was given royal assent.[15]

In the meantime, and despite considerable apprehension about the perils of the voyage,[16] Marmier was busy with last-minute preparations: packing his belongings (principally books) into crates, arranging for his

---

[13] François Pierre Guillaume Guizot (1787–1874) was a highly influential figure in French politics under the Restoration and the July Monarchy. Having been appointed to a chair in modern history at the Sorbonne in 1812, he was then secretary to the Ministre de l'Intérieur during the First Restoration (1814). From 1816–20 he held various important posts at the ministry of justice. After the fall of Decazes, he returned to education, but was suspended in 1822 because of his opposition to the government. Elected to parliament in 1830, he adopted a stance hostile to Polignac's reactionary cabinet, and then against the *ordonnances de St Cloud* on 25 July 1830, which brought about the July Revolution. Under Louis-Philippe, he became Ministre de l'Intérieur (1830), then Ministre de l'Instruction publique (1832–7), during which time he succeeded in having the *loi Guizot* on primary education passed in 1833. He was elected to the Académie française in 1836. From 1840 he was appointed Ministre des Affaires étrangères and effectively led the government, although he only held the post of Président du Conseil from 1847–8. His opposition to the campaign of banquets in February 1848 was a decisive factor in provoking the 1848 revolution which brought down the July Monarchy.

[14] François Villemain (1790–1870), from 1816 to 1830 professor of French literature at the Sorbonne, was elected to the Académie française in 1821. He published a *Cours de littérature française* (1828–9) emphasising the importance of the roles of social institutions and foreign literatures. He was elected to parliament shortly before the July Revolution, and was appointed as Ministre de l'Instruction publique (1840–4). Villemain was to be an important figure in Marmier's life and generally lent his support in professional matters. Marmier sent many letters to Villemain from Iceland reporting on his progress.

[15] AAf, Correspondance à l'Académie française, 5B15, 1836.

[16] Quinet wrote to Michelet that Marmier 'était très effrayé en partant'. Jules Michelet, *Correspondance générale*, ed. Louis Le Guillou, 12 vols. (Paris: Champion, 1994–2001), 2, 435, letter 1405, 25 May 1836.

mail to be collected by a friend, and for various objects (including a packing case and an umbrella!) to be sent to his father.[17] He had also started in
earnest on the intellectual task before him: he read books in French (so far
as these existed) and other languages in the National Library about
Icelandic language and literature;[18] and also (as already mentioned) set
about teaching himself Danish. To his mind, his mission was clear: he was
to observe the current state of literature and learning in Iceland in order
to compare the intellectual relationship between the ancient and the
modern—the Iceland of the sagas and the Iceland of the nineteenth century. Leaving Paris on Monday 9 May, Marmier travelled via Evreux, Caen,
Bayeux, and St Lô to arrive in Cherbourg on Wednesday 11 May. After
catching sight of *La Recherche* in dock for the first time, he spent the next
few days purchasing essentials for the expedition: trousers, boots, socks,
and a hat figure prominently in his accounts. His spare time was spent reading, working on his Danish grammar, and practising his newly acquired
language skills on two attractive young women: Mme Normand, a young
Norwegian, and Mme Kirkheim.[19]

La Recherche finally set sail on 21 May, and the crossing to Iceland
took nine days. For two days, Marmier was terribly seasick, but gradually
gained his sea legs, and was able to spend much of the remainder of the
voyage reading. On 30 May, the vessel arrived at Reykjavík, and a local
pilot (wearing a sealskin overcoat which greatly impressed Marmier)
guided the vessel into the port. Marmier's first impression of Reykjavík
was of an overwhelming stench which he attributed to a combination of
factors: the vast quantities of fish being dried in the open air, the unsani-
tary living conditions of the majority of the population, and the often
putrid foodstuffs which they were forced to eat. On the day of their arrival,
Marmier dined with Gaimard at the club in Reykjavík, which was soon to
become a regular haunt of the commission members (one of the expenses
noted in the accounts of the expedition is a sum of twenty francs to be
paid on 7 June to the Bishop's son, Hannes 'Steingrimsen' [*sic*] (for
Steingrímsson) Johnsen, who had paid their entrance fees[20]). On this first
day, Marmier's eyes fell on a beautiful young waitress, 18-year-old
Málfríður Sveinsdóttir (Fríða), who was soon to become the first of a

---

[17] Spoelberch de Lovenjoul, BIF, Lettres adressées à Sainte-Beuve, D606, 10, fo. 130. Although this
letter is conserved with the 'Lettres adressées à Sainte-Beuve', it is not in fact addressed to him, but
to Clerget.
[18] *Rapport de M. Paul Gaimard, président de la commission scientifique d'Islande et de Groënland,
à M. l'Amiral Duperré, ministre de la Marine et des colonies* [Paris: Imprimerie Royale, 1836].
[19] Bibliothèque Sainte-Geneviève, Fonds nordique (hereafter BSG, Fn), MS 3894, fos. 8 and 12.
[20] AnF, 5JJ181.

number of lovers in Iceland.[21] The members of the commission were invited to tea in the evening with the governor (Krieger), the doctor, an influential merchant, and a magistrate. The governor, who had travelled extensively in France and Italy, and who spoke perfect French, was an excellent host. Marmier also had the opportunity to try out his Danish and was delighted to be able to report to Sainte-Beuve in a letter written that very evening— obviously in a state of euphoria—that 'J'ai parlé danois [. . .] J'ai compris et j'ai été compris'.[22]

The following day, Marmier took his last two meals on board *La Recherche*, which was due to depart for Greenland, and moved his personal effects on shore, where he would spend the next three months. Krieger took them to visit the bishop, Steingrímur Jónsson, a former teacher of theology at the school of Bessastaðir, who communicated with the various members of the commission in Latin, English, and Danish. Marmier was excited to discover that the bishop possessed a rich library with collections of works by foreign authors, a number of rare editions, and manuscripts concerning the history of the country. The bishop, for his part, gratefully received a number of gifts sent with Gaimard on behalf of Louis-Philippe and the minister responsible for the navy and colonies, Admiral Duperré. His wife prepared coffee, wine, and port for the visitors, while a crowd of Icelanders gathered to view the Frenchmen and their gifts.

Marmier was greatly impressed by the hospitality he received every- where in Iceland, although he was soon to discover that the majority of the population lived in dire poverty. Behind the façade of elegant wooden Danish houses lining the seafront, he discovered the typical dwelling of the Icelander, which he refers to as a 'cabane islandaise' or 'bœr' [*sic*] (for 'bær') (see Plate 1). The walls of the dwelling, some four- or five-foot thick, were made of peat and moss, covered with earth, and hermetically sealed on all sides to keep out the cold. The roof, pointed like a tent, was made of turf. In the middle was a narrow door, so low that one had to stoop to enter, with a small window beside it, and a small opening in the top of the roof to allow smoke to escape. The floor inside was simply bare earth, and the cramped interior was divided into four sections. The furnishings were minimal: the hearth was composed of two stones placed on top of one another; whale- bones and horses' skulls served as seats. Some of the better off were able to

---

[21] BSG, Fn, MS 3894, fo. 15.
[22] Spoelberch de Lovenjoul, BIF, Lettres adressées à Sainte-Beuve, D606, 10, fo. 148. He wrote the same evening to Michelet in similar terms: 'A ma très grande joie j'ai parlé facilement danois—Me voilà sauvé, car tous les hommes un peu instruits, et une grande quantité des gens du peuple parl- ent cette langue [. . .]'. Michelet, *Correspondance générale*, 2, 436–7, letter 1408.

add to their home an extension of a few square feet, built of wooden planks, where fish could be hung to dry. Most Icelanders, however, were unable to manage such a luxury, and would simply hang the fish out to dry on the walls; yet, Marmier was intrigued to discover that, despite the terrible poverty, crime was virtually non-existent, and nobody seemed to have their fish stolen. This was perhaps all the more striking in view of the fact that most of the Icelanders would not be able to afford to keep these fish for their own consumption; after cutting off their heads which was the only part they would keep for themselves, the rest of the fish would be taken to the local fair and sold to the Danish merchants in exchange for goods such as salt, flour, and spirits. Marmier found the local people hospitable to a fault; they would offer the visitors the best of everything they had, obviously drawing on provisions that had been put aside for a special occasion—and despite this, would be offended by any offer of payment.

Fascinated by every new experience, Marmier soon began to put pen to paper, and addressed his first official progress report to Villemain on 15 June. This, and the subsequent letters addressed to Villemain, were published first of all by Buloz in the *Revue des Deux Mondes*;[23] in a volume under the title *Lettres sur l'Islande* in 1837;[24] finally, the sections on the history and literature of Iceland appeared virtually unchanged in the official report on the expedition, published under the collective title *Voyage en Islande et au Groënland exécuté pendant les années 1835 et 1836 sur la corvette 'La Recherche', dans le but de découvrir 'La Lilloise', publié par ordre du Gouvernement sous la direction de M Paul Gaimard.*[25]

---

[23] These articles appeared in *RDM* in the latter part of 1836: 'Reykjavík' appeared in August (4th ser., 7, 342–51); 'Le Geyser et l'Hécla' in September (4th ser., 7, 699–711); 'L'Instruction publique' in October (4th ser., 8, 163–70); 'Les Sagas' and 'Langue et littérature' in November (4th ser., 8, 287–99 and 478–94 respectively); 'Découverte de l'Islande' in December (4th ser., 8, 704–13); and 'Mythologie' in February 1837 (4th ser., 9, 318–29).

[24] Published by Bonnaire in Paris. New editions were brought out by Delloye and a fourth edition published by Arthus Bertrand appeared in 1855. Pirate Belgian editions (a mark of the book's success) appeared as early as 1837; Marmier discovered one while he was in Copenhagen, which he bought. Page numbers given in this chapter refer to another Belgian edition: *Lettres sur le Nord (Danemark, Suède, Norvège, Laponie et Spitzberg) et sur l'Islande*, 2 vols. (Brussels: N.-J. Grégoir, V. Wouters et Cie, 1841). The *Lettres sur l'Islande* (cited hereafter as *LI*) are presented as a separate single-volume item with discrete numbering, but bound in with the second volume of the *Lettres sur le Nord* in this edition.

[25] Marmier was responsible for *Histoire de l'Islande* (Paris: Arthus Bertrand, 1840) (cited hereafter as *HI*); and *Littérature islandaise*, 2 vols. (Paris: Arthus Bertrand, 1843). The latter is, however, expanded and slightly more up-to-date than the literature sections of the *Lettres sur l'Islande* (see above, n. 24). The *Lettres* contain more details of the journey and personal impressions: it was presumably because of the quality of this writing that Marmier was appointed as official 'rapporteur' on the subsequent expeditions of the commission.

In the volume entitled *Histoire de l'Islande*, Marmier treats history right up to the present day, and includes a survey of public and social institutions. In this text, he is far more outspoken than in his letters about a number of aspects of the Danish administration of the country. A major focus of his criticism is the Danish trade monopoly; he strongly favours opening trade up to outside competition. The merchandise brought in from Denmark is extremely expensive, he argues: the price for the Icelanders of such uncompetitive trade is a life of hardship and deprivation. In exchange for a few basic commodities, the impoverished Icelandic peasant must hand over to the Danish merchants 'tout le fruit de ses rudes travaux, des veilles de sa famille, des dangers que ses fils ont courus [. . .]'.[26] Fishing is a 'rude labeur', full of perils and carried out in the most primitive of working conditions, which leads to 'des maladies hideuses'[27] such as leprosy and elephantiasis. Healthcare, on the other hand, is one area where he expresses approval of a number of measures recently taken by the government. He was impressed by the recent appointment of seven doctors to treat the whole population; they would offer free medical care to those unable to pay. He also welcomes the promise to appoint a number of midwives in the near future; their services are much needed, according to Marmier, because of the high rates of infant mortality in the country. He is also full of praise for the postal service, which, although very limited in comparison to a country like France, offers a regular delivery.

The members of the commission had originally intended only to spend a few days in the capital before setting off to visit the more remote regions of Iceland during the more clement summer season. The expedition, however, proved difficult to organise. Since they needed to take tents and provisions, along with scientific equipment, horses were essential for the journey. The beginning of June was a difficult time to find good horses. In the winter, supplies would run so low that the Icelanders had to turn their ponies out into the wild to find their own food and shelter. Many would perish before the milder weather returned, and those that survived would be thin and weak until they had been able to build up their strength with the new grass. In 1836, the weather had been particularly severe, and ponies were in short supply, so that the party's departure was postponed until 20 June. They were accompanied on the first leg of their journey by the governor and a dozen dignitaries as far as a salmon farm, where they took an improvised lunch on the grass. Several bottles of champagne were drunk before the Frenchmen climbed back onto their ponies and continued on their way.[28] The first stage of the expedition was to visit the geyser, taking the party

---

[26] *HI*, 22.   [27] Ibid., 19.   [28] AnF, 5JJ182A (Bévalet's account).

across deserted plains of lava and volcanic rocks, marshes, and rivers. Marmier grew to respect the ponies of Iceland, which were surefooted and reliable. No doubt ahead of public opinion of his time, he was fond of animals in general, and he admits in his *Lettres sur l'Islande* that 'dussé-je faire rire ceux qui n'ont jamais compâti aux souffrances des animaux, j'avouerai que, dans mes excursions en Islande, j'ai souvent pressé entre mes mains, avec attendrissement, la tête de mon cheval qui me portait si patiemment'.[29]

The regions the party crossed were sparsely populated, and the Frenchmen would sometimes go for days without coming across a single dwelling. Marmier particularly enjoyed visiting the isolated farms and chatting with the owners, perched on a horse's skull in the smoke-filled kitchen. Apart from the warm hospitality of the Icelanders, Marmier was struck by two other particularities: the remarkable dexterity and resourcefulness of those living in remote parts who, despite or perhaps because of their poverty, had become extremely ingenious in using the few natural resources available to them; and the impressive level of education in the country. He was astonished to find that even those living in the most remote districts (where the organisation of schools for such a far-flung population would be impossible), and those living in the most wretched poverty, were literate; virtually all Icelanders could read and write. He decided that they had a natural penchant for study, and noted that even the least well-off possessed a number of books, normally including the Bible and a selection of sagas, which they would lend to neighbours, borrowing others in return. He was greatly impressed one day in Reykjavík, when the daughter of a local fisherman, who brought a weekly delivery of fish and seabirds, found him sitting in his room reading Njal's saga. She told him that she knew the text well, having read it several times when she was a child, and was immediately able to show him the finest passages. Where in France, he mused, would you find a fisherman's daughter with that kind of knowledge?[30]

Camping at Thingvalla (þingvellir) on 21 June and revelling in its history, the party was approached by a man dressed in pitiful rags who wanted to sell them milk and fish. It was the priest of Thingvalla, whose dwelling was the most wretched Marmier had yet seen. As well as accommodating the priest and his wife, the hut also provided shelter for their children, an old woman, and a man suffering from leprosy (probably Finnur Jónsson, who, according to the accounts kept, was paid four francs for allowing his portrait to be painted by Bévalet). Leprosy, Marmier notes, is quite frequent in Iceland, but the disease was regarded as hereditary rather than contagious,

---

[29] *LI*, 155.   [30] Ibid., 256.

so that lepers were not cast out from the rest of the population. Gaimard sent the priest, Björn Pálsson, five pairs of clogs, an ordinary knife, an elegant knife, a lighter and several boxes of matches, a pair of bellows, a tin plate, a pair of earrings for his daughter Solveig, and a framed portrait.[31] In the *Histoire de l'Islande*, Marmier condemns the fact that no measures have been taken to alleviate the poverty suffered by local priests, despite the problem having been officially brought to the attention of the Danish government in the last century. It is essential, he says, that a solution be found: most priests do not earn as much as 100 francs a year, which is insufficient to survive on. He contrasts this with the 3,600 francs paid to the Stiftsamtmand, a post always held by a Dane: an Amtmand receives some 3,000, and a Sysselmand between 900 and 1,000 francs. Such expenses, he says, are barely covered by the Icelandic revenue.

That night the party slept in the church, and the following day continued their route past the crater of Trenton and the hot springs of Laugarvatn, travelling through the night without stopping for rest. At sunset the following morning they crossed the wide waterfall of the Brúará on a rotten plank, and two hours later they arrived at Geysir. The temperature in the meantime had fallen from 12° to 0°, and a strong wind was blowing across the plain. As the geyser was not active on their arrival, they set up camp between the springs in order to get the best possible view, taking turns to keep watch as the others slept so as not to miss the spectacle. After waiting for two days, they became impatient, and threw stones and fired guns in an attempt to bring it to life; the result was spectacular:

> L'eau mugit tout d'un coup comme si elle eût ressenti dans ces cavités profondes l'injure que nous lui faisions, puis elle s'élança par bonds impétueux, rejetant au-dehors tout ce que nous avions amassé dans son bassin, et couvrant le vallon d'une nappe d'écume et d'un nuage de fumée. Ses flots montaient à plus de quatre-vingts pieds au-dessus du puits, ils étaient chargés de pierres et de limon; une vapeur épaisse les dérobait à nos regards, mais, en s'élevant plus haut, ils se diapraient aux rayons du soleil, et retombaient par longues fusées comme une poussière d'or et d'argent. L'éruption dura environ vingt minutes et deux heures après, le Geyser frappa la terre à coups redoublés, et jaillit à grand flots, comme l'eau du torrent, comme l'écume de la mer, quand le vent la fouette, quand la lumière l'imprègne de toutes les couleurs de l'arc-en-ciel.[32]

The eruption allowed Robert to gather a number of specimens of lava and silt, and Lottin was able to take a number of measurements including the temperature of the bubbling springs, which he discovered was well above

---

[31] AnF, 5JJ181.   [32] *LI*, 168.

100°C. Marmier, more poetic in his reactions, recalled that the author of *Kongs-Skugg-Sio* [*sic*] (for *Konungsskuggsjá*), an Icelandic text of the twelfth century, explained the phenomena by the hypothesis that the springs were 'autant de fournaises où le démon faisait bouillir les damnés'.[33]

From the geyser, the party moved on to Skálholt, one of the two most significant ancient episcopal sites in Iceland, whose history Marmier had studied in preparation for the visit. He was disappointed to find a miserable group of buildings inhabited by three families, and a rickety wooden church. He was, however, intrigued to discover that despite its dilapidated state, the church possessed a number of treasures, including splendid books and altar ornaments.

After visiting the cemetery and the ruins of the village, someone noticed that the pony carrying the provisions was missing. They asked the farmer for some bread, but it turned out that Icelanders did not normally eat bread. Instead, his wife made them some flat pancakes with rye flour, which were neither kneaded nor baked. Having eaten, the party all suffered from violent stomach upsets, and left weaker and hungrier than when they had arrived. On subsequent journeys, Marmier frequently describes local food; unless it makes him very ill (as on this occasion) he is normally open-minded and appreciative of even the simplest or most unfamiliar offerings.

Their next destination was the volcanic mount Hekla, which was the most dramatic sight they had yet visited:

> Partout le sol bouleversé, partout la terre enfouie sous ce déluge de feu; des blocs de lave comme des murailles, des montagnes de cendre engendrées par le cratère, et vomissant tour à tour d'autres montagnes, voilà ce que nous contemplions avec un sentiment d'effroi et de stupéfaction.[34]

After a trek of sixteen hours, they set up their tents on 28 June at the foot of the mountain; and the following day, accompanied by a local guide, they left camp at 9 a.m. (according to Marmier; at 11.20 a.m. according to Bévalet) to climb to the top.[35] Wearing thick boots and heavy clothing, the party set off up the steep and barren slopes. Since there was no vegetation to serve as a foothold, the steep gradient made progress slow, and they were obliged to take frequent breaks to recover their breath. Marmier took advantage of one of these pauses to lie flat out on the basalt rock, but as he stretched his legs out, the sharp coldness of the rocks caused an intense sensation of pain, as if he had broken the bone. Now the wind began to howl; the rain fell in torrents; and a thick mist shrouded the mountain so that visibility was extremely poor. The guide refused to go any farther, but the

[33] *LI*, 168.   [34] Ibid., 173.   [35] AnF, 5JJ182A.

members of the group, having struggled to arrive thus far, were reluctant to turn back. They persuaded the guide to take them just to the foot of the next ridge; once there, they talked him into going just a little farther, and so on, until they had reached the summit. In the meantime, the storm had abated, and a ray of sunshine penetrated the dense fog, but it served only to emphasise the darkness all around:

> Nous distinguions au-dessous de nous les montagnes comme des masses con- fuses, la plaine couverte d'une brume épaisse, et à travers cette brume, cette plaine, ces montagnes, le soleil projetait de loin en loin une lueur vague, une teinte blafarde. Et tout était morne, silencieux, comme le désert, profond comme l'abîme. Pas un cri ne se faisait entendre; pas un être vivant, pas une plante ne se montrait à nos yeux. On eût dit la nature morte, entourée par la nuit, plongée dans le chaos.[36]

Suddenly, the veil of cloud was torn asunder, the sky turned blue and the sun began to shine. Marmier instantly forgot the ardours of the climb, the cold, and the snow. Even the guide was enthused: it was only the second time he had ever climbed to the summit—and the first time he had escorted a party of Frenchmen. At the summit, the party and the guide shared a bottle of champagne which Bévalet had brought with him, and the bottle was left there with a message to record the event. Exhausted but exhilarated, the party finally arrived back at their camp at midnight after their fifteen-hour excursion.

They next moved on to Breiðabólsstaður, where they were received warmly on 1 July by the local priest Tómas Sæmundsson, who was to main- tain contact with Marmier, and offer him considerable help with his study of Icelandic language, literature, and history. At this juncture, on 3 July, the members of the group went their different ways. The main party, headed by Gaimard, was to continue the journey around the coast of Iceland, going east in the first instance. Marmier and Lottin made their way back to Reykjavík, Lottin to pursue his astronomical observations in order to com- plete a report for Arago,[37] and Marmier to take lessons in Icelandic so as to acquire enough proficiency to be able to read the sagas in their original form. He had learned Danish as a prelude to learning Icelandic, which turned out to be a wise move. The only grammar book he was able to find was written in Danish; the only foreign dictionary was a Danish one; and his lessons were also given in Danish. On Wedneday 6 July, he had a first one-hour lesson in the morning, with a teacher named Hjaltested, which

---

[36] *LI*, 174–5.
[37] Dominique François Arago (1786–1853) was an astronomer, physicist, and politician.

was followed by a three-hour session in the evening. The rest of the day he spent reading and making notes, happy to be able to study in peace. On 10 July, he notes in his diary, he came across a book in Swedish which he was able to read quite easily because of the similarities of the language with Danish and Icelandic. He decided that after learning Icelandic, he would apply himself to Russian, the Slavonic languages, and Arabic, in order to study the major branches of modern literature. Arabic was the only one of these languages he was to fail to master at all.

On Monday 11 July, he was delighted to receive a visit from Tómas Sæmundsson, the priest from Breiðabólsstaður, who later wrote him an extremely long and informative letter (an introduction in French and some sixteen pages in Danish).[38] In the evening, he dined with the governor and a number of priests, which turned out to be a jolly occasion: a great deal of wine was drunk. On returning to his quarters, Marmier attempted to resume his studies, but the wine had gone to his head and he was unable to concentrate. By 23 July, however, he was able to send an informal letter to Villemain (which was not subsequently published) revealing that he had by then learned enough to be able to read the sagas, 'qui sont écrites dans un style simple, héroïque pourtant, mais uniforme'.[39] Poetry, however, was still beyond him, 'parce qu'elle est hérissée de phrases métaphoriques et d'images'.[40] Although he had begun to learn Icelandic first and foremost in order to study the literature, he began to find an intrinsic interest in the study of the language:

> Cette langue islandaise m'intéresse extrêmement. C'est une langue [. . .] riche, expressive, [. . .] agréable à parler. C'est une chose vraiment merveilleuse de voir à quel degré de perfection cette langue est arriveée dès le 11ᵉ, le 12ᵉ siècle, car les Islandais de nos jours ne parlent pas une autre langue que celle de l'Edda.[41]

He also began to make a comparative study of Icelandic and the other languages of the Northern countries:

> entre le danois et le suédois qui viennent de la même souche, l'allemand qui s'en écarte un peu plus, mais qui y tient encore par plus d'un côté et l'anglais qui s'est imprégné de tant de couleurs différentes, mais qui est islandais par tous les mots essentiels. En apprenant encore l'anglo-saxon, ne pourrais-je faire un jour un dictionnaire étymologique de toutes les langues du nord? C'est là mon rêve ambitieux, mon rêve de jeune homme.[42]

Marmier did in fact begin work on this project. A notebook conserved with

---

[38] AnF, 5JJ180.   [39] AAf, Correspondance à l'Académie française, 5B15, 1836.
[40] Ibid.   [41] Ibid.   [42] Ibid.

his library in Pontarlier shows significant evidence of preliminary work. Eventually, however, he was forced to abandon it because he had so little spare time.

Meanwhile, in Reykjavík, Marmier was also spending his free time improving his Icelandic in a more unorthodox—although arguably also effective—manner. Before he had even left French shores, Sainte-Beuve (who obviously knew him well) had written him a rather prophetic warning: 'Soyez bien prudent avec les Islandaises, même quand vous les trouveriez écloses par le plus doux printemps'.[43] From his arrival in Iceland, however, he had been attracted to the women, whom he found to be 'gracieuses et jolies. Elles ont de beaux cheveux blonds, soyeux, qu'elles laissent flotter sur leurs épaules, et des yeux bleus qui donnent une grande expression de douceur à leur physionomie'.[44] In Iceland at that time, the French were reputed for their elegance and sophistication. Marmier was a particularly handsome man, who had a natural charm and made friends easily with people of all social ranks. His ability to speak Danish, and his increasing fluency in Icelandic (probably with a French accent, also considered attractive) would have helped with communication; and in his new outfit (boots, trousers, jacket, etc.) purchased in Cherbourg, he would have cut a dashing figure. On his first day in Reykjavík, he had noticed Málfríður in the club; the attraction was mutual, and three days later, on 2 June, he had kissed her for the first time. The following day, the two had a long talk together, and on 5 June, the couple were able to meet again, since Marmier was present as she sat for Mayer to draw her portrait, modelling the traditional Icelandic costume: a headdress in black and red silk; a green top with gold braid trimmings; skirts embroidered with red, and with silver and gold braiding; a silver necklace and belt; and calf-hide shoes.[45] She was presented with a pair of earrings as payment for her modelling.[46] Málfríður was an outstandingly beautiful young woman whose face is still familiar in Iceland today, for Mayer's portrait of her wearing the traditional Icelandic costume is an important document of social history (see Plate 2). The conversation during this session obviously became quite intimate (presumably not making Mayer's task any easier!), for Marmier noted in his diary: 'Désirs des deux côtés. Impossibilité de trouver une occasion'.[47] Two days later, on Tuesday 7 June, however, they found their first opportunity, at six o'clock in the

[43] AnF, 5JJ180.   [44] *LI*, 157.

[45] The portrait was published in *Voyage en Islande et au Groënland, publié par ordre du roi sous la direction de M. Paul Gaimard: Atlas historique*, 2 vols. (Paris: Arthus Bertrand, [1842?]), 1, 10. Two (complementary) descriptions of the outfit are to be found: the first with the portrait (as above), and the second in AnF, 5JJ182C.

[46] AnF, 5JJ181.   [47] BSG, Fn, MS 3894, fo. 20v.

morning. Some notes scribbled in Danish to record the event suggest that he found her to be uninhibited and sexually aware.[48] She came to see him again on 14 June, and the next day, as Marmier was preparing to leave on his excursion to the geyser, the manager of the club where Málfríður worked called on him to ask if he had any messages for her. The affair seems to have continued after his return from the excursion, since he noted in his diary at the end of July: 'b[aisé] le soir F[ríða]'.[49]

Málfríður was not, however, Marmier's only lover during his stay, for a note in his diary the same day adds rather cynically: 'Commencé hier d'autres a[mours]. Les pauvres femmes sont partout les mêmes. Celles que je croyais ici innocentes et ignorantes savent certaines choses depuis longtemps'.[50] On Tuesday 2 August he attended a ball held at the club. Although he found the music poor, the women were 'mal habillées, mais plusieurs très jolies', and he was able to have conversations with 'les plus belles fleurs du bal'. Despite this, he left early and retired to bed with his Icelandic dictionary; at midnight Málfríður paid him a surprise visit.[51] Three days later, he seemed to be wrestling with the temptation of further affairs: 'Oh! non, plus de ces am[ours] faciles et décevants comme je pourrais en avoir ici. Non, je veux travailler, garder la tranquillité du cœur, et faire mon bon devoir d'étudiant'.[52] This resolution, however, did not survive the weekend. An entry in his diary on Sunday, written in a curious mixture of languages, states clearly that his good intentions have not lasted. Three women (mentioned by initials only) are listed: one for Saturday evening (whose name began with a B), another with the initials AMTD for Sunday, and Málfríður the same evening! A further entry for Sunday consists of a poem addressed to a girl called Helga (whose initial is not included in the preceding list!), apparently a pretty girl with blue eyes. The gist of the poem suggests that he went to visit her at her home under the cover of darkness. Although the final stanza declares that 'Ton amour rend le cœur heureux', a note at the end of the poem, perhaps rather ironically placed, states: '11h.—Mauvais temps—le vent—la pluie—Mal à la tête—tristesse tout le jour'.[53]

Apart from his progress with the Icelandic language and his study of the literature, and despite these amours, he seems to have been generally rather bored and depressed, wondering when Gaimard would arrive back in Reykjavík from his expedition, and when *La Recherche* would return from its mission to Greenland so that they could go home to France. On Saturday 20 August, Marmier was woken at seven o'clock in the morning by the gov-

[48] BSG, Fn, MS 3894, fo. 21.   [49] Ibid., fo. 45.
[50] Ibid.   [51] Ibid., fo. 45v.   [52] Ibid.   [53] Ibid., fo. 46.

ernor coming in to report that the vessel had been sighted. Marmier rushed to the lookout post, and saw her sailing into port, having been delayed by bad weather and damaged in Greenland. No trace had been found of *La Lilloise* and her crew. The following day, Gaimard arrived back, having had to send Anglès, who had been taken ill, to Copenhagen.[54] Their departure date was fixed for 1 September. The 31 August was a day of farewells, particularly from his girlfriends: 'un dernier baiser à A, et un autre à F. Il n'y a qu'une femme que je ne puisse embrasser avec plaisir, et c'est celle-là qui a pleuré tout le jour—celle-là seule peut-être qui m'aime réellement'.[55]

If the 'F' here stands for 'Fríða', then this is the last reference to Málfríður in Marmier's personal papers. Even if there was another F., and Málfríður was the unfortunate young woman in tears all day, it would appear that Marmier did not view their affair as having been particularly significant.[56] Did he know that she was pregnant? The story of Málfríður is not well documented,[57] but it seems to have been a sad one, despite the fact that an illegitimate birth at that time in Iceland did not carry the social stigma that it might have done in other parts of Europe and although the affair appears to have been based on mutual attraction and consent. Málfríður's position in Icelandic society was already a difficult one. Although she was a bright and beautiful young woman, she came from a family whose reputation was tarnished before she was even born. Prior to marrying Málfríður's mother, her father had been married to a woman who had been convicted of stealing sheep, and then, more seriously, of assaulting and killing her sister-in-law, for which she was sent to prison. Iceland at that time had an exceptionally low level of crime, and this kind of behaviour was not tolerated. Sveinn, Málfríður's father, obtained a divorce, and settled in Reykjavík before remarrying. Although the woman concerned was not Málfríður's mother, and the episode had occurred some time before the young woman's birth, the family were all tarred with the same brush and

[54] A letter to Admiral Duperré from Gaimard reports that Anglès was suffering from inflammation of the abdomen (AnF, 5JJ179).

[55] BSG, Fn, MS 3894, fo. 48v.

[56] A comment made by Eugène Mequet in his *Journal de voyage* suggests that Fríða appeared not to have been overwhelmed by grief prior to the departure. He noted that on 30 August a party was held at the club, and 'il y a dans ce Club une servante nommée Frida qui est fort jolie, et aussi coquette que jolie. Elle a fait une poupée de femme en grand costume islandais, qu'elle a vendue soixante francs au docteur Robert' (Eugène Mequet, *Voyage en Islande et Groënland, exécuté pendant les années 1835 et 1836 sur la corvette 'La Recherche'* [. . .] *Journal de voyage* (Paris: Arthus Bertrand, 1852), 167).

[57] Unless otherwise indicated, information given here is found in Jón Helgason, *Íslenzkt mannlíf*, 2nd edn., 4 vols. (Reykjavík, 1984), 1, 30–3. I should like to record my thanks to Svanhildur Óskarsdóttir for drawing this work to my attention.

treated by and large as social outcasts. By 1836, Málfríður had already been engaged twice in succession. In both cases, however, the families of the young men in question were against the proposed marriage because of her family antecedents, and the engagements were broken off. Málfríður learned the art of dressmaking and became a seamstress, but gave this up to become a waitress in Maack's club in Reykjavík, where she had met Marmier.

With her family history and the two broken engagements behind her, Málfríður began to acquire a somewhat notorious reputation, which was probably bolstered by her flirtatious nature. Her friends worried that although many men were attracted to her, none would marry her because of this reputation. When *La Recherche* arrived in Iceland, she was apparently an instant success (witness the fact that she was chosen by Mayer to model the national costume for the famous portrait); there were also rumours that she had been in a relationship with a certain Kristian Müller that year. Correspondence shows that after the departure of the French, she became increasingly anxious and isolated. On 21 April 1837, she gave birth to a baby boy and declared Marmier to be the father, naming him Sveinn Xavier. The records of Reykjavík Cathedral show that the witnesses/godparents at the baptism on 30 April were Maack, the owner of the club; L[uðvig] Knudsen; and Davíð Helgason, together with the midwife, Madame Möller.[58] After the birth, Málfríður went to work in a bakery, and a couple of years later became pregnant by an assistant baker. It would seem that her life in Iceland had become very difficult, and in the course of 1839 she took the decision to leave definitively. In the summer of 1840 she went to live in Copenhagen to work as the servant of a former governor of Iceland. Here she eventually married a shoemaker, and the couple had two more children. Sveinn apparently died young, leaving no descendants.[59]

Neither Sveinn nor Málfríður are ever mentioned subsequently by Marmier,[60] although it is highly unlikely that he did not know of his son's existence; certainly his paternity was common knowledge in Iceland.

[58] The child's existence is mentioned in Gröndal's autobiography, *Dægradvöl*, in *Ritsafn*, 5 vols. (Reykjavík: Ísafoldarprentsmiðja, 1953), 4, 297; and in an interview with Pétur Pétursson, published in *þjóðviljinn*, 19 November 1978, 12–13; (my thanks to Finnbogi Guðmundsson of the National Library of Iceland for bringing this article to my attention). The precise information drawn from the cathedral register is published here for the first time, and I should like to record my thanks to Jón Torfason of the National Archives of Iceland and Svanhildur Óskarsdóttir for making this possible.

[59] See Pétursson, 12.

[60] Only two rather cryptic notes written in his diary on 12 and 13 March 1837 may possibly indicate that he was aware of the imminent birth. In a curious mixture of languages (which he often seemed to use during this period to record incidents pertaining to his love life) he indicates his relief at

Marmier's lack of interest in his own son contrasts sharply with the behaviour of Gaimard in Iceland, who took the young Icelandic boy who was selected for the scholarship, Guðmundur Sívertsen, back to France and virtually adopted him. Correspondence with the boy's parents and with the boy himself shows that Gaimard took the responsibility very seriously, and that the child seems to have been happy.[61] Guðmundur received a good education and eventually became a doctor.

In the meantime, at nine o'clock on the evening of 31 August, *La Recherche* set sail in a choppy sea by the light of the moon, which sparkled on the waves and cast a glow on the icy mountain tips. The departure was delayed by an unfavourable wind, and for two full days Reykjavík remained in view. Finally, on 2 September, the pilot came to guide them out of the estuary; the wind had turned, and by one o'clock the land was out of sight. The return journey took rather longer than the initial voyage had done: first a storm, then alternating periods of weather that was too calm to fill the sails, or a headwind—all made progress difficult; finally the vessel was caught in a dense fog off the coast of Portland. They eventually arrived back in France on 27 September—to Marmier's intense relief. His first reaction was to hurry to the post office, where he found letters from his father and a number of friends awaiting his return. On Thursday 29 September, he took leave of the other members of the commission, and set off for Paris by stagecoach. By coincidence, he found himself travelling with Schierbeck, a Danish officer who had been on an official visit to Iceland two years previously. They set off at two o'clock in the afternoon, and passed the time chatting in Danish until they arrived in Caen at nine o'clock the following morning (30 September). From here, Marmier went on to Rouen (a journey taking some twelve hours), where he found a hotel for the night; he then broke his journey to spend Saturday visiting the cathedral and the local bookshops. At 6 a.m. on Sunday he set off for Paris, arriving at eight o'clock that evening.

On Saturday 28 January 1837, Marmier finished the last page of his book on Iceland. His *Lettres sur l'Islande* constitute an important historical document in many respects. The descriptions of Icelandic life—particularly when read in conjunction with Mayer's illustrations—are still of great interest today as a record of social conditions at the time. It is also possible that this work (along with the *Histoire de l'Islande*) may have been instrumental in the decision to allow the Icelandic parliament to be re-established

---

something (unspecified) having been no more than a 'grosse maladresse', and yet also suggesting a considerable sadness (BSG, Fn, MS 3894, fo. 67).

[61] See particularly the correspondence in AnF, 5JJ179 and 5JJ180.

in 1843: certainly, in 1837 Marmier had offered a copy of the *Lettres* to Prince Christian, the future Christian VIII, under whose reign the Althing was restored. The *Lettres* also contain a remarkable survey of Icelandic literature encompassing the eddic and skaldic poetry, Icelandic mythology, the sagas, and a history of the Icelandic language. Perhaps influenced by Mme de Staël, he insists on studying a literature in its national context and on living amongst the people in whose language it is written: 'Il y a, entre la poésie d'un peuple et la terre qu'il habite, et la nature qui l'entoure, et le ciel sous lequel il vit, une alliance intime, alliance que peu de livres révèlent, et qu'il faut avoir observée sur les lieux mêmes pour les bien sentir'.[62]

The volume contains a detailed bibliography and consistent references to manuscript and source materials, both of which were rare in literary criticism of that era.[63] Indeed, Marmier's whole approach appears to have been extremely methodical. His mid-term progress report shows that his conscientious documentation was also critical: 'Je me suis fait un catalogue complet des livres anglais, danois, suédois, allemands écrits sur l'Islande, et j'ai compulsé ces livres, à mesure que je me les suis procurés, de manière à y prendre de nouveaux aperçus, et à noter les lacunes ou les défauts de composition que je croyais y trouver'.[64] And Marmier's study goes beyond what was at that time available in published form, in any language: 'Là où l'histoire m'a manqué, c'est-à-dire quand j'en suis venu à l'étude de la poésie et des institutions actuelles, j'ai cherché à suppléer aux livres imprimés par les notes que je rassemblais de chaque côté, par les séries de questions que j'adressais aux hommes les plus instruits'.[65]

Marmier's survey encompasses chapters on a history of the language, runes, and Icelandic mythology. There is a long chapter on the skalds ('les bardes du Nord') and their four types of verse formation; Odin and Suttung; Starkaðr (transcribed by Marmier as 'Starkoddr'); the song of Hárbarðr (transcribed 'Hagbard'); and the story of Ragnar Loðbrók. A chapter devoted to 'Les Deux Edda' explains the origin of the word 'edda' and relates a visit to Oddæ. Marmier further includes presentations of Sæmund the Wise and Snorri Sturluson; *Völuspá*; *Hávamál*; *Völsung*; and

[62] *LI*, 130.

[63] One of the sources cited is a work by Uno von Troil, who visited Iceland in 1770. His report on his visit was translated into French as *Lettres sur l'Islande* (Paris: Imprimerie de Monsieur, 1781). This version is more scholarly than Marmier's book of the same name (my thanks to François-Xavier Dillmann for drawing this work to my attention), in that it contains copious notes, statistics, lists, and bibliographies. On the other hand, the style is rather dry, the language is detached and 'scientific', and the volume offers few personal impressions. Marmier's work is obviously more accessible and up-to-date, and wider in its scope.

[64] AnF, 5JJ182C.   [65] Ibid.

Sigurd: the chapter includes summaries and translations of notable extracts. A further two chapters are devoted to the sagas; the first of these deals with their origins and significance, the itinerant bards, and the heroic, historical, and romanesque sagas, their form and antiquity; the second is devoted to the sagas of Njal, Gunnlaugr, and Friðþjófr.

The work finishes with an analysis of the works of Thorarensen,[66] 'un vrai poète par la pensée, par la forme, un poète qui aime son pays et qui le chante avec enthousiasme'.[67] Although the two men did not meet, they corresponded, and Marmier was touched by the candour and the modesty of the poet's letters. The volume concludes with a translation of two poems, *þú nafnkunna landið* and *Sigrún*. Marmier reports that although he feels it impossible to render the nuances of the language, Thorarensen has seen the translations and attested to their accuracy.

Contemporary reviews of the *Lettres sur l'Islande* were favourable. Antoine de Latour, for example, writing in the *Revue de Paris*, speaks of Marmier's 'brillant exposé de la mythologie scandinave';[68] his style is described as 'une langue vive et naturelle, élégante sans recherche, élevée sans prétention, attrayante sans coquetterie'.[69] A lengthy review in the *Revue germanique* (signed simply 'F. C.') describes the volume as 'fort remarquable', judging it to be worthy of the mandate from the Académie française. The author particularly praises the extensive documentation and the elegance of the translations offered. According to this reviewer, the work contains (amongst other qualities) '[des] souvenirs classiques sans pédantisme'; '[des] comparaisons littéraires enrichies d'une érudition de bon goût'; '[des] renseignements classés avec la précision d'une statistique rigoureuse'; '[des] faits historiques cités à propos' and '[des] narrations rapides et originales'. In summary, the work presents 'les vues élevées d'une intelligence qui, en politique, en littérature, en religion, plane au-dessus de tout dogmatisme mesquin, et saisit le véritable, l'unique principe du progrès de notre époque, la fusion harmonique de tous les éléments divers utiles à l'humanité'.[70]

---

[66] Bjarni Thorarensen (1786–1841); a portrait of him is to be found in the *Atlas historique* (see above, n. 45), 2, 125.

[67] *LI*, 310.

[68] Antoine de Latour, 'Critique littéraire: *Lettres sur l'Islande* par M. X. Marmier', *RP*, 39 (1837), 206–14 (211).

[69] Ibid., 214.

[70] F. C., 'Critique littéraire: Livres français: *Lettres sur l'Islande* par M. X. Marmier', *Rg*, 3rd ser., 11/33 (1837), 322–8.

The number of reprints and new editions of the *Lettres*[71] attest to their popularity and the interest that was generated in them in France and abroad. In addition to the *Lettres* and the associated works already mentioned, Marmier also devoted a section of his *Chants populaires du Nord* to Icelandic material, and his *Contes populaires de différents pays* included a tale by Thordz de Tharadz.[72] An indication of their literary significance can be gleaned from Alison Fairlie's convincing demonstration that Marmier's work on Iceland (particularly the *Lettres sur l'Islande* and the *Chants populaires du Nord*, but also possibly the content of his lectures at Rennes) provided an important source of inspiration for Leconte de Lisle's *Poèmes barbares*.[73] In a different vein, Daniel-Henri Pageaux shows that Jules Verne's *Voyage au centre de la terre* was directly influenced by the *Lettres sur l'Islande*.[74]

Apart from being effectively the first to introduce Icelandic culture and literature to France, Marmier also left his own marks on Icelandic literature of the era. Finnbogi Guðmundsson argues that Jónas Hallgrímsson's famous poem, *Til herra Páls Gaimard*, was influenced by Marmier's letter on 'Le Geyser et l'Hécla', which was first published in the *Revue des Deux Mondes* in September 1836, and subsequently translated into Danish for publication in the *Kjøbenshavnposten* on 11 May 1837, when Hallgrímsson was in Copenhagen. He further argues that Marmier's description of the Tindafjöll may also have influenced the composition of Hallgrímsson's *Gunnarshólmi*.[75] On a lighter note, the same author's *Gamanbréf til kun-*

---

[71] See above, n. 24.

[72] *Chants populaires du Nord* (Paris: Charpentier, 1842); *Contes populaires de différents pays recueillis et traduits par Xavier Marmier de l'Académie française*, 2nd ser. (Paris: Hachette, 1888), 185–8.

[73] Fairlie was not the first to note the influence of Marmier on Leconte de Lisle; she summarises and evaluates the comments of earlier scholars (such as Vianey and Souriau) in the course of her detailed exposition. See Alison Fairlie, *Leconte de Lisle's Poems on the Barbarian Races* (*Poèmes barbares*) (Cambridge: Cambridge University Press, 1947), esp. 65–119.

[74] See Daniel-Henri Pageaux, 'Voyages aux sources du voyage au centre de la terre', *Revue de littérature comparée*, 54/2 (1980), 202–12.

[75] *Chants islandais*, Íslenzk kvæði og ræða Paul Gaimard í Kaupmannhöfn 16. janúar 1839. Finnbogi Guðmundsson annaðist útgáfuna og ritaði formála ([Reykjavík]: Bókaútgáfan Örn og Örlygur, 1986), [no page numbers]. It may also be significant to note that in addition to the article, which is noted both by Finnbogi Guðmundsson and Dick Ringler (see below, n. 76), Marmier also wrote a poem which he variously entitled 'A X'; 'A une Islandaise'; 'Sur l'Hécla'; and 'En Islande'. Although Marmier's poem is of no great intrinsic value, its form and some of its vocabulary may be important in the context. The general descriptions noted in the article are present here, but in addition there are words such as 'héros' and 'altières'. Although the poem does not appear to have been published until 1874 (in *Poésies d'un voyageur 1834–1874* (Paris: Raçon), 24–5), Marmier was obviously quite pleased with it, since there are manuscript versions of it in his notebook, and also in the Archives nationales (5JJ179). It was written at the end of June 1836, and is dedicated to an

ningja ('A letter of fun to friends') contains a character named Marmier. The text was written in 1843 as a parody of contemporary newspaper accounts of the state visit of Queen Victoria to France, using points of reference familiar to Icelanders. Marmier here is a courtier who has been elevated to the title of earl, and it is he who spots Queen Victoria's ship arriving. This text in its turn influenced the composition of Benedikt Gröndal's famous satirical novel *Sagan of Heljarslóðarorrustu*, and this novel also contains a character called Marmier.[76] Gröndal's Marmier is a wise man and a captain in the army of Napoleon III at war with Austria. The Austrian emperor is the villain of the piece, but Napoleon is aided by Marmier, Lamartine, and Alexandre Dumas. Marmier knows everything that goes on in Scandinavia, and has a unique armour made of pages from the *Revue britannique*. In battle, Marmier is provoked to anger and to stabbing his opponent Gúníbrandus when the latter infuriates him by pulling off one of his boots; Marmier is then caught off balance and puts his foot on the battleground which is covered with blood. The dirt which soils his previously clean sock is more than he can bear.[77] Thus is Marmier's name handed down to posterity in Iceland.

---

anonymous Icelandic woman. It is therefore not impossible that he should have given her a copy; could this have found its way to Hallgrímsson?

[76] Stefán Einarsson, *A History of Icelandic Literature* (New York: Johns Hopkins, 1957), 235–6. There is an English translation and a commentary of the text by Dick Ringler available on the internet at the following address: <http://www.library.wisc.edu/etext/Jonas/Gamanbrefi.htm>, accessed 18 October 1998.

[77] See B. S. Benedikz, 'Napoleon III as a saga hero—thoughts on the end of an epoch', in M. Gravier (ed.), *Rencontres et courants littéraires franco-scandinaves* (Paris: Minard, 1972), 89. One cannot but wonder if the episode intentionally pokes fun at Marmier's attention to his appearance, particularly in view of the smart new outfit (including boots) purchased in Cherbourg—which may have contributed to his success with the women.

5

Denmark (1837): 'le bon, le noble pays du Danemark'[1]

The year 1837 marked a new departure for Marmier to the Scandinavian countries: an extended journey over the next eighteen months would take him to Denmark, Sweden, Norway, Finland, and Lapland. This visit would bring him into contact with a number of important figures from all spheres of society (notably the literary and the political, but also the scientific, the artistic, and the world of learning) and result in an outstanding series of publications marking Marmier as the most influential Franco-Scandinavian intermediary of the era.

The initial circumstances of his mission are not entirely clear from papers surviving. Notes in Marmier's diary for the month of January 1837 show that he was finishing his work on Iceland. At this time, he was romantically involved with an uneducated seventeen-year-old from a poor background whose name was Marie. Early in February he also became involved with an older woman named Adèle, with whom he spent happy afternoons in bed. This period of sexual bliss came to an abrupt end with the prospect of a new journey. Gaimard (the president of the Commission du Nord) had requested permission to travel to Copenhagen and Christiania (Oslo) with Marmier and Eugène Robert in order to complete the documentation necessary for the publication of the official report on the expedition to Iceland.[2] On 17 February, Marmier received a letter (presumably of an informal nature) from Gaimard, informing him that he was to be awarded 2,000 francs from the Ministère de la Marine.[3] A letter from Rosamel (who had been appointed Ministre de la Marine in 1836)[4] to Molé (at this time Premier ministre)[5] dated 22 March 1837 confirms that permission had already been granted for the journey.[6] Curiously, however,

[1] *Journal*, 1, 311.   [2] AnF, 5JJ187.

[3] BSG, Fn, MS 3894, fos. 66–7. This is noted in Marmier's diary: the letter has not survived.

[4] Claude du Campe de Rosamel, baron (1774–1848), admiral and French politician. Elected to parliament in 1833, he became Ministre de la Marine in 1836 and held the post until 1839. He oversaw the organisation of several scientific expeditions, including that of *L'Astrolabe*.

[5] Louis-Mathieu Molé, comte (1781–1855), French politician; Ministre des Affaires étrangères in the early days of the July Monarchy, then Premier ministre (1836–9).

[6] AnF, 5JJ187.

Rosamel himself wrote officially to Gaimard to approve the journey only on 24 June, and Gaimard does not appear to have visited Copenhagen before the end of 1838.[7] Marmier, for his part, acted with characteristic alacrity on hearing the news and immediately set to work seeking additional sponsorship. A note in his diary shows that he visited François Guizot (at this time Ministre de l'Instruction publique) on 5 March and again on 12 March, in order to offer his services as a researcher in Scandinavia on a paid basis.[8] Guizot accepted Marmier's proposition enthusiastically, and instructed him to investigate two main areas. On the one hand, he was to undertake a comparative study of the education systems in Denmark, Sweden, and Norway, from primary to higher education. He was also to investigate the relationship between education and the Church there. A second strand of his task was to look into the current situation regarding historical research in these countries; the progress made in the field in recent years; and the extent of government involvement in the various projects. Guizot suggested that Marmier should submit progress reports every fortnight and that his pay would be proportionate to the amount and quality of information presented. If the work lived up to expectations, Guizot promised, Marmier would receive 500 francs per trimester.[9] The enterprise continued to receive official support when Salvandy took over from Guizot at the ministry in the course of the year.[10]

In the meantime, Marmier had written to his old mentor Charles Weiss on 18 March, apologising for the fact that this change of plan would prevent him from travelling to Besançon, where he had previously arranged to visit both him and his brother Louis, whom Weiss had taken on at the library at Marmier's behest in order to enable him to earn his living while studying for the entrance examination to the École Normale.[11] The fortunes of the Marmier family had changed somewhat over the last year: his father had been appointed to a post with the customs at Colmar in June 1836, where he was to remain for some fifteen months. Marmier now decided to travel to Denmark via Alsace; in the letter to Weiss, he asks permission for his brother to take two days' leave for Easter to enable him to visit Colmar for a family reunion. Marmier planned to leave Paris on 19 March, which would allow him to reach Colmar on 22 March. The family were delighted

[7] Ibid.

[8] BSG, Fn, MS 3894, fos. 66–7. The diary at this point is particularly difficult to decipher owing to untidy handwriting, a curious mixture of languages (French, Danish, and German), and torn pages.

[9] AnF, F17/21256.

[10] Narcisse Achille de Salvandy, comte (1795–1856), influential politician who took over from Guizot as Ministre de l'Instruction publique in April 1837 and remained in post until March 1839.

[11] BmB, Collection Estignard, MS 1907, Correspondance de Charles Weiss, Lettres de X. Marmier, fos. 74[1]–2.

to see him, and they spent a happy week together towards the end of the month. Marmier's father, François-Xavier, recalls with pride in his *Souvenirs* that his eldest son's celebrity status had reached Colmar; at the local school prize-giving, where Joseph (the youngest) was a pupil, two of the books selected as prizes were the *Études sur Goethe* and *Lettres sur l'Islande*. During the week that Xavier spent with the family, he was fêted at the town hall and the préfecture.

On 2 April, Xavier left his family and headed for northern Germany. In the course of his long expedition between 1837 and 1838, he wrote letters outlining his progress and discoveries to a number of friends and colleagues. These were published in various journals (principally the *Revue des Deux Mondes* and the *Revue de Paris*) and then reproduced in a volume entitled *Lettres sur le Nord*.[12] The initial stages of Marmier's journey took him through Mecklemburg, stopping at Schwerin and Ludwigslust. He wrote a long letter to Antoine de Latour outlining the history of the region and the principal towns, the local customs and traditions, folklore, and mythology. His route then took him through Berlin and Hamburg. In a letter addressed to Paul Gaimard, he sketches a portrait of Hamburg, describing its different districts. His overwhelming impression was of the sharp divisions between rich and poor; he was particularly struck by the squalid basements in the old town where the less fortunate would live cooped up in dark and damp dwellings below street level, while the families of rich merchants carried on their more prosperous business above:

---

[12] *Lettres sur le Nord, Danemark, Suède, Norvège, Laponie et Spitzberg*, 2 vols. (Paris: Delloye, 1840). A number of different editions appeared up to 1890 when a sixth edition was published by Hachette. References are to a pirate edition published in Belgium (cited in chapter 4 in connection with the *Lettres sur l'Islande*): *Lettres sur le Nord (Danemark, Suède, Norvège, Laponie et Spitzberg) et sur L'Islande*, 2 vols. (Brussels: N.-J. Grégoir, V. Woutens et Cⁱᵉ, 1841) (cited hereafter as *LN*). The impact of the work was such that it was rapidly translated into Italian and Dutch: *Lettere sulla Danimarca, la Svezia, la Norvegia, la Laponia e li Spitzberg. Prima versione dal Francese di A. Zoncada* (Milan: 1841) and *Brieven over het Noorden* (Deventer: 1841). The catalogue of the Danish national library also lists a more recent translation: *Brev Nordfrå*, trans. Magnhild Svenheim (Tromsø: Universitetsbiblioteket, 1997). Articles appeared in the *Revue des Deux Mondes* as follows: 'Poètes et romanciers du Nord. 1. Oehlenschlæger [*sic*]', 4th ser., 10 (1837), 792–811; 'Organisation de l'instruction élémentaire et secondaire en Danemark', 4th ser., 12 (1837), 105–17; 'Du Mouvement des études historiques dans le Nord. I. Danemark', 4th ser., 12 (1837), 305–20; 'Les Etablissements littéraires et scientifiques de Copenhague', 4th ser., 13 (1838), 202–17; 'De l'Etat de la littérature et de l'instruction en Danemark, avant le XVIᵉ siècle', 4th ser., 13 (1838), 507–22; 'De la presse périodique dans les trois royaumes scandinaves', 4th ser., 21 (1840), 301–18. In the *Revue de Paris*, there are articles entitled 'Une vie de poète', 46 (1837), 250–7; 'Paysages danois. La Séelande', Nouvelle série, 53 (1838), 91–101; 'Holberg', Nouvelle série, 53 (1838), 253–73; 'Poètes danois du dix-huitième siècle', Nouvelle série, 60 (1838), 320–39.

C'est une triste chose que de voir ces pauvres gens entassés dans ces retraites humides, où jamais l'air salubre ne pénètre, où jamais leurs regards ne peuvent se réjouir d'un rayon de soleil [. . .]. Ces malheureux sont placés là comme ils le sont dans le monde: tout l'édifice qu'ils habitent pèse sur eux comme toute l'échelle sociale. La famille du riche danse sur leur tête, le riche chante en passant devant leur prison.[13]

The residents of Hamburg, in Marmier's eyes, were the most materialist of all the Germans he had seen, and the least inclined to the arts: 'on sent qu'il ne faut leur parler ni d'art ni de poésie. Leur livre de poésie, c'est le registre de recettes et de dépenses ouvert sur le pupitre'.[14] From here, he travelled to Altona, the capital of Holstein, the second city of Denmark, and was rather surprised at the lack of frontier formalities which allowed freedom of movement between the citizens of the two countries (Holstein was not annexed to Germany until 1864). Early in May, he went on a pilgrimage to the village of Ottenven, just outside Altona, where Klopstock was buried. As he contemplated the tomb, he was approached by an old man who talked to him about Klopstock and his family, and recited a number of poems, which he had learned by heart. Marmier was happy to give the man money, 'de payer ce dernier tribut à la mémoire de celui dont les œuvres m'avaient souvent causé tant de joie, heureux de trouver dans ce village du Nord un homme qui demandait un acte de bienfaisance au nom de la poésie, comme ailleurs on le demande au nom d'une sainte'.[15]

From here, Marmier made his way to Kiel, where he was to catch the steamer to Copenhagen. At four o'clock in the morning of Saturday 6 May the vessel arrived in dock, and when the cannon sounded at seven o'clock the same evening for its departure with its new cargo, Marmier was among the passengers on board. He felt rather excluded as the other passengers made their tearful farewells, leaving family and friends behind on the quayside waving white handkerchiefs as the ship cast off. Soon, however, the boat was at full steam, and he enjoyed the peaceful contemplation of the coast disappearing in the sunset, with the seagulls being rocked gently by the motion of the waves. Despite being impressed by the efficiency of the steamer, which sped with 'la rapidité de l'oiseau',[16] he nonethless characterised it as a 'navire de marchand',[17] and regretted the poetry of a voyage in a sailing boat. At dawn, the vessel was passing the Falster point and passed between Zealand and the small islands dotted around. Further on, some locals urged him to the fore end of the ship to see the white cliffs at Møen. From here to Copenhagen the sea was full of sailing ships, but the

---

[13] *LN*, 1, 44.

[14] Ibid., 1, 46.   [15] Ibid., 1, 50.   [16] Ibid., 1, 65.   [17] Ibid., 1, 66.

steamer sped past even the swiftest schooners. At two in the afternoon they moored in Copenhagen, where he was to remain until December, apart from a two-month preliminary visit to Sweden and Norway in June and July.

Relatively little was known in France at this time about Denmark, or indeed about any of the Scandinavian countries. As Marmier himself admitted, patriot though he was, the French would welcome those who came from abroad to study French culture and institutions, but showed little reciprocal interest: 'Un rideau de brouillard enveloppe l'esprit, et le Danemark, la Suède, la Norvège, la Laponie, le Spitzberg, la Finlande, la Russie même, nous apparaissent derrière ce brouillard avec des formes indécises et se confondent dans notre imagination'.[18]

Marmier was astounded to find Copenhagen an elegant, flourishing, lively city with excellent institutions. In a letter addressed to Sainte-Beuve, he describes life in the city and traces its history, noting that Copenhagen had always been the most advanced city in Scandinavia, overshadowing even those of Lund, Uppsala and Christiania (Oslo). Education was excellent and widespread, and the love of literature was shared by both merchants and 'intellectual' classes. All around him he found a refreshing enthusiasm for scholarship. He was impressed by the rich collections of the libraries and museums, and the activities of the numerous learned societies; a letter dedicated to Salvandy covers the contents of the collections and the history of its most important institutions. In addition to the collected letters, a separate volume on literature, *Histoire de la littérature en Danemark et en Suède*, was published in 1839.[19] Similar material was presented in Marmier's volume on *Littérature scandinave* in the series of official reports published under Gaimard's direction in the 1840s.[20] The second volume is very similar to the first. The most substantial differences can be seen in the two chapters devoted to modern Danish literature. In the *Histoire de la littérature en Danemark et en Suède*, the first chapter is devoted entirely to Oehlenschläger, and the second exclusively to Andersen. In the second volume, the chapter on Oehlenschläger remains (although in a slightly revised

---

[18] *LN*, 1, 73.

[19] *Histoire de la littérature en Danemark et en Suède* (Paris: Bonnaire, 1839) (cited hereafter as *HLDS*). This work was rapidly translated into Italian by Filippo de'Bardi: *Storia della letteratura in Danimarca e in Svezia* (Florence: 1841).

[20] *Voyages de la Commission scientifique du Nord en Scandinavie, en Laponie, au Spitzberg et aux Iles Féröe, pendant les années 1838, 1839 et 1840, sur la corvette La Recherche commandée par M. Fabvre, publiés par ordre du roi sous la direction de M. Paul Gaimard. Littérature scandinave, par M. Xavier Marmier* (Paris: Arthus Bertrand, [undated, probably 1849; the various volumes appeared separately]). Marmier also wrote the volume on *Histoire de la Scandinavie* (publication details as above, with the exception of '*gouvernement*' for '*roi*'; date possibly 1854).

form), and the second is expanded to cover all the modern period of Danish literature, with Andersen occupying a much more modest place. The official version was reprinted under the title *Histoire de la littérature scandinave* in 1848.[21]

One of Marmier's first visits in Copenhagen was to the poet Adam Oehlenschläger. It was perhaps the work of Oehlenschläger which first motivated Marmier's interest in Denmark and Danish literature. While he was working in Germany, he had read Oehlenschläger's German translation of *Correggio*; after corresponding with the Danish poet, he translated the German version into French.[22] Now he hastened to visit Oehlenschläger, whom he found to be a tall, handsome man with blue eyes and dark hair which was just starting to turn grey. Marmier noted that he was a good conversationalist and enjoyed talking. On 12 May he dined with the Oehlenschläger family, who made him very welcome, and he noted in his diary: 'Sa femme très bonne. Sa fille très belle'.[23] On 17 May, Oehlenschläger took Marmier on an outing to Frederiksberg. He showed Marmier where he had grown up, and took him to visit the graves of his parents, and, most poignantly, the grave of his daughter Charlotte who had died on 12 March 1835, shortly before her twenty-fourth birthday. The sight of his recently deceased daughter's grave brought tears to the eyes of the poet; Marmier squeezed his hand, and the two men walked on in silence. Oehlenschläger finally broke the silence by confiding in Marmier that his religious faith and the beauty of the park, which he visited almost every day, brought him some consolation: 'C'est là, me dit-il, qu'il a trouvé ses meilleurs poèmes'.[24]

An article on Oehlenschläger written by Marmier appeared in the *Revue des Deux Mondes* on 15 June 1837,[25] and was reproduced virtually intact in the chapter devoted to him in the *Histoire de la littérature en Danemark et en Suède*.[26] Two chapters of Marmier's *Histoire de la littérature scandinave* are devoted to modern Danish literature, and the first of these concentrates exclusively on Oehlenschläger, 'l'un des plus grands poëtes du Nord, et l'un des hommes les plus distingués de la littérature moderne'.[27] Danish literature,

---

[21] *Histoire de la littérature scandinave, par M. Xavier Marmier* (Paris: Arthus Bertrand, 1848) (cited hereafter as *HLS*).

[22] 'Littérature dramatique. *Corrège*, tragédie en cinq actes par Œhlenschlaeger [*sic*], traduite par X. Marmier, *NRg*, 15/57 & 58 [joint issue] (1833), 23–134. Marmier had also used Oehlenschläger's German translations of Holberg to produce a French translation of Holberg's 'Le Potier d'étain politique', in *Théâtre européen* [. . .] *Théâtres danois et suédois* (Paris: Guérin, 1835).

[23] BSG, Fn, MS 3894, fo. 88.   [24] Ibid., fo. 91.

[25] 'Poètes et romanciers du Nord. 1. Oehlenschloger [*sic*]', *RDM*, 4th ser., 10 (1837), 792–811.

[26] *HLDS*, 199–236.   [27] *HLS*, ch. 6, 237–64 (237).

according to Marmier, was slow to develop in its own right, and if the eight-
eenth century had seen the emergence of talented men of letters such as
Holberg, 'cet homme de génie',[28] Ewald, Wessel, and Baggesen, it was
Oehlenschläger who had regenerated the whole of modern Danish literature
in the nineteenth century. In terms of literary stature, he is compared to
Holberg; in terms of his prolific output in a variety of genres, to Goethe.
Marmier runs through Oehlenschläger's major works in the various genres,
summarising and translating—sometimes at length—from his favourite
pieces. One of his major achievements, for Marmier, is the creation of a
form of tragedy which is essentially national in character. In this context, he
cites *Nordens Guder*, which for him has a 'majesté homérique';[29] *Palnatoke*,
Hakon Jarl ('le chef d'œuvre de tous ces drames scandinaves'[30]), and the
tragedy of Saint Olaf, at that stage as yet unpublished.

Marmier is less enthusiastic about the tragedies not based on national
mythology. Although he appreciates the characterisation, the organisation
of plot and dialogue, and the astute mix of comic scenes and tragic situations ('Bien entendu qu'il est de la nouvelle école, et qu'il se soucie fort peu
des trois unités'[31]), he finds these pieces in general to be long and tedious. In
a section on 'poëmes', *Helge* is described as being one of Oehlenschläger's
finest works, displaying a 'grâce charmante'.[32] *Aladdin* is summarised and
its allegorical themes highlighted. In the section on lyric poetry, Marmier's
knowledge of other literatures and his propensity to comparison come to
the fore. Whilst greatly admiring Oehlenschläger's poetry, he is rather per-
plexed to find no trace of 'ce caractère de panthéisme rêveur, de mélancolie
religieuse, que l'on trouve habituellement dans le Nord, ou ces nuances délicates de poésie intime qui nous charment chez les lakistes'.[33] Oehlenschläger's
great achievement in this genre, he asserts, is his use of the ancient ballad;
again, it is the national character which seems to be rated most highly: 'Ce
que Uhland a fait pour quelques chants traditionnels de l'Allemagne,
Œhlenschläger l'a fait pour le Danemark'.[34]

Marmier soon became a regular visitor to the Oehlenschläger household. On Friday 19 May he dined early with the family, left to keep an
appointment, and then returned to spend the remainder of the evening with
them. He was very attracted to Marie, the daughter, but had mixed feelings
about her, and was unsure of her feelings towards him. In his diary that
evening, he noted:

---

[28] *HLS*, 248.   [29] Ibid., 250.
[30] Ibid., 253.   [31] Ibid., 256.   [32] Ibid.   [33] Ibid., 259.   [34] Ibid.

Elle ne m'aime pas. Elle n'a pas l'âme que j'avais cru voir dans ses yeux. Peut-être aimera-t-elle un jour. [. . .] Elle m'a dit des paroles froides qui m'ont blessé, puis elle est venue me demander pourquoi je paraissais triste. J'ai eu tort de rêver, j'ai eu tort d'espérer. Maintenant je voudrais ne plus la revoir, mais le trait est dans le cœur, et je m'en irai d'ici comme de Leipzig, avec un amer souvenir et une triste déception. [. . .] O pauvre fou que je suis, quand deviendrai-je donc plus ferme et plus sage?[35]

The following evening, he dined with the Icelandic scholar Finnur Magnússon, where he enjoyed chatting about Iceland and Greenland. The conversation brought back pleasant memories of his time in Iceland, and he concluded that it had been a pleasant evening, infinitely more so than the previous one, 'que j'ai passée dans ces folles tristesses d'amour auprès de la jeune fille qui ne m'aime pas, qui ne m'aimera jamais'.[36] Despite this, however, he returned to the Oehlenschläger household for the evening again on Monday, and it seemed as if she was perhaps beginning to show an interest in him after all. But, as he notes in his diary, 'à quoi sert? Je ne l'épouserai pas et je n'en ferai pas ma maîtresse'.[37] The relationship never appears to have been a smooth one, but to have been characterised rather by its *odi et amo* nature; Marmier seems to have been strongly attracted to Marie, but in his private notes and correspondence he states consistently that he has no intention either of seducing her or of marrying her. On 7 June, he was preparing to leave Copenhagen to travel to Sweden and Norway, where he would remain until the beginning of August. As he bade farewell to the family, he noted, both parents had been courteous and friendly, but Marie had been cold towards him, and he again regretted having spent so much time thinking about her. On his return to Copenhagen at the beginning of August, she was obviously still on his mind, for he went immediately to the house. Oehlenschläger and his wife, he notes, were both pleased to see him; their daughter was more beautiful than ever, but very sullen. On 8 September, he wrote a letter to Sainte-Beuve, who had asked for news of the relationship, in terms suggesting that it was definitely over: 'Tout ce que j'avais senti pour elle à première vue est passé. Elle est grande et belle, mais froide et capricieuse. C'est une de ces femmes qui attirent et repoussent, qui vous séduisent par un regard et vous glacent ensuite par leur maintien'.[38]

---

[35] BSG, Fn, MS 3894, fo. 92.   [36] Ibid.
[37] Ibid., fo. 95.
[38] Spoelberch de Lovenjoul, BIF, Lettres adressées à Sainte-Beuve, D 606, 10, fo. 139.

At the same time, however, he enclosed a poem which he had written for her (now lost, although a rough draft is to be found in his notes[39]). Four days later (12 September), he noted in his diary that he had spent

> une soirée de bonheur, une heure d'amour et d'enchantement, une de ces heures qui font redevenir jeune. Marie m'aime. Elle me l'a dit. Elle appuye sa tête sur mes mains et j'en baise avec amour et crainte les beaux cheveux. Je la croyais froide et indifférente. Elle est tendre et comme effrayée elle-même de l'aveu qu'elle vient de faire, elle cache son visage [. . .] et me regarde de temps en temps. Oui, je crois qu'elle m'aime, j'ai su qu'elle avait tant pleuré un jour où j'avais promis de venir et où je n'étais pas venu. Je baise le bout de ses doigts, et je m'en vais, rêvant d'elle [. . .].[40]

By Friday 15 September, the relationship appeared to be 'off' again; reading between the lines of notes in Marmier's diary, it would seem that he was disappointed to discover that she was sexually inexperienced and rosily idealistic about the nature of their relationship:

> Hélas! non, ce n'est qu'un enfant qui ne comprend ni ma position, ni la sienne, qui s'abandonne à des impressions, sans songer à ce qu'elles pourraient devenir. Si je voulais je pourrais peut-être abuser de cette candeur, de cette ingénuité d'une jeune âme qui commence à développer. Mais que Dieu m'en garde! Je serai pour elle comme un frère. Je serai bon, honnête, noble, et je renoncerais au bonheur plutôt que de la compromettre.[41]

On 19 September, a further letter to Sainte-Beuve relates the incidents of the evening of 12 September, adding a few extra details, and suggesting that the relationship was still 'on'. He tells Sainte-Beuve that her father and mother know that the couple are in love, and approve. Significantly, he still insists on the 'honesty' of his intentions towards her, admitting that 'j'aime malheureusement parfois jouer avec ces relations'.[42] He remains adamant, however, that he will not contemplate marrying her: 'la pauvre fille n'a rien. Veux-je l'arracher à sa famille pour ne lui donner en France qu'une existence précaire et semée d'ennuis. Non je ne peux pas l'épouser, et sur mon âme, je ne chercherai pas à la séduire'.[43] Another half page of the letter is devoted to a description of her attributes and qualities. A postscript to the letter, however, written on 22 September, suggests that his feelings were again blowing cold:

> Je suis retourné hier dans cette maison qui m'a tant fait rêver depuis deux mois et j'en suis revenu avec une sorte d'ennui et de lassitude dans le cœur. Cette jeune fille est vraiment une belle et gracieuse nature, mais une nature

---

[39] BSG, Fn, MS 3898, fo. 137.   [40] Ibid., fo. 130.
[41] Ibid.
[42] Spoelberch de Lovenjoul, BIF, Lettres adressées à Sainte-Beuve, D606, 10, fo. 141.
[43] Ibid.

froide et variable comme un ciel du nord. Et quand je songe à cette douce et jolie enfant de Paris que vous connaissez, j'ai honte d'avoir pu l'oublier un instant.[44]

After this, there is virtually no further mention of Marie in his diary or in his correspondence until the following year. It becomes clear, however, that he must have become engaged to her. At the beginning of the year, Marmier had returned to Sweden. In April 1838, he received a letter from Gaimard inviting him to join the forthcoming expedition of the Commission du Nord. Marmier began to prepare to depart, not without some regret, from three Swedish lovers: Lisinka, Alete, and Henriette. A note in his diary on 23 April suggests a fourth lover, and states simply: 'Lis[inka]. . .K. . .A. Après de longs efforts'.[45] The following day, 24 April, he notes: 'Ecrit à ma pauvre Marie une douloureuse lettre. Je prie le ciel de me donner la force de l'envoyer. Mon cœur saigne d'avance à l'idée des larmes que je vais faire répandre. Mais il le faut'.[46] Perhaps out of consideration for Marie's feelings, his letter made no mention of Lisinka, Alete or Henriette, or indeed of the fact that his heart had obviously not been in the relationship in the first place. Although that letter is now lost, we know from other letters still surviving that he claimed that his parents were against the marriage, and had obliged him to break off the engagement on religious grounds. His family were Catholic and the idea of his marrying a Lutheran would, he asserted, send his poor old mother to her grave. He also claimed to have reached the conclusion that it would be wrong of him to take Marie away from her family and the environment where she was so happy; her life in a foreign country, married to a journalist with no regular employment or income would be unstable. But, he insisted, she was a wonderful woman and he would always miss her.[47] On Saturday 5 May, Marmier noted in his diary, he received a letter from Oehlenschläger, which was, in

---

[44] Ibid.   [45] BSG, Fn, MS 3899, fo. 34.   [46] Ibid.
[47] The original letter was destroyed, but a letter from Marmier to Dahl published by Poul Høybye in *H. C. Andersens franske ven Xavier Marmier* (Copenhagen: Branner & Korchs, 1950, 34–5) appears to repeat much of the same material:

> Ak, min god Dahl, jeg er innerlig traurig. Min forlovelse med Marie er forbi. Jeg har skrivet for nogle Dager det slemmste, det traurigste Brev som jeg har skrivet i mit Liv. Min moder, som er en streng Katholik, og min Fader og mein Søster ville ikke at jeg gifter mig. Jeg har stridet länge, länge imod og nu jeg kunne ikke meer, og jeg [har] sagt det till den Stakkels Marie. Aldrig, aldrig jeg har lidet saa meget.—Thi det er en Engel, som jeg skall evig vermisse. Og nu jeg längser mig efter som efter stormen efter nordiske dunkle Kyster. Der jeg skall være bedre en I den Stad hvor jeg har faaet saa rene, saa gode saa ømme og oskyldige Breve af henne. Min Lykke er forbi.—Det tænkte jeg siden läng Tider.—Det veed jeg nu gansk säkkert.

his words, 'sévère et froide. Dieu sait qu'elle ne devrait pas l'être. Mais je veux bien tout accepter pourvu que le cœur innocent de la fille ne souffre pas trop'.[48]

A letter written by Oehlenschläger to his friend Dahl, a bookseller in Christiania, relates the episode, expressing disappointment with Marmier's behaviour, but apparently taking the whole affair quite calmly, and expressing relief that his daughter would not now be leaving the country.[49] A note in Marmier's diary on 11 May, however, suggests that Talleyrand, the French envoy in Copenhagen, may have become involved.[50] Marmier had received a letter from him that evening, and admits privately that 'toute cette histoire de mariage a dû bien l'ennuyer'.[51] But, he says, with some relief, Talleyrand defended him without complaint.

Whilst caution must obviously be exercised in drawing autobiographical inferences from works of fiction, it is nonetheless tempting to wonder whether something of this episode is referred to in Marmier's short story 'Un mariage suédois' in the collection *Les Ames en peine*.[52] The story is written as a first-person narrative, and the protagonist is interrupted during an embrace by the parents of the young woman whose head 'se penchait sur mon épaule, où ses longues boucles de cheveux effleuraient ma joue'.[53] The young couple are immediately declared to be engaged and offered effusive congratulations, much to the consternation of the young man: 'Je sortis de cette maison dans un état d'agitation inexprimable. D'après les coutumes sacrées du Nord, j'étais fiancé . . ., fiancé, sans avoir même eu l'idée que cela pouvait être'.[54]

The broken engagement had obviously caused something of a stir in Copenhagen, and Marmier seems to have judged it prudent to stay away, even when Gaimard was in Copenhagen after the expedition on board *La Recherche* at the end of 1838 and early in 1839. Writing to Gaimard on 6 January 1839, Marmier asks to be remembered to a number of friends, including the Baroness Pechlin, Pingel, Finnur Magnússon, Rafn, Countess Moltke, and, rather self-pityingly, to 'un excellent homme, Rosenvinge,

---

This version appears to be substantiated by Oehlenschläger's summary of the contents of that letter, in his own letter to Dahl (see Høybye, *H. C. Andersens franske ven*, 84–5). I should like to express my profound gratitude to Jannie Roed for bringing Høybye to my attention, and for all her help with Danish manuscript material and language.

[48] BSG, Fn, MS 3899, fo. 46.   [49] See Høybye, *H. C. Andersens franske ven*, 84–5.
[50] Alexandre de Talleyrand-Périgord, baron (1776–1839), French ambassador to Copenhagen.
[51] BSG, Fn, MS 3899, fo. 47v.
[52] 'Un mariage suédois', in *Les Ames en peine* (Paris: Arthus Bertrand, 1851), 305–66.
[53] Ibid., 350.   [54] Ibid., 351.

hélas! mais peut-être ne veut-on plus se souvenir de ce grand coupable, qui a commis le crime d'aimer et de ne pas se marier'.[55] Gaimard's reply on 1 February assured him that 'tout le monde vous aime encore, malgré votre *crime d'avoir aimé sans vous marier*' (Gaimard's emphasis), and names all those Marmier had mentioned in his letter. He also told Marmier that St Priest, who had replaced 'votre ami M. de Talleyrand' had introduced him to Oehlenschläger, and that he had dined with the family several times. Gaimard found Marie to be charming company, although he could sense a secret sorrow behind her cheerful exterior. Oehlenschläger, Gaimard reported, could now speak of Marmier without anger, and had even expressed the opinion that all things considered, it was better that the marriage had not taken place, especially since his daughter would have had to move away. Ever the conciliator, Gaimard added that 'j'ai parlé comme votre ami devait le faire [. . .], j'ai profité des occasions qui m'étaient offertes et de celles que je faisais naître pour jeter quelques bonnes paroles dans le cœur de Melle Marie et de sa mère. J'en réserve le détail pour notre prochaine entrevue'.[56]

Despite the fact that a good deal of Marmier's time and energy while he was in Copenhagen was devoted to his relationship with Marie, he had not allowed this to slow down his work. As well as learning about the history and institutions of the city, visiting the libraries and art collections, going to the theatre and enjoying a busy social life, he had also been busy meeting the leading figures of the literary world, many of whom he was to include in his second chapter on modern Danish literature in the *Histoire de la littérature scandinave*.[57] On Tuesday 23 May, he received a visit from Hans Christian Andersen. His first impressions were of 'un grand jeune homme maigre, très affectueux'.[58] The two men were of a similar age (Andersen was three years older than Marmier), and they soon became close friends; Marmier is frequently mentioned in Andersen's diary and correspondence. One notable reference seems to be particularly characteristic of Marmier. In the summer of 1837, Andersen was in love with Sophie Ørsted, but

---

[55] AnF, 5JJ188.

[56] Ibid. The tone of Gaimard's letter is friendly and kind, but a tactful warning is discernible against becoming involved with women on expeditions. In fact, Gaimard worked so hard in his role as president of the commission to maintain good public relations in the countries visited that Marmier's adventures in Iceland and Denmark may have caused him some embarrassment.

[57] *HLS*, ch. 7, 265–308.

[58] BSG, Fn, MS 3894, fo. 95v. This would appear to have been the first meeting between the two men. Elias Bredsdorff (*Hans Christian Andersen: A Biography* (London: Souvenir Press, 1993), 134) suggests that they had met in 1836, but this seems unlikely in view of the fact that Marmier was in Iceland and Paris in 1836; moreover, the diary entry for Tuesday [23] May 1837 is recorded in terms of first impressions (physical appearance, etc.).

feeling that he was too poor to be taken seriously as a suitor, had not voiced his feelings. Sophie became engaged to someone else, and Andersen noted in his diary that after the last time he had dined in her company with Marmier, the latter had said that he could see that Andersen was in love with her, and tried to encourage him to propose to her.[59]

Marmier wrote a biographical sketch of Andersen, based on what Andersen had told him, and narrated in the first person singular (thereby adding a flavour of authenticity whilst enabling the author to distance himself from any inaccuracies). This was published first in the *Revue de Paris* in October 1837,[60] and was then essentially reproduced in the *Histoire de la littérature en Danemark et en Suède* in 1839 and again in the *Histoire de la littérature scandinave*, although in the former, a whole chapter is dedicated to Andersen;[61] in the latter (as in the official *Littérature scandinave*), the second chapter on modern Danish literature includes the piece on Andersen, but also a number of other contemporary writers and men of letters.[62] The article resurfaced then as the preface to a translation of Andersen's tales in 1856,[63] and it forms the basis for a piece on Andersen in *De l'est à l'ouest* in 1867, although there are some significant modifications here.[64] Marmier senses at the time of writing that Andersen's work has not yet reached maturity, but notes that his latest novels and poetry demonstrate a clear progress. Andersen, for Marmier, was above all a novelist and a poet. As a novelist, his characterisation is original, his plots realistic and dramatic: 'il ne manque pas d'une certaine faculté d'invention'.[65] He is a keen observer, yet his fiction has a poet's touch. Marmier was particularly impressed by Andersen's capacity to 'pénétrer dans la vie du peuple, de la sentir, de la représenter sous ses différentes faces'.[66] Marmier compares *Improvisatoren* with *O. T.*, finding them to be complementary in that they portray the essences of the warmth of the south and the calm of the north. Andersen's

---

[59] *H. C. Andersens Dagbøger 1825–1875*, 12 vols. (Copenhagen: G.E.C. GAD, 1971–7), 2, 31; this is also mentioned by Bredsdorff (*Hans Christian Andersen*, 135).

[60] 'Une vie de poète', *RP*, 46 (1837), 250–7.   [61] *HLDS*, 237–53.   [62] *HLS*, 265–308.

[63] *Contes d'Andersen, traduits du danois par D. Soldi avec une notice biographique par X. Marmier*, 6th edn. (Paris: Hachette, 1856), 1–12.

[64] *De l'est à l'ouest, voyages et littérature* (Paris: Hachette, 1867), 45–63. This version does not seem to have been noted at all by Andersen scholars, but an addendum contains a strong element of personal criticism. The comment refers to an autobiography which had appeared in two volumes. The first, Marmier suggests, has a certain value, but virtually all of the second should be withdrawn, as it consists almost entirely of self-congratulatory material, lists of his successes and compliments paid to him. Such material, Marmier argues, has no place in print: 'Qu'on raconte mystérieusement en une heure d'abandon, à un ami fort prudent et fort dévoué, ces petits triomphes de l'arène littéraire, soit; mais prendre le public pour un ami de cœur, et la presse pour organe de ses confidences intimes, c'est trop de candeur ou de vanité' (*De l'est à l'ouest*, 63).

[65] *HLS*, 301.   [66] Ibid.

style, he notes, has 'souplesse' and 'abandon', but could be 'plus ferme et plus concis'.[67] As a poet, he belongs to 'cette école mélancolique et rêveuse'[68] to which Marmier was so attracted, Romantic in the French manner. He cites two poems which he finds particularly characteristic, 'Aftendæmring' and 'Hjemvee', and offers a translation of 'Det døende Barn' ('L'Enfant mourant').[69] This, for Marmier, is where Andersen's real talent lies:

> Sa vraie nature est de se laisser aller aux émotions du cœur, et de les dépeindre avec naïveté; sa vraie nature est de s'associer aux scènes champêtres qu'il observe. Il est poëte quand il chante les forêts [. . .] Il est poëte quand il représente la vie comme une terre étrangère, où l'homme se sent mal à l'aise, et aspire à retourner dans sa lointaine patrie. Il est poëte, surtout, quand il chante, comme les lakistes, la grâce, l'amour et le bonheur des enfants; car sa poésie est élégiaque, tendre, religieuse, mais parfois un peu trop molle, un peu trop négligée et trop enfantine.[70]

Marmier's only other negative remark about Andersen's poetry is of 'quelques pièces humoristiques'[71] which are not specified, and by which he was clearly not impressed: 'il nous semble que sa muse ne sait pas rire, et qu'elle s'accommode mal de ce masque d'emprunt qu'il a voulu lui donner'.[72] Kirsten-Elizabeth Høgsbro takes this remark as referring to Andersen's fairy tales (although it is firmly placed in the middle of a sentence about his poems, in a page devoted entirely to poetry).[73] Whether or not this is the case, there is certainly no other reference at this stage to the fairy tales, whose importance Marmier appears not to have anticipated; this is fairly unusual in Marmier's criticism, for he is frequently ahead of his time in seeing the merits of literary works which are not widely recognised at the time of writing.

Marmier's work may well, however, have contributed indirectly to their widespread popularity. It was certainly to a large extent due to his efforts that Andersen achieved international recognition during his lifetime, both in France and further afield. As we have already noted, the article had been widely circulated in France. When Andersen visited Paris in March 1843, he went to the opera. The man sitting beside him asked him where he came from; when he replied that he was Danish, his neighbour said that he knew

---

[67] Ibid.   [68] Ibid.   [69] Ibid., 303.   [70] Ibid., 302.
[71] Ibid.   [72] Ibid.
[73] Kirsten-Elizabeth Høgsbro, 'A French Visit to a Danish Idyll. Xavier Marmier's Visit to Copenhagen in 1837', in Bente Scavenius (ed.), *The Golden Age Revisited. Art and Culture in Denmark 1800–1850*, trans. Barbara Haveland and Jean Lundskær-Nielsen (Copenhagen: Gyldendal, 1996), 92–9 (93). My thanks to Tom Lundskær-Nielsen for bringing this article to my attention.

of two great Scandinavian poets, Tegnér and Andersen, from having read Marmier.[74] Marmier was moreover instrumental at a personal level in widening Andersen's contacts. On Andersen's visit to Paris in 1843, Marmier put him in contact with Hugo, Lamartine, Dumas *père*, Vigny, the sculptor David d'Angers, and staff at the *Revue des Deux Mondes*.[75] Andersen's reputation had also travelled abroad thanks to Marmier's work. In 1838, Andersen recounted proudly in a letter to Henriette Hanck that Byron's widow had read Marmier's article.[76] In 1838, the Russian periodical *Biblioteka dlja čtenija* published a translation of 'Une vie de poète'; and a translation of the chapter on Andersen in the *Histoire de la littérature en Danemark et en Suède* appeared in the Polish *Magazyn Powszechny*, based in Warsaw, in 1840. The year 1841 saw the publication of a translation of the *Histoire de la littérature en Danemark et en Suède* in Italy, and in 1845, Mary Howitt's translation of *Improvisatoren* was prefaced by a biography based on Marmier's article.[77] Ironically, Marmier may also have helped Andersen to make his way in Denmark as well, for he presented a copy of his article to Prince Christian (later to become Christian VIII) at a time when Andersen had not yet attracted attention in royal circles.[78]

Marmier had met Prince Christian on Sunday 14 May, just a week before his first meeting with Andersen.[79] He found the crown prince to be 'grand, fort et un peu gras. Une figure belle et pleine de bonté'.[80] Marmier presented Christian with a copy of his book, and the two men talked about Iceland and Marmier's journeys; Marmier was delighted with the meeting, and noted that the prince was very courteous and pleasant. In the *Souvenirs d'un voyageur* (1867), nearly twenty years after Christian's death, Marmier describes him as 'gracieux', 'savant' and 'excellent'.[81] On his return in

---

[74] *H. C. Andersens Dagbøger 1825–1875*, 2, 322. This incident is also recounted by Bredsdorff (*Hans Christian Andersen*, 156).

[75] See *H. C. Andersens Dagbøger 1825–1875*, 2, 323–57; Bredsdorff, *Hans Christian Andersen*, 156–8; and Poul Høybye, *Andersen et la France* (Copenhagen: Munksgaard, 1960), 17–20.

[76] Bredsdorff, *Hans Christian Andersen*, 135.

[77] For further details of these translations, see Sven Hakon Rossel, 'Hans Christian Andersen: The Great European Writer'; Niels Kofoed, 'Hans Christian Andersen and the European Literary Tradition'; and Aage Jørgensen, 'Hans Christian Andersen through the European Looking Glass', all in Sven Hakon Rossel (ed.), *Hans Christian Andersen: Danish Writer and Citizen of the World* (Amsterdam: Rodopi, 1996), 1–122; 209–56; and 257–83 respectively.

[78] See Kofoed, 'Hans Christian Andersen and the European Literary Tradition', 235–6; I have not been able to locate a more specific reference.

[79] Christian VIII (1786–1848), King of Denmark 1839–48 (not Christian XII, as Kaye writes in his edition of the *Journal* (1, 39)). His contact with the Commission du Nord may have been significant in view of the restoration of the Icelandic Althing in 1843 (see chapter 4).

[80] BSG, Fn, MS 3894, fo. 88.

[81] *SV*, 234.

August from his excursion to Sweden, Marmier again visited the prince, spending a pleasant evening in the royal apartment. He was particularly delighted to meet Christian's wife, Princess Caroline Amalie, whom he found to be 'grande et belle',[82] and who singled him out for a long conversation. One Thursday the following month, he spent a 'charmante soirée'[83] in the prince's household. As the prince was at the gaming table, Marmier spent the evening chatting on the sofa with Caroline Amalie until one o'clock in the morning. He was impressed by the fact that she had travelled and was well educated. Her religious sentiments pleased him, although he was rather astonished to hear a princess of Denmark utter some liberal political opinions. He returned the following day and they continued their conversation. Nor were these his only contacts in royal circles. On arrival in Copenhagen, he had met King Frederik VI, already an old man, and Marmier recalls his being physically frail and of rather sickly appearance, but gentle and kindly. He arranged for Marmier to be taken around Zealand by a Danish officer named Skiaerbeck, with whom he was to strike up a friendship lasting into old age. The encounter with the king made a profound impression on Marmier, and years later he devoted some ninety pages of the *Souvenirs d'un voyageur* to the childhood of 'l'excellent souverain Frédéric VI',[84] and the conspiracy surrounding his mother's exile and subsequent death. Shortly before his departure to Sweden in June, Marmier had also been intrigued to meet Fru Dannemand (Frederikke Rafsted), who had been the long-standing mistress of Frederik VI and borne him four children. Always tending to judge women first and foremost by their physical appearance, he noted that this woman (old enough, it should be said, to be his mother) was 'v[ieille] et l[aide]'. He nonetheless admitted that 'Elle a été pour moi très prévenante et aimable'.[85]

Marmier further met a number of writers who were to be mentioned in his second chapter on modern Danish literature in the *Histoire de la littérature scandinave*. In August, he made the acquaintance of Ingemann (1789–1862); the meeting is described in rather unflattering terms in Marmier's private journal: '[Visite à] Ingemann, gros homme, assez épais, qui fume sa pipe en parlant de poësie, sa femme fait d'horribles tableaux et s'habille d'une façon souverainement ridicule'.[86] In print, the episode is recounted quite differently, in rather poetic terms: 'En Danemark, Ingemann m'avait conduit dans les vertes allées de chêne qui entourent sa retraite de Soroe'.[87] He is described as 'l'un des écrivains les plus féconds et les plus

---

[82] BSG, Fn, MS 3898, fo. 100.   [83] BSG, Fn, MS 3894, fo. 116.
[84] *SV*, 242–331 (278).   [85] BSG, Fn, MS 3894, fo. 98.   [86] BSG, Fn, MS 3898, fo. 102v.
[87] *HLDS*, p. iii.

populaires du Danemark'.[88] Marmier particularly notes the local colour in
Ingemann's work, and emphasises the importance of the imagination in his
compositions. Imagination was of course a fundamental preoccupation of the
Romantics, particularly in Germany, although the importance of the concept
was not really to filter through to France until later on (particularly in the
works of Baudelaire); prior to this time, the word was little used, except as
a synonym for 'fantasy'.

Four pages in the *Histoire de la littérature scandinave* are devoted to the
life and works of Grundtvig (1783–1872), his historical essays, criticism,
studies in philology, poetry, and the *Nordensmythologia*.[89] He is described
as a 'vénérable prêtre [. . .] qui, depuis vingt ans, édifie sa communauté par
son noble caractère, l'instruit par ses sages enseignements, et répand dans le
monde littéraire des œuvres d'art et de science justement estimées'.[90] In the
Lettres sur le Nord, he is described perhaps a little less flatteringly as a
'poëte original, philosophe religieux, d'une nature parfois bizarre et con-
fuse, mais grandiose'.[91] Socially, Marmier met him several times, but seems
to have found him rather hard work. The image he retained was one of a
taciturn man sitting on his sofa smoking his pipe and contemplating in a
melancholy manner his collection of Anglo-Saxon books. He met Christian
Winther (1796–1876), whose *Træsnit* are described as 'les images les plus
gracieuses de la vie champêtre'.[92] Marmier did not take at all to Heiberg
(1791–1860), whom he met on only one occasion, and noted that he did not
believe he could ever get to like him. Heiberg was described as having a
'figure ardente, orageuse, fatiguée'.[93] Some twenty pages are devoted to
Heiberg in the *Histoire de la littérature scandinave*, in which Marmier
writes of the diversity of Heiberg's œuvre; his greatest contribution, for
Marmier, was the introduction of the vaudeville to Denmark. Marmier particularly liked *Pottemager Walther* (*Le Potier*), of which he presents a summary and a number of extracts in translation. It is characterised as 'une
œuvre pleine de sève, de fantaisie, d'*humour*, où les sombres légendes du
moyen âge se joignent aux gracieuses apparitions des contes féeriques, et les
scènes d'un idéal roman d'amour aux incidents d'une vie burlesque'.[94]
Henrik Hertz (1798–1870), mentioned briefly in the *Histoire de la littérature
scandinave* as the author of *Svend Dyrings Huus*, is described in his diary
as a 'petit homme faible, malade, un peu sourd'.[95]

Among Marmier's other contacts in Copenhagen were a number of the
most prominent thinkers in various fields. On 18 May, he dined for the first

---

[88] *HLS*, 269.
[89] Ibid., 265–9.   [90] Ibid., 265.   [91] *LN*, 1, 86.   [92] *HLS*, 291.   [93] BSG, Fn, MS 3894, fo. 89.
[94] *HLS*, 275 (Marmier's emphasis).   [95] BSG, Fn, MS 3894, fo. 88.

time with the lexicographer Christian Molbech (1783–1857), and was immediately impressed by his fascinating conversation, his lively imagination, and his quick wit. Molbech's wife, however, left him distinctly ill at ease on this first encounter. He had the impression that although they were evidently quite comfortably off, she begrudged him the food that he ate and counted the lumps of sugar that he put in his coffee. On subsequent visits, however, he revised this opinion, and spent a number of pleasant hours in their company. Molbech is one figure where Marmier's private impressions and published assessment seem to tally closely. Although very little space is dedicated to him in the *Histoire de la littérature scandinave*, he is described as 'l'un des esprits les plus actifs que nous connaissons';[96] in the *Souvenirs d'un voyageur* he is described as 'le sagace lexicographe et le vaillant critique'.[97] Marmier also spent a great deal of time in the company of two specialists in Icelandic archaeology and mythology, Finnur Magnússon (1781–1847) and Christian Rafn (1795–1864). Magnússon seemed to Marmier to live like a monk, but he found him to be 'bon et naïf',[98] and was extremely touched by his kindness. Rafn, Marmier noted, was a tall, thin, and rather dry looking man with a very pale complexion who spoke little. The two men were of great help to Marmier on his mission, taking him to visit various institutions including Copenhagen University library. Magnússon is described in the *Histoire de la littérature scandinave* as 'l'un des plus grans érudits qui existent';[99] Rafn is mentioned in connection with his 'excellentes éditions des principaux monuments de la littérature islandaise'.[100] Marmier published a French translation of Rafn's *Mémoire sur la découverte de l'Amérique* in 1838.[101]

Marmier also dined frequently with the political economist C. N. David; these occasions were particularly agreeable for Marmier, who was strongly attracted to the wife of the latter. He also spent much time in the company of the jurist Kolderupe Rosenvinge 'avec qui j'aime beaucoup causer',[102] who is mentioned in print as the author of 'de savantes appréciations des anciennes lois du Danemark'.[103] C. L. Müller, who was later appointed as curator to Thorvaldsen's museum, took him to see Moltke's collection of paintings; he was shown around the museum of Scandinavian antiquities by the antiquarian C. J. Thomsen (1788–1865), whose work is highly praised in

---

[96] *HLS*, 306.   [97] *SV*, 237.   [98] BSG, Fn, MS 3894, fo. 85v.   [99] *HLS*, 304.
[100] Ibid., 306.
[101] Carl Christian Rafn, *Mémoire sur la découverte de l'Amérique, traduit par Xavier Marmier* (Paris: Arthus Bertrand, 1838). This publication now seems to be extremely rare; the only copy I have seen is held by the Bibliothèque Sainte-Geneviève, Fonds nordique.
[102] BSG, Fn, MS 3894, fo. 88v.   [103] *HLS*, 306.

the *Lettres sur le Nord*; Gustav Hetsch (1788–1864), an architect, showed him the models for several of Thorvaldsen's works. Some three pages are devoted to Thorvaldsen (whom he also met, although he recorded no personal impressions), the 'grande gloire' of Danish fine art, in the *Lettres sur le Nord*,[104] and in 1867 Marmier was to publish a biographical study of the Danish sculptor in *De l'est à l'ouest*.[105] Marmier was also a frequent guest of the French envoy to Denmark, the baron A. de Talleyrand-Périgord, described as 'un homme très bon et obligeant'.[106] Talleyrand, as we have seen, appears to have been instrumental in smoothing things over when Marmier broke off his engagement to Marie Oehlenschläger.

One important literary figure whom Marmier was not able to meet, but who figures quite prominently in his chapter on modern Danish literature in the *Histoire de la littérature scandinave*, was Steen Steensen Blicher (1782–1848). Blicher is described as one of the most prominent of the 'second rank' figures in modern literature (after Oehlenschläger), and qualified as a 'tendre et mélancolique poète'.[107] Marmier mentions the cycle of Jutland novellas, and offers a translation of his poem 'Til Glaeden' ('A la Joie').[108]

The two chapters dealing with modern Danish literature, then, are well-informed and quite up-to-date in terms of recent literary production. The remaining five chapters devoted to Danish literature in the *Histoire de la littérature scandinave* trace the history up to the modern period. The first begins with a history of the Danish language, moving on to the advent of Christianity; the first schools and monasteries; the foundation of Copenhagen University; the shift from the national language to Latin and German; and the historian Saxo. Marmier is full of praise for Saxo's work, considering it to be 'l'une des plus belles œuvres du moyen âge':[109]

> Ce livre ressemble si peu aux froides et monotones annales qui s'élaboraient alors dans les écoles des chapitres et des cloîtres, il est composé avec une si vive intelligence du pays dont il relate les traditions, et écrit d'une façon si élégante, qu'il apparaît, dans son ignorant XIIᵉ, comme un de ces phénomènes littéraires isolés dans les phases d'une nation [. . .]. C'est une œuvre qui intéresse à la fois l'esprit et l'imagination: l'épopée s'y marie habilement à l'histoire, la poésie des lieux et des hommes à la critique des faits, la légende populaire au récit positif.[110]

A summary of the work and what he is able to discover about the life of Saxo is then followed by commentaries of the proverbs of Laale and Niels'

[104] *LN*, 1, 98–101.   [105] *De l'est à l'ouest*, 31–44.   [106] BSG, Fn, MS 3894, fo. 97.
[107] *HLS*, 271.   [108] Ibid., 272–3.   [109] Ibid., 25.   [110] Ibid.

Den danske Krønike ('Chronique rimée'); Mikkel's poetry; the comedies of Hansen; and the story of Ruus.

A second chapter is devoted to folk song, mythology, the *Kæmpeviser*, superstitions, legends, and songs of war, love, and of the combats of giants. Popular folklore was always a favourite subject of Marmier's. Raised on legends of his native Franche-Comté around the fireside at night, he actively sought out local folklore on his visits to new areas or countries. The nineteenth century in general had seen a new interest in mythology and folklore, which was symptomatic in the shift in literature from the classical, which took its models from classical antiquity, to the Romantic, which looked to its own roots for subject matter. Marmier characterises it as 'cette forte et touchante poésie du peuple, que les lettrés des écoles ont longtemps repoussée avec un superbe dédain', as opposed to the 'essais timides et confus d'une poésie factice, d'une poésie d'emprunt'.[111]

In his works on Iceland, Marmier had already outlined the story of Odin; here, he returns to the subject, which is 'pour les écrivains scandinaves ce que fut la théologie de l'Olympe pour les Grecs et les Romains';[112] without it, he claims, it is impossible to appreciate and understand the finest works of Oehlenschläger or Tegnér. He moves on to the scaldes and the *Kæmpeviser* ('Chants de combat'). Here the early comparatist comes to the fore again as he traces some similarities with Norwegian and Swedish *chants*, and suggests links with the Edda, the stories of the Niebelungen, in Iceland and in Germany. He traces the history of the *chant danois*, citing critics such as E. Müller, Molbech, and Grimm, before moving on to summarise and/or analyse a number of these, including the combats of Orm and the giant, Dietrich and the dragon, the ballad of Vonred, and the ballad of Axel and Valborg. He notes the symbolism of certain pieces, and the religious satire of others. Translations are given of seven pieces, including the combat of Langben with Vidrik, the Wasswermann, *Morten af Fuglsang*, and *Hagbard og Signe*.

The third chapter of the book is devoted to the Reformation in Denmark; religious comedy; and Hegelund and Ranch's versions of *Suzanne*. Marmier comments on the lack of Danish independence in literature at this time, and laments the fact that despite the numbers of poets working, there is nothing to be found but 'poésies de circonstance ou des imitations, pas une pensée indépendante, et pas un mouvement hardi'.[113] He singles out and analyses, however, the works of three men whose attention to form and technical qualities set them apart from the majority: Arrebo,

---

[111] Ibid., 41.   [112] Ibid., 43.   [113] Ibid., 108.

Bording, and Kingo. Sorterup, who, according to Marmier, 'n'avait ni le sentiment profond ni le talent d'expression de Kingo'[114] is nonetheless exceptional in that he was one of the first who attempted to 'se frayer une route indépendante, et d'éveiller par ses vers un sentiment national'.[115] Two pages are also devoted to the poetry of Dass, which, despite its superficial resemblance to a geographical dissertation in Marmier's eyes, stands out by virtue of the 'profond sentiment de nationalité qui anime l'écrivain, c'est la touchante sympathie envers ses compatriotes [. . .], c'est une émotion naïve et vraie qui touche l'âme des lecteurs'.[116] The final pages of this chapter deal with advances made in the historical sciences in the seventeenth century in Denmark, concentrating particularly on Ole Wurm, Barholin, and Torfesen. 'La nation danoise', he writes, 'se retourne vers son histoire lointaine, comme l'homme, arrivé à l'âge mûr, se retourne vers les souvenirs de son enfance. [. . .] Nous retrouverons, au XVIIe siècle, ce mouvement historique, mais plus large, plus ferme, et plus fécond en résultats'.[117]

The fourth chapter is devoted entirely to Holberg, 'le créateur de la poésie dans son pays'.[118] Some fourteen pages are taken up by a biography, for which the principal source cited is *Professor Ludwigs Lifs og Levnets Beskrivelse af ham selv forfattet* (In-12, Bergen, 1741). Marmier does not, however, idealise his subject:

> Pardonnons à l'homme de génie ces taches qui obscurcissent l'éclat de sa couronne. Holberg fut un esprit distingué, un poëte excellent. Il n'est personne qui, en le lisant, n'admire la variété de ses œuvres, l'étendue et la souplesse de sa pensée; mais il avait le cœur égoïste, l'âme sèche, et il n'a pas aimé.[119]

In analysing Holberg's achievements, Marmier first addresses the historical works. He underlines the fact that Holberg was the first to write in an accessible manner, and in Danish: 'Nul doute', he surmises, 'que ces ouvrages d'histoire, dispersés dans les demeures des paysans, n'aient contribué beaucoup au développement de l'intelligence et aux progrès de la langue parmi les classes inférieures'.[120]

An analysis is then given of *Peder Paars* and its critical reception in Denmark; for Marmier, it is a masterpiece, which he characterises as a 'poëme héroï-comique à la manière du *Lutrin*, de la *Secchia rapita*, de la *Boucle de cheveux enlevée*, du *Renommist*'.[121] Whilst recognising the social satire inherent in the piece, he judges it to be essentially a witty, jolly work. He particularly seems to enjoy the apparently incongruous application of

---

[114] *HLS*, 112.   [115] Ibid.   [116] Ibid., 114.   [117] Ibid., 121.   [118] Ibid., 125.   [119] Ibid., 141.
[120] Ibid., 143.   [121] Ibid.

poetics to the journey of a poor merchant, and the serious depiction of everyday incidents or scenes of farce. The work is, above all, 'essentielle-ment danois par le sujet, par l'expression, par la couleur'.[122] Several pages are also devoted to a detailed analysis of *Niels Klim*, in which similarities with *Gulliver's Travels* are noted. Marmier explains the allegorical nature of the work, and explains (in terms reminiscent of Molière) that Holberg's aim was 'attaquer les ridicules usages, les préjugés qu'il remarquait autour de lui; son but était de corriger son époque et de l'instruire'.[123] For Marmier, *Peder Paars* and *Niels Klim* are two of Holberg's best works, although, he claims, his reputation is based largely on his comedies.

Despite his emphasis on the essentially Danish character of the works, Marmier also argues that traces of the influence of Molière, Bidermann, and Gherardi can be identified. Brief analyses are offered of some half-dozen texts, including *Don Ranudo*; his favourite seems to have been *Erasmus-Montanus*, to which some fifteen pages are devoted, despite the fact that, according to Marmier, this is perhaps the least accessible of the comedies to the average Dane. A large part of the comedy, he argues, derives from the grotesque use of Latin phrases, and the contrast between the pedantic scholar of the Middle Ages and the honest simplicity of a peasant family. In stylistic terms, he notes the 'bonhomie du poëte dans le dialogue le plus comique, et son sang-froid inaltérable dans les situations les plus inattendues'.[124] For Marmier, the natural spontaneity and lack of stylistic pretention may lead to a 'dialogue moins vif que celui de Molière, mais plus naïf et parfois plus vrai'.[125] If he agrees with certain Danish critics that Holberg's comedies contain too much buffoonery, vulgarity, and *jeux de mots* in poor taste, he nonetheless concludes that 'dans la hiérarchie des poëtes comiques, il occupe une des premières places après Molière'.[126]

A chapter on the eighteenth century begins with an analysis of the grow-ing influence of Klopstock, particularly on Ewald, whose drama (specifi-cally the tragedy of *Rolf Krake*) is felt to be much inferior to his lyric poetry. The influence of Edward Young at this time, particularly on the Norwegian poet Tullin, is also discussed. A number of poems by Tullin are analysed; Marmier likes all of them, but prefers *Navigation*, and devotes three pages to a prose translation of its opening lines. He compares this poem with works by the Frenchman Esménard and the German Gessner on the same subject, but finds Tullin's to be greatly superior. Another Norwegian poet, Nordal Brunn, is mentioned before Marmier passes on to Wessel, whose *Kierlighed uden Strømper* ('L'Amour sans bas') is praised as one of the best,

---

[122] Ibid., 148. [123] Ibid. [124] Ibid., 172. [125] Ibid., 173. [126] Ibid.

most adroit parodies ever written, and this despite its satire on French theatre. Pram and Rahbek are singled out, and several individual works are
analysed. The critical works of Nyerup are examined before passing on to
Baggesen, to whom some twelve pages are devoted. Marmier dwells at some
length on the apparent inconsistencies of his character, and the disputes
with Oehlenschläger, Brunn, and Rahbek, 'tous ceux enfin qui admettaient
en poésie la moindre innovation'.[127] Yet, Marmier claims, Baggesen remains
unparalleled in Danish literature for his use of language; his style is elegant,
supple and correct; his prose and his poetry are equally pure. In terms of
content, the variety and the richness of his œuvre are outstanding:

> Quand on jette un coup d'œil sur l'ensemble de ses œuvres, on dirait au pre-
> mier abord qu'il n'y a là qu'une poésie légère et superficielle; mais, en y regar-
> dant de plus près, on s'étonne d'y trouver tant de variété et tant de charme.
> Ses œuvres sont comme ces tableaux des anciens maîtres, qu'il faut observer
> à différentes reprises pour en saisir toutes les nuances, ou comme ces globes
> de cristal qui présentent de nouveaux reflets à mesure qu'on les fait miroiter.
>   Il y a dans la nature de Baggesen quelques traits de l'esprit de Voltaire,
> de l'enjouement de Wieland, de l'humeur fine de Sterne. Il a ri comme
> Holberg [. . .].[128]

Translations are offered of a number of poems.

Returning to the earlier part of the century, Marmier concludes the
chapter with summaries of the work of a number of scholars during the
period. He includes Arne Magnussen, Schönning, Holberg, Schlegel,
Langebek, Suhm, Sandvig, and Nyerup.

After his visit to Denmark in 1837, he returned to Copenhagen in 1839
on his way back to France after the expedition to Spitzbergen; and again in
1842 when he was awarded the order of the Danebrog. There then appears
to have been a gap of over twenty years before his final trip to Copenhagen
in 1864.

As can be seen from his travels and his publications, Marmier retained a
strong fondness for Denmark and its culture. Indeed, in addition to the later
publications already mentioned, his *Chants populaires du Nord* included
sections of ancient and modern Danish poetry and a number of verse imitations (mostly reprints from earlier publications including Andersen and
Oehlenschläger).[129] He also published a collection of *Nouvelles danoises*
in 1859 (translations selected from *Noveller gamle og nye* and *Nye*

---

[127] *HLS*, 218.   [128] Ibid., 221.
[129] *Chants populaires du Nord* (Paris: Charpentier, 1842). Verse imitations included Andersen's
'L'Enfant mourant' and Oehlenschläger's 'La Harpe brisée' (317 and 316 respectively).

Fortællinger),[130] a collection of *Contes populaires de différents pays* translated by Marmier containing a number of Scandinavian pieces appeared in 1880,[131] and in 1885, a collection entitled *A la ville et à la campagne* included a number of Danish short stories in translation.[132] A second volume of *Contes populaires de différents pays* published in 1888 also contained two Danish pieces.[133] The volume of his total output on Danish subject matter and its popularity in France (not to mention its influence in countries beyond—see particularly the translations of his work on Andersen and their influence) mean that he was arguably the most important figure of the nineteenth century in Franco-Danish literary relations.

---

[130] *Nouvelles danoises, traduites par Xavier Marmier* (Paris: Hachette, 1859). In his preface, Marmier claims that the collections appeared anonymously and that the identity of the author remained a mystery. He states that the author is Heiberg. In this, he appears to have been slightly mistaken, as the collections were edited by Heiberg, but written by his mother, Thomasine Gyllembourg-Ehrensvärd. The error is understandable in that she wrote anonymously, and her identity was only revealed posthumously. My thanks to Jannie Roed and Tom Lundskær-Nielsen for this information.

[131] 'Contes scandinaves', in *Contes populaires de différents pays, recueillis et traduits par Xavier Marmier de l'Académie française* (Paris: Hachette, 1880), 99–240.

[132] *A la ville et à la campagne, nouvelles traduites de l'anglais, du danois, du suédois et de l'allemand* (Paris: Hachette, 1885). Includes pieces entitled 'Le Miroir' by L. Budde; 'L'Agent d'affaires' (described simply as 'nouvelle danoise par l'Auteur de l'Histoire d'une jeune fille'); and 'Trop vieux!' by Carit Etlar.

[133] *Contes populaires de différents pays, recueillis et traduits par Xavier Marmier de l'Académie française*, 2nd ser. (Paris: Hachette, 1888); contains two 'contes danois': 'Le Sapin' and 'Stora l'Ambitieuse' (211–21 and 221–9 respectively).

6

The Early Swedish Experience (1837–8): 'jours de paix, d'étude, d'amour'[1]

Marmier's residence in Denmark from May to December 1837 was broken by a two-month visit to Sweden and Norway in June and July. In the course of this preliminary short stay, he paid fleeting visits to Lund, Växsjö, Uppsala, Stockholm, Dannemora, Falun and Christiania (Oslo). He was to return to Sweden early in January 1838, where he worked principally in Stockholm and Uppsala before travelling on to Trondheim via Christiania in May to join *La Recherche* for its next expedition. The first visit was spent predominantly in finding his feet and in establishing contacts, while the second involved more intensive study and consolidation. He would visit Sweden again briefly in 1839 on his return from Lapland, and again in 1842, on his way to Russia.

His first trip to Sweden began on 7 June 1837 at 9 a.m., when he set off from Copenhagen for Malmö in a small craft with a simple shelter in the middle, which gave him the curious but not unpleasant sensation of sitting directly on the water.[2] A good wind carried them the eight miles in two and a half hours, which was all the more impressive to Marmier since a fellow traveller confided to him that the same crossing had once taken him twenty-one hours. A pleasant journey took him on to Lund, where he found a simple room in an inn. That same afternoon, he visited Henrik Reuterdahl, professor of theology and university librarian, 'l'un des hommes les plus distingués que l'université ait eu depuis longtemps',[3] whom he found to be courteous and most helpful. He made a number of other calls which proved to be fruitless and returned back to his room in a state of utter exhaustion, and after drinking half a bottle of porter—which he found rather good—retired to bed at nine o'clock.

Over the next five days, he spent a lot of time with Reuterdahl, visiting his prebend just outside the town. He was shown around the cathedral by Brunius, who had devoted six years of his life to restoring it after a major

---

[1] BSG, Fn, MS 3899, fo. 110v.   [2] BSG, Fn, MS 3898, fo. 41.   [3] *LN*, 1, 172.

fire; Bring took him around the museum of Scandinavian antiquities and invited him to a dinner party; and Christian Gleerup found him a number of books by local authors, including Reuterdahl, Lindfors, and Brunius. He was invited to a dinner party by Johann Henrik Thomander, a professor of theology. Marmier was intrigued by the system according to which eminent scholars were also priests; it resembled, in his view, 'les premiers temps du christianisme, où le peuple choisissait pour prélat l'homme en qui il avait confiance, sans s'inquiéter s'il était diacre ou laïque'.[4] He was also fascinated by the uniforms, which are described in some detail in *Lettres sur le Nord.*[5] At Thomander's party, Marmier entered into the proceedings with great gusto, enjoying the anchovies and spirits, and joining in the numerous toasts being drunk. Mindful of his mission from the Ministre de l'Instruction publique, Marmier made copious notes about the education system in Sweden, the libraries he visited, and the universities. On Monday 12 June, his last evening in Lund, he was invited to dinner by Engeström, a scientist and theologian. He noted rather ungraciously in his diary: 'Des femmes très laides et de longs toasts. Deux choses aussi ennuyeuses l'une que l'autre'.[6]

Apart from these signal disadvantages, however, Lund impressed Marmier greatly. He found it remarkable that a town with a population of only two thousand should have a botanical garden, a museum of Scandinavian antiquities, a small natural history museum, a library containing some forty thousand volumes, an excellent bookshop, and a prestigious university. He was particularly impressed with the diligence and sobriety of the students, whom he compared favourably to their German counterparts. An article on the Swedish universities of Lund and Uppsala in the form of a letter to Salvandy was published in the *Revue des Deux Mondes* on 1 September 1837.[7]

From Lund, Marmier travelled via Kristianstad and Marklanda to Växsjö. It had rained continuously, and he had travelled all day on horseback through muddy valleys and sparse hills, arriving just as the clock was striking midnight. A child guided the horse through the slippery streets to the inn where he was to stay. It took a while to rouse anyone, since the people in these parts usually retired to bed at around 9 p.m. When he eventually succeeded, he was shown to a cold room with a sofa but no bed; Marmier, however, found it wonderfully appealing, principally because the floor was strewn with the branches of fir trees. His last waking thought was

---

[4] Ibid., 1, 171. [5] Ibid. [6] BSG, Fn, MS 3898, fo. 44.
[7] 'Les Universités suédoises: I. Lund—II. Upsal', *RDM*, 4th ser., 11 (1837), 570–93.

that he had arrived in the town where the poet Esaias Tegnér lived.[8] The following morning, he went immediately to call on Tegnér, armed with a letter of introduction from Oehlenschläger. Tegnér is described in Marmier's diary as being 'un homme d'une soixantaine d'années, très gros, yeux bleus, expression ordinaire'.[9] He found the Swedish poet to be a little melancholic and quiet to begin with, but quite hospitable, and he invited Marmier for lunch. The meal was a simple affair, although the wine was good, and Marmier noted: 'Je crois qu'il aime à boire'.[10] Invited back for dinner in the evening, Marmier noticed that after a glass of punch, Tegnér became much more expansive and interesting. So, he wrote to Sainte-Beuve, he decided to enter into the spirit of the occasion: 'je me suis assis à côté de lui, j'ai fumé une grande pipe, j'ai bu tout ce qu'il m'a présenté, et nous sommes devenus si bons amis qu'il m'a fait promettre en nous quittant de revenir un jour m'installer chez lui'.[11] Tegnér for his part wrote the following day to Beskow, mentioning Marmier's visit, and describing him as a 'pleasant chap' ('hygglig karl').[12] Marmier thought that Tegnér took his episcopal duties rather seriously for a man who was a poet at heart. The Swede confided in him that he had begun to write several poems which had remained unfinished because he had had to write speeches for the consecration of twenty churches, which had occupied a great deal of his time: 'C'est un singulier métier pour un poète',[13] Marmier concluded.

In his *Histoire de la littérature scandinave*, Marmier devotes an entire chapter to Tegnér and his work. Tegnér is described as one of the most popular authors in Scandinavia; Marmier recalls that in Uppsala, he once saw a very poor woman producing what appeared to be her last wordly wealth in a shop to buy a canto of *Frithiofs Saga* on a sheet of cheap and badly printed paper. Yet, Marmier argues, 'cet homme, qui a fait en littérature un miracle unique, celui d'être aimé sans envie, d'être loué sans critique, n'est pourtant pas un grand poëte'.[14] In this respect, according to Marmier, he lacks two important qualities: 'la force et l'invention'.[15] *Axel* (a romance, one of Tegnér's best-known poetic works), he claims, is a 'fable invraisemblable', whilst 'La Saga de Frithiof est la reproduction exacte de la saga islandaise'.[16] Whilst he cannot be compared, in terms of literary stature, to Goethe or Shakespeare, 'il doit être rangé au premier rang de ces hommes

---

[8] Esaias Tegnér (1782–1846) was a Romantic poet and a leading member of the Gothic League.

[9] BSG, Fn, MS 3898, fo. 49.   [10] Ibid.

[11] Spoelberch de Lovenjoul, BIF, Lettres adressées à Sainte-Beuve, D606, 10, fo. 134.

[12] Uno Willers, *Xavier Marmier och Sverige* (Stockholm: Kungl. Boktryckeriet, 1949), 21. I should like to record my thanks at this point to Thomas Munch-Petersen for his help with Swedish language.

[13] BSG, Fn, MS 3898, fo. 49v.   [14] *HLS*, 488.   [15] Ibid., 489.   [16] Ibid.

aimés qui cherchent la poésie dans les émotions de leur cœur plutôt que dans les efforts de l'imagination'.[17] His popularity, according to Marmier, derives principally from a combination of Tegnér's choice of theme and subject matter, and his style, which is 'pur, limpide, riche d'images, et habilement coloré'.[18] This is the case for both his verse ('franc et correct, facile et sonore') and his prose, which displays the same 'harmonie de langage, la même finesse d'expression'.[19] The *Smärre Dikter* are divided into 'poésies de circonstance', 'chants patriotiques' and 'odes élégiaques'. The 'poésies de circonstance' are dismissed as being of little interest, although the 'chants patriotiques' display 'fermeté et énergie'.[20] The 'odes élégiaques' are the most valuable, however, in that they constitute 'une expression plus fidèle et plus complète de l'individualité du poète. C'est là qu'il épanche son âme, c'est là qu'il laisse toute sa vie intérieure se refléter comme dans un miroir'.[21] Marmier cites the most important lyric poems and translates a selection, including *Skaldens Morgenpsalm*. Maurice Gravier, in his study *Tegnèr et la France*, considers that Marmier translates 'assez fidèlement'.[22] In considering the epic, Marmier judges *Frithiofs Saga* to be Tegnér's 'chef d'œuvre', and summarises the work, offering a number of extracts in translation. Gravier points out that although the summary is correct, Marmier fails to highlight the philosophical and religious significance of this work, but acknowledges that these aspects had also escaped the Swedish critics at the time.[23] Marmier's chapter concludes with a short biographical sketch. Gravier judges that to a modern critic, Marmier's presentation of the Swedish poet may appear superficial, but that 'dans cette étude les notations fines et justes ne manquent pas'.[24] Gravier further notes that Sainte-Beuve, who refers to Tegnér in an article on *Jocelyn*, probably became acquainted with his work through Marmier.[25]

The day after his visit to Tegnér, Marmier set off again, this time for Stockholm, where he arrived on 18 June and stayed until 29 June. His route took him via Norköpping, where he caught the steamer. The first glimpse he caught of Stockholm persuaded him that it was 'la plus belle ville du Nord',[26] with its white houses and its magnificent castle bathed in the golden rays of the setting sun. The crowds waiting on the quayside were all decked out in their Sunday best and enjoying the summer sun, and the church bells were ringing. His positive impression was reinforced by the fact that there were no customs formalities and no crooks waiting to prey on the

[17] Ibid.   [18] Ibid.   [19] Ibid., 490.   [20] Ibid., 491.   [21] Ibid.
[22] Maurice Gravier, *Tegnèr et la France* (Paris: Aubier, 1943), 127. Gravier writes 'Tegnèr' (as opposed to the more usual 'Tegnér').
[23] Ibid.   [24] Ibid., 128.   [25] Ibid., 132–3.   [26] *LN*, 1, 155.

unsuspecting traveller. Having found himself a room, it seems that he was
soon up to his sexual antics again, for the entry in his diary for his first day
in Stockholm states that not only were the girls there very pretty, but that
'elles se laissent embrasser, prendre la gorge, le reste n'est pas difficile'.[27] In
a letter to Sainte-Beuve from Stockholm, written on 22 June, he reports that
'Les femmes ici sont très belles et très . . . du moins dans la petite bour-
geoisie. Il suffit de parler'. He also adds, with more than a little self-irony,
'Heureusement que je suis comme vous savez d'une nature sage'.[28]

Marmier packed a great deal into this first ten-day visit to Stockholm.
He met a number of figures in the intellectual world, including Bernhard
von Beskow (the author of historical dramas), for whom he had been given
letters of recommendation by both Tegnér and Oehlenschläger, and who is
described in the *Histoire de la littérature scandinave* as a 'littérateur instruit,
esprit actif, poëte élégant, qui a chanté avec un heureux enthousiasme les
anciennes gloires de la Suède [. . .] et composé plusieurs opéras et plusieurs
drames représentés avec succès'.[29] He met the bibliophile Carl Gustav von
Brinkman, visited the national library, the museum (which did not impress
him a great deal), and met Jöns Jacob Berzelius and his wife. Berzelius was
the eminent chemist who is remembered today for inventing the modern
chemical notation of elements, and for the discovery of silicon, selenium,
thorium, and cerium. Marmier visited Berzelius in his laboratory, and
thought that he looked like an incarnation of Faust. In general terms, however, his most important contacts during this initial visit were in court and
social, rather than intellectual, circles. In his *Lettres sur le Nord* he asserts
that in Stockholm, 'la vie du salon' is far more important than literary, scientific or artistic activity, which in Sweden is largely concentrated in the
university towns of Lund and Uppsala. The only real centre of intellectual
activity in Stockholm is the house of Berzelius. His letter to Sainte-Beuve
expresses the disappointment of his 1837 visit: 'Stockholm avec toutes ses
magnificences m'a beaucoup moins intéressé que je ne croyais. Je n'y trouve
ni savant ni poète'.[30]

This first visit did, however, see Marmier accepted in diplomatic and
royal circles. A letter of recommendation from Molé for the French legation
in Stockholm put him immediately into contact with Lavalette, Billecoq,
Montessuy, and Flageau. On his first day in Stockholm, he had bumped into
Eduard Woyna, the Austrian ambassador, with whom he was soon on very

[27] BSG, Fn, MS 3898, fo. 50.
[28] Spoelberch de Lovenjoul, BIF, Lettres adressées à Sainte-Beuve, D606, 10, fo. 134.
[29] *HLS*, 527–8.
[30] Spoelberch de Lovenjoul, BIF, Lettres adressées à Sainte-Beuve, D606, 10, fo. 134.

close terms; and on his second day, he had dinner in the company of Beskow, Moltke (the Danish envoy to Stockholm), and Christopher Hughes, the American chargé d'affaires, who, according to Marmier, was suffering from 'le spleen'.[31] On his second visit, in 1838, he would re-establish these contacts, and also meet and develop relationships with a number of other influential personalities. The highlight of this first visit, however, was undoubtedly his meeting the king. King Karl XIV Johan of Sweden was Charles Jean-Baptiste Bernadotte, the Frenchman who had led a controversial but distinguished career under Napoleon, having been elevated to the title of prince. When Gustav IV of Sweden was deposed in 1809, he was succeeded by Karl XIII (uncle of Gustav IV), who was aged and had no children. The Swedes, needing a successor, and mindful also of the need for an alliance with Napoleon, approached Bernadotte, who had impressed them by his sense and generosity whilst commanding in northern Germany. Bernadotte accepted, and became crown prince in 1810. From this time on, he played an influential role in Swedish affairs, most notably allying with Russia and taking up arms against the French in 1812. He acceded to the throne as king of Sweden in 1818.

On Saturday 24 June, Marmier recorded in his diary, under the title 'Un épisode dans ma vie', the following:

> Aujourd'hui le roi célébrait sa fête. Il y avait une grande parade au Rosendal. J'étais allé le voir avec M de Billecoq, notre chargé d'affaires, M de Montessuy et M de Flageau. Le roi après la revue s'est approché de notre voiture. Il a salué M de Billecoq et ces deux autres messieurs de la manière la plus cordiale, puis comme je me retirais derrière M de B. pour lui faire place, le roi s'est tourné de mon côté et a dit: n'est-ce pas M Marmier. Sur ma réponse il m'a tendu la main: Vous êtes modeste comme la violette, m'a-t-il dit. Vous verrai-je ce soir? Je me suis excusé sur ce que je ne pouvais me présenter à la cour sans uniforme. Eh! bien je vous verrai demain ou après. Je ne suis pas savant. Mais j'aime la science.[32]

On Tuesday 27 June he recorded in his diary that he was bored in Stockholm and wanted to move on to Uppsala, but was waiting for his audience with the king. Impatient for an appointment, he went to see Adolf Göran Mörner, the minister for foreign affairs, who, he noted, was obliging as ever, and introduced him to the chamberlain. As a result, his audience was fixed for that same evening.

---

[31] BSG, Fn, MS 3898, fo. 51.

[32] BSG, Fn, MS 3898, fo. 55. This extract is transcribed by Willers (*Xavier Marmier och Sverige*, 27–8), but there are a number of errors in the transcription.

By this time, the king was an old man. In his official report on the expeditions, Marmier summarises his meetings with the Swedish sovereign. He says that he refused to write anything about him while he was alive in case he were accused of currying favour.[33] He finally published an article entitled 'La Suède sous Jean-Charles XIV' in the *Revue des Deux Mondes* on 15 June 1844, to mark the occasion of his death.[34] Significantly, however, the published accounts differ both from each other and from the record of the conversation in Marmier's diary on a number of details. The diary is probably the most reliable version of the meeting for a number of reasons: it is the most immediate record (and it presents Marmier in a rather more modest light than the published article or the account in the record), and also provides the fullest account of the meeting. Marmier describes the king as being white-haired, but noble in appearance with a straight back and an alert expression, his mood varying between animation and sadness. The conversation is particularly interesting in terms of Bernadotte's thoughts with respect to France, Napoleon, Sweden, his own career, and his current position.[35]

At 8 a.m. on Thursday 29 June, Marmier left Stockholm for Uppsala. On this occasion, he was to stay there only until Wednesday 5 July, but was able to make a number of important contacts. The academic, theologian, and archaeologist J. H. Schröder took him to visit the church and the library, on which he made detailed notes for his letter to Salvandy. He was particularly impressed by the fact that the library had printed catalogues, and that Schröder had also catalogued the manuscripts. He met Sjöbring, a professor of oriental languages, with whom he had long conversations about theories of the formation of languages. He also made a brief initial contact with the Romantic poet Per Amadeus Atterbom. His first impression was of a 'tête fine, longs cheveux blonds, beau front, les yeux bleus mais malades, d'abord affectueux mais réservé'.[36] Atterbom had to leave Uppsala on the Saturday, so the two men were not able to spend much time together on this occasion, although as they made their farewells, Atterbom embraced Marmier and, according to Marmier's diary, promised to remain friends for ever.[37]

As he left Uppsala at 6 a.m. on 5 July, he expressed regret in his diary at leaving 'cette bonne ville paisible. J'y ai passé des jours de calme et j'y ai

---

[33] *Voyages de la Commission scientifique du Nord en Scandinavie, en Laponie, au Spitzberg et au Feröe pendant les années 1838, 1839 et 1840 sur la corvette La Recherche commandée par M. Fabvre, publiés par ordre du roi sous la direction de M. Paul Gaimard. Relation du voyage, par M. Xavier Marmier,* 2 vols. (Paris: Arthus Bertrand, [1844–7]) (cited hereafter as *VCN*), 2, 178.

[34] 'La Suède sous Jean-Charles XIV', *RDM*, new ser., 6 (1844), 1062–90.

[35] See Appendix at end of chapter.   [36] BSG, Fn, MS 3898, fo. 63v.   [37] Ibid., fo. 64.

bien travaillé'.[38] At Osterby, he stayed in an excellent inn at the edge of a pine forest which reminded him of his native Franche-Comté. But not far from the inn, a clearing in the forest was completely laid waste by the mines of Dannemora, which even on the surface presented an awesome spectacle with their array of machines and pulleys, the steep and seemingly bottomless shaft, the continuous sound of hammers and the sporadic detonations which rang out. The descent into the mine shaft was made in a kind of barrel which Marmier entered with some trepidation, imagining all kinds of potential disasters, until he noticed a group of workers casually lighting up their pipes on the way up to the surface in the same contraption. Marmier was horrified by the conditions in which the miners had to work: the galleries were dark, freezing cold, wet, muddy, uncomfortable, and obviously dangerous. He writes of miners 'condamnés à vivre tout le jour dans ces retraites ténébreuses',[39] earning a meagre wage and becoming increasingly demoralised. Worse still, the appalling conditions shortened life expectancy quite dramatically, most of the workers dying prematurely from pulmonary complaints. Marmier befriended one of the miners who gave him detailed information about the working of the mines; he had been working there for ten years, and already showed symptoms of advanced consumption:

> Il avait le regard terne, le visage amaigri, et sur les joues cette fausse teinte rosée qui annonce la fatigue intérieure [. . .]. Il sentait ses forces décroître, et il pouvait compter le nombre de ses jours par les coups de marteau qu'il donnerait encore. Il me conduisit dans sa demeure, pour me montrer quelques échantillons de minerai. Sa femme et ses enfans vinrent à notre rencontre, et il était triste de voir cette femme bientôt veuve et ces enfans bientôt orphelins s'asseoir auprès de lui.[40]

The following day, Marmier left Osterby early, passing through Älvkarleby, where he stopped to admire the magnificent waterfall, before continuing on to Gävle, where he stopped at 3 p.m. On Friday 7 July he set off at 8 a.m. on rough roads damaged by the transport of iron ore; as he crossed the border of Dalecarlia, he caught his first glimpse of Falun through the torrent of thick smoke which practically obscured the whole town. Arriving at eight in the evening, he found a room in a large but unwelcoming inn. On Saturday, he took a letter along to Kröningssvärd, the district judge, who informed him that the governor was expecting him, and had arranged for him to visit the mines. The mines of Falun would have rung an immediate bell with the French public because of the famous tale *Die*

---

[38] Ibid., fo. 73v.   [39] *LN*, 1, 136.   [40] Ibid., 1, 137.

Bergwerke zu Falun by E. T. A. Hoffmann, who was extremely popular in France at that time.

Marmier found Falun singularly unattractive. The buildings had originally been painted red, but had been blackened by smoke, as had also the paving stones and even the air. The countryside all around was enveloped in a dense black fog emanating from the copper workshops. The surrounding landscape presented a scene of utter devastation: not a single plant or weed survived—the earth was bare, eaten away by the smoke. Conditions for workers in the mines here were immeasurably worse even than those at Dannemora. The descent was one of the most horrifying experiences he had known, and is described in vivid—and indeed poetic—terms by Marmier. Dressed in a large black workman's overall and a wide-brimmed hat lent to him for the occasion, he walked between two guides, the leader carrying a blazing pinewood torch:

> L'escalier est étroit et fangeux; on y glisse souvent, et il faut prendre garde de s'en écarter. Près de là est une mare d'eau ou un abîme. Les murailles, contre lesquelles on s'appuie, sont humides et gluantes. L'eau filtre à travers les couches de terre; le soufre et le vitriol s'amassent sur les piliers de bois ou sur les rochers; et quand le flambeau les touche, une fumée noire s'élève sur ces parois de la voûte, et cette fumée exhale une odeur infecte [. . .]. A moitié chemin, c'est-à-dire à environ trois cents pieds sous terre, l'escalier cesse, l'espace se rétrécit; on aperçoit un trou dans le sol, on pose le pied sur une échelle [. . .]. On n'y entend plus le retentissement de ce qui se passe autour de la mine, la vague rumeur qui annonce la présence des êtres vivants; c'est la nuit dans toute sa profondeur, c'est le silence de la mort. L'ouvrier est là sur le sol fangeux, entre les murailles humides. Une lampe l'éclaire, une montagne de fer pèse sur lui. Si la lampe s'éteint, si les piliers de la mine chancellent, c'en est fait de lui. Quand on songe aux deux catastrophes des siècles précédens, n'a-t-on pas le droit d'en redouter une troisième?[41]

Marmier left the mine with a great deal of relief, and spent the afternoon at the country house of the mine owner. He departed the following morning (10 July) at 7 a.m., travelling via Naglarby and Filipstad to Brattfors, where he had hoped to meet Erik Gustav Geijer (the poet, writer, and historian), whom he had been looking forward to meeting for some time. In his letter to Sainte-Beuve from Stockholm on 22 June, he had expressed the hope of catching him in Uppsala. Geijer, Marmier wrote, had published a volume of poetry which impressed him greatly: he found Geijer to be 'plus fort, plus profond, en un mot plus grand poète que Tegner'.[42]

---

[41] *LN*, 1, 140–1.
[42] Spoelberch de Lovenjoul, BIF, Lettres adressées à Sainte-Beuve, D606, 10, fo. 135.

Unfortunately, Geijer had not yet arrived in Brattfors, although his cousin received Marmier courteously. Finally, he caught up with the poet in Karlstad, and the two met briefly before Marmier pressed on to Christiania. Geijer, like Atterbom, was to be one of the writers Marmier would get to know much more closely on his second visit to Sweden in 1838.

Arriving at Christiania shortly before midnight on Thursday 13 July, Marmier soon settled in. Oehlenschläger had given him a letter of introduction for the bookseller Dahl, who welcomed him courteously; he was also given an introduction to Count Wedel Jarlsberg, and he spent a lot of time with both these men over the coming fortnight. His priority on this visit, however, was on gathering information about the library, the university, and other educational institutions. Marmier was not greatly impressed by either the library or the university. The library, he noted, was well funded, and held some 120,000 volumes; but, according to him, they were indiscriminately chosen—a question of quantity as opposed to quality—and he was particularly shocked to find that the collection even included fashion magazines. To make matters worse, there was no coherent classification system. With the exception of the observatory and the botanical garden, and despite the 'mérite incontestable de plusieurs professeurs',[43] he found the other institutes of the university similarly lacking. However, he concluded, the university was only recently founded, and had not yet had time to 'prendre l'essor qu'elle prendra sans doute un jour'.[44] Norway, he states, is still in a position of inferiority with respect to Denmark and Sweden; its political capital is Stockholm, whereas its intellectual life emanates from Copenhagen.

Marmier was, however, greatly impressed with the high level of literacy in Norway. In his report on the expeditions of *La Recherche* in 1838, 1839, and 1840, he comments that

> tandis qu'en Angleterre, lord Brougham annonçait que, de 18 000 individus mariés à Manchester dans l'espace de six ans, pas un ne savait lire; tandis qu'en France, les longues taches noires de la carte intellectuelle tracée par M. Dupin sont à peine amoindries, en Norvège on ne trouverait peut-être pas un paysan qui ne sût lire, et il y en a a très-peu qui ne sachent écrire et compter.[45]

In his diary for July 1837, Marmier noted that this was all the more remarkable in view of the extreme poverty of the majority of Norwegian peasants, who are often reduced to a diet of bread made from the bark of birch or fir trees, mixed with snow. The impressive level of instruction, he maintained, derived from the fact that a great deal of importance was attached in their

---

[43] *LN*, 1, 191.   [44] Ibid.   [45] *VCN*, 1, 42.

society to the religious ceremony of Confirmation. In order to be confirmed, a child had to be able to read and write; failure represented a severe social stigma for the whole family.

On 1 August, Marmier departed at 6 a.m. on the return journey to Copenhagen, accompanied in the first instance by Dahl. As ever, his departure was melancholy and tinged with regret: he wondered if he would ever visit Norway again. This state of depression was compounded by a chance meeting at Götheburg with Tegnér, who did not recognise him.

Back in Copenhagen, Marmier was busy not only with his writing, putting the final touches to a number of articles and letters which would be published in the *Revue de Paris* and the *Revue des Deux Mondes* (notably on the mines of Dannemora and Falun; Tegnér; early Danish literature; the educational system in Denmark; and the literary and scientific institutions of Copenhagen),[46] but also, of course, with his affair with Marie Oehlenschläger. He continued, however, to toy with the idea of returning to Sweden. After he had been back in Denmark for only one week, he wrote to Sainte-Beuve on 8 August, saying that he was planning, if possible, to spend the winter in Copenhagen before returning to Sweden and Lapland the following year.[47] A month later, however, he wrote to Sainte-Beuve again, this time saying that he had changed his plans and was intending to return to France shortly; in this letter he even makes tentative plans to visit Sainte-Beuve.[48] In October, his plans had changed once again, for he wrote to Reuterdahl expressing the desire to return to Sweden:

> J'ai trop peu vu la Suède, je le sens, j'ai un vrai Längtan pour les lieux où je n'ai fait que passer. Si nul obstacle imprévu ne m'arrête, si nulle lettre ne me rappelle, j'irai encore chercher le miel de la science dans votre ruche d'abeilles à Lund, j'irai encore voir Upsal et Stockholm. J'ai commencé à étudier bien des choses dans ce pays, et ce serait pour moi un vrai chagrin si je devais m'en retourner sans avoir posé sur une bonne base ces études.[49]

---

[46] See chapter 5 for details of articles on Denmark. On this first visit to Sweden, he published only an article in the *Revue des Deux Mondes* on the Swedish universities of Lund and Uppsala (see above, n. 7) and another on 'Poètes et romanciers du Nord: III. Tegner', *RDM*, 4th ser., 13 (1837), 716–34. On his second visit, he also published 'Du Mouvement des études historiques dans le Nord: II. La Suède', *RDM*, 4th ser., 15 (1838), 336–54. In the *Revue de Paris*, he published the following on Swedish subjects: 'Voyages. Aspect de la Suède', new ser., 50 (1838), 178–87; 'Châteaux suédois. 1. Skokloster', new ser., 52 (1838), 57–67; 'Traditions finlandaises', new ser., 55 (1838), 52–66; 'Poètes suédois au XVIIIᵉ siècle', new ser., 55 (1838), 275–89; 'Souvenirs de voyage—Stockholm', new ser., 56 (1838), 196–206.

[47] Spoelberch de Lovenjoul, BIF, Lettres adressées à Sainte-Beuve, D606, 10, fo. 136.

[48] Ibid., fo. 138.

[49] Letter of 10 October 1837, cited by Willers (*Xavier Marmier och Sverige*, 33).

At the end of December he packed his bags and set off from Copenhagen to Helsinger in a covered carriage—which was being used for the first time—and a crowd of onlookers gathered around to view the novelty. The steamer from Helsinger to Helsingborg had stopped its regular service, and Marmier had to take a private Danish craft with three sailors, for which he paid twenty francs. An excellent wind took them across in twenty minutes, but the harbour was closed in by ice, and Marmier was put ashore unceremoniously on the rocks, and left to make his own way as best he could to his accommodation. The following day, he went to find the stagecoach that would take him to Stockholm. Only two routes at this time were served by the diligence in Sweden, the lines to Stockholm from Helsingborg and from Uppsala. The affair was, however, by French standards fairly primitive:

> Qu'on se figure un coucou de Versailles, un vieux fiacre, une de nos lourdes pataches de province, reliées comme un tonneau avec des barres de fer, trouées par le bas, fermées par de perfides rideaux de cuir qui ont perdu l'habitude de se rejoindre, et qui ne barrent plus le chemin ni à la neige ni au vent. C'était là notre voiture.[50]

He resisted advice to travel inside, preferring to brave the cold in order to see the countryside. He was joined by a travelling salesman from Germany, who turned out to be a highly uninspiring companion. The journey from Helsingborg to Stockholm took eight days; despite his travelling companion and the evident discomfort of the journey, Marmier enjoyed the experience. The stark countryside, the purity of the air, and the light all appealed to his romantic nature. But he was even more impressed by a further feature of the Swedish winter sky:

> quand l'atmosphère s'épure, quand les rayons de l'aurore boréale se croisent comme des lames d'argent, puis se découpent, se revêtent de diverses nuances, et flottent comme des écharpes de gaze ou comme des feuilles de roses à la surface du ciel; c'est lorsqu'au milieu d'un cercle d'azur élargi on voit briller l'étoile polaire.[51]

He arrived in Stockholm on 7 or 8 January 1838. He found it very different from the city he had left behind in the summer. He had enjoyed wandering by the sea in the purple twilight which marked the transition between one day and another. Now he found the roads covered in snow, the port closed, and the water in the docks covered by a thick layer of ice; even the scenery on the horizon had taken on a monotonous and dull aspect. But the sky was a compensatory factor, as was the social life which was more

---

[50] *LN*, 1, 130.   [51] Ibid., 1, 132.

hectic than ever with the rounds of dinner parties organised over the winter months.

Marmier was to remain essentially in and around Stockholm from January to mid-May 1838. Unusually (for this period of his life), he did not keep a diary of his activities over the first three months of his stay—or at least none has survived. Much can be learned, however, from correspondence, from remarks made in published reports, and also from Willer's work in the Swedish archives. He spent most of January in Stockholm; he then made visits to Uppsala in February and March. From around the beginning of April until mid-May (for which period a diary has survived), he was in Stockholm. On his excursions to Uppsala, Marmier became involved in literary circles. He renewed his acquaintance with Atterbom, whom he had met the previous year, and who is mentioned frequently in both his accounts of his journeys and in the studies of Swedish literature. One particular gathering is mentioned on the evening of his return from an excursion to Skokloster, which Brahe had invited him to visit in his absence; this is recorded in a letter addressed to Charles de Mornay and reproduced in the *Lettres sur le Nord*. On this particular occcasion,

> Le gouverneur avait eu la bonté de nous inviter à passer la soirée chez lui, et je note cette soirée au nombre des plus agréables instants que j'ai passés en voyage. Toute la société des fonctionnaires, des professeurs de la ville était réunie dans les vastes salons du château [. . .] les hommes, groupés de côté et d'autre, s'entretenant de ces nobles études, de ces douces œuvres de la poésie [. . .]—ici, le savant Geiier dépeignait en termes précis le caractère de quelque grand personnage historique, et le mouvement d'une époque lointaine. Là, l'aimable rêveur Atterbom distillait, dans le suave langage d'un vrai fils d'Apollon, le miel de la poésie scandinave; plus loin, un naturaliste comparant les merveilles du Nord à celles du Sud. On eût dit autant de leçons universitaires, mais placées complaisamment au niveau des gens du monde, animées, éclaircies à chaque instant par quelque intelligente question, et dégagées de toute espèce de pédantisme.[52]

Willers has demonstrated from surviving archival material that Marmier was not simply a passive listener during these literary debates in Uppsala, but that he took an active part in the discussions both orally and in writing.[53] As well as Atterbom and Geijer, who both welcomed Marmier into their homes, he also met Franzén and Wallin.[54] These meetings obviously helped him to prepare the chapters on modern Swedish literature which appear in both the *Histoire de la littérature en Danemark et en Suède*, and the *Histoire de la littérature scandinave*; they must also have ensured that

[52] VCN, 2, 143–4.   [53] See Willers, *Xavier Marmier och Sverige*, 37 ff.   [54] HLDS, p. iii.

the work was completely up to date. The fourth chapter of the *Histoire de la littérature scandinave* (which is virtually identical to one in the *Histoire de la littérature en Danemark et en Suéde*[55]) is dedicated to 'Littérature romantique', and begins with an appreciation of the works of Franzén. Franzén, according to Marmier, was an innovator but who 'n'était pas de force à tenter une révolution littéraire'.[56] His poetry is highly praised, and compared in various respects to Millevoye, Hölty, Matthisson, and Burns. A verse translation of 'Den enda kyssen' ('L'Unique baiser') is given, and also prose renderings of a number of others. For Marmier, Franzén is essentially a lyric poet; his poems on the marriage of Gustav Vasa and on the French Revolution are long and boring, and dogmatic and boring respectively; his dramatic writing is also dismissed.

The chapter then continues with an account of the disputes surrounding the poet and dramatist Leopold and the partisans of the *Polyphem*, *Phosphorous*, and *Iduna* literary movements. Atterbom is described as 'le chef des phosphoristes',[57] although Marmier has difficulty in communicating the nature of Atterbom's 'génie poétique', which is 'un de ceux qui échappent le plus à l'analyse. Ses œuvres ressemblent à un miroir à différentes facettes et à différents reflets, dont il est difficile d'indiquer la nuance essentielle'.[58] He notes motifs of fantasy, dream, melancholy, idealism, symbolism, and mysticism. Atterbom's masterpiece, in Marmier's judgement, is *Lycksalighetensö* (*L'Ile du bonheur*), 'ce poëme, dont nulle analyse ne peut faire sentir les beautés, dont nulle traduction ne pouvait rendre l'harmonie musicale'[59] to which a four-page summary is devoted:

> C'est là qu'Atterbom a jeté à pleines mains tous les trésors de sa riche imagination, toutes les nuances charmantes de sa palette de peintre, toutes les mélodies de son rhythme musical [. . .]. Il [ce poëme] est divisé en 5 parties comme les 5 actes d'un drame, coupé par scènes et dialogues; mais il ressemble à une ode magnifique, plus qu'à un drame. C'est, comme l'a dit un critique suédois, un splendide panorama lyrique.[60]

The chapter concludes with commentaries on the lives and works of Stagnelius and Vitalis, neither of whom Marmier had been in a position to meet, since they were deceased in 1823 and 1828 respectively. The section on Stagnelius is the longest in this chapter; although Marmier does not much appreciate *Sigurd Ring* or *Riddartornet*, he writes enthusiastically about the lyric poetry, which is compared in certain respects to Goethe's *Römische Elegien* or the poetry of Novalis: 'le mysticisme de Novalis était fondé

---

[55] Ibid., 359–96.   [56] *HLS*, 446.   [57] Ibid., 455.   [58] Ibid.   [59] Ibid., 462.
[60] Ibid., 458, 462–3.

sur la nature, et [. . .] celui de Stagnelius flotte dans les nuages'.[61] His poetry, according to Marmier, is 'une magnifique expression de ce rêve idéal, qui ne touche à terre que pour prendre son essor et planer dans les sphères célestes'.[62] Translations are given of a number of pieces, including 'Flyttfåglarna' ('Les Oiseaux de passage'). A smaller section is dedicated to Vitalis, most of which is occupied by biography. A short commentary of his poetry divides the work into 'poésies sérieuses' and 'poésies comiques'. Marmier prefers the former, which he characterises thus: 'Son style est ferme, sévère, riche d'images, mais inégal; c'est, comme l'a dit Geiier, le style d'un homme qui en est encore à chercher sa véritable expression'.[63] The 'poésies comiques', Marmier writes, are much appreciated in Sweden; but for him, 'quand on connaît la douloureuse destinée de celui qui a écrit ces fantaisies moqueuses, il y a dans cette voix épuisée qui essaye de rire, dans cette harpe mélancolique qui s'efforce d'amuser l'oreille, je ne sais quel son trompeur qui fait mal'.[64]

The final chapter of Marmier's history of Swedish literature is devoted principally to the works of Geijer, with a number of smaller sections on authors such as Ling, Grafström, Wallin, Frederika Bremer, and 'Poésie de Finlande' (principally Runeberg). Geijer is characterised not only as 'l'un des fondateurs de l'Iduna', but as 'l'un des écrivains les plus illustres de la Suède'.[65] Some six pages are devoted to a biographical study, which are followed by a brief commentary of the historical works. The poetical works, although small in number, are described as excellent. The historical and national character of the subject matter of the 'poésies' is emphasised, and in this sense they are compared to the works of Uhland in Germany, in that they are 'inspirées par le même patriotisme, mais elles sont plus énergiques encore et plus imposantes'.[66] Furthermore, significantly,

> J'ai entendu chanter ces odes dans la maison du poëte; et, l'esprit ému, l'oreille attentive en écoutant ces mâles modulations, il me semblait écouter un concert des anciens jours. Geiier a lui-même composé la musique de ses vers. Les deux expressions de l'art ont été réunies dans l'œuvre. Il a trouvé en même temps la pensée et le rhythme, l'hymne et la mélodie.[67]

A prose translation of 'l'ode du Vikingr' is chosen to illustrate the most characteristic aspects of Geijer's work. The chapter then moves on to a page on Ling ('ce que Geiier avait fait pour la poésie lyrique, Ling essaya de faire pour la poésie dramatique'[68]); and brief mentions of Fahlcrantz, Dahlgren, Nicander and Beskow. 'Au-dessus de ces illustrations', however, Marmier

---

[61] *HLS*, 470.   [62] Ibid.   [63] Ibid., 479.   [64] Ibid.   [65] Ibid., 513.   [66] Ibid., 521.
[67] Ibid.   [68] Ibid., 525.

places the works of Wallin, former Archbishop of Uppsala, 'un homme dont le nom seul inspirait le respect'.[69] Apart from his hymns, which Marmier says are sung everywhere in Sweden, he particularly admires Wallin's lyric poems, which belong to 'ce petit nombre d'œuvres choisies qui vivent dans tous les temps et sont admises par toutes les écoles'.[70] The style is qualified as 'ferme, serré, correct' whilst the thought is 'à la fois pleine de majesté et de souplesse'.[71] Marmier offers a prose translation (which he acknowledges cannot do justice to the original) of 'Hemsjukan' ('Nostalgie'), 'une des plus belles compositions poétiques de la Suède'.[72] The section on Wallin is concluded by a verse translation of what was obviously one of Marmier's favourites, for it appears in most of his anthologies, where he entitles it 'La Dernière Pensée de Wallin'.

A further author given brief consideration in this final chapter is the writer Frederika Bremer, whom Marmier met in Stockholm in the second half of January 1838, according to a letter written by her to Hans Christian Andersen.[73] In a letter written to Sainte-Beuve many years later (undated, but from its contents, it must be post-1852), Marmier recalls their meeting:

> J'ai vu Mlle Bremer en 1838 à Stockholm déjà célèbre.
>
> Une petite personne un peu rondelette, grosse figure qui n'offrait au premier abord qu'une expression de simplicité et de bonhomie, mais sur laquelle on voyait un courant scintiller de ses petits yeux très vifs et briller de temps à autre un fin sourire.
>
> Nous avons parlé de voyages, de littérature. Il m'est resté d'elle l'impression d'une bonne, franche, bienveillante nature, cachant sous une modeste apparence un profond élément de poésie. En un mot, chose assez rare, elle ressemble à ses livres.[74]

In print, he comments on the success of her work, but not without reserve. Often, he claims, the development of plot is bogged down in the plethora of minute detail, which becomes overwhelming. Elsewhere, the overall effect is diminished by the introduction of 'scènes étranges' and 'conceptions bizarres'.[75] The author's real talent, he claims, and one which is extremely rare, is to 'nous intéresser à la peinture des relations ordinaires de la société, aux moindres épisodes de la vie vulgaire, à l'analyse des sentiments les plus simples et les plus naturels'.[76] Her works, futhermore, communicate the character and the customs of life in Norway or Sweden more effectively than any text of travel narrative.

---

[69] Ibid., 531.   [70] Ibid.   [71] Ibid.   [72] Ibid.   [73] Willers, *Xavier Marmier och Sverige*, 47.
[74] Spoelberch de Lovenjoul, BIF, Lettres adressées à Sainte-Beuve, D606, 10, fos. 144–5.
[75] *HLS*, 542.   [76] Ibid.

Apart from meeting Frederika Bremer in Stockholm, Marmier also spent time with Arwidsson[77] and Rydqvist,[78] who offered him considerable help with his research (this is acknowledged in the introduction to the *Histoire de la littérature en Danemark et en Suède*[79]). But Marmier did not only rely on his friends, as is shown by the comprehensive notes and bibliographies given in his work. Records at the Swedish Royal Library show that he borrowed some hundred volumes during his stay.[80] On his previous visit to Stockholm in 1837, he had made a number of contacts in diplomatic and aristocratic circles. Mornay, Woyna, Davey, Moltke, Potocki, and von Platen continued to invite him. He was a regular guest at the Löwenhjelm household. He grew much closer to Brahe, through whom he probably met Ulric Gyldenstolpe, who was to become a close friend of Marmier. Brahe's half-sister, the countess Ebba Brahe, was married to A. F. Gyldenstolpe, a cousin of Ulric, in April 1838. Willers suggests that she is the bride described in the letter on Stockholm in the *Lettres sur le Nord*.[81] This is probably the case; chronologically, it is possible, for the draft version of this letter in Marmier's notebook is dated 1 May [1838]. She also figures on Marmier's list of 'Cartes de visite à envoyer p[our] p[rendre] congé' (which, incidentally, is headed by Brahe).[82] Ebba died in 1842 while Marmier was in Sweden, and he wrote a poem entitled 'Sur la mort d'une jeune femme', which was dedicated: 'A madame la comtesse Brahe'. It was published with the 1844 edition of *Lettres sur l'Islande*,[83] and then included in a number of Marmier's anthologies.

While Marmier was in Sweden, preparations were being made in France for a new expedition of the Commission du Nord on board *La Recherche*, which this time was to attempt to explore and study Spitzbergen. Marmier received letters in Stockholm, from Rosamel, Ministre de la Marine, and Gaimard, inviting him to join this new expedition. He was invited several times by both the king, and Prince Oscar, the prince royal (the future Oscar I) to discuss plans for the trip. On 18 April, the king made him a gift of a copy of Brooke's book about his journey to the North Cape, and on 6 May, he received an invitation to a formal royal dinner, which caused him something of a panic. He hurriedly visited his various friends and acquaintances to borrow the necessary components of the obligatory uniform for such occasions. After a long conversation with Prince Oscar, Marmier was

---

[77] Adolf Ivar Arwidsson (1791–1858) was a librarian and also a historian.

[78] Johan Erik Rydqvist (1800–77) was a librarian, philologist, and critic.

[79] *HLDS*, p. iv.   [80] According to Willers (*Xavier Marmier och Sverige*, 36).

[81] Ibid., 44–5. The letter appears in *LN*, 2, 167.

[82] The manuscript containing notes from 1838 is BSG, Fn, MS 3899 (this reference fo. 47).

[83] *Lettres sur l'Islande et poésies*, 3rd edn. (Paris: Delloye, 1844).

summoned to sit beside the king, who presented him with an inscribed gold medal. In the presence of Mornay and Löwenjhelm, the king also promised to add an honorary title on Marmier's return from the expedition. A letter to Weiss written on 14 May summarises Marmier's relationship with the king at this particular juncture:

> Le roi surtout me témoigne une bienveillance dont j'ai été très touché. Je lui avais offert mes Lettres sur l'Islande, et en échange de ce pauvre volume de voyage, il m'a fait remettre son portrait et plusieurs ouvrages précieux. Quand j'ai demandé à prendre congé de lui, il m'a invité à dîner à la cour et après dîner il m'a remis une magnifique médaille en or portant pour inscription 'Charles XIV Jean à Xavier Marmier'. J'ai ensuite pris congé de ses enfants [. . .].[84]

In this letter, Marmier also assures Weiss that he has not forgotten his 'chère fiancée intellectuelle, la bibliothèque de Besançon'.[85] Indeed, Weiss had asked Marmier to acquire a number of books for him; as always, Marmier was happy to comply, as much, probably, out of his love for books as from esteem for his friend, for books were a real passion in his life.[86]

The date of his departure was drawing nearer, and the intervening days were filled with an increasing flurry of social occasions—as also with an increasing flurry of sexual activity. In mid-April, he had noted in his diary that he was involved with three women, designated only by their first names: Lisinka, Alete (sometimes written Alethe), and Henriette. On 24 April, he had written to Marie Oehlenschläger, breaking off their engagement. From this moment on, the affair with Alete, a married woman, became increasingly intense. On 4 May, the first real summer's day, he had a memorable encounter with her, which he—unusually—describes in some detail in his diary. Also unusually, it is written in French (most records of such encounters in his diaries—in Iceland for example—are written in a mixture of languages):

> Dans l'après-midi. Trois heures d'attente et d'inquiétude. Au moment où je désespère de voir venir celle que j'implore—Je regarde par la fenêtre et elle est dans la cour—elle se précipite dans l'escalier. Je la reçois dans mes bras, je l'emporte sur mon lit. Elle est si belle, si tendre et si timide. Je l'embrasse avec transport, je me jette à ses genoux, je baise ses jolis petits pieds et puis je la regarde dans ses beaux yeux bleus pleins de larmes. [. . .] Il y a longtemps que je n'avais rien éprouvé de semblable.—Je suis heureux car je sais que je peux encore trouver la vie dans l'amour.[87]

---

[84] BmB, Collection Estignard, MS 1907, Correspondance de Charles Weiss, Lettres de X. Marmier, fo. 743.

[85] Ibid., fo. 744.   [86] Ibid., fo. 810.   [87] BSG, Fn, MS 3899, fo. 45v.

The following day, he joined Alete, her husband and mother, to visit the couple's country house. Alete and her husband spoke French, and Marmier notes in his diary that the conversation was conducted in Norwegian for the benefit of Alete's mother. The conversation was polite and routine, but Marmier noted that he managed to slip in 'de temps à autre quelques mots que ma jolie Al. comprend et dont elle me remercie par un sourire'.[88] He was nevertheless obliged to resign himself, 'comme c'est la coutume en pareil cas, à voir tout ce qu'il y a de chambres, d'alcoves et d'armoires arrangés par le mari'.[89] For the next three days, he seems to have thought of no one but Alete, declaring rather dramatically in his diary that 'je n'ai plus la force d'aller voir ni la Ctesse ni la B^onne—je ne pense qu'à Al. et je ne désire qu'elle. Les baisers des autres me glacent. Les siens m'enivrent et me donnent une nouvelle vie'.[90]

Attending a soirée hosted by Prince Oscar on 8 May, he noted that Alete, who was present, looked charming in a black velvet dress and a garland of blue flowers in her hair. Lisinka, who also attended the function, was taken ill. In his diary, Marmier noted that 'On dit que c'est parce que j'ai été causer de trop près avec Al.',[91] thus implying that at least two other people present in the room knew about his affair. On Thursday 10 May, however, he notes with a hint of surprise that Carolin, 'la plus charmante piga de Stockholm',[92] remained completely impervious to his advances. The same evening, he attended a gathering at the home of Count Potocki, where he was in trouble again with both Lisinka and Alete, and decided that the time was now ripe for him to leave Stockholm. His diary for Thursday evening and Friday is full of self-criticism—not concerning his sexual conduct, but because he realised that he had been wasting his time on philandering instead of serious study. The only writing he has spent time on recently, he says, are love letters of no consequence; he has fallen into an 'engourdissement intellectuel',[93] and is ashamed of himself.

Having made his mind up to leave, the next few days were taken up with farewell visits to the Löwenjhelms, the Moltke family, Ebba Brahe, Charles de Mornay, and other friends. On Wednesday 16 May, he saw Alete for the last time, and saw both Henriette and Lisinka on Friday 18 May. As he had done in Iceland, he rather self-centredly compared the farewells of his various lovers, and decided that Lisinka, who was tearful and hardly able to speak, was the most touching of the three. On Saturday 19 May, Woyna, Davey, and von Platen came to see him off at 8 a.m. He was accompanied

---

[88] BSG, Fn, MS 3899, fo. 46.   [89] Ibid.   [90] Ibid.   [91] Ibid., fo. 46v.   [92] Ibid.   [93] Ibid.

by Count Ulric Gyldenstolpe, who formed part of the Scandinavian contingent on the expedition, nominated by the kings of Denmark and Sweden.

Appendix

BSG, Fn, MS 3898, fos. 61v–63:

Une audience de deux heures chez le roi. J'arrive à 7. J'en sors à 9. Le roi m'entretient d'abord de l'Islande dont il a étudié l'histoire. Il m'interroge sur l'état du pays et les rapports qui existent entre le pays et la Suède. Puis de la France.

J'aime la France, me dit-il. C'est elle qui m'a élevé, c'est elle qui m'a illustré. J'ai toujours désiré que ma politique soit celle de la France. Je suis venu dans ce pays et j'ai dû remplir ma mission. J'ai fait tout ce que ma conscience me disait. Mais j'aurais mille royaumes à donner à la France que je ne m'acquitterais pas vers elle de la reconnaissance que je lui dois.

Souvent, me disait-il, on tente des moyens et le succès les justifie. Le succès m'a justifié parfois, mais je puis dire que je n'ai jamais travaillé en vue du succès.

Il me parle encore avec émotion de la France. C'est un si beau pays, me dit-il, un pays qui a tout: richesse, esprit, savoir. Je puis me rendre justice. C'est que je l'ai servie dans ses moments de crise, en 1789, et que lorsque je l'ai quittée, elle était grande, forte, respectée.

J'ai été attaqué, voilà la règle de ma conduite. Ne parlons pas de cette époque—mes entrailles en sont encore émues, j'ai éte attaqué. J'ai demandé qu'on suspendît l'invasion de la Poméranie. On ne m'a pas répondu.

La France ne doit pas désirer la guerre. Les hommes qui ont fait la guerre ont employé ou le fanatisme religieux ou le fanatisme de la liberté. Le fanatisme religieux est passé. Le fanatisme de la liberté emporte ceux qui s'y soumettent.

Si la France est victorieuse elle donnera par là l'élan à ces opinions et cet élan où s'arrêtera-t-il?

Personne ne songe à attaquer la France, je vous en donne la garantie. Mais si on attaque la France, elle peut remuer le monde.

La France tranquille, l'Europe ne sera pas agitée.

Si Napoléon avait voulu être sage, s'il n'avait tenu ni au système continental, ni à la guerre de Russie, il était César, il serait devenu Auguste.

Mouvement religieux. Je crois, me dit-il, et il faut croire. Qu'est-ce qui a fait cette route. La chambre n'était pas éclairée, et nous entrevoyons au pied du château la mer éclaircie par un rayon du soleil couchant, qu'est-ce qui a fait cela si ce n'est une intelligence supérieure? Qui est-ce qui a donné aux hommes l'intelligence nécessaire pour bâtir ce palais, cette ville, ces quais, si ce n'est Dieu.

Mes intérêts ne sont pas ceux des autres souverains. Je suis ici sur une terre indépendante. La Suède avec ses montagnes, ses lacs, ne sera jamais un champ de bataille et quand une armée ennemie intervenait à Stockholm, je me défendrais de l'autre côté du Melaren, je ne céderais pas. Mais personne ne songe à attaquer la France, on craint qu'elle attaque.

J'ai été patriote français, je parle à un compatriote, à un homme qui est né comme moi dans un bon pays, je dois le dire, je suis devenu patriote suédois. En mourant, mon premier soupir sera pour la Suède, mon second pour la France.

L'amour propre est le mobile de nos actions. A l'époque où je fus élu, on disait 'il est proposé, mais il n'osera pas accepter'. Ce mot vint d'en haut. Alors, j'aurais voulu abdiquer ma place, rentrer dans la vie privée. Mais ce mot 'il n'osera pas' m'entraîna et j'[acceptai?].

Vous avez, m'a-t-il dit, sur votre figure, dans vos manières, le caractère de l'honnêteté.

[. . .]

En me quittant, il me prit les mains, m'embrassa et me dit: Que le ciel vous bénisse. Il ne vous arrivera rien d'heureux dont je ne me réjouis et si vous désirez quelque chose donnez moi la préférence [?] je vous offre amitié et confiance.

Œil vif, corps droit, tête noble, couverte de cheveux blancs. Dans certaines occasions un regard animé. Parfois expression de tristesse touchante.

En le quittant je rencontre dans la galerie Brahe qui vient à moi et m'offre de la manière la plus aimable ses services.

7

Sweden II (1838): Norway, Lapland, and the Northern Star

The departure of Marmier and Gyldenstolpe from Stockholm to join *La Recherche* at Trondheim marked the beginning of the 1838 expedition of the Commission du Nord,[1] and Marmier was appointed to write the official report. The following section of his journey is described in some detail in the *Relation du voyage* of the official publication, which is full of historical data about the sites described, details of local customs, folklore, climate, population, political organisation, public institutions, statistics, different modes of transport, local curiosities, monuments, and various other information.[2] Reading the letters sent back to France from this part of his journey (published in the *Lettres sur le Nord*), the official report, and his own private notes, one is struck by the apparent ease with which Marmier seems to make the transition from life in presumably fairly luxurious and sophisticated circles at court, or intellectual circles in Uppsala, to contact with some of the least privileged in that society. He seems to have made friends on his travels at all social levels; what is more, he records those contacts in his official reports.

---

[1] Chapters 6 and 7 demonstrate that Le Guillou is mistaken in his claim, in his edition of Michelet's correspondence, that Marmier left Le Havre for Sweden on 13 June 1838. See Jules Michelet, *Correspondance générale*, ed. Louis Le Guillou, 12 vols. (Paris: Champion, 1994–2001), 2, 681.
[2] It is important to note that this account of the journey in *VCN* is not given in strictly chronological order, which is sometimes misleading. He also published the letters from this part of the journey (subsequently collected in the *Lettres sur le Nord*) in the *Revue des Deux Mondes* in seven parts beginning on 1 October 1838 (4th ser., 16 (1838), 227–97 and 843–52; 4th ser., 17 (1839), 133–52 and 609–27; 4th ser., 18 (1839), 357–75; 4th ser., 20 (1839), 45–62 and 646–66). Additionally, in January 1840, a piece appeared entitled 'De la presse périodique dans les trois royaumes scandinaves', *RDM*, 4th ser., 21 (1840), 712–25. The official publications of the expedition (published under Gaimard's direction) included volumes on geology, meteorology, astronomy, hydrography, metallurgy, etc. by the various scientific experts. The series also included five volumes of illustrations. A number of these very beautiful engravings are reproduced by Nils M. Knutsen and Per Posti in *La Recherche: En ekspedisjon mot nord: Une expédition vers le Nord* (Tromsø: Angelica, 2002) and *La Recherche: En ekspedisjon mot nord: Une expédition vers le Nord: Bilder fra Norge og Spitsbergen: Illustrations sur la Norvège et le Spitzberg* (Tromsø: Angelica, 2002).

The initial stage of the journey from Stockholm was to take them to Christiania (Oslo), through Enköping, Västerås, where they spent a night, Köping, Arboga, and Örebro. Arriving here at 9 p.m., they found the hotel deserted, so turned back to an inn they had passed en route, where they were able to share a room: Marmier let his companion have the bed. The following morning, they went to see Bergenskjöld, the governor, with a letter of introduction from Brahe. Bergenskjöld showed them the sights of the town and offered them a splendid meal. From Örebro, they travelled via Kristinehamn and Karlstad to the border, where they arrived at Magnor on 23 May. The only place available to stay here was a 'chétive demeure de paysans',[3] where there was a very rudimentary bed, and no food to be had:

> Mais, en voyant ces pauvres gens s'empresser autour de nous, et consulter nos regards d'un air inquiet, comme pour nous demander si nous ne nous trouvions pas trop mal, nous nous sentîmes émus par tant de bonne volonté, et nous oubliâmes facilement l'incommode structure des lits et l'exiguïté des provisions.[4]

From here they travelled on to Kongsvinger (24 May) and thence to Christiania. They had planned to reach the capital at 9 p.m., but arrived only at nine the following morning. A letter from Lisinka was already there awaiting Marmier, which he found 'bien triste et bien tendre',[5] and which gave rise to more reflections on which of his lovers cared the most for him. He visited his old friends Dahl and Jarlsberg; the latter arranged a meal in his honour with a number of his acquaintances from the previous year. On Saturday, he noted in his diary: 'Visite à S. E. pour la première fois. Jeune, belle, et coquette. Le soir, elle me demande si je veux la reconduire chez elle. Nous nous promenons dans la rue et enfin j'entre avec elle et je reste deux heures'.[6] They stayed some ten days in Christiania, and Marmier's time was crammed with outings, dinners, and visits to old friends and lovers. On 25 May and 1 June, he went to the theatre; on 27 May he set off on an excursion to Bergen; on 28 May, La Roquette, the French consul in Norway, gave a large reception in honour of the expedition, and on 2 June, he attended a lunch hosted by Jarlsberg, where he apparently got into an argument with Gyldenstolpe and La Roquette, over which he felt ashamed afterwards. He was also a regular visitor at the Sørenssen household.[7]

---

[3] VCN, 1, 28.   [4] Ibid., 1, 29.   [5] BSG, Fn, MS 3899, fo. 50.   [6] Ibid., fo. 50v.
[7] Marmier writes 'Sorenson', but Marie Wells kindly informs me that there were two eminent Sørenssen brothers living in Oslo at the time: Niels Berner Sørenssen (1774–1857) who was a leading politician, and Christian Sørenssen (1764–1845) who was a bishop, court chaplain, and university vice-chancellor. Of the two, the latter sounds to be the more likely contact, but I have been unable to locate any further details.

A few days after Gyldenstolpe and Marmier had arrived in Christiania, they were joined by Mayer and Anglès, two fellow members of the Commission, who had been to Iceland with Marmier. They now decided to travel to Trondheim together, and to this end, they purchased a large open carriage with two horses. They had two benches solidly fixed to it, and in this new vehicle they set off on Monday 4 June. They soon found the Norwegian roads to be completely unlevelled, which gave rise to some rather hair-raising moments: but Marmier was full of praise for the Norwegian horses, which

> sont parfaitement habitués à ce singulier système de grands chemins: à peine sont-ils arrivés péniblement sur une sommité qu'ils prennent le galop et descendent ventre à terre la pente la plus raide. Cette façon de voyager semble peu rassurante, surtout quand on voit ces pauvres bêtes maigres, attachés avec des bouts de ficelle. Mais ils savent leur métier, et on peut s'y fier.[8]

Indeed, Marmier continues, in the course of their long journey, they had only one accident, and that was the fault of the coachman rather than the horses. Their path took them along the edge of the Randsfjord and through Gran, where they stopped for lunch. The local inn was able to provide only four slices of rancid bacon and a pot of beer between the four travellers; but Marmier remarked that this would have seemed a splendid feast to the majority of Norwegians, who were pleased if they could eat dry bread and curdled milk. That evening, they stayed at an inn which was similarly lacking in provisions, and which possessed only two forks and three glasses; to add to this, there was only one bedroom, and they slept on a bundle of hay. Marmier, however, found that this added 'un nouveau charme à notre voyage poétique [...] et jamais je n'oublierai ces jours joyeux de la vie errante'.[9]

They now made for Lillehammer, Laurgaard, and Fokstua. They arrived at Fokstua at ten o'clock in the evening, but decided to press on, so depressing was the sight of the staging post: 'Les habitants de la maison étaient, comme en hiver, réunis dans une chambre puante, autour d'un feu de broussailles dont la lueur pâle se cachait sous des tourbillons de fumée'.[10] After hastily changing their horses, the party wrapped themselves up more tightly in their overcoats, which they buttoned up to the chin, and set off again. It was a good decision:

> La nuit était froide, mais claire et pure. A la clarté de la lune, nous voyions se dérouler devant nous de grandes masses de neige et scintiller la glace des lacs. Le silence le plus profond régnait autour de nous, et ce silence imposant, nul

[8] *VCN*, 1, 66–7.   [9] Ibid., 1, 69.   [10] Ibid., 1, 84.

de nous n'avait envie de le rompre, car nous éprouvions tous cette grave et
mélancolique émotion qui saisit le cœur à l'aspect des grands scènes du
Nord.[11]

Towards 2 a.m., they arrived at Hjerkinn, trembling with cold, and expecting to find the door locked at the staging post. But by a stroke of good luck,
a traveller arriving earlier who had overtaken them had alerted the
innkeeper to their imminent arrival; they were greeted by the landlady who
showed them into a warm room where a wood fire was burning brightly, and
who served them a good supper.

After a good night's rest, Anglès and Marmier decided to let the others
travel on ahead while they remained behind to climb Snøhetta. They hired
a guide who had already made the ascent nine times, although this was
apparently the first time he had accompanied a group of Frenchmen. From
the top, they were struck by the barren aspect of the surrounding landscape;
the view, Marmier decided, did not have the 'aspect terrible' of the mountains in Iceland, nor yet the 'aspect sublime' of those in Switzerland; but it
was nonetheless 'beau et solonnel'.[12]

Marmier was also concerned about the poverty in the area, and the barren nature of the soil where no cereal or even potatoes could be grown successfully. Conditions were even worse here, he thought, than in Iceland.
He was impressed that the innkeepers had, despite these terrible material
conditions, managed to make this one of the best inns on the road from
Christiania to Trondheim. During his stay, Marmier made friends as always,
and one morning as the landlady brought him his breakfast milk, he asked
her to tell him her life story. Although on this occasion the name is not mentioned in print, a page of the *Lettres sur le Nord* is devoted to the story of a
countrywoman born in a mountain chalet, and whose most memorable
experience was a visit to Trondheim some twenty years before.[13] It is a significant feature of Marmier's narrative that he accords as much space and
respect to the biography of this woman and others of similar or lesser social
rank as he does to some of the major personalities of the day.

As the time came to leave Hjerkinn, Marmier and Anglès had to find a
new mode of transport, since Mayer and Gyldenstolpe had taken the open
carriage. The only possibility open to them was the peasant's cart, which
would be changed at each staging post with the horse. The cart was a rather
primitive affair, composed of 'deux brancards posés sur deux roues; en travers de ces brancards, on établit, tant bien que mal, une planche fixée de
chaque côté par une poignée de deux clous, quelquefois par des cordes ou

---

[11] *VCN*, 1, 84.   [12] *LN*, 1, 210.   [13] Ibid., 211–12.

des lanières. Rien pour appuyer le dos, rien pour reposer les bras'.[14] The contraption would not have been too bad, Marmier surmised, on level roads, but they were travelling along some of the roughest and rockiest roads in Norway. On the heights of Kongsvold, something gave way, and the two men found themselves thrown onto the road. They made their way on foot to Kongsvold, where they found a welcoming inn; but they were unable to find a better quality cart, so the remainder of their journey continued in similar fashion, through Økdal and Byneset to Trondheim.

A few days after their arrival in Trondheim, during the evening of 26 June, *La Recherche* was sighted entering the fjord, and at seven o'clock the following morning, she was only four leagues away. Marmier's party hastily hired a boat to go out to meet the vessel. Their small craft was followed by another, in which Garmann, a local tradesman and French vice-consul, brought a band of some twelve musicians who welcomed the French party with alternate renderings of the French and Norwegian national anthems. It was a very emotional moment for Marmier as *La Recherche* drew nearer, flying the French flag, and bringing colleagues and friends he had not seen for two years as well as news from home.

That same day, the new Scandinavian members of the Commission were presented to Gaimard. The Commission was now twenty strong, and its new members included four Swedes: Siljeström (a physicist), Lilliehöök (naval officer and physicist), Sündevall (doctor and zoologist), and Gyldenstolpe (army officer, artist, interpreter, and facilitator). Three Norwegians also joined their number: Meyer (army officer), Boeck (geologist and zoologist), and Due (naval lieutenant), as did two Danes: Krøyer (zoologist), and Vahl (botanist). Laestadius, a Swedish pastor and botanist from Karesuando in Lapland, was to join them at Hammerfest.[15] The French contingent included Robert, Lottin, Mayer, Anglès, Bévalet, and Marmier, who had all been to Iceland; its new members were Martins (doctor and botanist) and Bravais, a scientist. Bravais was a physicist, astronomer, meteorologist, and crystallographer who is still remembered today for his work on the theory of crystals: Bravais lattices are named after him. The ship was now under the command of Fabvre. The presentations were made by La Roquette, who had made the journey from Christiania especially for the occasion. The following day, Garmann organised a big dinner in honour of the Commission, which was attended by all the local dignitaries. Marmier saw with satisfaction that the Norwegians spontaneously offered toasts to France and to Louis-Philippe. The next day, Riis, the governor, held a similar function.

---

[14] *VCN*, 1, 91.   [15] AnF, 5JJ187.

Marmier reflected that the residents of Trondheim were so hospitable that if the commission had been able to stay longer, they would have been invited by every citizen in turn.

As *La Recherche* prepared to set sail for Hammerfest, Gaimard wrote a letter to Freycinet[16] on 3 July, informing him that he had authorised Marmier, Mayer (the artist), Martins, and Anglès to take the steamboat from Trondheim to Hammerfest, since the service stopped two days at Tromsø, which would allow supplementary research to be carried out there.[17] In fact, Marmier and the others had already boarded the *Prinds Gustav* on 2 July. The new service, as Marmier was quick to point out, was not a commercial operation, and the income generated by passengers and cargo together would hardly cover the cost of the coal used to fuel the engines. But the advantage for passengers was enormous: prior to its introduction, the journey from Trondheim to Hammerfest would have taken at least a month in small open vessels, in which the passengers would have to sit huddled up together with their feet submerged in water, and exposed to all the elements. Now, the steamer covered the same ground in eight days, stopping off at various points. On 4 July, they crossed the Arctic Circle, and Marmier was struck by the fact that

> A mesure que nous avançons, toute la nature prend un aspect plus sauvage et plus imposant; des montagnes nues s'élancent par jets hardis du niveau de la mer, leurs flancs droits et escarpés, leur cime taillée carrément, effilée comme une aiguille ou dentelée comme une scie; la neige s'abaisse de plus en plus vers la mer, et les brouillards noirs jettent comme un voile de deuil sur cette surface blanche.[18]

Their next stop was at Bodø, the only town in Nordland, 'si l'on peut appeler ville un groupe d'une trentaine de maisons en bois et quelques magasins à moitié vides'.[19] After visiting the church and the pastor's house, they were back on board and steaming up the Vestfjorden, towards the Lofoten Islands (see Plate 3). Marmier gives statistics on the fishing industry and describes the methods employed there, but describes the life of these fishermen as 'wretched' ('misérable'):

> Rien qu'à voir ces cabanes en bois qui les abritent à peine contre le froid, ce sol nu où ils reposent avec leurs habits humides, on éprouve un profond sentiment de pitié. Et c'est là qu'ils restent trois mois au milieu de l'hiver, loin de

---

[16] Louis-Claude de Saulses (sometimes written de Saulces) de Freycinet (1779–1842), naval captain and navigator, founder of the Société de géographie, Membre de l'Institut de France (Académie des sciences), Membre du Bureau des longitudes. He was the brother of baron Louis-Henri de Saulses de Freycinet (1777–1840) who was an admiral in the French navy.
[17] AnF, 5JJ187.   [18] *LN*, 1, 239.   [19] Ibid., 1, 240.

leur famille, pauvrement vêtus et pauvrement nourris, couchés la nuit dans la boue, et s'en allant le jour tirer des filets hors d'une eau glacée. La malpropreté, l'humidité des vêtemens, la mauvaise nourriture, engendrent parmi eux des maladies graves dont ils ne guérissent presque jamais; c'est la gale, la lèpre, l'éléphantiasis, et surtout le scorbut.[20]

Despite Marmier's emotional response to the plight of these people, he is aware of the danger of judging uniquely by alien (French) criteria, and insists that despite their poverty, they are fiercely attached to, and extremely proud of, their way of life.

As the steamer pressed on northwards, the sea became increasingly rough, the sky black, and the wind cold; the deck was too cold, while the lounge was filled by 'la funeste odeur de mal de mer'.[21] As the temperature continued to drop, the island of Sandtorg suddenly appeared through the gloom; here they were to spend the night. The real power on this island lay with a rich merchant who seemed to control everything: even the fishermen are described by Marmier as his 'vassaux' ('vassals').[22] The other passengers made for the merchant's luxurious house, which also served as stock exchange, hotel, and point of contact with the outside world. Marmier, however, headed for the wooden huts inhabited by the working people. As he walked by, the pilot spotted him and invited him into his home to meet his family. There was only one room which had to serve as a bedroom, kitchen, and living room; on the outside was a rack for drying the fish, and a half-built barn. The family slept on skins on the floor, wore coarse clothes of sackcloth, and lived on watered-down milk, fish, and cheese; they had tried to grow barley, the only crop which stood a chance in that climate, but the harvest was unreliable, and often failed. Yet Marmier was made welcome and offered a drink of milk. The family seemed happy and contented, and the pilot himself showed an evident pride in the beauty of his surroundings. Leaving this family, Marmier made his way to the merchant's house, where the other passengers were having a lively party with the merchant. Marmier noted, however, that in the midst of the general merriment, the women of the family sat silently to one side, leaving their places only to serve more drink to the men. No comparison is articulated, but the clear implication is that the simple workers, albeit exploited and living in poverty, have more worthy values than the merchant class.

The next stop on the itinerary was Tromsø, which struck Marmier by its cosmopolitan nature. The artist Mayer was rather distressed to find that the local women had abandoned their traditional dress, which he had hoped to

---

[20] Ibid., 1, 242.   [21] Ibid., 1, 244.   [22] Ibid.

capture on canvas, in favour of poorly imitated Parisian fashions. The governor being absent, they were invited to dinner by the bishop, along with the captain of the steamer and a number of local schoolteachers. Marmier took the opportunity to find out about the local education system and schools, the reading circles, and the activities of the music and drama societies in the town. He was much struck by the fact that nothing seemed to grow here, not even barley in the valleys or fir trees on the mountainsides. He was profoundly touched by the sight of a young woman being moved to tears at the sight of a bunch of lilac which her husband had brought for her from Christiania. Passing through Talvik and Alta, Marmier and his companions decided to leave the steamer in order to visit the surrounding area in greater detail. At Kåfjord on 10 July, Marmier visited the copper mine which had been recently founded by an Englishman named Crowe. He was astonished to find a self-sufficient 'colony' of Russians, Germans, Norwegians, Sami, and Englishmen living together with their own church, school, shop, and doctor. He was impressed by the system according to which a small proportion of every salary was deducted at source to pay for the schoolteacher, the priest, and a form of health insurance; if a worker fell ill, he received free medical treatment and sick pay. It is unusual for Marmier to express approval of anything emanating from England (particularly a 'colony'), or of any capitalist enterprise; presumably here, the rudimentary welfare provision outweighs other considerations in his eyes.

From Kåfjord, the party set out again in a small sailing craft with five oarsmen. The steamer, which by this time was also departing from Kåfjord, towed them a little way, after which they initially made swift progress, carried by a good wind. When the wind dropped, the oarsmen set to work:

> Notre marche était moins rapide, mais elle était charmante. A minuit le soleil brillait encore à l'horizon: de grands jets de lumière couraient sur les vagues comme une fusée, et la mer, où le dernier souffle de la brise venait de s'endormir, était çà et là blanche comme de l'acier, rouge comme la lame de cuivre.[23]

At the edge of the land, they glimpsed a dwelling and steered towards it. It turned out to be a rough and ready shapeless shelter fashioned out of earth and clumps of turf. The owner was sitting beside the entrance, and Marmier settled down beside him and started chatting, so that the man told him his life story. He was born in the district of Tromsø, and since his early childhood had earned his living as a fisherman, like his father, both summer and winter. His father had been very poor, and had been able to leave him noth-

---

[23] *VCN*, 1, 163–4.

ing when he died. He had found that the fishing here was good, and decided to settle. His wife had brought him a cow as her dowry. The cow had borne two calves, and with his savings from a good season's catch, he had been able to buy half a dozen ewes. He showed Marmier the interior of his dwelling. There was no covering on the bare earth, and the walls were bare. There was no furniture; two stones in the centre served as a hearth, and a little straw and some skins on the floor served as beds. The man's only real possession was a crate of books, all of which he had read, with the exception of a Latin grammar. A page and a half of the *Lettres sur le Nord* and the official report[24] are devoted to the life of this individual who, Marmier records, was highly intelligent, and spoke a very pure Norwegian. Two other features struck Marmier with some force: the first was the man's reaction when Marmier naïvely asked him if he was a Laplander ('Lapon'), which he took as a profound insult. The second was an account book listing the money owed to the local merchant, on whom the individual appeared to be completely dependent. A few modest purchases, of which the most expensive seemed to have been a bag of flour, had put him in severe debt. Although the system is not overtly criticised, the merchant's monopoly is shown to be profoundly unjust.

A mile away from here, Marmier met his first family of real Sami. Their accommodation was similarly sparse; on one side of the room a few reindeer skins provided a bed for the whole family; a flock of ewes had their stable on the other. In the middle of the room was a fire, over which a woman was stirring a pot of boiling fishbones with a branch from a birch tree; a girl was sitting on a stone making thread from reindeer nerves; and half a dozen pale, thin, children sat listlessly around. All had sore red eyes from the smoke. Attempts to make conversation failed; Marmier at this stage had obviously not yet mastered the language. The only thing which produced any reaction at all was when one of the group happened to take some tobacco out of his pocket. The girl and the young woman sprang forward, their hands outstretched, and made gestures of profuse gratitude. This was the last stop the contingent made, and they returned to their small craft, anxious to rid themselves of the swarms of insects pursuing them. In the absence of a wind, the oarsmen again set to work; at 8 a.m. on 12 July, they rounded the point at Kvaløya, and some two hours later, they reached Hammerfest.

La Recherche arrived shortly afterwards, and preparations were made for the voyage to Spitzbergen. Marmier, however, after a good deal of

[24] *LN*, 1, 255–7; *VCN*, 1, 164–6.

reflection, requested permission not to join the expedition, which for him, in the circumstances, would merely have been a tourist excursion. His official mission was to conduct research on language, literature, and cultural institutions—none of which, quite clearly, was to be found at Spitzbergen.

In true Romantic fashion, Marmier shed several tears as *La Recherche* sailed off on 14 July. He returned sadly to his hotel, brooding on all the work he planned before his colleagues returned. He found some consolation with a woman named Margrete, but did not allow this to distract him from his research. His first self-appointed task was to visit some of the isolated dwellings scattered around the coast, in order to see how the people lived. To this end, he enlisted the help of Aale, the pastor of Hammerfest. Leaving Hammerfest together on 20 or 21 July, they climbed the mountain ridge and walked down to Ryppefjord before then proceeding on to Kvalsund. Here, a large crowd of Sami had gathered for one of the three annual religious services to be celebrated by the pastor. Marmier's description of the scene in both the official report and the *Lettres sur le Nord* is used to correct a number of prejudices concerning a people about whom relatively little was known in France at that time:

> En général, les pauvres Lapons ont été durement calomniés. Les voyageurs qui n'ont fait que voir de loin les sombres demeures où ils vivent, leur ont prêté bien des vices dont ils sont, pour la plupart du moins, très innocents. Il suffit de rester quelque temps parmi eux, de causer avec eux, de les suivre dans les diverses situations de la vie, pour être touché de tout ce qu'il y a de bon, de simple et d'honnête dans leur nature.[25]

If the final sentence of this short extract may sound patronising, the whole is in fact telling in terms of Marmier's writing in the context of the more conventional travel narrative of the era. The words 'voir de loin' summarise both the behaviour and the discourse of the typical 'traveller-as-hero' or 'traveller-as-coloniser'. The usually (but not necessarily) masculine subject in such a context seeks characteristically to preserve his or her distance from those who are 'other'. Such a strategy enables the subject to retain a position of superiority, which is normally already established by financial superiority, mobility, and possibly also superior physical strength, or weaponry. The apparently objective, although intensely subjective gaze reinforces the distance and confers power on the traveller who is looking, and judging everything according to his (or her) own pre-established national or social criteria. Thus factors of difference (for example, different types of clothes, standards of hygiene, or particularly disease) may be used

[25] *VCN*, 1, 191.

as pretexts to look (down) on others. The refusal to relinquish the position of superiority and power implies also a failure to exchange, to empathise, to understand.[26] Marmier, for his part, refuses, by and large, to 'voir de loin'. In many situations, where exchange or involvement of any sort is impossible, he actually refuses to look. The key words in his rhetoric here are conjunctions such as 'avec' and 'parmi', and words such as 'touché'; he seeks to break down the distance between himself and others. But this is not necessarily a selfless decision; although he may relinquish a part of his own cultural identity in the act, he is able to acquire in exchange the experience of a different life, of a different cultural identity.

After attending the church service held by Aale, Marmier joined a jolly gathering in the merchant's shop. From his account of the party, it would seem that the Laplanders, the lowest of the low in social terms, were excluded from any such gathering; their only contact with the merchant was for business, begging for credit when they had no other means to purchase necessities. One such man, who was moved by curiosity, put his head around the door, and Marmier soon engaged him in conversation. The man, Ole Olsen,[27] came from near the Russian border, but brought his herd of reindeer to Kvalsund every summer. He told Marmier about his life, and invited Marmier to visit him in Kitell the following year. The following day, as Marmier was about to leave, Olsen came to find him, made him a gift of a Norwegian coin in memory of their meeting, and reiterated his invitation.

Marmier's departure that day (22 July) was determined by the arrival of Per Nilsson, a fisherman from Finnmark who was also the schoolmaster at Rafsbotn for seven months of the year. He had to come to fetch Aale to administer last rites to his mother, who was dying from leprosy. They set off early in the afternoon, in a small vessel with three oarsmen, guided by Nilsson, and followed the east coast of Kvaløya. As the evening drew on, huge dark clouds built up in the sky, and soon nothing could be seen except the black waves and the outlines of the mountains. At 2 a.m. they reached

---

[26] The travel narrative published by Léonie d'Aunet about this same journey (undertaken the following year; see chapter 8), entitled *Voyage d'une femme au Spitzberg* (Paris: Hachette, 1854), offers a clear example of the author constructing herself in the role of 'traveller-as-coloniser'. In particular, d'Aunet's text subjects all 'others' encountered (most notably, but not only, the Sami) to a process of dehumanisation. Further details can be found in Wendy Mercer, 'Gender and *Genre* in Nineteenth-Century Travel Writing: Léonie d'Aunet and Xavier Marmier', in Steve Clark (ed.), *Travel Writing and Empire: Postcolonial Theory in Transit* (London and New York: Zed, 1999), 146–63.

[27] Marmier writes 'Ollsen' or 'Olssen', but Thomas Munch-Petersen kindly advises me that 'Olsen' would be a more usual spelling.

Rafsbotn; the sky was still laden with heavy clouds, but in a ray of pale red light from the horizon, a turf hut was just visible.

Shivering with cold, their garments soaked through with fog and sea water, Aale and Marmier followed Nilsson into the hut, a poor Sami shanty inhabited by two families. On one side were the reindeer skins, which served as beds, and on the other a weaving loom, a few wooden buckets resting on planks, and a pot hanging over the fireplace. Two women who appeared to have thrown their sackcloth tunics on in some haste sat on their bed, while the dying woman was crying out in pain from a dark corner. An incurable form of leprosy had eaten her palate away to such an extent that only her son was able to understand what she said. The priest, kneeling at her side, and not quite trusting his command of the Sami language, began to pray in Norwegian, while Per Nilsson, his hands together and his head bowed, translated his words. For Marmier, it was 'une scène que je n'oublierai jamais [. . .] c'est tout ce que j'ai vu dans ma vie de plus terrible et de plus imposant'.[28] Marmier's presence in this situation is undeniably inappropriate; he has no part to play in the proceedings other than as a distant observer. And yet he makes an emotional investment in the scene which diminishes the distance between himself and the other participants. By his own emotional investment, he also invites that of the reader; and the Sami here are presented as fellow human beings.

After the administration of the last rites, Marmier and Aale slept on reindeer skins in the barn outside. In the morning, the women served their guests a meal of fishtails which had been boiled up in a large tub, and oatcakes baked on a slab of stone over the fire. There was no cutlery, but the two men used the blade of a penknife to fish the tails out of the tub; the meal was washed down with water from a nearby torrent. Marmier heartily enjoyed the meal.

After spending a few more days in Hammerfest and the surrounding region, Marmier set out on 5 August to visit the North Cape, accompanied by a Frenchman named Saint-Maur who had recently arrived in Hammerfest. With a small boat and five local oarsmen they passed Masøya and Gjesvaer, where they found the last merchant of the north. The man of the family was ill, and the business was run by a woman named Kielsberg with her two daughters, Marthe and Marie. In contrast to the merchants Marmier had met earlier on his travels, this family lived in obvious poverty, but they gave him a warm welcome. Marmier as usual took the opportunity to find out all he could about his new friends, and Mme Kielsberg's life story is included in the official report on the journey.[29]

---

[28] *VCN*, 1, 197.   [29] Ibid., 1, 207–9.

They had intended to spend the night here, but at midnight the sky began to clear and a fresh breeze blew up from the south; these conditions were too good to be missed, and with a ration of spirits to fortify them the crew were persuaded to relinquish their night's sleep. As they sailed closer to the North Cape, the landscape became increasingly stark and barren, so that Marmier was quite astonished when the guide sailed the ship back around the cape into a small sheltered bay where flowers and grass were growing, 'comme un dernier rayon de vie sur cette terre inanimée'.[30] Saint-Maur suggested climbing to the summit of the cape, and Marmier readily agreed. Although the summit was not high, it was not an easy climb, since there were few reliable footholds, and they had to cling to the rocks to avoid losing their balance. The view from the summit was moving:

> Ailleurs la nature peut ravir l'âme dans la contemplation de ses magnifiques beautés; ici elle la saisit et la subjugue. En face d'un tel tableau, on se sent petit, on courbe la tête dans sa faiblesse, et si alors quelques mots s'échappent des lèvres, ce ne peut être qu'un cri d'humilité et une prière.[31]

This rather Romantic discourse contrasts strongly with the accounts of the ascent of a mountain in the traditional travel narrative, which tends to posit the traveller as hero triumphing over nature. This idiom is not, however, totally absent from Marmier's text; his portrayal of nature is much less original than his portrayal of people, alternating between the Romantic and the 'traveller-as-hero'.

The return journey took them back to Gjesvaer, where Mme Kielsberg was waiting with Marthe and Marie, all decked out in their Sunday best. Beds had been prepared for the travellers, but again the wind was favourable: much to Marmier's regret and the girls' disappointment, they decided to press on, arriving at Havesund at 9 p.m. where they spent the night before returning to Hammerfest.

La Recherche, meanwhile, had been to Bear Island (Bjørnøya) and on to Bell-Sund at Spitzbergen, whence they had hoped to make further explorations; but the deteriorating meteorological conditions had forced them to leave on 5 August, some five days earlier than they had intended.[32] On 12 August the ship sailed back into Hammerfest, and Marmier spent a happy day with his colleagues. A grand ball was organised by the commission to bid farewell to the people of Hammerfest and to thank them for their hospitality. A room of their inn was completely transformed for the

---

[30] *LN*, 2, 11.   [31] Ibid., 2, 12–13.
[32] Letter from Fabvre to Rosamel, Ministre de la Marine, 20 August 1838, AnF, 5JJ187.

occasion by the sailors who decorated it ingeniously with flags, torches made with bayonets, and stars from the blades of sabres.

Captain Fabvre and the crew of *La Recherche* now set sail for France, leaving the members of the commission to pursue their investigations on land. A number of letters from Fabvre to Gaimard from this period have survived; although these are generally of a formal nature, they include a number of pleasingly human touches.[33] One of the most surprising, in view of the relatively short time Marmier must have spent with the crew of the ship on this occasion, is that almost every letter contains a special greeting for Marmier, who obviously made something of an impression on the captain. But in the meantime, Gaimard and the others were busy with preparations for the next stage of their journey. Gaimard, Robert, Meyer the Norwegian, Marmier, and Gyldenstolpe and Sündevall the Swedes were to make their way across Lapland to Sweden, accompanied by Laestadius.[34] Lottin, Bravais, Siljeström, Lilliehöök, and a number of others were to spend the winter in the region in order to continue their scientific experiments and observations. On 22 August, they all boarded the steamer *Prinds Gustav* on which Marmier's small party had travelled north from Trondheim, and by evening they were back at Kåfjord. At Bossekop they found a suitable base for the scientists who were to spend the winter in the area. During the week spent here, Marmier wrote a poem entitled 'L'Arbre de Bossekop', which was subsequently published in a number of his anthologies.[35] This poem must have struck a chord with Mme Hanska (Balzac's lover and future wife), for it is copied out by hand in her 'carnet de lecture'.[36] As the scientists were settling into their new accommodation, preparations were being set in motion for those who were to make the long trek down through Lapland. They managed to obtain a tent large enough to shelter the whole party, and to hire a total of twenty horses, including twelve to carry the tent, luggage, and equipment; and they engaged a guide, Mickel Johansson. They were also to be accompanied by eight locals who would return the horses from Karesuando. On 29 August they bid farewell to their

---

[33] One particularly touching example is a letter from Brest on 26 September 1838, in which Fabvre regretfully informs Gaimard that the last of the four reindeer he had tried to bring back to France for him had died. Fabvre had managed to accustom the reindeers to a diet of bread, but they had perished because of the severe weather conditions on the return journey (AnF, 5JJ188).

[34] A copy of a book by Laestadius in Marmier's library in Pontarlier contains the inscription: 'Til Herr Professor Marmier vördnadsfullt af L. L. Laestadius'.

[35] Occasionally referred to as 'Le Pin de Bossekop', it appears in the *Poésies d'un voyageur* (Paris: Félix Locquin, 1844), in which it is dedicated to 'mon ami Amédée Pichot' (46–7); it appears again in the new 1874 and 1882 editions, and then again in *Prose et vers 1836–1886* (Paris: Lahure, 1890), 235–6.

[36] Spoelberch de Lovenjoul, BIF, MS A374, Carnets de lecture de Madame Hanska, fo. 52.

friends and set off on horseback on the first leg of their journey. The caravan had been joined by three additional travellers who would not have been able to make the journey alone: a Swedish workman, a girl from Torneå who had been working at Kåfjord, and an orphan who wanted to join some relatives at Karesuando.

The journey took them through swamps and rivers, up and down mountains and through untamed stretches of thick shrubbery. Where they came across a dwelling, they slept in Sami huts, but usually made their beds on reindeer skins under cover of the tent. The ground on which they slept was often wet, and the reindeer skins offered little protection, so that they would often wake in the morning numb with cold. Fire could only be made by burning dwarf birch trees which were young, green, and damp, and generally produced more smoke than heat. Laestadius would tell stories about the history of Lapland, or its myths and legends. One of Marmier's favourite memories is of an evening when Laestadius, sitting by the camp fire, recounted the tales of Stallo and Sotno, which are related in both the *Lettres sur le Nord* and the official report.[37]

After travelling for several days without seeing a single sign of human life, they were particularly pleased to spot a cloud of smoke on the horizon one evening. They made their way towards it, and soon came upon a Sami tent which was inhabited by two families who had been fishing on the Norwegian coast, and were now taking their herds of reindeer back to Kautokeino, where they would spend the winter. Here Marmier drank reindeer milk for the first time, and found it to be 'douce, onctueuse, légèrement aromatisée'.[38] Before moving on, the party negotiated the purchase of a reindeer for food. Aslack, the richer of the two men, killed the beast by plunging a knife between its legs in order to prevent any blood being lost. Marmier was horrified at the suffering caused to the animal by this method of slaughter ('une coutume atroce'), which is recounted in both texts.[39]

After five days on the road, Kautokeino came into view. Here they stayed at the priest's house, and although they had only a little hay to sleep on, the fact of sleeping under a proper roof made it seem very luxurious. Marmier was particularly delighted to note that Louis-Philippe had stayed overnight in the very same house in 1795, and went off to interview a 90-year-old woman who remembered the visit. From here, they went on to Galanito, the last habitation of Finnmark, and the following day, they were in Russian territory (Finland had passed from Swedish to Russian control in 1809). It had been raining solidly for several days, and the swampland was becoming

[37] *LN*, 2, 27–30; *VCN*, 1, 352.   [38] *VCN*, 1, 362.   [39] *LN*, 2, 34; *VCN*, 1, 363.

increasingly difficult to negotiate. Their problems were exacerbated by the fact that their initial guide, Mickel, had declined to accompany the party beyond Kautokeino, since he felt that he did not know the region well enough. Now his place was taken by an inexperienced guide, and the party found themselves being led through the thickest areas of shrubland and the most dangerous parts of the swamps; on more than one occasion, horses and men had to be rescued. Their next scheduled stopping place was Karesuando, and Laestadius went ahead of the group to make preparations; at the end of a particularly gruelling day, the party were guided to safety by a fire which Laestadius had lit as a beacon.

At Karesuando, they were able to sleep indoors, accommodated by Laestadius: although it was small and cramped, it seemed the height of luxury, particularly since they were able to eat at table with knives, forks, and plates for the first time in weeks. From Karesuando, Marmier wrote a slightly dispirited letter to Quinet on 6 September, saying that he had 'rien appris et rien acquis dans le cours de mon long voyage', and that he would return 'pauvre d'esprit et d'argent'.[40] He was also, he added, 'très las du campagnonage que j'ai eu pendant une partie de ma route'.[41] The positive side of the journey for him, he adds in vaguely Rousseau-esque terms, was the

> heures de calme et de solitude que je n'oublierai jamais. J'ai vu les ondes de l'océan glacial dans les heures de la tempête, j'ai gravi des rocs déserts, et les montagnes couvertes de neige et toutes les pensées qui m'ont accompagné dans ces pélérinages, toutes les rêveries qui m'ont bercé le soir sur la grève des îles du nord, toutes les charmantes résolutions qui m'ont éveillé le matin, tout cela est pour moi un monde de bons souvenirs que je chercherai à reforger quand je serai dans le monde mauvais.[42]

On 10 September, slightly later than anticipated, they set off on the water, travelling in four narrow craft which could each accommodate two passengers in addition to the two oarsmen and the pilot. They passed through Kättisuvando, Ofwer-Muonio, and Muonioniska, which lay close to the Eyanpaïkka falls (see Plate 4). Here the party were advised to leave their boats in the hands of an experienced helmsman and to follow in safety on dry land. There used to be four helmsmen here, but one had drowned the previous year, and two others had died prematurely, worn out by the arduous nature of their work. This rang as a challenge to the ears of Marmier and Gaimard, who were tempted to make the descent in the boat. Their decision was confirmed when they were told that only a few days previously,

---

[40] BnF, n.a.fr. 20792, Lettres d'Edgar Quinet, fo. 409.
[41] Ibid.   [42] Ibid.

two Englishmen had been tempted to make the descent, but had hastily reversed their decision when they had actually seen the danger of the falls. Marmier and Gaimard made the descent once, and then decided to do it again for good measure. Here, interestingly, Marmier presents himself in the role of 'traveller-as-hero', triumphing over the forces of nature. He also, through the references to the Englishmen, casts himself in the role of defender of French supremacy abroad. In the context of the rivalry between the two powers at that time, particularly in the sphere of colonialisation, the narration of this episode marks a change of emphasis in his writing.

From here, the journey took them down to Haparanda, which they left on 17 September for Umeå, where Marmier was invited to dinner by Grafström, a poet who was also the son-in-law of Franzén. The meeting is recalled in the *Histoire de la littérature scandinave*, where Grafström is classified simply as an 'écrivain de la génération présente': 'J'ai lu, par une mélancolique soirée d'automne, son recueil dans sa retraite septentrionale d'Umeå, et je cède à un agréable souvenir en en citant deux pièces'.[43] The two pieces, rendered in prose, are 'La Harpe' and 'La Vieillesse de la terre'. The following day, the party boarded the steamer *Nordland* to make the crossing from Umeå to Härnösand, Sundsvall, Hudiksvall, Söderhamn, and Gävle, where they travelled overland via Löfsta and Dannemora to Stockholm.

The travellers arrived in Stockholm on the evening of 28 September, and Marmier was again swept up in the social whirl of dinner parties, excursions, and love affairs. On his first night back he dined with Mornay, and met him for lunch again the following day with Gaimard, after visiting Lisinka. After supper, he spent the evening with Lisinka, and returned back to his room at 1 a.m., to spend a 'Kärleksnatt' ('night of passion') with someone referred to only as 'S' (here again reverting to a foreign idiom for sexual matters). He also made contact again with Alete. He dined a number of times with Prince Oscar, and was invited twice by the king. On 10 October, the day prior to Marmier's departure, he and Gaimard were presented with the Order of the Northern Star (Nordstjärna). On this occasion, Marmier had his last conversation with the king, and found him to be profoundly depressed and very tired. Still reflecting on events of his younger days, he expressed bitterness about having been forced into a position whereby he had had to abandon France; although he realised that it had been his own decision in part, and made through human weakness, he insisted that 'Quand le jour de la vengeance viendra [. . .], elle tranchera lourdement sur les coupables'.[44]

---

[43] *HLS*, 528.   [44] BSG, Fn, MS 3899, fo. 110.

Marmier was to retain his interest in things Swedish over the years. In addition to the literary and historical publications mentioned above, Swedish material was to figure prominently in a number of anthologies and collections. The *Chants populaires du Nord* (1842)[45] includes translations of Franzén, Tegnér, Wallgrin, and Anna-Maria Lenngren. In 1854 he published a collection of short stories in translation, *Les Perce-Neige*, which included tales by Almquist ('La Femme du pêcheur'), Emelie Flygare Carlén ('Une simple histoire de village'), and Wetterbergh ('Le Pasteur adjoint').[46] 1864 saw the publication of a further selection of short stories, *Histoires allemandes et scandinaves*, which included a tale by Wetterbergh ('Le Caporal Sigurd').[47] A similar collection, entitled *Sous les sapins*, appeared in 1865. This collection included works by Mellin ('La Fille du charbonnier'), Nepomuk ('Les prêtres auxiliaires'), 'Oncle Adam' ('Le Vieux Rask'), and two Norwegian authors: Mme Thoresen ('Un soir à Bergen' and 'Vorring') and Bjørnstjerne Bjørnson ('Le Père: Scène de la vie norvégienne').[48] In 1868, Marmier published a further collection entitled *Les Hasards de la vie*, which included 'Les adieux. Scène de la vie norvégienne'.[49] Wallin and Runeberg figure in *La Maison* (1876),[50] whilst a number of Swedish tales are included in the *Contes populaires de différents pays* in 1880;[51] a second volume appeared in 1888.[52] *Nouvelles du Nord*, published in 1882, contains a piece by Flygare Carlén;[53] and two short stories by the same author, along with others by Daniel Fallstrom appeared in *A la ville et à la campagne* in 1885.[54] A short novel with

[45] *Chants populaires du Nord* (Paris: Charpentier, 1842).

[46] *Les Perce-Neige, nouvelles du Nord traduites par X. Marmier* (Paris: Garnier, 1854). Uno Willers (*Xavier Marmier och Sverige* (Stockholm: Kungl. Boktryckeriet, 1949), 73) mentions a number of Marmier's translations of Swedish works, but this particular collection appears to have escaped his attention.

[47] *Histoires allemandes et scandinaves par X. Marmier* (Paris: Michel Lévy, 1860).

[48] *Sous les sapins, nouvelles du Nord traduites par X. Marmier* (Paris: Hachette, 1865). Marmier names the author of 'Le Père' as 'Biœrnson', and I am grateful to Marie Wells for bringing the correct spelling (Bjørnson) to my attention. The inclusion of more recent authors provides additional evidence that Marmier kept up to date with developments in Scandinavian literature later in life.

[49] *Les Hasards de la vie, contes et nouvelles* (Paris: Brunet, 1868).

[50] *La Maison* (Paris and Lyon: Lecoffre fils, 1876).

[51] *Contes populaires de différents pays, recueillis et traduits par Xavier Marmier de l'Académie française* (Paris: Hachette, 1880); includes eleven 'Contes scandinaves' (99–240).

[52] *Contes populaires de différents pays, recueillis et traduits par Xavier Marmier de l'Académie française*, 2nd ser. (Paris: Hachette, 1888). Contains 'Sigurd et Singorra, conte suédois' (189–209).

[53] 'La Douleur d'une femme', in *Nouvelles du Nord, traduites du russe, du suédois, du danois, de l'allemand et de l'anglais* (Paris: Hachette, 1882), 127–66.

[54] *A la ville et à la campagne, nouvelles traduites de l'anglais, du danois, du suédois et de l'allemand* (Paris: Hachette, 1885). Contains 'Jalouse après la mort' and 'Le Paradis sur terre' by Flygare Carlén (159–87 and 199–222 respectively); 'Le Destin d'une hirondelle' by Daniel Fallstrom (188–98); also a piece entitled 'La Vie d'un pauvre homme en Suède' (223–81) whose author is not identified.

a number of autobiographical features and set in Sweden, entitled *Deux émigrés en Suède*, was published in 1849.[55] The protagonists and setting of the novel *Les Voyages de Nils à la recherche de l'idéal*[56] are also Swedish.

In addition to bringing Swedish literature to France, Marmier also sparked off a renewed interest in French literature in Sweden. More particularly, he began by publicising the *Revue des Deux Mondes* (where a good number of his articles were published). A private letter to François Buloz, editor of the *Revue des Deux Mondes*, shows that Reuterdahl, the librarian in Lund, took out a subscription to the review, and hoped to buy a complete collection when his next budget became available; Tegnér also promised to take out a subsciption for the library at Växsjö.[57] Marmier hoped to obtain more orders before he left the country. He was also indignant to see Belgian pirate editions in circulation, and suggested that the Parisian book trade should take a joint initiative to send a salesman to the Scandinavian countries in order to put a stop to the 'infâme contrefaçon belge'.[58] Willers concludes that the growing interest in Sweden for French literature must be attributed in large part to Marmier's personal influence.[59]

An intriguing post-scriptum to this chapter lies in the shadowy world of political and diplomatic intrigue. Whilst most of Marmier's contribution to Franco-Swedish relations undoubtedly lies in the domain of literature, Willers tells us that in the mid-1840s, Marmier was able to render a further service to the country in a delicate matter. A number of dispatches sent by Stedingk, the Swedish minister at St Petersburg, before the Russian attack on Finland in 1808 were being prepared for publication in Paris; the publication to which Willers presumably refers is the *Mémoires posthumes [. . .] lettres, dépêches et autres pièces authentiques [. . .]*, which was published in three volumes between 1844 and 1847 by Björnstjerna.[60] The authorities in Stockholm were unhappy about the appearance of this publication because of the potential impact on Sweden's contemporary foreign relations. Gustaf Löwenhjelm, the Swedish minister in Paris, turned for assistance to Marmier, who played a most helpful role in the efforts of the Swedish authorities to suppress at least parts of the text. Marmier was thanked

---

[55] *Deux émigrés en Suède* (Paris: Administration du journal *Le Pays*, 1849).
[56] *Les Voyages de Nils à la recherche de l'idéal* (Paris: Hachette, 1869).
[57] Marie-Louise Pailleron, *François Buloz et ses amis: la vie littéraire sous Louis-Philippe*, new edn. (Paris: Firmin Didot, 1930), 146–7.
[58] Ibid., 147.
[59] Willers, *Xavier Marmier och Sverige*, 96.
[60] Curt-Bogislaus-Louis de Stedingk, *Mémoires posthumes [. . .] lettres, dépêches et autres pièces authentiques [. . .] par le général comte de Björnstjerna*, 3 vols. (Paris: Arthus Bertrand, 1844–7). French at this time was the language of international diplomacy.

personally by the now Oscar I for his help in the affair.[61] Magnus Fredrik Ferdinand Björnstjerna (1779–1847) was Stedingk's son-in-law, which is presumably why he had his papers; he served as Swedish minister in London from 1828 to 1846. Magnus's wife was Elisabeth Charlotta von Stedingk. Willers makes some reference to her being in correspondence with Marmier,[62] but no previous commentators appear to have noticed that she must have been Marmier's lover Lisinka (which itself must have been a pet name). This can be deduced from one of the parts of Marmier's private journal which was not included in Kaye's edition. In *Memorandum 2*, Marmier notes details of his return visit to Copenhagen in 1864. Amongst the people he saw was the Swedish envoy to Copenhagen, 'M. de Björnstjerna, fils de la chère Lisinka'.[63] The Björnstjerna in question here was Oscar Magnus Fredrik (1819–1905), the second son of Magnus and Elisabeth, who was 'minister ad interim' in Copenhagen between 1864 and 1865.

On 11 October 1838, the morning after he and Gaimard received their decoration, Marmier was to board the ship which was to take him to Lübeck on the first leg of his journey back to France. He had become so attached to Stockholm, he noted in his diary, that he almost decided not to leave. He stood on deck to bid farewell to 'la plus belle ville que je connaisse. J'ai des larmes plein le cœur en songeant à tous les jours de paix, d'étude, d'amour que j'y ai passés'.[64] The crossing was an unpleasant one, with a storm lasting five days which left him incapacitated by seasickness for most of the journey. Once in Lübeck, he travelled rapidly through Germany via Hamburg and Hanover to Alsace. He was anxious to reach Bourgfeld in order to rest and spend some time with his family, whom he had not seen since his departure at the beginning of April the previous year.

[61] Willers, *Xavier Marmier och Sverige*, 62–5.
[62] Ibid., 61.
[63] Académie des Sciences, Belles Lettres et Arts de Besançon, *Memorandum 2*, fo. 203. I am grateful to Thomas Munch-Petersen for biographical details about the Björnstjerna family.
[64] BSG, Fn, MS 3899, fo. 110v.

8

Star Status: Rennes and Spitzbergen (1839)

On 18 September 1838, while Marmier was still in Sweden, he was appointed, in his absence, to the newly created chair of Foreign Literature at the University of Rennes.[1] This was one of a number of new posts created in an expansion of provincial universities by an initiative of the Ministre de l'Instruction publique, Salvandy.[2] With remarkable foresight, Salvandy had created a new faculty of 'Lettres' at Bordeaux, Lyon, Montpellier and Rennes, each with chairs in Philosophy, History, Ancient Literature, French Literature, and Foreign Literature. Marmier's friend Quinet was simultaneously appointed to the University of Lyon.[3] Once back with his parents in Bourgfeld, Marmier learned with great satisfaction that Salvandy would allow him to spend the remainder of the year on sabbatical in Paris.[4] On 6 January 1839, he wrote to Gaimard from Paris, where he was staying in Gaimard's old accommodation, 35 rue de l'Odéon. He had itchy feet again, and urged Gaimard to organise a new expedition 'à la rencontre du pôle, ce qui fait déjà tressaillir d'aise mon âme de voyageur'.[5] With this new expedition in mind, and also a plan (unspecified) for another publication on Iceland, he was procrastinating about taking up his new post, which never really seems to have filled him with enthusiasm: 'Je me débats encore contre la volonté de Mr de Salvandy, qui persiste à vouloir m'envoyer là-bas, mais j'espère l'emporter'.[6]

In the meantime, Marmier had been increasing his social contacts. In mid-November, he was received by Louis-Philippe for the first time. Having visited the Scandinavian countries in his youth (1795), the king began the conversation with Marmier in Danish. This first audience lasted about an hour, and Marmier came away delighted and impressed at the clarity of

---

[1] AnF, F17/21256.

[2] Salvandy was Ministre de l'Instruction publique between April 1837 and March 1839, then from February 1845 until February 1848.

[3] Decrees, details, and appointments to be found in AnF, F17/13700 (no folio numbers).

[4] Letter from Marmier to Paul Gaimard, 29 October 1838, AnF, 5JJ188.

[5] Letter from Marmier to Paul Gaimard, 6 January 1839, AnF, 5JJ188.

[6] Ibid.

Louis-Philippe's memories of some forty years before. The following day, he was invited to dine with the royal family where he received a warm reception from the queen, Marie-Amélie, and the princes.[7] His *Chants populaires du Nord* bear a dedication to the duchesse d'Orléans.[8] He was chosen to instruct the princesses Marie and Clémentine in modern literature at the Tuileries,[9] and was to remain on close terms with the royal family for many years, neither forgetting nor being forgotten by them even long after 1848.[10] He visited Marie-Amélie in Claremont in 1850 after his trip to America, and in 1857, on his rounds of the second-hand bookstalls, he found a book belonging to her: suspecting that it had found its way there after the sacking of the royal apartments in 1848, he bought it and sent it back to her. A few days later, it was returned to him in Paris with a handwritten note: 'Conservez-le en souvenir de moi. M. A. Claremont, 17 août 1857'.[11] Marmier now also made his debut in the aristocratic circles of the Faubourg Saint-Germain. This was a very closed and socially elite world; acceptance here represented one of the highest aspirations of the 'nouveaux riches'. Marmier had been given a letter of introduction from St Priest for Mme de Chastenay, 'ma plus ancienne connaissance dans ce monde nobiliaire'.[12] From this moment on, Marmier's social career seems to have been launched:

> Elle m'invita à dîner avec M. le Chancelier, Mme de Boigne. C'est par elle que j'ai été ainsi introduit dans le monde du faubourg Saint-Germain, et elle a souvent eu la bonté de me dire qu'elle s'en applaudissait [. . .] je dois à la bienveillance que l'on me témoignait dans cette maison de Mme de Chastenay, la bienveillance de beaucoup de personnes.[13]

---

[7] F. Bonnaire, 'Bulletin', *RP*, 59 (1838), 217–24 (223–4).

[8] *Chants populaires du Nord* (Paris: Charpentier, 1842); no page number for dedication.

[9] See Arthur-Léon Imbert de Saint-Amand, *Les Femmes des Tuileries: Marie-Amélie et la société française en 1847* (Paris: Dentu, 1894), 49–50. In a letter to Michelet, Marmier also refers to his twice-weekly 'corvée littéraire' with 'Mme la Grande Duchesse de Mecklembourg chez Mme la Duchesse d'Orléans' (Jules Michelet, *Correspondance générale*, ed. Louis Le Guillou, 12 vols. (Paris: Champion, 1994–2001) 3, 276). The obituary in *Le Figaro* (12 October 1892, 2) signed by 'Etincelle' (whose relationship with Marmier is discussed at the end of this chapter) states furthermore that 'Le roi Louis-Philippe le choisit [Marmier] pour donner des leçons de littérature à ses filles, les princesses Marie et Clémentine. Les jeunes princes, leurs frères, furent souvent heureux d'aller écouter cette parole imagée et poétique'.

[10] Alexandre Estignard (*Xavier Marmier, sa vie et ses œuvres* (Paris: Champion, 1893), 57) claims that Marmier's personal correspondence (now lost) contained numerous letters and souvenirs from the royal family, including a bronze statuette and a medallion struck for the baptism of the comte de Paris.

[11] Bibliothèque Xavier Marmier, Pontarlier, item N455: *Tales of woman's trials by Mrs S. C. Hall* (London: Chapman & Hall, 1847). On the death of Marie-Amélie in 1866, Marmier noted in his private papers that she was a 'noble, sainte femme, justement aimée et vénérée' (*Journal*, 1, 351).

[12] *Journal*, 1, 188.

[13] Académie des Sciences, Belles Lettres et Arts de Besançon, *Memorandum 2*, fos. 196–7. In the *Journal* (1, 288), Kaye mistranscribes 'invite' for 'invita'.

In a manner which would have seemed exemplary to many a young Balzacian hero, Marmier was not only accepted, but became an extremely popular guest. Although in his youth he was away from Paris on his travels for long stretches of time, he was always welcomed back—rather to his own amazement:

> Il me semble que je n'y apporte aucune des qualités qui font rechercher un homme dans le monde, ni la naissance, ni la fortune, ni les dons de l'esprit, ni une position influente, ni même une agréable gaieté, et cependant on m'invite tellement dans ce monde riche, aristocratique, distingué, de telle sorte que depuis le 1er avril jusqu'au 25 mai (55 jours) je n'ai pu dîner un seul jour chez moi.[14]

But his new-found celebrity did not keep him from his old friends and his literary preoccupations. He dined regularly at Pinson's with Sainte-Beuve, and also entertained regularly in his 'chambrette'. Guests included Sainte-Beuve, Brizeux, Turquety, Antoine de Latour, and occasionally A. I. Turgenev.[15] Sometimes young women were also invited (Sainte-Beuve, for example, mentions the presence of the novelist comtesse Dash, although he also remarks that given the dimensions of Marmier's room, this could be rather a compromising situation for a young woman!) and the assembled company read poetry, drank punch, and engaged in various forms of literary debate.[16]

Meanwhile, Salvandy was calling and Rennes was waiting. On 16 January, Michelet wrote to the historian Dargaud, informing him that Marmier would be visiting on Thursday, before leaving for Rennes.[17] He in fact left Paris on 22 January, arriving in Rennes on 24 January.[18] He gave his first lecture (the first of a series of twelve) at 9 a.m. on 2 February. In this lecture, the only one of the series to have been published, Marmier argued that in order to appreciate literature, one must be open to the study of the literature of all countries, regardless of national boundaries: 'Chaque nation a eu tour à tour son grand siècle, dont les lueurs rapides se sont projetées de part et d'autre comme autant de rayons de l'aurore boréale qui se cherchent, se croisent, s'entrelacent et courent à la surface du ciel'.[19] The study of literature, furthermore, should not be limited to 'cette littérature

---

[14] *Journal*, 1, 188.
[15] Aleksandr Ivanovich Turgenev (1784–1845), historian and brother of the Decembrist Nicholas Turgenev.
[16] See, for example, Charles Augustin Sainte-Beuve, *Correspondance générale* [...], *recueillie, classée et annotée par Jean Bonnerot*, 19 vols. (Paris: Stock, 1935–83), 3, 24 and 34.
[17] Michelet, *Correspondance générale*, 3, 13, letter 1909bis.
[18] BSG, Fn, MS 3899, fo. 128.
[19] 'Discours prononcé à l'ouverture du cours de littérature étrangère à la Faculté des lettres de Rennes', *Nouvelle Revue de Bretagne*, 1 (1839), 305–21 (308).

savante, élaborée, fleurie, décrite dans les cours d'esthétique, couronnée dans les académies'.[20] An equal interest should be afforded to the study of folklore, 'la littérature populaire', which is perhaps 'plus humble', but also 'plus spontanée et plus vivace'.[21] Citing a number of examples from different countries, he pays particular attention to the serious studies of national folklore which have been undertaken in Germany, and expresses regret that the subject has been neglected in France. His survey of literature, he says, will take his audience on a long journey from the banks of the Rhine to the most northerly shores of the Scandinavian countries, whose literature is virtually unknown in France. Here again, Marmier can be seen to be making the way for the study of comparative literature.

Numerous reports of this first lecture survive, all of which show that it had the kind of success that we might nowadays more readily associate with a pop concert than an inaugural lecture, with Marmier being mobbed by enthusiastic women admirers. No room in the university was large enough to contain the crowds who arrived for the event, and a room had to be found in the town hall.[22] Firmin La Ferrière, who attended the lecture, hurried home immediately afterwards without waiting to congratulate Marmier, in order to write and tell Michelet about it:

> un nombreux et brillant auditoire avait été attiré par le désir d'entendre le voyageur et le littérateur qui peut nous inviter à cette poésie de l'Allemagne si gracieuse et si forte. Le discours de M. Marmier, écrit avec cette variété de style, ce bonheur d'images que vous lui connaissez [. . .], ce discours a mérité tous les suffrages: le succès du professeur a été complet, et tous les esprits sont avides de jouissances littéraires que promet un si beau début. [. . .] L'auditoire de M. Marmier n'était pas composé seulement des hommes studieux de la ville; les dames ont formé une belle couronne autour de la chaire du jeune professeur [. . .].[23]

Even the staid *Moniteur Universel* commented on the presence of the women, albeit in fairly neutral tones. Sainte-Beuve reported rather more salaciously that 'Les dames en ont raffolé, elles ont fait invasion dans la salle, au grand scandale de l'université; Cousin a tonné là-contre dans le Conseil. On a fait à Rennes une complainte sur certaine dame trop assidue [. . .]'.[24] *Le Moniteur Universel* spoke of Marmier's 'rare talent' and reported

---

[20] 'Discours prononcé à l'ouverture du cours de littérature étrangère à la Faculté des lettres de Rennes', 309.   [21] Ibid.

[22] See *Le Moniteur Universel* (1839), 274. The same article appears in the *Journal Général de l'Instruction publique*, 8 (1839), 143–4.

[23] Michelet, *Correspondance générale*, 3, 17–18, letter 1916. Le Guillou definitely transcribes 'inviter' in the first sentence, but the word 'initier' would appear more appropriate.

[24] Sainte-Beuve, *Correspondance générale*, 3, 85.

that 'L'impression de ce discours d'ouverture a été vive et profonde. C'est qu'à un savoir fort étendu, le professeur joint une grâce de diction et une vivacité d'imagination peu communes'.[25]

On 4 February, Marmier wrote to give his own account to Michelet. Although obviously flattered by his success (particularly with the women), he was already beginning to show signs of boredom, both with his post and with Rennes in general, and seemed to be seeking a new challenge:

> J'ai débuté, mon cher ami, samedi dernier, dans ma cathèdre universitaire, et tout s'est passé plus heureusement que je ne le croyais. Le public y a mis de l'empressement et de la bienveillance. C'était tout ce que j'osais espérer. Les belles dames du Parlement et de l'aristocratie ont rompu la barrière des préjugés et sont venues (chose inouïe!) s'asseoir en face de la tribune. Mais je n'avais qu'à lire un discours écrit et cela n'était pas à vrai dire bien effrayant. Samedi je veux essayer d'improviser. C'est là le redoutable passage du Raz, grand Dieu, [. . .].
>
> J'ai été très content de faire ici la connaissance de M. Laferrière et de parler de vous avec lui. [. . .] J'ai vu aussi dans cette ville un ou deux hommes qui m'ont paru intéressants. Du reste la société me paraît bien pauvre et toute la ville bien dénuée de monuments. On en est encore aux bonheurs du cancan. C'est là le grand mobile des femmes et la grande préoccupation des hommes. Depuis quinze jours que je suis ici je n'ai pas encore entendu autant de bonnes et sérieuses paroles que j'en entendrais chez vous dans un quart d'heure. Aussi je prie le ciel de me reconduire prochainement dans ma mansarde parisienne ou sur les bords des mers scandinaves. Le bruit du vent, le mugissement des flots valent mieux que le monotone retour de ces monotones conversations.[26]

Letters were written in similar terms to Sainte-Beuve and Weiss: indeed, much correspondence has survived from this period of Marmier's life; it is hard to say whether this is because he was so bored in Rennes that he spent a great deal of time writing letters, or whether his new-found fame made the recipients feel that his letters were worth keeping.

Evidence suggests that the remaining lectures on the course were equally well received, and that Marmier had no difficulty in rising to his self-imposed challenge of speaking without notes. *Le Moniteur Universel* reported that

> C'est à la seconde leçon que devait avoir lieu l'épreuve décisive. M. Marmier, par une modeste défiance de lui-même, avait lu la première. Restait à apprendre si, en s'abandonnant, il retrouverait par la parole ce bonheur d'expression qui distingue son style. Hâtons-nous de dire qu'il a heureusement triomphé dans cette difficile épreuve. Il a, on peut le dire, conquis son auditoire; conquête heureuse, car elle profite à la fois à l'enseignement et aux disciples.[27]

---

[25] *Le Moniteur Universel* (1839), 274.
[26] Michelet, *Correspondance générale*, 3, 20–1, letter 1919.
[27] *Le Moniteur Universel* (1839), 274.

Amongst the student body at Rennes at precisely this time was Leconte de Lisle, who was following a course in law. It is highly probable that he not only attended Marmier's lectures, but also that Marmier's work may have influenced the composition of a number of his better-known poems.[28]

In a letter to Quinet written on 15 February (presumably the Thursday following his second lecture), Marmier gave his own impressions of his performance and his post:

> Je me presse ici le cerveau de mon mieux pour en faire sortir un chapelet de paroles (notez que je ne dis pas d'idées) qui ressemblent à quelque chose de raisonnable et ma bonne étoile est encore venue cette fois au secours de ma faiblesse. Le public de Rennes, hommes, femmes, étudiants, et magistrats s'est pressé dans la salle où je n'ai pas craint de m'asseoir comme si j'allais lui distribuer la manne céleste. Je crois que je ne lui ai rien distribué qu'une assez plate improvisation, mais l'auditoire était bienveillant. Il a battu des mains et m'a loué. Merci! Je désirais faire cette épreuve de l'improvisation. C'est là à vrai dire la raison la plus déterminante qui m'ait amené ici. À présent, l'épreuve est faite, je la continuerai encore de mon mieux quelque temps et puis je m'en retournerai rejoindre ma mansarde parisienne, après laquelle il m'arrive souvent de soupirer.[29]

From surviving correspondence it appears that the attraction of his 'mansarde parisienne' very soon took precedence. Marmier wrote to Quinet on 22 March, saying that he had been in Paris on leave for the past two days, and hoped very much that the period of leave would be extended. The boredom of life in Rennes seems no longer to have been an issue, but he still felt that he was not cut out for lecturing: 'à vrai dire, j'éprouve peu de joie à monter dans la chaire. De tout ce chapelet de paroles que l'on débite très académiquement pendant une heure, que reste-t-il?'.[30] In addition to this, however, he had come to realise that however popular his lectures proved to be, he would never be a candidate for promotion because of his unconventional education. His appointment to the chair had been 'par un bond de côté'[31] as he put it, rather than by working his way through the system. In contrast to the majority of people in his position, he was largely self-taught, and had never attended university, let alone obtained a doctorate. Quinet wrote and suggested Marmier go to Lyon (where Quinet himself held a chair and had recently received his doctorate) in order to obtain the qualifi-

---

[28] See Alison Fairlie, *Leconte de Lisle's Poems on the Barbarian Races (Poèmes barbares)* (Cambridge: Cambridge University Press, 1947), esp. 25, 44–5, 59–61, 66, 70–6 and 144–5; and Charles-Marie Leconte de Lisle, *Articles, préfaces, discours. Textes recueillis, présentés et annotés par Edgar Pich*, Bibliothèque de la Faculté des Lettres de Lyon, Fascicule 23 (Paris: Société d'Édition 'Les Belles Lettres', 1971), 29–30.

[29] BnF, n.a.fr. 20792, fo. 411.   [30] Ibid., fo. 413.   [31] Ibid.

cations necessary for promotion. In a reply written on 7 May, Marmier thanked his friend, but refused his offer: 'C'est chose inutile. Je n'appartenais qu'à demi à l'université, je ne lui appartiendrai peut-être bientôt plus du tout'.[32] He had in the meantime applied for leave without pay to join the next expedition of the Commission du Nord to the Faroe Islands and Spitzbergen. In the first instance the application had been refused by the 'conseil royal', about which Marmier felt very bitter:

> Cousin et Villemain qui depuis dix ans ne font plus de cours et touchent 30000[fr] de traitement ont trouvé que de vouloir s'en aller dans le nord poursuivre des études commencées il y a longtemps n'était pas un motif valable pour me faire obtenir quelques mois de liberté *sans traitement*, car c'est là ce que je demandais.[33]

If the minister (i.e. Villemain) upholds the decision of the council, he adds, he will resign. A further letter addressed to Quinet by Marmier on the eve of his departure from Paris for Le Havre on 8 June confirms that his request for leave 'sans appointements' has been refused, 'quoiqu'il [i.e. le ministre] me promette de me rendre ma place à mon retour, je n'y compte pas. Il la veut pour quelqu'un des siens'.[34] Obviously, Marmier saw Villemain as the chief obstacle to retaining his post. Interestingly, however, it would seem that his friend Michelet may have played a part. Although there is no evidence to suggest that he was involved in the initial decision to refuse Marmier his leave, a draft letter from Michelet to Villemain, written in September 1839 (thus after Marmier's departure on board *La Recherche*), makes the case for *not* keeping Marmier's post open for him:

> Vous avez, je crois, promis à Marmier de lui laisser sa chaire de Rennes, jusqu'à ce qu'il soit revenu de ce rude voyage du Nord commencé depuis 2 ans sous les auspices de l'Académie, sous les vôtres. Il a été suppléé cette année par Le Huérou. Le Huérou a réussi. Il a commencé son cours de littérature galloise et bretonne par un résumé indisp[ensable] de l'hist[oire] d'Angl[eterre]. Si la suppléance de M[armier] lui était ôtée, il serait perdu à Rennes, obligé de quitter la Bretagne qui est son païs et de vous demander une chaire [. . .] dans une autre province, par exemple celle de Dijon.
>
> Cette même chaire de Dijon vous est demandée par le jeune et savant Weiss, reçu docteur ces jours-ci d'une manière très honorable.
>
> Le Huérou professe depuis onze ans. [. . .] Weiss et Huérou sont docteurs. Si l'on veut conserver quelque valeur à ces titres univ[ersitaires] il faut qu'ils influent sur le placement. Les concurrens qu'on leur oppose [. . .] ne sont pas docteurs [. . .].[35]

---

[32] Ibid., fo. 399.   [33] Ibid. (Marmier's emphasis).   [34] Ibid., fo. 415.

[35] Michelet, *Correspondance générale*, 3, 90, letter 2015.

Villemain, however, obviously decided not to act upon Michelet's suggestion, for a letter from Le Huérou to Michelet dated March 1840 refers to the retirement of Esch, who had been given the post, and also to Villemain's reluctance to appoint him. As Villemain was now to be succeeded by Cousin as Ministre de l'Instruction publique, Le Huérou asks Michelet if he would intercede with the new minister on his behalf. He claims that having to teach six classes a week is ruining his health as well as interfering with his own research. He does add, however, that 'je ne me serais pas permis de demander cette chaire si Mr Esch avait pu s'y maintenir, ou si Mr Marmier n'y avait pas absolument renoncé'.[36] Marmier seems to have held no grudge against Michelet (possibly not knowing of the latter's actions), but from this point on, he seems to have borne an implacable grudge against Villemain. In the published official report on the expeditions, he took the unusual step of making public his discontent:

> En l'année 1839, nous fûmes appelés par le ministre de la marine à faire une nouvelle expédition dans les parages du Nord. [. . .]
>
> Lorsque cette décision fut prise, j'occupais, à la faculté des lettres de Rennes, la chaire de littérature étrangère, créée par M. de Salvandy. Je regrettais de quitter une noble ville que j'avais en peu de temps appris à aimer [. . .]. J'espérais, en montrant l'ordre du ministre de la marine, qui voulait bien, pour la troisème fois, m'adjoindre aux travaux de la commission de Nord, être en droit d'obtenir de l'université un congé de quelques mois, et pouvoir, au retour de notre expédition, reprendre des fonctions qui m'étaient devenues chères [. . .]. M. Villemain me refusa ce congé; et le démon des voyages l'emportant dans mon esprit sur toutes les considérations d'avantages matériels, j'abdiquai l'honorable position que M. de Salvandy m'avait donnée pour m'élancer encore vers l'espace lointain.[37]

In the private papers forming Marmier's journal and memoirs in his later years, this event is not specifically referred to; but he repeatedly evokes Villemain's supposed meanness of spirit ('jamais il n'a eu le moindre plaisir de faire quelque bien, jamais il n'a cédé qu'à regret aux plus justes demandes').[38] Surprisingly, however, in view of this evident bad feeling, Marmier's employment record with the Ministère de l'Instruction publique et des Beaux-Arts, which was used to calculate his pension, shows that his period of employment as professor of foreign literature at the university was two

---

[36] Michelet, *Correspondance générale*, 3, 190–1, letter 2135.
[37] *VCN*, 2, 293–4.
[38] See *Journal*, 1, 318–19. Earlier, Villemain is described as 'très laid, difforme, bossu et sale [. . .]. Un affreux singe, et un méchant singe, taquin, fantasque, bizarre, bourru, vaniteux, quinteux, haineux' (*Journal*, 1, 318).

years, three months and twenty-three days as from 18 September 1838 (thus showing that he was credited with the full period of employment).[39]

The members of the Commission du Nord assembled at Le Havre in the second week in June. *La Recherche* was again to be captained by Fabvre, who had befriended Marmier on the expedition the previous year. The commission this time was composed of Gaimard, as leader; Durocher, a mining engineer; Delaroche, a hydrographer; Martins, the naturalist; Anglès; and the artists Lauvergne and Giraud (who were to replace Mayer and Bévalet). Bravais (the scientist from the previous expedition who was later to become a famous crystallographer) and the painter Biard were to join the vessel at Hammerfest. On 14 June, *La Recherche* set sail,[40] but they had not got very far when the wind turned against them, and they had great difficulty getting out of the English Channel. On 17 June, Marmier wrote to Michelet saying that they were anchored a mile off the English coast because of the adverse weather conditions. The previous day they had passed Hastings,

> une petite ville allongée sur les grèves au pied d'une colline couverte de bois çà et là. C'est au bout de cette colline que se livra dit-on la fameuse bataille que vous connaissez mieux que moi. C'est dans ce lieu aussi que Napoléon avait projeté de descendre en Angleterre. Sur toute la côte, on aperçoit encore une distance d'une demi-lieue ou une lieue des tours d'observation bâties par les Anglais pour repousser l'invasion préméditée.[41]

Marmier's principal interest on this expedition, he claims, is less the voyage to Spitzbergen than the planned visit to the Faroe Islands, 'dont je lis maintenant les chants populaires avec un vif intérêt'.[42] As it turned out, he had plenty of spare time on the outward journey for his reading; on their fifth day out of port, they had still not got beyond Dover. The adverse wind was followed by periods of calm and spells of rain, both of which prevented their progress. Finally, on 25 June, there was a change of wind, and a brisk southerly took them swiftly towards their destination. On the night of 28 June, through a grey mist, the snow-capped peaks and barren rocks of the islands loomed into view. They searched for any sign of a church tower or any other sign of a town, but none was discernible. Towards morning they fired a cannon to call a pilot; but there was no indication of the sound having reached anyone other than a flock of seagulls. An hour later, they

---

[39] AnF, F17/21256.
[40] See *VCN*, 2, 294 and *LN*, 2, 72. Le Guillou mistakenly claims that they had set sail on 8 June (Michelet, *Correspondance générale*, 3, 61). This error is surprising in view of the fact that it is given as a footnote to a letter from Marmier to Michelet written on 17 June in which Marmier says that they have 'fait peu de chemin depuis trois jours' (Michelet, *Correspondance générale*, 3, 62).
[41] Michelet, *Correspondance générale*, 3, 62, letter 1967.
[42] Ibid.

repeated the signal, and eventually spotted a small craft flying a red hand-kerchief on the end of a stick heading towards them. Marmier's initial impression of the pilot was of an open and honest face, but also of terrible poverty suggested by his sackcloth jacket and trousers which had been clum-sily darned and patched up so many times with such a variety of different scraps of material that it was hard to discern the form of the original gar-ment. His hat was made from a piece of sackcloth folded over on top, and his shoes were made from pieces of sheepskin wrapped around the foot and tied up with a strap. Rather overawed by *La Recherche*, the pilot climbed on board and guided the vessel to a bay facing Thorshavn (see Plate 5).

The things which struck Marmier most during his contacts with the local population were their hospitality, their honesty, their physical beauty, and their terrible poverty. On the whole, his comments about them are sym-pathetic and positive, although he condemns the treatment of animals there. Sheep are offered no shelter from the elements, and in winter are left to fend for themselves and frequently starve; it is not uncommon, he says, to see a sheep eating its own wool in desperation. Worst of all, sheep shearing is accomplished 'd'une manière barbare':[43] rather than cutting the wool, the farmer pulls it out in fistfuls, sometimes with such violence that the unfortunate beast is left with bleeding wounds. The traditional manner of catching dolphins is described as a 'carnage horrible': 'les pêcheurs frap-pent, égorgent, massacrent; le sang ruisselle à flots, la mer devient toute rouge [. . .]'.[44]

Marmier describes the superstitions of the islands, their legends and mythology; he also gives detailed information about the history of the islands, local institutions, customs, and a rundown of the economic situa-tion. On this subject, he is unusually outspoken. He condemns the com-mercial monopoly ('cette hideuse loi de monopole'[45]) to which the islands are subjected by the Danes, and compares it to a form of serfdom. 'Jamais nulle part', he asserts, 'une loi de monopole n'a été dictée avec aussi peu de ménagement et exécutée avec autant de rigueur'.[46] The Danish government, he explains, abuses its power by imposing a surcharge of 33 per cent on Danish goods, and a reduction on the sale price of Faroese goods of 50 per cent, thus leaving the Faroese with a deficit of 83 per cent on all transac-tions. He cites individuals who have been sentenced to heavy fines for minor infringements of the trade law, such as the case of a young woman who traded wool in exchange for a pair of earrings from a French fisherman.

---

[43] *LN*, 2, 83.   [44] Ibid., 2, 85.   [45] Ibid., 2, 93.   [46] Ibid., 2, 92.

The monopoly has further consequences: the first Danish ships arrive at Thorshavn in May and make their last voyage of the year in September, thus leaving the islanders completely cut off from the rest of the world for the remainder of the year. A request for permission to receive post and news-papers via the Shetland Islands was refused by the Danish government. It appears to be a Danish government policy, he writes, to keep the Faroese deliberately in a state of abject poverty and unending dependence. He astutely concludes his letter on the Faroes with a condemnation which is at once tactful and yet forceful:

> Ces pauvres gens, en me parlant de leurs souffrances, m'ont souvent répété que le roi les ignore, qu'il est juste, bon et compatissant; que s'il savait jusqu'où va leur détresse, il viendrait à leur secours. Mais ceux qui le savent et qui le lui taisent assument sur leur tête une triste responsabilité.[47]

From the Faroe Islands, a brisk wind took them northwards to Hammerfest, where they met up with Bravais, who had spent the winter at the Bossekop observatory, Vahl the Danish botanist, and Biard the painter, who was to join the expedition to Spitzbergen accompanied by his partner, Léonie d'Aunet.[48] The couple had travelled overland to join the expedition at Hammerfest; they had been given special dispensation for d'Aunet to accompany Biard, since women were normally not allowed on board any vessel of the French navy.[49] On 17 July, *La Recherche* set sail, and a southerly wind carried them rapidly northwards to Bear Island (Bjørnøya), which they reached on 21 July (see Plate 6). From here they sailed on alter-nately through wind, rain, fog, and snow. From time to time a whale would lift its enormous head above the waves to blow a waterspout which dispersed as a cloud of dust. As they drew further north, they became aware of a deepening silence as even the birds that had been following the ship turned back.

[47] Ibid., 2, 94.

[48] The couple were to marry in July 1840 and had two children; she left Biard around April 1844 dur-ing her second pregnancy. In 1845, Biard had her followed by the vice squad (adultery at that time being illegal for married women) and she was caught in the act of adultery with Victor Hugo and sent to prison, thus creating a public scandal. See Jean Savant, *La Vie sentimentale de Victor Hugo*, 6 vols. (Paris: chez l'auteur, 1982–5), vols. 2 and 3; Hubert Juin, *Victor Hugo*, 3 vols. (Paris: Flammarion, 1980–6); Louis Guimbaud, *Victor Hugo et Madame Biard* (Paris: Blaizot, 1927); and Wendy Mercer, 'Léonie d'Aunet (1820–1879) in the Shade of Victor Hugo: Talent Hidden by Sex', *Studi Francesi*, 109 (1993), 31–46.

[49] D'Aunet wrote her own account of the expedition: Léonie d'Aunet, *Voyage d'une femme au Spitzberg* (Paris: Hachette, 1854). See also my edition of this work: Léonie d'Aunet, *Voyage d'une femme au Spitzberg*, ed. Wendy S. Mercer (Paris: Le Félin, 1992) and Wendy Mercer, 'Gender and *Genre* in Nineteenth-Century Travel Writing: Léonie d'Aunet and Xavier Marmier', in Steve Clark (ed.), *Travel Writing and Empire: Postcolonial Theory in Transit* (London and New York: Zed, 1999), 146–63.

The weather on 28 July was miserable: a heavy sleet fell steadily and the temperature reached a maximum of 1°. But it was nonetheless a day of national celebration in France (the day on which Louis-Philippe reviewed the troops to mark the anniversary of the July Revolution), and the members of the commission were determined to celebrate in style. The officer in charge of the mess had kept a supply of fresh fruit in the hold especially for a banquet to mark the occasion. A number of toasts were drunk to France and to absent friends.

Finally, on 31 July, they were nearing their destination, but the approach to Magdalena Bay was hampered by a blizzard and a number of icebergs which had gathered there. It was the first time Marmier had seen icebergs:

> Les uns ressemblaient par leur lourde masse à des quartiers de roc; d'autres avaient pris dans le frottement continu des vagues les formes les plus bizarres. Ceux-ci étaient arrondis comme un œuf, ceux-là taillés comme une pyramide. Il y en avait qui étaient creusés à leur base comme une voûte, d'autres qui, sur leur surface plane, portaient des arcs-boutants ou de longues tiges tordues pareilles à des rameaux d'arbres. Tous étaient d'une couleur bleue limpide qui se reflétait dans les vagues, et dont les nuances délicates variaient sans cesse avec l'ombre d'un nuage ou la clarté du jour.[50]

At around 4 p.m. they were finally able to anchor. All around, as far as the eye could see, lay the jagged mountaintops which gave Spitzbergen its name. Wide streams of snow and glaciers ran down the flanks of the mountains like bands of silver; the sea, dark and menacing, was silent but for the whistling of the wind and the cry of the gulls (see Plate 7).

On the following day, all the members of the commission fell to their various tasks, setting up observation points and scientific experiments, seeking specimens and sites to sketch. Marmier, for once, had no official duties: but he was more than happy to contemplate the panorama, whose ever-changing colours and forms provided a fascinating spectacle. Occasionally a seal would clamber out of the water onto a sheet of ice and gaze around in astonishment at all the activity; from time to time a white dolphin would leap clear of the water, scattering clouds of spray as it plunged back beneath the waves. Some of Marmier's descriptions of these scenes are quite outstanding:

> Le fond de la baie, les plateaux de neige, les cimes des montagnes, tout était inondé d'une vapeur ténébreuse, sans lumière et sans reflet. A travers cette ombre épaisse on ne distinguait que des masses confuses, des chaînes de rocs interrompus, des cimes brisées, une terre sans soleil, une nature en désordre,

---

[50] *LN*, 2, 104.

une image du chaos. Si dans ce moment le vent venait à ébranler les parois des montagnes de glace, on entendait l'avalanche tomber avec un fracas semblable à celui du tonnerre, et ce bruit sinistre au milieu de l'obscurité, cette chute d'une masse pesante dont les éclats scintillaient dans l'ombre comme des étincelles de feu, tout portait dans l'âme une impression de terreur indéfinissable. Mais, lorsque le soleil venait à reparaître, c'était une magnifique chose que de voir sortir de la brume toutes les montagnes avec leurs pics élancés, et les plateaux de neige sans ombre et sans tache, et les glaciers qui, en reflétant les rayons de lumière, prenaient tour à tour des teintes d'un bleu transparent comme le saphir, d'un vert pur comme l'émeraude, et brillaient de tous côtés comme les facettes d'un diamant. Vers le soir les nuages remontaient à la surface du ciel; une ombre mélancolique s'étendait au loin. Une brise du nord ridait la surface de la mer [. . .]. Le soleil disparaissait peu à peu dans les plis ondoyans de la brume, et ne projetait plus à l'horizon qu'une lueur jaunâtre et vacillante, pareille à celle d'un cierge qui s'éteint dans la nuit. Alors l'eider cessait de se plaindre, la mouette de crier, et rien n'interrompait plus ce sombre repos du soir que le souffle de la brise courant par raffales entre les cimes des montagnes, et le retentissement des glaces flottantes que la vague ou le vent chassait l'une contre l'autre.[51]

The peninsula where the members of the commission had set up their equipment was on the site of a makeshift cemetery where previous explorers or fishermen trapped by the ice had been laid to rest by their companions. Each grave was marked by a single wooden cross bearing a date and a name. Marmier was moved to discover one such cross bearing the name of a Dutchman whose story he had read. Even sadder than this, however, in Marmier's eyes, was the north-eastern tip of Spitzbergen where there was no trace of life whatsoever—not even a grave to be found. The spot was even bereft of the meagre plants which had been found at Magdalena Bay; not a single bird was spotted. As his colleagues went about their research, Marmier sat on a rock and gazed out to sea:

Je ne voyais plus devant moi que l'immense espace des flots, coupé par les trois îles de Cloven Cliff, Fuglesang et Norway. L'Océan était sombre et immobile, le ciel chargé çà et là de quelques nuages lourds, et de tous côtés couvert d'un voile brumeux: seulement, sur un des points de l'horizon, on distinguait une lueur blanchâtre qui se déroulait sous les nuages comme un ruban d'argent: c'était le reflet des glaces éternelles. J'étais seul alors au milieu de la solitude immense; nul bruit ne frappait mon oreille, nulle voix ne venait m'interrompre dans mon rêve. Les rumeurs de la cité, les passions du monde, étaient bien loin. Mon pied foulait une des extrémités de la terre, et devant moi il n'y avait plus que les flots de l'Océan et les glaces du pôle. Non, je ne saurais exprimer toute la tristesse, toute la solennité de l'isolement dans un tel lieu.[52]

[51] Ibid., 2, 106–7.   [52] Ibid., 2, 117.

Thus ends the final letter of Marmier's *Lettres sur le Nord*. It is intriguing to see that in his official report of the same voyage, he adds to this description of Hakluyt an account of an attempt by the members of the commission to row to the great ice barrier. This account is written in a rather different register from the previous impressions (which are recorded, incidentally in both the *Lettres* and the official report of the expedition[53]):

> Nous aurions voulu quitter la dernière grève sur laquelle était amarrée notre embarcation, tenter au-delà des limites extrêmes du globe une aventureuse exploration, naviguer jusqu'au bord de cet éternel rempart qui entoure le pôle, et essayer d'y pénétrer. Mais des brumes épaisses voilaient à tout instant la surface du ciel [. . .]. La prudence du pilote expérimenté arrêtait l'élan de nos rames: 'Vous n'irez pas même, nous disait-il, jusqu'à cette barrière que vous désirez voir de plus près; et vous courez risque d'être, dans le trajet, surpris par une brume ténébreuse qui vous empêcherait de reconnaître la direction que vous devez suivre, et de vous trouver là enserrés, écrasés par les glaces flottantes'.[54]

Here Marmier sounds more like the typical nineteenth-century 'explorer as hero/celebrity' than he does in the bulk of his writing. The venture is glorified by the use of terms such as 'limites extrêmes', 'éternel rempart', etc. The narrative conforms to the tradition according to which nature is identified with the feminine, and is portrayed as something to be 'conquered', whilst the act itself is recounted in terms of active male domination ('exploration', 'vigueur', 'pénétrer', 'élan', etc.). The warnings of the pilot are referred to in terms reminiscent of an over-protective mother or nanny. This contrasts quite strikingly with the earlier predominance of terms suggesting the splendour of the spot and the emotions evoked, which include 'une terreur indéfinissable';[55] 'profond saisissement', 'mélange de terreur et d'admiration';[56] the final sentence in the *Lettres*, moreover, includes the phrase: 'J'ai courbé le front sous le sentiment de mon impuissance'[57]—rather different from the 'élan' and 'pénétration' of the official account. A possible explanation for this may be that in writing the official report, Marmier is attempting to conform to the more traditional form of travel writing in that era, according to which natural phenomena are seen as objects to be 'conquered' and exploration is associated with strength and virility. In this context it may be that Marmier did not consider it appropriate to present either himself, or more probably his colleagues on the expedition, as being in any way 'impuissants'.

---

[53] *LN*, 2, 117; *VCN*, 2, 349–50.   [54] *VCN*, 2, 351.   [55] *LN*, 2, 107.   [56] Ibid., 2, 104.
[57] Ibid., 2, 117.

By 13 August, winter was already setting in at Spitzbergen, and at four o'clock in the morning the anchor was lifted, and *La Recherche* set sail; by ten o'clock they had left the bay and were out at sea. The historic achievements of the expedition were recognised by the Arctic explorer Nordenskiøld, who was responsible for the naming of 'Recherche Bay' and the 'Pointe Xavier Marmier' as they still appear on maps today.

On the morning of 22 August, they entered the harbour at Hammerfest. Here Marmier was delighted to be greeted by his old friend Ole Olsen and his wife, whom he had met the previous year, and who had invited him to their tent. Olsen was anxious to know what had happened to the reindeer he had sold them the previous year: Marmier assured him that they were well (in fact, this must have been a white lie, since we know from Fabvre's unpublished and rather sad missive to Gaimard that they had all perished on the voyage to France[58]). The following day Marmier invited the couple on board *La Recherche*; at first they were reluctant to accept, since Olsen was frightened that he or his wife might be taken back to France, 'ce triste pays [. . .] où l'on ne trouve point de troupeau de rennes'.[59] Olsen was finally persuaded, and a good glass of eau-de-vie soon restored his good humour. If it is slightly patronising to derive humour from his position of 'superiority' in relation to Olsen, this is mitigated by the reciprocity and evident mutual respect of the encounter. Marmier does not cast himself as the distant outsider, travelling only to observe (and to judge, from his own ethnocentric point of view) the peoples of the regions. He enters into relationships and gives the individuals a certain stature by giving their names and recording their life stories, their opinions, their hopes, and their anxieties.

A few days later, *La Recherche* set sail for France, whilst Marmier, Gaimard, the Biards, Durocher, Bravais, Martins, Anglès, Lauvergne, and Giraud set off overland at the beginning of September across Lapland by the same route that Marmier had taken the previous year. At Haparanda, Gaimard, Lauvergne, and Giraud headed off towards central Finland, whilst Marmier travelled on towards Stockholm. From here, he made his way back to France via Copenhagen, Kiel, Hamburg, Lübeck, Schwerin, and Ludwigslust.

An important biographical question mark hangs over this last voyage to Spitzbergen. According to L. Guimbaud, Marmier boasted to Victor du Bled that he had been the lover of Léonie d'Aunet (the then partner of the painter Biard) during the expedition.[60] In Maxime Du Camp's papers,

---

[58] Letter from Fabvre to Gaimard, 26 September 1838, AnF, 5JJ188.
[59] *VCN*, 2, 353.
[60] Guimbaud, *Victor Hugo et Madame Biard*, 29.

moreover, which are conserved at the Institut de France, there is a copy of an obituary for Marmier, published in *Le Figaro* and signed 'Etincelle'. Alongside the obituary is a note handwritten by Du Camp, which reads as follows: 'Etincelle est la fille de Marmier et de Mme Biard (Léonie d'Aulnet [*sic*]), veuve d'un M. Pérony [*sic*], elle a épousé le baron Double. X. Marmier m'a dit qu'il ne savait pas si elle était sa fille ou celle de Victor Hugo'.[61]

The reference to Hugo here is totally misleading, as there is no evidence whatsoever to suggest that there was any hint of an affair between these two prior to 1843 at the earliest. Although it is impossible to be completely certain about such matters in retrospect and with only documentary evidence to go on, it would seem unlikely that Marmier was either d'Aunet's lover during the expedition, or the father of her daughter, particularly in the light of the faulty evidence presented by scholars to lend credence to the idea. During the time spent on board *La Recherche*, d'Aunet was accompanied by Biard, who by all evidence was an extremely jealous lover: he had her followed by the vice squad in 1845 and charged with adultery, even though the couple were at that time legally separated. It would seem that opportunities for sexual encounters between d'Aunet and anyone but Biard would have been extremely hard to organise. It is true that Marmier and the Biard/d'Aunet couple also crossed Lapland as far as Haparanda; but we know from various pieces of correspondence that Marmier travelled and shared accommodation with Gaimard; indeed, a number of notes from Biard to Gaimard which have been conserved show that Biard seemed to be very well-disposed towards Marmier—which, given his jealous nature, would presumably not have been the case had he suspected any infidelity.[62] After reaching Stockholm, the Biards left for Ystad and Greifswald, whereas Marmier went on to Copenhagen.[63] What is absolutely certain is that a

---

[61] Institut de France, Papiers Maxime Du Camp, 3748, 30, fo. 47. (Du Camp writes 'Pérony' for 'Peyronny'.) The article appeared in *Le Figaro* on 12 October 1892. The same suggestion about Marmier's putative paternity is made implicitly by Guimbaud (*Victor Hugo et Madame Biard*, 203–4).

[62] AnF, 5JJ189; see, for example, fos. 148–9, 150–1, 152–3.

[63] They probably did not even travel to Stockholm together, because Marmier, bored with the second trip through Lapland, says that 'Dès que nous fûmes à Haparanda, je me mis en route pour Stockholm' (*VCN*, 2, 354), whereas d'Aunet claims to have spent two days resting from the rigours of the journey before setting off (d'Aunet, *Voyage* (1854), 310). A number of notes addressed to Gaimard by Biard on 3, 10, and 12 September send compliments from him and his wife to Marmier (thus demonstrating conclusively that they were not travelling together at this stage); a further note from Marmier to Gaimard dated 16 October shows that even after Marmier and Gaimard parted company, Marmier was not travelling with the couple (AnF, 5JJ189, fos. 148–9, 150–1, 152–3, and 206 respectively).

number of scholars have been so eager to find 'evidence' of the affair that they have misinterpreted and misquoted Marmier's words to support the hypothesis. Guimbaud, for example, claims that after *La Recherche* arrived back at Hammerfest on 24 [*sic*] (for 22) August:

> Il y eut alors dislocation de la petite troupe. Marmier partit le premier. Il s'en alla rejoindre ses chers Lapons, non sans avoir adressé à la corvette un 'adieu' pathétique: 'Ah!' s'écriait-il,
>
>> Ah! je quitte avec toi notre pays de France,
>> Je te livre mon sort, mes regrets, mon amour!
>
> Biard et sa femme prirent congé de la mission officielle le 28 [. . .]. Le tête-à-tête conjugal recommença pour eux. Jusqu'à leur retour à Paris, il ne semble pas qu'il ait été troublé.[64]

Marmier's poem 'Adieu à la Recherche', dated 'Hammerfest, 24 août 1839', was obviously written shortly before leaving the ship to set off across Lapland with the other members of the team—who included Biard and d'Aunet. Marmier is not at this stage taking leave of her, nor is she implied by 'mon amour': the lines cited by Guimbaud are not only placed in a misleading context, but are also misquoted (presumably also in order to mislead), in that the tenses are completely altered. Marmier's original lines read:

> Je quittais avec toi notre pays de France,
> Je te livrais mon sort, mes regrets, mon amour,
> Les vœux de l'amitié nous suivaient dans l'absence [. . .].[65]

Eldon Kaye also wrongly reads references to d'Aunet into Marmier's poetry, presumably basing his supposition on Du Camp's faulty chronology. He claims that 'au retour du voyage, elle [Léonie] succombera au charme de Hugo', and claims that the following lines refer to d'Aunet, the 'autre amour' being Hugo:[66]

> Celle qui d'un seul mot m'avait rendu si fier,
> Celle dont j'adorais le nom et l'image,
> Déjà d'un autre amour a recherché l'hommage.[67]

---

[64] Guimbaud, *Victor Hugo et Madame Biard*, 34–5.
[65] *Poésies d'un voyageur* (Paris: Félix Locquin, 1844), 81–2. Nils M. Knutsen and Per Posti claim (without references, but presumably following Guimbaud, who is cited earlier) that Marmier wrote love poems for d'Aunet (*La Recherche: En ekspedisjon mot nord: Une expédition vers le Nord* (Tromsø: Angelica, 2002), 177, 183).
[66] *Journal*, 1, 29.
[67] 'Départ', in *Poésies d'un voyageur*, 83–4; the reference is not given by Kaye.

Kaye's reasoning is faulty on a number of counts: first of all, there is no question of the affair between Hugo and d'Aunet having started on their return to Paris.[68] Moreover, the poem is dated September 1839. At that time, Marmier and the Biards were certainly not in Paris, but setting off on their trek across Lapland. Guimbaud also uses these lines to support the hypothesis of the affair, although he claims that the 'autre amour' 'ne peut être que Biard'.[69] Even if d'Aunet had been the woman in question, it would seem highly unlikely that Marmier would refer to Biard as 'un autre amour', or used the word 'recherché', both of which would imply a new lover, rather than the man with whom d'Aunet lived and who was recognised as her husband.

Shortly after their return to Paris, d'Aunet did indeed discover that she was pregnant, and she and Biard were married in July 1840 (suggesting that he thought himself to be the father). Marie-Henriette Biard, as she was called, was born on 14 October 1840. This date suggests, at any rate, that the child was not conceived during the expedition, but probably around 14 January. This would not in fact rule Marmier out completely as the father, since the evidence suggests that he arrived back in Paris around 10 January after a prolonged stay in Copenhagen.[70] Whether or not the attraction on both sides was so strong that hasty assignations were made as soon as he returned to Paris must remain a matter for pure speculation.

---

[68] The different theories about the date when the relationship with Hugo began are summarised in Wendy Mercer, 'Léonie d'Aunet (1820–1879) in the Shade of Victor Hugo: Talent Hidden by Sex', *Studi Francesi*, 109 (1993), 31–46 (39).
[69] Guimbaud, *Victor Hugo et Madame Biard*, 36.
[70] See Sainte-Beuve, *Correspondance générale*, 3, 220; letter 1023, dated 15 January 1840, states that 'Marmier est revenu depuis cinq jours'.

9

Into Hostile Territory: Holland and Russia (1840–2)

Holland

Only a few months after his return from Spitzbergen, the attraction of the 'mansarde parisienne' seems to have dimmed, and Marmier was restless again. On 7 April 1840 he wrote to Edgar Quinet to say that he was planning to visit his father and then go on to Switzerland to get some fresh air. 'Après cela', he wrote, 's'il y avait un ministre qui prit réellement intérêt à moi, il m'enverrait bien loin d'ici je ne sais où et peu importe où pourvu que je revoie des lacs et des montagnes'.[1] Perhaps rather ironically in view of the latter part of this statement, his next journey would in fact take him to Holland on a mission for Charles de Rémusat, who at that time was Ministre de l'Intérieur.[2] The resulting volume of *Lettres sur la Hollande* is dedicated to Rémusat, 'l'homme d'état distingué qui a bien voulu me prêter son appui dans le cours de ce nouveau voyage'.[3] According to Sainte-Beuve, the mandate from Rémusat was in fact a pretext to allow Marmier to complete his studies on the northern countries, and also to write a book on Dutch literature which he forecast would be 'neuf et joli'.[4]

As Sainte-Beuve's remark suggests, Dutch culture was not widely known or appreciated in France at this time. Although it is perhaps not entirely accurate to describe Holland as 'hostile territory', there had been some tension between the two countries in the years immediately preceding Marmier's visit. The July Revolution in France in 1830 had also led to

---

[1] BnF, n.a.fr. 20792, fo. 417.

[2] Charles-François Marie de Rémusat, comte (1797–1875), politician and statesman. At this time he was Ministre de l'Intérieur, having been appointed by Thiers.

[3] *LH*, p. xv. The letters in this volume appeared in the *Revue des Deux Mondes* between 1840 and 1841, beginning with 'Une Visite au roi Guillaume', 4th ser., 24 (1840), 685–703. Interestingly, an article by Marmier had been published in this review as early as 1836 on 'Poésie populaire de la Hollande' (4th ser., 6, 488–503), demonstrating a prior interest in the country. Some thirty years later, Marmier noted in his diary that Rémusat was an 'esprit dogmatique, nuageux et prétentieux' (*Journal*, 2, 141).

[4] Charles Augustin Sainte-Beuve, *Correspondance générale* [. . .], *recueillie, classée et annotée par Jean Bonnerot*, 19 vols. (Paris: Stock, 1935–83), 3, 297.

insurrection in Belgium; this was a largely national movement, and the Belgians wanted independence from Holland. In September 1830, Willem I[5] sent Dutch troops into Brussels, but they were beaten back into Antwerp and Maastricht. On 3 February 1831 the Belgian National Congress elected the duc de Nemours, the second son of Louis-Philippe, as their king. The Great Powers, however, insisted that Belgium maintain its neutrality, and eventually the Congress revised its decision and elected Leopold of Saxe-Coburg-Gotha. Leopold worked out a settlement with the Great Powers, but the King of Holland refused to accept it and sent his troops back into Belgium. Louis-Philippe then responded by sending French troops into Brussels. At this point, the Russians and the Prussians threatened to invade in order to expel the French, who withdrew in September 1831. A provisional agreement was drawn up between the Great Powers and the Belgians in November 1831; but the Dutch king still refused to accept it, or indeed to leave Antwerp. Finally, the French and British joined forces to expel the Dutch and an armistice was concluded in 1833, but it was not until April 1839 that a treaty was signed by all the Great Powers giving independence to Belgium. It was against this background, therefore, that Marmier's visit took place.

He set off via Bourgfeld (the family home) as planned, but here he was taken ill with severe haemorrhaging which left him in a state of collapse and forced him to delay his departure by a few weeks.[6] His eventual route took him into Holland via the Rhine. He visited Nijmegen, Loevestijn, Gorcum, Dordrecht, Rotterdam, Delft, The Hague, Leiden, Haarlem, Zaandam, Alkmaar, Den Helder, Leeuwarden, Groningen, Utrecht, and Amsterdam.

The aim of his visit, he wrote in the preface to *Lettres sur la Hollande*, was to

> rechercher les analogies existant entre la langue, la littérature de ce pays et celle [*sic*] des contrées septentrionales. Je voulais voir quelle influence les habitudes industrielles et commerciales, le sol et le climat avaient exercé sur la race néerlandaise; jusqu'à quel point l'élément germanique s'était maintenu dans ses traditions poétiques [. . .].[7]

A further objective, in publishing the results of his observations, was to correct a number of mistaken but widely held views about the country and its people. A significant number of foreigners, he claims, visit the country every

---

[5] Willem I (b. 1772, The Hague; d. 1843, Berlin), King of Holland and Grand Duke of Luxemburg 1815–40.

[6] Jules Michelet, *Correspondance générale*, ed. Louis Le Guillou, 12 vols. (Paris: Champion, 1994–2001), 3, 276–7.

[7] *LH*, pp. vii–viii.

year and publish their travelogues. But the majority of these, he says, are '[des] voyageurs conduits dans ce pays par une curiosité de touriste',[8] who come with preconceived ideas which they then confirm by paying fleeting visits to The Hague and Amsterdam. 'Je ne connais pas un pays plus durement, plus injustement traité dans les descriptions de voyage que la Hollande',[9] he writes. He will not attempt to cover subjects in which he has no expertise (such as art or commerce), but

> J'ai dit ce que j'avais vu et observé pendant mon séjour en Hollande; ce que j'avais appris dans mes livres de prédilection ou dans la société des gens instruits qui ont daigné m'éclairer de leurs conseils. J'ai tâché de raconter sans emphase et sans prétention aucune ce qui m'avait frappé dans les habitudes et le caractère des Hollandais, intéressé dans leur littérature, ému dans leurs expéditions lointaines, et si ce livre n'a pas d'autre mérite, il a du moins, j'ose le croire, celui d'une entière sincérité.[10]

On his arrival in Holland, he admits, he was disappointed by the monotonous plain which surrounded him and stretched as far as the eye could see. Indeed, the word 'monotone' appears several times in the physical descriptions of the first letter. Yet the overall impression created is not one of monotony, but rather one of mists, silence, and calm. During his entire stay in Holland, he recalls, he rarely saw the sun at all; there are numerous references to a 'ciel chargé de brume'[11] or to the 'brouillard hollandais'.[12] The water of the canals is always decribed in terms of stillness (for example 'son onde pacifique' or 'cette onde paisible'[13]); even the mighty Rhine 's'écoule en silence et s'en va mourir tristement dans les sables de Katwijk'.[14] Everywhere, he says, 'vous ne trouvez qu'un grand silence [. . .]. Il y a du silence jusque dans l'activité et le mouvement'.[15] All motion is described in terms suggesting calm: the verb 'glisser' is used on a number of occasions to depict the boats on the canals;[16] and the cargo boats 'suivent mollement les sinuosités du canal'.[17] Even a disarmed frigate is pulled 'paisiblement' along the canal by twenty-four horses.[18] The windmills, so evocative of the Dutch countryside, 'tournent péniblement leurs longs bras au souffle léger qui les fait mouvoir'.[19] This general impression of calm applies also to the people: the fisherman returns home to his hut 'à pas lents';[20] even in the town, 'vous ne voyez point de curieux dans les rues,

---

[8] Ibid., 10.   [9] Ibid., 4.   [10] Ibid., pp. xiv–xv.   [11] e.g. Ibid., 7.   [12] Ibid., 64.   [13] Ibid., 62.
[14] Ibid., 21.   [15] Ibid., 8.   [16] e.g. Ibid., 7, 86.   [17] Ibid., 8.   [18] Ibid., 87.   [19] Ibid., 7.
[20] Ibid.

point de gens affairés qui courent çà et là et se heurtent sur les trottoirs, point de fenêtres qui s'ouvrent à l'arrivée de la diligence'.[21]

But if the overall impression received by Marmier on his summer visit was one of sleepy calm, he does not remain insensitive to the 'lutte incessante entre l'homme et la nature',[22] due to the geographical situation of the country: 'Il faut avoir parcouru cette terre marécageuse, menacée de tous côtés par les ondes fougueuses qui la dominent pour voir jusqu'où peut aller la hardiesse, la persévérance de l'homme aux prises avec les éléments les plus difficiles à subjuguer'.[23] He is full of praise for the 'labeur le plus opiniâtre et [. . .] l'industrie la plus éclairée'[24] which he sees all around him. It is because of this constant struggle with nature, which can be so unpredictable, he argues, that the Dutch have learned to be cautious. And caution is the cause of two national characteristics which have earned the country an unfavourable reputation with its foreign visitors: the general reserve and lack of hospitality on the one hand; and on the other, the apparent avariciousness of the general population.

Whilst acknowledging that the Dutch are not by temperament a sociable people, Marmier explains that the caution they have learned from an early age makes it difficult for them to trust new acquaintances. Indeed, in his letters he mentions a number of abortive attempts he has made to engage various individuals in conversation—most notably the taciturn captain of a *trekschuit* (canal boat) on his way from Alkmaar to Den Helder. Once, however, they have got to know a person and decided to admit them to their circle, he says, they become loyal and trustworthy friends. Similarly, he claims that there is truth in the statement that the Dutch are very careful with their money; children are given lessons in investment from an early age (the way in which this is recounted sounds remarkably similar to Grandet giving his daughter gold coins for her birthday every year in Balzac's novel). The reason for this, he argues, is that Holland is a country with very little in the way of natural resources; everything has to be imported, and the country has a large national debt. The only reason for the general wellbeing of the population is the national interest in finance and speculation. Furthermore, he adds, the obsession with money is quickly forgotten where charity is concerned, or at times of natural disaster. He cites the numerous

---

[21] *LH*, 9. Many of these terms are echoed in both the verse and prose poems versions of Baudelaire's *L'Invitation au voyage*. Holland became a fashionable subject in French literary and artistic circles in the 1840s.
[22] *LH*, 11.
[23] Ibid., pp. xi–xii.   [24] Ibid., 17.

orphanages and poorhouses, free schools and charitable organisations which are funded by private donation.

In Holland, according to Marmier, country folk, like town dwellers, are 'remarquables par leur esprit d'ordre [et] de travail'.[25] Levels of education and literacy are high, and he finds that a widespread interest in the Bible leads to much theological debate. On Sundays, he recalls, it is common to hear groups of people analysing the sermon they have just heard in church and picking out the flaws in the priest's arguments. This critical spirit, he says, leads to a great diversity of religious opinions and sects, but he notes that the general level of tolerance is high.

Just as the attitude to social life differs greatly between Holland and Germany, according to Marmier, so does the attitude to music. Whereas music had seemed to be important at all social levels in Germany, the Dutch remain generally uninterested in it; German workers love to sing, but not the Dutch. They do, on the other hand, enjoy their beer and gin.

The typical dwelling is described overwhelmingly in terms of order and cleanliness:

> Tout, dans cette demeure, est rangé avec soin, et entretenu avec une minutieuse propreté; les fenêtres sont lavées chaque semaine, les meubles essuyés et frottés chaque jour. Pour plus de propreté, on ne fait pas la cuisine dans le corps de logis habité par la famille, mais dans un petit bâtiment à part.[26]

He nonetheless emphasises (with a certain degree of light-hearted irony) the fallacy of certain preconceived ideas which exist on this matter in France and which have been spread through unreliable travel narratives:

> Il y a des gens qui croient encore sincèrement que le pavé de Broek est frotté chaque matin comme un parquet de la Chaussée-d'Antin, qu'il est défendu d'éternuer, et à plus forte raison de cracher dans les rues, que les poules et les chats sont bannis de cet Eldorado de la propreté, et qu'en arrivant là on est tenu d'ôter ses bottes.[27]

In the province of Drenthe, which he judges to be 'la plus triste, la plus aride de toutes les provinces de la Hollande',[28] he notes the poverty of the local population, even in Assen, its capital. Here the typical dwellings are described as 'pauvres cabanes' in which 'l'on ne distingue même plus aucune trace de la propreté hollandaise'.[29] In Noord-Holland, he is struck by the contrast between rich and poor, something which always concerns him on his travels; the prosperity of Haarlem and the 'luxe des grands seigneurs',[30] for example, is only a short distance from Zandvoort and its 'frêles cabanes

---

[25] Ibid., 45. [26] Ibid., 49. [27] Ibid., 5. [28] Ibid., 30–1. [29] Ibid., 31. [30] Ibid., 54.

en planches'.[31] He was, however, astonished to see the transformation of this population on Sundays. Those whom he had seen on working days dressed in miserable rags, soaked from head to foot and surrounded by their hungry, ragged children, now donned their traditional long blue jacket with bright silver buttons, a thick woollen waistcoat and a smart broad-rimmed hat. They seemed to be a different people, proud and independent.

He was also fascinated by the apparent temporary suspension of social rank on Wednesdays at The Hague when the king, Willem I, opened the doors of his residence to receive any subject who wished an audience. Marmier decided to join the queue one week, and was astonished to note that the order in which they were heard depended solely on who had arrived first: 'L'ouvrier avec sa veste de grosse laine et ses pieds poudreux passait avec l'élégant gentilhomme dont on entendait encore piaffer les chevaux dans la rue; l'élève passait avant le maître, et le soldat avant l'officier'.[32] He watched as each subject was received individually by the king, who listened to the request or grievance and then dismissed the individual with a courteous nod of the head. As he waited, Marmier reflected on the significant incidents of the reign of Willem I, and decided that his physical countenance and mannerisms all seemed in keeping with the type of character suggested by his deeds. Apart from his white hair, it appeared that not even old age had been able to temper the formidable man's appearance:

> Sa figure calme et régulière, ses lèvres légèrement serrées, offrent tout à la fois un type de force et de prudence; ses yeux vifs, brillant sous deux épais sourcils, annoncent la pénétration, et [. . .] toute sa physionomie semblait être [. . .] la vivante expression de cette devise de son royaume, qui fut surtout celle de son règne: *Je maintiendrai*.[33]

The following day, Marmier left The Hague for Amsterdam and two days later, to his astonishment, the *Handelsblad* newspaper reported the king's abdication. Marmier was therefore among the last to have attended one of these 'open' audiences. A large part of his second letter from Holland is devoted to a discussion of the possible reasons for the abdication. Marmier concentrates mainly on the recent amendments to the constitution and the reasons for these, which involves a potted history of the country dating back to Napoleonic times (which he characterises as an era of 'servitude profonde'.[34] In an even-handed manner, he summarises Willem I's major achievements, under which heading he includes the construction of roads and canals, most notably the North Holland canal; his support for industrialisation; and his reform of Dutch colonisation. His personal qual-

---

[31] *LH*, 53.   [32] Ibid., 105.   [33] Ibid., 107 (Marmier's emphasis).   [34] Ibid., 110.

ities, Marmier says, are representative of the Dutch people in general: patience, attention to detail, business acumen, and perseverance. The latter, however, according to Marmier, also brought about serious error: 'sa persévérance a été trop loin'.[35] By the time of his abdication, Marmier states, Willem had become unpopular on a number of counts: his obstinacy in wishing to reconquer Belgium; his plan to marry Henrietta d'Oultremont; and his attitude to the country's substantial debt.

A few biographical details are given of his son and successor, Willem II.[36] Although the Dutch are not very forthcoming with their views, Marmier finds public opinion to be in favour of the new king, who is seen as intelligent and dynamic. In contrast to his father, he is perceived as having a feeling for the arts, and also pleases by his affability, his polished manners, and the prestige associated with his military career.

One of the aspects of the constitutional charter of 1840 which Marmier felt to be particularly significant was article 225, which guaranteed the freedom of the press. He offers a survey of the country's newspapers and concludes that since the Belgian war, the Dutch have developed a new interest in political and current affairs. This could, he indicates in his conclusion to the chapter, have future repercussions: 'Que la monarchie s'engage dans une fausse voie, commette quelque grande faute, et à la longue il pourrait bien arriver que le peuple hollandais devînt un jour assez remuant, voire même assez difficile à gouverner'.[37]

The aspect of the country which appears to impress Marmier most, however, is the exploitation of its colonies. For one so critical of Danish rule in the Faroes and Iceland, or even of Napoleonic rule in Holland, this is perhaps rather surprising. He even suggests that the French learn from the Dutch example, and this in a hitherto (for him) unprecedented form of rhetoric:

> Ne pourrait-on se souvenir de cet exemple quand on discute la question d'Alger? Ici, je le sais, les conditions ne sont pas les mêmes. Le sol d'Afrique ne vaut pas celui d'Inde, et l'Arabe est plus difficile à dompter que le Javanais. [. . .] Nous ne luttons dans l'Algérie que depuis dix ans, et déjà nous y avons fait plus de progrès que la Hollande n'en avait fait dans le même espace de temps à Java. Qui sait jusqu'où la constance, secondant notre courage, pourrait nous conduire, quelle œuvre de conquête et de civilisation l'avenir nous réserve sur le sol barbare de l'Afrique?[38]

[35] Ibid., 126.
[36] Willem II (b. 1792 The Hague, d. 1849 Tilburg), King of Holland and Grand Duke of Luxemburg 1840–9.
[37] *LH*, 134.   [38] Ibid., 312–13.

This is the first occurrence of such polemic in Marmier's writing, although it recurs in a number of later works. The use of the word 'barbare' here as transferred epithet applied to the Algerian people is highly pejorative, and the use of the word 'dompter' at once denies respect and dehumanises (thus lending justification to the enterprise). The juxtaposition of 'civilisation' and 'progrès' to 'barbare' presents the French venture in the usual language of the coloniser, while the use of terms such as 'luttons', 'courage', and 'constance' glorify the participants. It is hard to judge the reason(s) for this departure from Marmier's normal respect for alterity. It may have to do with a Eurocentric bias (although that concept is perhaps even more complex in nineteenth-century terms than it is today); it may also be connected with the fact that in 1841, the year the letters were published, his brother Hyacinthe, now a 'sous-lieutenant' in the 3rd Regiment of Hussars, was sent to Algeria.

Less surprisingly, Marmier is also full of respect and admiration for the scholarship of the country, in particular for the University of Leiden and its classical traditions: he maintains that its excellence in these subjects is unparalleled, and that its students are better trained to speak Latin than in any other institution. He expresses mixed feelings, nonetheless, about the use of Latin as the only official language of scholarship. He witnessed an oral examination where a student was defending a thesis about an ancient Dutch poem. The unfortunate candidate, he says, was handicapped by his inability to translate neatly and spontaneously into Latin a number of phrases in old Dutch.

Two letters out of seven in the published volume are devoted to a survey of Dutch literature, which is divided quite simply into categories of 'ancienne littérature' and 'littérature moderne'. The former, according to Marmier, 'se compose d'imitations ou de traductions',[39] and is interesting only 'sous le rapport philosophique'.[40] He mentions the stories of Arthur and Charlemagne, the epic poetry, the 'contes facétieux de France' and the 'mélancoliques légendes d'Allemagne'.[41] Much to his disappointment, he finds a lack of popular folklore. This he attributes to the fact that mythology normally develops as a primitive explanation for natural phenomena, and cites examples from Sweden, Germany, Scotland, and elsewhere. But in Holland, he argues, there are none of those rocks, forests, caves or mountains which have given rise in other countries to 'cette mystérieuse terreur d'où naissent le conte fantastique et la légende populaire'.[42] In fact, the Dutch have worked so hard to fashion their own environment in order to make it habitable that it holds no more secrets from them: 'ce travail

[39] *LH*, 139.   [40] Ibid., 144.   [41] Ibid., 139.   [42] Ibid., 141.

matériel, continu, ne lui permet guère de rêver'.[43] He further maintains that the emergence of a strong middle class quite early on in Holland also inhibited the development of the genre, since these people were very practical and down-to-earth, with little time for such fantasy.

He mentions the work of Maerlant and Stoke, but the only items which really fire him with enthusiasm from this period are the poem of *Karel ende Elegast* (*Elegast et Charlemagne*) and *Van den vos Reinaerde* (*Roman du Renard*), of which he quotes an edition by Willems.[44] He analyses both of these in some detail, and translates a number of extracts. The latter, he says, is significantly different from versions in other countries, and he outlines the different arguments pertaining to its origin, although without pronouncing in favour of any particular theory. What he does note in the Dutch version is that 'Le récit est beaucoup plus dramatique, plus serré, que celui de nos anciens poètes, beaucoup moins licencieux, et l'ouvrage entier est empreint, comme l'a dit Jacob Grimm, d'une couleur toute flamande'.[45] The second part, he argues, is surely derived from the French version; but the first part forms a separate entity, 'une épopée complète, une comédie excellente écrite avec verve, avec une profonde connaissance des vices du temps et des subtilités du cœur humain'.[46]

The chapter on modern literature traces in some detail the history of the 'Rederijkerskamers' ('Chambres de rhétorique') and also mentions the emergence of 'Dichtgenootschappen' ('Sociétés de linguistique'),[47] but maintains that far from fulfilling their original literary goals, they were not even in a position to defend the purity of the language from external influences. The French influence, according to Marmier, brought nothing positive, whilst the enthusiasm for classical studies largely inhibited the development of Dutch language and literature—although it did produce some excellent classical scholars. Coornhert is mentioned as one author who did use his classical knowledge to develop a national form of literature: his works are described as 'l'expression fidèle des idées de dévouement et de fidélité qui l'occupèrent toute sa vie'.[48]

It is only in the seventeenth century, however, that Marmier sees Dutch literature as really coming into its own. After Hooft, he mentions Vondel

---

[43] Ibid., 142.
[44] Details of this 1836 edition of *Van den vos Reinaerde* are given by Marmier in a note at *LH*, 152.
[45] *LH*, 153.   [46] Ibid., 163.
[47] Not 'Sprachgesellshaften' as Marmier claims (*LH*, 192); here he seems to have confused the German and Dutch terms. I would like to record my thanks here to Diana Tyson for all her help with Dutch language and literature in this chapter.
[48] *LH*, 196.

who, according to Marmier, 'avait plus de génie poétique que Hooft et plus de goût'.[49] Several pages are devoted to his work, with particular attention to *Lucifer*. Whilst the Dutch are not fully justified in comparing this work to *Paradise Lost*, he argues, it is nonetheless 'une grande et belle œuvre qui suffirait à elle seule pour sauver la littérature hollandaise de l'injureux oubli auquel nous l'avons si longtemps condamnée'.[50] He further notes the admiration on the part of the Dutch for Cats. Whilst respecting the 'sentiment d'honnêteté, de vertu' which he finds in 'ces compositions didactiques et sérieuses', he is certain that in France, even the most intrepid reader would be put off by 'un tel déluge de vers'.[51] But what Hooft, Vondel, and Cats had in common, in Marmier's view, was the distinctive national character of their work, which he found to be largely lacking in the eighteenth century, which is characterised rather tautologically as one of 'froides et fausses contrefaçons'.[52] In this category he includes the works of Hoogvliet, Lucretia van Merken, Nomsz, and Juliana de Lannoy. Langendijk was the poet of this era who, in Marmier's eyes, had most 'verve' and 'esprit'—although even he shows 'peu d'invention' and also falls into 'des détails de mœurs par trop grossiers'.[53]

A presentation of the works of the van Haren brothers is followed by a grudging reference to Poot, the merit of whose work is greatly overestimated in Holland: Bellamy, according to Marmier, 'a plus de sentiment et d'animation'.[54] Van Alphen, whose work cannot be counted 'parmi les œuvres d'art',[55] is dismissed in a paragraph; Feith, 'l'un des poètes les plus mélancoliques que la Hollande ait jamais eus',[56] is treated rather more favourably.

The contemporary era is described as 'plus hardie et plus vivace'.[57] Bilderdijk is mentioned, although Marmier seems more impressed by his biography than by his publications; he admits nonetheless that he is 'le premier guide d'une foule de jeunes esprits studieux et entreprenants, il est le chef d'une nouvelle littérature'.[58] Van Lennep is described as one of the most productive and popular contemporary writers. The national flavour of his novels is his major achievement in Marmier's eyes, and although he cannot be compared in terms of literary stature with Walter Scott, 'il n'en a pas moins le mérite d'avoir frayé, dans la littérature de son pays, une nouvelle route et ravivé habilement des noms glorieux, des faits poétiques, des usages touchants'.[59] The poems of Bogaers are described as 'châtiés et corrects',[60] whilst Tollens, 'le poète le plus populaire de la Hollande',[61] is mentioned with reference to *Wien Neêrlands Bloed*, a well-known patriotic song, of which

[49] *LH*, 200.   [50] Ibid., 203.   [51] Ibid., 215.   [52] Ibid., 217.   [53] Ibid., 218.
[54] Ibid., 220.   [55] Ibid., 222.   [56] Ibid.   [57] Ibid., 224.   [58] Ibid., 227.   [59] Ibid., 229.
[60] Ibid., 230.   [61] Ibid.

Marmier translates five stanzas. The survey concludes with references to da Costa, 'écrivain austère et religieux',[62] Beets 'qui joint dans ses vers la mélancolie de la pensée allemande à la pûreté du style classique',[63] and Withuys.

Overall, however, Marmier does not rate Dutch literature very highly. He regrets the lack of sparkle, the 'capricieux élans, la fougue ardente et désordonnée'[64] which he occasionally finds in English, French or German literature. In Holland, he says, everything is taken very seriously, and even 'les œuvres de l'imagination sont dominées par la raison'.[65] The resultant literature may be worthy, he argues, but finishes by becoming somewhat monotonous. The letter finishes nonetheless on a positive note: 'Quoi qu'il en soit de ces lacunes, la littérature hollandaise, par cela même qu'elle n'a pas suivi le mouvement impétueux des autres, est importante à signaler, comme l'expression fidèle et constante de l'un des peuples les plus estimables qui existent'.[66]

From Sainte-Beuve's correspondence, it would appear that Marmier was back in Paris in October 1840.[67] He was appointed as librarian at the Ministère de l'Instruction publique in Paris on 11 January 1841.[68] There was an established tradition of offering these library posts to writers as a form of sinecure: certainly, in Marmier's case, it made minimum demands on his time, and left him with a relative degree of freedom to write and prepare works for publication.[69] Over the course of the next year, it is hard to find much evidence of his movements, other than a number of dinner parties to which he was invited by Michelet.[70] His friendship with Sainte-Beuve at this point appears to have waned somewhat, although there is no evidence of any quarrel between the two men. Bonnerot, the editor of Sainte-Beuve's correspondence, suggests that the relationship may simply have cooled because Marmier was so rarely in Paris.[71]

---

[62] Ibid., 231.   [63] Ibid.   [64] Ibid., 234.   [65] Ibid., 233.   [66] Ibid., 234–5.
[67] Sainte-Beuve, *Correspondance générale*, 3, 371.
[68] AnF, F17/21256.
[69] See John Lough, *Writer and Public in France* (Oxford: Clarendon Press, 1978), e.g. 306, 310–12.
[70] See Michelet, *Correspondance générale*, 3, 365, 399, 447, 506, 550, 553, 558.
[71] Sainte-Beuve, *Correspondance générale*, 4, 313.

Finland and Russia

Early in 1842 Marmier left Paris again, this time heading for Russia, Finland, and Poland.[72] His impressions were recorded in a series of outspoken and highly controversial articles in the *Revue des Deux Mondes* which were then published in book form under the title *Lettres sur la Russie, la Finlande et la Pologne*.[73] His travels here brought him into contact with many leading Russian writers and intellectuals, and aroused in him a passion for Russian literature which would later result in his ground-breaking publication of works by a number of authors virtually unknown in France at that time.

Marmier's initial motivation for this journey was to complete his exploration of the Scandinavian countries by visiting Finland, which at that time was under Russian rule.[74] He travelled first to Stockholm, where, early in May 1842, he boarded the *Murtaia*, a cargo boat bound for Finland. It was not a particularly comfortable mode of transport, since most of the vessel was loaded with livestock and provisions, and the passengers had to pile into the fore end of the deck amongst the carts, trunks, and bundles of goods. Towards evening, they arrived at the Aland Islands and cast anchor off Degerby while they waited for customs officials to inspect the vessel before giving authorisation to disembark. While a load of wood was being added to the ship's already considerable cargo, Marmier went ashore and struck up acquaintance with a family of local peasants who invited him into their home; while the wife offered him a cup of milk, the husband told him about his daily life, 'de ses jois [*sic*] et de ses travaux [. . .] c'était le tableau sans art d'une de ces existences paisibles, obscures, ignorées, qui s'écoulent dans la grande vie de l'humanité comme une goutte d'eau dans les vagues de l'Océan'.[75]

---

[72] Sainte-Beuve, *Correspondance générale*, 4, 209. This letter, dated 7 February 1842, says simply that 'Marmier est parti'. In vol. 3, p. 299, Bonnerot states that Marmier had left towards the end of 1841; several factors, however, suggest that he waited until the new year, not least the preface to his *Chants populaires du Nord* (Paris: Charpentier, 1842) which is dated 'Paris, 31 décembre 1841'.

[73] Marmier's letters from this new journey were published individually in the *Revue des Deux Mondes* between December 1842 and April 1843. See 'De la poésie finlandaise', 4th ser., 32 (1842), 68–96; 'La Russie: première partie: La Finlande—Pétersbourg—La Société russe', 4th ser., 32 (1842), 701–55; 'La Russie II: Moscou', new ser., 1 (1843), 95–123; 'La Russie III: Le Couvent de Troïtza: Le Clergé russe', new ser., 1 (1843), 619–44; 'La Russie en 1842 IV: Varsovie et la Pologne sous le régime russe: La Littérature polonaise', new ser., 1 (1843), 50–84. They appeared in book form under the title *Lettres sur la Russie, la Finlande et la Pologne*, 2 vols. (Paris: Delloye, 1843) (cited hereafter as *LR*).

[74] From the fourteenth century, Finland had been under Swedish rule, but was conquered in 1809 by Alexander I. Independence was only granted after the Russian Revolution.

[75] *LR*, 1, 18.

At daybreak they cast off again and a good following wind took them towards the mainland. Here the vessel was visited by both the customs officials and the police, whom Marmier was rather surprised to find were extremely polite. In Abo he soon found a hotel which was pleasant and clean, but packed with travelling salesmen from Holland, Belgium, Germany, and England, whose company he found uncongenial, and whom he did his utmost to avoid.

Abo, he explains, was the former capital of Finland, but power was transferred to Helsinki by the Russians, who were unhappy about a centre of power and learning situated too close to Sweden. Before leaving for Helsinki, Marmier was invited to visit the local prison, where the governor had made elaborate ceremonial preparations in honour of his visit. The prisoners were all lined up for inspection, and the women had cleaned and decorated their workshop with pine branches (the women, although apparently not the men, had to work). Of all the prisons and hospices ('ces douloureux refuges du vice et de la misère'[76]) he had ever visited, in any country, he found this the most distressing. He cut the visit short halfway through, 'car je ne me sentais pas le courage de contempler plus longtemps une telle infortune avec l'impuissance d'y apporter quelque adoucissement'.[77]

From Abo he travelled on to Helsinki in a comfortable carriage with two horses which he had borrowed from a new friend he had made since arriving in Finland. The journey seemed remarkably short given the distances involved, 'grâce à l'honnêteté, à la douceur des habitants'.[78] For Marmier, whereas Abo symbolised the country's distant past, Helsinki represented its recent history. Traces of Russian influence were in evidence everywhere. Even the shop signs were painted in the Russian manner: the names were Swedish, but the tradesman's title was written in Russian. During his stay in Helsinki, he had an audience with the tsar's heir apparent, the future Alexander II, accompanied by Prince Menshikov, governor of Finland.[79] On 3 June he boarded a small vessel named the *Helsinki*, which was bound for Vyborg, via Borgo, Louisa, and Frederikskamm. The journey was pleasant but slow, and the accommodation fairly basic. The only pieces of furniture

[76] Ibid., 1, 28.   [77] Ibid., 1, 30.   [78] Ibid., 1, 43.

[79] Michel Cadot, *La Russie dans la vie intellectuelle française (1839–1856)* (Paris: Fayard, 1967), 103–4. Cadot refers to Alexander as the heir apparent to the grand duke, but I am grateful to Robin Aizlewood for pointing out to me that this was a title given to the brothers of the tsar (Alexander was therefore heir apparent to the tsar). I am also indebted to Robin Aizlewood for his help with this chapter (particularly in respect of names and place names). Alexander II (1818–81) was tsar of Russia from 1855. Prince Alexander Sergeievich Menshikov (1787–1867) was later to be commander of Russian forces during the first half of the Crimean War.

on board were four wooden benches and a camp stool which were all occupied come nightfall. Marmier fortunately spotted the rowing boat suspended from the aft end of the vessel. It had taken in a small amount of sea water, but he threw his coat inside and settled down to sleep in his makeshift hammock.

At 4 p.m. the following day, they arrived at Vyborg, which at that time lay inside the Finnish border. Marmier was fascinated by the way in which the different languages were used here in different circumstances: Swedish was the language for legal and administrative matters; Russian was used by the military; and Finnish was spoken by the ordinary working people and the servants. As ever, Marmier chatted to everyone, 'le fonctionnaire et le marchand, l'officier et le bourgeois';[80] but more space is devoted in the text to his contacts with the ordinary working people. Here, he judges, they are generally better off than their counterparts elsewhere in Finland; the poor here, for example, are seldom reduced to eating the bread made from the bark of birch trees as they so frequently are inland. Many, he says, live from hunting and fishing, whilst others work as merchant sailors. On Finnish ships they earn the modest salary of between twelve and fifteen francs a month. The more ambitious are snapped up by English shipping companies, since the region produces good sailors; here they can earn sixty to seventy francs a month. Many are farmers who have the status of *torpars*, which Marmier describes as a kind of voluntary serfdom governed by a legal document. The *torpar* is allowed to cultivate land on his own behalf, but must work a certain number of days every week for his landlord. It may be a voluntary arrangement, Marmier states, but is nonetheless 'pénible', since the *torpar* must be prepared to abandon his own work, even at critical moments, if his master needs him. The typical Finn, he decides, is hardworking, patient, and resigned: 'et je l'observe avec un profond sentiment d'intérêt et de sympathie'.[81]

Marmier's record of this journey includes two letters addressed to Villemain (Ministre de l'Instruction publique), one on the University of Helsinki (history, scholarship, library, statutes, etc.) and another on Finnish literature. This includes sections on the Finnish language and versification, mythology, legends and folklore, folk song, and *Kalevala*, the national epic of Finland, of which he translates a page, 'une des plus belles et plus ravissantes pages qui existent dans la poésie ancienne et moderne'.[82] The *Kanteletar*, he says, contains verses written for all possible occasions, from engagement and marriage to mealtimes and work, for fishing and hunting,

---

[80] *LR*, 1, 231.   [81] Ibid., 1, 226.   [82] Ibid., 1, 142–3.

PLATE 1

Fishermen's dwellings in Reykjavík, probably 1836. Lithograph by Villeneuve from drawing by Mayer. Vol I, plate 6 from *Voyage en Islande et au Groënland, publié par ordre du roi sous la direction de M. Paul Gaimard. Atlas historique*, 2 vols (Paris: Arthus Bertrand [1842?]). By courtesy of the British Library.

PLATE II

Málfríður Sveinsdottír (Friða), 1836. Lithograph by Bayot from drawing by Mayer. Vol I, plate 10 from *Voyage en Islande et au Groënland, publié par ordre du roi sous la direction de M. Paul Gaimard. Atlas historique*, 2 vols (Paris: Arthus Bertrand [1842?]). By courtesy of the British Library.

PLATE III

Skraaven, Lofoten Islands, probably 1838. Lithograph by Guiaud from drawing by Mayer. Vol I, plate 101 from *Voyages en Scandinavie, en Laponie, au Spitzberg et aux Feröe, pendant les années 1838, 1839 et 1840, publiés par ordre du gouvernement sous la direction de M. Paul Gaimard. Atlas pittoresque, lithographié d'après les dessins de MM. Mayer, Lauvergne et Giraud*, 2 vols (Paris: Arthus Bertrand [1852?]). By courtesy of the British Library.

PLATE IV

Eyanpaïka (Äijänpaïkka) falls, probably 1839. Lithograph by Sabatier from drawing by Lauvergne. Vol II, 167 from *Voyages en Scandinavie, en Laponie, au Spitzberg et aux Feröe, pendant les années 1838, 1839 et 1840, publiés par ordre du gouvernement sous la direction de M. Paul Gaimard. Atlas pittoresque, lithographié d'après les dessins de MM. Mayer, Lauvergne et Giraud*, 2 vols (Paris: Arthus Bertrand [1852?]). By courtesy of the British Library.

PLATE V

View of Thorshavn (Faroe Islands), showing the departure of *La Recherche*, probably 1839. Lithograph and drawing by Lauvergne. Vol 1, 35 from *Voyages en Scandinavie, en Laponie, au Spitzberg et aux Feröe, pendant les années 1838, 1839 et 1840, publiés par ordre du gouvernement sous la direction de M. Paul Gaimard. Atlas pittoresque, lithographié d'après les dessins de MM. Mayer, Lauvergne et Giraud*, 2 vols (Paris: Arthus Bertrand [1852?]). By courtesy of the British Library.

PLATE VI

The corvette *La Recherche* near to Bear Island (Bjornoya), 1838. Lithograph and drawing by Mayer. Vol I, 141 from *Voyages en Scandinavie, en Laponie, au Spitzberg et aux Feröe, pendant les années 1838, 1839 et 1840, publiés par ordre du gouvernement sous la direction de M. Paul Gaimard. Atlas pittoresque, lithographié d'après les dessins de MM. Mayer, Lauvergne et Giraud,* 2 vols (Paris: Arthus Bertrand [1852?]). By courtesy of the British Library.

PLATE VII

La Recherche anchored at Bell Sound (Bellsund), Spitzbergen, with pinnacles of the glacier in the background, probably 1838. Lithograph by Sabatier (vessel by Mayer) from drawing by Mayer. Vol I, 134 from Voyages en Scandinavie, en Laponie, au Spitzberg et aux Feröe, pendant les années 1838, 1839 et 1840, publiés par ordre du gouvernement sous la direction de M. Paul Gaimard. Atlas pittoresque, lithographié d'après les dessins de MM. Mayer, Lauvergne et Giraud, 2 vols (Paris: Arthus Bertrand [1852?]). By courtesy of the British Library.

PLATE VIII

Portrait of Marmier in old age, c.1885. Oil on canvas, by Nicolas Xydias. Reproduced by the Museé municipal de Pontarlier from the original held in their collection.

for journeys in summer or winter, and to celebrate the beauties of nature. He notes their melancholy tone, which he ascribes to the fact that 'ils ont été inspirés par une pensée austère, ils sont nés sous un ciel sombre, au bord d'une mer inconstante'.[83] A letter on modern literature, addressed to Sainte-Beuve, concentrates largely on Franzén and Runeberg, and offers translations of a number of poems and extracts. He had in fact already met Franzén in Härnösand during his travels in Sweden, and had included material on his work in the *Histoire de la littérature en Danemark et en Suède*. He is described as a 'poète d'une nature tendre, rêveuse, idyllique, qui porte en lui tout un monde de pensées' and is compared in various ways to Millevoye, Hölty, Matthisson and Burns.[84] Runeberg's works are praised for their 'vérité locale', their 'couleur toute septentrionale et toute fin-landaise'.[85] The letter is concluded by a brief summary of the Finnish newspapers, which he says are too heavily censored to carry any significant political commentary. A number, however, are singled out for their contribution to the preservation of Finnish culture and literature and for encouraging the literary production of their country.

From Vyborg, Marmier was unable to resist the temptation of travelling on into Russia, although this was not a venture undertaken lightly by a Frenchman at this juncture in history. Under the Restoration, it had looked as though an alliance with Russia might be in prospect; but the July Revolution put paid to that, and Tsar Nicholas I only reluctantly recognised Louis-Philippe. In the 1830s, a number of tensions existed between the French and the Russians. The opposing Russian and French interests in the conflict between Holland and Belgium have already been mentioned. At the time of this crisis, there was also the Warsaw insurrection, which divided French opinion as to whether they should intervene on the side of the Poles; this problem was still being hotly debated in France. There was also the Near Eastern question, in which Russia and France had conflicting interests, and in which France had been marginalised by the other Great Powers, most notably England and Russia (particularly in the exclusion of France from the Convention of 1840 and in the Russian plans to divide Turkey, Egypt, and Crete between themselves and the English in 1841). All this meant that few Frenchmen ventured into Russia during the 1830s, and very little of interest was published about Russia in France. The only notable exception to this rule was Custine, who had visited Russia in 1839 and gathered the material for his famous book, *La Russie en 1839*; but this

[83] Ibid., 1, 171.   [84] Ibid., 1, 190–1.   [85] Ibid., 1, 196.

was not actually published until May 1843.[86] Marmier's collected letters appeared in book form in August 1843, but they had already been published in article form in the *Revue des Deux Mondes*, so they stole much of Custine's thunder by virtue of their novelty. When Custine's book finally appeared, it in fact eclipsed Marmier's work to a large extent. However, as Corbet concludes in his survey of *L'Opinion française face à l'inconnue russe (1799–1894)*, 'son infortune historique n'empêche pas le livre de Marmier de marquer une date importante dans l'histoire de la découverte de la Russie par les Français: la justice oblige même à dire que ce livre était à certains égards supérieur à celui de son concurrent plus heureux'.[87]

The stagecoach service which used to operate between Vyborg and St Petersburg had been discontinued, and no steamships made the journey. Marmier therefore had no option but to hire an uncovered, four-wheeled peasant's cart. He decided to travel with a fellow Frenchman whom he had met on the journey, a merchant from Lyon named Besson. Besson was a well-educated and cultured young man with a jolly disposition, which made him a congenial travelling companion. The journey was not comfortable, for the road was extremely rough; in fact, Marmier reflected, 'le meilleur carrossier de Paris n'inventerait pas, avec toute son habileté, des ressorts assez flexibles pour rendre supportables les secousses d'un landau dans cet atroce trajet'.[88] As they drew nearer to the Russian border, the roads became worse, the carts which they exchanged at the staging posts along the way became smaller and even more rudimentary, and the drivers became increasingly dishevelled in their appearance. Once at the frontier, his belongings were subjected to a rigorous search. Marmier had already taken the precaution of sending all the books on history and literature that he had acquired during his stay in Finland back to Stockholm; all he had kept for the journey was a Russian dictionary and a novel by Zagoskin. These books were passed on by the customs officers to a superior who inspected them closely, and then passed them to another colleague for confirmation before handing them back. Unfortunately, Marmier had inadvertently left a page from a French newspaper amongst his personal effects; this led to the journey being delayed for a further half-hour as the inspection was started again from the

---

[86] Astolphe-Louis de Custine, marquis, *La Russie en 1839*, 4 vols. (Paris: Amyot, 1843). This is undoubtedly the most important work of the era, although that is not to deny any Russian presence in the French cultural imagination before this (see, for example, the roles played by Voltaire and Diderot—albeit of a different nature from those played by Custine or Marmier—in Franco-Russian literary relations in the previous century).

[87] Charles Corbet, *L'Opinion française face à l'inconnue russe (1799–1894)* (Paris: Marcel Didier, 1967), 212.

[88] *LR*, 1, 235.

beginning. After this, the postmaster came to inspect their *podorozhnaia*, which Marmier describes as an official document permitting the traveller to hire horses along his route—or, in simple terms, another way of extracting taxes.[89] At every station along the way, the document was inspected, and he had to pay another tax instalment. Finally, the main barrier to St Petersburg came into view, defended by half a dozen guards and a batallion of grenadiers: a customs officer again searched all his belongings, and papers were checked by an officer. The city centre, however, was still an hour away by cart. The first thing Marmier did on arriving was to go in search of a public bath; one hour in the bath cost him five francs, and he concluded that the cost of living in St Petersburg must be higher than in any other city in Europe.

The long letter on St Petersburg addresses history, society, and government as much as pure physical description. Although Marmier pays tribute to the city's beauty, he finds it tiring after a while because its lack of history means that it is characterless. It is nonetheless, in his eyes, 'une ville toute jeune, qui se développe avec l'ardeur de la jeunesse et marche à pas de géant'.[90] The Winter Palace is described as one of the most imposing residences in the world. The ordinary people, he says, regard it with 'un singulier mélange de respect craintif et de confiance'.[91] The tsar, Marmier reminds his readers, is an

> empereur dont la domination s'étend sur les deux hémisphères, [. . .] qui gouverne soixante millions d'hommes, [un] souverain sans constitution, qui ordonne et qui est obéi, qui peut d'un trait de plume, d'un signe de tête, envoyer en Sibérie le plus puissant de ses nobles [. . .]. Auguste ne régnait pas sur un empire aussi vaste, et Louis XIV n'avait pas un pouvoir aussi absolu sur ses sujets.[92]

Always passionate about books and libraries, Marmier visited the Imperial Library, but was unable to forget that this 'pacifique institution, qui ne devrait reposer que sous les ailes des muses'[93] is for the Russians a symbol of military conquest. He also viewed with regret the precious French collections brought to Russia by Dubrovskii; but the French, he says, have no one to blame for this loss of their heritage other than their own short-sightedness.

He is extremely outspoken in this letter about the general lack of education in Russia, according to him, a privilege of the very rich. Four-fifths of the peasants, he estimates, are totally illiterate. He says that the Russian

---

[89] Marmier writes 'podovoshna'; I am grateful to Robin Aizlewood for bringing the correct spelling to my attention.

[90] *LR*, 1, 269.   [91] Ibid., 1, 271.   [92] Ibid.   [93] Ibid., 1, 285.

people are 'plongé dans une ignorance profonde, dans le sommeil de l'indifférence et les ténèbres de la superstition'.[94] Nonetheless, despite this terrible lack of education, his contacts with the local population led him to note an innate intelligence, 'une aptitude merveilleuse à comprendre et à saisir tout ce qui s'offre à son instinct'.[95] He remarks that the government finds itself in a dilemma of its own making: on the one hand, it is extremely progressive in terms of its public establishments, manufacture, and construction; on the other, it desires to maintain its authority by preserving the ignorance of the people. Marmier—rather prophetically—sees the tremendous potential of all the wasted talent:

> Qu'on observe avec impartialité tout ce qu'il y a de dons naturels, de force physique, de patience et de germes incultes chez ce peuple auquel nous appliquons encore journellement l'épithète de barbare; qu'on pense au développement que l'instruction même la plus restreinte pourrait lui donner, et je laisse à deviner jusqu'où il ira quand il aura porté la main à l'arbre de la science et trempé son esprit à la source vive de la civilisation.[96]

Apart from the state's withholding of education to preserve ignorance, Marmier explains, it also uses massive censorship of literature, science, and the press, as well as a highly developed intelligence network. Russian newspapers are so heavily censored, he says, that even a train crash two leagues from St Petersburg or the explosion of a steamship off the coast are passed over in total silence—as, of course, are military defeats. Those French newspapers and reviews which are not totally banned in Russia (for example the *Journal des Débats*) are frequently delivered in a more or less unintelligible form as uneven scraps of paper where the censor's scissors have been at work. But, he argues, even the strictest prohibitive measures will not ultimately be able to prevent the principles of analysis, discussion, and liberalism from entering the empire. If not in paper form, these ideals will be carried in the hearts and consciences of those who enter the country, 'là où la main de la police ni les ciseaux de la censure ne peuvent pénétrer'.[97]

The activities of the secret police are described vividly. Marmier was greeted by the officer responsible for foreigners with perfect civility and charm. But as soon as a Frenchman has been welcomed to the country, he claims, all the wheels of the intelligence network are set in motion: servants and hoteliers are instructed to observe and report on all their movements. All this is done, he says, with the utmost discretion, so that the object of surveillance is lulled into a false sense of security. Then one day, a man you have known well by sight for some time, because you have seen him in the street

---

[94] *LR*, 1, 251.   [95] Ibid., 1, 252.   [96] Ibid., 1, 259.   [97] Ibid., 1, 250.

or reading newspapers in a café, comes up to you. If you are a foreigner, he will ask you politely to leave the country within twenty-four hours; if you are a Russian citizen, he will make arrangements for your transportation to Siberia.

In Moscow, he saw the prisoners awaiting their departure for Siberia.[98] Many were sentenced to hard labour, and many would never return. A substantial number of them, according to Marmier, were not guilty of any criminal act. Some were there as a result of a straightforward error; others had been sentenced for political reasons; some had been convicted for a momentary rebellion against a despotic master; yet others were victims of a mere whim on the part of their master. Marmier explains with outrage that Russian landowners have the right to have their serfs transported to Siberia without legal formalities: all they have to do is to give the name of the alleged offender to the police. The only possible restraint on a master's impulse is the fact that he has to pay a notional amount for his prisoner's keep—hardly, in Marmier's view, a deterrent: 'Il y a là dans la législation russe une affreuse lacune, et, par les larmes de ceux qui en ont été les victimes, par les souffrances qu'ils ont subies, par *la loi de Dieu*, enfin, l'humanité entière demande qu'elle soit réparée'.[99]

Marmier's comments on the bondage of serfs may at first appear contradictory, but they raise a number of interesting questions. He says that those belonging to the Crown are in a worse situation than those belonging to individuals. On the face of it, they enjoy greater freedom in that despite the law 'qui les enchaîne au sol où ils sont nés',[100] they only pay a reasonably modest tax which gives them the right to farm a fixed piece of land— rather like an ordinary farmer paying rent, he says. But they are unfortunately also answerable to administrators, who treat them very harshly. In times of disaster or famine, he maintains, aid is sent to them by the Crown—but very little of this actually reaches its intended recipients because of the corrupt administration. Russian administration, in Marmier's eyes, is 'l'une des administrations les plus vénales, et tranchons le mot, les plus honteuses qui aient jamais existé'.[101] On his way from St Petersburg to Moscow, he is horrified by the spectacle of serfs begging by the roadside; crowds of women dressed in miserable rags, children with cadaverous complexions and emaciated limbs; and old people weakened by age and need. And yet this situation, he reports, however bad it may seem, is better than it had been in the summer of 1841 when there had been a famine.

---

[98] Marmier left St Petersburg on 14 June and arrived in Moscow on 17 June 1842.
[99] *LR*, 1, 374 (Marmier's emphasis).   [100] Ibid., 2, 106.   [101] Ibid., 2, 94.

The serfs tied to individual landowners, he says, have to work for their master, and also pay a higher level of taxation; yet these are generally better off in material terms, because here at least the owner is aware of the needs of his serfs. It is in the owner's interest to look after them, 'car ils sont une partie intégrante de sa propriété, et ils lui donnent la somme la plus nette de son revenu. Plus ils sont aptes au travail, et plus il a de bénéfices à attendre d'eux; plus leur bien-être s'accroît, et plus sa fortune s'affermit'.[102] Here Marmier inadvertently confounds his own faulty logic by reference to a young man he had met, a bachelor who had fifteen servants, having inherited them on the deaths of his mother and his brother. The young man in question states that he would be much happier and better looked after with only two servants, but the others have nowhere else to go.

The major apparent contradiction in Marmier's presentation of the subject lies in the assertion that while he is not in favour of serfdom (he in fact uses the emotive term 'esclavage' to make his point), the French should perhaps reflect a little before expressing their horror at the system. The life of a Russian serf, he says, is perhaps no worse than that of an ordinary worker in an industrialised nation. He urges his reader to consider the English working classes in particular,

> dans cet abyme de souffrances, de tortures journalières, de privations continues, de maladies sans remèdes, où sont plongés des millions d'infortunés que l'on honore du nom d'hommes libres. Que l'on compare ensuite ce qu'on appelle si débonnairement leur existence, à l'existence des plus pauvres serfs, et, je le demande, où est l'esclavage? où est la barbarie?[103]

The phenomenon of Russian bondage was not unknown in France at this time, and had already provoked negative comment. Here Marmier perhaps exploits this to raise awareness of the general plight of the working classes whose exploitation, in his eyes, was linked to the new capitalist ethic. The workers in England are described as 'victimes' and 'bêtes de somme', their condition determined by 'une spéculation infame', a trade in human life which he (perhaps rather exaggeratedly) considers to be 'plus atroce et plus ignominieux que la traite des nègres'.[104] We should not, he therefore concludes, be too hasty in our condemnation of Russia for the treatment of its serfs, 'car dans notre siècle de liberté, au milieu de notre civilisation, dans nos villes et nos manufactures, nous avons le plus affreux, le plus déplorable de tous les servages, le prolétariat pauvre, languissant et entaché, par le fait même de notre organisation'.[105]

---

[102] *LR*, 2, 108.   [103] Ibid., 2, 118.   [104] Ibid., 2, 117–19.   [105] Ibid., 2, 118–19.

But this is far from being an apology for serfdom. Russian serfs are completely in the power of their masters, who may have them transported to Siberia, enlisted in the military, or subjected to severe corporal punishments. As a system, Marmier says, it is 'monstrueux',[106] and robs the human being of his dignity and dehumanises him. Like a plant, the individual here is tied to the spot where he was born; a price may be placed on his head as if he were a cheap commodity; and he may be sold like livestock. He argues that a system based on such foundations cannot last: 'Un jour viendra où les serfs russes, instruits de ce qui existe dans les autres contrées, se révolteront contre le caractère abject de leur condition. Evidemment aussi, un jour viendra où la nation russe ne voudra plus fléchir la tête sous l'administration vénale qui la pressure aujourd'hui'.[107] Major social upheaval is perhaps unlikely during the lifetime of Nicholas I, he says, but when he dies there will either be major reforms or immense civil unrest. The most urgent reforms, he summarises, are the 'émancipation des serfs, formation régulière du tiers état, réforme des mœurs et de la hiérarchie administrative'.[108]

His outspoken criticism of the Russian state is perhaps surprising in view of the efforts made in public relations during his stay. We know that in St Petersburg, Marmier had met Viazemskii;[109] it would seem likely that an introduction had been effected by A. I. Turgenev.[110] Viazemskii appears to have arranged for him to meet Shevyrev[111] in Moscow; we know that he was also put into contact with Khomiakov[112] and Ivan Kireevskii.[113] These were all individuals associated with conservative Slavophile circles and who would actively put forward positive aspects of the regime. Marmier recalls in his *Lettres* having spent an 'heure charmante'[114] with Shevyrev and some of his friends. The aim of the *Muscovite* (Shevyrev's review), he writes, is to 'faire connaître tantôt par des traductions, tantôt par des critiques et des analyses, les principales productions de la littérature étrangère, et d'éveiller, de propager, par des recherches historiques ou biographiques et des chants

[106] Ibid., 2, 120.   [107] Ibid., 2, 120–1.   [108] Ibid., 2, 121.

[109] Petr Andreevich Viazemskii (1792–1878), Russian poet and critic, and friend of Pushkin.

[110] We know from Sainte-Beuve's correspondence (*Correspondance génerale*, 3, 129) that A. I. Turgenev had been a guest at Marmier's gatherings in his Paris flat; we also know that Turgenev had written to Viazemskii about Marmier and these gatherings as early as 1839 (see Cadot, *La Russie dans la vie intellectuelle française*, 103).

[111] Stepan Petrovich Shevyrev (1806–64), professor of history and Russian literature at Moscow University and considered as one of the most influential members of the Slavophile camp. He also edited the review the *Muscovite*.

[112] Aleksei Stepanovich Khomiakov (1804–60), leading thinker of the Slavophile movement, and strongly opposed to the Westernisers.

[113] Ivan Kireevskii (1808–56), theologian.

[114] *LR*, 1, 393.

populaires, le culte des souvenirs nationaux et le sentiment de la poésie russe'.[115]

It is true, as Cadot states, that at this juncture Marmier does not appear to have been aware of Shevyrev's article of 1841 denouncing the 'occident pourri'.[116] But this does not necessarily mean, as Corbet suggests on a number of occasions, that Marmier was 'taken in' on this issue by the propaganda.[117] It has to be remembered that Marmier's main interest was in literature; and that literature for him, as it had been for Mme de Staël, should be the expression of a society. Marmier always sought the national character of any literature he studied; it is therefore not surprising that he was not entirely condemnatory of what he had heard. He does not, however, ignore the wider implications of the goals the movement had set itself. He translates the final stanza of Khomiakov's poem addressed to the English: 'Et Dieu choisira une nation humble, pleine de foi et de miracles, pour lui confier les destins de l'univers, la foudre de la terre et la voix du ciel'.[118] Obviously, he writes, the nation referred to here is Russia: 'C'est une pensée que j'ai entendu souvent exprimer en Russie, dans les salons comme dans les sociétés universitaires. Les Russes n'hésitent pas à s'attribuer une mission de régéneration sociale et l'empire du monde'.[119] He was determined not to be unduly swayed by any one group. In a letter to François Buloz, he said that he had received a very warm welcome in Russia, 'mais tous les bons et affectueux souvenirs ne m'empêcheront pas d'en parler librement'.[120] He was also independent enough to meet Chaadaev,[121] whom he heard speaking against serfdom and against Khomiakov.[122]

The problems faced by the Catholic Church in Russia and Poland also incensed Marmier. From Moscow, he had visited the monastery of Troitsa at Sergiev-Posad,[123] and addressed a letter on the subject to Lamartine. Perhaps unsurprisingly in view of his religious background and the contemporary problems in Russia, he has some rather harsh words for the Orthodox Church. The clergy, he maintains, are ignorant and unable to help their congregations. The monks are well fed, but they live in a state of

[115] *LR*, 1, 392.

[116] Cadot, *La Russie dans la vie intellectuelle française*, 475.

[117] See, for example, Corbet, *L'Opinion française*, 215 and 216.

[118] *LR*, 1, 396.   [119] Ibid., 1, 397.

[120] Marie-Louise Pailleron, *François Buloz et ses amis: la vie littéraire sous Louis-Philippe*, new edn. (Paris: Firmin Didot, 1930), 158–9.

[121] Petr Iakovlevich Chaadaev (1794–1856), philosopher and author of the *Philosophical Letters*; the infamous first letter extolled western Europe and condemned Russia as a blank in world history.

[122] See Corbet, *L'Opinion française*, 213.

[123] Marmier does not specify the location of the monastery: for this I am grateful to Robin Aizlewood.

'saleté repoussante'.[124] The persecution of Catholics takes place 'sous le manteau de la censure et du despotisme'.[125] Censorship of the press and of private correspondence by the police have ensured that even the pope knew nothing about what was going on until recently. The tsar, however, is unlikely to heed the pope's displeasure, Marmier concludes: 'l'empereur de Russie veut avoir l'omnipotence absolue'[126] and he has the strategies in place to achieve this: 'il veut user du despotisme dans toute l'étendue du mot, il en usera'.[127]

For Corbet, Marmier's analysis of Russian society may be less detailed than that given by Custine, but it is nonetheless 'une description plus précise et plus juste'.[128] In terms of the presentation of Russian literature, however, Marmier's superiority is overwhelming. In the first place, it was mainly Marmier's love of literature which motivated his travels, and he had been teaching himself Russian. He also contrived to meet a prodigious number of intellectuals and writers during his time in Russia. As we have seen, A. I. Turgenev was probably responsible for introducing him to Viazemskii; in St Petersburg he also met, amongst others, Pletnev, Odoevskii, Countess Rostopshchina, Gogol, and Sologub.[129] In a letter to Buloz, Marmier also claimed that he could have stayed in St Petersburg: 'le ministre de l'Instruction publique [S. S. Uvarov] m'a fait les plus belles offres'.[130] In Moscow he was reunited with Turgenev, and also met Khomiakov and Herzen.[131] Here he was also introduced to a young teacher, Schewireff, who supplied him with the material for his chapter on 'chants populaires', which was always one of Marmier's favourite subjects.

In addition to a chapter on modern literature, addressed to Amédée Pichot, Marmier continued his work on Russian literature over the following decades, publishing translations of works by many major authors and contributing to a new interest in Russian literature in France. During the heat of the 1848 revolution, he shut himself away in his small flat with his Russian books, finding the challenge of the language therapeutic.[132] In 1854,

---

[124] *LR*, 2, 28.   [125] Ibid., 2, 67.   [126] Ibid., 2, 68.   [127] Ibid., 2, 69.

[128] Corbet, *L'Opinion française*, 214.

[129] Petr Aleksandrovich Pletnev (1792–1865), poet and literary critic; Vladimir Odoevskii (1804–69), author; Evdokiia Rostopshchina (1811–58), poet, playwright, and novelist; Vladimir Sologub (1813–82), author.

[130] Pailleron, *François Buloz et ses amis*, 158.

[131] Aleksandr Ivanovich Herzen (1812–70), thinker and writer. An anti-tsarist, he left Russia for western Europe in 1847.

[132] He notes in his private papers in 1855 that his good health was allowing him to continue to work diligently on his Russian, although 'un bon maître m'aurait été d'un grand secours'. In his edition of the *Journal* (1, 170), Kaye mistakenly transcribes 'aurait' as 'avait'. See Académie des Sciences, Belles Lettres et Arts de Besançon, *Memorandum 2*, fo. 90.

a collection of short stories appeared under the title *Les Perce-Neige*; the Russian section included tales by Pushkin and Pavlov.[133] 1856 saw the publication of *Au Bord de la Néva*, which included introductions to the works of Lermontov, Gogol, and Sologub.[134] In the preface to his rendering of Gogol's 'Le Manteau' ('une des productions caractéristiques de cet esprit original'[135]), he recalls meeting the author in 1842. Despite the resounding success of his recent novellas and of his *Ames mortes*, Marmier says, Gogol looked like one of his 'âmes mortes', even in a circle of loyal friends, 'n'écoutant que d'une oreille indifférente tout ce qui se disait autour de lui, ne répondant que par un froid sourire aux éloges sincères que l'on faisait de ses œuvres, et sortant d'une intéressante soirée, sombre et morne comme il y était entré'.[136] An introduction to Sologub's 'La Pharmacienne' also harks back to 1842, describing the author as one of 'les hommes les plus aimables de cette société russe si attrayante et si hospitalière'[137] which Marmier can never forget. He dedicates the volume to Sologub 'comme un témoignage de l'heureux souvenir que j'ai gardé de nos soirées chez le prince Viazemski et de nos promenades du dimanche à Paulovski'.[138] A volume entitled *Les Drames intimes*, another collection of shorter works by authors including Polevoi, Sologub, Bestuzhev, and Pushkin appeared the following year (1857);[139] and in 1858, a collection of novellas by I. S. Turgenev appeared under the title *Scènes de la vie russe*.[140] These were followed in 1859 by the publication of his translation of Vonliarliarski's *Une grande dame russe*.[141] *Les Hasards de la vie*, published in 1868, contained a tale by Zagoskin.[142]

From Moscow, Marmier returned to St Petersburg, whence he made his way towards Poland. Poland had been subjected to three partitions between

---

[133] *Les Perce-Neige, nouvelles du Nord traduites par X. Marmier* (Paris: Garnier, 1854); translations of 'Le Tourbillon de neige' and 'Le Coup de pistolet' by Pushkin and 'L'Anniversaire' by Pavlov.

[134] *Au bord de la Néva: contes russes traduits par X. Marmier* (Paris: Michel Lévy, 1856). Includes 'Un héros de notre temps' with a notice on Lermontov; 'Le Manteau' and a notice on Gogol; and 'La Pharmacienne' and a notice on Sologub. A luxury edition of Marmier's translation of Gogol's 'Le Manteau' appeared in 1961 (Paris: André Dérue).

[135] *Au bord de la Néva*, 212.   [136] Ibid., 214.   [137] Ibid., 264.   [138] Ibid.

[139] *Les Drames intimes: contes russes, par X. Marmier* (Paris: Michel Lévy, 1857). Includes a notice on Polevoi and Bestuzhev, and also a 'Note sur le poème de Pouschkine' ('La Fontaine de Baktschisaraï'). This collection was reprinted in 1876 (Paris: Calmann Lévy), and a new edition, entitled *Histoires russes. Polevoï, Lioudmila* [. . .] appeared in 1891 (Paris: Calmann Lévy).

[140] *Scènes de la vie russe: par M. J. Tourgueneff, nouvelles russes, traduites avec l'autorisation de l'auteur par M. X. Marmier* (Paris: Hachette, 1858). This was obviously a tremendous success: it was reprinted seven times until 1918. The volume contains 'Les Deux Amis', 'Jacques Passinkof', 'Moumou', 'Faust', 'Le Fe3ailleur', and 'Les Trois Portraits'.

[141] *Une grande dame russe: par B. A. Vonliarliarski, traduit du russe par X. Marmier* (Paris: Michel Lévy, 1859).

[142] 'L'Orpheline', in *Les Hasards de la vie, contes et nouvelles* (Paris: Brunet, 1868), 75–116.

1772 and 1795; it had been carved up again during the Napoleonic era, and had again been divided up by the Congress of Vienna in 1815. Western Prussia, the territory of Posen, Danzig, and Thorn were under Prussian rule; Galicia and Lodomeria fell to Austria; Cracow had been set up as a semi-autonomous republic; and the remainder was ruled by Russia through a constitutional link. Poland, writes Marmier, was 'livrée comme une proie sans force aux vautours qui la convoitaient'.[143] The two most shameful 'taches qui souillent l'histoire moderne'[144] in his view are the oppression of Ireland by the English and the division of Poland.

The road and transport between St Petersburg and Warsaw were excellent, and it would have been possible, he reflected, to make the journey in three days had it not been for the interminable stops for passports, visas, and customs which extended the travelling time to five days and five nights. The route was largely deserted apart from the occasional band of workmen on foot, or the odd peasant's cart. The only incessant activity along the way was that of the telegraphs, which Marmier found very sinister in the context. The telegraph is personified and referred to as a 'messager gouvernemental' whose 'longs bras' fold, cross over, and stretch out: the use of the verb 's'étendent' is well chosen to suggest the power of Russia stretching into Poland.[145] The communications carried on even into the night. It took just an hour and a half, Marmier reflected, for the emperor to learn everything that happened and everything that was said in Warsaw; likewise, he could transmit 'l'arrêt de sa volonté à l'infortunée nation qu'il a vaincue'.[146] In terms which almost seem to foreshadow Marx, he argues that 'Dans les contrées soumises au régime absolu, les œuvres de l'art et de l'industrie ne servent que les intérêts du despotisme. C'est la pensée du peuple qui les a créées, et c'est le maître qui les emploie pour le dompter et le châtier'.[147]

His route took him through Ostrow, Kowno, and Ostrolenko. The natural beauty of the countryside contrasted strongly with the wretched poverty of the local populations. The most miserable of all were the Jewish villages through which he went on the road between Ostrow and Kowno:

> Je vois encore ces frêles maisons en planches, éclairées par quelques vitres, partagées en soupentes, coupées par des cloisons où des familles entières s'entassent à l'étroit dans un air méphitique, ces ruisseaux fangeux où des enfants barbottent comme des animaux immondes, ces rues où l'on ne rencontre que des hommes et des femmes en haillons, regardant d'un air hébété le voyageur qui passe [. . .].[148]

---

[143] *LR*, 2, 219.   [144] Ibid., 2, 220.   [145] Ibid., 2, 215.   [146] Ibid.   [147] Ibid., 2, 215–16.
[148] Ibid., 2, 221.

A footnote inserted in the 1843 edition of *Lettres sur la Russie, la Finlande et la Pologne* at this juncture by Marmier states that after this letter was published in the *Revue des Deux Mondes*, he received a letter from a Polish author criticising him for presenting the Polish Jews in such a negative light. Marmier defends himself on the grounds that he has done nothing more than relate the truth of what he saw. His intentions, he declares, were not to 'insulter à la misère de cette population déjà si honnie et si maltraitée';[149] indeed, he sincerely hopes to see them liberated, emancipated, and happy. It is interesting both that Marmier should have received this letter and that he should have responded in print, and in such terms. Although there was a current of philo-Semitism in some quarters, anti-Semitic feeling and expression were commonplace in France at this time, and it is significant that Marmier did not wish to be associated with this.

On arriving in Warsaw, he visited the principal sights including the library, where he was quite shocked to discover that censorship in St Petersburg had been 'un modèle d'indulgence'[150] in comparison with what he found here. Despite the censorship and the police inquisitions, however, he was delighted to discover 'dans une société fermée aux regards suspects'[151] that Polish literature was flourishing. An unnamed 'écrivain très instruit' wrote Marmier a letter about developments in modern Polish literature, which is partially reproduced in his letter on Warsaw. After visiting a number of castles in the area around Warsaw, he made his way on to Cracow, 'l'une des cités les plus majestueuses et les plus désolantes qui existent'.[152] Cracow has been betrayed, he writes, by those nations responsible for protecting its constitution. Virtually nothing remains of the constitution, which has been flouted; Cracow has been subject to harsh oppression, while the signatories of the Congress of Vienna have stood by.

The Poles, he writes, must now put their own internal differences to one side and pull together. If they then wait for the right moment they will have a chance to throw off their oppressors. If they manage to do that, he says, Russia will turn to the East. In this context, Marmier concludes his text on a note of rather high-handed colonialist discourse: 'C'est là que nous voudrions la voir, et c'est là, c'est parmi les peuplades ignorantes et barbares, qu'elle aurait une grande et belle mission à accomplir. Les Russes qui ont le plus vif sentiment de patriotisme et d'orgueil national le disent hautement, et l'Europe entière devrait s'associer à leurs vœux'.[153]

This turned out to be one of his longer journeys: Marmier travelled back through Germany and Denmark (where he was awarded the Order of the

---

[149] *LR*, 2, 229.   [150] Ibid., 2, 262.   [151] Ibid., 2, 270.   [152] Ibid., 2, 308.   [153] Ibid., 2, 334–5.

Danebrog), arriving back in Paris in November 1842.[154] It was not long
before he was in circulation again, dining with his literary friends, including
Latour and Michelet.[155] The publication of his letters and of the collected
volume caused quite a stir both in France and in Russia. When the
December article appeared in the *Revue des Deux Mondes*, Viazemskii was
not impressed. He wrote to A. I. Turgenev that it was 'mince et pâle', and
suggested that it would please neither the French nor the Russians because
it was so insipid. A. I. Turgenev seems to have reacted rather more
favourably, for he replied that 'son coup d'œil sur votre société et d'autres
questions est assez juste. C'est écrit sans bile et raisonnablement'.[156]
Bulgarin and Pletnev also reacted negatively: the latter, in a letter to Grot,
speaks of 'des mensonges à la française', refers to Marmier as 'un Français
superficiel', and concludes that the article on the monastery and the clergy
is 'terriblement offensant pour la Russie'.[157] The volume was perhaps not
surprisingly banned in Russia. When the ban was officially announced,
Marmier's publisher received an urgent order for 300 copies from a bookshop in St Petersburg.[158] It was translated into German the following year,[159]
and was published in a new French edition in 1851.[160]

[154] Sainte-Beuve, *Correspondance générale*, 4, 311.
[155] Michelet, *Correspondance générale*, 3, 777.
[156] Both letters quoted by Cadot, *La Russie dans la vie intellectuelle française*, 105.
[157] Corbet, *L'Opinion française*, 217.
[158] Edmond Biré, *Études et portraits*, new edn. (Paris and Lyon: Librairie Catholique Emmanuel Vitte, 1913), 323.
[159] See Cadot, *La Russie dans la vie intellectuelle française*, 104.
[160] *Lettres sur la Russie, la Finlande et la Pologne*, 2nd edn. (Paris: Garnier, 1851).

10

From the Doubs to the Desert (1843–6)

A Wedding and Two Funerals

On 5 April 1843, Marmier addressed a rather vague request to his employers at the Bibliothèque du Ministère de l'Instruction publique for two or three weeks' leave to attend to 'une affaire de famille très importante' in the Franche-Comté. In the letter he offers to spend some of his time in the area visiting the public libraries of Dôle, Besançon, and Vesoul in order to prepare a report on their collections which he would submit on his return to Paris: he was granted leave of one month.[1] Nothing in the letter or on his employment file indicates the nature of the family affair. In fact, he wanted to take the leave in order to get married. It is not too difficult to see why he should have wished to keep the matter private. His broken engagement to Marie Oehlenschläger in 1838 had caused something of a scandal both in Denmark and in France; even long-standing friends such as Quinet had distanced themselves from him in its aftermath. 'Je regrette bien vivement', Marmier had written to Buloz, 'que les journaux aient livré au public un projet et un nom qui devraient être à jamais ensevelis dans un respectueux silence'.[2] This time, he seems to have gone to some lengths to ensure that news did not leak out. Even Marmier's old friend and mentor, Charles Weiss, whom he asked to witness the marriage, was not informed of arrangements until the week before.[3] It is difficult to know if Marmier simply wished to protect his fiancée from unwanted publicity and media attention, or if he was fearful of suffering from cold feet once again: it may well have been both. Indeed, he admits in his letter to Weiss that

> Je compte sur vous comme sur un père dans cette solonnelle occasion de la vie qui me réjouit et m'inquiète, qui m'ouvre un nouvel avenir et rejète dans l'ombre derrière moi tout un passé jeune, poétique, aventureux qui m'a tant de fois

---

[1] AnF, F17/21256.

[2] Marie-Louise Pailleron, *François Buloz et ses amis: la vie littéraire sous Louis-Philippe*, new edn. (Paris: Firmin Didot, 1930), 156–7.

[3] BmB, Collection Estignard, MS 1907, Correpondance de Charles Weiss, Lettres de X. Marmier, fos. 808–9. The letter is undated, but it says the wedding is 'pour lundi'.

à tort ou à raison charmé et que je regrette, comme on regrette un amour de cœur et d'imagination.[4]

At the time of the Oehlenschläger affair, he had confided to François Buloz that he had a number of reasons for breaking off the engagement: but above all, he wanted to retain his independence.[5] The woman for whom he was now preparing to renounce his precious freedom was Françoise Eugénie Pourchet (she used the name Eugénie), an eighteen-year-old orphan born in Maisons du Bois and living in Pontarlier. Her guardian was François Joseph Xavier Fauconnet, but she seems to have been adopted by the family of her conseil-adjoint to the guardian, Pierre Antoine Patel, a well-known lawyer and local politician. She was financially secure, having inherited a fortune of some three hundred thousand francs. This time, Marmier remained firm in his resolve, and the wedding went ahead. The civil ceremony took place in the town hall of Pontarlier at 10 a.m. on 8 May 1843, witnessed by Charles Weiss; his brother Louis Marmier; Antoine Marie Carbon; and Bernard Edmond Brossard.[6] It was followed by a religious service at the Doubs church, just outside Pontarlier. This church held a special place in Marmier's affections. One of his earliest memories was of being carried there in his mother's arms; it was also the church where he had been baptised.[7] The party extended until Tuesday evening when the bride and groom left for Frasne, and thereafter returned to Paris.

The marriage lasted such a short time that it is hard to find much documentary evidence about it; such as there is suggests that the couple enjoyed some eleven months of happiness together. An untitled poem recalls Marmier's happiness in unequivocal terms: 'oh! quel amour!/Le plus fervent,

---

[4] Ibid.

[5] See Pailleron, *François Buloz et ses amis*, 157.

[6] Ville de Pontarlier, État civil no. 22: 'L'an mil huit cent quarante trois, le huit du Mois de mai, à dix heures du matin, à l'Hôtel de la Mairie, par devant nous Etienne François Benoît Monnier, Maire [. . .] ont comparu Monsieur Jean-Marie Xavier Marmier [. . .] et Delle Françoise Eugénie Pourchet [. . .]. Chacun d'eux ayant répondu séparément et affirmativement avons déclaré au nom de la loi que Monsieur Jean-Marie Xavier Marmier et Melle Françoise Eugénie Pourchet sont unis par le Mariage'.

[7] A poem entitled 'A l'église de Doubs' in the *Poésies d'un voyageur* (Paris: Félix Locquin, 1844, 104–5) and dated 20 April 1843, concludes with the following lines:

> Conservez-moi votre soutien,
> Et protégez la jeune fille
> Dont le destin s'unit au mien.
> [. . .]
> Vous qui sonniez pour mon baptême,
> Sonnez, ô cloches, pour l'époux.

le plus sincère'.[8] During this time, Marmier seems to have lost touch with a number of his old friends. Mélanie Bixio (wife of Alexandre Bixio, the politician and co-founder of the *Revue des Deux Mondes*), for example, informed the Breton poet Auguste Brizeux in November 1843 that their friend Marmier had 'subi le joug du mariage', but that she had not yet met his wife, adding that she now considered him to be 'perdu pour ses amis'.[9] In the same month, the duchesse de Rauzan wrote to Sainte-Beuve, asking 'Que faites-vous de l'heureux M. Marmier? Comment fait-il pour se passer de mélancolie? Il en jouait si bien. Je fais mille vœux pour son bonheur'.[10] By this time, Eugénie was pregnant, and Sainte-Beuve's mother wrote to Marmier: 'J'espère que votre aimable épouse se porte bien pour son état de grossesse, et qu'elle vous donnera bientôt une joie de plus, qui complétera tout le bonheur que vous méritez: c'est le vœu que je forme pour vous jeunes mariés [. . .]'.[11]

Unfortunately, this was not to be, and the marriage ended in the tragic deaths of both mother and child, shortly after the birth on 17 April 1844 at their Paris home in the rue Saint-Thomas d'Aquin. The child, 'cet enfant tant désiré' died first, during the labour.[12] The terrible sense of loss must have been heightened—if such a thing is possible—in her case by the fact that apart from her husband, she had no family in the world. Distraught with grief and in the grip of a fever which was to prove fatal for her, Eugénie became confused, and believed that the child was alive and suffering the same physical symptoms as she was. She pleaded with Marmier to give him a drink to cool his burning brow and calm his racing pulse. She grew gradually weaker, and as the chill of death began to creep over her limbs, she grasped Marmier's hand to utter her final words: 'Vois-tu ce pauvre petit qui n'a pas de vêtements, il a froid, il grelotte'.[13]

On her death, Marmier inherited half of her fortune, and Sainte-Beuve wrote rather coldly to Mme Juste Olivier the following month that 'Marmier a perdu sa jeune femme après un an de mariage: il garde de la for-

---

[8] *Poésies d'un voyageur 1834–1874* (Paris: Simon Raçon, 1874), 104.

[9] Auguste Brizeux, *Un poète romantique et ses amis: Correspondance (1805–1858)*, ed. Jean-Louis Debauve (Brest: Centre de recherche bretonne et celtique, CNRS, Faculté des Lettres et sciences sociales, Université de Brest, 1989), 31.

[10] Charles Augustin Sainte-Beuve, *Correspondance générale [. . .], recueillie, classée et annotée par Jean Bonnerot*, 19 vols. (Paris: Stock, 1935–83), 5, 327.

[11] Pailleron, *François Buloz et ses amis*, 161.

[12] *Nouveaux souvenirs de voyage et traditions populaires: Franche-Comté* (Paris: Charpentier, 1845) (cited hereafter as *Franche-Comté*), 328.

[13] Ibid.

tune'.[14] Marmier may have had his faults, and he may not always have behaved correctly towards his women friends, but it is certainly unfair to suggest any mercenary motivation in his affairs: he was, in reality, quite disinterested in his attitude towards money. Certainly, at this juncture, he appears to have been overwhelmed with grief. He had been planning a trip to the Grande-Chartreuse, but now he returned to grieve in the Franche-Comté, 'au sein de mes montagnes natales, comme un enfant qui a besoin de consolations se retire auprès de sa mère, comme un cerf blessé se cache dans l'ombre de son taillis'.[15] The *Nouveaux souvenirs de voyage et traditions populaires: Franche-Comté*, published in 1845, is dedicated 'à la mémoire d'une femme bénie, que l'amour m'avait donnée au sein de mes belles montagnes, que la mort m'a enlevée dans la funeste atmosphère de Paris'.[16] Suffering from 'une lassitude extrême' and 'un profond découragement',[17] he was unable to settle to anything, or to find any consolation. 'Quand l'âme souffre', he wrote, 'elle se tourne dans l'espace comme un malade dans son lit; elle essaie par mille rêves aventureux d'échapper à la pensée constante qui l'enlace et se fuir elle-même'.[18]

Kaye, in the introduction to his edition of Marmier's *Journal*, suggests that the marriage represented a mere interlude for Marmier in his travels, and that his wife's death left him largely unmoved.[19] It is true (as Kaye also states) that her name occurs only once in the papers left by Marmier to the Besançon Academy; but this does not necessarily denote a lack of feeling on his part. A number of pieces of evidence would suggest that 'celle dont rien n'efface/L'image dans mon deuil, l'amour dans mes regrets' was never forgotten.[20] Bornier, who was elected to the French Academy following Marmier's death, made his maiden speech—as was the tradition—about the life and achievements of his predecessor. Bornier in this speech refers to the bereavement as 'cette grande douleur de sa [i.e. Marmier's] vie'. If Marmier very rarely spoke about it, he says, it was because the memory remained too painful for him: 'la blessure ne devait jamais se fermer'.[21] A number of implicit references to his short marriage in poems written later in life would appear to substantiate this claim. One such appears in *Dernières Glanes*, published in 1869:

[14] Sainte-Beuve, *Correspondance générale*, 5, 585.
[15] *Franche-Comté*, 174.　　[16] Ibid., p. xii.　　[17] Ibid., 173.　　[18] Ibid.
[19] See *Journal*, 1, 34.
[20] *Prose et vers 1836–1886* (Paris: Lahure, 1890), 304. The poem is dated 1844.
[21] *Discours prononcés dans la séance publique tenue par l'Académie française pour la réception de M. le Vicomte H. de Bornier le jeudi 25 mai 1893* (Paris: Firmin Didot, 1893), quotations 16 and 17.

> Mais quand l'homme a subi le deuil qui le désole,
> L'hiver de la douleur, l'hiver qui le flétrit,
> C'est en vain qu'il aspire au printemps qui console,
> Sous son fardeau glacé, plus rien ne refleurit.[22]

More explicitly, an autobiographical poem which was published in *Poésies d'un voyageur 1834–1874* follows the course of Marmier's career through the years of 'plaisirs du monde', 'voyages', and 'étude' until he found

> [. . .] un amour, oh! quel amour!
> Le plus fervent, le plus sincère,
> Le plus beau qui, par un beau jour,
> Fleurit jamais sur cette terre.
>
> [. . .]
>
> Hélas! celle à qui tu livras
> Ton ardeur et ta destinée,
> Qui finit tes rudes combats,
> N'a pu t'aimer toute une année.
>
> [. . .]
>
> Souffre donc, sans le laisser voir,
> Pleure, pleure sans injustice,
> Pleure sur ton dernier espoir
> Et sur ton dernier sacrifice.[23]

If Marmier was soon to resume his travels and his writing, it was not, as Kaye suggests, through indifference, but in an attempt to lose himself in his work as an antidote to the profound depression which gripped him. A letter addressed to François Buloz articulates this very clearly:

> Mon cher Buloz, je vous remercie bien cordialement du témoignage d'affection que vous m'avez donné, en assistant au convoi de ma pauvre malheureuse femme. Vous ne pouviez rien faire qui me touchât davantage, et m'imposât plus de reconnaissance, et je vous prie de vouloir bien remercier pour moi Bonnaire d'avoir pris part à la même action.
>
> Je pars dans quelques jours, pour m'en aller porter ailleurs le deuil de mon cœur. Je ne me sens plus en moi ni force, ni espoir, ni rien de ce qui m'aurait guéri, cependant je comprends bien que le travail peut être pour moi un utile remède.[24]

---

[22] *Dernières Glanes* (Paris: Simon Raçon, 1869), 43.
[23] *Poésies d'un voyageur 1834–1874*, 103–5 (untitled poem).
[24] Pailleron, *François Buloz et ses amis*, 162.

From the Rhine to the Nile

After his brief sojourn in the Franche-Comté, Marmier was granted leave in 1845 by Salvandy, Ministre de l'Instruction publique, in order to undertake a new journey.[25] Turning away from the melancholy associated with the northern climes, he now set out to travel from the Rhine to the Nile via the Holy Land. The idea for this change of direction may have been in part inspired by his friend Brizeux, whose poem 'Les Fleurs sombres' in *Les Ternaires* is dedicated to Marmier.[26] The poem probably refers to an on-going debate between the two about the use of classical or northern models in literature. On 6 January 1839, Sainte-Beuve had written to M. and Mme Juste Olivier that

> Chez Marmier, l'autre jour, nous avons eu le petit punch [. . .]. Nous avons dit des vers, courts, vifs, comme le punch qu'à petits coups nous buvions. Brizeux en a dit de jolis, pareils à des fleurettes franches et sauvages [. . .]. En qualité de *Grec* par le goût, il est, à un certain moment, entré dans une violente colère contre le Nord, et contre les sapins.[27]

Marmier replied to this poem by one of his own, dedicated to Brizeux, and entitled 'Mélancolie', which was published in 1844.[28] One of Marmier's better poems, it accepts the notion that melancholy can be a dangerous and undesirable muse, but also emphasises her attractions. Although Marmier rejected his friend's literary argument, it would seem that he now accepted the poem's admonition on a personal level. His expedition to the warmer southern countries would take him away from the 'ciel souffrant', the 'froid calice inondé de pluie' of Brizeux's poem, presumably in an endeavour to 'Écrase[r] à [s]es pieds la mélancolie/Cette fleur du nord'.[29]

The pilgrimage to the Holy Land was a fashionable tourist excursion in the nineteenth century; writers such as Chateaubriand, Lamartine, Nerval, and Ampère had been there before Marmier and recorded their impressions. He was aware that his destination lacked originality and that

---

[25] Detail found in the preface to Marmier's published record of his journey, *Du Rhin au Nil*, 2 vols. (Paris: Arthus Bertrand, [1846]) (cited hereafter as *RN*), p. ii. A number of the letters had been published in newspapers and periodicals in 1846 prior to their inclusion in these volumes: see *Le Moniteur Universel*, 1070, 1865–6, 2147–8, 2352, 2488; *L'Illustration* (September), 38–9; and *Le Correspondant* (10 April).

[26] Auguste Brizeux, 'Les Fleurs sombres. A Xavier Marmier', *Les Ternaires*, in *Œuvres complètes de Auguste Brizeux, précédées d'une notice par Saint-René Taillandier*, 2 vols. (Paris: Michel Lévy frères, 1860), 2, 66–7. *Les Ternaires* was first published in 1841 (Paris: Masgana).

[27] Sainte-Beuve, *Correpondance générale*, 3, 129.

[28] 'Mélancolie. A mon ami Brizeux', in *Poésies d'un voyageur*, 10.

[29] *Œuvres complètes de Auguste Brizeux*, 2, 66.

he was unlikely to make any startling discoveries on this journey. His motivation, he writes in the preface to his record of this expedition, was somewhat different this time:

> Le désir d'aller, de voir, ce vague et inextinguible désir qui ne fait que se développer à mesure qu'on s'abandonne à son essor, a été le premier mobile de mon voyage. Un rêve poétique m'a conduit sur les rives du Bosphore; une espérance studieuse dans les principales possessions de la Turquie, un sentiment religieux dans l'aveugle enceinte de Jérusalem, et la grandiose image des anciens temps au sommet des pyramides.[30]

He travelled first of all through Switzerland, which at this time was undergoing a period of civil unrest. There had been a conflict between the liberal cantons, which aspired to being a unitary federal state, and the conservative/ Catholic cantons which wanted to retain the confederation. Many of the liberal cantons had become radically anticlericalist and sought the closure of convents and the expulsion of Jesuits. Lucerne had responded to the radical anticlerical measures of the recent past by appointing Jesuit teachers. In March 1845, the radicals had tried unsuccessfully to invade the territory of Lucerne. The Catholic cantons joined forces, and in December 1845, shortly after Marmier's passage through the country, their separatist league, the Sonderbund, would come into being.

Crossing Switzerland in these conditions was a depressing business for Marmier, who contrasted the 'vertige des novateurs' to the 'épouvante des gens de bien'.[31] Education, he feared, had suffered a severe setback; he particularly regretted the demise of the Academy of Lausanne, which he found impoverished, disorganised, and existing in name only. The new measures, he argues, had led to a general lowering of standards in the name of political expediency. The troubles in the country were also taking their toll on the economy: according to him, Switzerland normally derived a good deal of its income from the tourist trade—particularly from rich English visitors; this year (1845), he found hotels and restaurants deserted, and the people anxious. Only one other traveller took the coach to Constanz with him, and the 'Hôtel du brochet', usually one of the busiest hotels in the town, had only six guests, including the two new arrivals. From Constanz, he took the steamer on to Bregenz. The transition to Austrian territory was very clear; the boat was greeted by police and customs officials. Marmier first had to present his passport and then open up his trunk and spread his clothes and belongings out in the open air for inspection. Fortunately, his passport

---

[30] *RN*, 1, p. ii.   [31] Ibid., 1, 2.

was in order and none of his books appeared offensive, so he was able to continue on his way.

The hotel was peaceful, and the guests all appeared to be 'dans un état de béatitude parfaite'.[32] Austria, he reflected, was altogether a haven of 'quiétude d'esprit et du bien-être matériel'.[33] A reasonably priced stage-coach service took him on to Innsbruck, and he was very aware of the improvements to roads and communications in the Tyrol area which had been made over the last few years. He remarked ironically that

> Il faut rendre cette justice au gouvernement autrichien, que par tout ce qui tient au *confort* matériel de ses sujets, il est on ne peut plus accommodant. Qu'on lui demande routes, canaux, édifices publiques; rien de mieux, pourvu qu'au nom du ciel, on ne lui parle ni de constitution, ni de cette abominable liberté de la presse, qui n'enfante que désastres et révolutions.[34]

Despite all this material progress, he was delighted to note that the Tyrol was exceptional in its preservation of local colour, traditions, and dress. One local custom, however, appeared to shock him. Once a couple here have become engaged, he recounts, they are able to spend the night together; and, he notes with some astonishment, 'la jeune fille n'en est moins considérée et le mariage dignement conclu après ces dangereuses séries de promenades nocturnes'![35] A rapid overland journey of only fourteen hours took him from Innsbruck to Salzburg, whence he made his way on to Linz, and then by boat down the Danube to Vienna.

From Vienna he travelled on to Pressburg (now Bratislava), which at that time was in Hungary. He admired its wide, regular streets and enormous buildings. He stayed at the 'Hôtel des trois arbres verts', where he had to negotiate corridors a quarter of a league long in order to reach his room. Unsure as to whether the same police formalities would be required here as in Vienna, he asked a local whether he should hand his passport in at the police station. He was proudly informed that 'La Hongrie est une terre libre; nous n'avons ici ni douane ni police'.[36] For Marmier, however, it seemed that the freedom from police restrictions had gone a little far: 'Certaines réunions nocturnes qu'on n'admet point dans les bons hôtels de Paris, et qu'on ne tolère qu'à peine dans d'autres, sont ici trop facilement acceptées'.[37]

From here, he travelled by boat to Gran via Raab and Komorn. He had no letters of introduction, but within minutes of disembarcation had made friends with a young priest named Lipovniczky. On Marmier's first day in Gran, Lipovniczky took him to a hotel, found him a room, and then gave

---

[32] Ibid., 1, 11.   [33] Ibid., 1, 12.   [34] Ibid., 1, 15 (Marmier's emphasis).   [35] Ibid., 1, 35.
[36] Ibid., 1, 108.   [37] Ibid.

him a tour of the new cathedral, 'l'un des plus beaux monuments modernes de l'art catholique'.[38] The following day, after mass, Marmier's new friend offered to introduce him to the prince primate, the archbishop of Gran. Marmier accepted the invitation with enthusiasm, although he was rather worried that his travelling outfit might be inappropriate for such an occasion. Lipovniczky helped him out by lending him a black hat in place of his Tyrolean straw hat. Thus clad, Marmier was shown into a drawing room where 'un beau vieillard, à la physionomie noble et douce, à l'attitude majestueuse'[39] rose to greet him, addressing him in French. Marmier expressed his admiration for the work being done on the cathedral; the conversation then turned to political and religious questions in France, and Marmier was surprised to find the Hungarian prelate so well informed about French current events.

From here, Marmier's travels took him on to Buda and Pest. A number of aspects of life here shocked him for various different reasons. Censorship he found to be just as harsh as in Vienna. He was disappointed to find the university poor, run down, and with very low standards of scholarship. His moral sensibility was offended by the 'honteux spectacles' presented by the mixed bathing at the thermal baths: 'Quelques planches', he suggests, 'suffiraient pour séparer les deux sexes et prévenir des scènes qui révoltent'.[40] There were, however, more pressing reforms to consider. As in Russia, he found the gap between rich and poor striking. He presents information about the Hungarian opposition and separatist movements, but argues that the nobility forming the official opposition would be more credible if they had set about reforming some of the more abusive of their own privileges. The nobility still retained, he explains, exemption from taxation; this of course meant that the burden fell on those least able to pay. He had gained first-hand experience of life for those at the bottom of the social hierarchy by making an extended sojourn in one particular village in order to gather detailed information. He witnessed the poverty of a local population doubly enslaved to both their lord and his creditors. He saw a young man being flogged in public for having demanded to be paid wages due to him; this so distressed Marmier that after having attempted to console the victim and his family, he made hasty excuses to leave the village the following day.

The need for reform in Hungary, he concludes, was urgent. The Austrian government could have lent their support to a gradual system of improvements, but seemed, in Marmier's eyes, 'n'être occupé que du désir de comprimer et d'étouffer en Hongrie tout projet de réforme et tout essai de

[38] *RN*, 1, 112.   [39] Ibid., 1, 117.   [40] Ibid., 1, 126.

progrès'.[41] The current situation was such, he argues, that Austria had now reached a point where it must decide whether to reinforce or to break off all links with Hungary:

> Que l'Autriche donc y prenne garde! Le système de précautions qu'elle a employé en Bohême, en Italie et dans le Tyrol, pourrait fort bien échouer en Hongrie. Je ne suis pas assez clairvoyant pour prévoir ce qui arrivera, mais je suis entièrement convaincu que la Hongrie ne peut rester dans l'état où elle est avec un gouvernement qui ne veut point tenir compte de ses besoins, une oligarchie qui s'affranchit de tout impôt, et un peuple réduit à un inique état de vasselage.[42]

From Pest, Marmier boarded a steamer bound for Mohacz (Mohács), Vukovar, Illok, and Petervaradin (Petrovaradin), before reaching Semlin (Zemun). The only thing which really interested him here was the local leech trade: Semlin itself, Marmier concluded, would hardly be worth visiting were it not for the fact that it lay on the opposite bank of the Danube from Belgrade. He was delighted to learn that there were no quarantine restrictions, but Belgrade turned out—initially, at least—to be something of a disappointment:

> Ce qui m'a paru si beau à un quart de lieue de distance, est affreux de voir de près. Une population sale et déguenillée sur le rivage, des Turcs dont la mâle stature et la belle physionomie contrastent avec les hideux haillons dont ils sont revêtus, des rues tortueuses, escarpées qui ressemblent à des escaliers brisés.[43]

Thanks to the French consul in Belgrade, Marmier was able to meet the chief rulers of the Turkish and Serb sectors of the city. In the Turkish sector, Durand de Saint-André arranged an audience with the pasha, 'ce courageux et malheureux Hafiz pacha'.[44] Marmier found the pasha to be a man of about sixty, straight-backed and sturdy, and with noble and honest features. He was wearing a blue frock coat buttoned up to the chin; a silvery beard fell to his chest, and on his head he wore a red fez decorated with an enormous blue silk tassle. He invited the Frenchmen to stay for dinner. The consul had alerted Marmier to the fact that the pasha was very interested in geography. Once engaged in conversation through the intermediary of a German interpreter, the pasha sent for an atlas so that Marmier could point out Iceland, the Faroes, Norway, and Sweden; he then asked numerous questions about the nature of the countries, the character of their populations and their national customs.

---

[41] Ibid., 1, 179.   [42] Ibid., 1, 186.   [43] Ibid., 1, 220.   [44] Ibid., 1, 225.

Two days later was a national day of celebration in honour of Alexander Karadjordjevic, the prince regent of Serbia. The consul invited Marmier to a reception at the palace. The prince is described as a man in his thirties, with dark hair and eyes, a bronzed complexion, and a generous and gentle expression. He welcomed the Frenchmen, who were given hookahs and introduced to a number of dignitaries including Vučić, Petronievič, and a number of senators. Marinovič, the prince's secretary, spoke French and offered to show Marmier around some of the city's public institutions. Everyone rose, Marmier noted, as the Russian consul walked proudly into the room 'comme un seigneur souverain chez son vassal'.[45] Serbia, Marmier states, belongs now in name only to the Turkish empire; but in its struggle for freedom from Turkish rule, it has fallen under the influence of Russia. Austria, England, and indeed France are criticised for giving Russia a free hand in 'une question qui est étroitement liée à toute la grande question d'Orient': indeed, he continues, '[i]l faudrait ne pas avoir la moindre idée de la Russie pour ne pas voir à quel but elle aspire en faisant tant d'efforts'.[46]

A steamer took him from Semlin to Moldova, Drencova and Orsova. Here he met up with a young Frenchman who was also heading for Valachia, so they hired a carriage together. At Tourno-Severin they stayed in a very basic hostel before leaving for Craïova. Along this road, Marmier was appalled by the scenes of poverty and degradation surrounding them on all sides: colonies of Bohemians crouching around brushwood fires, their children, brown and bushy-haired, some evidently in their teens, running around entirely naked. Further on, he was horrified to find that in the heart of Europe, Valachian families sheltered under shacks which would be considered unfit for animals in France. In all his travels, he could not recall seeing such extreme destitution as in Valachia. The situation was all the more shameful, he claimed, in that the country was one of the most fertile lands in Europe; the poverty was caused by social and political interests. The people were dehumanised and robbed of their dignity, 'ne possédant rien, ou presque rien, soumis à l'autorité absolue d'un maître qui fait peser sur lui le poids des impôts, le fardeau des corvées, lui prend la meilleure part de sa récolte, et le traite avec un profond dédain'.[47]

He also noted that the Valachian women were particularly downtrodden; the men took out on them all their frustrations for the way in which they were treated: the women, Marmier writes, are subjected to an 'esclavage de second ordre'.[48] While the men laze about in the sun, the women do most of the work. The Russians have designs on Valachia, Marmier concludes, and

---

[45] *RN*, 1, 236.   [46] Ibid., 1, 251.   [47] Ibid., 1, 289.   [48] Ibid., 1, 292.

the countries have much in common: 'aristocratie hautaine et peuple misérable, luxe extravagant des nobles et des princes, servage des paysans, ignorance partout'.[49] It came as a great relief to Marmier to climb back on board
the steamer in order to leave 'une région barbare pour rentrer dans les
domaines de la civilisation'.[50]

Three days after leaving Skala Gladowa, the boat arrived at Braila;
Marmier then visited Galatz, where he was horrified at the way heaps of
rubbish and rotting corpses of dead animals were left in the street for the
swarms of scavenging crows that gathered around. At Sulina, he boarded
the *Ferdinand*, the only Austrian boat able to navigate the Sulina canal. From
here, his route took him down the Black Sea coast and on to Constantinople
(Istanbul). Since no shipping was allowed into the Bosphorus before sunrise,
Marmier was able to appreciate the 'merveilleux tableau'[51] by daylight. The
splendour of the scene from afar, however, was matched by the squalor of
the city at close quarters. He was particularly anxious about the packs of
wild dogs roaming the streets, which he found to be something of a nuisance
in the daytime; at night, these 'bandes voraces'[52] constituted a real danger.

Entering Turkey during the period of Ramadan, he noticed the oarsmen
on the Bosphorus who were not allowed to eat or drink all day growing vis-
ibly thin, weak, and pale. It seemed to him also that religious tradition
was responsible for the way women were treated here: 'c'est le Coran qui
fait de la femme un être inférieur, qui l'asservit comme un esclave à la
volonté de l'homme et autorise le dégradant usage de la polygamie'.[53] In
Constantinople, Marmier boarded the *Tancrède*, a fine and swift vessel
which whisked him across the Sea of Marmara towards the Dardanelle
Straits. As he watched Turkey disappear into the distance, he contemplated
the 'ombre sinistre du despotisme turc', the 'malheureuses populations', and
'en admirant cette magique création de Dieu, je maudissais le stupide
pouvoir qui la régit, l'iniquité qui la désole, la lèpre qui la ronge'.[54]

In his writing on the Middle East and on Turkey and its empire in particular, Marmier constructs himself very much as a representative of French
colonialism: this aspect of his writing was to become more pronounced as
he ventured to countries where France had interests or aspirations. Here, he
repeatedly resorts to references to dirt, disease, idleness, and the failure of
the Turks to exploit natural resources. These are all features frequently
found in the writing of those in favour of colonisation in order to justify
their enterprise. Marmier is quite open about his colonialist views. A visit
to Rhodes, for example, prompts the following reflection:

[49] Ibid., 1, 293.　[50] Ibid., 1, 296.　[51] Ibid., 1, 331.　[52] Ibid., 1, 333.　[53] Ibid., 1, 382.
[54] Ibid., 2, 8.

> Quand les derniers liens qui soutiennent encore la Turquie viendront à se
> rompre, et quand les puissances occidentales auront à se partager les débris
> de cet autre Bas-Empire, la France n'aura-t-elle pas le droit de revendiquer
> cette belle île de Rhodes [. . .]. Rhodes, Chypre, la Syrie, les berceaux de la
> civilisation et du christianisme à la France civilisatrice, à la France chrétienne
> [. . .] qu'on laisse à la France [. . .] les contrées qui ont été grandes et qui
> doivent le redevenir, les pauvres races opprimées dont il faut briser les
> chaînes et renouveler la vie. C'est à la France à les prendre sous son généreux
> patronage, à les ranimer par sa propre force, à les éclairer par son génie.[55]

On the boat from Rhodes to Cyprus, he found himself travelling in the
company of a harem of forty Turkish women accompanied by 'une cohorte
de eunuques noirs et blancs'.[56] Judging the women from his masculine,
European standpoint, he concluded that 'pas une n'était jolie, et toutes
avaient des habitudes d'une saleté révoltante'.[57] This form of colonialist
rhetoric contrasts with the other form which was very popular at the time,
in which the oriental was equated to the exotic and frequently eroticised,
portrayed as the object of European masculine desire.[58] The harem of
course typified this trope. Although Marmier's response debunks this particular colonialist myth, it nonetheless serves to debase the women in question, falling back onto an alternative Eurocentric stereotype. It is interesting
that on previous journeys (for example, to Lapland), he may have judged
women by their appearance in terms of his own sexual desire, but avoided
falling into the clichés of ugliness, filth, and so on. The comments on
'others' generally, and on women in particular in his writing, are imbued
with a certain respect based on empathy which is lacking in his comments
on the Arab and Muslim worlds. Further colonialist rhetoric is employed by
Marmier in direct calls for control of the Middle East in the course of the
narrative. France, he says, has a 'magnanime devoir' to defend Catholicism
in the region where, according to Marmier, it is 'entouré d'ennemis, opprimé,
persécuté'.[59] In practical terms, the region is presented as backward and in
need of modernisation:

> Pour moudre le blé, on n'emploie que la meule antique à la main. Pour faire
> le vin, on use de si mauvais procédés que les raisins succulents des pentes du
> Liban ne donnent qu'une boisson amère et souvent impotable. L'olive même,
> le premier fruit du pays, est si mal préparée que les marchands ont toujours
> soin de faire venir, pour les Européens, des bocaux d'olives de Provence.[60]

---

[55] *RN*, 2, 59–60.   [56] Ibid., 2, 31.   [57] Ibid., 2, 32.
[58] See, for example, the writings of Richard Burton; or the paintings of Ingres or Delacroix.
[59] *RN*, 2, 115.   [60] Ibid., 2, 117.

After Rhodes, he went on to Cyprus in the company of Mas Latrie and Wœhrmann, with whom he had decided to continue his pilgrimage, where he met up with an old schoolfriend, Irénée Foblant, who was working as a doctor in a lazaret. From Cyprus, a steamer took him overnight across to Beirut. Here the ship was greeted by Péretier, chancellor of the French consulate. Marmier was immediately struck by the beauty of the country, 'cette nature si colorée et si chaude, si nouvelle pour ceux mêmes qui viennent de voir les beautés de l'Archipel [. . .] cette campagne couverte de figuiers, d'orangers, et cette mer étincelante'[61] and by the bustling cosmopolitan population. He had done a good deal of reading in preparation for his visit and had hoped to study 'questions d'origine, de dialecte, de culte, de coutumes anciennes et modernes qui se rattachent aux peuplades chrétiennes, musulmanes, schismatiques du Liban'.[62] He was deterred from these objectives, he writes, not by the potential dangers or the physical obstacles, but by the fear of adding to the already considerable diplomatic tensions in the region.

The French had supported Méhémet-Ali, viceroy of Egypt, in the Eastern crisis of 1840 when he initially resisted the British, Austrian, and Russian moves to limit his power in Syria. This led to British and Austrian fleets imposing a blockade on Syria, and to the British bombarding Beirut and ultimately sailing for Alexandria. As a result of this, Méhémet-Ali was forced to abandon Syria in return for which he would retain hereditary possession of Egypt. Thiers, who had been in charge of foreign affairs in France at the time, resigned over the affair. In the years immediately following this crisis, the Ottomans were unable to restore order in Lebanon, and there was an ongoing power struggle between the various communities (particularly the Maronites and the Druzes) with serious hostilities breaking out in 1842 and again in 1845, the year of Marmier's visit. These hostilities served as a pretext for the various countries to intervene in order to protect particular groups: in general terms the British lent their support to the Druzes and the Jews, the Russians supported the Orthodox, while the French moved to protect the Maronites and the Catholics. Marmier witnessed a number of incidents which prompted him to criticise in print not only the 'ambition effrénée de l'Angleterre et les intrigues de la Russie'[63] but also the failure of the French government, in his view, to provide its diplomats abroad with sufficient support and authority to fulfil their responsibilities.

It was in the light of these problems that the party made preparations for their pilgrimage through the Holy Land. In the past, Marmier laments, Ibrahim Pasha, son of Méhémet-Ali, had kept the marauding Bedouins

[61] Ibid., 2, 98.   [62] Ibid., 2, 102.   [63] Ibid., 2, 106.

firmly in check: now the road to Damascus was a no-go area, and even the route to Nazareth and Jerusalem was not considered safe. The travellers were accompanied by three officers from the *Belle-Poule* (Fontanges, Morand, and Lefebvre), local guides, and a guard supplied by the governor, 'un grand gaillard de six pieds de haut, portant à la ceinture un demi-quintal de sabres et de pistolets',[64] although they were warned that his presence would act more as a deterrent than as protection since despite his fearsome appearance, he would probably be the first to take flight if any Bedouins were spotted. Valuables were sent on in advance to Alexandria as a precautionary measure, and each member of the party was armed with two pistols and numerous letters of recommendation from the governor and the French and Russian consulates.

From Beirut they passed through El Khulda, crossing the river and making their way to Neby Yunas and then Seïda (Sidon la Grande) where they were offered lodging by Conti, the French consul. At this point in the narrative, Marmier again calls indirectly for French intervention by stressing the sufferings of the Maronites and the French role in their protection:

> Une quantité de Maronites forcés de fuir leurs demeures envahies par les Turcs, et leurs champs ravagés, erraient dans les rues, portant sur leurs figures l'empreinte d'une misère profonde et d'une cruelle souffrance. M. Conti en avait recueilli un grand nombre, et les pauvres gens étaient couchés là dans les galeries du khan, admirant encore la France qui leur donnait un asile dans leur abandon [. . .]. Mais le khan était trop petit pour tant de malheureux, et les dons de la France trop restreints.[65]

Their route took them next through Tyr, Ras-el-Beyad, and then St Jean d'Acre where they stayed in a Franciscan monastery. Whilst praising the work of the Franciscans, Marmier again took the opportunity to call for a greater Catholic influence in the area, notably the establishment of Lazzarist institutions along the coast of Syria and Palestine. From here they travelled through Saphori and on to Nazareth, Caïffa and Mount Carmel, Jaffa and Ramleh, accommodated largely by religious communities and diplomats. From Ramleh, they went on to Jerusalem.

Before reaching their destination, they made an obligatory visit—not without some trepidation—to Abou Ghosh, the head of one of the most important Palestinian families.[66] Marmier describes him as 'le chef d'une

---

[64] *RN*, 2, 120.   [65] Ibid., 2, 144.
[66] The name is transliterated variously as Abou Ghosh or Abū Ghūsh; Marmier writes Abou-Gosh or Abou Gosh. I am grateful to Nadia Sirhan for her help in finding out about this family. It would appear that their fortunes had been varied in the years immediately preceding Marmier's visit. Traditionally, they had derived their income from controlling the main roads to Jerusalem (see

des plus redoutables tribus de la Syrie',[67] a powerful leader who had 1,800 men under his command and could muster 6,000 in case of need; it was also in his power to close all the roads to Jerusalem if he so decided. The party had been given a letter of introduction for Abou Ghosh, who welcomed them into his palace and offered them fresh water, grapes, and pipes. Initially, the conversation was rather awkward, since they feared that 'le moindre mot imprudent pouvait éveiller une de ses rancunes, froisser une de ses susceptibilités',[68] but Abou Ghosh soon seemed at ease and shook hands warmly with each party member before they left, inviting them to stay with him on their return journey. Marmier was disappointed that they were unable to accept the invitation and remarked humorously that 'Abou Gosh est un très-aimable brigand, un de ces brigands qui font l'ornement d'un opéra et la fortune d'un romancier'.[69]

In the course of their journey through Palestine, the various sites are described in terms of their biblical connotations. In Jerusalem the party visited all the main biblical sites including the Via Dolorosa and the Church of the Resurrection. Here Marmier was shocked to see that while pilgrims were praying all around, Turkish soldiers were sitting drinking coffee, smoking, and chatting. The Turkish presence is described in terms such as 'honte', 'scandale', and 'iniquité musulmane'.[70] From Jerusalem there was a pleasant excursion to Bethlehem, although here he was disappointed by what he saw as the misguided redecoration of the grotto of the nativity in slabs of marble. He was also struck by the cramped and unhealthy conditions in which entire families lived and worked, producing crosses, rosaries, and other artefacts for the tourist industry. He also visited the Mount of Olives, the tomb of Lazarus, the plain of Jericho, and was able to bathe in the river Jordan (the site of Christ's baptism by John the Baptist according to biblical tradition and a popular destination for pilgrims).

Mordechai Abir, 'Local Leadership and Early Reforms in Palestine 1800–1834', in Moshe Ma'oz (ed.), *Studies on Palestine during the Ottoman Period* (Jerusalem: The Magnes Press, The Hebrew University Institute of Asian and African Studies, 1975), 284–310, esp. 289; and Donna Robinson Divine, *Politics and Society in Ottoman Palestine: The Arab Struggle for Survival and Power* (Boulder and London: Lynne Rienner Publishers, 1994), 16 and 20). During the Egyptian occupation, the family had joined the revolt in the early stages because the Egyptians had abolished their collection of fees from travellers on the road to Jerusalem, but Ibrahim Pasha then appointed some of the family's leaders to important administrative posts as compensation and in order to secure their support (Divine, *Politics and Society in Ottoman Palestine*, 60). New reforms followed the restoration of Ottoman power which limited the benefits enjoyed by the family and resulted in outbreaks of violence as the family sought to recover their losses in the early 1840s (Divine, *Politics and Society in Ottoman Palestine*, 101).

[67] *RN*, 2, 235.   [68] Ibid., 2, 237.   [69] Ibid., 2, 241.   [70] e.g. Ibid., 2, 268–9.

From Jerusalem, the party set off again for Jaffa, where they were met by Damiani (the French consul who had taken care of so many other visitors including Chateaubriand and Lamartine), then made their way to Ibna, Geth and Mejdal, Ascalon and Gaza. Here Marmier seized the opportunity to visit the local markets in order to sample the everyday life of the general population, before entering into protracted negotiations with a camel driver to take them across the desert to Cairo. The following day, the camels were brought to the door and Marmier climbed onto the back of his beast with a certain amount of trepidation. He soon took to this new means of transport, however, and noted that the camel is 'l'une des plus douces, des plus sûres, et des meilleures bêtes qui existent'.[71] The camel drivers also impressed him a great deal, yet this gives rise to more of Marmier's Eurocentric stereotyping: 'Le paysan arabe est, de sa nature, insoucieux et indolent; caractère de lazarone, peu difficile pour le présent et oublieux du lendemain, mais soumis en esclave à la main qui lui promet un salaire ou la menace d'un châtiment [. . .] et d'un zèle étonnant si on le force à l'action'.[72]

The clear suggestion is that here lies a hitherto untapped resource in the form of an as yet unexploited workforce. The 'paysan arabe', according to Marmier, is both lazy and irresponsible, and by implication therefore neither worthy of respect nor fit to be left to his own devices. As a group they could, however, quite easily be coerced to provide slave labour for an external power, either on the promise of financial reward, or indeed by threat of physical violence. This overtly capitalist-colonialist rhetoric is reinforced in slightly different terms a few pages later. The emphasis is shifted to one of supposed pity for the Arabs, who are victims of their past history, in need of rescue from the outside world:

> L'esclavage d'un millier de siècles l'a, de génération en génération, humilié, opprimé, écrasé. Mais que cet esclavage cesse, qu'un bras ferme le relève de sa chute, qu'une voix compatissante le rappelle à l'œuvre, le guide dans ses efforts, le soutienne dans son travail, et l'Arabe, enfant de ces races poétiques qui ont peuplé le midi de l'Europe de tant de monuments admirables, et l'Egyptien, dont les aïeux donnaient des leçons à la Grèce, reprendraient leur place dans la marche de l'humanité.[73]

These two sentences are brimming with colonialist cliché. The phrase 'reprendraient leur place dans la marche de l'humanité' effectively dehumanises the people described. At best they are represented as children (the word 'enfant', although used with a different emphasis, is significant in the context; it also reinforces the sense implied above of an individual unable to

---

[71] *RN*, 2, 368.   [72] Ibid., 2, 377.   [73] Ibid., 2, 381.

take responsibilty for himself) in need of a firm yet sympathetic guiding hand to be supplied, of course, by (French) colonial power.

The journey across the desert was largely uneventful, although at the frontier town of El-Arîsh, where they were obliged to set up camp for a week in order to comply with quarantine regulations, the party witnessed a storm which completely changed the topography of the landscape. Shortly after this break, it was discovered that the water container had leaked and there was no water left. Marmier became quite ill until a travelling merchant who joined the caravan kindly offered him his remaining supply of thick, green, warm water, which he drank greedily and which gave him the strength to continue on as far as Salahieh where they joined the Nile and were overjoyed to be able to gulp down large jarfuls of its yellow, muddy water. In Hanka they hired donkeys for the final stage of their journey.

Cairo fascinated Marmier, and he was overwhelmed by the cosmopolitan crowds and the mix of cultures. For him, it compared favourably with Constantinople (perhaps partly through his prejudice as a Frenchman). He notes that the advent of Méhémet-Ali's rule in Cairo brought with it an 'ère de grandeur et d'embellissement'[74] although he found much to criticise in social terms. Prominent among his concerns were the slave markets and the continuation of slavery. He was also profoundly shocked by the use of physical beating as a means of repression, which, he claims, reflects badly on the regime of Méhémet-Ali. He furthermore repeatedly criticises the wide gap between the opulence of the ruling classes and the extreme poverty and ill-health characterising a large sector of the population. It is curious, in the light of his comments about the 'paysan arabe' above, that he should have written with such passion about the abuses of power in Egypt: obviously to him there was no blatant inconsistency in his views.

One of the highlights of his visit to Cairo was an invitation to meet Méhémet-Ali, organised by the new French consul, Barrot.[75] Marmier found the viceroy reclining on a pile of cushions smoking a hookah, a servant fanning him with a palm leaf. Conversation was not difficult, since Méhémet-Ali was a good raconteur and took a keen interest in European politics. Marmier noted that he possessed a remarkable intelligence and outstanding diplomatic skills. The visit left him with a lasting impression 'de cette figure si vivace et si intelligente, l'éclair de cet œil scrutateur, et les modulations de ce langage en même temps si adroit et si animé'.[76] This is the last eyewitness

[74] Ibid., 2, 426.
[75] The brother of the politician Odilon Barrot: see J. M. Carré, *Voyageurs et écrivains français en Egypte*, 2 vols. (Cairo: Imprimerie de l'Institut français d'archéologie orientale, 1956), 2, 71.
[76] *RN*, 2, 441.

description to be written in French of Méhémet-Ali, who, by this time, was 76 years old and whose health was failing rapidly.

In December 1845, Marmier visited Méhémet-Ali's residence in Choubra, and made excursions to Heliopolis and to the pyramid of Cheops at Gizeh (al-Jizah). Marmier and his two companions paid for the services of Bedouin guides to take them up to the top of the pyramid, and then to view the interior. The visit turned out to be more exhausting than he had anticipated. No sooner were the guides engaged than Marmier was frog-marched at great speed, a guide on either arm, to the corner where the climb to the top began. The guides sprang nimbly from step to step dragging Marmier along behind them, not heeding his calls for a rest to catch his breath. It transpired that his guides were racing those accompanying Marmier's travelling companions to the top. Marmier records that his guides won, reaching the top of the 238 steps, some 136 metres according to Marmier, in five minutes flat. Marmier confessed to feeling that such visits to a place of burial were not entirely appropriate, although he was impressed by the grandeur of the edifice. More pointedly, though, in terms of Marmier's own social and political views, is his reflection that 'Quelle autre œuvre d'une utilité immense pour le pays Chéops n'eût-il pas pu faire avec les hommes, l'argent, les matériaux employés à celle-ci?'[77]

Marmier began to prepare for his departure from Cairo to Alexandria just as preparations were getting under way for the marriage of Méhémet-Ali's daughter. Barrot invited him to the festivities, but he had to decline as he had booked a passage back to France and time was running short. He was sad to leave Cairo: despite the glaring social inequalities and the poverty, he had found a certain peace of mind amidst the palm trees, in the gentle climate, and even in the immensity of the desert.

The voyage up the Nile in a small hired sailing boat took much longer than the forty-eight hours anticipated: four days after leaving Boulaq, they found themselves at Fouah, and resolved to leave the sailing boat at Hatfeh to hire an expensive—but fast—horse-drawn vessel from an English company. This mode of travel speeded things up considerably, and in only eight hours they had reached Alexandria. This, however, turned out to be a great disappointment since so little remained of the city's ancient origins. Marmier left without too much regret to board the *Luxor* for his voyage to Marseille.

This was the first region Marmier visited as a simple tourist 'et d'où je ne rapportais ni la traduction de quelque texte antique et ignoré, ni une

---

[77] *RN*, 2, 457.

découverte archéologique, ni une rare merveille enfouie pendant des siècles [. . .] et où je n'ai fait, dans mon ignorance, que regarder et rêver!'[78]

Although this work is indisputably one of Marmier's least original travel narratives—particularly in terms of the visit to the Holy Land and Egypt— it nonetheless has distinct merits. J. M. Carré notes that Marmier's *Du Rhin au Nil* is the first travel narrative of the region to be prefaced by 'une abondante bibliographie'.[79] He notes Marmier's learned references to the works of scholars such as Maillet, Savary, Volney, Marmont, and Clot-Bey. He judges that in comparison to Ampère's (admittedly more detailed) account of his journey the previous year, Marmier is the better 'tourist' in the sense that '[il] regarde mieux que Jean-Jacques Ampère, un peu gêné par sa myopie et sa littérature, et s'attarde avec complaisance auprès des conteurs, des bateliers, dans les bazars et dans les bains, il ne s'embarrasse pas de drogman et fait ses achats lui-même'.[80] Carré furthermore rates the eloquent and poetic style of the descriptions favourably even in comparison to descriptions of the same scenes by Nerval.[81]

Algeria

On his return to France, Marmier decided to stand for election in the ward of Pontarlier in the general elections to be held at the beginning of August 1846. The idea of standing for election seems to have been in his mind at least since 1843, when his wife was still alive. A letter that month from Mélanie Bixio to the poet Auguste Brizeux states that

> Je lui [i.e. à Marmier] en veux beaucoup pour sa conduite envers la famille Demesmay. Il a l'idée fixe de supplanter Auguste à la députation et il a commencé par se brouiller, dès son mariage, c'est décidément ce que je n'avais jamais voulu entendre jusqu'ici: un garçon sans cœur et plein d'ambition.[82]

Although Marmier's motives for standing against Demesmay may not have been entirely straightforward, this letter is clearly written without knowledge of the wider circumstances.

Auguste Demesmay had been elected to parliament on 9 April 1842 to represent Pontarlier, filling the seat vacated by Jouffroy. Best remembered for his support of the reduction on salt tax, he also penned some minor works

---

[78] Ibid., 2, 466.
[79] Carré, *Voyageurs et écrivains français*, 2, 71.
[80] Ibid., 2, 72. Ampère's *Voyage en Égypte et en Nubie* was first published in 1868.
[81] Ibid., 2, 70. Nerval's *Voyage en Orient* was published in 1851.
[82] Brizeux, *Un poète romantique et ses amis*, 31.

on the Franche-Comté. Some of Marmier's antipathy to Demesmay, a former friend, can be explained by a long handwritten note attached to a copy
of Demesmay's *Traditions populaires de Franche-Comté* (1838) conserved
in Marmier's library. According to Marmier, Demesmay was working on
this book when Marmier returned from Germany with a collection of
German legends, several of which he translated into French for Demesmay,
at the latter's request. Demesmay then, according to Marmier, unscrupu-
lously included these almost verbatim in his book, as if they originated in
the Franche-Comté. Not content with this first piece of fraud, Demesmay
then had the temerity to ask Marmier to review the book in the *Revue de
Paris*: when he refused, Demesmay was apparently furious. This note also
mentions Demesmay's fury over the 1846 elections, but without details,
although Marmier concludes that 'en l'un et l'autre cas, j'ose dire que de
mon côté était la raison'.[83]

Within a month of the elections, however, Marmier addressed a letter to
the voters of Pontarlier informing them of his decision to withdraw his candidature.[84] He declares that he is standing down in favour of Demesmay in
order that the latter may see through Jouffroy's bill on the salt tax;
Demesmay was duly elected.[85]

Between the dates of announcing his candidature and then withdrawing
it, Marmier had set off on his travels again. On 22 June, *Le Moniteur
Universel* announced that Marmier would be departing the following day
for Port-Vendres, where he would meet up with the Ministre de l'Instruction
publique, Salvandy, whom he was to accompany, with Salvandy's family, on
a ministerial mission to Algeria.[86]

France at this time was heavily involved in Algeria: colonisation had
begun in the last days of the reign of Charles X in 1830 and had continued
under Louis-Philippe. A strong resistance movement had sprung up which
the Armée française d'Afrique had been fighting in a very controversial war.
One of the most brutal French generals, whose methods had been widely
criticised in the French press, was Bugeaud. Bugeaud had made himself
unpopular in France by his heavy-handed repression of the insurrection of
April 1834. In 1836, he was sent to Algeria, where he set about crushing the
Arab resistance. In 1840 he was made Governor General of Algeria and continued his relentless and ruthless agenda. The brother-in-law of Salvandy,

---

[83] Bibliothèque Xavier Marmier, Pontarlier, note attached to a copy of Auguste Demesmay,
Traditions populaires de Franche-Comté (no folio nos.).
[84] The letter is dated 3 July 1846. 'Chambre des Députés. Elections Août 1846. A Messieurs les
électeurs de l'arrondissement de Pontarlier' (Paris: Crapelet, [1846]).
[85] *Le Moniteur Universel* (4 August 1846), 2117.
[86] *Le Moniteur Universel* (22 June 1846), 1865.

Henri-Louis Feray, was due to marry Bugeaud's daughter Éléonore, and Salvandy's trip to Algeria appears to have been due, at least in part, to the forthcoming wedding. Marmier's published account of the trip, *Lettres sur l'Algérie*, makes scant mention of this wedding (although it is recorded in some detail in his private papers); he simply states that Salvandy was on a fact-finding mission to Africa in preparation for a parliamentary debate on the subject.[87]

Marmier's role in this journey appears not to have been—on the surface at least—an official one, in the sense that he claims not to have been asked to write an official record of the tour. He emphasises at length in his letters that he is writing in a personal and unofficial capacity, in that Salvandy 'n'attendait point de ceux qui s'en allaient de plage en plage, de fête en fête avec lui, une narration complaisante'.[88] He nonetheless admits that

> je m'estimerais heureux s'il se trouvait dans mon humble livre assez d'obser-
> vations vraies pour justifier la faveur que M. de Salvandy a bien voulu m'ac-
> corder en m'associant à son excursion, en ajoutant ce nouveau témoignage de
> bienveillance à tous ceux qui depuis longtemps me lient à lui par une loyale
> reconnaisance.[89]

Such statements read in conjunction with the body of the text bring into serious doubt Marmier's claims to be writing 'avec une entière indépendance'.[90]

On 30 June 1846, a fine morning, Marmier boarded *Le Météore* at Port-Vendres, along with Salvandy and family, for the crossing to Algeria. On the morning of 3 July the vessel sailed into the port of Algiers to be greeted in person by Bugeaud amidst tremendous pomp and ceremony to the accompaniment of bugle fanfares and cannon salutes.[91] This was in effect to set the tone for the entire visit. It would appear from his letters that Marmier had little or no contact with the indigenous population, but that he travelled as part of Salvandy's retinue accompanied by huge military escorts and receiving the kind of treatment normally associated with royalty. It was, as Marmier points out,[92] the first official ministerial visit to the Algerian

---

[87] *Lettres sur l'Algérie* (Paris: Arthus Bertrand, [1847] (cited hereafter as *LA*), 5–6. The letters were previously published in *Le Correspondant* on 25 October and 25 December 1846, and 10 February and 10 May 1847. The wedding was, however, mentioned in *Le Moniteur Universel* (17 July 1846), 2046; see also *Journal*, 2, 9–10.

[88] *LA*, p. xli.   [89] Ibid.   [90] Ibid.

[91] The date is given as 4 July according to *L'Alchbar* quoted in *Le Moniteur Universel* (12 July 1846), 2026. Marmier says 3 July (*LA*, 35), and his letter to the voters of Pontarlier is dated 3 July and purportedly written in Algiers (see above, n. 84).

[92] *LA*, 36.

colony. The pomp and show of strength were of course all part of the demonstration of supremacy on the part of the French.

The ministerial visit was based on a tour of the areas or positions which were in some sense considered strategic to the programme of colonisation. The first few days were spent in and around Algiers; the party soon settled into a routine, with excursions in the daytime and evenings spent as guests of the Bugeaud family at the governor's official residence. Marmier thoroughly enjoyed these gatherings and found Bugeaud to be 'un vrai capitaine de l'Empire, qui unit au courage, à l'intrépide résolution des généraux de cette époque, un bon sens pratique et un jugement admirable'.[93]

Marmier appears to have been reasonably sincere in this judgement: we know from his private papers that he still kept in touch with Bugeaud after the latter's return to France;[94] in 1868 Marmier still refers to him as 'l'excellent maréchal Bugeaud'.[95] Although Bugeaud enjoyed great popularity amongst his men, he was less well thought by many of his officers[96] and today he is largely remembered for his unashamed brutality.[97]

The wedding took place on 7 July 1846, and the next visits scheduled for Salvandy's party were to Plida (Blida) and Médéa, leaving on 8 July.[98] Unusually for him, Marmier was unable to leave his sickbed, having come down with a bout of 'fièvre intermittente',[99] probably some form of malaria, which was rife in Algeria at this time.[100] Marmier was dosed with quinine which effectively reduced the fever, but which caused characteristic side effects: 'la quinine vous enflamme les entrailles, vous trouble la vue, et dérange tellement le système auriculaire, qu'il semble qu'on ait trente-six

[93] *LA*, 70.   [94] See, for example, *Journal*, 1, 59.   [95] Ibid., 2, 92.

[96] See Marc Michel, 'Une guerre interminable', in *L'Histoire: L'Algérie des Français: présentation par Charles-Robert Ageron* (Paris: Seuil, 1993), 39–51 (44).

[97] See, for example, Sadek Sellam, 'Algérie: des colons aux colonels: camps, extermination, éradication', in *Parler des camps, penser les génocides: textes réunis par Catherine Coquio* (Paris: Albin Michel, 1999), 322–48, quoted at http://www.algeria-watch.de/farticle/sellam.htm, accessed 18 January 2006; see also Michel, 'Une guerre interminable', 44–6; and Charles-Robert Ageron, *Histoire de l'Algérie contemporaine (1830–1988)*, 9th edn. (Paris: Presses universitaires de France (collection *Que sais-je?*), 1990), 15.

[98] *Le Moniteur Universel* (12 July 1846), 2046.

[99] *LA*, 91.

[100] Malaria was an important cause of mortality amongst French troops and settlers alike at this time. Michel ('Une guerre interminable', 43) claims that in the first few months of 1840, 4,200 troops died from disease of one sort or another; in particular, according to Philip D. Curtin, 13.2% of all deaths caused by disease, and 6.87 in every thousand deaths between 1837 and 1846 were ascribed to 'remittent fever' (overall deaths from disease during this period accounted for 81.54 per thousand). See Philip D. Curtin, *Death by Migration: Europe's Encounter with the Tropical World in the Nineteenth Century* (Cambridge: Cambridge University Press, 1989), 36.

mille sonnettes dans les oreilles'.[101] Quinine, he concludes, is a 'remède souvent pire que le mal'.[102]

Fortunately, by the time Salvandy and Bugeaud had returned from Médéa around 16 July, Marmier was on the road to recovery, and was able to join the group as they boarded the *Panama* for the day's voyage to Tenez. From here they travelled on to Orléansville (El-Asnam) via Dahra. On this leg of the journey Marmier was enthralled to travel with the colourful Yousouf who had reached an almost legendary status in France at this time.[103] As Marmier remarks, 'tout le monde connaît l'étonnante histoire de cet officier intrépide, ses amours romanesques avec la fille du bey de Tunis, sa condamnation, sa grâce obtenue par une victoire incroyable, puis sa fuite audacieuse, et les actes de courage par lesquels il a gagné ses grades dans notre armée'.[104] Arriving back in Tenez, they were greeted by a national guard of four hundred men standing to attention. The *Panama* now took them in just a few hours to Cherchell, where Marmier was proud to be present as Salvandy announced that the treasure in the museum would be left there 'afin que les archéologues vinssent eux-mêmes les voir là, et que Cherchell gardât tout l'honneur de son passé, toute la jouissance de ses trésors'.[105]

The party returned thence to Algiers where a ball was being held in honour of the newlyweds (Feray and Éléonore Bugeaud), after which they boarded the *Montezuma* for a trip to Bougie (Béjaïa), 'l'une des situations les plus pittoresques qu'il soit possible d'imaginer'.[106] Here they were greeted with the now familiar pomp and ceremony: 'Les troupes étaient rangées sous les armes; le clairon sonnait gaiement dans les rues. Tous les habitants en habits de fête étaient sortis de leurs demeures pour jouir du spectacle d'une parade militaire éclairée par un jour splendide'.[107]

In the evening they returned aboard the *Montezuma* for the overnight journey to Bône (Annaba), after which the party set off for Hippone (the ancient Numidia). An elegant carriage prepared for Mme de Salvandy travelled under heavy escort ('le général avec ses aides de camp; le colonel Clerc avec les principaux officiers de son régiment, un escadron de hussards'[108]). Marmier, who was an experienced horseman, having travelled long distances across Lapland and Iceland on horseback, joined the escort, but

---

[101] *LA*, 92.   [102] Ibid.

[103] The *Petit Robert* entry for Yousouf gives a taste of the life that had so captured the public imagination: 'YOUSOUF (Joseph VANTINI, dit). Général français (île d'Elbe, v.1810–Cannes, 1866). Esclave à Tunis, il se mit au service de la France, à la tête d'un corps d'armée indigène. Il prit part à la prise de Bône, fut à l'origine de l'expédition contre Constantine et joua un rôle important dans la prise de la smala d'Abd al-Qādir [Abd-el-Kader] (1843) [. . .]'.

[104] *LA*, 105.   [105] Ibid., 146.   [106] Ibid., 154.   [107] Ibid., 166.   [108] Ibid., 172.

found his equestrian skills unequal to the 'chevaux africains impétueux, fougueux, se cabrant sous le mors et piaffant dans un tourbillon de poussière'.[109] He was saved from total humiliation by colonel Clerc, a fellow Franc-comtois, who took Marmier's horse by the reins and led it.

From Hippone, the tour continued on to La Calle (El Kala) on the Tunisian frontier, then the *Montezuma* sped them via Bône (Annaba) on to Philippeville (Skikda). From here they took the Constantine road and made their first halt at El-Arouch. A pleasant surprise awaited Marmier here: his brother Hyacinthe (Mami) had travelled from his garrison at Sétif via Constantine to El-Arouch to meet him. Hyacinthe had joined the army at the age of eighteen as a volunteer in the 3rd regiment of hussars. By 1834 he was a 'sous-officier' in Saumur; he was eventually promoted to 'sous-lieutenant' in 1840 and then posted to Africa the following year in the 3rd regiment of chasseurs. In 1844 he suffered serious injury when a bullet went through his thigh.[110] As a result of this he was promoted to the rank of lieutenant and awarded the cross of the Légion d'Honneur. Apart from the wound, Marmier notes, his brother 'n'a eu qu'une quinzaine de fois la fièvre'[111] since arriving in Algeria.

The following day, the party was off again, en route for Constantine via Smedou. The two carriages transporting the official party were escorted by a party of chasseurs which included Hyacinthe; horses and escort were changed at Smedou, and the party was again greeted by a great deal of pomp and ceremony on arrival at Constantine, this time by General Bedeau,[112] in whom Marmier noted a 'heureux mélange de qualités sérieuses et de qualités aimables. Au courage du soldat, il unit la perspicacité d'un administrateur habile et prudent'.[113] Having spent a few days at Constantine, the party was whisked back to Philippeville (Skikda) and back on board the *Montezuma* for the next stage of the visit. Salvandy ordered a stop at Djidjelli, 'pauvre garnison cernée, comme celle de Bougie, par les kabyles, mais plus solitaire encore, plus abandonnée à elle-même',[114] in order to boost the morale of the troops stationed there.

---

[109] *LA*, 173.

[110] See *LA*, 205 and François-Xavier Marmier, *Souvenirs de famille pour mes enfans* (Paris: Plon, 1896), 26. The footnote added in the latter appears to be erroneous in the dates given for Hyacinthe's various exploits. The expedition at the oasis of Zaatcha, for example, happened in November 1849.

[111] *LA*, 204.

[112] Marie-Alphonse Bedeau (1804–63), French general who had a distinguished career in Algeria from 1836 and was made Governor General in 1847. He was later Ministre de la Guerre in the provisional government in 1848 and went into exile after December 1851.

[113] *LA*, 220.   [114] Ibid., 222.

Now the party were to move on to the 'districts d'Algérie qui ont été le théâtre de la guerre la plus acharnée [. . .], la région où la voix d'Abd-el-Kader a toujours soulevé contre nous un fanatisme ardent'.[115] At Mostaganem they were greeted by General Pélissier[116] and the party travelled hence to Oran on board the *Montezuma*. At Mers-el-Kebir (Marsa al-Kābir) they met up again with the *Montezuma* and prepared to visit Djemma-Gazouat (Ghazaouet) on the Moroccan frontier in the company of General Cavaignac,[117] whom Marmier describes as 'un de ces hommes vers lesquels on se sent de prime abord attiré par une indéfinissable séduction: une belle tête blonde, une physionomie d'une rare distinction, d'une expression grave, mélancolique, un peu maladive'.[118] Here the party were to witness at first hand an army in the field; for Marmier, a stirring sight:

> l'artillerie, la cavalerie, l'infanterie rangées symétriquement par bataillons, par compagnies, les munitions et les bagages au milieu, un amas de petites tentes grises qu'on prendrait de loin pour une nuée d'oiseaux, d'autres tentes plus hautes et plus élégantes pour les officiers, un pêle-mêle de chevaux, de mulets, de faisceaux d'armes, d'ustensiles de cuisine, et tous les hommes en mouvement, ceux-ci se rendant à l'appel du matin, ceux-là attisant en plein air le feu qui fait bouillir la gamelle, d'autres astiquant les sabres et leurs buffleteries, chacun à sa besogne de chaque jour. Au premier abord, on ne voit qu'une image confuse, un tourbillon de diverses couleurs.[119]

After an inspection of the troops and a tour of the camp, it was back on board the *Montezuma* for the return journey to France via Gibraltar— which Marmier did not like because of the heavy English presence, and which he left 'avec joie, comme on sort d'une boutique où l'on n'a trouvé ni un objet attrayant, ni une figure avenante, comme on sort d'une citadelle où l'on a peur de se voir enfermé'.[120] The following day they stopped at Cádiz to reload with coal, then it was on to Tangiers where they were all carried ashore piggyback-style by local Moors. Marmier's final reflection on Morocco before the *Montezuma* departed for the two-day voyage to Port-Vendres, summarises the tone of the entire volume of letters: 'l'empire du Maroc est dans un état de barbarie grossière qui ne se doute d'aucune idée

---

[115] Ibid., 277.
[116] Aimable Jean-Jacques Pélissier (1794–1864), Maréchal de France. He took part in the Spanish expeditions in 1823, served in Algeria from 1839 to 1854, then took over (from Canrobert) charge of the Crimean army; he won the title of Maréchal at Sébastopol in September 1855. He ended his days as Governor General of Algeria (1860–4).
[117] Louis-Eugène Cavaignac (1802–57), general and politician who was sent to Algeria in 1832 and was made Governor General in 1848. As Ministre de la Guerre, he crushed the insurrection of June 1848.
[118] *LA*, 277.   [119] Ibid., 273–4.   [120] Ibid., 290.

intelligente et vit au jour le jour, sous le régime despotique et rapace de ses pachas, sous le poids de son ignorance'.[121]

Although here applied to the Moroccans, this is the kind of vocabulary used systematically about the Maghrebins in general and the Algerians in particular throughout the text. If the record of Marmier's visit to the Middle East already showed signs of colonial rhetoric (dirt, idleness, incapacity for self-determination, etc.), the *Lettres sur l'Algérie* show a harsher side yet. The Algerians are referred to variously as 'brigands', 'fripons', 'barbares',[122] and as being inveterate cheats and liars. Even an apparently friendly gesture when a group of 'Arabes' come to offer welcome refreshment to the party consisting of Bugeaud, Salvandy, Marmier, and various officers of the military on their way to Dahra gives rise to the received views that 'plus un Arabe proteste de son dévouement [. . .], plus il faut se défier de lui' and that 'la première qualité indispensable à quiconque a des relations avec eux, est de ne jamais croire un mot de ce qu'ils disent'.[123]

The French army, on the other hand, is generally glorified, both by the arguments presented and the language used. In the preface to the volume of letters, Marmier states that

> il m'était doux d'entrer dans un pays où la vieille et historique pensée de la France éclate dans toute sa mâle énergie, où le soldat renouvelle chaque jour par son courage et sa patience, les grandes pages de notre histoire chevaleresque où l'armée donne une nouvelle gloire à cette devise qui faisait palpiter le cœur de nos pères: Honneur et patrie![124]

Terms such as 'gloire', courage', 'patience', 'mâle', and so on are used repeatedly in the text to refer to the French occupying forces. We might also add to the list 'hardiesse', fermeté', and 'résignation';[125] 'mission céleste'[126] or 'troupe brillante'[127] amongst others.[128] These were not opinions necessarily shared by all Frenchmen at this time: indeed, opinion in France was deeply divided about the methods employed by the military. Marmier's comments take account of a number of these criticisms, albeit rather speciously at times. Bugeaud, for example, whose portrait is penned in the most glowing terms, is, according to Marmier, 'un homme dont les actes ont été tant de fois amèrement critiqués, et souvent dénaturés par une presse partiale et hostile'.[129] For the indigenous population, however, the years of Bugeaud's

---

[121] *LA*, 307.   [122] e.g. Ibid., 37 ('brigands', 'barbare'); ibid., 171 ('fripons').   [123] Ibid., 129.
[124] Ibid., pp. xxxvii–xxxviii.   [125] Ibid., p. xxxviii.   [126] Ibid., 51.   [127] Ibid., 208.
[128] The only criticisms ever voiced by Marmier about the army in Algeria are in fact criticisms of their treatment and conditions, in particular of their uniforms, which he feels are ill-adapted to the climate and cause unnecessary discomfort.
[129] *LA*, 69.

leadership are now generally recognised to have been 'seven years of violence [. . .] at the hands of an army of more than 100,000 men, during a
campaign known as the *razzia*'.[130]

Pélissier likewise, according to Marmier, is a man 'dont l'aimable et gracieuse physionomie ne ressemble guère à celle que lui ont faite les journaux'.[131] Most worryingly, a long defence is offered in justification of
Pélissier's actions at Dahra the previous year. In 1845 an insurrection of the
Ouled-Riah instigated by Bou-Maza led to confrontation with French
troops and hundreds of people seeking refuge in the mountain caves of
Nekmaria. Pélissier ordered brushwood fires to be lit and burned at the
mouths to the caves in order to asphyxiate the besieged rebels. The following day, several hundred corpses of men, women, and children were discovered. Sources disagree about the actual body count: figures given by
historians range from five hundred to a thousand victims. Even Marmier's
account, which seeks to justify the action, mentions 'un millier de cadavres
humains, mêlés sur le sol à des cadavres d'animaux'.[132] Parliamentary questions were asked in France about the incident; Bugeaud took full responsibility, claiming that the French military had no other possible course of
action in the circumstances. This phrase summarises the second part of
Marmier's long (four-page) but unconvincing argument. Marmier claims on
the one hand that the fires lit at the entry to the caves were intended only to
'répandre une crainte salutaire',[133] but that once they were lit, they were
fanned by the wind and impossible to extinguish.[134] He acknowledges that
all the victims had perished 'd'une mort affreuse';[135] he adds, however, the
following qualification:

> Cependant il n'est peut-être pas inutile d'observer que la guerre contre les
> Arabes oblige à des rigueurs que l'opinion publique condamnerait en Europe
> comme des monstruosités. Les Arabes ne sont que trop disposés à regarder
> tout ménagement d'humanité comme un signe de faiblesse, et ils usent envers

---

[130] Peter Dunwoodie, *Writing French Algeria* (Oxford: Clarendon Press, 1998), 10. According to
Dunwoodie, Bugeaud 'decades later, still epitomized in popular memory the violence of the
implantation of French colonialism in North Africa' (10).

[131] *LA*, 231.

[132] Ibid., 234. See Ageron, *Histoire de l'Algérie contemporaine*, 16; Michel, 'Une guerre interminable', 46; Sellam, 'Algérie', 2.

[133] *LA*, 234.

[134] It appears that asphyxiation was a fairly systematic policy at the time. Sellam claims that
Cavaignac had already used the same method against the Sbéahs the previous year, and Saint-
Arnaud used precisely the same technique just a few weeks after the Dahra massacre, again against
the Sbéahs. See also Benjamin Stora, *Algeria 1830–2000: A Short History*, trans. Jane Marie Todd
(Ithaca and London: Cornell University Press, 2001), 5.

[135] *LA*, 234.

nous, chaque fois que l'occasion s'en présente, d'un régime de cruauté qui nous conduit forcément à des représailles de même genre. Qu'on suppose à la place des Ouled-Riah quelques-uns de nos bataillons renfermés et cernés dans les cavernes du Dahra; il est certain que les Arabes ne leur auraient pas offert la moindre capitulation, ou les auraient, après de perfides promesses, traités sans pitié.[136]

Pélissier himself, according to Marmier's account, 'parle sans embarras de la catastrophe [. . .]. L'insurrection du Dahra [. . .] résistait encore [. . .] aux efforts de nos troupes. Il fallait à tout prix écraser ce foyer de révolte.'[137] Words such as 'oblige', 'forcément', 'à tout prix' are used in the context of the massacre to convey the notion that Pélissier's action was necessary or inevitable. The phrase maintaining that 'la guerre contre les Arabes oblige à des rigueurs que l'opinion publique condamnerait en Europe' constructs the 'Arabes' quite clearly on a different plane from Europeans; cruelty against them, it is suggested, is not only justified but necessary, and this should not be measured against what is acceptable or not in Europe. Marmier in any case confounds his own (clearly disingenuous) argument presented in these lines by his earlier claim that the fire had spread accidentally and that the massacre was unintended; the two parts of his argument are therefore contradictory.

Marmier rejoices that Algeria, described variously as a 'côte barbare', or a 'repaire de brigands', has been 'conquis par nos armes'.[138] Yet the French, he warns, must not be complacent. The Arabs are not yet 'subjugués'[139] and must be kept firmly in their place:

> En attendant que ces continuelles velléités de révolte soient non pas anéanties, ce qui ne peut être le résultat de quelques années, mais suffisamment comprimées, en attendant que les Arabes s'habituent à ne pas se lever [. . .] nous regardons le gouvernement militaire comme une nécessité inévitable pour l'Algérie, comme le seul qui puisse maintenir l'ordre par son unité et inspirer par sa force une crainte salutaire à nos ennemis.[140]

Thus although Marmier elsewhere passionately condemns colonialist injustices (particularly, it must be said, those perpetrated by England, Turkey, or Russia, but even by Denmark, a country he otherwise loved), he here sides firmly with the French military. And rather than pass over some of the more outstanding atrocities, he attempts to justify them.

Just a few apparently minor asides cause the reader to look behind the rhetoric, although even then with no degree of certainty. The first occurs in

---

[136] *LA*, 235.   [137] Ibid., 232.   [138] Ibid., 37.   [139] Ibid., 74.   [140] Ibid., 77.

the body of the text as Marmier describes a military display in honour of the ministerial tour in Tenez:

> une garde nationale de quatre cents hommes rangés sous les armes. Bufleteries blanches, fusils brillants, shakos vernis, fifes et tambours, rien n'y manquait [. . .] nous n'épargnons aux Arabes aucune de nos richesses: s'ils ne finissent pas par être contents de nous, c'est qu'ils sont vraiment d'une nature bien endurcie et bien ingrate.[141]

It seems difficult to take the final clauses at their face value, and to believe that such a strong irony could have been unintentional. Most striking, however, is the rather stark but enigmatic conclusion to the book: 'J'ai fini mon itinéraire algérien. Pardonnez les fautes de l'auteur'.[142] None of Marmier's other travel narratives finish on a similar note. What exactly is the reader being asked to forgive? The fact that this is perhaps the one text in which Marmier has no new information to offer on any of the peoples or locations visited—a fact of which the reader was made aware in the introduction? Or could it be that Marmier is aware that whilst defending the military and the plan of colonisation, he is hardly encouraging the government plan for colonisation? Certainly his accounts of sickness, heat, dirt, squalor, hostility of the indigenous populations, and reciprocal military atrocities would not have been reassuring to a prospective French settler.[143] It is most tempting, of course, to read it as a plea to forgive the author his greatest fault: an unquestioning adoption of the racist right-wing colonialist discourse, and a clumsy attempt to defend indefensible brutality. And yet the colonialist and military line are given such emphasis throughout that this seems improbable. The matter is evidently not clear cut.

The party was back in France by 13 September 1846, when *Le Moniteur Universel* announced that Marmier would be accompanying Salvandy on a

---

[141] Ibid., 144.   [142] Ibid., 312.

[143] From 1841 a policy of settlement had begun in earnest: 'Frenchmen were settled on the State lands confiscated from the Bey and from other leading Algerians, or in strategic centres [. . .]. In the same way French soldiers in Algeria were encouraged to visit France towards the end of their period of service, to procure a wife and to bring her back to Algeria and settle there. Free land was given by the Government, and intermarriage with natives discouraged': A. J. Grant and Harold Temperley, *Europe in the Nineteenth and Twentieth Centuries (1789–1950)*, ed. Lillian M. Penson, 6th edn. (London, New York, Toronto: Longmans, Green & Co., 1953), 311. Although written over a hundred years later, the political overtones of these lines are remarkably similar to those found in Marmier and other nineteenth-century writers. The final clause about intermarriage is interesting in the context of the Marmier family. Obviously social interaction at any level between an army of occupation and an indigenous population is likely to decrease alienation and hence levels of hostility. Hyacinthe Marmier later married an Algerian, Fathma ben Massaoud ben Nezzar, the daughter of a chief. Hyacinthe appears to have been in every other sense a model of conformity in French military terms, working his way up to become brigadier general.

tour of the departments;[144] he spent some time preparing *Du Rhin au Nil* for publication in book form (the preface to this work is dated September 1846), and presumably also preparing the volume on Algeria. On 22 November he was appointed to the post of 'conservateur' at the Bibliothèque Sainte-Geneviève in Paris.[145]

[144] *Le Moniteur Universel* (13 September 1846), 2365.
[145] AnF, F17/21256.

11

Revolution and Republic (1848–50)

From Paris to New Orleans

On 9 February 1848, Marmier wrote to Salvandy (at this point still Ministre de l'Instruction publique), requesting a year's paid leave of absence from his post at the Bibliothèque Sainte-Geneviève as from 15 March in order to visit South America. Here, he intended to 'continuer des études comparatives d'ethnographie et de géographie que j'ai déjà poursuivies dans diverses régions, [. . .] d'achever par là un livre dont j'ai depuis plusieurs années préparé quelques premiers matériaux'.[1] In his diary, however, he notes with disappointment:

> J'avais fait faire un livre pour y écrire la relation de mon voyage au Brésil. Quelles douces heures j'ai passées à rêver à toutes ces splendides régions que j'allais voir! Que de fois le matin, dans la journée, le soir, j'ai erré d'avance par la pensée sur les flots de l'océan Atlantique, sur les crêtes des Cordillères, dans les îles de l'Océanie! Tout était résolu. J'avais une feuille de route officielle. J'allais dire adieu à mes parents, puis m'embarquer à Toulon! Quel doux songe de voyageur! Et quel réveil, mon Dieu.[2]

The events to which he refers are, of course, the February days of the 1848 revolution, and Marmier found himself confined to Paris. Salvandy lost his portfolio in the change of government, and was replaced by Falloux, a liberal Catholic. On 25 December 1848, Marmier addressed a similar letter to Falloux, asking Falloux to ratify Salvandy's decision to allow him to take paid leave for his voyage (this time extending the period to fifteen months!), postponing the departure date by one year to February 1849. He emphasises that he is not requesting any additional grant, and that the additional expenses over and above his salary of 3,000 francs would be met by him personally. He even advises the new minister that 'toutes les pièces concernant la décision prise envers moi par M. de Salvandy se trouvent dans les cartons de la division de lettres de votre ministère, et sont enregistrés au bureau du secrétariat'.[3] Such a request could not fail to move a minister who was in any case an old acquaintance of Marmier's, and an 'arrêté' of

---

[1] AnF, F17/21256.   [2] *Journal*, 1, 59.   [3] AnF, F17/21256.

6 January 1849 authorises the leave as from 1 March. An official letter written the same day to inform him of the minister's decision ends in a friendly
unofficial greeting: 'J'espère cependant que vous reviendrez: mille vœux!'.
Marmier is also informed that he will be expected to return to his post on
1 June.[4]

An undated letter to Sainte-Beuve written shortly before his departure
invites the latter to a farewell dinner:

> Cher ami, je vais me rejeter encore une fois dans ce sentiment que vous avez si
> poétiquement appelé la Volupté des regrets. Je pars à la fin de la semaine
> prochaine pour l'Amérique du Sud. En me préparant à cette nouvelle fuite, je
> ne puis oublier qu'autrefois vous me tendiez la main au moment suprême, et
> que vos bonnes paroles me fortifiaient le cœur. [. . .] Voulez-vous venir me dire
> adieu vendredi 25 à 6 heures. Vous trouverez à ce dernier banquet notre fidèle
> Demandre et quelques autres de mes amis.
>   Mille compliments de cœur à votre chère mère.[5]

Despite the good wishes of his friends and even the minister, Falloux,
Marmier set out with a heavy heart. The events of 1848 had depressed him
profoundly. The royalist sympathies he had inherited from his family had
been confirmed and strengthened by his relationship with Louis-Philippe.
For Marmier, the revolution was 'l'action de quelques centaines d'individus
échappés en partie des bagnes ou des prisons'.[6] He could discern no possible virtue in the republic as he saw it: 'en haut comme en bas, je ne vois que
la passion égoïste ou l'intérêt individuel qui hier se parait d'une cocarde
monarchique'.[7] He had always dreaded the advent of a republic in France,
and 'maintenant que la voilà venue, je la crains plus que jamais'.[8]

It was therefore in low spirits that he finally boarded an American
steamer bound for New York at Le Havre on 9 September 1849.[9] Although
by this time the wave of European emigration towards the Americas was in
full swing, and a transatlantic crossing was not regarded as a particularly
novel adventure, it was nonetheless still an uncomfortable and unpleasant
experience for most passengers. Marmier was first of all struck by the stark
contrast between the conditions available to first- and second-class ticket
holders, which he saw as representative of American society ('la société
américaine n'admet guère que deux classes, les riches et les pauvres').[10] The

---

[4] AN, F17/21256.
[5] Spoelberch de Lovenjoul, BIF, Lettres adressées à Sainte-Beuve, D606, 10, fo. 159.
[6] *Journal*, 1, 64.   [7] Ibid., 1, 75.   [8] Ibid., 1, 61.
[9] *New York Herald* (14 October 1849); discovered and quoted by Jean Ménard, *Xavier Marmier et le Canada* (Quebec: Presses de l'Université Laval, 1967), 1.
[10] *Lettres sur l'Amérique: Canada, États-Unis, Havane, Rio de la Plata,* 2 vols. (Paris: Arthus Bertrand, 1851) (cited hereafter as *LAC*), 1, 16.

first-class passengers (including, for once, Marmier, who normally chose the simplest means of transport available) paid 650 francs for the crossing. For this sum, they had the privilege of a comfortably furnished cabin, the use of a lounge, a spacious deck on which to take fresh air, and copious (if not very appetising) meals served four times a day. With a couple of exceptions, he found his travelling companions in the first class extremely dull, but was simultaneously fascinated by the variety of characters in the second class, and horrified by the conditions in which they were forced to travel, which he compared to conditions on slave ships. The price of a second-class ticket was 60 francs: for this, two hundred and forty German emigrants were piled into a small space below the dog kennels, chicken cages, and cow stalls in the depths of the steerage. Here, thirty mattresses were arranged on planks in two layers; two foot above these was another layer of thirty straw mattresses. Each mattress had to be shared by four people, and each was surrounded by a clutter of belongings, including packing cases, food, and cooking implements: their tickets included only water and a primitive means of heating food; they had to provide their own meals. Apart from this 'sombre cavité',[11] as Marmier refers to it, the second-class passengers had access only to a narrow strip of the deck between the two masts, amidst cargo and a double line of barrels. This was the only space where these passengers could see the sky or take a breath of air. It was here that they also had to do all their cooking, 'se disputant une place pour leur poêle ou leur cafetière, puis emportant leur déjeuner à moitié cuit pour ne point trop irriter ceux qui attendent'.[12] Marmier hints at how dreadful the living quarters can become during a storm, and says that even on a calm day, 'la lumière pénètre à peine aux deux extrémités. On s'avance à tâtons à travers un amas de sacs, de caisses sur un plancher humide et boueux où gisent tous les pauvres êtres débiles, las de rester sur leur couche et trop faibles cependant pour sortir de cet antre de douleurs'.[13]

The primitive nature of the arrangements even by the middle of the century was emphasised by the death of a small child during the crossing in stormy weather. Marmier remarks justly that although seasickness on its own is not fatal, the combined factors of cramped and unhygienic quarters and a storm can, and often does, prove fatal. The mother and father of the child, working people from Wurtemberg, wept helplessly as the child's body was wrapped in sailcloth, bound to a plank, and slid into the sea:

> Le navire ne s'arrête même pas pour la cérémonie funèbre. La même lame qui le pousse en avant emporte dans son repli le mort qu'on lui abandonne. En un

[11] *LAC*, 1, 18.   [12] Ibid., 1, 19.   [13] Ibid., 1, 18–19.

clin d'œil elle s'est ouverte sous le poids du cercueil, en un clin d'œil elle s'est renfermée et rien à sa surface n'indique qu'elle vient d'engloutir une victime humaine.[14]

The horror of the conditions on board that vessel were to haunt Marmier for years to come. In the introduction to his translation of Gerstäcker's *Aventures d'une colonie d'émigrants en Amérique*, published some fifteen years later, he recalls that

Ce que j'ai vu là de misères morales et physiques, chaque fois que je descendais du large espace des premières places au milieu de cette pauvre légion d'ilotes, ce que j'ai entendu, pendant une traversée de trente jours, de soupirs et de lamentations, d'accents de regret et de cris d'angoisse, jamais je ne l'oublierai.[15]

Before even setting foot on American soil, Marmier was firmly against American capitalist values and the priorities that these implied, particularly in view of the fact that the previous year, the shipping company concerned had made an enormous (at that time) profit of 150,000 dollars:

On ne comprend pas qu'une compagnie qui réalise sur les voyages de ses navires de si larges bénéfices qu'une de ces compagnies d'Américains, qui affectent de si bien connaître la Bible et qui parlent si haut de philanthropie, puisse tranquillement laisser subsister un tel état de choses, et traiter comme un gouvernement ne traiterait pas des repris de justice, une cohorte de gens dont l'unique crime est de n'avoir qu'un trop petit nombre de dollars à offrir au Mammon des Etats-Unis.[16]

After a thirty-five-day crossing—'cinq mortelles semaines'[17]—the ship finally arrived in New York on 14 October. After a very brief spell in New York, Marmier took a steamer called the *New World*, which turned out to be extremely luxurious, to Albany. From on board the steamer, he watched New York disappearing rapidly into the distance:

Derrière nous, les églises, les maisons en briques des riches quartiers de New York s'effacent rapidement, mais à notre droite longtemps encore apparaissent les chantiers, les fournaises de ses faubourgs, vraie cité de Vulcain, où sans cesse la fumée du charbon de terre s'échappe en nuages épais des hautes cheminées, où l'acier siffle dans l'eau qui le trempe, où le fer est tordu, effilé, arrondi sous toutes les formes, où des milliers d'ouvriers façonnent à grands coups de marteau les énormes machines qui bientôt subjugueront les vagues des deux océans.[18]

[14] *LAC*, 1, 36.
[15] Friedrich Gerstäcker, *Aventures d'une colonie d'émigrants en Amérique, traduites de l'allemand par Xavier Marmier* (Paris: Hachette, 1881), p. vii. This text was first published in 1855.
[16] *LAC*, 1, 19.   [17] Ibid., 1, 39.   [18] Ibid., 1, 45–6.

He spent his free time on the trip observing American manners, and was clearly unimpressed by what he saw. Marmier, normally so open-minded and well-disposed to the customs of the countries he visited, could find little of interest in the American character. The average American, according to Marmier, 'est en ce monde pour faire circuler des dollars et des billets de banque'.[19] The capitalist ideal has, in Marmier's eyes, transformed materialism into a national religion: 'la banque est son temple, le registre en partie double sa loi, et l'or californien son soleil. Qui prononce ici ce grand mot d'argent est sûr de tenir les esprits attentifs et les oreilles éveillées'.[20] This, according to Marmier, is the only subject which can arouse the Americans out of their normal state of stupor. Even the most simple request for information, he says, is met with a blank gaze; at one point, on a train journey, he concludes that 'les Américains ne lisent rien et ne regardent rien. Ils ruminent en silence quelque spéculation. C'est la seule différence qu'il y ait entre eux et les coffres qu'ils ont déposés dans le wagon des bagages'.[21]

The greed of these 'chiffres ambulants et dévorants qu'on appelle des Américains',[22] who are also compared to sharks and pike,[23] is also exhibited at mealtimes. As on the transatlantic ship, on board the *New World* four meals were served daily, the first between seven and eight in the morning. At the sound of the gong, these 'animaux affamés'[24] would rush to the dining room to pounce on their breakfast of haunches of roast beef, whole ox-tongues, ducks, and chickens, all accompanied by dishes of potatoes, loaves of bread, and other 'mets légers' (light delicacies).[25] The scene was not a pleasant one:

> Sans s'inquiéter de son voisin, sans se soucier d'une des règles des plus banales de notre politesse européenne, chacun tire à soi tout ce qui se trouve à sa portée et entasse sur une ou deux assiettes des pyramides monstrueuses de viandes, de beurre, de légumes. Puis le voilà travaillant des mains et des dents, comme si chaque seconde lui était comptée, ne parlant pas.[26]

After this snack, they would all fill in time at the bar until the next meal was served. This lack of grace in table manners is matched, in Marmier's eyes, by an equally unattractive physical appearance:

> Imaginez, s'il vous plaît, une maigre stature avec des poignets osseux, des pieds d'une dimension qui ternirait à jamais le blason d'un gentilhomme, un chapeau renversé sur le derrière de la tête, des cheveux plats, une joue enflée, non point par une fluxion accidentelle, mais du matin au soir par une boule de tabac, des lèvres jaunies par le suc de cette même plante, un habit noir aux

---

[19] Ibid., 1, 47.   [20] Ibid., 1, 269.   [21] Ibid., 1, 236.   [22] Ibid., 1, 61.   [23] Ibid., 1, 55.
[24] Ibid., 1, 56.   [25] Ibid.   [26] Ibid.

pans effilés, une chemise en désordre, des gants de gendarme, un pantalon à
l'avenant;

and he finishes with the droll comment: 'et vous aurez, je puis le dire, l'exact
portrait d'un Yankee pur de sang'.[27]

On arrival at Albany, Marmier immediately caught the 'chemin de fer
égalitaire' to Montreal. This mode of transport was less luxurious than the
New World: the passenger accommodation consisted of two long benches
placed lengthways in a carriage in the form of an omnibus. The behaviour of
his travelling companions was, however, true to form, and he found himself
wedged between two individuals with a propensity for spitting. It was with
tremendous relief that he eventually arrived in Montreal, where he immediately felt at home, attributing this to the civilising French influence. The fact
that Marmier was already quite well-known in Canada by this time may also
have contributed to feeling at ease. *Le Canadien* announced his visit, describing him as 'trop connu de nos lecteurs pour qu'il soit nécessaire de leur faire
l'historique du poëte et du nouvelliste dont les douces et suaves inspirations
leur ont fait passer des moments si agréables'.[28] Despite the satirical humour
of his American descriptions, his experiences in the United States had left
him profoundly depressed:

> Je ne puis vous dire les douces émotions que j'ai éprouvées à mon entrée dans
> ce pays, au milieu de ces fidèles commémorations de la France. Mon rapide
> passage parmi les froids Américains m'avait littéralement gelé le cœur et la
> langue. Je n'osais plus m'approcher d'un de ces ours de comptoir qui ne
> répondent à mes avances que par une sorte de grognement, je sentais qu'il n'y
> avait aucune espèce d'aimant, ni de point de jonction entre les mercantiles
> pensées de cette race additionnante et multipliante, et les fantaisies de ma
> pauvre nature de voyageur. J'avais fini par me tirer à l'écart, et malgré mon
> horreur pour cette romantique situation, j'entrais forcément dans la classe des
> êtres incompris [. . .] Ma pensée se ravive; mon cœur se dilate. Je commençais
> à me croire à demi mort. Je suis ressuscité.[29]

In Canada, he was able to fulfil a dream he had held ever since his journey through Lapland: to visit a settlement of native Americans ('une de ces
vaillantes tribus [. . .] que les Européens ont écrasées ou refoulées au fond
des forêts'[30]). He was particularly anxious to discover whether their physical characteristics, their customs, their superstitions and their lifestyle bore
any resemblance to those he had witnessed in Laplanders. He wished, in

---

[27] *LAC*, 1, 60–1.
[28] *Le Canadien* (9 November 1849); discovered and quoted by Ménard (*Xavier Marmier et le Canada*, 80).
[29] *LAC*, 1, 97–8.   [30] Ibid., 1, 123.

short, to 'faire une curieuse comparaison ethnographique entre eux et mes amis les Lapons'.[31] Having travelled to the St Louis Falls (about ten miles from Montreal) to visit the Iroquois tribe, he was therefore greatly disappointed to find a village of a thousand people living in houses built in well-ordered streets; the houses had windows, beds, chairs, and all manner of European furniture. To complete his disappointment, two young Indian girls spoke to him in English, 'la langue de leurs maîtres. L'idiome de la perfide Albion nous poursuit jusqu'au milieu d'une tribu iroquoise'; whereupon he hastened to take leave of 'ces enfants dégénérés'!'[32]

He next travelled up to Quebec, where he was warmly welcomed; he sent a cable for the first time in his life, and was highly impressed by the way in which a message to New York, which would normally take three days to be received and a further three to be returned, could now be conveyed in six hours. From here, he took the train back to Saint-Hyacinthe where he admired the scenery bordering the Yamasha river, which he could see from his window: 'les rives agrestes de l'Yamasha, l'immense plaine silencieuse, parsemée de forêts sombres, coupée seulement d'un côté par les cimes bleuâtres de la montagne de Belœil, et fuyant au nord comme un océan sans fin'.[33] Here he stayed with someone referred to simply as M. de S., who introduced him to a rich neighbour whose two children entertained him one evening by singing Canadian folk songs. He also visited several ordinary country people: as always, it was here that he felt most at ease, and wrote of the 'chaste simplicité, [. . .] le calme bienfaisant qu'on y respire'.[34]

The eve of his departure from Canada was spent in Montreal, where a dozen local residents had collaborated to prepare a farewell dinner for their French visitor. Sad to leave Canada, he departed reflecting on what the future might hold in store for the country in the light of its current failure to attract immigrants. The first possibility which struck him was that of annexation to the United States, which, he wrote, would be disastrous, in that the Canadian national identity and culture would simply be swamped 'comme l'eau de leur Saint-Laurent dans les vagues de l'Océan'.[35] An alternative envisaged was a continued association with England, which, although regrettable, would be preferable to annexation 'à son odieuse fille, la république des États-Unis'!'[36] He concludes these speculations, however, on an optimistic note:

> Pour moi, je me plais à croire à l'avenir du Canada. Je vois là un sol fertile qui tôt ou tard ne peut manquer d'attirer des colonies de laboureurs, et sur son

---

[31] Ibid., 1, 125. [32] Ibid., 1, 129. [33] Ibid., 1, 185. [34] Ibid., 1, 186. [35] Ibid., 1, 199.
[36] Ibid., 1, 196.

sol une population honnête au sein de laquelle il est agréable d'habiter. C'est vers cette région que les émigrants français devraient se diriger; ils y trouveraient tout aussi aisément qu'aux États-Unis un moyen d'existence, et de plus leur langue, les souvenirs vivaces de la France, l'image de la lointaine patrie.[37]

Marmier was to maintain his contacts with Canada throughout his life. In Paris, a steady stream of Canadian visitors would climb the flights of stairs to his little flat in the Latin quarter. In 1860 he published a novel, *Gazida*,[38] based on his experiences in Canada, for which he was awarded a prize by the French Academy the following year.[39] In 1881, he was to write to Maxime Du Camp deploring France's indifference to the disaster in Quebec, which he refers to as 'notre sœur' and 'notre France par delà l'Atlantique'.[40] In 1883, he published a volume entitled *A la maison*, which includes a chapter on 'La littérature française du Canada';[41] the work of Chauveau is referred to here, and Marmier recounts the 'douces heures que j'ai passées avec lui et quelques-uns de ses amis à Québec'.[42] In 1883, the French Academy was invited by the Governor General of Canada to send a representative to the second annual session of the Canadian Royal Society; Marmier was elected to represent the Academy, an invitation which he accepted gladly. At the last minute, however, his ill health (and presumably his age, since he was now seventy-five years old) prevented him from making the journey, to his intense disappointment. Further details of Marmier's association with the French Academy are given in subsequent chapters, and further particulars of his Canadian contacts and his work on Canada are to be found in Jean Ménard's *Xavier Marmier et le Canada*.[43] In particular, Ménard concludes that 'Marmier fut un des premiers écrivains français de quelque envergure qui s'intéressa à la colonie après la conquête'.[44] To this effect, he quotes an obituary of Marmier published in Canada in 1892 which claims that 'ce fut M. Marmier qui révéla le premier à la France, après un siècle de conquête, qu'il existait encore au Nord de l'Amérique des

---

[37] *LAC*, 1, 192–3.

[38] *Gazida* (Paris: Hachette, 1860).

[39] 'Rapport de M. Villemain, secrétaire perpétuel de l'Académie française sur les concours de l'année 1861', in Académie française, *Recueil des discours, rapports et pièces diverses 1860–1869* (Paris: Firmin Didot, 1866), 413–28 (419).

[40] Institut de France, Fonds Maxime du Camp, MS 3748, 30, fo. 2.

[41] *A la maison, études et souvenirs* (Paris: Hachette, 1883), 260–99.

[42] Ibid., 294.

[43] See above, n. 9.

[44] Ménard, *Xavier Marmier et le Canada*, 172.

Canadiens-Français'.[45] Ménard further claims that 'grâce à Marmier et à Ampère, la France découvrait le folklore du Canada'.[46]

On leaving Montreal, Marmier travelled by ship to Kingston (Lake Ontario) and then on to Rochester on board the *Dame du lac* which, despite its name, was a most inhospitable vessel whose staterooms were glacial, and where supper consisted of mouldy bread and rancid butter. The Canadian ships, mused Marmier, have less poetic names, but are more pleasant. Obliged by a feeling of nausea to leave the 'longue et ténébreuse cellule décorée du titre de salon',[47] he went up on deck. Although he had to run up and down to keep his feet warm, he was nonetheless able to contemplate the spectacle of Lake Ontario. He was perhaps a little disappointed to discover that on one side he could distinguish only the hazy blue outline of New York State, and on the other, the sight of waves stretching to infinity as on the open sea.

In Rochester, he was not prompted to revise the opinion he had formed of the Americans six weeks before: 'mêmes figures moroses, même rudesse et même saleté'.[48] Despite the 'tourment' and 'ennui mortel'[49] of having to dine among them, he was able to console himself with the thought that the following day, he would visit the Niagara Falls. Nor was he to be disappointed. The seasoned traveller who had by this time visited a good part of the globe, from the geysers of Iceland and the icy peaks of Spitzbergen to the deserts of Algeria and Palestine and the Egyptian pyramids, and who held a strong antipathy by this time for anything American, was moved to tears by the sight of the Niagara Falls: 'En face de la cascade, j'ai été saisi d'une telle surprise, d'un tel ravissement, que je suis resté comme cloué sur le sol, ne poussant qu'un cri d'admiration. Puis, l'émotion a paralysé ma voix et m'a rempli les yeux de larmes'.[50]

After viewing the falls, he went on to visit the home of a German immigrant family. Although he had no letter of recommendation, he was not one to stand on ceremony, and simply addressed the father of the family in German, introducing himself and explaining that he had not yet been able to visit a German farm in America. The man was delighted to hear his native language and welcomed Marmier into his home like a long-lost friend to talk about Germany and German politics.

The next stage of his journey took him from Buffalo to New York. The first leg of the journey was by train, and Marmier, now forewarned and thus

[45] E. Rameau de Saint-Père, 'Lettre de France, La Mort de Xavier Marmier', *La Minerve* (3 November 1892), 2; quoted in Ménard, *Xavier Marmier et le Canada*, 173.
[46] Ménard, *Xavier Marmier et le Canada*, 72.   [47] *LAC*, 1, 215.   [48] Ibid., 1, 218.   [49] Ibid.
[50] Ibid., 1, 220. Chateaubriand had of course famously described the falls in *Atala* (1801).

forearmed, was able to put his waistcoat and travelling bag out of the spitting range of his fellow passengers. These precautionary measures taken, he opened a book, read, and then watched the countryside; his fellow travellers did neither. By evening, he was on a boat bound for New York, which pleased him no more on his second visit than on his first. Turning his attention to the press, he comments on the quality of the 2,400 newspapers available in the United States, which he says consist of nothing more than a mass of personal diatribes, vulgar chronicles, puerile anecdotes, and a confused medley of political and commercial notices, the whole swamped in a sea of advertisements. The typical American attitude to literature is summarised for him by an anecdote about an American who was told that Murray paid Byron 1,600 guineas for a canto of *Childe Harold*, whereupon he exclaimed enthusiastically that he wished that he could have written *Childe Harold*. But when he was told that Béranger occupies only a modest house in Passy, and that his entire fortune extends only to a modest annuity, he ridiculed the achievements of the latter, suggesting that he would have been better advised to go into commerce.[51]

Marmier also reflects on the reasons for the unparalleled crime rate in New York, and comes to the conclusion that the principal cause is the fact that so many criminals wanted by the police in Europe are able to take refuge there. Since no passport is necessary for entry, and American citizenship and all the rights that this bestows are open to all, there are, according to Marmier, many arch-criminals pursuing their lives of crime quite openly in the States: 'Nulle part, j'en suis convaincu, il n'existe dans la proportion de la population autant de fripons patentés et de filous de grandes rues qu'à New York. L'étranger y est à tout instant exposé à se voir très doucement dupé, ou audacieusement volé'.[52]

From New York, he travelled on to Philadelphia, where the sight of the penitentiary kept his mind on the subject of crime. Here he gives expression to one of the flashes of quite modern liberal insight which characterise his work together with the more reactionary views expressed elsewhere, confirming the impossibility of relegating Marmier to a particular political or indeed human 'category'. For him the penitentiary is

> de tous les genres de châtiments inventés par les sociétés humaines pour punir l'infraction à leurs lois [. . .], le plus froidement barbare. Oui, je crois que les tortures du moyen âge, les plombs de Venise, étaient moins redoutables que ce sépulcre dans lequel on ensevelit ici le condamné. Les bourreaux alors n'attaquaient que le corps, ne laceraient que la chair; ici, c'est l'âme même que l'on livre au plus affreux supplice; on enlève au captif l'usage des trois organes

[51] *LAC*, 1, 274.   [52] Ibid., 1, 284–5.

par lesquels la pensée s'alimente: l'ouïe, la vue, la parole [. . .] il me paraît que ce système est on ne peut mieux conçu pour conduire une partie de ses victimes à la folie, et d'autres à l'idiotisme.[53]

In Washington, Marmier visited the Capitol, where he found the spectacle very similar to the Palais Bourbon, with the exception that the members of the American parliament spit with remarkable aim at a distance of fifteen paces. After watching a vote being taken three times which left the issue in question quite unresolved, he went to visit the library and the other rooms of Congress. His tour ended with a visit to the home of the American president (presumably Zachary Taylor), which was open once a week to any American citizen who cared to visit. Of all Marmier's encounters with national leaders, this must surely have been the least memorable: 'L'aimable étrangère qui m'avait fait l'honneur d'accepter mon bras, s'est avancée devant le président qui lui a tendu la main, en lui disant: "How do you do?". Elle m'a nommé, il s'est tourné vers moi, en me tendant la main, et en me disant: "How do you do?" '.[54]

Marmier's next stop was in Baltimore, whence he boarded the train for Cumberland; for once, this was a journey he rather enjoyed, spending pleasant hours contemplating 'une nature qui n'a point encore été scalpée par l'industrie'.[55] At Cumberland, he faced a new experience: the American stagecoach. Generally, he preferred the stagecoach to the train; by this stage of his career, he had experienced numerous different modes of transport, but the latest appears to have been in a class of its own:

> une caisse en bois posée sur quatre roues et destinée à charrier les voyageurs sur les routes que la locomotive n'a point encore favorisées de ses bienfaits. Mais quelle caisse! et quelle route! Nous étions neuf serrés l'un contre l'autre comme des harengs, et tombant dans les ornières, et sautant sur les cailloux comme si nous avions été affligés de la danse de Saint-Guy.[56]

The torture of this twenty-four-hour journey was exacerbated by the behaviour of his fellow-travellers:

> sept gracieux Américains, chiquant, crachant, et pour se mettre plus à l'aise, ôtant leurs bottes. Une faible timide jeune fille assise à l'un des angles de cette infâme boîte souffrait sans mot dire, et le lendemain matin, nous l'avons trouvée évanouie. Quant à moi, j'ai passé la nuit à rejeter d'un côté ou de l'autre un énorme corps sale qui sans cesse retombait sur moi et deux énormes jambes qui semblaient avoir juré d'écraser les miennes.[57]

From Cumberland he travelled on to Pittsburg via Brownsville, and then down the Ohio to Cincinnati, a journey of forty hours, this time in a

---

[53] Ibid., 1, 302–3.   [54] Ibid., 1, 330.   [55] Ibid.   [56] Ibid., 1, 340.   [57] Ibid., 1, 340–1.

magnificent boat. After a short stay here, he was about to buy a ticket for New Orleans on board the '*splendid and fast-running*'[58] steamer the *John Hancock*, when he overheard a conversation between two Americans from which he gathered that such a move would be ill-advised. The boilers of the said *John Hancock* had apparently been condemned by the inspectorate, and the general state of the vessel was so bad that it had been refused insurance cover. Marmier thus purchased a ticket for travel on the rival *Western World*, in the hope that it would prove at least to be in a fit state of repair. The whole incident provoked a good deal of thought on Marmier's part about the irresponsible nature of a government which imposes no binding obligation on shipping companies to ensure that their vessels are seaworthy, or their crew capable:

> Il n'y a point de loi qui puisse empêcher un bateau avarié d'exposer la vie de ceux qui se confient à lui. Bien plus, il n'y a point d'examen pour ceux qui sont appelés à diriger dans les parages les plus dangereux un bâtiment gigantesque. Le capitaine est ordinairement un associé de la compagnie qui lance le bateau, un négociant qui de son comptoir sédentaire passe sur un comptoir ambulant, et l'ingénieur, le pilote, le machiniste, sont ce qu'il plaît à Dieu.
>
> Aussi, que d'explosions! que de catastrophes! et sur les fleuves de l'ouest plus encore que dans les autres parties des Etats-Unis! La navigation de ces fleuves, abstraction faite de la qualité des bateaux, est par elle-même très dangereuse.[59]

He estimates at thirty or forty the number of steamers lost in western waters, and the average existence of a boat there about four years. During that period it must recover the initial outlay and make the profits anticipated: any active service beyond four years is an unexpected bonus for its owner. And yet, he reflects, the American is not dissuaded from his travel. About one month previously, the *Louisiana* had exploded, depositing the remains of her boilers along with hundreds of corpses on the quayside at New Orleans. The following day, not a steamer had a passenger less. 'Je devrais admirer une telle intrépidité', Marmier muses, 'et dans mes vieilles idées européennes, j'ai regret de songer que les séductions de la fortune peuvent inspirer le même courage que les sentiments chevaleresques de gloire, de religion, d'amour'.[60]

Marmier's journey happily passed off without incident, leaving him time to register with astonishment the ignoble way in which the American men relegate their wives to a rocking chair after dinner, and then neglect them for the remainder of the evening: 'Et les Américains se vantent de leur respect pour les femmes!'.[61] The *Western World* meanwhile steamed on

---

[58] *LAC*, 1, 364.   [59] Ibid., 1, 364–5.   [60] Ibid., 1, 368.   [61] Ibid., 1, 373.

peacefully past Tennessee, where the sight of the cotton plantations reminded Marmier that this 'terrible culture, après avoir alimenté notre industrie, menace de la détruire'.[62] The cotton plantations of Tennessee were succeeded by the sugar plantations of Louisiana. He expresses regret that 'deux fois ce pays nous a appartenu, et [. . .] deux fois nous l'avons abandonné; la première je ne sais pour quelle raison, la seconde pour une somme de soixante-quinze millions, la quinzième partie de nos budgets annuels'.[63] Arriving in New Orleans, he is struck by the thought that the journey he has made from Quebec has been like 'un voyage à travers les ruines de l'ancienne France, partout les traces d'une domination qui n'est plus, d'un empire plus grand que celui d'Alexandre, dont les Américains et les Anglais se sont partagé les dépouilles'.[64]

In New Orleans, he found the same warm welcome that he had experienced in Canada. This is attributed to the fact that both were former French colonies and had retained the civilising French influences. If Marmier's overall attitude towards colonisation appears rather illogical, his attitude towards French colonisation remains quite consistent. His stand on the issue of slavery is even less clear. In his *Lettres sur l'Amérique*, in the chapter devoted to Washington, he claims to put forward his unreserved opinion. He says that the free black man who in theory enjoys civil liberties in the northern states, is in fact condemned by the colour of his skin to 'l'état de domesticité [. . .] comme un paria enchaîné dans un état d'abjection dont il ne lui est pas permis de sortir'.[65] In many ways, he maintains, the lot of the Russian serf, who belongs to his lord, is preferable to that of the 'free' black man in the northern states of America. Whilst admitting that those of African origin are happier 'sur leur sol natal, sous le soleil d'Afrique, qui est leur foyer héréditaire, qu'aux colonies', he nonetheless argues that they are 'plus heureux cent fois dans le paternel esclavage des colonies que dans l'ignominieuse liberté qui leur est octroyée par une partie de l'Amérique'.[66]

Even this highly dubious defence of slavery in the South is belied, however, by the doubly inconsistent diatribe launched in New Orleans, in which no pretence is made of having the best interests of the slaves at heart. Here, Marmier, like the materialist Americans whose unbridled form of capitalism he claims to despise, reduces the whole subject to a matter of finance. Despite professing to have been profoundly disgusted at the sight of a slave auction, where he witnessed a mother being sold separately from her child, he claims that as things stood at that time, slavery is, for economic reasons, a necessary evil: 'Il n'est pas possible de songer à cultiver sans les nègres sous

---

[62] Ibid., 1, 379.   [63] Ibid., 1, 383.   [64] Ibid., 1, 423–4.   [65] Ibid., 1, 312.   [66] Ibid., 1, 314.

l'ardent climat des États du Sud, ni le coton qui exige un travail très-assidu, ni la canne à sucre, qui dans la Louisiane doit être renouvelée chaque année'.[67] Exploitation of one's fellow man, he seems to imply, is acceptable in the economic interest if his (or her) skin happens to be black. In an astonishingly materialistic and inhumane manner, he discusses slaves purely in terms of their monetary value:

> Un nègre représente par la somme qu'il a coûté un intérêt annuel de deux cents à deux cent cinquante francs. Le maître lui doit de plus la nourriture et le vêtement. A ce prix, jamais on n'aurait des ouvriers libres. A supposer cependant qu'on augmente les prix du coton et du sucre, qu'on puisse employer à la culture de ces deux plantes des manœuvres qu'il faudrait payer fort cher, il n'est pas possible d'admettre qu'on puisse sans un grave péril affranchir tout à coup trois millions d'individus, dont les passions éclateraient sans doute dans l'ivresse de la liberté au milieu de la société qui les a trop longtemps contenus. Enfin, on doit penser que les nègres sont une propriété acquise en vertu des lois.[68]

He goes so far as to criticise the provisional government which he sees as having betrayed its principles of fraternity by the compulsory emancipation of slaves. This, he claims, has 'ruiné des blancs',[69] who received only an average indemnity of four hundred francs for slaves who had originally cost three or four thousand each. Whilst they retain ownership of their plantations, he continues, these are virtually useless to them without the slaves. The newly freed slaves, for their part, he declares indignantly, 'veulent jouir de la vie en hommes libres. Ils ne travaillent que quand il leur plaît et comme il leur plaît, aux conditions qu'ils imposent, au prix qu'ils exigent pour les labeurs auxquels ils étaient naguère patiemment soumis. La culture du sucre devient peu à peu impossible'.[70] Furthermore, he warns, one day, the freed slaves 'ne se contenteront plus de leur salaire. Avec les idées d'égalité qui leur sont prêchées [. . .] ils s'indigneront de leur état d'ouvriers mercenaires. Ils voudront avoir aussi leurs terres. Pour les avoir plus vite, ils les prendront'.[71] He foresees 'une catastrophe sanglante, terrible' if a 'répression énergique' is not imposed.[72] As a conclusion to this offensive tirade, Marmier predicts the rupture of the union between North and South on the issue of slavery, thus hinting at some of the tensions which were to give rise to the civil war in just over ten years' time.[73]

---

[67] *LAC*, 1, 446–7.   [68] Ibid., 1, 447.   [69] Ibid., 1, 422.   [70] Ibid., 1, 423.   [71] Ibid.
[72] Ibid.

[73] 'Rupture de l'Union! Tel est en effet le danger qui menace la république américaine. Quand les deux moitiés de cette immense contrée auront acquis plus de développement [. . .] le sentiment de son pouvoir rendra ses susceptibilités plus vives, elle repoussera avec colère ce qu'elle tolère

From New Orleans to Montevideo

On 31 December 1849, Marmier parted with much regret from his new friends in New Orleans, and boarded the *Ohio*, bound for Cuba. New Year's Day saw the *Ohio*, the 'léviathan des bateaux américains',[74] steaming at the full speed of her 1,000-horsepower engines through the blue waves of the Gulf of Mexico. On the fourth day after their departure, all the passengers gathered together on deck. At first light of dawn they could see towering above them the ramparts which guarded the entrance to the port of Havana. In contrast to the USA, immigration controls here were strict. Even with a Spanish visa and having surrendered their passports along with a fee of eight dollars, all passengers were forcibly detained on board ship until a resident of the island had guaranteed their respectability and their behaviour during their stay. This problem was resolved by a crowd of islanders each offering their services. Marmier paid four dollars for a certificate of his worthiness from an individual he had never seen before. It was then necessary to hire a boat and a porter to reach the hotel. In total, it cost approximately twenty dollars to disembark from the ship and reach his hotel. This, for Marmier, was money well spent. Despite arriving in midwinter, he was enchanted to discover a blue sky, warm weather, and beautiful landscape. The only inconvenience was an outbreak of yellow fever, common there in winter months, which he managed to avoid. The local people, who were open, hospitable, generous, and carefree as 'une couvée d'alouettes'[75] made a complete contrast to the 'bas peuple américain'.[76] Aware of machinations afoot to bring about the annexation of Cuba to the United States, he hoped fervently that any such plan would be resisted. Cuba's prosperity and well-being would be threatened by annexation or indeed any other constitutional change: the Cubans had only to look around them to see 'à quel degré de démoralisation et de misère le Mexique en est venu avec sa constitution calquée sur celle des États-Unis, dans quelle débilité sont tombées les régions de l'Amérique du Sud scindées en république'.[77]

By a happy coincidence, Marmier was in Havana for the 'Jour des Rois', a national festival when all the black people turned out in their traditional costumes with musical instruments. Nowhere else had Marmier been present at such a spectacle, which he obviously thoroughly enjoyed, despite his initial shock at the lack of inhibition:

---

aujourd'hui. Une circonstance fortuite fera éclater une animosité longtemps comprimée, et l'esclavage est peut-être la paille par où se brisera la barre d'acier' (*LAC*, 1, 449).
[74] *LAC*, 2, 2.   [75] Ibid., 2, 15.   [76] Ibid., 2, 20.   [77] Ibid., 2, 24.

Hommes et femmes se rangent l'un en face de l'autre, et dansent. Non; le mot de danser ne peut donner aucune idée d'une telle scène. C'est un frémissement nerveux, un tressaillement de tous les membres; des corps qui s'agitent, se tordent, se replient, se relèvent, et sautent comme des salamandres dans le feu. Les pieds, les bras, les hanches, la poitrine, tout est en action, dans les attitudes que je ne puis décrire et dont la moindre ferait rougir la vertu de nos sergents de ville. Un cercle de curieux des deux sexes assiste pourtant, en plein jour, à cette étonnante choréographie et n'en paraît nullement choqué.[78]

Marmier's entertainments also extended to a visit to the theatre, where he was struck by the elegant fashions of the Havanese ladies; and to a coffee house, where he was intrigued to hear a customer ordering a drink called a 'President Taylor',[79] and another ordering a 'President Jackson'.[80] With characteristic curiosity, Marmier ordered both, and declared that the drinks were aptly named: the Taylor was a sweet and refreshing long drink, whereas the Jackson was a rather strong punch.

As a final comment on Havana society, Marmier declared that nowhere had he seen fewer beggars than in Havana; that the black people were on the whole happier and lived in better conditions than thousands of ordinary working-class people in France and England, and were sure to be fed and clothed until their dying day; and that a poor white man would easily find shelter and work.

One morning, a French merchant in Havana, a M. Segrestan, came to fetch Marmier to take him to visit a coffee plantation owned by another Frenchman, named Beguerie. They travelled by the local railway which, as Marmier happily remarked, bore less resemblance to the American railways than a 'salon de bonne compagnie ne ressemble à une taverne de carrefour'.[81] Immediately on arrival, they were served lunch, which Marmier found more interesting than appetising. He then visited the coffee plantation and saw various other crops (bananas, coconuts, etc.), then a vast sugar plantation belonging to an individual referred to simply as 'M. le comte d'Ib. . .',[82] where he was also treated to a splendid dinner. A later visit to a tobacco plantation, where he learned about the process of cigar manufacture, prompted him to write that the tobacco plant is a 'vilaine herbe [. . .] et vraiment, à voir sa livide figure, on peut aisément lui attribuer toutes sortes de vices dangereux'.[83]

---

[78] *LAC*, 2, 42.
[79] Zachary Taylor (1784–1850), twelfth president of the United States (Whig), elected in 1848 after his triumphs in the war with Mexico.
[80] Andrew Jackson (1767–1845), seventh president of the United States (Democrat); remembered for his authoritarian style of leadership, and his expansionist and isolationist policies.
[81] *LAC*, 2, 54.   [82] Ibid., 2, 62.   [83] Ibid., 2, 86.

Back in Havana, Marmier could not resist the temptation to join the *Ambiorix*, a Belgian vessel which sailed into port en route for Montevideo and Buenos Aires. It was a decision he was to regret more than once in the course of the two-month sea voyage—principally at mealtimes. The food consisted of potatoes, beans, salt beef, and occasionally a kind of paste made from flour and rice, which was given the rather grand name of 'pudding'.[84] Despite Marmier's culinary experiences in some more under-developed countries, he had to declare himself beaten by the salt beef, the smell of which could induce sickness at a distance of twenty paces:

> J'essayai de toucher à la viande salée, et dès la première tentative, je recon-nus qu'il fallait totalement y renoncer. J'ai pourtant partagé la mauvaise nourriture des pêcheurs du nord, mangé la morue d'Islande, bouillie dans une fumée de tourbe infecte; le pain de la Dalécarlie, mélange d'écorce de bouleau; le pain d'orge de Muonioniska, moitié farine et moitié paille; la chair de renne découpée par les mains des Lapons et cuite dans leur chaudière, le couscoussou des Arabes préparé dans des vases d'un fort triste aspect. De plus, je me rappelle les vingt-quatre heures que j'ai passées dans un misérable village de Pologne, sous le toit d'un cabaretier juif et l'assiette ébréchée sur laquelle une effroyable vieille me servait je ne sais quel ragoût sans nom. Ce fut ma plus rude épreuve.
>
> Mais j'ai eu beau, pour m'enhardir, invoquer mon courage d'autrefois, mon courage a failli devant ces terribles pièces de bœuf plongée dans une amère saumure depuis trois à quatre ans, enfouies dans la cale depuis vingt mois, tellement décolorées qu'on ne peut dire que par tradition de quel pauvre animal elles ont recouvert les os.[85]

Apart from the diet, however, Marmier quite enjoyed this voyage, as he was by and large left to his own devices, and spent a great deal of time reading.

In the course of the two months, he was astonished to experience every extreme of climate: snow, rain, hurricane, and burning heat. At two degrees above Bermuda, he could not lay hands on enough overcoats, blankets, and woollens to withstand the cold. Six weeks later, at the beginning of March, the deck of the boat was like a white-hot furnace, with never a breath of wind to refresh. Crossing the Equator was a particular disappointment, for Marmier had read many accounts of celebrations on crossing the line. He experienced the Equator in a thick fog, accompanied by heavy showers. The sailors had no need of fancy dress, he says, clad as they were in their cos-tumes of waterproof trousers, sou'westers and fur-lined jackets; as for the symbolic baptism, this was more than adequately provided for by the very ample cloudbursts. Another surprise came later on, as they were sailing

---

[84] Ibid., 2, 99.   [85] Ibid., 2, 99–100.

through much calmer weather. One evening, the sun set with rays so red that the entire sea took on the warm glow. Shortly afterwards, with no other warning, the pampero blew up, as from nowhere.[86] Fortunately, this was its gentler season, and it raged for only a few hours before the clouds parted and dispersed, leaving the ship to sail through calmer waters.

Seventy-five days after setting sail, just 'un souffle de vent propice'[87] was needed to reach Montevideo where, he admits candidly, he was hoping to find a French vessel, enjoy some decent conversation and, above all, a decent meal. By this time, he declares, he was ready to sell his inheritance for a cutlet after his diet of potatoes and dried beans. His hopes were dashed, however, by the captain's decision to anchor for less than an hour, leaving him time only to salute the officers on board the frigate *La Constitution*. They now left the ocean and sailed up the Río de la Plata towards Buenos Aires. This relatively short stretch of the journey, which Marmier had expected to take only a few hours, in fact took five days of sailing quite as unpleasant as anything he had experienced on the open sea, including a pampero much more dangerous than in the Atlantic.

Once arrived at Buenos Aires, his suffering was not completely over, for the vessel was obliged to spend eight days offshore in quarantine and exposed to the full force of the pamperos since the city had no conventional port. Fortunately, this discomfort was mitigated by the presence of the nearby vessel *Astrolabe* whose commander, Montravel, sent Marmier fruit, milk, and French newspapers. On 4 April 1850, Marmier wrote to Sainte-Beuve, giving an account of his journey to date, and outlining his plans for his South American visit. According to the letter, he planned to be back in France in three months' time 'plus riche d'un amas de notes géographiques, et plus triste'.[88] The expedition, he says, has generally been a disappointment: 'sauf le Canada, et la Havane, je n'ai eu dans cette traversée de plusieurs milliers de lieues que de tristes émotions [. . .] je n'ai trouvé dans la riche puissante république des Etats-Unis que de mœurs qui m'ont glacé le cœur'.[89]

The eventual disembarkation in Buenos Aires was a novel affair. As there was no natural harbour, and no docks had been constructed, the vessel had to anchor some quarter of a league offshore. Along this stretch of water came troops of horses harnessed to carts (which Marmier compares to those used to take calves to Poissy market), driven by children. The passengers had

---

[86] The pampero is a meteorological term for a severe line squall occurring over the pampas of Argentina and Uruguay.
[87] *LAC*, 2, 125.
[88] Spoelberch de Lovenjoul, BIF, Lettres adressées à Sainte-Beuve, D606, 10, fo. 143.
[89] Ibid., fo. 142.

to pile up their luggage on one of these carts, then hoist themselves up on top of their trunks. The horses, up to their chests in the water, would then be driven to the shore where a band of black men in red trousers carried the trunks to the customs. This rather primitive procedure is ascribed by Marmier to the oppressive nature of the Rosas regime, an 'atroce dictature',[90] which is summarised in two words: 'férocité' and 'imbécillité', defined thus: 'Férocité de la bête fauve, imbécillité sauvage, non en ce qui touche à l'accroissement de sa propre domination, mais en ce qui tient aux intérêts, à la prospérité de son pays'.[91]

The failure to develop this primitive country is evident at every juncture: the grass growing on the pavements; the streets with no cobbles or paving stones, which blow up clouds of sand and dust in the summer and form a virtual mire in the winter; the ignorance of the *porteños* (inhabitants), who have relinquished all general curiosity for fear of reprisals; the transport provided by enormous wooden crates placed on wooden shafts, and harnessed to eight or ten horses. Yet the people are found to be 'd'une variété curieuse et d'un caractère original'.[92] Having arrived without letters of introduction, Marmier at first found it hard to make contact, but soon struck up a friendship with a local doctor who introduced him to many of his patients. After visiting La Bocca and Santos Lugares, he went out to the countryside where he found the gauchos and was invited into a number of homes to share meals. He was particularly impressed by *azado*, the local speciality:

> Le véritable azado est le quartier de bœuf cuit dans sa peau. Un vigoureux garçon apporte au bout de sa broche cet homérique rôti, et chacun en coupe tour à tour une tranche qu'il prend entre ses doigts et mange d'un bon appétit, ordinairement avec un peu de sel, presque toujours sans pain. Je suppose qu'un habitué du café des Anglais éprouverait un profond sentiment de pitié en entendant narrer les détails d'un tel souper, et pourtant je ne sais s'il y a dans les officines culinaires les plus renommées, un disciple de carême capable de composer avec toutes les ressources de son art, un mets plus savoureux que cette pièce de viande grillée dans son enveloppe de cuir. On me l'avait dit, et j'en ai fait plusieurs fois l'expérience avec un vrai plaisir gastronomique.[93]

Otherwise, Marmier's reflections on the area are almost exclusively centred on the sufferings arising from its bloody dictatorship, and the shameful role France has played by recognising and negotiating with Rosas. Marmier is quite outspoken in his criticism of French foreign policy in this area:

---

[90] *LAC*, 2, 244. Juan Manuel de Rosas (1793–1877) assumed overall power of Argentina and headed a bloody dictatorship from 1835 to 1852. Marmier therefore witnessed the last years of this regime.
[91] *LAC*, 2, 244.   [92] Ibid., 2, 221.   [93] Ibid., 2, 281.

> C'est cet ignoble saltimbanque près de qui nous envoyons en ambassade de
> nobles officiers de marine, c'est cet homme couvert de sang et de boue avec
> lequel nous poursuivons patiemment le cours d'une interminable négociation,
> c'est le gaucho que nous avons nous-mêmes grandi par notre condescendance
> et avec lequel la France traite pour ainsi dire d'égal à égal. Nous disons que
> notre honneur national est intéressé dans la question de la Plata. Si notre hon-
> neur est compromis, c'est dans les égards que nous avons depuis sept ans pour
> ce tyran de bas étage.[94]

The problem arose, according to Marmier, from Argentina breaking away
too soon from its ties with Spain, and being unable to cope with premature
independence, thus leaving itself open to domination and abuse. This led to
a failure to attract immigration, despite its being in most respects of its climate and geography a more favourable location for settlement than the
United States. Hence a downward spiral in which underpopulation combined with unenlightened leadership leads to a lack of capital investment;
this in turn leads to a failure to develop communications or to exploit
agricultural or geographical resources—all of which of course make the
country unattractive to a prospective immigrant.

Marmier next visited the Banda Oriental (Uruguay), a country in the
grip of a civil war; Oribe, backed by Rosas, had returned from exile, and
had been laying siege to Montevideo since 1843.[95] Uruguay is described as a
country trapped between two hostile powers: on the one hand, the Brazilian
empire, on the other, the Rosas dictatorship. Here he was struck by the
beauty of nature unspoiled by human hand; he also visited the Charrúas, a
primitive tribe virtually untouched by Western civilisation. They did not,
however, live up to the rather poetic mental image he had formed of them.
The national costume, for example, was somewhat unexpected: the typical
male 'se promène au grand air dans le simple appareil de notre père Adam
avant la catastrophe qui lui fit chercher la feuille de vigne'.[96] The women,
too, were disappointing in all traditional 'feminine' respects, and he depicts
them in Eurocentric terms as having 'pas la moindre idée élémentaire de
propreté; les belles dames sauvagesses ne se lavent ni les mains ni le visage.
[. . .] Elles ne nettoient non plus jamais leur demeure'.[97] Not, however, that
these dwellings were constructed in a manner conducive to norms of
Western civilisation in terms of the houseproud wife and mother:

---

[94] *LAC*, 2, 327–8.
[95] Manuel Oribe (1792–1857) was president of Uruguay from 1835 to 1838; he subsequently went
into exile and initiated the civil war which gave rise to the eight-year siege of Montevideo (1843–51).
[96] *LAC*, 2, 348.   [97] Ibid.

Dans l'endroit où il veut se fixer, le Charruas coupe quelques branches du premier arbre qu'il rencontre, les plante en terre, les recouvre d'un cuir de bœuf,
et voilà l'édifice où il repose sa femme et ses enfants. [. . .] Il n'a point de devis
d'architecte à payer, et point de journées de maçon.[98]

To complete this picture of Indian life, Marmier adds that they do not trouble themselves with agriculture or industry. They live quite simply on the
meat of wild cattle which are found in abundance on the plains where they
live.

The descriptions of this tribe incorporate a significant number of the
colonialist clichés so frequently found in travel writing of the time—clichés
which have been shown to prepare the way for domination and exploitation.
Judging these people by a European norm he finds them to be dirty,
immoral, and lazy; thus falling again into a colonialist discourse. Andrea
Pagni in her study of 'Fließende Übergänge zwischen Orient und Okzident'
highlights the clichés normally associated with Orientalism in Marmier's
writing on South America.[99]

In June 1850, Marmier decided to visit Montevideo. Despite its proxim-
ity to Argentina, this was not a journey to be undertaken with ease because
of the ongoing blockade. Choosing the overland route, the putative traveller
would first have to cross the Río de la Plata opposite Colonia, and would then
find himself on a deserted strip of land with no paths, guarded only by the
hostile soldiers of Oribe. This route was deemed to be totally impracticable.
By the river, only three vessels made the journey. The best option was the
English steamer which left Buenos Aires every month for Falmouth, stopping
at Montevideo en route. However, since it was a warship, it was at the diposal
of the English chargé d'affaires; he might postpone its departure as he saw fit,
depending on the current situation, the mood of Rosas, or the political climate. The second vessel, whose owners took out expensive advertisements in
all the newspapers announcing the regular and rapid service, in reality only
made the voyage when sufficient travellers had bought tickets. The third vessel, owned by the Argentinian republic, did not accept passengers from
Buenos Aires to Montevideo. Marmier points out that anyone sending a
letter from Buenos Aires to Montevideo, a distance of only forty-five leagues,
would have to wait three weeks for a response. Fortunately, he was able to take
the English ship. Thanks to a favourable wind, the voyage, which had taken
five days when he arrived, was accomplished this time in a matter of hours.

[98] Ibid., 2, 348–9.
[99] Andrea Pagni, 'Fließende Übergänge zwischen Orient und Okzident', in *Post/Koloniale Reisen:
Reiseberichte zwischen Frankreich und Argentinien im 19. Jahrhundert* (Tübingen: Stauffenburg
Verlag, 1999), 119–29 (124).

Once there, Marmier found himself a pleasant room opposite the Cerro (hill) and overlooking the port. The month of June is a winter month in this region, but Marmier reports that the weather was clement and springlike. Despite its troubled political situation of virtual siege, he found the locals to be hospitable and friendly. Although he had no letters of recommendation, he never found himself short of invitations and made many friends. He was particularly impressed by the intellectual activity, which had been virtually non-existent in Buenos Aires. Despite stringent laws of censorship, he concludes, literary production is flourishing here, and an entire chapter of his *Lettres sur l'Amérique* is devoted to 'Les journaux et la littérature'. He writes about, and translates, extracts of works by Jean Varela; Florencio Varela ('une de ces natures d'élite qui de loin en loin apparaissent comme l'idéal d'un être complet'[100]); Vicente López;[101] Domingo; Mármol,[102] and Echeverría, whose *Consuelos* is described by Marmier as 'un reflet de notre littérature élégiaque passant par plusieurs nuances, depuis la molle stance de Millevoye, jusqu'à l'accent plus grave des *Méditations* de M. de Lamartine'.[103] Echeverría is seen in a positive light as an innovator in literature, but severely criticised for the innovations he attempted to bring about in politics, since his ideas were founded on a 'principe démocratique'.[104] He also met Figueroa, whose works he greatly admired, and whom he found to be 'affable et jovial, spirituel et tendre, plein d'indulgence envers les autres et de défiance envers lui-même, simple et timide'.[105] He concludes that 'C'est un plaisir de lire ses vers. C'est un plaisir de le connaître'.[106]

Marmier fears for the future of literary and cultural activity in Montevideo. Already material conditions have degenerated due to the war: buildings lie disused and fall into disrepair; others are abandoned half-built. There is widespread poverty among the population. He visited one family to find a wretched woman with emaciated limbs cooking a few grains of maize for her children who were lying listlessly and half-naked around her. The windows of the dwelling had disappeared and been replaced by rags. In one dark corner a man lay on a sack of straw, his gaze haggard. As Marmier

[100] *LAC*, 2, 420.

[101] Vicente López (1815–1903) was a novelist; his best-known work is *La Novia del Hereje* (1846). A book bearing a handwritten dedication to Marmier from López and dated 25 May 1850 is conserved at the Bibliothèque Xavier Marmier in Pontarlier (item K562).

[102] José Mármol (1818–71) was banished from Argentina by Rosas in 1839; he is now generally recognised to have been one of the most versatile writers of his generation.

[103] *LAC*, 2, 428–9. Esteban Echeverrría (1805–51) is now remembered for having introduced Romanticism to Argentina.

[104] *LAC*, 2, 433.

[105] Ibid., 2, 436. Francisco Acuña de Figueroa (1791–1862) was a Uruguayan poet.

[106] *LAC*, 2, 436.

left, he handed one of the children some money, which the child examined with stupefaction as if he had never seen money before. However poor conditions may be, he argues, they will be much worse if the regime of Rosas, or indeed Oribe, take it over. The French intervention may have brought the hostilities to a provisional standstill, argues Marmier, but they have failed in their promise to defend the interests of Montevideo. He concludes by calling on the French government to negotiate a proper peace settlement which will guarantee the security of the Banda Oriental, and will assure the stability and the prosperity of the region. This is not a purely altruistic call, however; by such a treaty, France stands to gain 'un riche comptoir, une colonie industrielle et agricole que nous n'aurons pas besoin de faire garder par des canons'.[107] In point of fact, Montevideo was liberated by Anglo-French forces the following year (1851).

On 25 June, Marmier boarded *La Triomphante* for his return to France, returning to Rochefort on 26 August 1850.[108] His trip had therefore taken much longer than he had anticipated (his leave was granted until 1 June), and had given rise to some anxiety in France. On 28 May, his brother Joseph, then studying at the seminary of Saint-Sulpice, wrote to the minister expressing his concern. The last letter he had received from Xavier was sent from Havana in January; in this letter, he had stated his intention of visiting Rio de Janeiro and Brazil. Since then, the family had received no news of him, but had read in the newspapers of a severe epidemic of yellow fever in Rio, which had caused a large section of the population to flee the coast.[109] Joseph states that if, as he hopes, Marmier has survived the epidemic, he must have encountered severe difficulties since he has neither returned, nor sent any news to friends or family. He begs the minister to continue the discretionary payments of his brother's salary until further news is received. In the meantime, however, the library had suffered a cut in funding, and it was not possible to continue paying the salary.[110] The wandering librarian finally reported back to work on 3 September.[111] On 17 December, an irate letter was addressed to Marmier by the ministry, informing him of their displeasure at receiving a bill for 208 francs and 12 centimes from the Navy for the cost of his fare back to France, and ordering him to settle it himself.[112]

The *Lettres sur l'Amérique* were well received in France, and also

---

[107] Ibid., 2, 457.

[108] The crossing therefore took two months, rather than the one stated by Ménard (*Xavier Marmier et le Canada*, 109).

[109] Marmier had also voiced this intention to Sainte-Beuve; see Spoelberch de Lovenjoul, BIF, Lettres adressées à Sainte-Beuve, D606, 10, fo. 143.

[110] AnF, F17/21256.   [111] Ibid.   [112] Ibid.

favourably reviewed in England. The various reviews dwell more on
Marmier's account of North America, but in 1852, he was awarded the
honour of Knight of the Order of Charles III of Spain.[113]

A long review by Adolphe Joanne in *L'Illustration* in 1851 provides a
balanced assessment of the work which is generally positive. While indicat-
ing that Marmier is perhaps unjust to the Americans (although he does not
specify or substantiate the claim) he also points out Marmier's inconsistencies on the question of government. He argues that

> Aux États-Unis, il [Marmier] déteste et maudit la liberté; à Buenos-Aires, il
> l'adore et l'invoque; à Cuba, il bénit et encense l'absolutisme; dans le Rio de la
> Plata, il l'a en horreur et le voue à l'exécration de tous les peuples. La tyrannie
> de Rosas lui a semblé encore plus détestable que la démogagie américaine.[114]

Joanne nonetheless also points out that Marmier's book stands out above
others on America by virtue of its solid documentation; 'peu de ses
prédécesseurs s'étaient livrés aux mêmes recherches historiques, et avaient
eu comme lui l'heureuse idée de les résumer pour le plaisir et l'instruction
de leurs lecteurs'.[115] The *Lettres sur l'Amérique*, he concludes, 'offrent une
lecture aussi agréable qu'instructive. M. X. Marmier y exploite avec bonheur
ce fonds inépuisable de sensibilité, d'esprit, de finesse d'observation et
d'érudition, dont la nature l'a doué ou qu'il a acquis par son travail'.[116]

A further review appeared in *Blackwood's Edinburgh Magazine*.[117] For its
author, Marmier is an 'experienced and literary Frenchman', whose 'work on
America is an improvement on his previous publications', which contains
'pointed and interesting passages, and occasionally an original view of men
and things Transatlantic'.[118] A number of substantial extracts are included in
translation. Whilst acknowledging that 'it may be said that M. Marmier is
hardly indulgent enough to the honest Yankees',[119] the author argues that
'substantially [. . .], it is true enough'.[120] In conclusion, s/he notes that

> the verdict passed upon the citizens of the Great Republic by an educated and
> intelligent Frenchman must always possess weight and interest. Were M.
> Marmier an irritable or grumbling traveller, one might think it right to receive
> his impressions with caution; but, on the contrary, in all his previous books that
> we have seen, he has shown himself so indulgent and easy to please, that it is
> impossible to refuse him credit when he adopts a different tone, and abandons
> his habitual suavity for one of sarcasm.[121]

---

[113] AnF, LH.1747.018.
[114] Adolphe Joanne, 'Bibliographie. *Lettres sur l'Amérique*', *L'Illustration* (1851), 174–5.
[115] Ibid., 174.   [116] Ibid., 175.
[117] [Anonymous], 'Transatlantic Tourists', *Blackwood's Edinburgh Magazine* (May 1851), 545–63.
[118] Ibid., 546.   [119] Ibid., 547.   [120] Ibid., 549.   [121] Ibid., 550.

Ironically, one of the aspects of the book which found the least favour in this article was Marmier's prophecy about the issue of slavery being the catalyst to the rupture of the union. This is characterised as an 'ominous valediction' and the reviewer adds that 'M. Marmier [. . .] must be admitted to form his own opinions and to speak them out boldly, whether right or wrong'.[122]

Cuvillier-Fleury, writing in 1856, is perhaps more harsh in his judgement, although he makes some enlightening points. He declares that Marmier left France for the USA 'plutôt en misanthrope qu'en touriste',[123] less willing to be tolerant of a republican society than he might otherwise have been because of his frustration at the events of 1848 in France. Marmier himself was aware of the political dimension of his dislike of America, although it would seem from a letter to Sainte-Beuve that his visit had merely confirmed his political stance: 'Je n'étais pas républicain en quittant la France, je le suis moins que jamais après avoir vu l'adoration du matérialisme dans la plus florissante des républiques'.[124] Cuvillier-Fleury qualifies the book as an 'odyssée amusante de tous les désagréments, de toutes les misères, de tous les dégoûts qui l'attendent':[125] Marmier, again, had already admitted to Sainte-Beuve that 'tout mon récit de voyage n'a tourné qu'à la raillerie'.[126] Perhaps in an attempt to soften the tone of his criticism, Cuvillier-Fleury concludes that Marmier is unreliable in his judgement of America 'par toutes les qualités mêmes que je lui connais; il aime trop les arts et la poésie, les bons livres et les doux loisirs [. . .]. Il est donc trop poëte, trop sensible, et à la fois trop civilisé et trop rêveur pour être un juge impartial de l'égoïste et impatiente Amérique'.[127]

A new edition of the *Lettres sur l'Amérique* was brought out in 1881 to coincide with the centenary of American independence.[128] The new edition was largely unchanged, but bore a preface paying tribute to a number of men of letters from America, most notably Longfellow, whom Marmier had met in the meantime (their relationship and Marmier's translations of Longfellow are discussed in chapter 12). A review article by P. Douhaire in *Le Correspondant* underlines the fact that Marmier had witnessed some of

[122] Ibid., 557.
[123] Alfred-Auguste Cuvillier-Fleury, *Voyages et voyageurs* (Paris: Michel Lévy frères, 1856), 267.
[124] Spoelberch de Lovenjoul, BIF, Lettres adressées à Sainte-Beuve, D606, 10, fo. 143.
[125] Cuvillier-Fleury, *Voyages et voyageurs*, 269.
[126] Spoelberch de Lovenjoul, BIF, Lettres adressées à Sainte-Beuve, D606, 10, fo. 142.
[127] Cuvillier-Fleury, *Voyages et voyageurs*, 278.
[128] *Lettres sur l'Amérique: nouvelle édition*, 2 vols. (Paris: Plon, 1881). In the meantime, he had also brought out two volumes composed largely of extracts from *Gazida* and the *Lettres*: *Les États-Unis et le Canada* (Tours: Alfred Mame, 1874); and *Récits américains* (Tours: Alfred Mame, 1874).

the problems which were to lead up to the civil war (and indeed, in a sense, actually anticipated it). He also insists on the accuracy of Marmier's descriptions:

> M. X. Marmier a vu les lieux qu'il décrit et les hommes qu'il peint, et il les a bien vus les uns et les autres; car nous retrouvons encore tous leurs traits dans les peintures qu'on nous en fait aujourd'hui. Entre l'Amérique que M. Marmier nous a montrée et l'Amérique que les voyageurs nous montrent en ce moment, il n'y a d'autres différences que celles qu'offrent les portraits d'un même homme pris à deux âges différents.[129]

---

[129] P. Douhaire, 'Revue critique', *Le Correspondant*, 125 (Oct.–Dec. 1881), 775–6.

12

The Transitional Years (1851–69)

From Paris to the Balkans

If the years 1849–50 brought a degree of disappointment in the Americas and in the wake of the French revolution of 1848, they also brought a new love into Marmier's life. He had for some time known the Panckouckes. Ernest Panckoucke was the editor of *Le Moniteur Universel* and Marmier sympathised with his plight when he ran into financial and organisational difficulties with the publication of the paper in the wake of the 1848 revolution.[1] In his editorial role, Panckoucke had been able to give Marmier entrance tickets to parliamentary debates during the turbulent May sessions. Marmier found the household to be 'une des plus charmantes maisons que j'aie connues depuis que je suis à Paris'.[2] He particularly appreciated the warm welcome always extended by Mme Panckoucke even when financial difficulties obliged her to offer a much simpler menu than the sumptuous fare she had always served in the past: 'Qu'importe ce qu'on servira sur sa table, tant qu'elle sera là avec son inaltérable gaieté, sa grâce parfaite, et sa bienveillance si douce'.[3] Such utterances already hint at Marmier's feelings for her. He had fallen in love, but did not dare to make his feelings known to her. Indeed, an affair with a married woman in those days could be a risky business, even if a woman were separated from her husband: only a few years before, Léonie d'Aunet, whom Marmier knew well, had been sent to prison after being caught in the act of adultery with Victor Hugo despite the fact that she was separated from her husband. Marmier thus maintained his silence while the marriage survived, and Mme Panckoucke apparently remained unaware of his secret passion.

However, this situation did not last long. The object of his affection, born Louise-Adelaïde Amélie Viéz-Lefebvre-Gineau, had apparently tolerated an unhappy marriage for some fifteen years and suffered numerous infidelities on the part of her husband. Around this time, according to Marmier's diary, the marriage broke down irretrievably, and the couple decided to break all contact and lead separate lives. It would seem to be at

---

[1] See entries for March 1848 in *Journal*, 1, 78 and 84–5.
[2] *Journal*, 1, 85.   [3] Ibid.

this point that Marmier made his move, and the two became very close.[4] Marmier gave her the pet name Ebba (a Scandinavian name). He became convinced that he would spend the rest of his life with the woman he describes as 'jeune', 'belle', 'chaste', 'charmante d'esprit et de grâce' and endowed with a 'délicate et généreuse nature'.[5]

On his return from the Americas, he took Ebba on an excursion to London; they also went to Esher and Claremont, where he visited the exiled Marie-Amélie.[6] Although he had never liked England, he was free and in love, and declares in his private papers that 'jamais je ne fus plus complètement heureux'.[7] On their return to France, they went to Ebba's house in the country at Etrépigny for two months.

The year 1851 began on a happy note: a winter spent with little social contact cloistered indoors with his books, the old love of his life, and Ebba, the new. Spring and summer passed in gentle excursions to Neuilly, Passy or Saint-Cloud in the environs of Paris, made all the more agreeable by companionship. Even the coup d'état on 2 December did not seem so bad at first: Marmier had been so outraged by the 1848 revolution and the republican government that, in the early days, he felt that any change would be preferable. Soon, however, he was disenchanted by the hypocrisy of individuals who had claimed loyalty to previous regimes (in particular, but not exclusively, to Louis-Philippe, with whom his own sympathies lay) and now sycophantically courted the favours of the empire: 'Chaque révolution les vomit dans ses orages. Ebranlés un instant par la secousse imprévue, bientôt on les voit se rejoindre et tourbillonner comme des insectes dans les rayons du soleil du pouvoir'.[8] In fact his extreme disillusion with the bad faith of his compatriots was to colour his outlook on French society to the end of his days.

The year finished even more unhappily for him. A letter from his sister informing him that his father was unwell sent him back to his parents' home at Saint-Louis in Alsace. Concerned, but not unduly anxious, he arrived at 9 p.m. on 28 December to find the last rites being administered with his mother, sisters, and younger brother gathered around. Once the ceremony

[4] In his private papers, Marmier recollects that in 1848 Ebba came to meet him in Mézières (Académie des Sciences, Belles Lettres et Arts de Besançon, *Memorandum* 2, fo. 181). The incident is included in Kaye's edition of the *Journal* (1, 253) but loses much of its sense due to faulty transcription.

[5] *Journal*, 1, 162. It is probably also significant that after 1848, Marmier's name disappears from *Le Moniteur Universel*, although he had been a regular contributor and his name was also frequently mentioned in its pages prior to this date.

[6] *LAC*, 1, 9.

[7] *Journal*, 1, 163.

[8] Ibid., 1, 164.

was finished, Marmier went to kneel beside his father's bed; his father was able to smile at him, and Joseph took his father's hand and placed it on Xavier's head. No longer able to speak, the father then lost consciousness and died the following morning.

The Marmiers had always been a close family, and Xavier felt his father's loss keenly: 'le meilleur père, le cœur le plus tendre, qui ne vivait que par nous et pour nous, qui, pour nous élever, avait souffert tant de privations'.[9] With his father, he writes, he had lost all his ambition, and also 'toutes les joies du foyer, du pauvre humble foyer où nous revenions avec tant de bonheur'.[10] On 5 January 1852 he was granted a month's leave from his duties as librarian at the Bibliothèque Sainte-Geneviève,[11] but the same winter also saw the death of Ebba's mother. In the spring of 1852 the couple went south on an excursion to try to distract their grief, taking in Lyon, Marseille, Hyères, Grenoble, and the Grande-Chartreuse. In the summer, Xavier was visited by his brother Hyacinthe whom he had not seen since their brief meeting in Algeria in 1846. In the intervening years, his brother had received a head injury and lost an eye at Zaatcha, and been promoted to squadron leader. Whilst admiring his brother's bravery and his promotion, Marmier was obviously shocked by the physical suffering Hyacinthe had endured.

Now Marmier was preparing to set off on what was effectively to be his last real expedition to a little-known territory. A letter in his employment file dated March 1852 begs permission to take paid leave from his post at the library for eighteen months in order to 'partir encore pour un lointain pays, consacrer un dernier reste de jeunesse à un courageux travail'.[12] His intention was to travel down to the Balkans and visit Slovenia, Dalmatia, Montenegro, and Albania. He had already visited Serbia, Moldavia, and Valachia and the eastern side of the Balkans on his way to the Holy Land in 1845:[13] now he was to turn his attention to the western reaches of the Ottoman empire.

His proposed itinerary was a courageous one, and also highly topical, since the end of 1851 and the early part of 1852 had seen the principality of Montenegro at war with Turkey. This conflict seems to be largely forgotten today—partly, no doubt, because it is eclipsed in retrospect by the Crimean War. At the time, however, it was widely reported in France, and

---

[9] Ibid. [10] Ibid. [11] AnF, F17/21256. [12] Ibid.

[13] Not 1855 as stated by Liljana Todorova in 'Xavier Marmier et les Slaves du Sud: A l'occasion du 80ᵉ anniversaire de sa mort', in Académie des Sciences, Belles Lettres et Arts de Besançon, *Procès-verbaux et mémoires, années 1972–3*, 180 (1974), 185–98 (192). The contents of this paper are expanded in *Les Slaves du sud au XIXᵉ siècle* ([Paris]: Publications orientalistes de France, 1980).

was generally held to be one of the factors which indirectly gave rise to the Crimean War.[14]

Prince Peter II, Vladika of Montenegro, died on 18 October 1851 and his successor, Danilo,[15] obtained permission from Tsar Nicholas I of Russia to separate the civil and ecclesiastical offices of the ruler (thus enabling him to marry). Turkey felt that its support should have been sought, and war was declared. Omar Pasha was sent to invade Montenegro, but he was defeated; the Turks lost around 4,500 men on the battlefields alone. Through Austrian mediation, peace was restored, although hostilities continued in the border regions.[16]

Marmier sent letters from the journey back to France where they were published first in the *Revue contemporaine* before appearing in book form as two volumes.[17]

Permission to take leave for one year was granted on 24 June 1852,[18] and Marmier left Strasbourg in September after visiting his mother and made his way through Karlsruhe, Heidelberg, Stuttgart, and Friederickshafen—towns which he knew well from previous visits—and thence to Saint-Gall where he was outraged by the contrast between the opulence of the houses built and occupied by the owners of the broderie businesses and the squalid conditions and starvation wages paid by them to their workers. From here, he travelled on to Ragatz, where he stayed in an excellent hotel before visiting the spa at Pfeffers: 'ce puits d'eau brûlante dont une foule de malades subissent la chaleur et l'odeur sulfureuse pour reconquérir la joie de la santé'.[19] He then made his way via Lake Lucerne and Saint-Gothard to Milan, which he had not previously visited. He was particularly struck by the splendour of the cathedral, a 'tableau sans pareil':

> Si le Saint-Pierre de Rome a des proportions plus grandioses, si la cathédrale inachevée de Cologne étonne l'esprit par ses masses colossales, si plusieurs cathédrales d'Espagne, de Belgique étalent dans leurs chœurs, sur leurs arceaux, sous leurs portails des chefs-d'œuvre de ciselure, il n'en est point qui présente une image plus solennelle que celle de Milan, un ensemble plus harmonieux et une telle profusion d'ornements.[20]

[14] See, as a minor example, V. de Mars, 'Revue littéraire', *RDM*, 2nd ser., 5 (1854), 856–64 (859).
[15] Danilo (1826–60), nephew of Peter II, was sovereign ruler of Montenegro from 1851 until his assassination in 1860.
[16] Details from: William Denton, *Montenegro: Its People and their History*, reprinted from the edition of 1877 (New York: AMS Press, 1982).
[17] See *Revue contemporaine*, 7 (1853), 49 and 208; 8 (1853), 57 and 383; 9 (1853), 29 and 385; and 10 (1853), 573 and 606. These appeared in book form as *Lettres sur l'Adriatique et le Monténégro*, 2 vols. (Paris: Arthus Bertrand, 1854) (cited hereafter as *LAM*).
[18] AnF, F17/21256.
[19] *LAM*, 1, 43.   [20] Ibid., 1, 108.

He was, however, scandalised by the profane behaviour of the Milanese at the cathedral on holidays, which he finds not only 'peu édifiant', but 'la brutalité mise en contraste auprès du spiritualisme'.[21] From Milan, Marmier went on to Venice (which was still under Austrian occupation) before arriving in the 'mercantile cité de Trieste'.[22] He left Trieste in a carriage pulled by two horses up the steep slopes of the Karst mountain range. From its peak he went down into Laybach (Ljubljana), thence making his way back along the valley towards Veldes (Bled). On the way to 'ce charmant Veldes',[23] they came to a bridge which had come down the previous winter and been the object of such very minimal reconstruction work that the travellers were obliged to get out of the coach, unharness the horses, and pull the coach themselves while leading the horses over the rickety planks. Not the least discouraged by this 'difficulté accidentelle',[24] Marmier felt that the beauty of the destination, and in particular the lake, was more than worth the effort.

Another visit he was determined to make in the region was to the abode of the Zichi (Ćiribirci/(Ćići), who had caught his eye in Trieste as they brought their coal to sell. Numerous attempts to dissuade him from this plan had failed, and he set off in the stagecoach from Rijeka at eight o'clock one evening. At one o'clock they reached Castelnuovo; the following day, a five-hour journey in a rickety trap took him and his travelling companion to Mune and Seniane (Zejane), the home of the Zichi. They were welcomed by the local priest, a friend of Marmier's travelling companion, who gave them lunch and took them on a tour of his parish. Shocked by the poverty and squalor in which the people lived, Marmier judged their living quarters to be amongst the worst he had seen, comparable only to the 'antres infects occupés par les ouvriers de Liverpool, de Manchester, et dans les campagnes de la malheureuse Irlande'.[25] Their 'chétives cabanes couvertes en chaume'[26] are divided into two parts to accommodate animals and family; they are muddy, damp, dark, and smoke-filled, and have no windows or sleeping quarters of any sort. The people make their own clothes out of sheep's wool—brown for jackets and white for trousers. Young men buy themselves a wife in exchange for a number of sheep; she will become 'leur compagnon et surtout leur esclave'.[27] Marmier seems quite horrified at the way women here are dehumanised: 'leur donner le nom de femmes, c'est profaner ce mot [. . .] elles travaillent d'une façon terrible. Pour elles, toutes les fonctions les plus pénibles, pour elles tous les fardeaux. Ce sont les bêtes de somme de la maison. [Elles sont] habituées dès leur enfance à cet état de servitude'.[28]

[21] Ibid., 1, 116.   [22] Ibid., 1, 197.   [23] Ibid., 1, 218.   [24] Ibid.   [25] Ibid., 1, 242.
[26] Ibid., 1, 243.   [27] Ibid., 1, 244.   [28] Ibid., 1, 244–5.

Marmier now made his way towards the Monte Maggiore (Učka Gora) in Istria and from here travelled over to the Gulf of Kvarner to begin his voyage down the Dalmatian coast. He had long wished to visit 'cette vieille romantique Dalmatie'[29] and see for himself the Morlaques. The people of Dalmatia, he concludes, are amongst the most primitive in Europe. Although Dalmatia is only a narrow strip of land with poor-quality soil stretching from Croatia down to the Albanian border, it has been highly prized because of its strategic position and subjected to a series of occupations down the centuries. This, he argues, has hindered the land in its material and intellectual progress. There is not a single institution of higher education in the whole of the land; there is no industry or manufacture to speak of; the people lack the means and the knowledge to exploit their agricultural land to the full; and there is only one main line of communication. A postal service links Cattaro (Kotor) with Trieste three times a week: from Cattaro the postman carries the bag of letters on his shoulder to Ragusa; from here the path is more practicable, and the bag is carried over hill and dale by a donkey to Zara; there it can be placed on a cart. If all goes well, it arrives at its destination in about nine days. Marmier quite took to the Morlaques, whose dwellings, clothes, customs, folklore, and religious observance are described in some detail. He was particularly struck by the tradition of 'pobratimi' (and 'possestrime') which he explains as 'frères et sœurs, non de naissance, mais d'adoption', describing the ceremony as something like a wedding, and similarly binding.[30]

He summarises thus the condition of Dalmatia: 'comme on rencontre souvent de par le monde des individus qui passent leur vie à faire la fortune des autres, sans pouvoir travailler à la leur, on voit aussi des États qui semblent condamnés au même sort. Telle est l'Irlande. Telle est, dans une condition infiniment moins dure, la Dalmatie'.[31]

One of the most important developments in recent years, he claims, has been Lloyd's inauguration of a regular steamboat service linking the principal coastal towns. Thanks to a letter from von Bruck, director of Lloyd's of Austria, one of the company's employees found Marmier a cabin on the boat about to depart, and which already appeared to be full. His couchette seemed to him like 'une sorte de tiroir',[32] but this did not detract from his fascination with the whole proceedings: 'Dans chaque pays, le bateau à vapeur a sa physionomie particulière. C'est un petit monde ambulant,

---

[29] *LAM*, 1, 249.

[30] Todorova shows that Marmier is the first foreign traveller to the region to represent this correctly (*Les Slaves du sud au XIXe siècle*, 104).

[31] *LAM*, 1, 272–3.   [32] Ibid., 1, 309.

détaché de la contrée que l'on parcourt ou des contrées voisines, et qu'on ne retrouve point dans d'autres parages. C'est une peinture locale en voyage'.[33]

Very soon after they had set sail, however, the sirocco started to blow strongly and the ship was obliged to shelter in the Bay of Lussino (Lošinj) until the sea had calmed. The steamer made its way past Veglia (Krk) and Arbe (Rab) and Segne (Senj), which brought to mind the Uscoques and their past.[34] From Senj it then made its way down to Zara (Zadar),

> tourn[ant] et serpent[ant] entre ces îles, comme le fil d'Ariane dans le labyrinthe, et en naviguant ainsi, on n'a pas même l'aspect de la grande mer. Tantôt on entre dans un canal qui a l'apparence d'une rivière, tantôt dans une enceinte plus large qui ressemble à un lac, et les bords de cette rivière et les contours de ce lac sont également monotones.[35]

As they approached Zara, the landscape became less monotonous, giving way to clearly defined mountains, forests of fruit trees and picturesque villages. After giving a brief history of the town, Marmier describes its then political situation, government, and administration. He was received by the governor of Zara, baron Mamula, whom Marmier found to be highly intelligent and dedicated to his work. A letter of introduction from a friend in Trieste to two locals resulted in Marmier being given a guided tour and allowed him to gather information on not only the customs and the economic situation, but also the intellectual life of the city.

From here, the steamer passed Wrana (Vrana) and made its way to Sebenico (Šibenik). The history of Sebenico is presented in some detail, particularly its intellectual history. The present, for Marmier, is interesting, but not without its inconvenience. Access to the centre of the town is via 'des défilés d'une saleté pareille à celles des plus sales villes turques', the streets which are 'hideuses', and the staggered slopes which are 'boueux', 'brisés', and 'glissants'.[36] But the market to which they lead fascinates him by its cosmopolitan nature and the different tongues and costumes of those who mingled there. He comments on the importance to the local economy of fishing, coral, and sponge industries, and the coal mining which provides fuel for the Lloyd's steamers. He is profoundly shocked, however, to note that whilst the men sit chatting and smoking their pipes, their wives and sisters carry the weighty baskets of coal on their heads down to the boats and load them on. Marmier's comments on the place of women in this society are consistent with his views expressed elsewhere (particularly on women in Muslim

[33] Ibid., 1, 309–10.
[34] Todorova notes that the Uscoques had figured in French works by George Sand, Musset, and Balzac (*Les Slaves du sud au XIXᵉ siècle*, 105).
[35] *LAM*, 1, 352–3.   [36] Ibid., 1, 381.

countries), and can be divided into two main strands. On the one hand, religion, for him, unquestionably has an important role: 'le christianisme a affranchi, ennobli la femme'.[37] Furthermore, and in this he sounds remarkably modern, 'là où l'homme met encore son orgueil dans sa force physique, la femme est esclave. Là où il en est venu à se complaire dans les vraies émotions du cœur, dans les délicates conceptions de l'esprit, la femme a sa couronne'.[38]

The boat now steamed on to Spalato (Split), replete with the history of Diocletian, which Marmier still found to be very much in evidence—although he disapproved of much of the new building, in part because it did not sit easily beside the old town. He also found basic amenities such as a hostel or a good bookshop to be lacking. In a Franciscan monastery, however, he was delighted to be allowed to view two beautiful manuscripts, and he was most impressed by the archaeological collections in the museum.

The next main stop was at the attractive island of Curzola (Korčula), with its rich forests which were exploited for the shipbuilding industry. Here, he explains, many of the Lloyd's ships are built. This leads to an active population of engineers, carpenters, and sailmakers in full employment by the waterside in the shadow of the ancient town, whose history he then proceeds to trace. The local women impressed him a great deal; not only by their physical beauty, but by their expert sailing skills and also their striking headgear which contrasted strongly with their simple black clothes: 'la plus plaisante, la plus bizarre, la plus carnavalesque coiffure qu'il soit possible d'imaginer; des amas de bouquets de fleurs, des flots de rubans, des gerbes de paillettes, des masses de verroteries, des pièces d'or étrangères, tout ce qu'un père généreux ou un fiancé prodigue leur a rapporté de ses voyages'.[39]

After a short stop at Raguse (Dubrovnik), Marmier was impatient to arrive at the Cattaro (Kotor) estuary. By the time they arrived, a storm had brewed up: 'le ciel était noir; des masses de nuages noirs flottaient autour de nous, et si nous n'avions su que les hautes crêtes au pied desquelles nous naviguions portaient depuis longtemps le nom de Tzernagora, de Montenegro, de montagne Noire, nous n'aurions pu leur donner une plus juste dénomination'.[40] Although there was no hostel or hotel here, Marmier was fortunate enough to have a letter of introduction to Doimi, whom Marmier describes as 'le capitano des Circolo'.[41] Doimi found him some lodgings with an old lady and pressed Marmier to dine with him every day.

---

[37] *LAM*, 1, 385. This comment must of course be taken in a relative and historical context. It was a popular notion in the nineteenth century (shared by, amongst others, Mme de Staël).
[38] *LAM*, 1, 385.   [39] Ibid., 2, 31.   [40] Ibid., 2, 89–90.   [41] Ibid., 2, 119.

The town of Cattaro, he notes, has two main markets, the 'Marché de la Marine' for the 'Bocchesi', of whom he presents a detailed ethnological and sociological description, and a bazaar reserved for the Montenegrins. The diverse origins and customs of the Bocchesi made them particularly fascinating to Marmier. Their extreme loyalty to their roots may make them prone to intense rivalry and animosity amongst themselves, but it also means that they have clung to many of their ancient traditions. Not least among these is their resistance to 'l'universel étranglement de notre uniforme habit',[42] which results in every village having its own costume; in the market it is possible to identify any individual with their home village simply by their clothes.

Their essentially combative nature, he argues, means that here also women are relentlessly exploited by the male population. When one day he chanced upon a wedding, he found himself moved by the ceremony, although his foremost thought was for the bride, and could almost have been adopted as a twentieth-century feminist slogan: 'Reine un jour, esclave ensuite'.[43] The Marché de la Marine held many curiosities for the traveller, not all of which were of the most enticing:

> un boulanger étale sous son auvent des pains noirs, difficiles à mâcher; un marchand de liqueurs pose avec orgueil sur une table quelques flacons d'une affreuse eau-de-vie, et une cuisinière, accroupie par terre, tient entre ses genoux une corbeille d'où s'exhale, avec un tourbillon de fumée, une nauséabonde odeur. Il y a là un amas de pieds de bœuf, bouillis avec leur corne, qu'elle vient de tirer d'une chaudière dont elle tâche de conserver la chaleur en les couvrant d'un haillon.[44]

And yet despite the manifest signs of poverty, the men nonetheless sport a hugely valuable collection of arms, and the women are adorned with costly gold and silver jewellery.

At the other market, reserved for the Montenegrins, the race he had travelled so far to see, he realised that he had fallen prey to misplaced and romanticised stereotypes in imagining them to be 'quelque peu comme de romantiques chevaliers, chrétiens en croisade perpétuelle contre les Turcs, quelque peu aussi, je dois le dire, comme des pillards, mais des pillards d'une énergique beauté, que j'habillais d'un costume scénique'.[45] Indeed, he found a thin, jaundiced, and ragged population resembling beggars more than anything else and more wretched in their poverty than 'la populace la plus déguenillée des pauvres bazars de l'Orient'.[46] As amongst many of the other peoples he had visited on this journey, he found the women to be

---

[42] Ibid., 2, 99.   [43] Ibid., 2, 125.   [44] Ibid., 2, 120–1.   [45] Ibid., 2, 136.   [46] Ibid.

treated as 'bêtes de somme',[47] prematurely wizened and aged by their harsh existence. Even in the winter they walk barefoot over pebbles and through rain so as not to wear out their shoes, carrying heavy goods down the mountainside to the market. So thoroughly inculcated is their sense of inferiority that they may not even greet a man directly: they have to bow to any man they happen to meet, even their own husband, and kiss his hands. 'Les pauvres femmes!' exclaims Marmier; 'à quel état d'humilité et de servitude elles sont astreintes'.[48] The Montenegrins' treatment of women, he concludes, is arrogant, disdainful, and downright cruel.

In Cattaro, Marmier waited for a break in the bad weather to set off for Cétinié (Cetinje), the old capital of Montenegro. It was now nearing the end of November, which marked the onset of the rainy season in the region. Marmier had a letter of introduction to Prince Danilo written by Doimi,[49] and another from the marquis de Salvo.[50] When he heard that Janko, one of the prince's messengers, was in town, he persuaded him—for a small consideration—to act as his guide. A peasant from Scagliari hired him his horse, sending a young farmhand along to bring the animal back. The rain continued to fall relentlessly as the threesome set off; and Marmier, although a little uneasy in the realisation that both Janko and the boy would have been much happier to stay at Cattaro, was determined to press on to his destination. At first they made a reasonable pace, but weather conditions rapidly worsened:

> tout prenait autour de nous un aspect d'un caractère lugubre. A gauche, un précipice profond où roulaient des flots écumeux; à droite, une cime perpendiculaire sillonnée de distance en distance par de bourbeuses cascades. Derrière nous le golfe de Cattaro couvert d'une masse de brouillards pareille à une cloche de fer, et devant nous un cercle de rochers où je cherchais en vain à entrevoir une issue. Parfois la lueur d'un éclair déchirait comme une flèche enflammée la voûte de nuages amassés sur notre tête. Puis le tonnerre éclatait, et de rocher en rocher, de ravin en ravin se répercutait au loin comme le fracas d'un mine qui éclate ou le gémissement d'une voix lamentable. Et pas un être sur la route, et pas un signe d'espoir sur un horizon meilleur.
>
> C'était une de ces scènes imposantes et terribles qui frappent le cœur d'un homme d'une sorte de commotion électrique, qui lui donnent un instant, comme à l'aigle, une sorte de joie sauvage, puis le font fléchir, dans la conscience de sa faiblesse, sous le sentiment de l'écrasante puissance de Dieu.[51]

---

[47] *LAM*, 2, 136.   [48] Ibid., 2, 141.
[49] Todorova tells us that the letter of introduction is dated 22 November (*Les Slaves du sud au XIXe siècle*, 82, 83, 120).
[50] See *LAM*, 2, 170 and 263.   [51] *LAM*, 2, 150–1.

At this juncture, the boy seized the chance to grab the horse and run back off in the direction of Scagliari.

Janko and Marmier carried on through the pouring rain, wading through streams and across waterfalls, even at one point having to improvise a crossing for a fierce torrent which swept along uprooted trees, rocks, and clods of earth. They managed to push some large boulders into the middle of the torrent which they then used as giant stepping stones. Leaping from one rock to another like goats, Marmier kept up with Janko, sometimes even going a few leaps ahead, which seemed to surprise the Montenegrin; Marmier must have appeared at first sight, after all, like a rich, elegant middle-aged Parisian gentleman. But, as Marmier mused,

> il ignore, le brave Janko, que je suis comme lui, un fils des montagnes, des hautes montagnes de Franche-Comté. La montagne est pour celui qui y est né la terre d'Antée. Il y a dans la vivacité de son atmosphère, dans ses escarpements et jusque dans ses aspérités une vertu qui nous ravive, un ressort qui nous rend l'agile mouvement de l'enfance.[52]

Eventually, they arrived at Niégouss (Njeguši), where Marmier asked Janko to take him to see the interior of a house. At one of the larger buildings, labelled 'hosteria', four men were absorbed in a task which Marmier was initially unable to make out because of the thick smoke. In a hole in the ground, a brushwood fire was being vigorously fanned by a small child with the blade of his dagger. The landlord ordered his wife to bring some rather unappetising food, and as Marmier's eyes grew gradually accustomed to the smoke, he realised that two of the men were placing dozens of bullets in cardboard cylinders, while the other two, leaning on the brazier with a chibouk between their lips, were calmly taking gunpowder out of an open bag between them and making cartridges. 'Une très-guerrière occupation, fort peu amicale pour les Turcs, fort indifférente pour moi', he reflected; 'il faut venir dans le Montenegro pour jouir d'un tel spectacle'.[53]

As Cétinié finally came into view, Janko uttered a piercing cry. At first, Marmier assumed that this was a spontaneous expression of his joy at arriving home, until another similar cry replied from the distance. Janko had merely been alerting his wife to his imminent arrival home. After a brief visit to Janko's wife and children, they pressed on towards the Vladika's palace at the far end of the valley. On their arrival, however, they found that the prince was absent, having set out to Zabliak on a military expedition 'qui a mis en émoi toute la diplomatie russe, turque, autrichienne, et dont les péripéties ont alimenté pendant plusieurs mois la presse européenne'.[54]

---

[52] Ibid., 2, 155–6.   [53] Ibid., 2, 162–3.   [54] Ibid., 2, 171.

Before setting out, however, Danilo had called on his brother George Petrovitch to take care of his affairs in his absence. When Marmier arrived, George was at table with his brother's secretary, tucking into a hearty meal of beef and cabbage. Although Marmier realised that he must have cut a rather eccentric figure in his simple frock coat, cap, and walking stick beside these warriors bristling with arms which they did not even remove when they sat down to dinner, he was made welcome and the prince's brother moved over to make room for him to join them at table. Even the servant who brought potato salad and cheese to supplement the meal had two large pistols and an 'effroyable poignard' on his belt.[55] After the meal, the party all retired to the kitchen where a good fire was blazing in a huge fireplace which reminded Marmier of those to be found in the mountain chalets of the Jura. 'Si, à la fin de ma diluvienne journée, il m'eût été donné de choisir moi-même une agréable place pour passer la soirée, je n'aurais pu en trouver une meilleure', he reflected.[56] In the kitchen they were joined by a succession of visitors; a cousin of the prince and his brother in simple peasant attire; a tailor whom the prince had summoned from Cattaro to make his formal outfits; a young Dalmatian who gave the prince Italian lessons; and a carpenter. Marmier was struck by the lack of formality: everyone sat together as a large family; the royal cousin gave the carpenter tobacco and the latter lent the royal cousin his pipe. Of the two easy chairs in the kitchen, Marmier was offered one while the prince's brother occupied the other; but as soon as the latter rose to fetch his pipe, Janko the messenger immediately slipped into his place.

Conversation turned to the latest military skirmishes, and how the Turks had been soundly beaten in the recent encounters. The following day, George assured his visitor, he would see the heads of thirty-two Muslims on the wall of the tower: 'Le dernier Vladika [i.e. Peter II] qui avait rapporté de ses voyages en Europe des idées toutes nouvelles pour nous, ne voulait plus qu'on leur coupât la tête; mais, comme les Turcs continuaient à décapiter les Monténégrins [. . .] nous avons repris le même usage'.[57] For every Turk's head brought to the capital, Marmier explains, 'ils reçoivent une prime comme nos paysans de France pour une tête de loup'.[58]

---

[55] *LAM*, 2, 172.   [56] Ibid., 2, 174.

[57] Ibid., 2, 178. Todorova remarks: 'Marmier ne pouvait point comprendre que cet acte des Monténégrins n'exprimait qu'une vengeance contre les massacres du même genre' (*Les Slaves du sud au XIXᵉ siècle*, 31).

[58] *LAM*, 2, 179. Todorova objects to these comments: 'Ne se montre-t-il un peu trop sévère lorsqu'il juge de leur brigandages qui ne sont, en réalité, que représailles contre les sanglantes violences de leurs ennemis?' (*Les Slaves du sud au XIXᵉ siècle*, 166).

The following morning, Marmier awoke to find the whole house in a commotion. News had arrived overnight that Danilo had won a first victory, and was now calling for ammunition. Janko had departed in haste, and the vice-president and several other officials had left the capital to join their ruler. Danilo's brother George, the secretary, and the language teacher nonetheless found time to show Marmier around the palace and the surrounding district, including the Scutari lake which was the subject of a border dispute.

A disappointment was in store, however. Marmier's plan had been to go from Cétinié to Scutari and thence to return via Budua to Cattaro. But the prince's brother now warned him—in friendly enough terms—that they would be unable to guarantee his safety in the valley; and that even if he were to succeed in reaching Scutari in one piece, it was highly unlikely that he would be able to gain access to the city itself. He thus prepared reluctantly to retrace his steps towards Cattaro, this time accompanied by the tailor and an 83-year-old Montenegrin named Marco who was carrying a bag of vegetables to sell at the market. The weather for the return journey could not have been more different from the day of his arrival. The sun was shining, the puddles and mud had dried out, and even the torrents had calmed down; the path was busy with people who had waited for the end of the storm to go to market.

Although Marmier could not but admire the courage of this little-known people ('un courage qui s'élève jusqu'à l'héroïsme'[59]), and although he felt a good deal of respect for a number of the individuals he had met, he was relieved to be away from Montenegro:

> Je ne me passionne point pour les Monténégrins, non, je dirai même que leur aspect et leurs mœurs m'ont inspiré plus de répulsion que de sympathie. Près des domaines de la bénigne Autriche, je les vois avec leur ardeur de pillage et de razzias comme une bande d'Uscoques retranchés sur une montagne. [. . .] Leur pays m'apparaît comme une île barbare au sein des flots de la civilisation, et leur existence comme un fait anormal qui ne peut subsister.[60]

Marmier completes his narrative with surveys of the topography, administration, judiciary, statistics, ethnography and a description of the life and customs of the country, including sections on marriage, the position of women, and an analysis of the total annual transactions made by Montenegrins at the Cattaro market. A chapter on the history of the country concludes with a commentary on the new government. Peter II, according to all Marmier's sources, was a great and just ruler whose untimely

[59] *LAM*, 2, 224.   [60] Ibid., 2, 223.

death in 1851 prevented him from implementing a number of 'généreux pro-jets'[61] which would have been of great benefit to the country. Although he insists that it is too early to be able to judge Danilo, the present ruler, Marmier makes it clear that his actions to date are not auspicious. Already, he claims, schools founded by the two previous Vladika, the national press, and the library have all been abandoned. Marmier clearly disapproves of Danilo's immediate abdication from his religious duties in order to marry, and what Marmier sees as his subsequent military aggression on Zabliak: 'De là une nouvelle guerre avec les Turcs, de là une rumeur européenne'.[62]

One prediction turned out to be mistaken. In the preface to the text, written in November 1853, he argued that Montenegro would rapidly become involved in the Crimean War:

> Le Montenegro[63] est par sa situation destiné à faire plus d'une fois à l'avenir résonner ses coups de fusil. C'est un avant-poste de guérillas entretenus par la Russie entre l'Albanie et la Herzégovine. C'est un obus toujours chargé dont le tzar tient la mèche. Déjà la question d'Orient a mis en émoi les Monténégrins. Déjà ils aiguisent leurs poignards, ils préparent leurs car-touches, et le bruit se répand que leur prince a peine à contenir leur impa-tience. Pour peu que cette nouvelle complication des éternels embarras de la Turquie se prolonge, on verra les guerriers de la Montagne Noire jeter aussi leur fer dans la balance. Tandis que les Russes combattront sur le Danube, les Monténégrins s'élanceront sur l'Herzégovine, la Bosnie et l'Albanie.[64]

Two contemporary reviews picked up on this point. For an anonymous reviewer in the *Nouvelles annales des voyages* (who also found the work to be 'un livre intéressant' and 'un livre tout-à-fait de circonstance'), it was a persuasive argument:

> Avec son flair de touriste expérimenté, M. Marmier est allé là où il a pressenti que l'attention publique devait le suivre. Ces rudes habitants de la Montagne Noire, Slaves par le sang, indépendants par nature, batailleurs et pillards par besoin et par instinct, il a deviné qu'ils ne pourraient pas rester froids et pais-ibles quand tout bouillonne autour d'eux, et il a voulu voir de près cette race curieuse et peu connue qui doit inévitablement jouer un rôle dans le terrible drame qui va s'ouvrir. De ce côté-là, du moins, nous serons bien préparés.[65]

V. de Mars, writing in the *Revue des Deux Mondes*, was less impressed:

---

[61] *LAM*, 2, 265.   [62] Ibid., 2, 267.

[63] Marmier's spelling alternates between 'Montenegro' and 'Monténégro'.

[64] *LAM*, 1, p. ix.

[65] [Anonymous], 'Analyses critiques et extraits d'ouvrages récents', *Nouvelles annales des voyages*, 5th ser., 37 (1854), 170–201 (170–1).

Marmier n'a [. . .] point prétendu recueillir des impressions politiques dans le nouveau pays qu'il vient de parcourir; autrement il eût remarqué un fait sur lequel on ne saurait trop insister lorsque l'on parle des Slaves: c'est que le penchant qu'ils ont pu par instants témoigner pour la Russie n'a jamais été qu'un pis-aller.[66]

Although Marmier turned out to be mistaken about the role of Montenegro in the Crimean War (in which it remained neutral), it could perhaps be argued that some of his comments foreshadow some of the late twentieth-century conflicts in the region.

Rather curiously at first sight, the final chapter of his *Lettres sur l'Adriatique et le Monténégro* returns to the subject of Serbia, reminiscences of his journey seven years previously to Belgrade, and in particular, 'les chants serbes'. This is not, however, he argues, as one might imagine, 'la propriété exclusive de la petite principauté danubienne dont Belgrade est la capitale; c'est la guirlande champêtre, c'est le romancero, c'est l'Iliade des différentes peuplades qui jadis formaient la royauté serbe'.[67] He divides the 'chants' into the categories of 'chants lyriques' and 'chants épiques', which he presents in comparatist style, in the context of equivalent genres in other European countries. A number of summaries and extracts are given in translation. Todorova judges that 'son compte rendu sur notre poésie populaire, qu'il analyse et traduit tour à tour, est très intelligent'.[68]

From Marmier's diary, we know that he spent the remainder of the winter in Hamburg and returned to Paris in the spring of 1853 via Bavaria and the Tyrol. He must have arrived back in Paris sometime in June: Charles Weiss had written a letter of introduction for Auguste Castan[69] to Marmier, and Castan was eager to seek him out. A letter from Castan to Weiss dated 14 June says that Marmier has not yet arrived back in Paris, but that he is expected shortly. A further letter, dated 24 June, suggests that although Castan has not yet managed to meet Marmier, he suspects that Marmier 'a bien soin de cacher sa retraite puisque la portière le croit encore en voyage'.[70]

1854 was not a particularly happy year: the winter saw him suffering from a mysterious ailment which left him tired, listless, and unable to work—a most unusual state of affairs for Marmier. The great traveller

---

[66] V. de Mars, 'Revue littéraire', *RDM*, 2nd ser., 5 (1854), 856–64 (859).

[67] *LAM*, 2, 339.

[68] Todorova, *Les Slaves du sud au XIXᵉ siècle*, 166.

[69] Auguste Castan (1833–92) was a Bisontin who, like Marmier, was a protégé of Charles Weiss. Unlike Marmier, he made his career as librarian in Besançon. He published a number of works on the Franche-Comté.

[70] BmB, Collection Estignard, MS 1902, Correspondance de Charles Weiss, Lettres de Auguste Castan, fo. 182.

found that it now took him all his strength to walk down to the Tuileries, sit on the terrace and listen to a barrel organ for an hour or so. A part of the trouble may have been grief, depression, or some sort of mid-life crisis. In his diary, he reflected that although he had lived in Paris for some twenty-five years and made friends and acquaintances up and down the social scale, he was very much alone: 'il n'y a peut-être à présent pas une âme qui pense à moi, pas un être qui se demande ce que je fais et où je suis'.[71] Although his relationship with Ebba was positive in that she was affectionate and attentive towards him, it distressed him that they could never be married. He refers to such relationships as 'unions de cœur' and concludes that although they can certainly bring much joy,

> à tout instant on les voit entravées dans leur libre essor par un grain de sable, gênées par une froide convenance, obligées de s'abaisser jusqu'à prendre un masque aux yeux mêmes des indifférents, [. . .] subjuguées tout à coup par la loi qui n'a pu les sanctionner, ou par la religion qui les condamne, ou par le monde qui les tolère, un jour qui s'en égaye peut-être, et à une certaine heure les traite impitoyablement.[72]

Yet his general health began to improve in the springtime, and he finally felt that he was cured in the summer after spending time with Ebba at her country home. In October he made a journey to Alsace via Lorraine, Metz, and Strasbourg, where he met up with his brother Louis and treated him to dinner; the two spent a happy evening before Xavier made his way, the following day, to Saint-Louis where he spent five days with his mother and sister, days 'de joie si pure, d'épanchements si purs, de causerie si douce'.[73] His mother wept as he left for Paris, and he promised to come back and visit her again, never suspecting that this would be the last time he would see her.

A Journey to the Baltic

1855 started inauspiciously, with a further attack of the ailment which had affected him so badly the previous year; this time the lassitude and depression were accompanied by searing pains in his legs and stomach. Early in January he was forced to take to his bed for a fortnight during which time he had no fewer than one hundred and twenty hot poultices applied to his chest. While he was thus incapacitated, he learned that his brother Joseph was ill in Besançon, and then suddenly, and quite unexpectedly, he further received a telegram announcing that his mother was on her deathbed. His

---

[71] *Journal*, 1, 165.   [72] Ibid., 1, 165–6.   [73] Ibid., 1, 168.

doctor advised him that he should not attempt to make the journey, and warned Marmier that he thought it unlikely in his present condition that he would survive as far as Strasbourg. His younger sister Léocadie set off from Lons-le-Saunier and joined their elder sister Maria at their mother's bedside as she drew her last breath on 31 January 1855. Léocadie had attempted to persuade her mother to move to Lons-le-Saunier and live with her and her family after the death of Marmier senior, but the mother had refused, saying that she wished to die in the same place as her husband. Marmier remembers her as a 'douce, tendre, sainte femme' and judges that 'c'est sans doute une punition de mes fautes que je n'aie pu la revoir encore et lui demander sa bénédiction'.[74] His condition was diagnosed by the eminent Tardieu[75] as a 'gastralgie avec appauvrissement du sang et affaiblissement général' and he was prescribed sea bathing.[76] Marmier began to feel a little stronger in the spring, and in May wrote to his employers at the ministry to request permission to take paid sick leave in June and July, when the library was generally quiet, and to combine his doctor's prescription with a research trip to the island of Rügen in northern Germany. Here, he writes, 'il y a [. . .] des monuments de l'ancien paganisme scandinave, une histoire, des traditions qui m'occupent depuis plusieurs années, et qui peuvent être l'objet d'un intéressant récit'.[77]

His request was approved, although the volume produced as a result of this trip of relatively short duration would suggest that Marmier cannot have had a great deal of free time to devote to sea bathing, as the doctor had ordered.[78] He does offer rapid descriptions of the spa facilities in both Rügen and Heligoland, but on the whole he seems unenthusiastic about the concept of the spa. They are referred to (and he cites numerous spa towns in both France and Germany in this context), as '[des] plages arides, des collines infructueuses' where nature happens to have provided 'un filet d'eau très désagréable, une source sulfureuse, bitumineuse, ferrugineuse'.[79] The main attraction of the spa for Marmier appears to have been that of a

---

[74] Ibid.
[75] Ambroise Auguste Tardieu (1818–79) was a distinguished professor of medicine who is best remembered today for his pioneering work on battered child syndrome (1860). Marmier may have met him through his brother Amédée Tardieu, who was a fellow librarian (at the Institut de France). For further details, see *Les Professeurs de la Faculté de Médecine de Paris: Dictionnaire biographique 1794–1939* (Paris: Éditions du Centre national de la recherche scientifique, 1991).
[76] AnF, F17/21256.   [77] Ibid.
[78] *Un été au bord de la Baltique et de la mer du Nord* (Paris: Hachette, 1856). References here are to the second edition (Paris: Hachette, 1883) (cited hereafter as *EB*). Two extracts were published in *Le Correspondant*: 'Le Couvent d'Oliva [. . .]' and 'Dantzig, géographie et histoire' on 25 September 1855 and 25 February 1856 respectively.
[79] *EB*, 319.

spectacle, a sociological phenomenon worthy of study; in terms of the common good he sees the benefits they bring mainly in terms of economic stability: 'Il y a des districts entiers qui doivent leur avenir, leur prospérité, à la savante et généreuse Faculté de médecine'.[80]

In comparison with some of his other travel narratives, there is relatively little here in terms of personal comment or physical details of his journey. He appears to have travelled from Berlin to Danzig (Gdansk, now in Poland, but which at this time was Prussian territory),[81] then back along the Pomeranian coast via Stettin (Szczecin) and Stralsund to Rügen. He also went to Heligoland. For the first time in his life, Marmier tells us, he was grateful to be able to catch a train that would whisk him from Berlin to Danzig in just fifteen hours. The advantage of speed notwithstanding, however, he was still far from being converted to the 'affreux chemins de fer' which, in his words, 'ont anéanti la poésie et l'agrément des voyages'.[82] Furthermore, in his opinion, as well as being responsible for a general decline in culinary standards by initiating a sort of nineteenth-century fast-food culture, they would ultimately be shown to have contributed to an epidemic of stress-related diseases, ulcers, general impatience, an overall tendency to self-centredness, a decline in old-fashioned courtesy and manners, and an increase in the importance placed on material wealth with attendant degeneration of the moral fabric of society. The construction of the railways has moreover laid waste numerous 'lieux consacrés par de religieux souvenirs ou par une poétique pensée',[83] created pollution, and generally ravaged areas of outstanding natural beauty:

> [Le chemin de fer] se lève dans sa force gigantesque, et dévore l'espace comme un conquérant dont rien ne peut arrêter la marche [. . .] il va sans s'arrêter dans son essor impétueux, scindant les montagnes, comblant les vallées, renversant les chênes séculaires et les roches pyramidales, rasant les tourelles du moyen âge et les colonnades de l'antiquité [. . .] et entrant dans les villes de guerre comme un conquérant, par une brèche ouverte au milieu des remparts. De ses noirs tourbillons de fumée, il voile l'azur du ciel, le gazon des prairies; sous ses rails il engloutit plus de fleurs que les jeunes filles d'Allemagne n'en cueilleraient en plusieurs générations pour leurs jours de fiançailles, et le sifflet de sa locomotive retentit comme un rire méphistophélique sur les tranchées qu'il a faites.[84]

---

[80] *EB*, 319.
[81] The border between Poland and Prussia shifted significantly at each division of Poland, but Dan(t)zig/Gdansk remained within Prussian boundaries from the second division of Poland (1793) throughout the nineteenth century with the exception of 1807–14 when it became a free town under the French occupation.
[82] *EB*, 5.   [83] Ibid., 3.   [84] Ibid., 3–4.

The above is a short extract from a diatribe that runs to eleven pages. Interestingly, although all manner of evils are attributed to the railway system, Marmier does not touch on the most widespread fear about railways at the time, namely the physical dangers of travelling at speed. However crude this extract might seem at first glance with its demonisation of the locomotive, the contrast between the engine's whistle as a 'rire méphistophélique' and the old 'cor du postillon'[85] which is now likened to the 'Wunderhorn'[86] of yore, the antithesis between the 'noirs tourbillons de fumée' on the one hand, and the 'azur du ciel', 'le gazon des prairies' and the flowers picked by young girls on the other, it also seems remarkably perceptive—in retrospect at least—in terms of some of the vocabulary used. Combined with words simply connoting power (e.g. 'force gigantesque') are numerous terms suggesting war or aggression, including 'remparts', 'villes de guerre', 'renversant' 'dévore', 'scindant', and 'conquérant' used twice in the space of a few lines, once with the qualification 'dont rien ne peut arrêter la marche', thus communicating relentless inevitability. Some fifteen years later, the Prussians would use their well-organised railways to their advantage in the Franco-Prussian War (which of course turned out so disastrously for the French). Berlin even now is presented in such terms as 'cette capitale d'un peuple essentiellement guerrier';[87] the geometrically precise roads are compared to 'des régiments de maisons prêtes à s'ébranler à un roulement de tambour, à se mettre en marche'.[88] Even the city's layout has 'une empreinte de rêve belliqueux'.[89] More threatening yet is

> cet arsenal qui s'élève en face du musée, ces canons alignés près de l'académie, ces officiers qu'on rencontre à chaque pas en grand uniforme, ces parades perpétuelles, et ces troupes à pied et à cheval qui, pour faire leurs exercices, envahissent jusqu'aux allées du parc, on sent qu'il y a là un esprit martial plus puissant encore que l'esprit scientifique.[90]

Marmier's depiction of Prussia in 1855 therefore bears little resemblance to 'la rêveuse, la poétique, la mélancolique Allemagne'[91] he had presented to the French public in the early 1830s; rather, it foreshadows the Prussian threat to France in 1870.

He found Danzig, by virtue of its physical situation, to be picturesque, but by the layout of its streets and its architecture, to be 'une des villes les plus originales et les plus bizarres'.[92] He was also struck by the mixture of profane and religious imagery in statues and public buildings, of which he

[85] Ibid., 2.　　[86] Ibid.　　[87] Ibid., 12.　　[88] Ibid., 13.　　[89] Ibid.　　[90] Ibid.　　[91] Ibid., 1.
[92] Ibid., 32.

cites the old stock exchange as an example. The Pomeranian coast he found to be 'morne et terne',[93] although fascinating for its geology, ethnology, and social anthropology. Rügen was not at all as he had imagined, and he has some fun in the narrative, ostensibly at his own expense (although probably, by implication, at the expense of other travellers less honest in their accounts):

> Je m'étais figuré une île d'un aspect sinistre, sauvage, une de ces contrées que l'on contemple avec un doux saisissement d'effroi, et dont on se réjouit de décrire, un soir, au coin du feu, d'un air modeste, les magnifiques horreurs, à des amis qui n'ont point quitté la ligne des boulevards et qui admirent votre courage.[94]

He had known Hamburg well in the past, but now particularly enjoyed his stay at the Hotel Victoria with its view over the Alster. He very much approved of the rebuilding which had taken place after the great fire of 1842 and declared Hamburg to be 'une véritable, une éclatante image du fabuleux phénix'.[95] He also enjoyed the resources of the rich libraries, and spent happy hours with the enormous choice of newspapers from all corners of the globe. His narrative then covers the Elbe estuary, Blankenese and Cuxhaven before turning to Heligoland. Heligoland is a small rocky island in the North Sea off the Elbe estuary and the Holstein coast. From 1714 to 1807 it was a Danish possession, and was then taken by the English (who only relinquished it to the Germans in 1890 in exchange for Zanzibar). Marmier, always mistrustful of the English, emphasises the potential strategic importance of its location in the event of war: Heligoland would be

> un point d'observation capital. Là, elle peut élever une forteresse redoutable et abriter une flotte sous ses canons; de là, elle peut surveiller au loin les mouvements de ses adversaires, dominer les quatre vastes artères fluviales, bloquer Brême et Hambourg, menacer le Hanovre, pénétrer dans les parages du Danemark.[96]

But if the book reveals relatively little of Marmier's personal impressions of the trip or of his travel arrangements, this is more than compensated for by the depth and breadth of the information presented. As a whole, the volume reads like a particularly erudite kind of guidebook to the region. Marmier spared no trouble in his fact-finding mission, and all available sources appear to have been exploited: the train journey from Berlin to Danzig was spent with a railway engineer whom Marmier quizzed about crops grown in the region, its industrial progress, and its current economic

---

[93] *EB*, 188.   [94] Ibid., 222.   [95] Ibid., 262.   [96] Ibid., 312–13.

situation. In the stagecoach from Stettin (Szczecin) to Stralsund he learned about local folklore and history from a priest. He left Stralsund for the ten-minute crossing to Rügen armed with a collection of books; indeed, the extraordinary range of sources consulted and quoted is perhaps the most impressive angle of the work. A three-page bibliography precedes the narrative, composed mainly of works in German, but also including French, English, and Latin texts. The body of his text contains a significant number of footnotes with references to additional works and authors ranging from Tacitus, Sir Walter Raleigh, the Irish poet Thomas Moore, and Tieck, to lesser-known figures such as Adolphe Joanne (itineraries) or Quatrefages (natural history). Each location visited is discussed in terms of its history, ancient and modern; its language; its geographical peculiarities; its physical appearance and architecture (where applicable); its current economic and political situation; its social institutions; its folklore and legends (Marmier was of course a pioneer in this field in France).

Even in this context, however, there is evidence of a certain world-weariness on the part of the traveller. In a comparative discussion of *Sagas* and *Märchen*, for example:

> Dans les rêves qui nous viennent de ces trésors du passé, n'y a-t-il pas souvent une grave réflexion? Ces légendes, qui nous représentent des cités ensevelies sous les vagues et subsistant encore au fond des océans, ne sont-elles pas une image des empires que les révolutions du temps ensevelissent dans leurs abîmes, et dont le mouvement, les mœurs, se perpétuent par la chronique et par l'histoire? Et nous-mêmes, à une certaine époque de l'existence, ne sommes-nous pas des exemples de ces ruines vivantes? N'avons-nous pas au fond de notre cœur les magnifiques édifices de notre jeunesse, les palais d'or de nos illusions, qui se conservent sous le voile de l'âge, qui se perpétuent par la mémoire [. . .]?[97]

His general dissatisfaction with the state of the world and the fabric of society surfaces at several junctures. He laments, for example, 'les nouveaux instruments de guerre, les petits salaires des pauvres condamnés à un juste mépris, et les grands jeux de la Bourse honorés d'une respectueuse considération; les consciences qui, pour mieux dormir, s'abritent dans des billets de banque [. . .]'.[98] Although no reference is made to his recent bereavements, the text certainly bears witness to his depressed state. Even more strikingly, and probably in part as a consequence of the above, this is the first of his books which reads as the work of an older man. From the summit of a lighthouse near Danzig he gazed out onto the Baltic Sea so intently that the lighthouse-keeper's wife asked him if he was concerned about any

[97] Ibid., 184–5. [98] Ibid., 221.

particular ship: 'Oui, me disais-je, j'ai là le navire de ma jeunesse; et celui-là, nulle compagnie d'assurances ne peut payer la cargaison et jamais il ne reviendra'.[99]

1855 saw the publication of Marmier's translation of Gerstäcker's *Fahrten und Schicksale* (*Aventures d'une colonie d'émigrants en Amérique*).[100] After a spell in the Ardennes writing up his material, Marmier set off in October 1855 on a pilgrimage to Saint-Louis in Alsace to visit his parents' graves, 'qui renferment tout ce qu'il y a eu pour moi en ce monde de bonté impérissable, de tendresse infinie, de dévouement que rien ne peut remplacer'.[101] By chance he met his elder sister Maria who had also come to pay her respects; the two siblings spent a few hours together, and then Marmier made his way via Mulhouse and Belfort to Besançon. Still in melancholy mood, he wandered the streets on his own and spent hours sitting on the rocks of the citadel as he had done when he first lived in Besançon, 'dans les rêves de ma jeunesse. Ah! ma chère, pauvre, idéale, ardente jeunesse, qu'êtes-vous devenue?'.[102]

In November he returned to Paris where he resumed his study of Russian language and literature, which 'pacifique étude'[103] brought him some satisfaction and comfort. There is a certain irony in his choice of adjective here, since, as he noted, at the time of writing, France was at war with Russia. In Marmier's words, 'nos journaux par complaisance ou par ignorance répandent dans le public, en parlant de ce pays, [. . .] de[s] mensonges ou de[s] sottises'.[104] Marmier in fact seems to have made little specific reference to the Crimean War in either his work for publication or his private papers, although the above suggests a note of scepticism on his part. In his *Un été au bord de la Baltique et de la mer du Nord*, he indicates that Danzig had suffered considerably from the blockade of the Russian ports and that the war had caused a bad season for the Heligoland spa, with consequent hardship for its inhabitants, as potential visitors had been dissuaded from travelling by the knowledge that England had established a garrison of mercenaries there. More importantly, a strong pacifist—and indeed at some points almost socialist—ethos emerges from that text. The mercenaries are largely 'innocents'[105] who have no interest in either England or Russia, and no interest in the war itself. He roundly condemns a state of affairs in which

[99] *EB*, 70.
[100] Friedrich Gerstäcker, *Aventures d'une colonie d'émigrants en Amérique, traduites de l'allemand par Xavier Marmier* (Paris: Hachette, 1855).
[101] *Journal*, 1, 169. This is a further episode where details are deformed by Kaye's faulty transcription. See Wendy Mercer, 'Xavier Marmier and the Contraband Vegetables: Notes on the Published Version of Marmier's *Journal*', *Australian Journal of French Studies*, 28 (1991), 29–38 (1).
[102] *Journal*, 1, 170.   [103] Ibid., 1, 174.   [104] Ibid., 1, 171.   [105] *EB*, 339.

one of the most prosperous regions of Europe should find within it 'des malheureux qui, pour la misérable somme de cent cinquante francs, sacrifient leur liberté, qui pour vivre vont se faire tuer'.[106] Elsewhere in the text, war is referred to as 'cette cruelle passion de l'homme'[107] and Marmier asks in rhetorical mode if 'la guerre même que l'on appelle la plus glorieuse, peut-on vraiment s'en réjouir quand on songe au sang qu'elle fait verser, aux calamités qu'elle répand sur le sol qu'elle traverse?'.[108] He quotes Raleigh's argument about the majority of men slaughtered on the battlefield having no idea of what they were fighting for or why. As an avowed Christian he further questions the appropriateness of the *Te Deum* which he describes as a 'hymne de reconnaissance sur l'arène sanglante [. . .] pour tant de coups de canon qui ont détruit tant d'existences'.[109]

The last years of the decade brought mixed fortunes for Marmier. On the professional front, it was a successful period. The time he had recently devoted to his study of Russian resulted in the publication of three volumes of translations (*Les Drames intimes*, a collection of Russian tales; *Scènes de la vie russe* by Turgenev which would be reprinted seven times; and *Une grande dame russe* by Vonliarliarski).[110] As well as Turgenev, he had also met Lev Tolstoi. Troyat tells us that in 1857, Tolstoi mixed very little outside his Russian circle of friends. In the French literary world, the only people he knew were Marmier, Louis Ulbach, and the chansonnier Pierre Dupont.[111] In his *Journal intime* for that year, Tolstoi suggests that he did not appreciate these contacts: on 16 (28) March, he notes: 'dîné en compagnie de Tourguéniev et de Marmier chez Miss Pancouk [*sic*], avec des académiciens. Mesquin, banal, stupide'.[112] A volume of Danish novellas also appeared in 1859.[113] An excursion undertaken with Ebba 'dans la Forêt-Noire, et en Allemagne'[114] in 1856 or 1857 provided the basis for two articles in *Le Correspondant*.[115] It would seem that this excursion, together with notes from his travels in 1852 and 1855, as well as memories of his

---

[106] Ibid.   [107] Ibid., 18.   [108] Ibid.

[109] Ibid., 19. This sentiment is frequently echoed in Marmier's work. See, for example, *Prose et vers 1836–1886* (Paris: Lahure, 1890), 141–3.

[110] *Les Drames intimes: contes russes, par X. Marmier* (Paris: Michel Lévy, 1857); *Scènes de la vie russe: par M. J. Tourgueneff, nouvelles russes, traduites avec l'autorisation de l'auteur par M. X. Marmier* (Paris: Hachette, 1858); *Une grande dame russe: par B. A. Vonliarliarski, traduit du russe par X. Marmier* (Paris: Michel Lévy, 1859).

[111] Henri Troyat, *Tolstoï* (Paris: Fayard, 1965), 202.

[112] Léon Tolstoï, *Journal intime (1853–1865)*, [trans. Jean Chuzeville and Wladimir Pozner], 2 vols. (Paris: Fasquelle, 1926), 2, 18.

[113] *Nouvelles danoises, traduites par Xavier Marmier* (Paris: Hachette, 1859).

[114] *Journal*, 1, 175.

[115] 'La Forêt-Noire', *Le Correspondant* (December 1857 and January 1858); these also appeared as *La Forêt noire* (Paris: Charles Duniol, 1858).

extended period of residence in Germany in the 1830s, all brought up to date by copious reading and scholarly references, supplied the substance for the two very splendid volumes of *Voyage pittoresque en Allemagne* which were published in 1859 and 1860.[116] In addition to extensive information on history, myths and legends (some of which, but not all, had already been published), literary anecdotes, and reminiscences, the volumes contained forty-six stunning engravings. Many of the anti-Prussian statements made in *Un été au bord de la Baltique et de la mer du Nord* are repeated almost verbatim in this later work.[117] The aims of his work and also its necessary limitations (despite its broad coverage) are summarised in his conclusion:

> Dans ces deux volumes consacrés à l'Allemagne, j'ai essayé de dire de mon mieux ce que j'avais vu et observé dans cette contrée, ce que j'avais appris par l'étude, ce qui s'était gravé dans mon souvenir par mes émotions. Puis-je penser que j'ai fait une description complète de l'Allemagne? Non, certes, je n'ai point une telle présomption. L'Allemagne est un pays trop étendu, divisé en trop d'États distincts et présentant trop de points de vue différents pour qu'un seul homme puisse en faire en un seul livre un tableau complet. Mais je me suis efforcé au moins de saisir dans l'aspect de son sol et de ses cités, dans ses mœurs et sa littérature, les traits les plus caractéristiques d'un pays que j'ai traversé en tous sens, où j'ai vécu à diverses reprises et que je n'ai cessé d'aimer.[118]

The Novelist

At the behest of Templier, Hachette's son-in-law, Marmier wrote his first major novel, entitled *Les Fiancés du Spitzberg*, which appeared in 1858.[119] *Les Fiancés du Spitzberg* has a relatively simple plot. The *Rosa-Marie*, pride of the fleet of a rich shipowner in Dunkirk, is sent on a whaling expedition to Spitzbergen. The vessel docks at Hammerfest to restock and engage a pilot. As the ship has arrived relatively late in the season, all the experienced pilots have already left. The only decent pilot still available is Lax, a very experienced, although ageing, Swede. He is highly recommended, but will consent to join the expedition only on condition that he be accompanied by his daughter, Carine. Carine (in the best Romantic tradition) suffers from delicate health and Lax is convinced that the rigorous climate of Spitzbergen is beneficial to her. At Spitzbergen, a number of misfortunes

---

[116] *Voyage pittoresque en Allemagne*, illustrations by the Rouargue brothers, 2 vols. (Paris: Morizot, 1859–60) (cited hereafter as *Voyage pittoresque*).

[117] *Voyage pittoresque*, 2, 175 ff.   [118] Ibid., 2, 512.

[119] *Les Fiancés du Spitzberg* (Paris: Hachette, 1858). The BnF catalogue lists a copy dated 1856, but I have never been able to see the book to check; I have found no other reference to publication before 1858; certainly the *Bibliographie de la France* makes no mention of the title prior to 1858.

culminate in the mutiny led by the thuggish Tromblon. Owing to the commotion caused by the mutiny, the ship becomes frozen in for the winter with
only six people on board, including the fragile Carine and a young cabin
boy. Thanks largely to the good sense and innate qualities of leadership dis-
played by the second-in-command, Marcel Comtois (Marmier's alter ego),
but also to the resourcefulness and determination of the others, they survive
the winter and manage to return to Hammerfest. During the time away,
Marcel falls in love with, and becomes engaged to, Carine. She, unfortunately, does not survive the experience, and dies as the ship sails into
Hammerfest. This rather romanticised plot is spiced up by a number of dramatic elements including not only details of the mutiny and the drunken
exploits of Tromblon, but also an encounter with a hungry polar bear and
the killing of a number of seamen by a mother walrus whose baby they have
unwittingly slaughtered while hunting the adults.

It would be easy to dismiss the novel as naive and sentimental—which
in some respects, it certainly is.[120] Its interest lies more in the abundance of
information presented about a vast range of subjects connected with
Scandinavia, and Spitzbergen in particular. At times the amount of information presented is *too* copious and perhaps resembles an ill-disguised
lecture. Indubitably, however, the text offers a wealth of fascinating information, from Scandinavian myths and legends to Sami language and customs; details about reindeer farming which include, quite intriguingly for
the non-specialist, a vivid description of the noise made by a herd of reindeer on the move ('un craquement pareil à une détonation [. . .]'[121]); a list of
the fourteen nautical terms used in English to express different forms or
movements of ice;[122] the art of manœuvring a sailing boat through different
kinds of ice-fields;[123] detailed descriptions and scientific explanations of
icebergs[124] and of the aurora borealis.[125] The latter are divided into two
categories, 'l'une fixe, l'autre mobile':

> La première apparaît quelquefois comme un sillon de pourpre dans les champs
> célestes [. . .] mais sa lumière est douce et calme comme celle du crépuscule,
> et elle garde longtemps la même forme.
>
> La seconde est plus brillante, plus variée, et en quelques instants elle
> présente toutes les nuances [. . .]. Peu à peu le nuage qui la revêt se détache sur
> un fond azuré, se couronne d'un cercle lumineux [. . .] puis soudain, de la
> sommité de cette aurore jaillissent des gerbes de feu qui éclatent comme des
> fusées [. . .] Du milieu de son foyer, tantôt on voit ruisseler des flots de

---

[120] For example, Carine is given a cabin to herself with the only stove while the five others shiver next door in their hammocks without any form of heating in the Arctic winter!

[121] *Les Fiancés du Spitzberg*, 127.   [122] Ibid., 189–90.   [123] Ibid., 191–3.   [124] Ibid., 221–4.

[125] Ibid., 368–9.

> lumières pareils à la lave ardente qui s'échappe des entrailles d'un volcan [. . .]
> tantôt on voit surgir les colonnes de feu [. . .].[126]

Also to be found are less pleasant descriptions of the harpooning of a whale
and the techniques involved; the flora and fauna (predominantly, of course,
the latter) of Spitzbergen; and a survey of tasks carried out by working dogs
all over the world.

Marmier notes in his private papers that he put his heart and soul into
the writing of this 'histoire demi-réelle, demi-fictive'.[127] The plot appears to
be largely imaginary, but is clearly based on Marmier's experiences on board
La Recherche and the character of Marcel Comtois is semi-autobiographical
('ce jeune homme, c'était moi [. . .] c'est ma jeunesse que j'ai représentée
en lui, ce sont mes désirs d'étude, mes émotions de cœur et mes rêves'[128]).
He also took a great deal of trouble with documentation to ensure the exactitude of the scientific details. The work enjoyed a significant success.
Although, as Marmier notes, it received scant attention in the press, it was
appreciated by the people who mattered to him personally. It also caught
the attention of the people who mattered professionally: the French
Academy awarded Marmier a prestigious Prix Montyon for the novel in
1859.[129] The annual report, written by Villemain, summarises the novel as
'un récit romanesque fondé sur une étude attentive des mœurs et des
lieux'.[130] In stylistic terms, it is judged by the Academy to have 'un style
naturel et pur, un intérêt sans effort, l'image des vertus que donne une vie
simple sous un ciel sévère [. . .] une étude saine avec agrément'.[131]

Marmier's reaction at winning the prize was to characterise his reaction
to any major event in his life henceforth:

> Ah! si mon pauvre père vivait encore, lui qui était si occupé de mes moindres
> succès, quelle joie il aurait eue de cette décision de l'Académie! Chaque fois
> qu'il m'arrive quelque chose d'heureux, je pense plus vivement à lui et à ma
> mère. Nulle affection ne peut remplacer la leur.[132]

His personal life over these years was less happy. Already grieving for his
parents, he now entered a turbulent period in his relationship with Ebba. In

---

[126] *Les Fiancés du Spitzberg*, 366–7.
[127] *Journal*, 1, 176.   [128] Ibid.
[129] The Prix Montyon were intended 'aux ouvrages les plus utiles aux mœurs, publiés par des
Français'. See comte de Franqueville, *Le Premier Siècle de l'Institut de France: 25 octobre 1795–25
octobre 1895*, 2 vols. (Paris: Rothschild, 1895), 2, 384. Marmier's award for this novel is listed on
page 386.
[130] 'Rapport de M. Villemain, secrétaire perpétuel de l'Académie française sur les concours de l'année 1859', in Académie française, *Recueil des discours, rapports et pièces diverses 1850–1859* (Paris:
Firmin Didot, 1860), 685–704 (694).
[131] Ibid.
[132] *Journal*, 1, 184.

1857, Ebba's daughter Sarah, who had apparently previously been of a sweet and gentle disposition, became obsessed with the idea of marriage, and subjected her mother to all manner of tantrums because she did not have a husband. Ebba, in despair, turned to Marmier, who found an eligible young man, a decent person from a good family who had a modest fortune to his name. Both mother and daughter took to the young man in question, who soon became a regular visitor. Marmier rapidly began to feel that he had been supplanted in the household, and that he was no longer so welcome. Very soon, however, the marriage plans fell through when Ernest Panckoucke failed to give his consent. Marmier had apparently warned them that he would have to be approached tactfully, but his advice had been ignored. Marmier was now sought out again: the affection was genuine, he believed, on the mother's part, but not so on the part of the daughter. In his private papers, he declares that the latter 'n'a ni cœur ni âme [. . .], n'est bonne envers les autres que lorsque son amour-propre ou son intérêt dépend de leur volonté'.[133] She is, he concludes, 'la plus mauvaise, la plus dangereuse, la plus détestable nature'.[134] He underlines her lack of sincerity by recording her reaction when she was told, three months after the wedding was called off, that her ex-fiancé had died: 'Ah! vraiment! [. . .] cela m'est bien égal'.[135]

The following spring, Amédée Pichot introduced Marmier to a young man named Oscar Devallée (later de Vallée) who had apparently repeatedly requested an introduction.[136] Marmier's initial impressions were favourable, although he admits in his private papers that this may have been because he was so flattered to have been sought out. De Vallée then assiduously cultivated Marmier, who in turn introduced him to Ebba and Sarah. After a courtship of six weeks, wedding plans were in the offing, and Panckoucke would have to be approached again with this new suitor. It was decided that he would be unlikely to assent if he realised that the relationship had been instigated by Marmier and Ebba. It was thus arranged that de Vallée would call on Panckoucke's lawyer stating simply that Sarah had caught his eye, and ask whether there would be any opposition in principle to their marrying. Panckoucke questioned de Vallée as well as his daughter—who both dissembled convincingly—and eventually gave his consent. Now de Vallée's demeanour towards both Ebba and Marmier altered significantly—the former being treated with disdain as some kind of servant, the latter totally

---

[133] Ibid., 1, 175.   [134] Ibid.   [135] Ibid.
[136] De Vallée was authorised to separate the particle in his name in July 1860 according to Kaye's footnote (*Journal*, 1, 199).

ignored. This created scenes between mother and daughter, with the mother threatening to reveal all to her husband in order to scupper the marriage. Marmier dissuaded her from this course of action, and the wedding went ahead as planned on 1 July 1858.[137] Marmier subsequently discovered the extent of de Vallée's machinations. He had learned, through a mutual acquaintance, of Marmier's relationship with Ebba and of the fact that Sarah would be a rich catch. It was at this point that he began begging to be introduced to Marmier. The same mutual acquaintance had also been approached with a view to increasing the dowry that Sarah would bring. Marmier realised that he had been used : 'Je lui avais servi d'escabeau. Son but était atteint, il a commencé par rejeter l'escabeau'.[138] Marmier classes de Vallée as 'l'homme le plus méprisable que j'aie rencontré'.[139]

What really hurt Marmier, however, was that the affair was to cause a rift between himself and Ebba from which the relationship would never fully recover. Although at the time of the wedding and in the months that followed, Ebba was disgusted at the behaviour of both her daughter and her son-in-law, a reconciliation was gradually effected. While Marmier claims that she realised that the couple had ulterior motives for this, and she admitted that she had to buy their respect, she now spent more and more time with them and increasingly neglected Marmier. He was quite devastated by her coldness to him, but he could not bear the thought of losing her. Over the course of the following year, she behaved inconsistently, seeking him out for consolation whenever she had an argument with her daughter, and then dropping him as soon as they were reconciled. He recalls her summoning him to the Ardennes from Paris, then summarily dismissing him when her daughter decided to come and visit; she asked him to leave Besançon and break off a journey in order to meet her in the Ardennes, only then to depart for Paris; by the time he had managed to reach Paris, she had become reconciled with her daughter again, and had left Paris for the country. Here she was again abandoned by her daughter, and prevailed upon him to join her, but as he prepared his departure, she wrote to say that she had received a conciliatory note from the young couple and would now be returning with them to Paris, so that his presence would not now be required.

Not surprisingly, Marmier became tired and depressed; he was consumed with passion, despair, unable to sleep and generally suffering both emotional and physical pain. He had enough insight to realise that he should break off a relationship which was making him so unhappy, but admits in his diary that 'un mot et un regard d'E. me ramenaient tremblant

---

[137] See Kaye's footnote in *Journal*, 1, 199.
[138] *Journal*, 1, 178. Kaye's 'avait' is a transcription error.   [139] *Journal*, 1, 199.

à ses pieds'.[140] He recalled his parents' advice to him to remarry, and decided that in disregarding their wish, he had neglected his filial duty: 'J'ai lié mon sort et ma vie à une femme qui ne peut être ma femme. Je suis puni. Je l'ai mérité. J'expie mon erreur. Mais quelle cruelle expiation!'.[141] He saw the new year in on his own, regretting the past and fearful of the future. In the course of the day, he became more positive, deciding to put his mistakes behind him, and made a number of New Year's resolutions:

> Je vivrai donc seul. Je travaillerai tant que je pourrai. J'ai été souvent mauvais. Je tâcherai de devenir bon, de faire un peu de bien chaque fois que je le pourrai. Je ne serai pas heureux, mais peu à peu je reprendrai le calme et peut-être le contentement. Que Dieu bénisse ma résolution et que la mémoire de mes bons chers parents me vienne en aide![142]

Later in the year, he made his almost annual trip to Alsace, Franche-Comté and Lons-le-Saunier to see his two sisters and Léa's children. He was distressed to find his brother-in-law, Nicolas Guichard, whom Marmier considered very highly, was suffering from a serious illness, but enjoyed seeing the family.[143]

The following year (1860) saw him undertake more foreign travel, although this time closer to home. In June 1860 he was in Switzerland, which he already knew well, in order to gather material for a new travel book, *Voyage en Suisse*, which would be published in 1861.[144] The travel narrative also gave him the opportunity to write about his home town, Pontarlier (which lies very close to the Swiss border) which he describes as 'une des plus jolies villes de nos quatre-vingt-neuf départements'.[145] On his return journey he learned that his brother-in-law's illness had proved fatal—as had been feared—and he stopped off at Lons-le-Saunier to attend the funeral before spending some time in Besançon with his old friend and mentor, Charles Weiss. In November he returned to the Franche-Comté, visiting Pontarlier and Neuchâtel, and then returned to Paris to finish writing up his book on Switzerland.

---

[140] Ibid., 1, 180.   [141] Ibid., 1, 181.   [142] Ibid., 1, 183.

[143] A number of details concerning this family are given in André Pidoux de Maduère, *Le Bon Curé de Dôle 1892–1925. Le Chanoine Xavier Guichard 1849–1925* (Dôle: Edition de la Vie dôloise, 1926). I am grateful to M. André Damien, Membre de l'Institut, for drawing this work to my attention. Nicolas Guichard is characterised here as a 'juge', 'président du tribunal civil' and 'colonel de la garde nationale'. The couple had two daughters and a son, born on 29 June 1849, whom they called after Xavier Marmier, and who became a priest, the subject of the book.

[144] *Voyage en Suisse* (Paris: Morizot, 1861). The volume contains beautiful engravings by the Rouargue brothers who had provided the illustrations for the *Voyage pittoresque en Allemagne*.

[145] *Voyage en Suisse* (Paris: Morizot, 1862), 458.

On New Year's Day 1861 he remained at home alone by the fireside, having declined all invitations in the vain hope that Ebba might come to join him. On 20 January, he had an unfortunate accident: ignoring warnings about black ice on the streets, he went out to visit Pasquier,[146] who had become a very close friend over the years. He then decided to visit another friend, walking briskly, as was his wont. On the rue de la Ville l'Évêque he slipped on the pavement and broke his elbow. Somehow, he managed to summon the strength to walk to the doctor in the rue de la Paix and was lucky enough to find him at home. The doctor bandaged his arm and escorted him home, prescribing bed rest for a month. Thanks to a large stack of books, and to the visits of friends and acquaintances, the time passed quite quickly. Ebba visited him briefly five days a week, but Marmier could sense that she considered these visits to be a duty and was counting the minutes until she could decently leave. At the end of February, he was able to get outside with a walking frame, although when he dined out he still had to have his food cut up for him. At Easter, the relationship with Ebba, which had been steadily deteriorating, finally came to an end. Marmier asked her to dine with him on Easter Day, and told her that it was very important to him: she refused.

Although he was now profoundly depressed, he was shortly to receive some good news. On his return to Paris in the beginning of autumn 1859, Marmier had begun work on a new novel, *Gazida*, which he finished in 1860.[147] *Gazida* is set in Canada and is written in epistolary form. The letters are written by a young Franc-comtois travelling to Canada and relate his experiences on the ship and his adventures in the USA and Canada. The plot concerns the love of a European settler, Bertrand, for a young Native American, Gazida; the novel concludes with the marriage of Bertrand to Gazida and of the protagonist, Henri de Vercel, to the daughter of his Canadian host (who also happens to be of Franc-comtois origin).[148] As with *Les Fiancés du Spitzberg*, the principal interest lies arguably in the various digressions. The novel includes numerous references to old French customs, folklore, and songs that have been forgotten or abandoned in France, but which have survived amongst the French settlers and their descendants. There are numerous lengthy but lively digressions on Native American-Canadian history, folklore, and superstitions. Marmier also presents a good

---

[146] Étienne Pasquier (1767–1862) had an interesting career in that he served successively in the governments of the First Empire, the Restoration and the July Monarchy; under Louis-Philippe he was made chancelier de France.

[147] *Gazida* (Paris: Hachette, 1860).

[148] Chateaubriand's *Atala* (1801) had of course been set in North America (Louisiana) with Native American protagonists.

deal of political comment in the form of condemnation of the various ways
in which the Native Canadians/Americans have suffered at the hands of the
European settlers: not only in terms of the massacres and the expropriation
of lands, but the exploitation of the survivors through their cultivated and
growing dependence not only on alcohol but on guns, fabrics, and other
commodities for which they previously had no use, but for which they now
pay outrageous prices to the merchants: 'Voilà dans quel état de vasselage ils
sont tombés ces Indiens, dont les aïeux ont été les possesseurs de la terre
d'Amérique'.[149] A number of asides in the text also demonstrate elements of
what might nowadays be referred to as elements of 'écriture féminine' (as
opposed to the traditional mode of 'masculine' discourse of the explorer or
colonialist writer).[150] The missionary preaches respect for the difference of
'others' (here the Native Canadians/Americans): 'nous devons prendre
garde que les apprivoisements de la civilisation ne nous aveuglent aussi sur
les qualités réelles des peuples que nous appelons barbares et sauvages'.[151]
One of these qualities is the relationship that these people have with nature,
which stands in contrast to the modern impulse to measure and rationalise
as a means of subjugation:

> Ils ne s'enorgueillissaient point, comme nous le faisons aujourd'hui, d'en
> expliquer les phénomènes; mais ils les observaient à tout instant, dans toutes
> ses saisons, et par cette attention continue, ils acquéraient les connaissances
> nécessaires pour régler leurs actions et assurer leur bien-être. [. . .] La nature
> était leur première et leur constante institutrice.[152]

In addition to the more inevitable autobiographical features of a novel
about travel in a foreign country, there are also two clear references to the
personal trauma Marmier had suffered in his personal life with Oscar de
Vallée. Early on in the novel the protagonist declares that

> Un jour je me suis trouvé sur le chemin d'un habile homme qui aspirait à faire
> un riche mariage, dans une maison où l'on avait confiance en moi, et très-
> innocemment je lui ai servi de pont. A l'aide d'un beau petit masque de vertu
> et de désintéressement, et de plusieurs jolies scènes de comédie, il a décroché
> la dot, décroché le trousseau, quelque chose de plus encore.[153]

Furthermore, a humble country farmer, Jean-Baptiste, is given a puppy by a
fisherman. He initially decides to call it Oscar 'à cause d'un méchant

---

[149] *Gazida*, 355.
[150] For a discussion of these terms in relation to Marmier's travel writing, see Wendy Mercer,
'Gender and *Genre* in Nineteenth-Century Travel Writing: Léonie d'Aunet and Xavier Marmier', in
Steve Clark (ed.), *Travel Writing and Empire: Postcolonial Theory in Transit* (London and New
York: Zed, 1999).
[151] *Gazida*, 183.   [152] Ibid., 158.   [153] Ibid., 13.

hypocrite que j'ai eu le malheur de connaître'; but he then decides that this would constitute an insult to the dog rather than to 'ce mauvais garnement', and names it Brisquet instead.[154]

The novel was another great success for Marmier. A review by Antoine de Latour in *Le Correspondant* criticises the abundance of quotations in old Danish, Dutch, and Russian, but is otherwise overwhelmingly positive.[155] For this reviewer, Marmier is an 'écrivain abondant, d'une facile élégance, d'une grâce attrayante'.[156] The combination of autobiography, fact, and fiction is seen to be particularly successful: 'le voyageur ne se borne plus à recopier les notes de son agenda et à coordonner ses impressions fugitives; un art à la fois élevé et simple s'empare des souvenirs et les transforme; l'homme enfin épanche son cœur'.[157] The whole is characterised, for Latour, as 'cette réalité du souvenir, ce relief exact du paysage et des mœurs éclairé d'une juste et vive lumière ce qui est ici la part de l'invention'.[158]

On 20 June 1861, the Académie française decided to award him a second Prix Montyon. Jules Sandeau went immediately to tell Marmier that the Academy had been unanimous in the decision, and that the duc de Broglie, Mignet, Vitet, Patin, Ampère, Sainte-Beuve, and Vigny had spoken strongly in favour of the work. Villemain's report of the deliberations states that

> Une fiction très-simple qui sert à rendre plus vivante l'exacte description d'un pays lointain et tout français [...]. Le ton naturel du récit, l'intérêt délicat des sentiments, la pureté du style sont des mérites qu[e l'Académie] doit distinguer pour le bon exemple des lettres. Elle choisit, à ce titre, *Gazida*, par M. Marmier.[159]

Apart from the accolade of the Academy, the novel also brought him in some welcome additional income, thanks to the honesty of his friend Templier at Hachette. When Marmier had submitted to him the manuscript of *Les Fiancés du Spitzberg*, Templier had offered him a contract according to which he would receive royalties of thirty centimes per copy sold. Marmier was then delighted when Templier subsequently insisted that fifty centimes should be paid for *Gazida*; this, he calculated, would amount to a substantial increase on 4,000 copies sold.[160]

---

[154] *Gazida*, 242.
[155] Antoine de Latour, 'Bibliographie', *Le Correspondant*, 50 (1860), 615–18 (618).
[156] Ibid., 615.   [157] Ibid., 618.   [158] Ibid., 617–18.
[159] 'Rapport de M. Villemain, secrétaire perpétuel de l'Académie française sur les concours de l'année 1861', in Académie française, *Recueil des discours, rapports et pièces diverses* [...] *1860–1869*, Part 1 (Paris: Firmin Didot, 1866), 413–28 (419).
[160] See *Journal*, 1, 289. Although Marmier claims that the increase was offered the following year, he definitely recalls it as being for his second novel, so it seems most likely that the work in question is *Gazida*. Hachette do not unfortunately keep archives this far back.

Marmier had found further distraction from his separation from Ebba that spring in a hectic social whirl, noting in his diary that in the fifty-five days between 1 April and 25 May 1861 he had not once dined at home. The people he frequented belonged, on the whole, to a 'monde riche, aristocratique, distingué'.[161] In his private papers he lists the salons where he was invited the most regularly: for the most part, they are nobility, and monarchist, either Orleanist or legitimist.[162] In this company, he picked up a huge amount of gossip about the major figures of his day, much of which is published (albeit with very high levels of inaccuracy) in Kaye's edition of the *Journal*.[163]

One of the people he visited the most assiduously, and for whom he appears to have held a genuine respect and admiration, was the ex-chancellor ('chancelier') Pasquier. He had become close to Pasquier after the latter's retirement in 1848, and in the years before his death visited him on an almost daily basis. On 10 April 1861 he confided to his friend Weiss that his old friend was 'malade et affaissé. Le 21 de ce mois il entrera dans sa 95e année. Cette date l'inquiète'.[164] Invited to Pasquier's ninety-fifth birthday celebration, Marmier marvels that although the older man had lost his sight and was deaf in one ear, he was still intellectually sharp, had an excellent memory, made excellent conversation, and had remained very popular: 'l'idéal d'une belle, noble, intelligente vieillesse', he notes.[165] Despite Pasquier's advanced age, Marmier was thus devastated at his death in July 1862. A letter to Charles Weiss on 20 July describes the scene:

> Oui, mon cher ami, la mort de M. Pasquier m'a fait un grand chagrin, et me laisse un grand vide. Depuis plusieurs années, je n'ai guères passé de jours sans dîner avec lui, et sans rester tout le soir près de lui, et je l'ai vu jusqu'à son dernier moment. Le jour de sa mort [...] il m'a pris la main en me disant: vous allez perdre un bon ami; cela me fait bien de la peine pour vous. A 10h j'ai été chercher le prêtre qui l'a administré. Il avait sa pleine et entière connaissance. Dans la journée, il s'était encore fait lire le procès présenté par M. de Montalembert à l'académie, et la veille, je lui avais lu jusqu'à 10 heures du soir une histoire de la révolution. Après avoir reçu les sacrements, il s'est endormi d'un sommeil paisible. Je l'ai quitté à minuit, comptant le revoir le lendemain. Une heure après mon départ, il avait exhalé le dernier souffle, il ne s'était pas réveillé.[166]

---

[161] *Journal*, 1, 188.   [162] See *Journal*, 1, 188–96.

[163] For details of the inaccuracy of Kaye's edition, see Mercer, 'Xavier Marmier and the Contraband Vegetables'.

[164] BmB, Collection Estignard, MS 1907, Lettres à Charles Weiss, Lettres de X. Marmier, fos. 776–7.

[165] *Journal*, 1, 190.

[166] BmB, Collection Estignard, MS 1907, Lettres à Charles Weiss, Lettres de X. Marmier, fos. 780–1.

In June 1862, on his now annual trip to visit the graves of his parents in Alsace, he lingered a little longer than usual in Strasbourg, buying books, paying daily visits to the cathedral, and soaking up the atmosphere in preparation for his next project, a novel entitled *En Alsace: L'Avare et son trésor*.[167] In the meantime, he had been busy working on another novel, situated in the Franche-Comté, and entitled *Hélène et Suzanne*, which appeared in July 1862.[168] In this text he again attacks Oscar de Vallée, who appears thinly disguised as d'Entremonts.[169] D'Entremonts is portrayed as an odious character who displays many of the character traits ascribed by Marmier in his private papers to de Vallée; he too is an unscrupulous fortune-hunter in search of a rich marriage partner. In this novel, however, Marmier has his revenge as d'Entremonts is shot in the jaw in the course of a duel provoked by his dastardly behaviour and left horribly disfigured, thus severely disadvantaged in the marriage market.

In September 1862, he set off on a journey to rekindle happy memories of times with his parents in Lorraine, where he spent some time visiting old haunts.[170] October saw him back in the Franche-Comté, visiting Weiss in Besançon and his two sisters and Léa's three children in Lons-le-Saunier. He was delighted to see that Gabrielle, one of his nieces, appeared to have a flair for languages: after he had given her just three English lessons she started to translate unaided.

Back in Paris, his spirits were lifted both by the sense of a new freedom from his 'déplorable amour'[171] and by the welcome extended to him by people from the top to the bottom of the social scale. Towards the end of the year he became friendly with Thiers;[172] the two men had often been present at social gatherings together, but had never spoken. Now Thiers invited him to dinner, and Marmier found the statesman to be 'séduisant au plus haut degré, surtout chez lui, d'une politesse parfaite, et vif et animé, causant avec

---

[167] *En Alsace: L'Avare et son trésor* (Paris: Hachette, 1863). In his journal he notes that 'c'est un bon petit livre et il m'est doux de penser que je l'ai fait en mémoire de mes parents' (*Journal*, 1, 273).

[168] *Hélène et Suzanne* (Paris: Hachette, 1862).

[169] In his *Journal* he states (perhaps somewhat superfluously) that the novel contains 'le portrait de l'ignoble Oscar de Vallée sous le nom d'Entremonts' (*Journal*, 1, 252).

[170] This passage is included in Kaye's edition of the *Journal* (1, 254), but the errors of transcription are so numerous and so nonsensical that it becomes almost comical. See Mercer, 'Xavier Marmier and the Contraband Vegetables'.

[171] *Journal*, 1, 255.

[172] Louis Adolphe Thiers (1797–1877) was a historian and prominent politician who had a long and controversial career. He held numerous cabinet posts under the July Monarchy but retired temporarily from political life after the coup d'état of December 1851 until 1863 when he effectively became head of the Liberal opposition. In February 1871 he became Chef du Pouvoir exécutif de la République, and Président de la République from 1871 to 1873. For further details on Marmier's relationship with Thiers and his family, see chapter 13.

un merveilleux entrain, et racontant les choses les plus intéressantes'.[173] An excellent conversationalist, Thiers could speak on matters as diverse as science, politics, art, and literature. Marmier soon became a regular visitor to the household, where he mingled with politicians and members of the French Academy including Mignet, whom he liked very well. Thiers' mother-in-law he found rather serious although quite outgoing; his wife was another matter. Marmier thought her cold, taciturn, and socially difficult. But he was to become an ardent admirer of her younger sister Félicie, whom he at once declared to be 'belle, gracieuse, instruite, distinguée, pleine de bonté, de douceur, fort attachante'.[174]

The year 1863 passed quite happily with social visits, and a journey through Nancy and Lorraine, Metz, and Alsace. He also went to Basle where he was delighted to meet up with the comte de Paris and the duc de Chartres, whom he had not seen for some fourteen years.[175] They spent a day together, and Marmier noted his impressions. The comte de Paris had his mother's attractive and rather dreamy eyes, with a handsome, intelligent face. His younger brother was smaller and more alert, and very attached to his brother. Later in the year, Marmier also went on an excursion to Normandy, visiting Cherbourg, Saint-Vaast, Caen, and Trouville. Back in Paris, he resumed his social round of dinner parties and salons while setting to work on his latest novel, *Le Roman d'un héritier*, which is set in 'l'humide vallée de Saulnes'.[176] His old enemy de Vallée reappears in this novel as 'un individu qu'on appelait par dérision le vertueux Oscar, qui prétendait se faire considérer comme un type de générosité et de désintéressement, et qui en même temps voulait devenir riche à tout prix'.[177]

In 1864 Marmier retraced his footsteps to places he had visited earlier in his career. In August he set off for Denmark for the first time since 1842, travelling through Germany: this is the journey upon which his *Souvenirs d'un voyageur* is based. It was not, however, a happy juncture to visit Denmark, which was in the midst of war. When Christian IX succeeded to the throne in 1863, Frederik of Augustenberg contested his succession. Christian, as one of his first acts, had ratified a new constitution which

---

[173] *Journal*, 1, 255.   [174] Ibid., 1, 275.

[175] Grandsons of Louis-Philippe, sons of the duc d'Orléans (1810–42).

[176] *Le Roman d'un héritier* (Paris: Hachette, 1864), 319. It is curious to note that this was the first book to be advertised in the *Journal populaire* at Zola's instigation in his post as head of advertising at Hachette, in the 'Bibliographie' rubric (10 February 1864). The reviews were taken almost verbatim from *Le Bulletin du libraire*. For further details, see Émile Zola, *Correspondance*, 10 vols. (Montréal: Presses de l'Université de Montréal, Éditions du Centre national de la recherche scientifique, 1978), 1, 338.

[177] *Le Roman d'un héritier*, 148.

repealed the traditional autonomy of Schleswig and Holstein; this naturally displeased the German Confederation, who decided to support Frederik's claim to the throne. Bismarck then made an alliance with Austria, and Prussia and Austria declared that they would carry out the resolution of the German Diet. Joint Austrian and Prussian forces invaded Denmark and the Danish government was driven from the mainland. In the treaty of Vienna, signed in October 1864, Schleswig, Holstein, and Lauenburg were handed over to Prussia and Austria. Marmier was horrified by the war, which he qualified as 'inique'.[178] The dismembering of the country, he declared, was 'un des faits les plus monstrueux qu'on puisse imaginer'.[179] In his *Souvenirs d'un voyageur*, he strongly criticises the French refusal to intervene, which he found 'shameful' and also compromising: 'Comment osons-nous proclamer si haut nos principes de justice, si nous laissons tranquillement s'accomplir près de nous les plus flagrantes iniquités, les actes de violence les plus monstrueux?'[180] He was further saddened by the reflection that 'Bien des gens que j'ai connus autrefois dans cette ville sont morts, d'autres naturellement ont vieilli, et moi aussi, je sens comme j'ai vieilli en me rappelant les poétiques émotions que j'éprouvais là autrefois et que je n'éprouve plus guère'.[181]

He was nonetheless cheered by visits to a number of old friends, including the dowager queen Caroline Amalie, Mme de Moltke, Björnstjerna (the Swedish envoy in Copenhagen and son of Lisinka), and his friend Skiaerbeck, with whom he had visited the royal residences in 1837.[182] He had hoped also to revisit some other parts of Denmark and then travel to Sweden and Finland. But the weather was terrible; a glacial rain fell continuously in Copenhagen, so that he hardly left the city. He spent one day at Lyngby with the queen and a further day visiting Helsinger and Helsingborg before returning to Hamburg, which had become a favourite retreat in recent years, and where he spent a day with the comte de Paris and his wife. Two days later he travelled out to meet them at Ludwigslust, where the dowager grand-duchess Auguste-Friederike, Princess of Mecklenburg, was pleased to see Marmier again: she remembered that he had brought her a flower back from Spitzbergen in 1839. He was also invited to a big dinner party with the duke and his family (Friedrich-Franz) before setting off for Leipzig, whence he returned to Paris via Frankfurt and Metz. This journey served to deepen still further Marmier's dislike and fear of Prussia, and the *Souvenirs d'un voyageur* is unambiguous in its warnings about the military

---

[178] *Journal*, 1, 311.   [179] Ibid.   [180] *SV*, 240.   [181] *Journal*, 1, 312.
[182] Académie des Sciences, Belles Lettres et Arts de Besançon, *Memorandum 2*, fo. 203 (omitted by Kaye from the *Journal*).

might and the political ambitions which are presented as a direct threat to France.[183]

The remainder of 1864 was spent largely in trying to shake off a persistent cold he had picked up in Denmark. In November, a new novel, *Les Mémoires d'un orphelin*, appeared.[184] Marmier did not feel it was one of his better works. He had written it, he recalls, the previous winter, 'lentement et péniblement, et cependant avec amour et avec grand soin'.[185] He was afraid that despite his care it might appear 'monotone et froid',[186] but was reassured by friends and also by Templier, his editor at Hachette.

In April 1865, Marmier stood for the first time for election to the French Academy. Two places had fallen vacant: the seats held by Ampère and Vigny. Marmier stood as candidate for Ampère's chair against—amongst others—Jules Janin, Philarète Chasles, and a latecomer, Prévost-Paradol.[187] Prévost-Paradol was eventually elected after three rounds of voting, winning fourteen votes on the first and second rounds and sixteen on the third. Marmier received only two votes on the first round, one on the second, and none on the third.[188] Although he had not expected to be elected at the first time of standing, he was disappointed not to have received more votes: according to his diary, he had hoped for at least seven or eight.[189] Initially, a number of members had pledged him their support, including Broglie and his father. Things had changed, however, with Prévost-Paradol's return to the country from Egypt, and many of Marmier's former supporters, he believed, had switched their allegiance. In the event, he surmised, Lebrun, Laprade, and probably Ségur had kept their word and voted for him.[190] Elections for the French Academy were of course highly political, and Marmier felt that although the successful candidate was young and had never written a book, he was talented, and, more importantly, had published a number of articles against the government. Marmier recalls with some glee that the very day when Paradol was elected to the Academy, Marmier met him running down the rue Taranne in a panic. When asked what had happened, Paradol replied that he had met a pretty and flirtatious girl on the rue Saint-Dominique. He started to follow her and she had

---

[183] See Wendy Mercer, 'From Idyll to Arsenal: The Changing Image of Germany in France as seen through the Work of Xavier Marmier [. . .]', *New Comparison*, 6 (1988), 176–93.

[184] *Les Mémoires d'un orphelin* (Paris: Hachette, 1864).

[185] *Journal*, 1, 314.   [186] Ibid., 1, 315.

[187] Lucien Anatole Prévost-Paradol (1829–70) wrote for the *Journal des Débats* and the *Courrier du dimanche*. Until the late 1860s he held and expressed strong views against the empire.

[188] Figures taken from AAf, 4B9 (no page/folio nos.).

[189] *Journal*, 1, 336.

[190] He may have been mistaken in this assumption: since he received three votes in all, two on the first round and one on the second, there were not necessarily three individuals voting for him.

seemed happy enough. But when she entered a building and he followed her down a corridor, she suddenly screamed, bringing forth neighbours who began calling out for the police. There was a pleasing irony, he felt, that Montalembert, Noailles, and Dupanloup were even at that very moment voting for him. 'Il est assez joli garçon, mon ami Paradol', he reflected, 'et passionné par les femmes'.[191]

The year 1865 was otherwise unremarkable in Marmier's life except for a succession of ailments which might have been enough to prove fatal to someone less robust. In the winter he caught a 'violent' cold[192] which gradually grew worse, although he refused to succumb to bed rest. He continued his social visits until May when he went to Alsace where he met his niece Gabrielle, of whom he was very fond. But he was growing weaker, and he developed an exhausting cough. He lost his appetite, suffered from insomnia and broke out into a sweat at the slightest physical effort. Every night he suffered from a high temperature. When he visited Thiers at Vrigny in June and July everyone expressed concern at the physical deterioration which seemed to have occurred over the past months. At first Marmier believed himself to be suffering from a recurrence of malaria ('fièvre intermittente'[193]) which he had picked up in Algeria, and dosed himself with quinine. When this proved to be ineffective, he decided that it must be a 'fièvre de faiblesse'[194] and eventually consulted a doctor, who diagnosed chronic bronchitis and recommended Marmier to take the waters at Allevard. He was delighted to find Allevard only two leagues away from the railway, in a picturesque valley dominated by high mountains. His stay was an enjoyable one, and as he left in October to return via Switzerland, he felt completely recovered. In Geneva, however, he fell ill again, this time probably suffering from cholera. With great difficulty he made his way via Basle and Strasbourg back to Paris, where he gradually regained his health.

At the end of 1865, his new novel, *Histoire d'un pauvre musicien*, began to appear in serial form in *L'Union*.[195] In February 1866 he lost his old friend and mentor from Besançon, Charles Weiss. In June of the same year, problems of the joint administration of Schleswig-Holstein by the Prussians and Austrians, combined with Bismarck's ambitions, led to war between those two countries. Marmier had consistently made his fears about Prussia public for more than a decade, and now, in his diary, he notes 'la Prusse contre

---

[191] *Journal*, 1, 341.
[192] Ibid., 1, 332.   [193] Ibid.   [194] Ibid.
[195] It was published in book form the following year: *Histoire d'un pauvre musicien* (Paris: Hachette, 1866).

l'Autriche; la Prusse, arrogante, ambitieuse, avide, insatiable; l'Autriche honnête, loyale, brave'.[196] French public opinion generally favoured Austria, but Napoleon III—after some dithering—committed the country to neutrality, later claiming compensation from Bismarck: his lack of clear-sightedness in this affair would be a contributory factor in the eventual French catastrophe of the Franco-Prussian War.

In 1869, three seats fell vacant at the French Academy in April and Marmier stood for election to two of them, although unsuccessfully. For the seat vacated by Viennet, he stood against d'Haussonville, Jules Lacroix, Léon Halévy, Auguste Barbier, and Théophile Gautier: d'Haussonville was elected with nineteen votes, and Marmier obtained three.[197] For the *fauteuil Empis* there were four rounds of voting. Marmier obtained nine votes in the first round, six in the second, two in the third and none in the fourth. Barbier was elected with eleven, twelve, sixteen and eighteen votes in the first to fourth rounds respectively.[198] On this occasion, Marmier recalls, it was Lebrun who urged him to stand for election, advising him to declare his intention to stand much earlier than on his previous attempt, and to campaign incessantly right up until the elections. For two months he had encouraged Marmier, discussing tactics and possible chances. Shortly before the election, however, he admitted slightly shamefacedly to Marmier that he would be voting for Gautier at the behest of Princess Mathilde. Marmier was rather shocked at Lebrun's 'lâcheté' and 'tricherie', but concluded that 'J'en étais, il est vrai, un peu péniblement surpris, mais j'en éprouvais en même temps un sentiment de fierté, par la pensée que j'étais injustement traité et que je ne m'étais point condamné, par une indigne ambition, à faire une vilaine action pour complaire à une princesse'.[199]

The decade closed with the birth of a new friendship and the deaths of two people close to him. In October 1869 Marmier lost another old friend: Sainte-Beuve. In the 1830s the two had been inseparable friends, but had drifted apart until Marmier heard that Sainte-Beuve had spontaneously spoken at the French Academy in favour of his novel *Gazida* for the Prix Montyon. Marmier had visited him to thank him in person, and the two had again become close. During Sainte-Beuve's final illness, Marmier was

---

[196] *Journal*, 1, 352.
[197] AAf, 4B9: Jules Lacroix obtained five votes, Halévy four, Barbier and Gautier one each.
[198] AAf, 4B9: Gautier received eleven votes in the first round, thirteen in the second, and fourteen in each of the third and fourth rounds. Halévy and Léon Laya each obtained one vote in the first and second rounds and none in the third and fourth. The other vacant seat (*fauteuil Berryer*), for which Marmier did not stand, was won by Champagny.
[199] *Journal*, 2, 106.

one of the few friends to whom his door was always open. In remembering his old friend, Marmier disapproved of Sainte-Beuve's lack of religion and also some of his sexual activities,[200] but nonetheless insisted that he was an 'homme de grand talent, le plus fin, le plus sage, le plus pénétrant des critiques [. . .]. Très passionné, très irritable, mais avec un fond de cœur plus sûr et meilleur qu'on ne le croit généralement'.[201]

The year before Sainte-Beuve's death, Marmier had been able to introduce him to his new friend, the American poet Longfellow.[202] It is not entirely clear whether Marmier and Longfellow knew each other before Longfellow's visit to Paris. Stéphen Liégeard claims that Marmier had visited him at Craigie House on his American trip (1849–50),[203] but there appears to be little evidence to substantiate this claim. Certainly there is no correspondence extant between the two men prior to Longfellow's visit to Paris; and no mention is made in Marmier's *Lettres sur l'Amérique* of the American author. Strikingly, the new edition of the *Lettres* published in 1881 bears a preface stating that 'dans la turbulente mêlée des adorateurs du dollar, il y a des hommes d'un esprit élevé', and concludes by addressing his friend directly: 'Et vous, cher poëte d'Évangeline, cher Longfellow, qui pourrait dire les sentiments de sympathie et de respect que de toute part au loin vous conquérez en modulant vos vers, au bord de la rivière Charles, à l'ombre de vos ormes, sous votre toit de Craigie House?'[204] Certainly, according to Samuel Longfellow, his brother met Marmier while on the European trip of 1868–9; according to the biography, the two men then spent a good deal of time 'haunting the booksellers and the stalls of the quais', and visiting the historic streets of Paris.[205] These excursions are recalled both by Marmier in *La Maison*, in which he goes into some detail about the places they visited together, and also

[200] Marmier recalls that Sainte-Beuve was 'grossièrement libertin, courant après les filles des rues, les plus dodues l'appétant plus que les autres. Il aimait à me raconter ses aventures et aurait voulu me donner les mêmes goûts' (*Journal*, 2, 126). He also notes slightly disapprovingly that in his will, Sainte-Beuve leaves 'une pension de 4000 francs à une fille publique qui vivait habituellement chez lui, bien que depuis longtemps il ne pût se livrer à ses désirs de libertinage' (*Journal*, 2, 126).

[201] *Journal*, 2, 127.

[202] Charles Augustin Sainte-Beuve, *Correspondance générale* [. . .], *recueillie, classée et annotée par Jean Bonnerot*, 19 vols. (Paris: Stock, 1935–83), 18, 200–1: 'J'ai eu le bonheur de voir Longfellow qui passait à Paris [. . .]. C'est un de mes amis, Marmier, qui m'a procuré l'honneur et le plaisir de cette visite'.

[203] Stéphen Liégeard, *Au caprice de la plume* (Paris: Hachette, 1884), 228.

[204] *Lettres sur l'Amérique: nouvelle édition*, 2 vols. (Paris: Plon, 1881), pp. vii–viii.

[205] Samuel Longfellow (ed.), *Life of Henry Wadsworth Longfellow, with Extracts from his Journals and Correspondence*, 2 vols. (London: Kegan Paul, Trench and Co., 1886), 2, 445–6.

includes an impressive physical description of Longfellow;[206] and also by Longfellow in letters to Marmier.[207]

It is perhaps not surprising that the two men should have struck up a friendship. Despite the differences between them in creative literary terms, they had a good deal in common, in respect of both private and professional careers. Of similar age (Longfellow was born in 1807, Marmier in 1808), both had travelled extensively and were fascinated by the literatures of other cultures. Both were avid collectors of old books; both were interested in translation (and each would translate works by the other). If it is correct to assume that the two met in the springtime of 1868, it can safely be stated that Marmier had become an admirer of Longfellow's work somewhat earlier. In 1867, he had published a volume entitled *De l'est à l'ouest* which includes a chapter on 'Souvenirs du Canada' containing a lengthy prose translation of an extract of 'Évangeline', which Marmier describes as 'un des plus charmants poëmes des temps modernes'.[208] Further translations would appear later: in 1872 Marmier published an anthology[209] whose contents were reproduced in the *Prose et vers* (1890).[210] Longfellow later wrote to thank Marmier for the 'beautiful translation'.[211] A further collection published posthumously also included an article on 'La Vie rurale en Suède' by Longfellow.[212] Longfellow, for his part, translated Marmier's 'A la Chaudeau'.[213]

The decade closed with the death of Marmier's brother Louis on 2 November 1869. Curiously, there is no mention of this in Marmier's personal papers: the details given here are to be found in Louis's employment file.[214] Prior to his death, Louis had held the post of school inspector in Dijon. His file shows that for some months prior to his death he had been

[206] *La Maison* (Paris and Lyon: Lecoffre fils, 1876), 86–7.

[207] *The Letters of Henry Wadsworth Longfellow*, ed. Andrew Hilen, 6 vols. (Cambridge, Massachusets: Belknap Press of Harvard University Press, 1966), 5, 271–2, 288, 397–8, 707.

[208] *De l'est à l'ouest, voyages et littérature* (Paris: Hachette, 1867), 404.

[209] Henry Wadsworth Longfellow, *Drames et poésies, traduits avec l'autorisation de l'auteur, par X. Marmier* (Paris: Hachette, 1872). The collection contains 'Wenlock Christison'; 'Giles Corey ou la sorcière de Salem'; 'Le Psaume de la vie' (which had also been published in *L'Union* during the Siege of Paris); 'Le Jour de pluie' (this had already appeared in *Dernières Glanes* (Paris: Simon Raçon, 1869), 29); 'Fatigue'; 'Consolation'; and 'Excelsior'.

[210] *Prose et vers 1836–1886* (Paris: Lahure, 1890). This collection also includes 'The Arrow and the song, imité de Longfellow'.

[211] See *The Letters of Henry Wadsworth Longfellow*, 5, 397.

[212] *A travers le monde: diverses curiosités* (Paris: Firmin Didot, 1893), 19–25.

[213] *The Poetical Works of Henry Wadsworth Longfellow* (London: Henry Frowde, Oxford University Press Warehouse, 1893), 782.

[214] AnF, F17/21256.

seriously ill and unable to work; he was suffering from liver cancer and consequent haemorrhaging. He was swiftly followed to the grave by his widow Jeanne-Lucie (née Longchamps) on 11 December. The couple left an 18-year-old daughter, Jeanne Marie Honorine Marthe (always known as Marthe). A note from Marthe attached to the file written in Dijon on 27 December states her intention of travelling to Lons-le-Saunier to live with her aunt (Marmier's sister Léa) and cousins.

13

A Decade of Tumult (1870–9)

The year 1870 was to prove momentous both in terms of French life and history and for Marmier personally. His joy at being elected to the Académie française would be set against the grim backdrop of the Franco-Prussian War, the Siege of Paris, and the bloodbaths at the end of the Commune.

The year did not start auspiciously for his personal well-being. One evening in March as he was returning home after dining with Thiers and his family, he suddenly suffered a violent pain in his back which grew worse overnight and the following day. A doctor diagnosed pneumonia which turned into a serious bout of pleurisy that kept him in his bed for the next two months. His condition was so serious that his brother Joseph and his sister Léa hurried to his bedside from the Franche-Comté, the latter to nurse him, the former to make sure that he would receive the last rites if need be.

In the meantime, his friends rallied round to help with his renewed candidature for the latest round of elections to the Académie française. He had originally intended to stand for the *fauteuil Lamartine* in the elections of March 1870, but discussions minuted in the Procès-Verbaux show that a decision was taken by the Academy to defer his candidature on account of his ill-health.[1] In May 1870, new elections were held to replace Pongerville and Marmier's old friend the duc de Broglie.[2] Marmier stood for Pongerville's seat against Loménie, Rousset, About, Laya, Lacroix, Halévy, and Duvergier de Hauranne. In the deliberations on 12 May prior to the elections on 19 May, mention was made of the fact that distinguished members recently deceased, including Pasquier, Broglie, and Sainte-Beuve had supported him in the past. The early interest shown by the Academy in Marmier's work and the fact that it had sponsored his first major expedition (to Iceland) was considered relevant. The first speaker maintained that Marmier

> n'a pas seulement visité en touriste les contrées les plus diverses, il a voyagé en philologue, en critique, dans les littératures étrangères; de là de nombreux ouvrages où comme dans ceux d'Ampère, dont on peut aussi le rapprocher, se

---

[1] AAf, PV, 2B13, fos. 272–4.
[2] Achille Charles Léonce Victor, duc de Broglie (1785–1870) was a statesman and diplomat.

mêlent heureusement les impressions reçues des lieux, des appréciations morales et littéraires.[3]

The prizes awarded to Marmier by the Academy for his novels were also mentioned by this speaker in his support. Another member made further reference to the parallels between the contributions to learning made by Ampère and Marmier; to Marmier's knowledge of foreign languages and literatures (his translations and criticisms of Schiller's work were singled out by this speaker); and to the tremendous contribution that Marmier would be able to make to the work of the Academy 'par la variété de ses connaissances philologiques et la finesse d'un goût très exercé'.[4] This speaker also quite astutely pointed out the fact that 'ce mélange heureux d'impressions de voyage et de critique' in Marmier's work constitutes a 'genre à part de littérature'.[5]

On 19 May, Marmier was elected to fill the seat vacated by Pongerville after five rounds of voting, at the end of which he achieved sixteen votes as against six to Loménie, four to Rousset, and two to About.[6] At four o'clock that afternoon, Albert de Broglie, Mignet, and Lebrun called round to visit the invalid and announce the good news.[7]

Elections to the Academy at this time had a very prominent public profile and were thus always highly charged—which led to much string-pulling and wrangling. Despite his victory, Marmier was disappointed by the lack of support from old acquaintances. Guizot (the historian and influential politician who had helped Marmier earlier in his career), Vitet (the archaeologist), and the poets Laprade and Barbier had stated their intention of supporting Loménie in the first round, but had promised Marmier that they would support him subsequently if Loménie were not decisively elected in the first round. In the event, they had held out for the other candidate until the end. Marmier was particularly upset with Laprade 'qui m'a fait tant de protestations d'affection quand il venait déjeuner quatre fois par semaine chez moi, et que je négociais ses marchés de livres avec Didier qui n'en avait nulle envie'[8] and Barbier 'qui doit sa nomination à Montalembert et à qui Montalembert avait fait promettre de voter pour moi'.[9] But he was nonetheless delighted to have won the election, and he was immensely cheered by

---

[3] AAf, PV, 2B13, fo. 291.   [4] Ibid., fos. 291–2.   [5] Ibid., fo. 291.

[6] AAf, 4B9. In the previous rounds, Marmier gained 9, 11, 13, and 14 votes respectively before gaining 16 in the fifth. Loménie achieved 7, 7, 7, 7, and 6; Rousset 4, 4, 3, 4, 4; About 2, 5, 5, 3, 2; Halévy 1, 0, 0, 0, 0; and Duvergier de Hauranne 1, 0, 0, 0, 0.

[7] Jacques-Victor-Albert, duc de Broglie (1821–1901) was the son of Victor (see above, n. 2); François Auguste Marie Mignet (1812–1884) was a historian; Pierre-Antoine Lebrun (1785–1873) was a poet and a politician.

[8] *Journal*, 2, 158.   [9] Ibid.

the congratulations which poured in, not only from family and close friends, but from all corners of the globe.

Although the *Journal pour tous* approved heartily of his election, maintaining on the front page that 'personne n'en était digne autant que lui', reactions in the press on the whole were hostile.[10] Both *Le Figaro* and *Le Gaulois* put a political gloss on the result, maintaining that Marmier was elected because of his allegiance to Thiers; *Le Figaro* even went so far as to claim that 'M. Thiers a battu cette fois M. Guizot'.[11] Both *Le Gaulois* and *Le Moniteur Universel* claimed that About should rightfully have won the contest, *Le Moniteur* in rather more restrained terms. In its opening account of the election, *Le Moniteur* claimed that 'l'Académie française a recruté hier, deux vieux soldats qui avaient plus de chevrons honorables que de campagnes brillantes'.[12] This was followed by the pronouncement that 'l'esprit le plus vif, le plus français, l'écrivain qui sent le mieux le coude à Voltaire, le normalien le plus applaudi et le plus attaqué (c'est un double honneur en ce temps-ci), M. Edmond About, est resté à la porte'.[13]

Le Gaulois and *Le Figaro* were much more outspoken and highly personal in their attacks on Marmier. An article in *Le Figaro*, signed simply 'Masque de fer' (presumably P. Gille), criticises the election of

> ce pauvre M. Marmier, si inconnu quand il écrivait, et combien plus inconnu encore depuis qu'il s'est rendu justice en se condamnant au silence! N'est-il pas cruel de l'enlever à ses oreillers, à ses laits de poule, à ses gilets de flanelle, à son bonnet de coton, de lui faire courir les risques d'un rhumatisme—toujours dangereux à cet âge—pour faire savoir au public, qui n'en a cure, qu'il existe encore! Qu'il boive à son aise de la tisane, mais qu'il ne nous en fasse pas prendre sous forme de discours.
>
> Ah! l'Académie! quelle belle occasion elle a perdu là d'éviter une sottise, de fatiguer un pauvre homme qui à sa faiblesse d'esprit d'autrefois ajoute aujourd'hui celle du tempérament, et qui se contentait, pour toute ambition, de caresser son chien Oscar, cet Oscar qui lui rappelle une vengeance satisfaite et un doux rêve envolé![14]

A series of articles in *Le Gaulois* by Francisque Sarcey were even more vitriolic. In electing Marmier, Sarcey claims, the Academy had 'travaill[é] de

---

[10] [Anonymous], 'Courier de Paris. Élections à l'Académie française', *Journal pour tous,* 2nd ser., 16 (25 May 1870), 145–6 (145).

[11] *Le Figaro* (23 May 1870), 2. There was, of course, a political dimension to the elections, and Marmier himself acknowledged that Thiers had helped him (see *Journal*, 2, 277).

[12] *Le Moniteur Universel* (1870), 720.

[13] 'Baronne Jenny d'Erdeck', 'Souvenirs politiques et littéraires d'une vieille femme: les visites académiques', *Le Moniteur Universel* (1870), 739.

[14] 'Masque de fer', *Le Figaro* (21 May 1870), 2.

ses propres mains à sa déconsidération' and brought its reputation into disrepute. Whereas About enjoyed '[une] grande célébrité', Marmier's 'macédoine de volumes' was unknown: 'il écrivait déjà incognito pour la génération qui nous a précédés; à plus forte raison n'est-il point connu à la génération à laquelle nous appartenons, ni de celle qui nous suit'.[15] In a satirical piece in poor taste entitled 'Les Bons Morts', Sarcey continues his campaign against Marmier by maintaining that his election was due to his being considered a 'bon mort' in the parlance of the Academy.[16] Sarcey claims, tongue-in-cheek, that a fixed sum is allocated to pay members' expenses at meetings. If fewer members attend a particular meeting, the share of the pot of money to be distributed is therefore proportionally higher. The same system works, he claims, for attendance at funerals of members of the Academy. Thus the death of a celebrity such as Lamartine, Guizot or Thiers, which would be well attended, would result in a smaller allowance. The funeral of a nonentity, therefore, which would be more sparsely attended, would result in payment of a higher allowance to those present. This, he facetiously claims, is a factor taken into account at elections. In order to qualify as a 'bon mort', a candidate should therefore be 'un inconnu avéré, authentique, un inconnu qui a fait ses preuves'. He should also have a short life expectancy: 'Et c'est ainsi que M. Marmier obtint ses seize voix. Il fut nommé en qualité de bon mort'. In respect of this last quality, however, Sarcey claims that Marmier was guilty of deliberately misleading the members of the Academy. Referring no doubt in ironical terms to Marmier's recent illness, Sarcey maintains that he visited the members of the Academy to canvass votes 'coiffé d'un abat-jour vert, branlant la tête, courbé sur sa canne, et exhalant avec un effort pénible chacun de ses mots, comme s'il poussait le dernier soupir'. On the very evening following his election, Sarcey maintains, 'on le vit rajeuni [. . .]. Le faux mort avait jeté sa béquille comme le Sixte-Quint de la légende'.

Two days later, the front page of the same newspaper featured a series of spoof letters purportedly received by Sarcey from a number of fictitious individuals such as 'Besuchet, Empailleur ordinaire de l'Académie française', all objecting to various aspects of the article on 'Les Bons Morts', but continuing nonetheless to cast ridicule on Marmier's election.[17] A 'letter' signed 'Pingouin fils' argues that 'l'élection de M. Marmier n'est pas un fait si anormal que vous semblez le croire. L'Académie a depuis longtemps témoigné de son goût pour les médiocrités'. The 'letter' concludes that 'on

---

[15] Francisque Sarcey, 'Illustres ganaches', *Le Gaulois* (22 May 1870), 1.
[16] Francisque Sarcey, 'Les Bons Morts', *Le Gaulois* (26 May 1870), 1.
[17] Francisque Sarcey, 'Mes Lettres', *Le Gaulois* (28 May 1870), 1.

ne s'est point inquiété de savoir si M. Marmier serait un bon mort. C'était un bon vivant; et cette considération a suffi'.

In addition to decrying Marmier's literary and intellectual achievements, both *Le Figaro* and *Le Gaulois* attribute his election to his successful networking. *Le Figaro* writes that

> M. Xavier Marmier se délassait de sa gloire dans quelques salons influents, de ceux où, tout en se gardant comme du feu de lire un auteur, on le prône, on le pousse, on le *palme* d'immortalité, le cas échéant. Les femmes excellent à ce jeu qui consiste à mettre en branle les amours propres: ce sont d'actives ouvrières en brigues académiques. [. . .] La nomination de M. Marmier aurait été soufflée, dit-on, tout bas, par les Égéries de quelques salons politiques, à l'oreille des Numa qui ont fait prévaloir leur vote.[18]

Sarcey, in *Le Gaulois*, parodies the response (traditionally an enumeration of the newcomer's achievements) which could be made in the name of the Academy to Marmier's inaugural speech:

> Personne n'a plus et mieux que vous mangé chez les autres. Vous avez accepté plus de dîners que vous n'avez composé de volumes, et vous avez montré plus d'esprit encore en soutenant les uns qu'en produisant les autres. [. . .] Vous avez su dîner, monsieur, don précieux, don rare, et qui serait le premier de tous, s'il ne fallait pas mettre avant l'art de dîner chez les autres celui de donner aux autres à dîner chez soi.
>
> Vous avez dîné sous la hutte du Scandinave; vous avez dîné dans le wigwam de l'Indien; vous avez mangé assis par terre chez les rois de l'Afrique centrale; mais ce qui a plus touché encore les académiciens, c'est que vous avez, dînant chez eux, conté tous ces dîners que vous aviez faits dans les quatre parties du monde.[19]

Marmier was rather bemused to have been singled out for such a sustained campaign of criticism and ridicule. He guessed that the comments in *Le Figaro* had probably been either written or at least instigated by Pontmartin, a former friend who, having failed in the past to get himself elected to the Academy, had not stood again, and begrudged Marmier his success.[20] The more sustained and vitriolic articles in *Le Gaulois*, he concluded, were almost certainly written by Sarcey at the behest of his friend About.[21] Marmier himself had no contacts on that newspaper, and had never met, or had any sort of correspondence with Sarcey. 'Ainsi la louange ou l'outrage dépend du caprice, de la mauvaise humeur d'un écrivain' he mused. 'C'est ce qu'on appelle la royauté du journalisme'.[22]

---

[18] *Le Figaro* (23 May 1870), 2.   [19] Sarcey, 'Illustres ganaches', 1.   [20] *Journal*, 2, 159.
[21] Ibid., 2, 158.   [22] Ibid., 2, 358.

Despite his delight at winning the election, his health was slow to recover. By mid-June he was still having trouble in walking and found stairs extremely difficult. His doctor prescribed a rest in the country, and Ebba, with whom he had not been in close touch for some time, invited him to stay at her country house in Etrépigny, for the first time in ten years. For the first time also, Marmier felt at ease in her presence; the passion had disappeared from the relationship and been replaced by a steady friendship.

As Marmier convalesced in the country, however, Napoleon III was preparing to declare war on Prussia. The tension between the two countries had been growing for some time. Marmier supported the anti-war stance of Thiers—not because of any pro-Prussian sentiment, as has sometimes been claimed; indeed, he had been making his feelings about the Prussian threat clear since the early 1850s—but because he feared the consequences of war and the probability of defeat at the hands of Prussia.[23]

War was finally voted for on 15 July and the declaration sent to Prussia on 19 July. In the meantime, Marmier had left the Ardennes and was making his way towards Alsace on his now annual pilgrimage to his parents' graves. By 16 July he had reached Nancy, but was able to go no further. The majority of the trains had been requisitioned to carry troops and cannons to the front, and travel for civilians was soon to cease. Reluctantly, he decided to make his way back to Paris.

Marmier's brother Hyacinthe was among the troops recalled from the colonies for the war, and he arrived back from Algeria to command a cavalry division at Verdun. On his arrival he wrote to tell his brother how ill-prepared he found the French army. Very soon, of course, it became apparent that Hyacinthe's initial assessment was only too accurate. After an early French victory at Saarbrücken on 2 August, defeats followed rapidly at Wissembourg, Wörth, Spicheren, Forbach, and Froeschwiller. On 18 August Bazaine's army was defeated and driven back from Metz to Gravelotte on their way to Verdun. On 2 September, Marmier received a letter from his brother written a few days previously at Verdun, recounting how

> J'ai été assez heureux pour être chargé de la défense de cette ville bloquée, assiégée, rebloquée. J'ai dirigé cette défense pendant une attaque furieuse, au milieu d'une grêle d'obus, n'ayant pour toute garnison que de très jeunes sol-

---

[23] Probably the strongest and most ill-founded criticism of Marmier for his supposed role in the French defeat is to be found in the works of Louis Reynaud: see *Français et Allemands: histoire de leurs relations intellectuelles et sentimentales* (Paris: Fayard, 1930); and *L'Influence allemande en France au XVIIIᵉ et au XIXᵉ siècle* (Paris: Hachette, 1922). For an example of Marmier's private fears about defeat, see for example *Journal*, 2, 160.

dats. Ce qui m'a valu cette honneur, c'est que le général qui commande ici était cloué dans son lit. Hier, j'ai enlevé aux Prussiens un convoi important.[24]

Other news was slowly reaching Paris, very little of which brought any cheer. Also on 2 September, Marmier reflected that 'nulle langue humaine ne peut dire le deuil produit par cette guerre sans raison'.[25] The Prussian bombardment of Strasbourg was 'la plus infâme, la plus horrible action des temps modernes'.[26] News of the earlier defeats had caused French ministers responsible to be replaced and the war effort thereafter became increasingly chaotic, culminating in the overwhelming defeat of the French forces at Sedan and the surrender of Napoleon III on 2 September. When this news filtered through to Paris, France was declared a republic on 4 September. At six o'clock that evening, Marmier calmly set out for Passy where he had been invited to dinner and was surprised to find the roads deserted despite a revolution having occurred: 'Tout cela s'est fait tranquillement, sans la moindre collision, ni la moindre résistance, et le lendemain décret sur décret comme en 1848'.[27] Having lived through a turbulent period of political change in France, Marmier thought he had seen it all before and viewed the proceedings with a certain weary cynicism. Despite his hatred of 'ce lâche et misérable empereur',[28] the image of crowds tearing down the eagles, symbols of the empire, led him to sigh: 'Toujours les mêmes niaiseries'.[29]

Most evenings since the outbreak of hostilities, Marmier had been going over to the Thiers salon to hear the latest news. On 5 September, however, he was put out of circulation temporarily by an accident at home in his flat. Tripping over, he fell heavily on his left shoulder which caused him a dislocation and a fractured humerus. As he convalesced at home, Thiers' efforts to broker peace failed, and the new French Republic found itself still at war, with the Prussian army marching on Paris. A siege of the capital now seemed inevitable. Wealthy Parisians began to flee to their country homes, and by 19 September the siege proper had begun: all train stations had been closed, and an announcement was made to the effect that postal services to the rest of the country could not be maintained. That very morning, Marmier was surprised to receive a visit from a messenger who had succeeded in crossing Prussian lines surrounding both Verdun and Paris in order to deliver a dispatch from his brother to the Ministère de la Guerre, having made a detour of some 200 leagues to avoid other Prussian detachments.

---

[24] *Journal*, 2, 164.   [25] Ibid., 2, 165.   [26] Ibid., 2, 164.   [27] Ibid., 2, 166.
[28] Ibid., 2, 170.   [29] Ibid., 2, 166.

Before the onset of the siege, Marmier had supported Thiers' efforts to negotiate peace, and when the Germans refused to recognise the new government, Marmier felt that this was simply 'un absurde prétexte pour écarter toute tentative de conciliation ou de traité de paix'.[30] At this stage, the siege of Paris in his eyes represented 'notre dernière chance de salut, notre dernier espoir'.[31] As the situation developed, however, his views modified. Although he felt that the government proclaimed on 4 September did contain 'de braves gens, au moins Trochu et Jules Favre',[32] it was in essence nonetheless a government 'issu d'une émeute',[33] and by 23 September he was moved to declare in his diary that 'Les Trochu, les Gambetta et aussi leurs collègues n'avaient pas plus que le dernier tapissier de Paris le droit de régir les provinces. Le roi de Prusse ne veut pas traiter avec eux, et il a raison. La France ne les reconnaîtra pas sans hésitation, et ne les secondera pas'.[34]

Kept at home by his injury, he passed his time reading: in addition to newspapers as and when available, he re-read Gibbon's *Decline and Fall of the Roman Empire* and received visits from friends such as Vuillemin, Cochin, and the duchesse de Galliera. By the end of October he was able to get out and about again, and one of his first engagements was a dinner party given by the duchesse de Galliera where they ate 'un magnifique morceau de viande qu'on nous a présenté comme une culotte de bœuf et qui était une culotte de cheval. C'est la première fois que j'en mangeais, et c'était très bon, grâce surtout à l'habileté du cuisinier'.[35] Horse meat had not been widely eaten in France prior to this war; it had been available for the previous few years, but only as a cheap alternative bought by those who could not afford beef. By 12 October ration cards had been distributed authorising holders to purchase 100g of meat per person a day, but prices soared and meat became scarce, so that even the better-off who could actually afford it found it increasingly difficult to buy their ration. By 23 October the ration had been cut to half a pound of meat per person for three days. On 6 November, Marmier was almost overwhelmed to be invited to dinner by a 'Mme D' (possibly Mme Duchâtel) who 'grâce à sa fortune' was able to provide 'un brochet et du veau, deux invisibles prodiges à présent à Paris'.[36] On 29 November he became very excited when he was invited to a dinner at which it was promised that pheasant would be served. Although he was rather disappointed when it turned out that there was one pheasant to be divided between twenty 'affamés',[37] he nonetheless enjoyed the dinner which was supplemented by spinach and horse steak.

---

[30] *Journal*, 2, 170.   [31] Ibid.   [32] Ibid., 2, 204.   [33] Ibid., 2, 177.   [34] Ibid.
[35] Ibid., 2, 186.   [36] Ibid., 2, 189.   [37] Ibid., 2, 191.

On 6 December news reached Paris that the Loire army had been defeated and Orléans regained by the Prussians. 'Douloureuse nouvelle', Marmier wrote in his diary, 'hélas! de tout côté! Quelle déception, quel malheur'.[38] The following morning he awoke to find everywhere covered in snow, and the snow still falling heavily. It angered him to think of

> nos pauvres soldats qui sont sur les remparts, sans abri ou avec de si chétifs abris. Mal vêtus en outre, mal nourris et obligés de prendre à tout instant les armes. Pauvres innocentes victimes de la plus abominable folie du plus infâme gouvernement. Et il est tranquillement dans le château de Wilhelmshöhe, le misérable qui a jeté la France dans un tel abîme d'humiliation et de douleur.[39]

By 14 December, Marmier noted in his diary that the government had requisitioned all the horses remaining in Paris. Cat and dog meat were now being sold for public consumption; at his local dog butcher, he records, you have to arrive very early in the morning to be able to buy dog cutlets or steaks for two or three francs a pound.[40] Although life was obviously not easy for Marmier during the siege, he does not appear to have suffered the terrible hunger experienced by the working people, many of whom were unable even to afford rat meat over the final weeks. He was delighted when the duchesse de Galliera presented him with a flannel jacket, a tin of beef, and a pound of Gruyère cheese for his Christmas present. He estimated that the tinned beef would probably have cost thirty francs, whilst the cheese was so rare as to be priceless: if he were to sell it, he estimated, he could easily ask forty or fifty francs. Gifts of this kind, he explains, are now given in place of the sweets or luxury items of previous years.

Amongst the generally affluent circles he frequented, he noted that because of the shortages, 'on en est venu à faire de tout ce qui tient à la nourriture une grosse affaire. On en parle très longuement et très gravement'.[41] On 10 January 1871, he noted in his diary that thanks to his contacts he had managed to purchase two pounds of mutton on the black market for thirty francs, but he realised that 'ni pour or ni pour argent je n'en pourrais acheter deux encore'.[42] From the beginning of January the Prussians began to bombard Paris, with shells falling close to many of Marmier's haunts: one fell on 8 January in the duchesse de Galliera's garden, and a number fell on and after 6 January around the Panthéon; by

---

[38] Ibid., 2, 193.   [39] Ibid., 2, 193–4.

[40] In 1870 the average wage of a Parisian worker was less than 5 francs a day; National Guards during the war in Paris were paid 1.50 francs a day. See Alistair Horne, *The Fall of Paris: The Siege and Commune 1870–71* (London and Hong Kong: Papermac, 1990), 182 and 185. Horne also states that during the same period, cheese cost 30 francs a pound and cat 6 francs a pound.

[41] *Journal*, 2, 199.   [42] Ibid., 2, 201.

14 January most of the businesses around the Panthéon had shut up shop; only the Bibliothèque Sainte-Geneviève, where Marmier worked, was still open. Curiously, as the siege progressed, he noted that were it not for

> les calamités et les deuils qu'on entend raconter chaque jour, les douleurs de cœur, les misères matérielles et l'incertitude de l'avenir, je serais très heureux de la vie de Paris telle que le siège de Paris me l'a faite. Jamais je ne l'eus si régulière, et si dégagée d'une foule d'odieux petits soucis. Plus de visites [. . .] plus de lettres à écrire, ni bals, ni soirées. Silence complet, solitude paisible au milieu de mes livres.[43]

Despite Marmier's firmly stated views on the essential futility of the war, his diary entries reveal by their language and tone a genuine support for the French effort: phrases such as 'nos soldats', 'brave garçon', 'bravement conduits' or 'une bonne bataille' are used to describe French victories; whereas expressions like 'douloureuse nouvelle', 'grande tristesse' or 'malheur' denote setbacks. This tone is fairly consistent. There is, however, clear criticism of the management of the war and of the siege in particular. As early as 6 October, Marmier recorded the general opinion that 'on s'étonne que le gouvernement militaire ne tente pas de faire une vigoureuse sortie, mieux combinée que celle de Chevilly'.[44] As the later attempts failed and the promised relief from the provinces failed to materialise he became pessimistic. He had never had very high hopes of the government of 4 September despite his sympathy for Favre and Trochu;[45] apart from being the result of a revolution, it contained individuals whose stances, he felt, could not work well together. Those of whom he disapproved are fairly predictable: 'ce stupide Etienne Arago'[46] or 'un stupide arrêté de M. Jules Ferry'.[47] By 22 December he foresaw that

> dans un mois, si nous ne sommes secourus, il faudra capituler, et à de rudes conditions, et alors quelles récriminations contre le gouvernement qui aurait

---

[43] *Journal*, 2, 206.   [44] Ibid., 2, 183.

[45] Jules Favre (1809–80) was a lawyer and politician. A republican, he had opposed the Empire and spoken out against the declaration of war on Prussia. He was Ministre des Affaires étrangères in the Gouvernement de la Défense nationale. Louis-Jules Trochu (1815–96) was an army general who had served in Algeria, in the Crimean War, and in Italy, but fell from favour after criticising the state of the French army in 1867. He was governor of Paris and then head of the Gouvernement de la Défense nationale.

[46] *Journal*, 2, 191. Étienne Arago (1802–92) was a republican who held various posts of responsibility after the fall of the Empire.

[47] Ibid., 2, 194. Jules Ferry (1832–93) was a republican who became mayor of Paris after the fall of the Empire; he was responsible for food distribution during the Siege of Paris. He later (in the 1880s) saw through reforms to the education system (for which he is now remembered), insisting on the need for compulsory and free primary education of a secular nature.

pu, dès le commencement de septembre, faire la paix! Que de sang et de larmes on aurait épargnés! Que de ruines et de désastres irréparables![48]

As Trochu came in for general reproach for his apparent lack of strategy, Marmier noted:

Le malheureux Trochu, dans quelle situation il est mis, et dans quelle fatale erreur il nous a maintenus! Si, comme c'est probable, nous devons capituler, que de fois on pensera avec douleur que si on avait eu la paix il y a quatre mois, les conditions n'en auraient pas été plus dures et nous n'aurions point eu à déplorer le ravage, la spoliation des environs de Paris, tant de ruine et tant de sang.[49]

On 20 January, he made his way in the dark to the residence of the duchesse de Galliera, carrying a lantern and his bread ration. As they dined, they agreed that 'il était temps d'en finir et que ce serait peut-être une terrible folie que de vouloir prolonger une défense impossible'.[50] On 26 January he noted simply 'finies les dernières illusions', adding bitterly that his friend the vice admiral de Langle had told him that the outcome could have been quite different if provisions had been managed sensibly: 'cet idiot de gouvernement n'a rien su prévoir, ni rien ménager [. . .]. Maintenant, à quelque prix que ce soit, il faut céder, il faut faire la paix'.[51]

One of Marmier's main preoccupations in the immediate aftermath of the war was to dicover what had happened to his brother at Verdun. Enquiries even to the highest level bore no fruit until on 4 February he received a letter from Hyacinthe written at Frankfurt-am-Main, where he was a prisoner of war. The letter gave no details of his surrender or captivity, but at least Marmier knew his brother was still alive.

A clause in the armistice signed on 28 January had stipulated that elections be held in France as a condition of the agreement. Under the circumstances, the election really boiled down to a referendum on whether to accept peace or to fight on. In general terms, all the monarchists (whether legitimists or Orleanists) were in favour of peace and the restoration of 'law and order'. Republicans were divided: the more moderate (such as Ferry) favoured peace, whilst the more radical, such as Gambetta or Rochefort, would not countenance surrender.

The elections were held on 8 February. Despite the differences on constitutional form between the different monarchist factions, the combined monarchists won a clear majority, taking more than half the seats, and more than twice as many as the republicans. Because candidates were allowed to stand in more than one department, Thiers (at this stage still an Orleanist)

---

[48] Ibid., 2, 196–7.   [49] Ibid., 2, 201.   [50] Ibid., 2, 205.   [51] Ibid., 2, 207.

was elected in twenty-six wards and was appointed 'chef du pouvoir exécutif de la République française'. By the terms of the armistice, Thiers had
until 19 February to conclude a definitive peace treaty with Prussia, but he
obtained various extensions until 26 February. On 20 February, he arrived
back in Paris from Bordeaux (where the new government had been set up);
that evening Marmier had called round to the house to see Thiers' sister-in-
law, Félicie, to whom he had always been profoundly attracted. Now he still
found her to be 'la plus charmante, la plus attachante personne du
monde'.[52] She told Marmier that Thiers would begin negotiations in
Versailles at midday on the following day. The following evening, Marmier
again attended the Thiers salon, but noted that Thiers himself arrived back
from Versailles only very late, ate rapidly, and then, after shaking hands
silently with all the friends present, left for a meeting with the peace commission. Over the next few days, Marmier continued to attend the salon
assiduously. Slightly hesitant about Thiers' choice of members of the new
cabinet, he was impressed by the new ambassadors named. He felt sure that
the new men would change the reputation of French diplomats abroad by
contrast with their predecessors,

> des joueurs de fifre ou des cyniques, des bilboquets comme Bendetti, des
> carotteurs comme le général Fleury, des chevaliers d'industrie comme Morny
> et Lavalette, et avant l'empire, pendant la république, des Bixio, des Arago,
> des pantins comme mon petit prétentieux compatriote Grenier, des tailleurs
> en faillite, des musiciens de Bobino, des commis voyageurs sans emplois, et
> plusieurs voleurs.[53]

On 25 February, Thiers invited a number of friends for dinner, but at
8 p.m. he had still not returned from Versailles. The party waited until
10 p.m. when Thiers arrived, 'triste et fatigué';[54] when he withdrew without
speaking a word, the company feared that the negotiations had not been
successful. On 26 February it was announced that France was to lose Alsace
and most of Lorraine, but was to keep Belfort, a concession obtained by
Thiers in exchange for the Prussians holding victory celebrations in Paris
between 1 and 3 March. France was also to pay an indemnity of six billion
francs and submit to a partial occupation until the debt was paid. Although
shocked by the harshness of the terms, Marmier could see no way around
the treaty. Whilst he felt that the refusal of the treaty on the part of the
deputies of Alsace and Lorraine was a 'protestation naturelle et touchante
à laquelle tout vrai Français s'associe', he concluded that 'il faut reconnaître
que, toutes nos armées étant en déroute, il nous est impossible de continuer

---

[52] *Journal*, 2, 214.   [53] Ibid., 2, 216.   [54] Ibid.

la guerre'.[55] He was less sympathetic to the protestations of those broadly in agreement with the opinions of Hugo (who 'n'a pas manqué cette occasion de faire encore un de ses discours pompeux, sonores, vides de sens'[56]) and his former friend Quinet:

> Les démocrates ont crié et beuglé que la France était trahie. Les misérables! Ils savent bien que nous ne pouvons continuer la guerre, et s'ils avaient un brin de conscience, ils pourraient bien reconnaître aussi qu'ils ne se sont exposés à aucun péril dans cette guerre, et que les folies qui ont été commises tant qu'elle a duré, c'est en grande partie à eux et à leur ami Gambetta et à cette stupide république du 4 septembre qu'il faut les attribuer.[57]

As for the 'démagogues de Belleville', he claims, 'pas un de ces braillards n'a montré pendant la guerre le moindre courage, ils fuyaient à qui mieux mieux les champs de bataille'.[58]

The Prussian entry into Paris—for which Thiers and the monarchist Assembly were held responsible by the Parisian working classes—combined with a number of thoughtless and heavy-handed decisions taken by the Assembly concerning Paris and the Parisians, was to lead to new rioting and the eventual declaration of the Commune. On 18 March, the government's decision to send in the army to reclaim the cannons from Montmartre and Belleville (which had been bought by public subscription) led to rioting and the executions of Lecomte and Clément Thomas.[59] On 19 March, Marmier was again astonished to find that although another revolution seemed to have taken place, all was quiet. Since it was a fine day, he went wandering along the banks of the Seine, scouring the booksellers' stalls for a bargain, which was one of his favourite pastimes. He bumped into Delescluze (a committed republican who had participated in the revolutions of 1830 and 1848 and who would shortly become a leader of the Commune) with whom he had a brief conversation. Delescluze assured Marmier that although he had not been involved in the recent events, he was sure that there was no reason why the organisation of the Commune might not happen peacefully. Marmier objected that if the Prussians were not paid, they would continue the war. The Prussians, Delescluze replied, 'sont foutus';[60] they would not get a penny, and would not keep an inch of French territory. 'Telle est l'espérance de l'indomptable républicain',[61] concluded Marmier, unable to

---

[55] Ibid., 2, 217.   [56] Ibid.   [57] Ibid.   [58] Ibid., 2, 216–17.

[59] General Lecomte headed one of the brigades sent to reclaim the cannons, and had ordered his men to fire on an unarmed crowd but was not obeyed; General Clément Thomas had recently resigned as head of the National Guard and was massively unpopular for his part in the repression of insurgents in June 1848.

[60] *Journal*, 2, 221.   [61] Ibid.

share his conviction. For Marmier, the recent revolution conjured up echoes of 1793, and he feared that a bloodbath was imminent.[62] A general exodus of the better-off from the capital had already begun, and Marmier predicted that the numbers leaving would increase rapidly. He, however, decided to stay put, 'à la garde de Dieu'.[63]

On 28 March, Hyacinthe arrived from Frankfurt, full of praise for the organisation of the Prussian army. The following day, the brothers went on an excursion to Versailles. The station was mobbed so that they had to fight their way to the ticket desk, and the huge train was packed full. As it made its way slowly past Viroflay and Charville into Versailles, Hyacinthe noted critically that troops were left standing idle—a dangerous state of affairs, he commented, which would not have been tolerated by the Prussians. At Versailles, they met Beugnot (a captain who had been taken prisoner on 18 March and had witnessed the executions of Lecomte and Thomas at the rue des Rosiers) and, of course, Thiers. Marmier found his friend well, but thought that he had aged considerably since thay had last met. On 30 March, the Marmier brothers were out and about in Paris, but Xavier insisted that they travel in a closed carriage. He felt that walking in the street would be far too dangerous for his brother who, despite being simply clad in civilian attire, was instantly recognisable as a military man. The following day, Marmier was intensely relieved to be able to see Hyacinthe off safely on the train to Lyon. That same evening, he also bade farewell to his friends the duc and duchesse de Galliera as they departed for Italy with substantial amounts of cash and valuables in their suitcases.

Despite his sympathy for the lot of the less fortunate in other countries, Marmier appears to have had little to spare for the Parisian working classes. No mention is made in his diary, for example, of the harsh laws on the payment of rent arrears and debts passed by the Assembly; on the other hand, the decree passed by the Commune declaring an amnesty on rent during the siege is one of two decrees which, in his words, 'ne sont pas faits pour rétablir la confiance publique, ni réjouir les honnêtes gens'.[64] Life under the Commune seemed more miserable to him than it had during the siege: 'la vie est complètement désenchantée. On ne peut plus avoir aucune joie, car on n'a plus aucune sécurité'.[65] Many decent people, he wrote, were now feeling anger at Thiers' failure to act, and believed that he should have asked immediately for help from the Prussians to deal with the situation. He received two letters from his adored Félicie on 22 April and 7 May; the first was 'bonne et affectueuse',[66] and the second proved that she was still the

---

[62] Although the worst bloodbath which did eventually occur was the work of Thiers and his troops.
[63] *Journal*, 2, 221.   [64] Ibid., 2, 226.   [65] Ibid., 2, 232.   [66] Ibid., 2, 239.

same 'douce, charmante dame',[67] but both were extremely vague and left Marmier doubting as to whether any relief was to be forthcoming from Versailles. From Marmier's point of view, the Commune was simply being allowed to continue its 'cours de despotisme et de bouleversement'.[68] He was tremendously upset when Thiers' grand residence on the place Saint-Georges was first seized (15 April) and then later demolished, with all the property confiscated. He could not help remembering the works of art and the rare books he had discovered there when he was first invited to the house some ten years before; most of all, of course, he recollected how he went to visit Félicie in the mornings and then returned in the evenings. Between 13 May and 15 May he indignantly witnessed workmen getting drunk on the fine wines plundered (as he saw it) from the cellar; and precious books and works of art being flung around as they were loaded onto wheelbarrows: 'Tout cela doit faire une peine extrême à M. Thiers [. . .] tout cela doit bien affliger Mme Thiers, et encore plus sa sœur, la tendre, religieuse Mlle Félicie qui attachait tant de prix à tout ce qui venait de sa mère'.[69]

Finally on 21 May in the evening, news arrived that the Versaillais had reached Paris; on the morning of 22 May, barricades were hastily erected in Marmier's quarter and the shops were closed. Fortunately Annette, his housekeeper, was able to buy bread and a few provisions in haste. For the next two days sporadic gunfire and then intense streetfighting made it impossible to leave the flat. Marmier noted that his little dog Saga trembled with fear while his canaries huddled together quivering in the corner of their cage. Marmier, as was his wont in times of crisis, turned to his work for consolation: the challenges of the Russian language provided distraction from the tragic events unfolding outside which he felt powerless to influence. He was nonetheless relieved early on the morning of 24 May to see from his window a company of regular soldiers replacing the red flag of the Commune with the tricolore. At 8 a.m. he was even more pleased to see a substantial detachment of sailors whose uniforms reminded him of happier times in his seafaring days. Within a short time, the place Saint-Thomas-d'Aquin had become a hive of military activity—to Marmier's intense relief:

> J'ai été heureux aussi lorsqu'au mois de juin 1848 j'ai vu réapparaître les sol-dats qui allaient combattre ces hordes révolutionnaires, ces hordes effroy-ables, moins effroyables pourtant que celles qui, depuis deux mois, s'étaient emparés de tout Paris, et qui de plus en plus épouvantaient les honnêtes gens.[70]

[67] Ibid., 2, 243.   [68] Ibid.   [69] Ibid., 2, 248.   [70] Ibid., 2, 254.

At ten o'clock the troops moved on and at midday Marmier could no longer resist the urge to set foot outside. A scene of desolation met his eyes: all the shops were closed, all the windows broken; barricades which had been abandoned lay in ruins, and many buildings had been badly damaged by gunfire. He tried to visit a friend in the rue de Lille, but was prevented by the numerous fires.

Marmier's reaction to the bloody repression of the Communards by the Versaillais seems extraordinarily harsh. Early suggestions in the press that the repression might have been unnecessarily heavy-handed are dismissed in surprisingly brutal terms:

> Très bien. Nous en viendrons dans quelques semaines à plaindre cette race d'êtres sans nom, ces hordes de brigands, d'assassins, de voleurs, d'incendiaires. Je vois venir l'heure où les journaux républicains comme le *Siècle* diront que parmi ces satellites de la Commune, il y avait beaucoup d'égarés et beaucoup d'innocents. [. . .] Ah! malheureux France, où les crimes les plus épouvantables trouvent encore des écrivains pour les excuser![71]

Although Marmier here cites *Le Siècle* (and also *Paris-Journal*) it is relevant to note that his views were not necessarily shared in conservative quarters. Even his friend, the right-wing Louis Veuillot, writing in *L'Univers*, argued strongly that summary executions were unacceptable, not least since justice was a fundamental necessity in a Christian society.[72] Marmier's own views from now on seem to become increasingly reactionary. On 9 June, he heard the news that between 21 May and 28 May some 20,000 (probably a conservative estimate, as we now know) had been killed by government troops. His initial reaction was to exclaim 'c'est beaucoup. Mais ce n'est pas tout'.[73] He feared that enough 'rouges' had survived who, with help from their contacts in the International and throughout Europe, would rise again to begin their struggle afresh:

> Pour écarter de nous ces mortels périls, il nous faudrait un gouvernement rigoureux [. . .]. Il faudrait qu'on rayât nettement des programmes de nos institutions, et la liberté de la presse, et le droit de réunion, et tant d'autres fatales inventions. Le régime absolu, pourvu qu'il fût juste et honnête, voilà ce qui peut relever la France de l'abîme où elle est tombée, et lui rendre la sécurité.[74]

His hatred of the Communards was reinforced when he apparently discovered on 14 June that according to one of the last decrees of the Commune,

---

[71] *Journal*, 2, 257.   [72] *L'Univers*, 30/31 May 1871, 1–2.   [73] *Journal*, 2, 263.
[74] Ibid.

he was to lose his post as librarian and be taken as hostage 'et probablement occis'.[75]

The July elections had shown a significant swing from the monarchists to the republicans and many on the right wing felt that Thiers was making too many concessions to the republicans. Marmier at this stage tried to separate his friendship with Thiers from his political allegiances. He had deliberately kept his distance since Thiers had come to power because he knew that the new leader had been besieged by acquaintances clamouring for favours. Marmier had no wish to be viewed as one who would deliberately seek to exploit a friendship. On 3 July he accepted an invitation to dine with the family at Versailles and found himself in the company of Galliera (now returned from Italy), the nuncio Saint-Aignan, maréchal Canrobert, Falloux, and Trochu. He found Thiers in good form, although he had lost a lot of weight; but the highlight of the evening for Marmier, as always, was the company of Félicie. As well as a further dinner with Thiers on 15 July, this time in the company of members of the Académie française, he also dined regularly with the Gallieras. On 12 July and 19 July, they invited him along with the various members of the Orléans dynasty who were back in Paris.[76] Despite his close links with Louis-Philippe and family, however, Marmier's politics had moved to the right and he now sympathised much more readily with the legitimists. At this time, the monarchist factions in France were trying to reach a compromise between the comte de Chambord and the Orléans dynasty in order to restore the monarchy. The proposal was that the comte de Chambord should take the throne, and that after his death (as he had no successor) the throne should revert to the Orléans. On 6 July, Chambord had published a manifesto agreeing to the proposal, but on the major condition that the white flag of Henri IV be retained (thus rejecting the tricolore and all it symbolised); this was effectively a refusal on his part, as the flag was a major point of principle. Marmier's sympathies lay with

---

[75] Ibid., 2, 265. Marmier notes this in his private papers, but does not give his source, and I have been unable to find any evidence to support the claim. The *Journal officiel* certainly lists public sector workers including librarians (principally from the national library and the Mazarine) who have been dismissed; the *Procès-Verbaux* of the Commune also list decisions made about the taking of hostages and their eventual fate; but Marmier's name does not appear to be mentioned either in a decree or in minuted discussions. See *Procès-Verbaux de la Commune de 1871*, ed. Georges Bourgin and Gabriel Henriot, 2 vols. (Paris: Leroux, 1924 (vol. 1) and Paris: Lahure, 1945 (vol. 2)); see particularly 1, 125 ('séance du 5 avril 1871') and 2, 387–8 ('séance du 17 mai 1871').

[76] The duc d'Aumale and the prince de Joinville had been elected to the Assembly in the February elections, but, as political exiles, were unable to take their seats. In June, Thiers pushed through a compromise vote allowing them to return to France on condition that they did not take their seats (although this condition was then repealed in December).

the position adopted by Chambord, commenting that 'depuis un temps immémorial rien en France ne s'était fait de si beau et de si noble'.[77]

Marmier's social calendar was broken just briefly over the summer by a short trip in August to Etrépigny, where he stayed at Ebba's house, and then to Lorraine. At Longwy he was quite overcome with grief at the devastation caused by the war in the quiet village where he had so many happy memories of time spent with his parents. In the meantime, he had also suffered another bereavement. On 4 July he received news that his brother Joseph had died on 28 June. For Marmier, Joseph had been almost like a son in the sense that there was an age gap of twelve years; their parents had sent Joseph to Paris to finish his studies with his elder brother, first at the university and then at Saint-Sulpice before he returned to Besançon. Marmier noted in his diary that his brother had been a 'saint prêtre, d'une charité et d'un zèle sans pareils', who had 'épuisé ses forces dans l'excès de ses bonnes œuvres'.[78]

On 7 December, Marmier made his inaugural speech at the Académie française—a hugely important event in his personal life and also one which was widely reported in the press. It was a bitterly cold day, and snow was falling heavily. As chance would have it, Thiers was making a presidential address at the Assembly at exactly the same time. But this did not deter a large audience. Admission was restricted to ticket holders, but even so extra benches and chairs had to be brought into the huge amphitheatre to accommodate the audience, many of whom arrived an hour early in order to find good seats. Receptions to inaugurate new members of the Academy were always an important event, but the list of dignitaries and celebrities who turned out to support Marmier was nonetheless impressive. Those present included his old friend the duchesse de Galliera; the comte and comtesse de Paris; the duc de Nemours; the duc d'Alençon; the duc d'Aumale; the duc de Guise; the prince de Joinville; the generals La Ruë, Dumas, and Hyacinthe Marmier; and the journalists Louis Veuillot and Louis Ratisbonne. The presence of the duc d'Aumale and the prince de Joinville was particularly remarkable, since it was widely anticipated that they would have been at the Assembly to hear Thiers' address.[79]

---

[77] *Journal*, 2, 270.   [78] Ibid.

[79] See, for example, 'Bulletin', *Le Moniteur Universel* (9 December 1871), 1229; or the article by Eugène Asse, 'Académie française. Réception de M. X. Marmier' in the same issue, 1230. The presence or otherwise of the princes at the Assembly was of course a big question at the time, since their permission to return to France from exile had originally been conditional upon their not taking their seats; this condition was then revoked by Thiers.

According to the tradition of the Academy, the inaugural speech of a newly elected member pays tribute to the life and works of his predecessor. Marmier's seat had previously been held by Pongerville, who had made his literary reputation largely by translating Lucretius; he had also been a librarian. Some years previously, Marmier had made his feelings about Pongerville quite clear in his diary. The latter, he wrote, was a 'bête adroite'[80] who had obtained advancement by calculated changes in political allegiance and generally sycophantic behaviour towards anyone in power. Thus Marmier claimed that although his predecessor had been in charge of the maps department at the national library, he would have been incapable of distinguishing north from south on a map. His two translations of Lucretius, Marmier judged, were 'aussi mauvaises l'une que l'autre'.[81]

On his big day, however, Marmier's speech gave little hint as to his true feelings about his predecessor. 'J'ai connu aussi M. de Pongerville', he declared: 'En vous parlant de lui, je joins à ce devoir un sentiment affectueux. Ceux qui l'ont connu l'ont aimé'.[82] Two newspaper reviews (the *Journal des Débats* and *Paris-Journal*), however, picked up on the fact that Marmier had spent a disproportionate amount of time talking about Lucretius rather than Pongerville himself.[83] Louis Ratisbonne, writing in the *Débats*, obviously noted the irony of Marmier, who was well known as a socialite; a devout Catholic; a professional traveller; and an author of numerous and diverse publications, being required to write an appreciation of a man who was in many ways his opposite. Pongerville had been a man who preferred solitude to company; a freethinker; a man who had not travelled; and whose literary reputation rested largely on a specialised knowledge of one Latin author.

Marmier himself was quite pleased with his performance, and felt that it had all gone well. He had put a lot of work into preparing his speech, and had been careful to read clearly. A review in *Le Gaulois* (the newspaper which had published the scathing articles by Sarcey about Marmier's election to the Academy only months before) confirmed that 'ce discours, prononcé d'une voix ferme, est plusieurs fois interrompu par des applaudissements'.[84] Eugène Asse, in *Le Moniteur Universel*, claimed that Marmier

---

[80] *Journal*, 2, 52.   [81] Ibid.

[82] *Discours prononcés dans la séance publique tenue par l'Académie française pour la réception de M. X. Marmier le 3 décembre 1871* (Paris: Firmin Didot, 1871), 3.

[83] See Louis Ratisbonne, 'Académie française. Réception de M. X. Marmier', *Journal des Débats* (8 December 1871), 3; Jehan Valter, 'Académie française. Réception de M. Xavier Marmier', *Paris-Journal*, 4ᵉ année, no. 331 (9 December 1871), 1–2 (1).

[84] [Anonymous], 'Académie française. Réception de M. X. Marmier', *Le Gaulois* (9 December 1871), 3. Valter, however, in the *Paris-Journal*, claims that 'Marmier se rassied au milieu d'applaudissements modérés' ('Académie française, Réception de M. Xavier Marmier', 2).

read 'd'un timbre assez net, sa voix un peu faible'.[85] Alfred d'Aunay, in *Le Figaro* (which had also been hostile to Marmier's election) reported that his speech was 'aussi bien conçu que remarquablement écrit', although it had been read in too quiet a voice for the audience to hear it all.[86] Only *Le Gaulois* (which nonetheless gave a favourable review of the speech) could not resist poking fun in a separate article claiming that

> Hier, dans le parcours de l'Institut au Louvre, les agents ont relevé plusieurs académiciens complètement gelés.
>
> Les médecins appelés en toute hâte au poste de police où ces malheureux immortels avaient été transportés ne pouvaient pas s'expliquer ce phénomène de congélation.
>
> Ce n'est que lorsqu'ils eurent appris que les moribonds venaient d'entendre le discours de M. X. Marmier que les hommes de l'art furent complètement édifiés [. . .].[87]

On 24 December, in accordance with traditional procedure, Marmier was formally presented to Thiers in his capacity as head of state, at an official Academy luncheon. Over the next few days, however, he was to learn that membership of that learned body could create stress in itself. A new election was already in the offing, and Marmier spontaneously promised Mignet that he would vote for Littré. This was an unexpected decision for a man of Marmier's beliefs and personal connections, particularly since standing against Littré (an agnostic philosopher) was the duc d'Aumale (the son of Louis-Philippe). Immediately, the old networks swung into action, and Marmier found himself bombarded with letters, messages, and unannounced visits to his home from individuals such as the bishop of Orléans, Falloux, and numerous members of the aristocracy. Emotional blackmail was also brought to bear: the archbishop of Besançon, for example, begged him to change his mind out of respect for his recently deceased brother; others told him that he would dishonour the memory of his parents by voting for Littré. Reluctant to break his initial promise, he nonetheless found the pressure hard to bear, and turned to his friend the duchesse de Galliera for advice. On her recommendation, he simply abstained, and instead of attending the Academy on 30 December, when the elections were held, he walked over to the Bastille 'dans un état de chagrin profond'.[88] In the event, the duc d'Aumale was elected to Montalembert's former seat; but Littré was also elected to replace Villemain. The episode was noted and raked up again

---

[85] Asse, 'Académie française. Réception de M. X . Marmier', 1230.
[86] Alfred d'Aunay, 'A l'Académie', *Le Figaro* (9 December 1871), 3.
[87] Un Domino, 'Ce qui se passe', *Le Gaulois* (9 December 1871), 3.
[88] *Journal*, 2, 283.

by Marmier's old enemy Francisque Sarcey over four years later in an attempt to discredit Marmier in his bid to stand for parliament.[89]

In the meantime, Marmier maintained his hectic social life, continuing his close contacts with not only Thiers and his family, but also monarchists of both persuasions (from whom Thiers was now becoming increasingly distanced). He blamed Thiers to some extent for the continuing failure of the negotiations to unite legitimists and Orleanists, arguing (privately in his diary, at least) that although Thiers claimed to support the proposed union, it was not actually in his own best interest for him to do so. If the union were to go ahead, Thiers would find his own powers diminished. Marmier also felt that the Orléans princes were hindering the process, particularly the duc d'Aumale.

In September 1872, when Thiers was in Trouville, Marmier was invited by Mme Thiers to stay with the family. He left Paris on 13 September, which was a fine day, and he enjoyed the journey through Evreux, Lisieux, and Bernay, which all brought back happy memories, before arriving in Trouville. Here he had a small but pleasant room with a sea view at the Hôtel de Paris. He was greeted warmly that evening by Thiers, his wife, and Félicie. The following morning he had an early start, leaving the hotel at 8 a.m. to meet Thiers and his entourage on the quay for the short sea journey to Le Havre: this trip had been announced in the newspapers for some time and repeatedly postponed.[90] The voyage began with a small detour to pass between two magnificent English ships (the *Northumberland* and the *Sultan*, a pair of armoured frigates) which had been sent in honour of Thiers. Marmier was moved to tears by the sight of the two impressive vessels—one of which he thought must be vastly larger than even the biggest ship in the French navy—flying the French flag, firing cannon salutes and playing the Marseillaise. The weather was superb as they sailed into Le Havre to the cheers of a huge crowd gathered around the port. An official reception was held at the town hall where Marmier particularly appreciated the company of one Mme Siegfried, an Alsacienne by birth, whom he found to be 'jolie', 'gracieuse' and 'charmante'.[91] On his return to Trouville that evening, he reflected that Thiers had every reason to be pleased with his reception: 'jamais aucun souverain n'en eût une plus éclatante et plus spontanée'.[92] The remaining three days were spent in walks on the beach and excursions with various dignitaries. On Wednesday 18 September he travelled back to Paris and on Thursday evening visited Thiers at the Élysée palace.

---

[89] Francisque Sarcey, 'L'Enfant de Pontarlier', *XIXᵉ siècle* (13 February 1876), 1–2 (2).
[90] See, for example, 'Lettres de Trouville', *Le Moniteur Universel* (6 September 1872), 984.
[91] *Journal*, 2, 299.   [92] Ibid.

Shortly after this episode (on 13 November 1872), Thiers made his controversial announcement to the effect that France was now officially a
republic. Despite his political sympathies with the right wing, and his
friendship with Broglie and Pasquier, Marmier still maintained his relationship with Thiers. When on 24 May the following year news came that the
latter had been forced to resign, Marmier was extremely touched to discover
that one of his old friend's last actions as head of state was to sign a decree
promoting him to the rank of Officier de la Légion d'Honneur.[93] But
Marmier felt profoundly for his friend. Although he realised that he could
not bring him much comfort, he made a point of calling in to see him on a
regular basis. He found it particularly striking how few of Thiers' erstwhile
fairweather friends now made the effort to seek him out. He was also worried that the few who did make the effort were left-wingers, which he felt
would create a vicious circle and alienate Thiers even further from his
former allies.

Marmier was soon to meet MacMahon, the new president of the
Republic, in an official capacity. On 16 June, he was called upon by
the Académie française to replace d'Haussonville (then chancellor of the
Academy) in accompanying the director and secretary (Champagny and
Patin) as—in keeping with tradition—they presented the newly elected
Littré to the head of state. Marmier felt that MacMahon seemed a little ill
at ease, possibly intimidated by 'ces grands savants qu'on appelle des
Académiciens'.[94] He fortuitously managed to break the ice on this occasion
by mentioning his brother Hyacinthe, which gave MacMahon the opportunity to talk with great animation about the latter's role in the capture of
Touggourt. Marmier later learned that MacMahon was always known to be
a poor conversationalist, but also discovered that Algeria or rabbit hunting
were two subjects almost guaranteed to stir him from his silence!

On 27 November it fell to Marmier, then director of the Academy, to
respond to the inaugural speech of Viel-Castel, elected on 2 May to replace
the historian Ségur.[95] This normally routine task was to create a great deal
of controversy for which Marmier was initially blamed, although subsequently completely exonerated. The row was in fact something of a storm
in a teacup. In his speech, Marmier referred to Ségur's eight volumes of

---

[93] See *Journal*, 2, 312. He actually received it on 6 June 1873: see AnF, LH.1747 018.
[94] *Journal*, 2, 312.
[95] Louis de Viel-Castel (1800–87) was the author of an *Histoire de la Restauration* published
between 1860 and 1878; his predecessor, Philippe-Paul, comte de Ségur (1780–1873) had published
an *Histoire de Napoléon et de la Grande Armée de 1812* in 1824.

memoirs having been published 'par les soins de ses fidèles légataires'.[96] The comte and comtesse de Ségur d'Aguesseau took exception to his use of the plural in the phrase, claiming that Ségur d'Aguesseau was his uncle's sole heir. In a long letter to Marmier, they also appear—somewhat illogically—to hold Marmier in some way responsible for the fact that they had received only fifty copies of the memoirs instead of the five hundred which they claim to have been promised. They demanded that Marmier make a public statement at the Academy to correct his error.[97] Marmier stuck to his guns, replying on 26 December to the lengthy letter in just a few incisive lines:

> Madame,
> Avant-hier, 24, j'ai reçu la lettre que vous m'avez fait l'honneur de m'écrire le 16 de ce mois.
> Vous me reprochez d'avoir mis dans mon discours sur M. le général de Ségur un pluriel au lieu d'un singulier; j'ai dit *ses fidèles légataires*, etc.
> Permettez-moi, Madame, de vous faire observer que je ne pouvais dire autrement, sachant toutes les dipositions par lesquelles l'illustre Général a confié l'entière publicité et la possession de son œuvre, non point à un seul légataire, mais à son fils et à ses autres enfants.[98]

The countess was not to be silenced so easily, however: she now circulated to all members of the Academy a brochure which she said was a 'protestation contre l'injuste persistance de Mr X. Marmier dans l'affirmation d'un fait qu'il sait être absolument faux'.[99] Eventually, in February 1874, the general's son, the comte Paul de Ségur, wrote a lengthy letter to Marmier, exonerating him completely. Referring to Marmier's 'excellent discours', he explains that he and his sisters were the only heirs to their father's estate; and that d'Aguesseau had been upset when the contract with the publisher of his uncle's memoirs had stipulated that he should receive only ten copies of his uncle's work. Ségur concludes his letter with an expression of regret at the episode: 'Je déplore, Monsieur, que votre sincérité bien connue et votre bienveillance pour ma famille ne vous aient pas mis à l'abri des ennuis de réclamations aussi étranges'.[100]

---

[96] Institut de France, Académie française, *Discours prononcés dans la séance publique tenue par l'Académie française pour la réception de M. Le Baron de Viel-Castel, le 27 novembre 1873* (Paris: Firmin Didot, 1873), 71.

[97] AAf, *Copies de lettres et documents divers adressées à MM les membres de l'Institut de France par la C^{sse} de Ségur d'Aguesseau née Lubomirska, à l'occasion d'un passage du discours de Mr X. Marmier, de l'Académie française, pour la réception de M. le Bon de Viel-Castel, successeur de M^r le Général Cte de Ségur* (Tarbes: Larrieu, 1874), 3–7.

[98] Ibid., 12–13.   [99] Ibid., 15.

[100] Ibid., 'Lettre du Cte Paul de Ségur à Monsieur X. Marmier, de l'Académie française, en réponse à la brochure adressée par Mme la Ctesse de Ségur d'Aguesseau, à M^{rs} les Membres de l'Institut'. See also AAf, PV, 2B14, fos. 18–20.

The year 1875 began rather sadly for Marmier. For some time he had attempted to retain his friendships with a number of individuals whose political differences were constantly widening, and his social life became increasingly harder to balance. Although Marmier himself did not approve of the way Thiers was moving in political terms, he endeavoured to maintain their relationship outside the political sphere, but many of his aristocratic friends reproached him for this. The first to break off a friendship on these grounds was the comte de Pozzo, in an outburst which left Marmier shaken and distressed. He also felt trapped in the middle of the growing antipathy between Broglie and Pasquier. His attachment to the Orléans family, too, had been rapidly fading. He felt that the princes—and particularly the duc d'Aumale—showed a marked lack of respect for religion. He was furthermore shocked in the summer of 1874 when the history of the American Civil War, written by the comte de Paris, began to appear. For Marmier, the fact that the comte de Paris and the comte de Chartres had enrolled in the Northern army was a disgrace which they should have tried to cover up or to excuse as a folly of youth, rather than drawing attention to it. By the end of 1875, he recorded in his diary that

> Les princes d'Orléans s'en vont de plus en plus s'amoindrissant, s'affaiblissant par leurs défauts de caractère, par la malhabileté de leur conduite. Ils n'ont pas su en rentrant en France y prendre une digne attitude de prince, et ils n'ont pu réussir à être de bons bourgeois. Ils ont successivement cajolé tous les partis, tendu la main à Gambetta, rendu hommage au comte de Chambord, invité à leurs soirées les ducs et les duchesses du faubourg Saint-Germain, et courtisé les rédacteurs des journaux républicains. A la Chambre, on a vu le prince de Joinville et le duc d'Aumale voter avec la gauche [. . .]. Au temps de leur exil, il y avait en France un parti orléaniste. À présent, c'est fini.[101]

After the division of the Assemblée nationale, elections were called in February 1876. Early on the morning of 2 February, Marmier was sitting quietly at home by his fireside when he received an unexpected visit from Gros, the mayor of Pontarlier, who had travelled overnight with a colleague to bring Marmier a letter exhorting him to stand for election in the ward of Pontarlier. The signatories of the letter claimed to be 'conservateurs dévoués aux idées d'ordre et de paix, pleins de confiance dans le gouvernement du maréchal Mac-Mahon'. They appealed to the 'patriotisme et au dévouement d'un enfant de Pontarlier, aujourd'hui une illustration de la France' to 'servir la société et la patrie'.[102]

---

[101] *Journal*, 2, 356.
[102] Letter published in *L'Union* (6 February 1876); text reproduced by Kaye (*Journal*, 2, 364).

At first, Marmier refused, having no wish to enter the cut-throat world of politics, preferring his peaceful existence divided between the Academy, the library and his writing. The two visitors insisted, however, promising that they would organise a committee to do all the spadework, and would require him only to travel to the Franche-Comté ten days before the election. Reluctantly, Marmier allowed himself to be persuaded. No sooner had his fellow Pontissaliens departed than he began to regret his decision bitterly, and fell into a profound depression. He felt that he was completely unsuited to life as a politician, both in terms of temperament and aptitude. If elected, his life would be turned upside down and he would be in a state of 'trouble perpétuel'.[103] These reflections caused him three weeks of insomnia, indecision, and anguish.

In the meantime, on 6 February 1876, he published his manifesto, in which he claims to represent 'les idées conservatrices de notre arrondissement'.[104] In recent times, he argues, France has undergone a series of terrible catastrophes from which it has not yet recovered. Its prestige cannot be restored, he continues, by 'de violentes commotions' or 'de monstrueuses utopies'.[105] In short, what is needed is 'l'ordre et la paix, les sages institutions qui favorisent le vrai développement de l'intelligence, protègent le travail, encouragent l'industrie. Il [. . .] faut les lois, sans lesquelles nul Etat, république ou monarchique, ne peut subsister, les saintes lois de la religion, de la famille, de la propriété'.[106]

His candidature evoked a mixed reception. He received letters of support from various clerics and local dignitaries. *Le Courrier de la montagne* in Pontarlier and *L'Union franc-comtoise* supported him, but he was vehemently opposed by the *Journal de Pontarlier*. The latter concentrated largely on the claim that despite Marmier's alleged attachment to his native region, he had returned there infrequently and had done little to help its inhabitants. *Le Courrier de la montagne* riposted by digging out an article apparently published in *Le Nouvelliste* in February 1842, reporting a banquet held in Marmier's honour at Morteau. Three 'friends', who had previously organised a reception for him in Pontarlier, accompanied him to the banquet at Morteau: one of the three was Colin, Marmier's rival in the election. According to the report in *Le Nouvelliste*, Colin proposed a lengthy toast to Marmier at the banquet, dubbing his future rival 'l'enfant du pays par la naissance et par le cœur'.[107]

---

[103] *Journal*, 2, 363.
[104] *Journal de Pontarlier*, 24ᵉ année, no. 7 (13 February 1876), 1.   [105] Ibid.   [106] Ibid.
[107] [Anonymous], *Le Courrier de la montagne* (13 February 1876) [no page numbers: front page]. The issue also contained a piece drawing attention to Colin's changes of allegiance with the advent of new political regimes.

In the meantime, Marmier's old enemy Francisque Sarcey (referred to in Marmier's diary as a 'crapaud venimeux'[108]), now writing for the *XIXe siècle*, took up his pen; two articles, entitled 'L'Enfant de Pontarlier' and 'L'Illustration de Pontarlier' appeared on 13 February and 18 February respectively, the former eagerly reproduced by the *Journal de Pontarlier* on 18 February.[109] Both of Sarcey's articles are characterised by the same biting tone as his earlier pieces criticising Marmier's election to the Académie française. Harking back to the letter inviting Marmier to stand, in which Marmier is referred to as 'un enfant de Pontarlier, [. . .] une illustration de la France',[110] Sarcey begins his first article by declaring that 'il faut être diantrement mal informé pour croire sérieusement que ce pauvre M. Marmier soit une illustration de la France' (the point is reinforced by the exclamation 'Marmier, une illustration!').[111] According to Sarcey, Marmier's works are virtually unknown; they are outstanding by their capacity to bore. In a reworking of some of his earlier articles on Marmier's election to the Academy, Sarcey goes on to claim that his victim's unique talent is to make friends in the right places through accepting dinner invitations (referring punningly to his 'profession de dîneur en ville'[112]). Those to whom he owed his election to the Academy, Sarcey adds, were Orleanists, although this had not stopped Marmier from failing to support the duc d'Aumale in his turn. As to whether Marmier is still an Orleanist, Sarcey concludes, Marmier's manifesto is too vague for anyone to judge.

The only thing that Marmier had promised his electoral committee was that he would return to the area ahead of the election. Electoral banquets were organised in advance at Pontarlier and Morteau. Despite his promise, however, he found himself repeatedly postponing his departure, and finally realised that he was subconsciously trying to sabotage his own chances, because 'en réalité je n'ai point envie de réussir'.[113] Circumstances finally conspired to allow him to stay in Paris. Around 10 February, a severe cold front swept over France which brought heavy snow even to Paris, while Pontarlier, high up in the mountains, was virtually cut off. Marmier caught a chill which brought back memories of his severe attack of pleurisy five

[108] *Journal*, 2, 365.
[109] Francisque Sarcey, 'L'Enfant de Pontarlier', *XIXe siècle* (13 February 1876), 1–2; and 'L'Illustration de Pontarlier', *XIXe siècle* (18 February 1876), 1; the former reproduced in *Journal de Pontarlier* (18 February 1876), 2–3.
[110] See above, n. 102.
[111] Sarcey, 'L'Enfant de Pontarlier', *Journal de Pontarlier* (18 February 1876), 3.
[112] Ibid.   [113] *Journal*, 2, 364.

years previously, and the doctor (his friend Barth[114]) forbade him to attempt the journey. The opposition, naturally, made the most of his absence. A front-page headline in the *Journal de Pontarlier* on 18 February announced that

> M. X. MARMIER, qui, DE LOIN, aime tant nos montagnes, nos sapins, nos sillons [an ironic reference to the manifesto] n'a pas DAIGNÉ venir, DE PRÈS, visiter les électeurs dont il sollicite les suffrages. Aujourd'hui, il n'est pas encore arrivé à Pontarlier où sa présence serait désormais inutile avant le vote de dimanche.[115]

Unsurprisingly, at the elections on Sunday 20 February, Marmier was defeated, winning 4,731 votes against 5,893 achieved by Gustave Colin, the republican candidate who had represented Pontarlier since 1871.[116] Four of the five cantons turned out a majority in favour of Colin; only Montbenoît (presumably because of its religious community) gave Marmier a majority of 1,045 to 499. The *XIXe siècle*, probably prompted by Sarcey and/or About (still smarting over his defeat in the elections to the Académie française), reported that Marmier had won only 473 votes (conveniently omitting the final digit) to Colin's 5,893![117]

The news reached Marmier on the morning of 21 February that he had not been elected. 'Dieu soit loué!'[118] he exclaimed in relief; the failure had lifted a terrible weight from his shoulders. Now, he wrote, he would be free to stay in his 'tranquille demeure'[119] surrounded by his books, far from the commotions of the Assembly. His election campaign had only cost him 1,500 francs ('avec lesquels j'aurais pu acheter de beaux livres, ou faire un joli voyage'[120]) but had earned him insults from papers in Paris and Besançon, and stirred up so much hostility in Pontarlier 'où je ne croyais avoir que des amis'[121] that he feared he would be unable to return there.

The elections of 1876 had given the republicans a large majority in the Assembly. MacMahon made Jules Dufaure (an Orleanist) leader of the government (président du conseil), but, faced with the hostility of the republican majority, he was soon replaced by Jules Simon. The latter found it impossible to reconcile the conflicting demands of President, Senate, and Chamber. When the republicans, following Gambetta, criticised his stance on the influence of the Church and the policy of 'ordre moral' and pushed

---

[114] Presumably the well-known doctor, Jean-Baptiste Philippe Barth, member of the Académie de Médecine.

[115] *Journal de Pontarlier* (18 February 1876), 1 (original emphasis).

[116] See Archives de Pontarlier, K10, Élections législatives; *Journal de Pontarlier* (27 February 1876), 1–2; and *Journal*, 2, 365.

[117] *XIXe siècle* (23 February 1876), 2.   [118] *Journal*, 2, 365.   [119] Ibid.   [120] Ibid.   [121] Ibid.

through a motion on 4 May 1877 condemning 'manifestations ultramontaines', the Catholic faction, spearheaded by Dupanloup, forced the President to react. On 16 May, MacMahon criticised Simon, who resigned and was then replaced by Broglie, who formed a conservative government. On the evening of 19 May, Marmier dined with Thiers, who was wholeheartedly against the latest change of direction. It was no secret that Marmier sympathised with the aims of the conservatives, although he had always made a point of avoiding political discussions with Thiers. He listened quietly to all the passionate debates and criticisms among Thiers' acolytes and refused to participate. His only comment was to ask Félicie, in jest, what she would do if he were appointed 'sous-secrétaire d'Etat'. Her response: 'je ne vous reverrai[s?] de ma vie'[122] hurt him profoundly. He had been a loyal friend and admirer of hers for years; he was not about to abandon her now, but things had changed significantly.

Famously, 363 members of the Assembly voted for a motion of no confidence in the new government; with the consent of the Senate, MacMahon dissolved the Chamber. Without having first been consulted, Marmier found that his name had been included once again on the list of official candidates in the forthcoming elections. His supporters in Pontarlier turned to him again, urging him to accept the nomination and do his duty. Once again, he agreed, albeit reluctantly:

> non toutefois sans m'effrayer de la tâche qu'il m'impose, de la lutte dans laquelle je vais entrer, et sans songer que si je suis élu, comme on le dit, c'est le bouleversement de ma vie si régulière, si paisible, si honnêtement et doucement arrangée. Mais que faire? L'ennemi est là, c'est-à-dire le radicalisme.[123]

Marmier felt that if 'le monstre' (i.e. 'le radicalisme') were to win, 'Dieu sait à quels nouveaux périls, à quelle catastrophe la France est exposée!'.[124] In his letter to the voters of Pontarlier, he warns that if the 363 were to be re-elected, 'c'est un nouveau conflit entre la Chambre des députés et le Sénat et le Pouvoir exécutif, un nouvel élan révolutionnaire, peut-être la guerre civile et le renversement de nos institutions'. In a remarkably alarmist manner, Marmier claims that if the 'radicaux' were elected, they would wish to dismantle the army and the magistrature; confiscate private land and property; and forcibly remove children from the care of their parents to be brought up by the state: 'il n'y a plus ni pères, ni mères, ni frères, ni sœurs. Il n'y a plus que des troupeaux de citoyens et de citoyennes séparés des grandes lois de l'humanité, asservis à l'inepte ou féroce pouvoir de leurs élus'. Recalling the atrocities visited upon the Church during the first revolution, including

---

[122] *Journal*, 2, 380.   [123] Ibid., 2, 382.   [124] Ibid.

'prêtres égorgés', he affirms that the radicals of the new generation are subject to the 'mêmes haines et les mêmes passions que ceux des temps de la Terreur. Ils abhorrent l'Eglise et n'aspirent qu'à l'écraser'.[125]

Not surprisingly, the opposition press took him to task. The *Journal de Pontarlier* claimed that 'ce candidat serait peut-être excusable s'il disait de bonne foi des choses aussi monstrueusement fausses. Mais étant académicien, et par conséquent censé savoir ce qu'il dit, il n'est pas excusable'.[126] An article in an earlier number of the same newspaper asked

> Où M. Marmier a-t-il vu que les républicains, les candidats ses adversaires, les 363 enfin, aient jamais rêvé de bouleverser la magistrature, l'armée, le clergé, de supprimer le mariage, la famille, la propriété, la religion, etc. Tous ces *épouvantements* (oh, oh!) sont terriblement usés, M. l'académicien, et vos compatriotes ne feront que d'en rire.[127]

Numerous other articles returned to Marmier's residence in Paris, to his lack of involvement in affairs of the Franche-Comté. Others protested at his being presented as the candidate representing family life, property owners, and religion. Much was made of his being unmarried with no family, owning no property in the Franche-Comté (as opposed to Colin, his rival, who was both a family man and a householder). Colin, moreover, it was repeatedly claimed, far from wishing to massacre priests, had actually voted for a pay rise for priests in small parishes.[128]

In August, Marmier noted in his diary that Thiers was now the 'chef de file' of the 'radicaux'[129] as they prepared their election campaign. Even though Thiers was now directly and openly a political opponent, Marmier could never talk about him in the same terms as, for example, a figure like Gambetta:

> Pauvre homme! A son âge, entrer dans de telles machinations! Sa haine pour le maréchal et pour le duc de Broglie lui trouble le cerveau, et l'idée d'être encore une fois président l'éblouit. Il ne voit pas, le malheureux, qu'il n'est que l'instrument de l'ambition de Gambetta, qu'il sera choyé et adulé par ses amis les radicaux tant qu'ils auront besoin de lui, et sans ménagement rejeté, outragé, proscrit peut-être dès qu'ils seront les maîtres.[130]

---

[125] Lettre aux électeurs de l'arrondissement de Pontarlier'; pasted into *Night Side of Society*, 5, fos. 290–2 (held at the Académie des Sciences, Belles Lettres et Arts de Besançon).

[126] 'Un académicien', in supplement to *Journal de Pontarlier* (12 October 1877), 2.

[127] 'Un électeur de Pontarlier', *Journal de Pontarlier* (7 October 1877), 2 (original emphasis).

[128] See, for example, *Journal de Pontarlier* (12 October 1877), 2–3.

[129] *Journal*, 2, 382–3.   [130] Ibid.

Perhaps significantly, however, this is the last mention of Thiers in Marmier's diary until after Thiers' death, when elections were being held at the Académie française to fill his seat in 1878.

In the meantime, Marmier set off for Pontarlier on 26 August 1877 to begin his new campaign against Colin (one of the 363). He worked hard between then and the elections, campaigning in all the cantons of the ward (Pontarlier, Mouthe, Montbenoît, Levier, and Morteau). Basing himself in Pontarlier, he tried to visit all the potential voters in both town and country. He was touched to be greeted warmly like a long-lost friend in many households; he enjoyed visiting the religious communities; and he enjoyed himself at a number of the electoral dinners. But his visits to the countryside depressed him greatly, and reveal a huge change in his character. His own background had been modest, and as a younger man he had found contact with simple working people enriching and rewarding. Now its charm seems to have worn thin:

> Il y a si longtemps que je n'avais vu les villages de mon pays! Et jamais je ne les avais vus si complètement. Ah! les affreux chemins si durs ou si boueux, les amas de fumier de chaque côté, les maisons si sales, les vêtements si sales. J'en suis souvent écœuré, et souvent aussi je m'humilie d'avoir à parler à des gens qui m'écoutent d'un air stupide.[131]

As the day of the election grew closer, however, he grew more confident of his chances, and as the polls closed, his last thought before falling into a sound sleep at the Hôtel de l'Europe at Besançon was that perhaps at that very moment he had become the member of parliament for Pontarlier.

In point of fact, he was mistaken. In the elections of 14 October 1877, Colin was again elected with a similar majority to the one he had achieved in 1876.[132] Despite an initial surprise, he was not too disappointed with his performance. He concluded that 'j'ai eu pour moi toute la vraie, bonne, honnête population de l'arrondissement et, sans les fonctionnaires et les ouvriers, j'aurais eu une grande majorité'.[133] He confided to his diary that he did not regret having stood; he felt that despite the result, he had done his duty and even with hindsight would have done the same thing. But as at the previous election, he was secretly relieved at not having been elected: 'Que ferais-je dans la minorité du parti conservateur? Quelle lutte pénible,

---

[131] *Journal*, 2, 383.

[132] The exact vote count is difficult to determine, the official document apparently no longer being extant. The *Journal de Pontarlier* (21 October 1877) gives 6,689 to 5,830; *Le Moniteur Universel* (16 October 1877) 6,683 to 5,425; whilst Kaye, in an undocumented footnote, gives 6,696 to 5,435 (*Journal*, 2, 384).

[133] *Journal*, 2, 385.

hélas! et totalement infructueuse! La Providence, en écartant de moi ce fardeau, m'a fait une grâce dont je la remercie sincèrement'.[134]

Overall, the republicans did not win all the seats they had hoped for, but nonetheless managed a majority of 327 to 208 (held by the conservatives). The extent of Marmier's growing reactionary streak can be measured by a comment in his diary to the effect that 'pour avoir de vraies bonnes élections, il fallait après la dissolution mettre la France en état de siège et supprimer les journaux radicaux'.[135]

The following year (1878) saw elections to the Academy to fill the seats left vacant by the deaths of Thiers and Claude Bernard. Marmier had grown increasingly to detest the political wranglings and frequent unpleasantness associated with the rivalry of these elections. At this time, Henri Martin and Taine were standing for the seat left vacant by Thiers. Marmier was naturally disinclined to vote for Martin and decided that in view of Taine's recent work, he would vote for the latter. Mignet, however, reminded him that a vote for Taine would be an insult to the memory of Thiers, who had always detested the man. Marmier therefore decided to abstain, a decision which brought him condemnation from both d'Haussonville and Broglie, two men he respected greatly, and with whom he had always been on excellent terms. Marmier reflected, however, that on balance he had made the correct decision.

In January 1879 he was temporarily distracted from affairs of the Academy by the news that the elections in that month had given the Senate a republican majority. The resignation of MacMahon and the election of Jules Grévy ('l'avocat de troisième ordre'[136]) as President of the Republic, all made a depressing start to the year for a man of Marmier's political persuasions. His attention was soon, however, fully occupied by new problems at the Academy. Henri Martin had been elected to replace Thiers, and Émile Ollivier was to make the customary speech in reply. Paying tribute to the life and work of Thiers was always going to be a controversial task; but with two individuals of such widely differing political opinions, the affair became something of a hot potato for the Academy. As was customary, a committee (Marmier, Dufaure, Legouvé, and Doucet) was appointed to give the two speeches a preliminary vetting. The ceremony being scheduled for 29 May, the committee meeting was held on 20 May.[137] The committee

---

[134] Ibid.   [135] Ibid.   [136] Ibid., 2, 389.

[137] In Kaye's edition of the *Journal* (2, 392) the date of the ceremony is given as 21 May; but this is an error in Kaye's transcription, rather than one on Marmier's part. For further details, see AAf, PV, 2B14, fos. 685–758.

unanimously decided that although both speeches had their own merits, 'ils ont paru, l'un et l'autre, avoir dans leur ensemble un caractère trop politique et trop passionné'.[138] Both speakers were asked to make certain alterations and cuts, and present their speeches again to an extraordinary meeting of the committee on 22 May (normally a public holiday for the Ascension). Henri Martin was found to have satisfied the commission; Émile Ollivier had made some alterations, but refused resolutely to modify a passage in which Thiers' patriotism was brought into question. The committee therefore decided that they had no option but to postpone the reception ceremony for six months. In the meantime, however, Ollivier had published an open letter to which the Academy took exception.[139] On 5 June, Mézières put forward a motion to the effect that since the differences between Martin and Ollivier were now deemed to be irreconcilable, Ollivier would be relieved of the responsibility of receiving Martin; Marmier, as current Chancelier, would be delegated to make the speech.[140]

Marmier was justifiably nervous about this 'lourde tâche';[141] indeed, *Le Moniteur Universel* described the ceremony at the Academy as 'assurément l'une des plus importantes qui aient jamais convié le public à ses solennités'.[142] It was a challenge he could not avoid for two reasons: first, he took his reponsibilities at the Academy very seriously, and did not want to create further disruptions; second, he felt a 'devoir de cœur envers M. Thiers qui, pendant de longues années, m'a donné de nombreux témoignages de bienveillance et d'affection'.[143]

The reception was finally held on 13 November, and apparently passed off smoothly, if not with a great deal of enthusiasm. The celebrity of Thiers and the scandal surrounding the ceremony ensured that it was well attended: *Le Moniteur* noted that crowds gathered early at the Institut, and by midday there was not a seat to be had for the ceremony which was to begin at 1 p.m. The audience included Mme Thiers and Mlle Dosne (Félicie); general Charlemagne, Martel, Lefranc, Lefebvre-Pontalis, de Rémusat, de Choiseul, Vian, Paul Lacroix, Ratisbonne, Spuller, La Pommeraye, Mounet-Sully, Worms, and Plon. Henri Martin's speech glorifying Thiers was not a

---

[138] AAf, PV, 2B14, fo. 703.

[139] See AAf, PV, 2B14, fo. 709; also Émile Ollivier, *Thiers à l'Académie et dans l'histoire*, (Paris: Garnier, 1879), 30–1.

[140] AAf, PV, 2B14, fo. 713 [Minutes of the meeting of 5 June 1879].

[141] *Journal*, 2, 392.

[142] Eugène Asse, 'Académie française: Réception de M. Henri Martin, *Le Moniteur Universel* (15 November 1879), 1585–6 (1585).

[143] *Journal*, 2, 392.

success. Jules Brémond, writing in *Le Figaro*, decared that 'Il y a longtemps qu'on n'avait entendu à l'Académie un discours plus insignifiant et plus lourd que celui de M. Henri Martin. Aussi l'assistance entière a-t-elle poussé un long soupir de soulagement quand elle l'a vu se rasseoir à son banc'.[144] Eugène Asse, in *Le Moniteur*, noted the 'froideur glaciale', the 'étonnante indifférence qui a régné, presque sans interruption, pendant toute cette séance'.[145] Never in living memory, he adds, has a speaker at the Academy received so little applause. The lack of enthusiasm is attributed by this critic to a combination of the recent change in public opinion towards Thiers, and the fact that Martin was excessive and unobjective in his praise. For Francis Charmes, writing in the *Journal des Débats*, Martin's speech 'aurait certainement produit un effet considérable s'il avait été lu d'une voix meilleure'.[146]

Marmier's speech studiously avoided reference to Thiers as politician, concentrating on the private individual; his passion for science, art and literature; his charm and his wit.[147] Charmes claims that having seen Ollivier becoming enmeshed in controversy for the political content of his speech, Marmier 'a eu peur', 'parlant de tout pour faire oublier qu'il ne disait rien du vrai sujet'.[148] Asse, on the other hand, found that the first part of Marmier's speech had been a 'modèle de cette critique courtoise comme on l'aime à l'Académie'.[149] In the tribute to Thiers, he continues,

> M. X. Marmier s'est surtout attaché, comme nous avons dit, à l'homme, et son auditoire lui en a su gré. En faisant descendre M. Thiers de l'Empyrée sur la terre, il a vraiment rendu service à sa mémoire, et l'auditoire a été infiniment plus charmé, plus ému, du portrait qu'il lui a présenté du causeur merveilleux, du lettré, de l'amateur passionné pour les choses de l'art, qu'il ne l'avait été du personnage olympien qu'on avait d'abord offert à ses adorations et à son culte.[150]

Brémond in *Le Figaro* also writes favourably of Marmier's speech, praising the decision to talk about 'M. Thiers intime', and singling out excerpts which were particularly warmly received. Brémond expresses regret, however,

---

[144] Jules Brémond, 'Requiescat in pace', *Le Figaro* (14 November 1879), 1–2 (2).
[145] Asse, 'Académie française: Réception de M. Henri Martin', 1586.
[146] Francis Charmes, 'Académie française: Réception de M. Henri Martin', *Journal des Débats* (14 November 1879) [no page nos.].
[147] 'Réponse de M. Xavier Marmier, Directeur de l'Académie française, au discours de M. Henri Martin', *Recueil des discours, rapports et pièces diverses lus dans les séances publiques et particulières de l'Académie française, 1870–1879*, 2 vols. (Paris: Firmin Didot, 1880), 2, 447–76.
[148] Charmes, 'Académie française: Réception de M. Henri Martin', [no page nos.].
[149] Asse, 'Académie française: Réception de M. Henri Martin', 1586.   [150] Ibid.

that 'la mauvaise impression produite par M. Henri Martin avait littérale-
ment glacé l'assistance'.[151] The affair was finally laid to rest on 27 November
when the Bureau of the Academy presented the newly received Henri
Martin to the President of the Republic at the Élysée palace.[152]

[151] Brémond, 'Requiescat in pace', 2.
[152] AAf, PV, 2B14, fo. 761.

14

The Last Years (1880–92)

Marmier was now over 70 years old, and the coming decade saw him limiting his activities to the Parisian sphere. He had naturally experienced a decline in his physical vigour, although his mind remained active and his general state of health permitted him to pursue many of his former interests. He maintained a steady flow of publications and settled into a new routine centred principally on his sessions at the Bibliothèque Sainte-Geneviève on Saturdays, and his Thursday meetings at the Académie française, which he attended assiduously right up to the end of his life. He also became involved with various good works: in 1880, for example, he was the guest of honour at the speech day of the parish school of Sainte-Clotilde;[1] in 1884, he gave a speech at the annual general meeting of the 'œuvre de l'hospitalité de nuit', a religious charity which had already set up three hostels for the homeless.[2]

His publications over these years include new volumes of translations, and revised editions of some of his earlier works as well as prefaces and editions of the works of others. He also published a large number of translations and other articles (principally about travel or foreign countries) in periodicals and newspapers. The index of the *Revue britannique* alone lists some thirty-three articles which appeared between 1880 and 1890. Two short stories came out in *Le Petit Moniteur illustré* (a supplement to *Le Moniteur Universel*) in February and May 1892, only months before his death.[3] In 1888 he also became an honorary member of the editorial board of *La Paix sociale*, a newspaper founded in June of that year proclaiming itself to be an 'organe de la ligue nationale contre l'athéisme'.[4] Between July 1888 and December 1889 he published some eleven articles here (some

[1] Paroisse Sainte-Clotilde, École paroissiale libre, tenue par les frères des écoles chrétiennes, *Discours prononcé à la distribution des prix par M. Xavier Marmier de l'Académie française* (Paris: Imprimerie de l'œuvre de Saint-Paul, Soussens et Cie, 1880).

[2] *Allocution de M. Xavier Marmier de l'Académie française prononcée à l'assemblée annuelle de l'œuvre de l'hospitalité de nuit le 16 mars 1884* (Paris: Éthiou-Pérou, 1884).

[3] 'Les Émigrés en Suède' on 21 February 1892 and 'Le Trébuchant' on 23 May 1892. He had previously published two other pieces in this review: 'Mistress Macfarlane' on 25 July 1886 and 'L'Anniversaire' on 24 July 1887.

[4] See 'Manifeste de *La Paix sociale*', *La Paix sociale*, no. 1 (2 June 1888).

of which appear to be extracts taken from *Prose et vers 1836–1886*, an anthology which appeared in 1890).[5]

In the meantime, he was attending meetings of the Académie française regularly. In April 1883, an invitation was received by the Institut de France from the Marquis de Lorne, Governor General of Canada, on behalf of the Royal Society of Canada, to send a delegation to attend its second annual general meeting in Ottawa on 22 May. Marmier (now nearly 75 years old) accepted a nomination to represent the Académie française, and an announcement was made at the meeting of 17 April that the government had offered to contribute 2,000 francs towards expenses. The following week, however, Marmier declared to the meeting that he had been unwell since the last meeting and had decided that, with the greatest regret, his current state of health would not allow him to make the voyage to Canada. The meeting supported his decision: 'L'Académie s'inquiétait d'avance de voir M. Marmier entreprendre pour elle un pareil voyage. Comprenant et approuvant les motifs qui le retiennent, elle renonce à demander qu'un de ses membres aille la représenter si loin, au risque de compromettre sa santé, sa vie peut-être'.[6] On 5 July, an extract of the minutes of the meeting of the Royal Society was read out at the Academy. The extract contained a vote of thanks to the Académie française for its response to the invitation,

> et des remerciements particuliers pour M. Xavier Marmier qui s'était chargé de représenter ses confrères. La société, qui aurait été heureuse de revoir M. Marmier, un ancien ami du Canada, a appris avec regret la raison qui ne lui a pas permis d'accomplir le voyage, et elle fait des vœux pour le rétablissement de sa santé.[7]

According to a physical description at about this time, Marmier had thick hair with hardly a touch of grey, pushed back off his face to reveal a broad forehead, 'l'œil vif, avec des reflets glauques de cet océan tant de fois traversé'; an expression of gentle melancholy, and a smile both kindly and engaging.[8]

In December of the following year, Marmier (now aged 76) received an unexpected promotion to the post of 'administrateur' at the Bibliothèque Sainte-Geneviève. The appointment letter is dated 20 December, and Marmier's reply to the Ministre de l'Instruction publique dated 22 December contains a formal acceptance of the post along with thanks for the confidence shown in him. Two days later, however, on 24 December, he

---

[5] *Prose et vers 1836–1886* (Paris: Lahure, 1890).
[6] AAf, PV, 2B15, fo. 444.   [7] Ibid., fo. 469.
[8] Stéphen Liégard, 'M. Xavier Marmier', in *Au caprice de la plume* (Paris: Hachette, 1884), 195–250 (211).

appears to have had second thoughts, and sent a second letter in which he resigns from the post he had accepted just two days before. In a very shaky hand, he explains that whilst he is extremely honoured by the decision to promote him,

> A l'âge où je suis, dans ma vie sédentaire, dans l'habitude régulière d'un silencieux et tranquille travail, je ne puis songer sans crainte aux complications, aux difficultés, aux diverses péripéties d'une administration comme celle de la Bibliothèque Sainte-Geneviève.
>
> Ma conscience ne me permet pas d'accepter, si désirable qu'il soit, un emploi dont je ne crois pas pouvoir remplir complètement les obligations.
>
> Je me suis donc décidé, non sans regret, à me démettre du grade que vous avez eu la bonté de me conférer [. . .].[9]

In later years, Marmier may have regretted his decision. Evidence suggests that his relationship with the man promoted above him was rather strained. An undated letter in his file, but with a date stamp suggesting it was received in November 1887, registers a formal complaint about Marmier. Although it would appear that Marmier was probably in the wrong in this particular instance, the letter itself is unpleasant and speaks volumes about the writer and his attitude to Marmier:

> Monsieur le Directeur,
>
> J'ai l'honneur de porter à votre connaissance un fait qu'il est de mon devoir de vous signaler, au nom de la bonne discipline de la Bibliothèque Sainte-Geneviève.
>
> Le 15 août dernier, M. Marmier, administrateur adjoint de la Bibliothèque Sainte-Geneviève, a pris son congé régulier qui devait durer jusqu'au 1er octobre.
>
> A cette date, M. Marmier n'est pas revenu prendre son service d'*une* séance par semaine; je n'ai reçu aucun avis m'expliquant la cause de cette absence. Une convocation avait été adressée à M. Marmier pour la séance du 29 octobre du Comité consultatif; notre collègue n'est pas venu et ne s'est pas fait excuser.
>
> En revanche, M. Marmier a écrit au conservateur chargé de la comptabilité pour lui demander un rendez-vous et s'est présenté en personne à la caisse le 31 octobre. Il avait trois mois d'arriéré à toucher.
>
> Je n'ajouterai à ces faits aucun commentaire; tout au plus prendrai-je la liberté, Monsieur le Directeur, de vous demander si l'Administration ne serait pas en droit de considérer M. Marmier comme démissionaire. [. . .][10]

---

[9] AnF, F17/21256.   [10] Ibid. (original emphasis).

A further letter in the file, this time from Marmier and addressed to the 'administrateur', presumably written as a result of the complaint, is dated 2 December:

> Depuis quelques semaines, je suis dans un état de malaise qui, en raison de mon âge, m'assujettit à de rigoureuses prescriptions.
>   Malgré mon bon vouloir, il ne m'est pas encore possible de retourner à la Bibliothèque.
>   J'en suis très peiné.[11]

The following month (January 1888), Marmier—now almost 80 years old—addressed a further letter to the Ministre de l'Instruction publique, requesting permission to retire. In this letter, he enumerates the various posts he has held under the aegis of the ministry and concludes that

> Il y a donc, Monsieur le Ministre, plus d'un demi-siècle que je suis au service de l'état.
>   Il y a quarante-huit ans que je remplis une tâche régulière dans la bibliothèque.
>   J'ai près de quatre-vingts ans.
>   Quoi qu'il m'en coûte de quitter un établissment où j'ai passé les meilleurs jours de ma vie, je crois devoir demander ma retraite.[12]

A reply dated 26 January 1888 from the minister agrees to his request and assures Marmier that his contribution and years of service would not be overlooked. Although the letter is couched in kindly and respectful terms, it states that his retirement had in fact been anticipated and that various changes in the staffing of the libraries had been planned; but that reorganisation had been put on hold out of respect for Marmier's long service and his eminent reputation until such time as he would decide to retire of his own free will. As a token of recognition, he is offered the title of 'administrateur honoraire'.[13] Calculations for Marmier's retirement pension in his employment file show that he was credited with a service of forty-nine years, four months and thirteen days payable from 10 June 1888 and backdated to 1 February of the same year.

In fact, 1888 saw a great deal of turmoil in Marmier's life in other respects. Already the previous year, he had written to Maxime Du Camp (with whom he seems to have become very friendly after the election of the latter to the Académie française in February 1880) that 'à mesure que nous avançons dans la vie, le cercle de nos relations mondaines se rétrécit, celui de nos affections encore plus, et nous attachons le plus grand prix aux

---

[11] AnF, F17/21256.   [12] Ibid.   [13] Ibid.

affinités électives qui nous restent'.[14] On 10 December 1888, he lost one of his closest and longest-standing friends, the duchesse de Galliera. They had known each other for some forty-five years, although the relationship had had its ups and downs over the preceding decade. He had disapproved strongly of her only surviving son, Philippe Ferrari, to the extent that he refused even to shake his hand, and claimed that the very sight of the younger man gave him a 'sentiment de révolte'.[15] The reasons for his antipathy appear to have been partly religious and political (Ferrari's alleged disrespect for the Church; his disdain for conservatives of all colours, including his parents; and his 'tendre penchant pour la démocratie, voire même pour les communards'[16]). This was topped, perhaps, by a degree of homophobia on Marmier's part. Marmier seems, perhaps unsurprisingly in view of his other reactionary tendencies in his old age, to have been quite outraged that 'nulle femme n'a pu lui donner encore la moindre émotion. Je l'ai vu assis à table près des plus jolies personnes, il ne leur accordait même pas un regard'.[17] The true object of the young man's passion, Marmier continues, was the son of a hosier whom he had brought home to meet his parents and with whom he had wanted to set up home under his parents' roof. But this was apparently not what brought about tension between Marmier and his friend, for he notes that he continues to regard her as 'une âme d'élite, généreuse, tendre, élevée'.[18]

By the end of the 1870s, however, he seems to have lost some of the huge respect he had always shown her (even in his private papers). She had been widowed in 1876 and had inherited her husband's immense personal fortune, reputedly in the region of 220 million francs. According to Marmier, she began to put the money to good use by founding two religious institutions, but then became irritated by the constant flow of begging letters and virtually ceased her good works, handing over a good proportion of her wealth to the Orléans princes. Not only did Marmier disagree with her that the Orléans were a deserving cause, he was also frustrated by the fact that she 'ne veut pas chercher à voir les vraies misères qui l'entourent et s'efforcer de les secourir'.[19] He was presumably even more disapproving in 1883 when, on the death of the comte de Chambord, whom she had allowed the use of her magnificent mansion in the rue de Varenne, she made it over to the comte de Paris, who used it as his political headquarters. The activities of the latter, however, led to a further political exile and displeased the duchesse, who cut the Orléans out of her will and bequeathed the mansion to the Austrian embassy. Presumably in the meantime, she and Marmier had

---

[14] BIF, Fonds Maxime Du Camp, MS 3748, 30, fo. 11.
[15] *Journal*, 2, 373. [16] Ibid. [17] Ibid. [18] Ibid., 2, 373–4. [19] Ibid., 2, 390.

become reconciled; Marmier was the last person she recognised before she died, and he was the recipient of the telegram of sympathy sent by Karl Alexander, Grossherzog (Grand Duke) of Weimar.[20]

In the meantime, he had other more practical worries. For nearly forty-five years he had lived in a modest apartment at no. 1, rue Saint-Thomas-d'Aquin. Stéphen Liégeard describes the interior of the third-floor flat as something between a museum and a library, but closer to a library; the walls of all the rooms appeared to be covered in bookshelves, from floor to ceiling. Everywhere 'des bahuts sculptés, des armes exotiques, des bronzes figurant les diverses parties du monde; des reliques recueillies un peu partout sur le long chemin de la vie, égayent, en la peuplant, cette studieuse solitude'.[21] The study was small with a single window overlooking a garden; in front of the window stood a tropical plant flourishing in a Chinese vase. Even in 1883–4, Liégeard noted that all the buildings around had been relentlessly demolished to make way for development, leaving Marmier's humble building standing 'comme si quelque divinité protectrice eût veillé à ce que rien n'y troublât pour lui la religion des souvenirs'.[22] Finally, however, some few years later, the decision was taken that Marmier's building also was to be demolished. The prospect naturally dismayed him: a move is always a major upheaval, and all the more so for a man of over 80 years old with a vast collection of books and memorabilia. It appears furthermore to have provoked more fundamental feelings of insecurity. In an article entitled simply 'Paris', published in August 1888, he reflects on the transitory and uncertain nature of life in the city:

> Les mille et mille habitations de Paris appartiennent à tout le monde et ne sont en réalité à personne. En revenant des lointaines régions, la cicogne retrouve son nid; l'homme à Paris, n'est pas sûr de garder longtemps le sien, pas même celui qui a le bonheur de posséder une maison. Son quartier peut, d'un jour à l'autre, être transpercé par une compagnie de spéculateurs, ou transformé par un arrêt du conseil municipal.[23]

He found a new flat on the first floor of 10 rue de Babylone, overlooking the square outside the 'Bon Marché'. According to Charles Formentin, the main room was square, its walls covered in books and pictures. The floor was covered by a luxuriously thick carpet, and Marmier had a couch, so that he could sit with his feet up, his legs covered by thick blankets and with

---

[20] Information taken from *La Grande Encyclopédie* (Paris: Société anonyme de la Grande Encyclopédie, [no date]); and an article in *Le Soleil* (13 December 1888). I have not managed to locate a copy of the newspaper, but the article is pasted into *Night Side of Society*, 6, fo. 293 (held at the Académie des Sciences, Belles Lettres et Arts de Besançon); it is reproduced, but with no reference, by Kaye in his edition of the *Journal* (2, 391).
[21] Liégeard, 'M. Xavier Marmier', 209.   [22] Ibid., 207–8.   [23] *La Paix sociale* (25 August 1888).

two plump cushions to support his back.[24] It was, Marmier conceded, a much more pleasant flat than his former residence, and the stairs were much easier for a man of his age. But, he wrote to Auguste Castan, 'le déménagement! Quelle calamité! J'y ai employé de longues heures et ce n'est pas encore fini. Comme on est toujours puni de ses passions, je suis puni de ma passion de bouquinage. Que de volumes, grand Dieu!'[25]

Despite the turbulence in his private life, he was still attending the meetings of the Académie française regularly when his health allowed, and continued to take a lively interest in its affairs. In May 1890, Zola stood for election for the first time (unsuccessfully). A number of contemporaries recount stories of Zola's visits to Marmier in order to canvass his vote. That September, Charles Formentin went to interview Marmier at home and asked him why he had campaigned so vigorously against Zola and voted for Pierre Loti. Marmier admitted that Zola had 'un talent immense' and that he was a 'puissant écrivain qui a renouvelé le roman moderne, et créé dans la littérature comme un frisson nouveau', even recognising that some of his work contained the mark of sheer genius. However, he told the journalist, he had also told Zola that: 'Vous avez fait, monsieur, des livres superbes, mais je ne vous pardonne pas d'avoir jeté dans vos œuvres des grossièretés et des horreurs. Dans *La Terre* et dans *L'Assommoir*, dans *Germinal*, vous avez sali des tableaux admirables par des taches que la morale et le bon goût condamnent'. Apparently, pushed by Formentin to justify this viewpoint, Marmier replied candidly: 'Quand vous entrerez au journal tout à l'heure pour raconter notre entretien, irez-vous, s'il vous plaît de décrire mon appartement, faire la description de mes water-closets?'.[26]

Adolphe Brisson recounts what may well be the same anecdote in slightly different terms — although the message remains the same. According to this version, Marmier gave Zola a warm welcome, spending about an hour showing his visitor his collection of rare books and manuscripts before showing him all around his new apartment, even including the dining room, bedroom, and kitchen. As Zola was about to leave, Marmier

> lui désigna de la main une porte bâtarde, sur laquelle se détachaient ces deux lettres fatadiques, W.C., puis, d'un air narquois:
> — Cher monsieur, lui dit-il, vous connaissez maintenant mes humbles pénates. Il n'est que cet endroit où je n'aie pas osé vous conduire, car j'ai l'habitude d'y pénétrer seul, et de ne point l'ouvrir au public.[27]

[24] Charles Formentin, 'La Vieillesse d'un académicien', *L'Echo de Paris* (21 September 1890).
[25] BmB, Collection Estignard, Correspondance de A. Castan, fo. 103.
[26] Formentin, 'La Vieillesse d'un académicien'.
[27] Adolphe Brisson, *Portraits intimes*, 1st ser. (Paris: Armand Colin, 1894), 22.

For some years now, Marmier had adopted a rather austere lifestyle, drinking only pure water and eating nothing but vegetables supplemented by the occasional egg (this the man who, it was alleged, owed his election to the Academy to his talent for dining out!). He had also decided to avoid doctors or medicines. The regime, he declared in 1890, appeared to be working as he felt quite healthy for his age: his stomach was in perfect working order. Only his legs—the supreme irony for the indefatigable traveller of yore—had given out, and he left his apartment only to go to church, or to the weekly meetings of the Academy. At this point in his life, contemporaries describe him as thin, always clean-shaven, with long white hair which he tucked behind his ears, but which fell forward over his neck. He had a dreamy, rather melancholy gaze, and a kindly face; he was often smiling, but his smile revealed gaps in his teeth. He was easily recognisable by his flat, wide-brimmed hat, his cane, and his outsized frock coat with long coat tails, into which he crammed the treasures that he picked up from the 'bouquinistes'.[28] He continued to relish the thrill of searching for a rare book or a bargain at the stalls of the 'bouquinistes' along the Seine as he made his way to and from the Institut de France. A number of inscriptions in books in his personal library show that he was still actively buying books in 1892.[29] His books had always brought him consolation in times of distress or illness. During a period of ill-health in November 1888 he wrote to Maxime Du Camp that 'je ne puis pas me plaindre quand je songe qu'il y a tant de braves innocents êtres qui souffrent, et qui n'ont pas comme moi, bon gîte, bon feu, une belle collection de livres, des yeux pour les lire, et la paix de l'âme'.[30]

But he was becoming increasingly aware that his time was running out. As early as June 1888 he wrote rather sadly to Maxime Du Camp, who was then holidaying in Germany:

> Je ne reverrai plus cette [*sic*] Jugendland où j'ai tant rêvé et fait tant de
> mauvais vers. Je ne reverrai plus les régions du nord lointain avec leur
> enchantement mélancolique, ni les splendides floraisons des Antilles, ni le

---

[28] See A. Mézières, 'X. Marmier', *Le Temps* (13 October 1892); Victor Fournel, 'Les Œuvres et les hommes: Courrier du théâtre, de la littérature et des arts', *Le Correspondant*, 169 (October 1892), 364–87 (378); and also BIF, Fonds Maxime Du Camp, MS 3748, 30, fo. 41.

[29] The Procès-Verbaux of the Académie française for this period (2B14, 2B15, 2B16) show that he missed three consecutive meetings in November 1888, but otherwise attended more or less regularly until his final illness in 1892. Books purchased and inscribed in 1892 showed that his interests were still very wide; they include a copy of Michelet's *Précis de l'histoire moderne*; Coxe's *History of the House of Austria*; Rodd's *History of Charles the Great*; Léon Gozlan's *Scènes de la vie littéraire*; John Parker Lawson's *Legends and Traditions* [. . .] *in the Old Testament*; and *The New Calendar of Great Men*, edited by Frederic Harrison, and purchased on 24 March.

[30] BIF, Fonds Maxime Du Camp, MS 3748, 30, fo. 17.

soleil de l'équateur. Je ne reverrai plus là-bas l'étoile polaire, là-bas la croix du Sud. Ah! Dieu, ces jours de voyage, ces beautés de la nature, c'est tout ce que je regrette.

Peut-être après la mort! Je voudrais errer à travers l'espace, dans un nuage tour à tour lumineux et noir, lumineux quand je passerais près de ceux que j'ai aimés et près des braves gens; noir, fulgurant, terrible, près des faux patriotes et des brigands.[31]

In April 1890 he wrote again to Maxime Du Camp telling him that in his will he had left him an oil painting; and in August 1891 he wrote a long letter, two thirds of which is devoted entirely to trying to lift his friend's spirits and concentrating entirely on Du Camp's affairs. In conclusion, Marmier says that he misses seeing Du Camp on Thursdays and adds that 'A mon âge on vit au jour le jour. Ainsi soit. Tant de choses sont déjà mortes autour de moi et en moi, que la dernière ne sera qu'une petite secousse. J'espère cependant vous revoir au mois de novembre'.[32]

He nonetheless continued to attend the meetings of the Academy assiduously, although by January 1892 he was sometimes forced to take a carriage, no longer able to walk from the rue de Babylone down to the Institut de France. He missed a couple of sessions in April and June of that year: a rhyme scribbled in a book purchased from one of the bouquinistes in June tells us that he was suffering from catarrh, anaemia, and 'un asthme bizarre'.[33] The anaemia might presumably have been a consequence of his vegetarian diet; but he was obviously now also suffering from breathing difficulties. That summer, his health seems to have deteriorated quite significantly. Jules Claretie notes in his memoirs that the meeting of the Academy on 23 July was 'macabre'; Doucet arrived, himself coughing and suffering from a heavy cold, and pointed to Marmier, who was extremely thin and red in the face, leaning heavily on the arm of an escort, and then remarked to Claretie that 'Il [Marmier] n'ira pas loin . . . D'un moment à l'autre . . .'.[34]

Marmier did manage to attend again on 4 August, but that was to be his last meeting at the Academy. His intellect, however, seems to have remained clear, and on 16 August he wrote to Maxime Du Camp to congratulate him on an article which had recently appeared in the *Revue des Deux Mondes*. He also retained a remarkably clear insight into his own condition:

---

[31] Ibid., fo. 15. [32] Ibid., fo. 31.

[33] Inscription in a copy of George Bruce Malleson, *Final French Struggles in India and on the Indian Seas* [. . .] (London: Wm H. Allen, 1878), conserved in the Bibliothèque Xavier Marmier in Pontarlier.

[34] 'Souvenirs d'un Académicien, mémoires inédites par Jules Claretie', in *Les Œuvres libres* (Paris: Fayard, 1934), 23.

> Pour moi, mon cher ami, je ne ferai plus aucun travail. Je ne ferai plus rien. Ces chaleurs désordonnées m'ont achevé. Je suis dans un tel état de faiblesse que je ne puis chavirer dans ma chambre qu'à l'aide d'un bâton, ou en allant d'un meuble à l'autre comme un enfant qui essaye de marcher.
>
> Grâce au ciel, j'ai encore l'usage de mes mains, de mes yeux, et je ne souffre pas. Je pense que par l'effet de l'âge, je m'en irai peu à peu languissant, dépérissant en silence sans crise et sans agonie. C'est mon rêve. Il n'est pas mauvais. Je voudrais cependant vous serrer encore la main.[35]

When he felt the time had come, he had a telegram sent to his old friend Le Rebours, parish priest of La Madeleine, who had just arrived in Rome. The priest promptly returned to Paris, arriving in good time to administer the last rites. Marmier apparently remained calm and clear as he spoke to Léa, his younger sister—now of course an old woman herself—who had come to his bedside. On 11 October, he lost consciousness at around 1 a.m. and died at about four o'clock that morning.[36]

News of his death spread rapidly, and on 12 October obituaries began to appear; the earliest announcements were carried in the *Journal des Débats*, *Le Moniteur Universel*, *Le Figaro*, *Le Temps*, and *Le Matin*.[37] In *Le Temps*, the initial announcement was followed by two full obituaries on 13 October and 16 October, by A. Mézières and Anatole France respectively.[38] Other tributes followed in the popular press and various periodicals, including *L'Illustration*,[39] the *Revue de France*,[40] the *Journal des voyages et des aventures de terre et de mer*,[41] *Le Journal illustré*,[42] *L'Univers illustré*,[43]

---

[35] BIF, Fonds Maxime Du Camp, MS 3748, 30, fos. 38–9.

[36] Mairie du 7e arrondissement de Paris: 'L'an mil huit cent quatre-vingt-douze, le douze octobre, à dix heures et demie du matin, acte de décès de Jean-Marie Xavier Marmier, âgé de quatre-vingt-quatre ans, membre de l'Académie française, Officier de la Légion d'Honneur, né à Pontarlier (Doubs), décédé en son domicile à Paris, rue de Babylone 10, hier matin à quatre heures, fils de François-Xavier Marmier et de Marie-Gabrielle Honorine Maillot, épouse décédée, veuf de Françoise Eugénie Pourchet [. . .]'.

[37] 'Nécrologie. M. Xavier Marmier, *Journal des Débats* (12 October 1892); 'Dernières nouvelles. Mort de M. Xavier Marmier', *Le Moniteur Universel* (12 October 1892), 1119; Étincelle, 'Xavier Marmier', *Le Figaro* (12 October 1892), 2; 'Dernières nouvelles', *Le Temps* (12 October 1892); 'Xavier Marmier', *Le Matin* (12 October 1892).

[38] A. Mézières, 'X. Marmier', *Le Temps* (13 October 1892), [no page nos., but first and second page]; Anatole France, 'La Vie littéraire. Xavier Marmier', *Le Temps* (16 October 1892), [no page nos., second page].

[39] *L'Illustration* (15 October 1892), 312.

[40] *Revue de France*, 4e année, no. 185 (15 October 1892), 33–4.

[41] *Journal des voyages et des aventures de terre et de mer*, no. 804 (4 December 1892), 366.

[42] *Le Journal illustré*, no. 344 (23 October 1892), 342.

[43] *L'Univers illustré*, no. 1961 (22 October 1892), 512 (portrait, 508).

L'Entr'acte,[44] *La Petite Revue*,[45] *Le Correspondant*,[46] *Polybiblion*,[47] the *Revue des traditions populaires*,[48] and *La Revue hebdomadaire*.[49] Several of these obituaries included portraits, and a number featured wholly or partly on the front pages of the publication.

Almost all the obituaries mention his travels, his role in introducing foreign literature to France, his membership of the Académie française, and his personal qualities. The *Revue de France*, for example, claimed that Marmier 'protesta toute sa vie contre notre indifférence à l'égard des écrivains étrangers et [. . .] il appuya sa protestation incessante de nombreux travaux'.[50] Anatole France, perhaps with greater detail and incisiveness than most, insists that it is easy to underestimate the significance and impact of Marmier's work on foreign literatures and cultures in France, since 'il faut replacer les productions de l'esprit dans le temps de leur éclosion pour juger de leur mérite et de leur utilité'. Marmier, he considers, 'fut pendant trente ans, avec beaucoup d'exactitude et de grâce, le professeur de littérature étrangère des Français et des Françaises'. In terms of personality, the deceased is recalled as 'fort savant et il l'était avec agrément; il contait à merveille; c'était un vieillard bienveillant, spirituel, infiniment gracieux et bon'.[51] Mézières covers similar ground, in particular highlighting Marmier's generosity in encouraging and helping the younger generation. This particular point is reiterated by François Coppée, the poet and dramatist, in *La Revue hebdomadaire*. Marmier and Coppée had been very friendly; Coppée recalls their first meeting in the passage Choiseul at the premises of the publisher Lemerre. Marmier, Coppée recalls, was a 'bon et charmant vieillard',[52] who 'aimait la jeunesse et la poésie'.[53] He took the younger man under his wing, and Coppée pays tribute to 'la bonté de son cœur et la grâce de son esprit'.[54] For Étincelle, writing in *Le Figaro*, Marmier was 'un vieillard exquis, une de ces âmes dont notre monde positif n'est peut-être plus digne, une vraie âme de poète et de chrétien', who loved children. In respect of the Académie française, she claims that he had friends of all political

---

[44] Fernand Bourgeat, 'Xavier Marmier', *L'Entr'acte*, 61e année (1892), 285.

[45] *La Petite Revue*, no. 231 (22 October 1892), front page and 257–8.

[46] Victor Fournel, ' Les Œuvres et les hommes. Courrier du théâtre, de la littérature et des arts', *Le Correspondant*, 169 (October 1892), 364–87 (377–9).

[47] Visenot, 'Chronique. Nécrologie', *Polybiblion*, 2nd ser., 36 (Paris: 1892), 463–5.

[48] P. S. in *Revue des traditions populaires*, 7e année, 7/11 (1892), 701–2.

[49] François Coppée, 'Xavier Marmier', *La Revue hebdomadaire* (October 1992), 615–20.

[50] *Revue de France*, 4e année, no. 185 (15 October 1892), 34.

[51] France, 'La Vie littéraire. Xavier Marmier'.

[52] Coppée, 'Xavier Marmier', 615.

[53] Ibid., 618.   [54] Ibid., 619.

colours and persuasions; in particular, his favourites, 'MM. Maxime Du Camp et Rousse peuvent le pleurer, ils en étaient profondément aimés'.[55]

Marmier had expressly stated in his will that he should have a pauper's funeral with a minimum of fuss: no delegations, no official invitations, no military honours, and no speeches. Instead of vast expenditure on the funeral, he asked that the sum of 2,000 francs (from his estate) be distributed to the poor of his parish by the priest. The funeral was held at the church of Saint-Thomas-d'Aquin at 10 a.m. on Friday 14 October. Marmier's wishes were largely respected: no speeches were made, the hearse was fifth class and the religious ceremony third class. Mass was celebrated by Father Ravaill, parish priest of Saint-Thomas-d'Aquin, and the absolution given by Father Le Rebours, parish priest of La Madeleine. The chief mourners were Marmier's nephews, Father Guichard and Henri Marmier (son of Hyacinthe). Wreathes were sent by both individuals and organisations, including the Alliance française of Stockholm, the Norwegian and Swedish communities in Paris, the Canadians (dedicated simply 'A Xavier Marmier, les Canadiens') and the 'bouquinistes'. Although Marmier had not wanted any official delegations, the funeral was massively attended by friends and colleagues wishing to pay their last respects. The list of dignitaries present (despite his request) is indicative of Marmier's status in the intellectual world at this time, and includes many individuals still famous today. Amongst the most distinguished intellectuals listed by journalists were Alexandre Dumas (fils); Leconte de Lisle; François Coppée; Ludovic Halévy; Charles Gounod; Ernest Legouvé (poet and dramatist); Joseph Bertrand (mathematician); Albert Sorel (historian); Auguste Daubrée (geologist); Léon Say (political economist); André Theuriet (poet); Le Châtelier (chemist and metallurgist); Henri Régnier (poet and novelist); Carolus-Durand (painter); Victor Duruy (historian and politician); Gaston Darboux

---

[55] Étincelle, 'Xavier Marmier'. All the evidence indeed suggests that Marmier was very attached to Du Camp, but the latter was obviously less enthusiastic about the friendship. A note about Marmier in Du Camp's personal papers claims that Marmier was poor, but a scrounger ('pique-assiette') who managed to dine out frequently because he was the darling of so many rich old ladies. Conversation with him could be awkward, Du Camp continues, because Marmier's sole topic of conversation was women. On the whole, Du Camp found him to be a rather spineless individual who was very susceptible to influence from those around him. His general benevolence, he continues, could be seen as banality—although, in private, Marmier did not hesitate to indulge in backbiting and gossip about his fellow Académiciens. In intellectual terms, Du Camp describes Marmier as 'woolly' ('nuageux'). He does acknowledge that Marmier has been consistent in his friendship towards him, and somehow, after this list of personal failings, concludes that he is 'un homme recommandable et d'une grande mansuétude' (BIF, Fonds Maxime Du Camp, MS 3748, 30, fos. 41–2). In the same document (fo. 47), he also sticks the cutting of Étincelle's obituary from *Le Figaro* with the aforementioned claim that the journalist is the daughter of Marmier and d'Aunet (see chapter 8).

(mathematician); Jules Simon (politician and philosopher); Eugène Melchior Vogüé (author, Russian specialist); and Stéphen Liégeard (author). The directors of some of the most prestigious national museums and learned institutions also attended: Jules Cousin (musée Carnavalet); Kaempfen (musées nationaux); Benedite (musée du Luxembourg); Darcel (musée de Cluny); Bergeron (secrétaire perpétuel de l'Académie de Médecine); and Ribierre (chef du cabinet du Ministre de l'Instruction publique). The town of Pontarlier was represented by Mercier (the mayor); Cardon (his first deputy); Hugon (a councillor); and Dionys Ordinaire (local member of parliament). There was also a delegation from the 'bouquinistes'.[56]

After the religious service at Saint-Thomas d'Aquin, the coffin was placed in a hearse and transported to the Gare de Lyon, whence Marmier would make the journey to his final resting place. The coffin and those accompanying it were met at Pontarlier station at midday on Saturday, and a brief religious ceremony preceded burial in the cemetery at Pontarlier. Marmier's grave is adorned by a copy of the medal by David d'Angers, and bears the inscription 'A XAVIER MARMIER, DE L'ACADÉMIE FRANÇAISE. LA VILLE DE PONTARLIER RECONNAISSANTE'.[57]

Marmier left an estate worth some 200,000 francs, a considerable sum for one who lived modestly and shunned the trappings of fortune. His heir was his nephew Xavier Guichard, the priest of Dôle, but Marmier had made a large number of smaller bequests (which must have left his executors with a good deal of work).[58] Apart from numerous mementoes left to colleagues and friends (books, paintings, artefacts, etc.), he had left a sum of 30,000 francs to the Académie française; the interest from the capital, he stipulated, was to be awarded to a writer (male or female) in financial distress. He left a sum of 10,000 francs to the Academy of Besançon in order to award a gold medal annually for a study on the Franche-Comté, its ancient monuments, customs, or village dialects. A large number of personal papers and diaries, forming the basis for his *Journal*, were also left to the Academy of Besançon. He left his personal library (some 6,000 books, including some

---

[56] See *Journal des Débats* (15 October 1992) and 'Informations. Obsèques', *Le Figaro* (15 October 1992), 3. Others less well-known now, but important and influential figures in their time, who were also listed as present include Jules Claretie; Santeiller; E. Gauthier, E. Hervé; Delaborde; Boissier; d'Estampes; comte d'Haussonville; comte de Labord; Aucoc; Picot; Maurice Hachette; Templier; Mézières; John Lemoinne; de Mazade; Charpentier; and Roger Balin.

[57] Official tokens of recognition in Pontarlier today include the rue Xavier Marmier and the Lycée Xavier Marmier.

[58] His executors were Choppin d'Arnouville (former attorney general); Pingard (of the Académie française) and Templier (of the Hachette family and business). The information given here on Marmier's bequests is taken from an extract of his will conserved in the Archives de Pontarlier, AX53066/R40.

very rare specimens and a small number of manuscripts) to the town of Pontarlier, where it is still kept. The parish of Pontarlier received 4,000 francs, the interest of which was to be used 'au soulagement des pauvres vieillards'. He left 3,000 francs to the 'école des frères de la doctrine chrétienne' in Pontarlier, and an identical sum to the 'école des sœurs'. His housekeeper received a pension of 800 francs. A number of other smaller bequests included a sum of 200 francs to the church at Doubs (the original building is no longer standing) in memory of his mother. One item in his will gave rise to numerous headlines and newspaper reports: a sum of 1,000 francs was left to the 'bouquinistes' to have a 'joyeux dîner' and 'une heure pleine d'entrain' in his memory; this was intended as a 'remerciement pour les nombreuses heures que j'ai vécues intellectuellement dans mes promenades presque quotidiennes sur les quais' and which he counted as some of the 'moments [. . .] les plus agréablement mouvementés de mon existence'.[59]

This dinner initially proved a little difficult to organise, owing to bickering about who was and who was not invited.[60] It was eventually held on 20 November 1892 at the Grand-Véfour, a restaurant at the Palais-Royal, and was attended by some ninety-five booksellers. A gargantuan meal was served, accompanied by fine wines, champagne, coffee, and cognac.[61] A speech was made by Choppin d'Arnouville (one of the executors), which seems to have hit an appropriate note for the occasion. Touching just briefly on Marmier's fame and achievements, it concentrated more on the importance to him of the 'bouquinistes' and their work, particularly in his last years. Choppin d'Arnouville urges the 'bouquinistes' to resist pressures from developers to modernise their practices; Marmier, he says, would certainly have offered the same advice:

> Conservez à vos quais, vous eût-il dit, leur aspect original et unique; ces longs parapets, tout garnis de livres, véritable ceinture du palais de la science, seront toujours un attrait pour les curieux et les lettrés, et pour tous un moyen d'apprendre. Dans un temps d'impitoyable démolition, gardez-nous, messieurs, ce souvenir utile du passé, gardez-nous ce coin charmant de notre vieux Paris.[62]

---

[59] See, for example, France, 'La Vie littéraire. Xavier Marmier'; Roger Roux, *Xavier Marmier bibliophile* (Besançon: Jacquin, 1910), 26 (Roux omits the 'joyeux').

[60] See, for example, 'Réunion de bouquinistes. Le legs de M. Xavier Marmier. Beaucoup d'appelés et peu d'élus. Séance orageuse', *Le Matin* (15 October 1892); and [no title], *Le Matin* (17 October 1892).

[61] The full menu, as well as details, guest lists, and text of the speech are given in Roux, *Xavier Marmier bibliophile*, menu, 27–8. See also 'Le Banquet des bouquinistes', in Octave Uzanne, *Bouquinistes et bouquineurs, physiologie des quais de Paris du Pont Royal au Pont Sully* [illustrations by Émile Mar] (Paris: Quantin, 1893), 307–14.

[62] Roux, *Xavier Marmier bibliophile*, 30.

The speech concludes, befittingly, that: 'Vous entouriez, messieurs, de vos attentions et de vos respects le bon et aimable vieillard qui a voulu vous en remercier; vous n'oublierez pas, j'en suis sûr, ni cet ami des livres, ni le témoignage d'estime et de sympathie qu'il vous a réservé'.[63]

Elections to the Académie française were very soon under way to replace Renan (who had died shortly before Marmier) and Marmier himself. Charles Normand, writing in *La Petite Revue*, predicted that Zola would be elected to one or other of the seats;[64] Gaston Calmette, writing in *Le Figaro*, was more specific, reporting that general rumour had it that Zola would replace Marmier.[65] This result would have been highly ironic, not only in view of Marmier's opposition to Zola, but particularly in view of the alleged exchange between Marmier and Zola related by Formentin in *L'Echo de Paris*:

> La maison fondée par Richelieu a toujours été un salon de bonne compagnie, où tous les talents ont leur place quand ils sont bien élevés. M. Emile Zola m'a déclaré que ses échecs ne le décourageront pas, et qu'il sera candidat jusqu'au succès, fût-il reculé à des calendes lointaines. Son opiniâtreté est louable, mais elle ne sera récompensée que le jour où l'Académie aura changé ses habitudes et ses goûts.[66]

In the event, Henri de Bornier (1825–1901), a poet and dramatist who is now largely forgotten, was elected. Marmier's opposition to Zola may not have been well founded, but his judgement of the ethos of the Academy was impeccable. Zola was to stand for election nineteen times, but—as Marmier predicted—was never successful.

Bornier made his inaugural speech at the Academy on 25 May 1893: as was customary, he paid tribute to his predecessor.[67] On the whole, the speech appears to have been rather sentimental and vague (reference to Marmier's enthusiasm, his melancholy, his delight in the company of women), although a number of valid points are made about Marmier's work.[68] In terms of the travel writing, Bornier notes the conscientious

---

[63] Ibid.

[64] Ch. Normand, 'Chronique de la semaine', *La Petite Revue* (22 October 1892), 258.

[65] Gaston Calmette, 'Candidatures académiques', *Le Figaro* (21 October 1892), 1.

[66] Charles Formentin, *L'Echo de Paris* (21 September 1890).

[67] *Discours prononcés dans la séance publique tenue par l'Académie française pour la réception de M. le Vicomte H. de Bornier le jeudi 25 mai 1893* (Paris: Firmin Didot, 1893).

[68] See Henry Michel, *Le Quarantième Fauteuil* (Paris: Hachette, 1898), 74: 'Je ferai pour ma part, au discours de M. de Bornier, deux reproches: le premier, c'est d'avoir, tout compte fait, traité un peu sommairement la partie essentielle du sujet. Il ne nous a pas appris grand'chose sur Marmier. Comment se fait-il que ce portrait, qui est pourtant d'un ami, et d'un ami sincère dans son affection comme dans sa reconnaissance, soit si incomplet, si peu vivant, si peu fouillé?'

documentation, the variety of sources consulted, the range of areas of inter-est covered, and the general erudition of the works. Interestingly, from a sociohistorical point of view, he pinpoints one feature of the travel narra-tives which in retrospect seems to be one of the more original and impor-tant, but which does not seem to have struck many contemporaries: 'il nous raconte aussi bien l'existence d'un roi ou d'un grand poète que la vie du plus humble artisan ou d'une bergère de la montagne'.[69] Marmier, he further argues, created a new genre of novel, the 'voyage extraordinaire'.[70] This is defined as a novel with a simple plot, the interest of which lies in the profusion of information conveyed about local history, customs, and so on.

The reply to Bornier's speech was made by the comte d'Haussonville. D'Haussonville also emphasised how fundamental travel was not only to Marmier's career, but to his very existence. Marmier found a new direction, according to d'Haussonville, after his election to the Academy, where he played an important part: 'aimable et souriant, étranger aux querelles, aux rivalités, aux passions, détaché des choses sans y être devenu indifférent [. . .]. C'est une noble vie que la sienne, vouée tout entière aux délicates joies de l'esprit'.[71] Outlining the breadth of Marmier's achievements, d'Haussonville claimed that: 'il n'a pas été seulement un voyageur et un traducteur. Il a été aussi un romancier, un poète, un historien, un critique, un naturaliste même à ses heures'.[72] D'Haussonville also appropriately emphasised Marmier's significance as a precursor in a number of fields—a somewhat thankless role, he argues, since once the public attention is drawn to an area of study, others come along whose work soon eclipses that of the precursor. In this context, he highlights Marmier's work on Iceland, Canada, Russia, and Russian literature, reminding his audience that 'c'est à lui qu'on doit les premières traductions de Gogol et de Lermontof'.[73] As this biography has shown, the list of areas in which Marmier was an innovator could have been continued—perhaps not quite to infinity, but a very long way. Indeed, his achievements in bringing to France the multi-lingual, multi-cultural, and multi-social fruits of his explorations would change forever the French attitudes to and understanding of what lay beyond their national boundaries, and lead to a new richness in their own culture.

---

[69] *Discours prononcés* [. . .] *pour la réception de M. le Vicomte H. de Bornier*, 6.
[70] Ibid., 7.
[71] Ibid., 46.
[72] Ibid., 45.
[73] Ibid., 44–5.

Index of People